Politics in the European Union

Develop your understanding of Europe's extraordinary experiment in international cooperation with the New European Union Series, created to give you clear and comprehensive coverage of essential topics in the area.

THE NEW EUROPEAN UNION SERIES

Series editors: **Dermot Hodson and Sophie Vanhoonacker**

The European Union is a crucial and compelling subject for students of politics, economics, history, law, and the social sciences. It is the most successful experiment in modern international cooperation but also a target of fierce criticism in Europe and abroad. Decisions taken by the European Union affect the daily lives of its 500 million citizens and many more worldwide.

The European Union of the twenty-first century faces multiple crises, not least Brexit – the United Kingdom's departure from the EU – as well as core policy challenges, particularly in transnational arenas such as migration, management of the eurozone, and climate change. The European Union, as it reshapes itself anew in response to these and other challenges, requires continuous reassessment.

THE NEW EUROPEAN UNION SERIES brings together the expertise of leading scholars and practitioners to analyse EU politics and policies for an international readership. Established by John Peterson and Helen Wallace, the series has encouraged generations of students, researchers, and policy makers to think critically about Europe's extraordinary experiment in politics beyond the nation state. Build your knowledge with regularly updated editions on:

ORIGINS AND EVOLUTION OF THE EUROPEAN UNION

POLICY-MAKING AND THE EUROPEAN UNION

THE EUROPEAN UNION: HOW DOES IT WORK?

THE INSTITUTIONS OF THE EUROPEAN UNION

THE MEMBER STATES OF THE EUROPEAN UNION

INTERNATIONAL RELATIONS AND THE EUROPEAN UNION

For more information on the titles available in the New European Union Series, visit the OUP website at: **https://global.oup.com/academic/content/series/n/new-european-union-series-neu**

MAKE YOUR VOICE HEARD: JOIN THE OUP POLITICS STUDENT PANEL.

To help us make sure we develop the best possible books for you, the student, we have set up a student panel to hear your opinions and feedback.

To find out more, visit
www.oxfordtextbooks.co.uk/politics/studentpanel

Politics in the European Union

Fifth Edition

Simon Bulmer, Owen Parker,
Ian Bache, Stephen George,
& Charlotte Burns

OXFORD

UNIVERSITY PRESS

OXFORD
UNIVERSITY PRESS

Great Clarendon Street, Oxford, OX2 6DP,
United Kingdom

Oxford University Press is a department of the University of Oxford.
It furthers the University's objective of excellence in research, scholarship,
and education by publishing worldwide. Oxford is a registered trade mark of
Oxford University Press in the UK and in certain other countries

2nd edition 2006
3rd edition 2011
4th edition 2015

Impression: 1

Published in the United States of America by Oxford University Press
198 Madison Avenue, New York, NY 10016, United States of America

British Library Cataloguing in Publication Data
Data available

Library of Congress Control Number: 2020938422

ISBN 978–0–19–882063–5

Printed in Great Britain by
Bell & Bain Ltd., Glasgow

Contents in Brief

Contents in Detail

Part Two History   87

5 From the End of the War to the Schuman Plan (the Late 1940s to the Early 1950s)   89

6 The 'Other' European Communities and the Origins of the European Economic Community (the Early 1950s to the 1960s)   107

Map of Europe

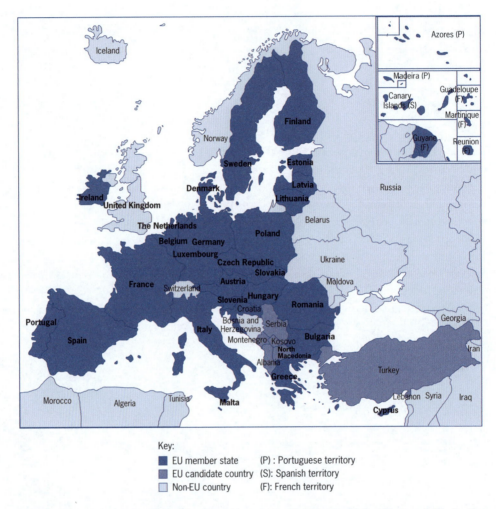

Key:

■ EU member state	(P) : Portuguese territory
■ EU candidate country	(S): Spanish territory
■ Non-EU country	(F): French territory

Adapted from the original published on http://europa/eu © European Union. Responsibility for the adaptation lies entirely with Oxford University Press.

 Go to the online resources to explore an interactive map, with data, and social and political information for countries in the European Union www.oup.com/uk/bache5e.

About the Authors

Simon Bulmer is Emeritus Professor of European Politics at the University of Sheffield. Having held lectureships at Heriot-Watt University and the University of Manchester Institute of Science and Technology (UMIST), he moved to the University of Manchester in 1989, and was Professor of Government from 1995. He has held a Jean Monnet *ad personam* chair since 1999 and has been an Academician of the Social Sciences since 2001. He retired from Sheffield in summer 2020. He has been a Visiting Professor at the College of Europe Bruges, the Autonomous University of Barcelona, the Stiftung Wissenschaft und Politik (the German Institute for International and Security Affairs), Berlin, and at LUISS Guido Carli University, in Rome.

Simon has published in key academic journals, such as the *British Journal of Political Science*; *European Journal of International Relations*; *International Affairs*; *Journal of Common Market Studies*; *Journal of European Public Policy*; *Journal of Public Policy*; *Public Administration*; and *West European Politics*. He has written or edited eighteen books on European politics, working with a range of co-authors. Recent publications include *Germany and the European Union: Europe's Reluctant Hegemon?* (co-authored with William Paterson: Macmillan/Red Globe, 2019); *The Politics and Economics of Brexit* (co-edited with Lucia Quaglia: Routledge, 2019); and *The Member States of the European Union* (3rd edn, co-edited with Christian Lequesne: Oxford University Press, 2020). He has supervised twenty Ph.D. students to completion. Between 1991 and 1998 he co-edited the *Journal of Common Market Studies*.

Owen Parker is Senior Lecturer in European Politics and a Research Fellow at the Sheffield Political Economy Research Institute (SPERI) at the University of Sheffield. Before moving to Sheffield, he completed his doctoral studies and was a Research Fellow at the University of Warwick (2007–2012). Prior to that, he worked for the European Commission in Brussels, Directorate General for Enlargement (2003–2006), on Turkey's bid for EU membership.

Owen has published widely on EU politics, political theory, and political economy. Recent projects have focused on the eurozone crisis; EU citizenship and the free movement of people; and Brexit. His publications include *Cosmopolitan Government in Europe: Citizens and Entrepreneurs in Postnational Politics* (Routledge, 2013) and *Crisis in the Eurozone Periphery: The Political Economies of Greece, Spain, Ireland and Portugal* (co-edited with Dimitris Tsarouhas, SPERI: Palgrave, 2018). He is currently working on a book with the provisional title, 'Europe and the British Left'.

Owen has contributed a number of chapters to edited volumes and published in a wide range of academic journals, including *British Journal of Politics and International Relations*; *Comparative European Politics*; *Constellations*; *Co-operation and Conflict*; *International Studies Quarterly*; *International Theory*; *Journal of Common Market Studies*; *Journal of European Public Policy*; *New Political Economy*; and *Public Administration*. He has taught EU politics and political economy at Sheffield and Warwick and also as a visiting teacher in Spain. In 2016, Owen was invited to give the University Association of Contemporary European Studies (UACES) keynote lecture at the UK Political Studies Association (PSA) teaching and learning annual conference. He has supervised (and supervises) a number of Ph.D. students working on the EU and European political economy. He currently leads two undergraduate modules on the EU: one on the politics and governance of the contemporary EU and one on Britain and the EU, with a focus on Brexit.

Ian Bache is Professor of Politics at the University of Sheffield. He has published widely on the EU and related issues, including: *The Politics of European Union Regional Policy* (UACES/Sheffield Academic Press, 1998); *Politics in the European Union* (co-authored) (Oxford University Press, 1st edn 2001; 2nd edn 2006; 3rd edn 2011; 4th edn 2015); *Multi-Level Governance* (co-edited) (Oxford University Press, 2004); *The Europeanization of British Politics* (co-edited) (Palgrave Macmillan, 2006); *Europeanization and Multilevel Governance* (Rowman and Littlefield, 2008); *Cohesion Policy and Multi-Level Governance in South East Europe* (co-edited) (Routledge, 2011); *Multi-Level Governance* (co-edited) (Edward Elgar, 2015); *Multi-Level Governance and Climate Change* (co-authored) (Rowman and Littlefield, 2015); *The Politics and Policy of Wellbeing* (co-authored) (Edward Elgar, 2015); *The Politics of Wellbeing* (co-edited) (Palgrave Macmillan 2018); and *Evidence, Policy and Wellbeing* (Palgrave Macmillan 2019).

He has published in a range of academic journals, including: the *British Journal of Politics and International Relations*; *Current Politics and Economics of Europe*; *Governance*; *Journal of Common Market Studies*; *Journal of European Public Policy*; *Journal of Public Policy*; *Journal of Southeast European and Black Sea Studies*; *Local Government Studies*; *Political Studies*; *Public Administration*; *Public Policy and Administration*; *Regional and Federal Studies*; *Scandinavian Political Studies*; *Social Indicators Research*; and *West European Politics*. In 2008, he received a University of Sheffield Senate Award for Sustained Excellence in Teaching and Learning and in 2014 he was awarded Fellowship of the Academy of Social Sciences (FAcSS).

Stephen George taught in the Department of Politics at the University of Sheffield for thirty years, the last ten as Professor. During that time, he authored or co-authored four major books on the European Community/EU, two of which—*An Awkward Partner: Britain in the European Union* and *Politics and Policy in the European Union*—went into multiple editions. He also edited books on Europe, and contributed some two dozen chapters to edited books and articles to several academic journals, including *The Annals of the American Academy of Political and Social Science*; *The British Journal of International Studies*; *Contemporary Record*; *Current Politics and Economics of Europe*; *European Access*; *International Affairs*; *Journal of European Integration*; *Journal of European Public Policy*; *Millennium: Journal of International Studies*; *Modern History Review*; *West European Politics*; and *The World Today*. He has given innumerable talks, guest lectures, and conference papers throughout the world, mostly on aspects of the EU. Between 1997 and 2000, he was Chair of the University Association for Contemporary European Studies (UACES). As a teacher he successfully supervised eight Ph.D. students, and devised innovative teaching materials on the EU for undergraduate students, including a simulation exercise in European decision making. Since 2003, he has been Emeritus Professor of Politics, retired from active teaching and administration, but still involved in research and writing.

Charlotte Burns is Professor of Politics at the University of Sheffield. She has taught at the Universities of Aberystwyth, Leeds, and York on EU and European politics and policy, and environmental politics and policy. Before entering academia, she worked in the European Parliament in Brussels for the Chair of the Environment Committee. She has published widely on EU decision making, the powers and the environmental behaviour of the European Parliament, and the impact of the economic crisis upon European environmental policy. She has recently worked on the impact of Brexit upon UK and EU environmental policy. She has published three jointly edited books, a range of book chapters, and articles in journals, including *Environmental Politics*; *Global Environmental Change*; *Government and Opposition*; *Journal of Common Market Studies*; *Journal of European Integration*; *Journal of European Public Policy*; and *Political Studies*.

About the Book

The EU has been the most successful experiment in international integration. However, in the 2010s it has been challenged by a series of crises, notably the eurozone crisis, the refugee crisis, Brexit, and the rise of populism, and Euroscepticism. While the book was in production, the Covid-19 pandemic presented a further challenge for the EU. On the face of it, integration has run into considerable turbulence and there is even a possibility of disintegration, highlighted most clearly by the departure of one of the largest member states, the United Kingdom (UK). However, amidst the turbulence of the 2010s, the EU has also proved remarkably resilient, for example by strengthening eurozone governance and developing a new European Border and Coast Guard. Moreover, the Brexit process brought the other twenty-seven member states closer together, with several Eurosceptic parties in other member states dropping their aspiration to imitate Brexit. The EU is once again in a state of flux, thus making this textbook of continuing salience.

The EU is a subject for analysis from several disciplinary perspectives, most obviously politics, economics, and law. This book is focused on politics, and specifically the EU's location at the intersection of international relations and comparative politics. In order to understand the EU of today we consider it important, first of all, for students to have a strong foundation in theory and analysis (Part One). Nevertheless, there are different approaches used in the teaching of the EU. Some courses are based around integration theory; others regard the EU as a political system to be studied using comparative politics approaches. We provide chapters on both, as well as considering thematic issues such as Europeanization and democratic legitimacy. The crises that have struck the EU have placed it under considerable scrutiny. In line with this, we place particular emphasis on critical approaches in academic literature, for they help address the questions of power, and whose interests the EU serves.

A comprehensive analysis of the EU also needs to be rooted in its history. Part Two therefore charts European integration from 1945 through to the 2010s. The EU's development has not been linear. It has suffered setbacks and advances at different stages in line with changing external and internal circumstances. It is important to have the varied dynamics of the past in mind when considering the present, for it is not new for European integration to experience turbulence.

The EU's institutions are an indispensable component of studying the EU. Their distinctive character as an amalgam of the collective and individual member-state interests places them at the intersection of international and domestic politics. Together with organized interests, they are addressed in Part Three.

Finally, in Part Four we cover the key EU policy areas: internal and external. We consider the range of EU policy responsibilities, the different balances of EU and member-state power across them, and the economic and political purposes of policies, and the policy instruments deployed. These considerations set up chapters covering the internal market, monetary union, agriculture, environment and climate policy, justice and home affairs, trade and aid, foreign and security policy, and enlargement.

This fifth edition of the book was written against the backdrop of the protracted process of the UK leaving the EU. The December 2019 election gave Prime Minister Johnson a clear majority so as to be able to complete the Brexit process at the end of January 2020, albeit with a transition period and the negotiation of a new British relationship with the EU to follow. The complexity of Brexit for British politics—its continued divisiveness and its challenge to the UK's territorial integrity—was not fully anticipated at the time of the June 2016 referendum. Whilst the twenty-seven EU member states were united in facing the challenge of Brexit, they have divisive issues of their own, including in relation to the refugee crisis, further reforms to put eurozone governance on a more stable footing, and the task of transitioning to a zero-carbon economy by 2050. The approaching end of the Merkel era in German politics, the salience of populism in some states, and rule-of-law challenges in central Europe are amongst challenges that the EU will face in the coming period. Together, these factors will intersect to shape the impact of the UK's departure on the EU27.

There will, therefore, be much more for students and instructors to explore in the period ahead.

Given our aspiration to be comprehensive and up to date with this co-authored textbook on the EU, so the authorship team has evolved to meet the challenge. We welcome Charlotte (Charlie) Burns to the team for this edition. Simon, Owen, and Charlotte have taken the lead with this edition, with Ian and Stephen having already invested much in the book, in addition to acting as reviewers of the new material.

New to this Edition

Charlotte Burns joins Simon Bulmer and Owen Parker, Ian Bache, and Stephen George as the team of authors for the fifth edition.

We have refreshed the theory section to take into account new developments such as postfunctionalism, politicization, the salience of Euroscepticism, and the possibility of disintegration in the EU. The history section has been updated to include the main recent developments, notably the eurozone crisis, the refugee crisis, and Brexit. Institutions have been updated to reflect the European Parliament elected in 2019 and the appointment of the Commission under President Ursula von der Leyen. The policy chapters have been fully updated, and in some cases given more fundamental 'refreshes'.

The online resources, which accompany the text, have also been updated with new materials for students and lecturers. Readers can also find in them a full account of Brexit, updated from a supplement that was bundled in print form with later print-runs of the fourth edition.

 Visit the online resources for access to the Brexit Supplement
www.oup.com/uk/bache5e.

Acknowledgements

This is the fifth edition of a textbook that appeared previously in 2001, 2006, 2011, and 2015. In revising it we have been helped enormously by the comments of colleagues and students who used these previous editions or acted as anonymous referees.

We would like to thank Paul Cardwell, Neil Carter, Viviane Gravey, Tammy Hervey, Andrea Lenschow, and Gabriel Siles-Brügge for their help and advice on various points. We also would also like to thank once again Vasilis Leontitsis, who wrote the chapter on environmental policy in the last two editions. This chapter has now been taken 'in house'. We are also grateful for the anonymous reviews by academic colleagues on how to strengthen the book generally, as well as specifically the re-shaped Chapter 18. We have been tremendously encouraged by the positive feedback that we have received from users and reviewers of our previous editions. We hope that it will continue to prove a stimulating textbook for all who use it and will lead to stimulating and critical debates in the classroom.

Finally, we would like to thank all of the editorial staff at Oxford University Press—Katie Staal, Sarah Iles, and Francesca Mitchell—as well as the production team of Elakkia Bharathi, Fiona Barry, Michael Janes, and Nicola Lennon, for their help, advice, and patience.

Simon Bulmer
Owen Parker
Ian Bache
Stephen George
Charlotte Burns
December 2019

Copyright disclaimer

Guided Tour of Textbook Features

We have developed a number of learning tools to help you develop the essential knowledge and skills you need to study EU politics. This guided tour shows you how to get the most out out of your textbook.

Chapter overviews

Chapter overviews set the scene for upcoming themes and issues to be discussed, and indicate the scope of coverage within the chapter.

Chapter 1
Theories of European Integr

Chapter Overview

The dominant approaches to understanding the early phase of European integ international relations (IR). In particular, the study of integration was dominate ing approaches of neofunctionalism and intergovernmentalism. Although neofu neatly fitted events in the 1950s and early 1960s, subsequent events led to d and the rise of intergovernmentalist explanations. While theorizing Europea moved on significantly from these early approaches, much of what followed by this debate or developed as a rejection of it. The debate about whether th ized by intergovernmentalism or supranationalism still informs academic work the late 2000s, postfunctionalism emerged as a new rival theory that helps e political controversy surrounding integration in recent times, particularly durin

Insight boxes

Throughout the book, insight boxes provide you with extra information on particular topics and define and explain key ideas, helping you to build on what you have learned from the main chapter text.

Insight 21.1 Main Reforms to the Common Agricultural Policy

Reform	Year	Driver for change	Main changes
MacSharry reforms	1992	External trade (Uruguay GATT round)	Decrease in price support to bring European products in line with world prices
		Costs	Initial move towards decoupling of production funding: direct support was introduced for inco rather than production
			Land taken out of production
			Retirement scheme to encourage older farmers

End-of-chapter questions

At the end of each chapter, questions allow you to reflect on the subject matter, apply your knowledge, and critically evaluate what you have learned.

QUESTIONS

1. How did federalism and functionalism contrast in their approaches to creating peace in western Europe through integration?
2. How do neofunctionalism and intergovernmentalism differ on their assumptions about the role of the state in international relations?
3. Why is spillover so important to the neofunctionalists' understanding of European integration?
4. Do you agree that LI is now the baseline theory against which to assess other theories?
5. How does postfunctionalism differ from neofunctionalism and LI in its assessment of the dynamics behind integration?

Glossary terms

Key terms appear emboldened in blue in the text and are defined in a glossary at the end of the book, helping you to understand technical terms as you learn, and acting as a useful prompt when it comes to revision.

...periences in this task that Monnet came to appreciate the economic inadequacy of he European nation state in the modern world. He saw the need to create a 'large and namic **common market**', 'a huge continental market on the European scale Monnet 1962: 205). He aimed, though, to create more than just a common market. Monnet was a planner (see Insight 5.4): he showed no great confidence in the ee-market system, which had served France rather badly in the past. He placed hi th in the development of **supranational institutions** as the basis for building a nuine economic community that would adopt common economic policies and tional planning procedures. Coal and steel were only intended as starting points. The n was to extend integration to all aspects of the western European economy—but ch a scheme would have been too ambitious to gain acceptance all at once.

There was also a new factor in the equation, the key factor prompting Monnet's plan e emergence in 1949 of a West German state. For Monnet, the existence of the deral Republic of Germany posed two problems in addition to that of how to create integrated western European economy. The first problem was how to organize anco–German relations in such a way that another war between the two states would come impossible. To a French mind, this meant how to control Germany. The pool g of coal and steel production would provide the basis for economic development as a st step towards a 'federation of Europe'. Stimulating the expansion of those industrie

Key points

Each chapter concludes with a set of key points that reinforce your understanding and act as a useful revision tool.

KEY POINTS

History

- When the EEC was set up in the 1950s, world economic relations were governed by the 1944 Bretton Woods agreements. Trade relations were governed by the GATT.
- A key principle of the GATT was MFN: members had to offer to all other member states terms of trade as favourable as the best terms they offered to any other state. The EEC gained exemption from MFN for the internal common market and for its relations with former colonies of EEC members.
- Relations with the former colonies initially continued their dependence on France in particular. When Britain joined the EEC, the Lomé Convention provided the ACP states with a fairer deal.
- Following the collapse of communism in eastern Europe, the EU concluded special trade and aid agreements with the CEECs in an attempt to ensure the stability of its near neighbours. For the same reason, special agreements were reached with the states of the southern Mediterranean.

External Trade Policy

- Trade negotiations are conducted by the Commission on behalf of the EU as a whole, working to a mandate agreed by the Council of Ministers and supervised by a committee of national representatives.
- Until the Lisbon Treaty came into force, trade in services and intellectual products were not automatically covered by this arrangement: the governments of the member states had to agree ahead of each round of negotiations to allow the Commission authority in these areas.
- Trade policy traditionally covered trade in goods, but has expanded to cover trade in services and 'behind-the-border' areas pertaining to regulations and intellectual property. The competence of the EU has expanded accordingly.
- Under the terms of the Lisbon Treaty, trade in services and intellectual products are an EU competence, but unanimity remains the voting rule where sensitive domestic issues are concerned.
- The Commission has the power to impose duties and other restrictions on imports of goods to the EU where dumping or unfair subsidies are suspected.
- Member states are often divided over trade issues both by conflicting economic interests and by their general attitude to free trade.
- Since the introduction of the WTO, the EU has been involved in a series of trade disputes, mainly with the United States, which took a protectionist turn with the Trump presidency.

Development and Trade

Further reading

Annotated recommendations for further reading at the end of each chapter identify the key literature in the field, helping you to develop your interest in particular topics.

FURTHER READING

C. Roederer-Rynning provides an excellent review of the literature and overview of the ev of the CAP in 'The Common Agricultural Policy: A Case of Embedded Liberalism', *Oxford R Encyclopaedia Politics* (2019). DOI: 10.1093/acrefore/9780190228637.013.1032. **C. Da and P. Feindt's** special issue 'Post-Exceptionalism in Public Policy: Transforming Fo Agricultural Policy', *Journal of European Public Policy* 24 (2017), provides a useful colle articles reviewing whether and how agricultural policy has changed in recent years. On g the CAP, **G. Alons** provides a detailed account of the limits of greening reform in 2 'Environmental Policy Integration in the EU's Common Agricultural Policy: Green Greenwashing?', *Journal of European Public Policy*, 24 (2017): 1604–22. A comprehensive sis of the key reforms pre-2013, drawing on the evidence of some of those involved in the decisions (including Ray MacSharry and Franz Fischler) is presented in **A. Cunha**

Guided Tour of the Online Resources

Bulmer, George, Bache, Parker, Burns, Politics in the European Union 5e

Description

Accessible and engaging, this is a complete guide to the past, present, and future of the European Union. An expert author team examine in detail the theory and history behind the EU, before moving on to explore the institutions and policies at work, giving readers a valuable insight to this complicated political body.

⬇ CC v1.0

Resources for Politics in the European Union 5e

Politics in the European Union 5e Instructor Resources ⭐

Bulmer, George, Bache, Parker, Burns

Lecturer resources to accompany *Politics in the European Union*, 5th edition

www.oup.com/uk/bache5e

The online resources that accompany this book provide students and instructors with ready-to-use learning and teaching materials. These resources are free of charge and have been created to take student learning further.

For students

Interactive map of Europe

An interactive map provides a wealth of social and political facts about each EU member state. Simply click on the state you are interested in and the information appears in a separate window.

Interactive timeline

Use the interactive timeline to improve your knowledge of the history of European integration. Key events are summarized when you click on each date.

Multiple-choice questions

A bank of self-marking multiple-choice questions has been provided for each chapter of the text to reinforce your understanding, and act as an aid to revision.

Flashcard glossary

A series of interactive flashcards containing key terms allows you to test your knowledge of the terminology of EU politics.

Web links

A selection of annotated web links, which accompanies each chapter, will point you in the direction of important treaties, working papers, articles, and other relevant sources of information on EU politics.

Additionally, you can access a supplement on Brexit via the online resources.

For registered adopters of the book

PowerPoint slides

PowerPoint slides complement each chapter of the book and are a useful resource for preparing lectures and handouts.

Essay and seminar questions

A range of essay and seminar questions has been devised to be used in assessment, or to stimulate class debate.

Boxes, tables, and figures from the text

Boxes, tables, and figures from the text have been provided in high-resolution format for downloading into presentation software or for use in assignments and exam material.

Late News Page

The Covid-19 Pandemic and the EU

At the time of writing, in April 2020, it was becoming increasingly clear that the ongoing Covid-19 pandemic constituted a major crisis for the EU. Rapidly rising death tolls, at first in Italy and Spain, made for grim reading. Government lockdowns aimed at limiting the spread of the virus were having an enormous economic impact throughout the EU (and far beyond). And the social and political consequences were already starting to be felt.

Early EU Responses

On 26 March 2020, the new Commission President, Ursula von der Leyen, lamented that, 'when Europe really needed an "all-for-one" spirit, too many initially refused to share their umbrella'. Indeed, at the end of February and in early March, as the situation quickly deteriorated in Italy, member state responses consisted mainly of closing borders and seeking to manage the crisis at the national level. The Schengen free travel area covering much of continental Europe (Chapter 23, Insight 23.2, 'The Schengen Area') was effectively suspended.

That said, by mid-March the EU had begun to play a role; it led joint efforts to procure medical equipment and it established 'green lanes', which facilitated the free movement of goods across borders, even as Schengen was suspended. On the economy, the EU established an investment fund worth €37 billion to mitigate the impact of the crisis. It effectively suspended rules limiting 'state aid' (public support for private enterprise), which in normal times are considered to be a 'non-tariff barrier' that impedes fair competition in the single market (see Chapter 19). And it removed the strict limits on public spending linked to the economic governance regime's Stability and Growth Pact (SPG) (see Chapter 20).

Divided on the Economy

Even as these initiatives were unveiled, it was already evident that they would not be enough to deal with the socio-economic impacts of the crisis. On the economy, many of the debates that had arisen during the eurozone crisis (see Chapters 11 and 20) resurfaced. This included a discussion around the creation of a common debt instrument, so-called 'coronabonds' (comparable to 'eurobonds'—see Chapter 11, 'The Unfolding Eurozone Crisis' and Chapter 20, 'The Eurozone Crisis'). The coalition in favour of such a step—which included the European Central Bank (ECB) and 'debtor' states such as Spain, Italy, and France—was larger than it had been during the eurozone crisis. But Germany's initial reaction was one of opposition, and it was supported by other traditional 'creditor' states, including the Netherlands and Austria.

Germany was willing to contemplate deploying the firepower of the European Stability Mechanism (ESM) (see Chapter 20, 'Long-Term Reforms') to support member states through the crisis. However, debtor–creditor divisions also existed on the timing of such support and on the question of whether the recipients of funds would be subject to the same tough conditionality that had long been applied to so-called 'memorandum' states (most notably, Greece) during the eurozone crisis (see Chapter 20, 'The Eurozone Crisis').

As the member states debated these issues, the ECB stepped in, as it had done during the eurozone crisis. In mid-March, it announced a €750 billion government bond-buying scheme (the 'Pandemic Emergency Purchase Programme', PEPP). This would effectively permit the eurozone states to borrow significant sums in order to fund their crisis responses. There was also some discussion of the ECB finally deploying 'outright monetary transactions' (OMTs) (announced by Draghi during the eurozone crisis, but never put into effect—see Chapter 20, 'The Eurozone Crisis'), which would allow for more directly targeted and far more extensive purchases of particular government bonds. However, this would require states to initially request support from the ESM, something that Italy and Spain, for instance, were not willing to accept with the aforementioned conditionality attached.

The Politics of Covid-19

The political implications of the crisis were still far from clear. Divisions on economic governance reforms led not only to private disagreement, but also to some very public and ill-tempered exchanges between ostensibly pro-EU governments in debtor and creditor states. Unveiling PEPP, the new ECB President Christine Lagarde, stated that, 'there are no limits to our commitment to the euro', echoing her predecessor Mario Draghi's infamous 2012 'whatever it takes' intervention during the eurozone crisis (see Chapter 20, 'Crisis Management'). But whether the ECB could continue to make good on that commitment in the absence of greater member state solidarity was certainly being questioned by some analysts at the time of writing. Any resolution to the divisions threatened to play into the hands of populists and Eurosceptics on one side, and the debtor–creditor divide on the other (see Chapter 3, 'Euroscepticism' and Chapter 11, 'The Populist Challenge').

Where populists were already in power, they used the crisis as a pretext to substantially increase their executive authority. This was most notable in Hungary, where, in mid-March 2020, parliament gave an increasingly autocratic Viktor Orban the powers to effectively rule by decree and (further) suppress opposition to the free press (see Chapter 11, 'The Populist Challenge'). In a thinly veiled critique of Hungary, Commission President von der Leyen said at the end of March that, 'it is of utmost importance that emergency measures are not at the expense of our fundamental principles and values as set out in the treaties'.

Early on in the crisis, some populists and nationalists tried to exploit the pandemic to justify the tough immigration policies that they had long supported. This happened against the backdrop of Turkey's decision in late February to open its borders for refugees to travel to Greece (in apparent contravention of the terms of the EU–Turkey deal) (see Chapter 11, 'The Refugee Crisis' and Chapter 23, 'The Refugee Crisis').

It was too early to judge whether these anti-migrant arguments would gain political traction with the public or, indeed, whether a broader populist and Eurosceptic politics would become more or less attractive as a consequence of the crisis. Support for mainstream parties was strong in March, but the crisis could certainly provide opportunities for populists. Whatever the direction of travel, the politics of the crisis would clearly have important implications for the capacity of the EU to respond, just as the responses of the EU would impact on the unfolding politics.

What Will Covid-19 Mean for the EU?

Covid-19 derailed normal and ongoing EU business. Discussions on the post-Brexit EU–UK relationship slowed and the prospect of an extension to Britain's transition period beyond the end of 2020 was seriously mooted (see the online Brexit Supplement). Discussions on the multi-annual financial framework for the period 2021–27 were also stalled as the financial implications of the crisis were considered. And the von der Leyen Commission's plans for environmental considerations to underpin its economic programme—contained in the Green Deal for Europe (see Chapter 22, Insight 22.1, 'The European Green Deal')—were called into doubt.

The pandemic brought into sharp focus the deeper existential questions that the EU was still confronting in the aftermath of other recent crises (see Chapter 11, 'Conclusion'). At the time of writing, it was impossible to predict with any certainty whether the responses to Covid-19 would mean further and much deeper integration or whether they would precipitate some kind of disintegration of the European project. As with previous crises, in the end, we may see an element of both. It was already clear, however, that the Covid-19 crisis would be uniquely grave and at once intimately connected with the various other crises that the EU had confronted over the previous decade.

 Visit the online resources for access to the Brexit Supplement
www.oup.com/uk/bache5e.

Part One
Theory

This part of the book consists of four chapters. Its purpose is twofold: first, to review the main theories used in the study of the European Union (EU); and second, to identify themes that will inform our analysis of subsequent chapters. We do not see this exercise as being an optional extra for a textbook: it is fundamental to the academic study of the EU.

Our understanding of the world is guided by our particular conceptual lenses or theoretical frameworks, whether we are aware of them or not. The theoretical frameworks we adopt determine the questions we ask, and so the answers that we find. As Rosamond (2013: 86) suggests: '. . . being conscious about the theoretical propositions chosen by authors is vital because alternative "readings" of the EU and European integration follow from alternative theoretical premises'.

There has been no shortage of theoretical models and frameworks applied to the study of EU politics and we provide an overview of what to us appear to be the most important. One way of considering the wide variety of approaches considered in these chapters is in terms of different phases of theorizing and the central questions that were asked during these phases. Table I.1 summarizes these phases and should serve as a useful reference point for students throughout their engagement with these theory chapters and other chapters. It should be noted that these phases and the questions posed are not mutually exclusive, but overlapping in a variety of ways. The table makes clear the wide variety of approaches that have sought to engage with the EU (and its antecedents) as an object of study.

The first phase of study, during the early stages of co-operation between western European states, was dominated by approaches from the study of international relations (IR). From the end of the First World War, academics had grappled with the question of how to achieve peace in war-torn Europe, and such issues became even more acute following the Second World War. In particular, federalist and functionalist theories identified the ways in which nationalism in Europe might be overcome and peace achieved. Federalists in particular were politically active in *promoting peace* via a federal Europe. As the EU's antecedent organizations evolved, albeit not along strictly federalist lines, IR scholars became increasingly interested in *explaining integration* as a potentially generalizable phenomenon. In the 1960s, neofunctionalists and intergovernmentalists placed the accent on, respectively, non-state and state actors in driving processes of integration. The question of how integration occurred and its key drivers has remained central for scholars of the EU and many have followed in the footsteps of these early or classical theories of integration. Liberal intergovernmentalism (LI), for instance, offered a refined version of early intergovernmentalism in the 1990s, and neofunctionalism was also subject to revision. From the late 2000s a further theory of explaining integration gained a foothold: postfunctionalism. It draws on the growing politicization of European integration that was expressed initially in public opposition to ratifying the Maastricht Treaty in 1992 but became an established pattern in the 2010s, such as in popular responses to the eurozone crisis, the refugee crisis, and the 2016 vote by the British people to leave the EU (Brexit). These theoretical approaches are considered in Chapter 1, 'Theories of European Integration'.

As the EU became more established and institutionalized, IR approaches were increasingly accompanied by insights from the study of domestic and comparative politics which asked, in particular, *'How does the EU and its governance work?'* The most straightforward way of understanding this theoretical shift is to see it as a move away from treating the EU as an international organization similar to others (such as the North Atlantic Treaty Organization—NATO) to seeing it as something distinctive, with some features more akin to those of national political systems. While there were important precursors to such work as early as the 1970s, it was in the 1990s that those with backgrounds in the study of domestic and comparative politics really became dominant in the study of the EU. Such work analysed the institutions and governance of the EU,

Table I.1 Phases in Theorizing and Key Questions

Phase	When	Main questions	Main theories	Chapter
Promoting peace through integration	1920s onwards	How can peace be achieved in Europe (and beyond)? How can nationalism be overcome?	Federalism Functionalism	1
Explaining integration	1950s onwards	How can integration processes be explained? What are the drivers of European integration?	Neofunctionalism (late 1950s) Intergovernmentalism (1960s) Liberal intergovernmentalism (1990s) Postfunctionalism (from late 2000s)	1
Analysing the EU as political system	1990s onwards	How does the EU and its governance work? How do its institutions work? What kind of political system is it? How can political processes be described?	New institutionalism Policy networks Governance approaches Multi-level governance EU governance approaches Differentiated integration	2
Analysing consequences of EU	1990s onwards	What is the impact of the EU on member states? What are the consequences of the EU for democracy and legitimacy? Could increasing controversy relating to the EU lead to its break-up?	Europeanization Politicization Euroscepticism Normative/democratic theories Disintegration literature	3
Critiquing EU and/or 'mainstream' approaches to its study	Late 1990s onwards	Which ideas/ideologies predominate in the EU? How and why? Where does power lie within the EU? In whose interest does the EU act and with what political and social consequences?	Social constructivism Critical integration theory Critical political economy Critical social theory Gender approaches Post-structural approaches	4

Adapted from Diez and Wiener (2004: 7).

adopting a variety of approaches, such as new institutionalism and policy networks, that had been applied to domestic politics. Theories based primarily on domestic and comparative politics approaches are set out in Chapter 2, 'Theories of EU Governance'.

Also in the 1990s, scholars from similar backgrounds began to consider *the consequences of the EU* on its member states. They did so by asking how it had impacted upon or 'Europeanized' its member states' domestic polities in various domains. Scholars also considered age-old questions about legitimacy and democracy in the context of the new governing realities precipitated by the developing EU. In Chapter 3, 'Theorizing Consequences', we consider the contribution of the *Europeanization* literature and approaches to understanding the challenges posed by the EU for *democracy*. Yet we also look at emerging literatures reflecting growing resistance to integration, namely literatures on *politicization* and *Euroscepticism*. Finally, in this chapter we cover analyses that investigate whether the EU is beginning to experience *disintegration*, which is a possible interpretation of EU politics in the 2010s.

These approaches provide important contributions to the study of the EU, but they have been joined by a wide range of more explicitly critical perspectives that question many of the assumptions on which these approaches are based. Such approaches are disparate, but all tend to take a more critical position, questioning the assumptions upon which other theories are largely based (see Chapter 4, 'Critical Perspectives' and Table 4.1, 'Mapping Approaches on a Positivist/ Post-Positivist Continuum'). The majority of these approaches have also been critical of various aspects of the EU status quo, although that is not to say that they are anti-EU per se. They ask such questions as: '*Which ideas or ideologies* have prevailed in EU governance?' and '*Which actors have been most powerful* and *whose interests* has integration served, and whose has it undermined?' Through considering these questions we also seek to engage theorizing the EU with contemporary debates concerning 'biases in the academic curriculum'. In Chapter 4, we consider several approaches that offer a flavour of this emerging critical work: social constructivism, critical political economy, critical integration theory, critical social theory, critical feminism, and post-structuralism.

In later parts of the book we refer back to these theory chapters where relevant, and we strongly encourage students to consider the connections between theory and the material discussed in other parts of the book.

Chapter 1

Theories of European Integration

Chapter Overview

The dominant approaches to understanding the early phase of European integration came from international relations (IR). In particular, the study of integration was dominated by the competing approaches of neofunctionalism and intergovernmentalism. Although neofunctionalist theory neatly fitted events in the 1950s and early 1960s, subsequent events led to declining relevance and the rise of intergovernmentalist explanations. While theorizing European integration has moved on significantly from these early approaches, much of what followed was either framed by this debate or developed as a rejection of it. The debate about whether the EU is characterized by intergovernmentalism or supranationalism still informs academic work on the subject. In the late 2000s, postfunctionalism emerged as a new rival theory that helps explain the greater political controversy surrounding integration in recent times, particularly during the 2010s.

European Integration and the First Attempts to Theorize It

The signing of the Treaty of Paris in April 1951 by the governments of Belgium, France, Germany, Italy, Luxembourg, and the Netherlands (see Chapter 5, 'The Schuman Plan for Coal and Steel') began the process commonly referred to as European integration (see Insight 1.1). This process meant that the economies of participating states became increasingly managed in common. Decisions previously taken by national governments alone were taken together with other governments, and in specially created European institutions. Governments relinquished the sole right to make legislation (national sovereignty) over a range of matters in favour of joint decision making with other governments (pooled sovereignty). Other tasks were delegated to European institutions.

It was something of a departure from mainstream IR theory when governments in the resultant European Coal and Steel Community (ECSC) began to surrender their national sovereignty in these policy areas. For the first half of the twentieth century, the nation state seemed assured of its place as the most important unit of political life in the western world, especially in Europe. Thus, the process of European integration constituted a major challenge to existing IR theories and generated an academic debate about the role of the state in the process. The two competing theories that emerged

Insight 1.1 European Integration

European integration has a number of aspects, but the main focus of Chapter 1 is on *political* integration. Ernst Haas (1968: 16) provided a definition of European political integration as a *process*, whereby:

> political actors in several distinct national settings are persuaded to shift their loyalties, expectations and political activities toward a new center, whose institutions possess or demand jurisdiction over the pre-existing national states. The end result of a process of political integration is a new political community, superimposed over the pre-existing ones.

Lindberg (1963: 149) provided a comparable definition of political integration as a process, referring to the transfer of power to 'new central organs':

> political integration is (1) the process whereby nations forego the desire and ability to conduct foreign and key domestic policies independently of each other, seeking instead to make *joint decisions* or to *delegate* the decision making process to new central organs; and (2) the process whereby political actors in several distinct national settings are persuaded to shift their expectations and political activities to a new center.

The first part of Lindberg's definition refers to two 'intimately related' modes of decision making: sharing and delegating. The second part of the definition refers to 'the patterns of behaviour shown by high policy makers, civil servants, parliamentarians, interest group leaders and other elites' (Lindberg 1963: 149), who respond to the new reality of a shift in political authority to the centre by re-orientating their political activities to the European level.

from IR to dominate the debate over early developments in European integration were neofunctionalism (Haas 1958; Lindberg 1963) and intergovernmentalism (Hoffmann 1964, 1966).

Before discussing these two main positions in the debate, it is necessary to consider the intellectual context from which the idea of European integration emerged. Below in 'The Intellectual Background' we look first at the functionalist ideas of David Mitrany on how to avoid war between nations, then at the ideas of the European federalists, and finally at the 'federal-functionalism' of Jean Monnet, arguably the main architect of early integration. We then turn in 'Theories of European Integration' to look first at neofunctionalism and then at intergovernmentalism and a later variant, liberal intergovernmentalism (LI). Finally, we focus on postfunctionalism, a more recent attempt at theorizing European integration that emphasizes integration's conditionality on consent from the wider public.

The Intellectual Background

To understand the ideas that fed into the first attempts to theorize European integration, it is useful to consider some important theoretical predecessors, which were prominent in the period after the Second World War. Particularly important among these were functionalism and federalism. While these theories differed in important respects, both were geared towards ending war and achieving peace in Europe (see Table I.1). As described in this section, while functionalists such as David Mitrany emphasized primarily technical solutions, federalists such as Altiero Spinelli saw the solutions as primarily political in nature. The pragmatic and political ideas of the functionalists and the federalists respectively were brought together in the proposals for integration that were put forward by one of the founding figures, Jean Monnet. His approach has been termed 'functional-federalism', reflecting the influence of two sets of ideas.

Mitrany and Functionalism

David Mitrany (1888–1974) was born in Romania, but spent most of his adult life in Britain and the United States. He was not a theorist of European integration. His concern was with building *A Working Peace System*, the title of his Fabian pamphlet (Mitrany 1966; first published 1943). For Mitrany, the root cause of war was nationalism. The failure of the League of Nations (established after the First World War) to prevent aggression prompted debate about a new type of international system even before the outbreak of the Second World War. Mitrany's response was that the League had not gone far enough and the same mistake should not be repeated: henceforth, nations should be tied more closely together.

Mitrany proposed the creation of a whole series of separate international functional agencies, each having authority over one specific area of human life. His scheme was to take individual technical tasks out of the control of governments and to hand them over to these functional agencies. He believed that governments would be prepared to surrender control because they would not feel threatened by the loss of sovereignty over, say, healthcare or the co-ordination of railway timetables, and they would be able to appreciate the advantages of such tasks being performed at the regional or world level. As more and more areas of control were surrendered, states would become less capable of independent action. One day, the national governments would discover that they were enmeshed in a 'spreading web of international activities and agencies' (Mitrany 1966 [1943]: 35).

Mitrany did not agree with the idea of federation as the means of tying states together. He opposed the idea of a single world government because he believed that it would pose a threat to individual freedom. He also opposed the creation of regional federations, believing that this would simply reproduce national rivalries on a larger scale. Any political reorganization into separate units must sooner or later produce the same effects. His proposal of creating functional agencies sought to have the opposite effect, of subduing political division.

These international agencies would operate at different levels depending on the function that they were performing. Mitrany gave the example of systems of communication. Railways would be organized on a continental basis; shipping would be organized on an intercontinental basis; aviation would be organized on a universal basis. Not only would the dependence of states on these agencies for their day-to-day functioning make it difficult for governments to break with them, but the experience of the operation of the agencies would also socialize politicians, civil servants, and the general public into adopting less nationalistic attitudes and outlook.

Spinelli and Federalism

A completely different approach to guaranteeing peace was devised during the Second World War in the ranks of the various Resistance movements. It was a specifically European movement, and whereas Mitrany aimed explicitly to depoliticize the process of the transfer of power away from national governments, federalists sought a clear transfer of political authority.

The European Union of Federalists (EUF) was formed in December 1946 from the war-time Resistance movements. It was particularly strong in Italy, where the leading figure was Altiero Spinelli. Federalism appealed to the Resistance groups because it proposed superseding nationalism. It is important to bear in mind that whereas in Britain the Second World War was a nationalist war (in the former Soviet Union, it was 'the great patriotic war'), in countries such as France and Italy it was an ideological war. Resistance fighters drawn from communist, socialist, and Christian democratic groups were in many cases fighting their own countrymen—Vichy supporters in France, Italian Fascists in Italy.

While being held as political prisoners of the Fascists on the island of Ventotene, Spinelli and Ernesto Rossi (1897–1967) produced the Ventotene Manifesto (1941), calling for a 'European Federation'. It argued that, left alone, the classes 'most privileged under old national systems' would seek to reconstruct the order of nation states at the end of the war. While these states might appear democratic, it would only be a matter of time before power returned to the hands of the privileged classes. This would prompt the return of national jealousies and, ultimately, to renewed war between states. To prevent this development, the Manifesto called for the abolition of the division of Europe into national, sovereign states. It urged action to bring together the separate national Resistance movements across Europe to push for the creation of a federal European state.

The EUF adopted the Ventotene Manifesto, and began agitating for an international conference to be called that would draw up a federal constitution for Europe. The strategy of the EUF was to exploit the disruption caused by the war to existing political structures in order to make a new start on a radically different basis from the Europe of nation states that was seen as the root of two world wars starting on the European continent. They aimed for a complete break from the old order of nation states, and to create a federal constitution for Europe. Their Congress took time to organize, though. It eventually took place in The Hague in May 1948 (see Chapter 5, 'The End of the War, Federalism, and the Hague Congress'). By that time, however, the national political systems had been re-established, and what emerged from the Congress was an intergovernmental organization, the Council of Europe, not the new federal constitutional order for which the federalists had hoped. Many federalists then turned to the gradualist approach that was successfully embodied in the ECSC (see Chapter 5, 'The Schuman Plan for Coal and Steel').

We have focused here on federalism as a mobilizing force behind European integration. However, analysis of EU governance through federal theory is a related contribution (see Kelemen 2019) that we shall return to in Chapter 2 (see Chapter 2, 'Multi-Level Governance').

Monnet and Functional-Federalism

The plan for the ECSC was known as the Schuman Plan (Chapter 5, 'The Schuman Plan for Coal and Steel') because it was made public by the French Foreign Minister Robert Schuman, but it is generally accepted that it was drawn up within the French Economic Planning Commission (*Commissariat du Plan*), which was headed by the technocrat Jean Monnet. It was the task of the Planning Commission to guide the post-war reconstruction and modernization of the French economy, and it was through his experiences in this task that Monnet came to appreciate the economic inadequacy of the European nation state in the modern world. He saw the need to create a 'large and dynamic **common market**', 'a huge continental market on the European scale' (Monnet 1962: 205). He aimed, though, to create more than just a common market.

Monnet was a planner (see Insight 5.4): he showed no great confidence in the free-market system, which had served France rather badly in the past. He placed his faith in the development of **supranational institutions** as the basis for building a genuine economic community that would adopt common economic policies and rational planning procedures. Coal and steel were only intended as starting points. The aim was to extend integration to all aspects of the western European economy—but such a scheme would have been too ambitious to gain acceptance all at once.

There was also a new factor in the equation, the key factor prompting Monnet's plan: the emergence in 1949 of a West German state. For Monnet, the existence of the Federal Republic of Germany posed two problems in addition to that of how to create an integrated western European economy. The first problem was how to organize Franco–German relations in such a way that another war between the two states would become impossible. To a French mind, this meant how to control Germany. The pooling of coal and steel production would provide the basis for economic development as a first step towards a 'federation of Europe'. Stimulating the expansion of those industries for peaceful purposes would provide an economic alternative to producing war materials for those regions of Europe that had been largely dependent on providing military material. The second problem facing Monnet was the very practical one of how to ensure adequate supplies of coking coal from the Ruhr for the French steel industry. The idea of pooling Franco–German supplies of coal and steel would tie the two states into a mutual economic dependency, in addition to taking out of the immediate control of the national governments the most basic raw materials for waging another war.

Mitrany (1966) described Monnet's strategy as 'federal-functionalism'. It is not clear, though, how far Monnet was a federalist at all. He might be seen as a supreme pragmatist who proposed the ECSC as a solution to the very practical problems described above. To solve these problems, Monnet adopted a solution similar to that of Mitrany: remove control of the strategically crucial industries—coal and steel—from the governments and put it in the hands of a free-standing agency. This was the High Authority of the ECSC, and in Monnet's original plan it was the only institution proposed. The development of other supranational institutions came from other pressures (see Chapter 7). The High Authority was the prototype for the later Commission of the European Economic Community (EEC), which became central to the neofunctionalist theory of European integration.

Theories of European Integration

Monnet and the EUF were practitioners of politics seeking peace in the post-war context. The challenge for IR theorists working on European integration in the 1950s and 1960s was different: how might it be explained and what were its key drivers (see Table I.1)? In many ways these theorists were responding to realism, the dominant approach to explaining IR in the 1950s. It assumed that sovereign states formed the fundamental units of analysis for understanding IR. The appearance of the ECSC and later the European Community (EC) departed from the principles of realism and prompted the emergence of alternative analyses. Neofunctionalism was the name given to the first attempt to understand European integration. Its implied critique of realism led to a counter-theory from within a broadly state-centred perspective, which became known as intergovernmentalism. The debate between these two broad positions has evolved over time, but the central issues of dispute remain much the same today as they were in the 1950s.

Neofunctionalism

Starting with the analysis of the ECSC by Ernst Haas (1958), a body of theorizing about European integration known as neofunctionalism was built up in the writings of a group of US academics (see Insight 1.1). These theorists drew on the work of Mitrany and Monnet in particular. In addition to Haas, the main figures in this school of analysis were Leon Lindberg (1963, 1966), and Philippe Schmitter (1970).

In the first period of European integration, neofunctionalism appeared to be winning the theoretical debate. Neofunctionalism sought to explain 'how and why they (states) voluntarily mingle, merge and mix with their neighbours so as to lose the factual attributes of sovereignty while acquiring new techniques for resolving conflict between themselves' (Haas 1970: 610). There were four key parts to the neofunctionalist argument, as follows:

1. The concept of the 'state' is more complex than realists suggested.
2. The activities of interest groups and bureaucratic actors are not confined to the domestic political arena.
3. Non-state actors are important in international politics.
4. European integration is advanced through 'spillover' pressures.

Neofunctionalism was a **pluralist** theory of international politics. In contrast to the more traditional realist theories, it did not assume that a state was a single unified actor; nor did it assume that states were the only actors on the international stage. In the concepts that it used, it anticipated later writings on global interdependence (Keohane and Nye 1977). Neofunctionalists argued that the international activities of states were the outcome of a pluralistic political process in which government decisions were influenced by pressures from various interest groups and bureaucratic actors. In essence, neofunctionalists were drawing on patterns of domestic politics within the United States to understand and seek to predict European integration.

Using the concepts that were later called 'transnationalism' and 'transgovernmentalism' (Keohane and Nye 1977: 129–30), neofunctionalists expected nationally based interest groups to make contact with similar groups in other countries (transnationalism), and government departments to forge links with their counterparts in other states, unsupervised by their respective foreign offices (transgovernmentalism). A particular form of transnationalism that was on the rise was the emergence of multinational corporations—often US ones, such as Ford. They helped neofunctionalists illustrate their argument that non-state actors are important in international politics.

However, the European Commission was the most important non-state international actor for neofunctionalists. It was believed to be in a unique position to manipulate both domestic and international pressures on national governments to advance the process of European integration, even where governments might be reluctant. This contrasted with realist explanations of IR, which focused exclusively on the international role of states.

At the heart of neofunctionalism was the concept of spillover because it sought to explain the dynamics of integration: how, once national governments took the initial steps towards integration, the process took on a life of its own and swept governments along further than they anticipated going. As Lindberg (1963: 10) put it:

> In its most general formulation, 'spillover' refers to a situation in which a given action, related to a specific goal, creates a situation in which the original goal can be assured only by taking further actions, which in turn create a further condition and a need for more action, and so forth.

Two types of spillover were important to early neofunctionalist writers: functional and political. The notion of 'cultivated spillover' was added by later theorists to explain the part played by the Commission in fostering integration (Tranholm-Mikkelsen 1991) and the concept of 'exogenous spillover' was added subsequently to explain enlargement (Niemann 2006).

Functional spillover argued that modern industrial economies were made up of interconnected parts. As such, it was not possible to isolate one sector from others. Following this understanding, neofunctionalists argued that, if member states integrated one functional sector of their economies, the interconnectedness between this sector and others would lead to a 'spillover' into other sectors. Technical pressures would prompt integration in those related sectors, and the integration of one sector would only work if other functionally related sectors were also integrated. For example, if a joint attempt were made to increase coal production across member states, it would prove necessary to bring other forms of energy into the scheme. Otherwise, a switch by one member state away from coal towards a reliance on oil or nuclear fuels would throw out all of the calculations for coal production. In addition, any effective planning of the total energy supply would involve gathering data about future total demand, implying the development of overall plans for industrial output across member states.

To this technical logic of functional spillover, the neofunctionalists added the idea of political spillover, and set perhaps more store by this than by functional spillover in explaining the process of integration. Political spillover involved the build-up of political pressures in favour of further integration within the states involved. Once one

11

sector of the economy was integrated, the interest groups operating in that sector would have to exert pressure at the supranational level, on the organization charged with running their sector. So the creation of the ECSC would lead to the representatives of the coal and steel industries in all of the member states switching at least a part of their political lobbying from national governments to the new supranational agency, the High Authority. Relevant trade unions and consumer groups would follow suit.

It was argued that, once these interest groups had switched the focus of their activity to the European level, they would rapidly come to appreciate the benefits available to them as a result of the integration of their sector. Further, they would also come to understand the barriers that prevented these benefits from being fully realized. As the main barrier would be that integration in one sector could not be effective without the integration of other sectors, these interest groups would become advocates of further integration and would lobby their governments to this end. At the same time, they would form a barrier themselves against governments retreating from the level of integration that had already been achieved. This was important because such a retreat would be the one alternative way in which pressures caused by functional spillover could be resolved. In addition, governments would come under pressure from other interest groups who would see the advantages accruing to their counterparts in the integrated sector and realize that they could profit similarly if their sectors of the economy were also integrated. For Haas, the driving force of political integration was the calculated self-interest of political elites:

> The 'good Europeans' are not the main creators of the regional community that is growing up; the process of community formation is dominated by nationally constituted groups with specific interests and aims, willing and able to adjust their aspirations by turning to supranational means when this course appears profitable.
>
> (Haas 1958: xiv)

Neofunctionalists looked for spillover pressures to be encouraged and manipulated by the Commission. It was expected both to foster the emergence of EC-wide pressure groups and to cultivate contacts behind the scenes with national interest groups and with bureaucrats in the civil services of the member states, who were another group of potential allies against national governments (Tranholm-Mikkelsen 1991). This was the third type of spillover, which was known as cultivated spillover because it involved the Commission cultivating the contacts and the pressure on governments.

While Haas (1958) mentioned the concept of 'geographical spillover', in particular to draw attention to the external effects of integration on Britain, the main contributions to neofunctionalism paid little attention to enlargement—understandably, given that they were written before the first enlargement in 1973 (see Chapter 7, 'The Hague Summit'). More recently, Niemann (2006) has argued that neofunctionalism does provide tools for understanding this process: integration leads to some contradictions and demands that cannot be satisfactorily resolved by increasing the intensity or policy scope of integration, but instead requires territorial expansion (see also Niemann and Schmitter 2009: 62).

In the 1950s, neofunctionalist theory neatly fitted events, particularly in explaining the transition from the ECSC to the EC (detailed in Chapter 6). Events in the 1960s were less supportive (see Chapter 7). Neofunctionalist theory's value delined sharply with the use of the veto by de Gaulle, leading to the 'empty chair' crisis of 1965–66 (see Chapter 7, 'The 1965 Crisis'). National governments had power and were clearly prepared to use it to determine the nature and pace of integration.

> By 1967 Haas was already attempting to cope with the possibility that De Gaulle had 'killed the Common Market' by revising his theory to account for the prospect of 'disintegration', and by 1975 he was announcing the 'obsolescence of regional integration theory'.
>
> (Caporaso and Keeler 1995: 36–7)

Neofunctionalism Revised

Although its applicability was severely weakened by politics in the 1960s and the declaration by Haas of its obsolescence, neofunctionalism did not disappear. Philippe Schmitter, a former student of Haas 'refused to accept his mentor's declaration of "obsolescence"' (Niemann et al. 2019: 51). In particular, he rejected the automaticity of spillover and instead identified other responses to integration, such as 'spill-around' (where integration entails power being delegated to strictly intergovernmental institutions rather than the Commission) or 'spillback', where the integration process is reversed (Schmitter 1970).

The relaunch of integration from the mid-1980s, with the development of the single market and then moves towards monetary union (see Chapters 8 and 9), led to a revival in neofunctionalist thinking (for instance, Tranholm-Mikkelsen 1991). In the mid-1990s, Stone Sweet and Sandholtz (1997) proposed a theory that drew on neofunctionalism, known as supranational governance. It sought to cut through the dichotomy between neofunctionalism and intergovernmentalism. It drew on elements of neofunctionalism, namely its 'understanding of the development of transnational society, the role of supranational organizations with meaningful autonomous capacity to pursue integrative agendas, and the focus on European rule-making to resolve international policy externalities' (Stone Sweet and Sandholtz 1997: 301). However, supranational governance was more eclectic in approach, drawing on the importance of social exchanges as driving integration: an earlier transactionalist approach to integration developed by Karl Deutsch 1953; Deutsch et al. 1957). And whilst presenting itself as a theory of integration, it arguably had more purchase in encapsulating patterns of supranational governance consistent with new institutionalism (see Chapter 2, 'New Institutionalism').

A further revision of neofunctionalism came in the work of Niemann (2006). As with Schmitter's earlier reformulation, he rejected the notion of the automaticity of spillover. He also drew on some of the developments of more recent political science, such as constructivist research (see Chapter 4, 'Social Constructivism') to incorporate learning and norms into his revision.

What was clear from the revisions made by Schmitter, Stone Sweet/Sandholtz, and Niemann was that the original straightforward model of neofunctionalism needed refinement but became more complex as a result. In the process, it lost some of its appeal. Nevertheless, it remains relevant today, as will be seen later in the chapter.

Intergovernmentalism

In response to the neofunctionalist analysis of European integration, a counter-argument was put forward by Stanley Hoffmann (1964, 1966). This argument drew heavily on realist assumptions about the role of states, or, more accurately, the governments of states in IR. Essentially, there were three parts to Hoffmann's criticism of neofunctionalism:

1. European integration had to be viewed in a global context. Regional integration was only one aspect of the development of the global international system. The neofunctionalists predicted an inexorable progress to further integration— but this was all predicated on an internal dynamic, and implicitly assumed that the international background conditions would remain fixed. This criticism became particularly relevant in the light of changes in the global economic situation in the early 1970s.

2. National governments were uniquely powerful actors in the process of European integration: they controlled the nature and pace of integration, guided by their concern to protect and promote the 'national interest'.

3. Although, where 'national interests' coincided, governments might accept closer integration in the technical functional sectors, the integration process would not spread to areas of 'high politics' such as national security and defence.

Hoffmann rejected the neofunctionalist view that governments would ultimately be overwhelmed by pressures from elite interest groups to integrate. He claimed that the neofunctionalist argument was based on 'false arithmetic' that assumed that the power of each elite group (including national governments) was approximately equal, so that if the governments were outnumbered they would lose. In addition, he argued that government decisions could not be understood simply as a response to pressure from organized interests, but that, often, political calculations led governments to take positions to which powerful groups were hostile (Hoffmann 1964: 93). These political calculations were driven by domestic concerns, particularly in relation to the impact of integrative decisions on the national economy and on the electoral implications for the governing party. Hoffmann's argument thus departed from classical realism, in which states were treated as unified rational actors, with little importance attached to domestic politics.

Hoffmann recognized that in the 'low-politics' sectors (e.g. social and regional policy) interest groups *did* influence the actions of governments—but, as he pointed out, they were not the only influence. Other influences included government officials (particularly on economic matters) and also the electoral considerations of the party or parties in office (Hoffmann 1964: 89). However, he considered national governments to be the ultimate arbiters of key decisions. The governments of states were said to be uniquely powerful for two reasons: first, because they possessed legal sovereignty; and, second, because they had political legitimacy as the only democratically elected actors in the integration process. In this view, where the power of supranational institutions increased, it did so because governments believed it to be in their national interest.

In Hoffmann's picture of the process of European integration, governments had much more autonomy than in the neofunctionalist view. The integration process therefore remained essentially intergovernmental: it would go only as far as the governments were prepared to allow it to go. Moreover, Hoffmann, like the realists, stressed the external limitations on autonomy: states were seen as independent actors, but their governments were constrained by the position of the state in the world system.

Liberal Intergovernmentalism

Building on Hoffmann's work, Andrew Moravcsik (1993) developed a revised version of the intergovernmental explanation of integration. Moravcsik's approach, like that of Hoffmann, assumed that states were rational actors, but departed from traditional realism in not treating the state as a **black box**. Instead, it was assumed that the governments of states were playing what Putnam (1988) called 'two-level games'. A domestic political process determined their definition of the national interest. This constituted the first part of the analysis and determined the position that governments took with them into the international negotiation.

This approach built on the undeveloped argument of Hoffmann about the role of domestic politics, but in some ways it was less sophisticated in its account of domestic politics than Hoffmann's. Moravcsik's 'liberal' view of domestic politics was that the primary determinant of the preferences of a government was the balance between economic interests within the domestic arena—a narrow conception of domestic political process that has been frequently criticized (e.g. see Wincott 1995: 601; Forster 1998: 357–9; Caporaso 1999: 162; Wallace 1999: 156–7; Hooghe and Marks 2019a).

The second part of the analysis was to see how conflicting national interests were reconciled in the negotiating forum of the Council of Ministers. This process was divided into two logically sequential stages. The first stage was to reach agreement on the common policy response to the problem that governments were trying to solve and often entailed 'hard bargaining' where the relative power of EU states would come into play. The second stage was to reach agreement on the appropriate institutional arrangements, delegating power to the EU institutions in order to ensure credible commitments, i.e. that individual governments would stick to the agreements reached.

The analytical framework of liberal intergovernmentalism was applied by Moravcsik (1998) to five key episodes in the construction of the EU:

- the negotiation of the Treaties of Rome (1955–58);
- the consolidation of the common market and the Common Agricultural Policy (CAP) (1958–83);
- the setting up of the first experiment in monetary co-operation and of the European Monetary System (EMS) (1969–83);
- the negotiation of the Single European Act (SEA) (1984–88);
- the negotiation of the Treaty on European Union (TEU) (1988–91).

On the basis of these case studies, Moravcsik came to the following conclusions:

1. The major choices in favour of Europe were a reflection of the preferences of national governments, not of the preferences of supranational organizations.

2. These national preferences reflected the balance of economic interests, rather than the political biases of politicians or national strategic security concerns.

3. The outcomes of negotiations reflected the relative bargaining power of the states; the delegation of decision making authority to supranational institutions reflected the wish of governments to ensure that the commitments of all parties to the agreement would be carried through rather than a belief in the inherent efficiency of international organizations.

However, he was criticized for his choice of case studies. As Scharpf (1999: 165) put it:

> Since only intergovernmental negotiations are being considered, why shouldn't the preferences of national governments have shaped the outcomes? Since all case studies have issues of economic integration as their focus, why shouldn't economic concerns have shaped the negotiating positions of governments? And since only decisions requiring unanimous agreement are being analysed, why shouldn't the outcomes be affected by the relative bargaining powers of the governments involved?

The alternative would have been to look at the smaller-scale day-to-day decisions that constitute the bulk of the decisions made within the EU. Here, the picture might be very different. Supranational actors might have more influence, and national preferences might be less clearly defined and less vigorously defended. We look at some of these arguments later in the book (Chapters 13, 14, 15). Moravcsik and Schimmelfennig (2009) provided a response to such criticisms, which were said to have 'small kernels' of theoretical truth, but were generally 'overstated'. Thus, while it was accepted that LI 'works best when decision making is taking place in decentralized settings under a unanimity requirement rather than in settings of delegated or pooled sovereignty under more complex and nuanced decision rules', it was also suggested that 'the theory applies far more broadly than is commonly supposed, including much everyday EU decision making' (Moravcsik and Schimmelfennig 2009: 74).

Liberal intergovernmentalism has in many respects come to be seen as the 'baseline theory' of European integration against which its competitors are to be assessed (Moravcsik 2018: 1648; Moravcsik and Schimmelfennig 2019: 64) and retains considerable relevance to explaining the EU of today (see Insight 1.2 below).

New Intergovernmentalism

In the 2010s, a new version of intergovernmentalism joined the theoretical debate: new intergovernmentalism (Bickerton, Hodson and Puetter 2015a, 2015b). However, we consider it to be a set of propositions about how EU governance works in the twenty-first century, and discuss it in Chapter 2 ('New Intergovernmentalism').

Postfunctionalism

The final theory that we examine in this chapter is postfunctionalism, which is of more recent origin (Hooghe and Marks 2009). Like neofunctionalism and LI it is concerned with explaining the genesis and evolution of integration. It supports both theories' assertion that pressure from various elite actors—whether business interests, supranational institutions, or national governments—can be important drivers of integration. However, its added value lies in its focus on the ways in which integration and EU policy has become more politically salient with the public and subject to political clashes in recent decades, as highlighted by conflicts in relation to the eurozone and migration crises and the politics of Brexit (see Chapter 11). Whereas neofunctionalism and LI assumed that integration would bring sufficient benefits for public opinion to be supportive (in other words, to grant their permissive consent to integration), postfunctionalism questions such an assumption.

Hooghe and Marks (2009) shared with intergovernmentalists and neofunctionalists the view that European integration was triggered by a mismatch between efficiency and existing structures of authority, but differed from them in believing that the outcome of this process would only reflect functional pressures. Instead, they suggested that political conflict was a crucial part of the explanation and that communal identities were central to this conflict. Hence their argument proceeded in three steps:

1. In their first step they noted the functional pressures in an interdependent world that led to the EU being made responsible for policy areas where its scale made it more efficient at delivering public goods than member states (Hooghe and Marks 2019*b*: 1116-17). This part of Hooghe and Marks' work derived from their earlier research on multi-level governance that reflected on how the functional needs of delivering public goods can result in the reconfiguration of decision making across levels and types of governance, from the local to the global levels (see Chapter 2, 'Multi-Level Governance').

2. Their focus then turned to the political arena in which decisions are taken. Departing from the elite-focused approaches of neofunctionalism and LI, they noted that decision making may be insulated or it 'may enter the arena of mass politics where it is subject to mass media, political parties, social movements, and government coalitions' (Hooghe and Marks 2019*b*: 1117). This step opened up the scope for their exploration of the politicization of European integration.

3. They then argued that European integration 'activates identity issues' (Hooghe and Marks 2019*b*: 1117) that have a polarizing effect on a cultural divide, resulting in constraints on integration or EU policy making. In other words, some citizens placed more emphasis upon national identity and self-rule than on the functional benefits of European integration and EU policy making, thereby acting as a brake on these processes. In separate work, Hooghe and Marks argued that a new cleavage had opened up in party systems, activated by the 'perforation of national states by immigration, integration and trade' (2018: 109). In this way, a new 'transnational cleavage' had developed that could be evidenced in the 2016 UK referendum on leaving the EU or the breakthrough in 2017 into the federal parliament of the Alternative for Germany right-wing party following the European migration crisis.

How does postfunctionalism fit in with other integration theories? Neofunctionalism and liberal intergovernmentalism share an understanding that changing international and European challenges may result in the need for a transfer of power to the EU level in order better to deliver public goods. However, they disagree on the mechanisms by which this comes about: specifically, whether it is socioeconomic groups and supranational elites (neofunctionalism) or national governments (LI). Postfunctionalism departs from this economic rationalization of integration and also draws on mass politics to identify the countervailing forces that have become so evident in EU politics in the 2010s. Indeed, Hooghe and Marks used the term *post*functionalism to stress that integration is not inevitably driven by functional or economic imperatives: those factors might be in tension with countervailing and contingent political pressures (Hooghe and Marks 2019*b*: 1117).

This is not to say that the theoretical debate is over. Each theory continues to offer insights, and contestation between the theories continues. For example, Moravcsik claims that the kind of populism captured by postfunctionalist analysis does not have much consequence. He claims that 'populists have rarely been successful in recent general elections, referendums and European elections, and in exceptional cases of success, they soon moderate general opposition to the EU' and that *'Brexit is an exception that proves the rule'*, pointing out that a hard Brexit would be 'impractical and unsustainable' (Moravcsik 2018: 1663—italics in original). Suffice it to say that this general position was challenged by Hooghe and Marks. They responded by fundamentally disagreeing that politicization is of secondary importance and not having a causal effect on integration (Hooghe and Marks 2019*a*). They argue that Moravcsik is stretching the theory to encompass new developments, thereby weakening LI theory.

Contestation between theoretical approaches has been the hallmark of the study of European integration for almost as long as the integration process itself. Each body of work offers important insights into the complex process of integration and policy making in the EU. We can illustrate by brief reference to the refugee crisis and the insights offered by LI, neofunctionalism, and postfunctionalism (see Insight 1.2).

Insight 1.2 Integration Theory and the Refugee Crisis

The migration crisis became acute in late summer 2015, fuelled by refugees from Syria and elsewhere seeking asylum in EU member states (see also Chapter 11, 'The Refugee Crisis'; and Chapter 23, 'The Refugee Crisis'). By the end of 2015 over a million refugees had reached Germany alone. The response of the EU itself was divided and limited, with some states taking a welcoming approach (notably Germany), while Hungary erected a fence to try and secure its borders. The common asylum system broke down and temporary border controls were introduced, weakening the Schengen system of passport-free travel. Member states had divergent interests. Those at the front line of migration flows, such as Greece or Italy, had different interests from those which were ultimately receiving the most asylum applications, such as Germany and (on the basis of applications in relation to population size) Sweden or Austria. 'Non-affected states' with few applications, such as Slovakia or Romania had different interests again, and formed a third category (Biermann et al. 2019: 255–7).

The immediate policy response was limited. The Commission had proposed reforms to the common asylum system but they were blocked by deadlock between governments. A very limited Commission proposal to redistribute migrants trapped in Italy and Greece was passed by a qualified majority in the Council in September 2015 but had been opposed by the Czech Republic, Hungary, Romania, and Slovakia. These states, joined by Poland after a change of government in October 2015, were highly critical of the policy and neglected its implementation, resulting in their being taken to the European Court of Justice, where they lost the case. In the meantime, the welcoming states began to experience a change of heart on the part of their voters, resulting in Germany in a surge of support for the Alternative for Germany and the adoption of a harder-line policy by Chancellor Merkel (Bulmer and Paterson 2019: 243–6). The main common policy response that could be reached by member governments was to offer a 'cash for cooperation' agreement to the Turkish government in return for it limiting the flow of refugees arriving in Greece.

The migration crisis presented a complex set of circumstances and a major challenge to the EU. All three theories had some insights to offer. Liberal intergovernmentalism was particularly insightful into the failure to really reform the policy regime to solve the crisis, despite the obvious need. Policy became deadlocked. As Biermann et al. (2019: 216) put it:

> the EU member states did not share on [sic] overarching preference for a joint policy response. While the group of affected states was pressing for reforms owing to its exposure to migratory pressures, the non-affected states could effectively block demands for reform, given its low non-agreement costs.

Postfunctionalist analysis, by contrast, could point to the way in which publics reacted adversely as the flow of migrants seemed to continue unabated over months, thereby creating problems of domestic assimilation and contributing to a widening gap between more multicultural countries such as Germany and opponents such as Hungary. As a result, postfunctionalism sees the domestic pressure on governments explaining their failure to reach agreement on an asylum policy response at EU level, other than the deal with Turkey (Hooghe and Marks 2019*b*: 1122).

At first blush neofunctionalism looks the least insightful of the theories because of the failure to reform and strengthen the common asylum regime. However, Niemann and Speyer (2018) argue that neofunctionalism can indeed offer insights to one area where supranational capacity was strengthened, namely the creation of an enhanced border force: the European Border and Coast Guard, which was proposed by the Commission and later agreed by the member governments (see Chapter 23, 'Europol, Eurojust, and Frontex'). Moreover, Niemann and Speyer (2018: 30) also point to the endurance of the Schengen regime (see Insight 23.2) in the face of severe challenge, reflecting a wish to preserve one of European integration's achievements. Thus, the vitality of the three main integration theories is evident in evidence from the migration crisis.

CONCLUSION

Until the late 2000s the same 'intergovernmental–supranational debate' about the process of European integration had been going on since the very early stages of the process. Central to this continuing debate was a disagreement over the central drivers of the integration process. In intergovernmental perspectives, European integration is a process whereby national governments are the central actors: they voluntarily enter into agreements to work together to solve common problems. The alternative supranational perspective—associated with neofunctionalism and supranational governance approaches—suggests that, although governments started the process, integration soon took on a life of its own that went beyond the control of the governments. The motivation was similar but the actors more pluralist in kind. Postfunctionalism added a new dimension to the debate from the late 2000s and quickly established itself during the eurozone and migration crises, and with the British referendum choice to leave the EU. It underlines the conditionality of integration on its acceptance in wider domestic politics.

This three-way debate forms the first of the themes that recur throughout this book. Although, as highlighted in this chapter, these theories are primarily explanatory, they have not been neutral in their effect (some scholars would argue that no theory can be—see Chapter 4). In the 1950s and 1960s, neofunctionalist ideas were eagerly embraced by members of the Commission as a blueprint for constructing a united Europe. Intergovernmentalist arguments are more likely to be voiced by the advocates of further steps, who echo Hoffmann and Moravcsik in reassuring hesitant European public opinion that the governments of states remain in charge: that sovereignty is only 'pooled', not lost. Eurosceptic parties, opponents of further integration, and the supporters of the UK leaving the EU implicitly invoke the identity cleavage that is at the heart of postfunctionalism.

While, as is discussed in subsequent chapters, theorizing about the EU has not been confined to these 'grand theories' that focus on the overall trajectory of integration, a number of themes that are central to the integration theory debate—state power, the influence of supranational institutions, and the importance of domestic politicization—continue to resonate in much research.

KEY POINTS

European Integration and the First Attempts to Theorize It

- European integration involved national economies being managed in common.
- This partial surrender of sovereignty by the participating states led to a reassessment of existing theories of IR.

The Intellectual Background

- Functionalism and federalism are two important precursors to European integration theory. Both addressed the problem of how to overcome war between nations.
- A key proponent of functionalism, David Mitrany, sought to prevent war between states by taking routine functional tasks out of the hands of national governments and giving them over to international agencies.
- Mitrany argued that world government would limit freedom, and that regional federations would reproduce on a larger scale the conditions that produced wars between states.
- European federalism attracted strong support among Resistance groups in war-time Europe. The leading intellectual figure was Altiero Spinelli, who advocated a 'constitutional break' at the end of the war to supersede the system of sovereign states with a federal constitution for Europe.
- By the time the Congress aimed at adopting this new constitution had been arranged, national political elites had been re-established in European states. While the (Hague) Congress did produce the Council of Europe, this was an intergovernmental body that fell far short of federalist aspirations.
- The Schuman Plan for the ECSC was devised by Jean Monnet, the head of the French Economic Planning Commission, who believed the European nation state was inadequate as an economic unit in the modern world and argued for a Europe-wide economy.
- The pooling of coal and steel resources was the first step towards a Europe-wide economic zone. It also removed strategic industries from German control and ensured adequate supplies of coal for the French steel industry: both were concerns for Monnet.

Theories of European Integration

- IR theory in the 1950s was dominated by realism. This theory treated nation states as the fundamental units of IR. It did not lead to any expectation that governments would voluntarily surrender their sovereign control over policy. As such, the first European integration theorists posed a direct challenge to realist assumptions.
- *Neofunctionalism* suggested that European integration was a process that, once started, would undermine the sovereignty of states beyond the expectations of governments.

- Neofunctionalism argued that states are not unified actors, but that national interests are determined through a pluralistic process in which governments interact with organized interests. Organized interests were also seen to be important transnational actors.

- The concept of spillover was central to the neofunctionalist theory. Functional spillover, political spillover, and cultivated spillover would lead the process of European integration to run out of the control of national governments. The concept of 'exogenous spillover' was added later to theorize enlargement.

- In the 1970s, neofunctionalism was declared obsolescent by one of its key authors. Others subsequently revised and revived the theory.

- Hoffmann's *intergovernmentalism* argued that neofunctionalists had made three mistakes: (i) regional integration was not a self-contained process, but was influenced by a wider international context; (ii) governments were uniquely powerful actors because they possessed formal sovereignty and democratic legitimacy; and (iii) integration in low-politics sectors would not necessarily spill over into high-politics sectors.

- Moravcsik's *liberal intergovernmentalism* incorporated the neofunctionalist insight that national interests are defined as part of a domestic pluralist political process; within this domestic process, economic interests were seen to be dominant.

- Moravcsik proposed a two-level analysis of EU bargaining, in which governments' preferences were determined at the domestic level and were then used as the basis for intergovernmental negotiations at the European level.

- Moravcsik denied the importance of supranational actors as independent actors in EU decision making and insisted that governments remained in control of the process of European integration.

- The postfunctionalism of Hooghe and Marks emphasized the importance of identity in the process of European integration and the need to go beyond the preoccupation with economic interests and functional pressures that had characterized much of the intergovernmental–supranational debate.

- Postfunctionalism brought important insights into the integration process, particularly during the 2010s when the EU became much more politically contested.

- Each of the theories offers valuable insights into the complex process of integration today.

For additional material and resources, please visit the online resources www.oup.com/uk/bache5e.

QUESTIONS

1. How did federalism and functionalism contrast in their approaches to creating peace in western Europe through integration?

2. How do neofunctionalism and intergovernmentalism differ on their assumptions about the role of the state in international relations?

3. Why is spillover so important to the neofunctionalists' understanding of European integration?

4. Do you agree that LI is now the baseline theory against which to assess other theories?

5. How does postfunctionalism differ from neofunctionalism and LI in its assessment of the dynamics behind integration?

FURTHER READING

Useful coverage of integration theories is offered in three books: **A. Wiener, T. Börzel, and T. Risse (eds),** *European Integration Theory*, 3rd edn (Oxford: Oxford University Press, 2019); **S. Saurugger**, *Theoretical Approaches to European Integration* (Basingstoke: Palgrave Macmillan, 2014); and **B. Rosamond**, *Theories of European Integration* (Basingstoke: Macmillan, 2000). The first two books also cover theoretical approaches which we address in Chapters 2–4. A useful overview article that highlights the relevance of the three integration theories today by applying them to the eurozone, migration, and rule-of-law crises, along with Brexit is: **L. Hooghe and G. Marks**, 'Grand Theories of European Integration in the Twenty-First Century', *Journal of European Public Policy*, 26 (2019*b*): 1113–33.

A good starting point on neofunctionalism, including its revisions, can be found in **A. Niemann, Z. Lefkofridi, and P. Schmitter**, 'Neofunctionalism', in **A. Wiener, T. Börzel, and T. Risse (eds)**, *European Integration Theory*, 3rd edn (Oxford: Oxford University Press, 2019), 43–63. Also of continuing value is an article that highlighted neofunctionalism's revival following the relaunch of integration in the mid-1980s: **J. Tranholm-Mikkelsen**, 'Neofunctionalism: Obstinate or Obsolete? A Reappraisal in the Light of the New Dynamism of the European Community', *Millennium*, 20 (1991): 1–22. For a book-length development of 'revised neofunctionalism', see **A. Niemann**, *Explaining Decisions in the European Union* (Cambridge: Cambridge University Press, 2006). The foundational texts on the early development of neofunctionalist theory are: **E. B. Haas**, *The Uniting of Europe: Political, Social and Economic Forces 1950–57* (London: Library of World Affairs, 1958), with two later editions published, and **L. Lindberg**, *The Political Dynamics of European Economic Integration* (Stanford, CA: Stanford University Press; London: Oxford University Press, 1963).

On intergovernmentalism, the main early contribution is: **S. Hoffmann**, 'Obstinate or Obsolete? The Fate of the Nation State and the Case of Western Europe', *Daedalus*, 95 (1966): 862–915. The earliest statement of liberal intergovernmentalism is **A. Moravcsik**, 'Preferences and Power in the European Community: A Liberal Intergovernmentalist Approach', *Journal of Common Market Studies*, 31 (1993): 473–524. A longer statement and application of the theory is given in **A. Moravcsik**, *The Choice for Europe: Social Purpose and State Power from Messina to Maastricht* (London: UCL Press, 1998). Of interest most recently are: **A. Moravcsik and F. Schimmelfennig**, 'Liberal Intergovernmentalism', in **A. Wiener, T. Börzel, and T. Risse (eds)**, *European Integration Theory*, 3rd edn (Oxford: Oxford University Press, 2019), 64–84; and a re-statement by Moravcsik himself in a journal special issue on LI: **A. Moravcsik**, 'Preferences, Power and Institutions in Twenty-First-Century Europe', *Journal of Common Market Studies*, 56 (2018): 1648–74.

The postfunctionalist theory of integration is set out in **L. Hooghe and G. Marks**, 'A Postfunctionalist Theory of European Integration: From Permissive Consensus to Constraining Dissensus', *British Journal of Political Science*, 39 (2009): 1–23. Postfunctionalism's argument about a new 'transnational cleavage' that is constraining integration is set out in **L. Hooghe and G. Marks**, 'Cleavage Theory Meets Europe's Crises: Lipset, Rokkan, and the Transnational Cleavage', *Journal of European Public Policy*, 25 (2018): 109–35. These articles are important because not all books on integration theory have incorporated postfunctionalism, which is the 'new kid on the block'.

Chapter 2

Theories of EU Governance

Chapter Overview

As European integration progressed, the academic focus began to shift from explaining the integration process to understanding the European Union (EU) as a political system (see Table I.1). EU scholars increasingly drew on approaches from the study of domestic and comparative politics, in part to escape the supranational–intergovernmental dichotomy. These contributions broadened the study of the EU beyond the traditional international relations (IR) debate, with many scholars referring to a 'governance turn' in EU studies in the 1990s. This chapter surveys a number of approaches that focus on the EU as a political system. These approaches are quite varied and include new institutionalism, governance, and policy network approaches. While they diverge in some important ways, what brings them together is their focus on the EU as a system of governance. At the end of the chapter we focus on some of the overall characterizations of EU governance that also offer valuable insights: supranational governance; new intergovernmentalism; and differentiated integration.

A Shift of Focus

Approaches from the study of domestic and comparative politics turn away from the focus of IR theories on the process of European integration, and instead treat the EU as a political system, and try to explain 'the nature of the beast'. This shift of attention to concerns with institutional and policy analysis first appeared with Lindberg and Scheingold's book *Europe's Would-Be Polity* in 1970 (Lindberg and Scheingold 1970). It gathered pace with the acceleration of integration in the 1980s through the single market programme (see Chapter 19), and was strengthened by Simon Hix's (1994) call to scholars within the discipline of comparative politics to wake up to the existence of the EU as a suitable subject for study using their established concepts and toolkits. Instead of asking questions such as how far the EU was dominated by the member states and how far it operated as an autonomous entity, Hix (1999: 1) asked questions that derived from the study of comparative politics:

> How is governmental power exercised? Under what conditions can the Parliament influence legislation? Is the Court of Justice beyond political control? Why do some citizens support the central institutions while others oppose them? How important are political parties and elections in shaping political choices? Why are some social groups able to influence the political agenda more than others?

Comparative politics approaches succeeded in shifting the focus away from the study of European integration as a process to '*how the EU works today*' (Hix 1999: 1; emphasis in original).

An increasing number of concepts are applied to the EU that originated from the study of comparative and domestic politics. Here, we look at three influential sets of analytical approaches that come under the headings of new institutionalism, governance, and policy networks. While we identify these as separate approaches, and there are variants within each approach, there is also overlap between them. We pull these approaches together at the end of the chapter as a way of highlighting broad characteristics of governance in the EU today. In this final section, we look at supranational governance, new intergovernmentalism, and differentiated integration. This final section is therefore concerned with characterizations of EU governance rather than the more widely applicable analytical approaches earlier in the chapter.

New Institutionalism

One approach that was originally applied to the study of domestic and comparative politics that found favour among EU scholars was new institutionalism (NI) (March and Olsen 1984, 1989, 1996). It developed as a reaction to the behavioural approaches that had come to dominate political science in the 1960s and 1970s. It was a return to older concerns with institutions but it departed from the formal, constitutional, and rather descriptive character of earlier institutionalist analysis by widening the scope of analysis. It was one way in which the governance turn in EU studies was operationalized.

Bulmer (1993) set down a marker in arguing that institutions matter in the EU context, identifying the different institutions and instruments of EU governance and how they shape political action. The article further argued that the profile of instruments and institutions differed within discrete 'governance regimes' situated within an overarching EU structure that had pronounced regulatory characteristics. In work with a lawyer, Kenneth Armstrong, he applied NI to the governance of the single market, including a set of six case studies that featured discrete governance regimes (Armstrong and Bulmer 1998).

As NI became more prevalent in political analysis generally and in the literature on EU studies, its 'value added' became clear. NI not only argued that institutions matter in understanding EU politics and policy making, but also sought to explain how they matter. What was 'new' about NI was that institutions were not only defined as formal organizations as they were traditionally understood—such as parliaments, executives, and courts—but also extended to categorize informal institutional features: rules, norms, and even institutional culture. Understood in this way, institutions constrained or shaped political action: whether at a macro (EU) level or in particular governance regimes concerned with specific policy issues. New institutionalists argued that institutions thus defined were not neutral arenas, since they biased access to the political process in favour of some actors and societal groups over others. Second, they argued that institutions could be autonomous political actors in their own right.

While, collectively, this reassertion of institutionalist perspectives is known as NI, it became common to distinguish between three varieties: rational choice institutionalism; historical institutionalism; and sociological institutionalism (Hall and Taylor 1996). These approaches emerged at around the same time, but in relative isolation from each other. In particular, the three variants display different approaches that derive from divergent understandings of institutions. Rational choice institutionalism has the 'thinnest' understanding of institutions: typically, as formal rules. At the other end of the spectrum is sociological institutionalism, which assumes the widest understanding of institutions, including culture, norms, and values. Moreover, sociological institutionalism assumed that political action followed a logic of appropriateness: following conventions, for instance, rather than simply trying to maximize self-interest, as with rational choice institutionalism. Historical institutionalism occupied a hybrid position between the two poles but was often especially concerned with developments across time: the causes and effects of policy change, for instance, or the 'stickiness' of policy; that is, its resistance to reform. NI therefore opened up new research agendas on the EU (see Schneider and Aspinwall 2001: Chapter 1).

Rational Choice Institutionalism

Rational choice institutionalism focuses on the constraints that formal institutional structures impose on actors. It suggests that, in trying to understand the behaviour of political actors, it is important to identify the parameters that are set by the specific framework of rules within which politics takes place. So, for example, the activities of interest groups reflect the procedures that prevail for the passage of the legislation that affects them, and the access points that are available to them in that process. Thus, in the case of the EU, whether interest groups choose to try to influence legislation through national governments or through the Commission and the European Parliament (EP) would reflect:

- the extent to which the process is supranational or intergovernmental (e.g. what decision rules apply within the Council of Ministers);
- in the case of a supranational process, what role the EP has in the final decision; and
- in the case of a more intergovernmental process, access to national governments.

For policy areas that are more supranational in character, such as the EU's trade policy (see Chapter 24), interest groups are more likely to turn to the Commission because it has the key powers in negotiating with other states; for instance if such states are using trade practices that conflict with international rules. Similarly, if **qualified majority voting (QMV)** in the Council of Ministers applies to the particular policy issue, the potential influence of the Commission is greater, making it a more attractive target for lobbying. Moreover, as the powers of the EP have increased over successive reforms (see Chapter 15, 'The Struggle for Power'), interest groups began to lobby the EP more extensively than they had previously.

By contrast, in a policy such as taxation policy, where unanimity applies in the Council of Ministers, it is important for interest groups to lobby at the national level because one member state's vote against an EU proposal could block it. There are consequently strong incentives for lobbying at the national level. Interest groups therefore are 'shooting where the ducks are'; that is, they lobby where they are most likely to get the desired results—a classic assumption of rational action.

Rational choice institutionalists have also made a significant contribution to understanding the ways in which supranational actors might obtain a degree of autonomy from national governments, allowing them to make their own input to the policy process (Pollack 1997). Applying what is known as **principal–agent theory**, rational choice institutionalists have highlighted the difficulties of principals (the national governments) in keeping control over the activities of their agents (the supranational institutions).

- As the range of delegated tasks has increased, so the difficulties of monitoring what the agents were doing has increased.

- As the number of principals increases with successive enlargements of membership, so the agents may play off the preferences of different coalitions of principals against the attempts of other principals to restrain them.

- As QMV has expanded, so the constraints on the Commission in constructing a winning coalition in support of its proposals have been reduced.

Pollack (2003) applied rational choice theory to test hypotheses about the delegation of power by the member states to the EU's supranational organizations (mainly the Commission, the Court of Justice, and the Parliament) and the efforts of these organizations to shape the process of European integration. Pollack's first concern was with the types of function that governments delegate to supranational organizations and the conditions under which greater or less discretion is allocated to these agents. Here, principal–agent theory suggested that governments would delegate to supranational agents to reduce the transaction costs of EU policy making. The evidence suggested that this was the case with the Commission and the Court of Justice, but delegation to the EP was motivated more by governments' attempts to reduce the EU's democratic deficit (see Chapter 3, 'Democracy and Legitimacy') and was thus more effectively explained in terms of the logic of appropriate behaviour identified by sociological institutionalists (see 'Sociological Institutionalism' below), rather than by rational choice explanations.

The principal–agent debate extends to a concern with how control is maintained over regulatory agencies that are a key component of modern governance in the EU and beyond (see 'Regulatory Governance' below). The proliferation of agencies in the EU context has been important to the development of governance approaches to understanding the EU (see 'Regulatory Governance' below) and has also raised important issues relating to the accountability of EU decision making (see Chapter 3, 'Democracy and Legitimacy').

Historical Institutionalism

Historical institutionalists place emphasis on the argument that political relationships have to be viewed over time. Their approach argues that decisions are not made according to an abstract rationality, but according to perceptions and within constraints that are structured by pre-existing institutional relationships. Historical institutionalists also take a broader definition of institutions to incorporate informal constraints on behaviour such as values and behavioural norms. As Hall and Taylor (1996: 938) note, 'they define them as the formal or informal procedures, routines, norms and conventions embedded in the organizational structure of the polity or political economy'.

Central to historical institutionalism is the concept of 'path dependence'. This is the argument that once one decision is made, it tends to make it more likely that policy continues to develop in a particular direction. Or, as Hall and Taylor (1996: 941) put it, 'forces will be mediated by the contextual features of a given situation often inherited from the past'. In extreme cases, path dependence can turn into 'lock-in' (Pierson 1996), whereby other avenues of policy are entirely blocked off by the bias towards the existing route that is built into the system. This could be one explanation of why policies such as the Common Agricultural Policy (CAP) proved so resistant to reform even after their negative effects (such as the policy's cost and distortion of trade with non-EU states) had become obvious in the 1980s (see Chapter 21).

Applying historical institutionalism to the EU led to a critique of liberal intergovernmentalism (LI), suggesting that national governments might not be entirely in control of the process of integration (Pierson 1998: 34–50). Intergovernmental analyses tended to focus on the major order decisions, represented mainly by revisions to the Treaties (see Chapter 1, 'Theories of European Integration'). Intergovernmentalists treated what happened between these historic decisions as simply the working through of the decisions. Historical institutionalists argued that, after the decision had been taken, it would be likely to produce unanticipated and unintended outcomes. This might be because of a simple failure to think through the implications—but it might be for one or both of two other reasons (Pierson 1998: 41).

First, the preferences of governments might change over time. For example, the preference for a CAP based on price support might have been a rational response to conditions in the 1960s in Europe, when security of food supplies was a paramount concern, but no longer appropriate in the changed circumstances of the 1990s, when technological advances had removed this concern. Also, national governments might change. For example, the EC directives on social policy to which a British Labour government had agreed in the 1970s were not to the liking of the Conservative governments between 1979 and 1997. However, even where preferences change, governments would find it extremely difficult to change decisions: policy sectors became institutionalized and various incentives emerged for maintaining the status quo.

A second reason why governments find it difficult to change decisions is because the voting rules in the Council of Ministers might make it difficult to reform the character of a policy once it has been agreed. Where the rule is subject to unanimity, it is impossible to make major reform so long as one member state benefits from the status quo and refuses to move from it. For example, France was reluctant to reform the CAP in the 1980s; yet its agreement was necessary due to the need for unanimity in the Council of Ministers. This situation is sometimes called 'the ratchet effect'. Even where QMV applies, in order to effect change it is necessary to construct a coalition representing more than a simple majority of states (the exact number depending on the weighting of the votes of the members of the coalition, and therefore on the identity of the states involved: see Chapter 12, 'The Council of the EU (the Council'). Not only do the necessary votes for reform need to be gathered but there also has to be agreement on the preferred policy revision.

In a similar vein, and working from the understanding of the EU's evolution as a timescape, Bulmer (2009: 313–14) also argued that intergovernmental bargains represented only one dynamic of integration; what happened between the historic decisions represented another, while the impact on politics and policy of the rulings of the Court of Justice of the EU introduced a third that was neglected by LI. Bulmer (2009: 314–17) also took issue with the critique often directed at historical institutionalism, namely that it could only explain continuity but less so policy change. He noted that some characteristics of EU politics were cyclical, such as the five-year elections to the EP now aligned with changes to the Commission composition and other posts. This cycle refreshed the internal politics of the EU, with the potential for policy change. Moreover, some policies are cyclical, such as the EU budget and the structural and investment funds. Both are subject to seven-yearly reviews. The policies therefore have inbuilt opportunities for reform, and contrast with others that incorporated no such opportunity for change, notably the CAP.

Sociological Institutionalism

The emergence of sociological institutionalism was closely linked with the 'constructivist turn' in the study of the EU and international politics (see Chapter 4, 'Social Constructivism'). Like constructivism, sociological institutionalism takes as its starting point a rejection of the rationalist approach to the study of politics that characterizes rational choice institutionalism and some contributions to historical institutionalism, and places more emphasis on broadly 'cultural' practices (see Chapter 4 for more on this debate).

Hall and Taylor (1996: 947) identified three features of sociological institutionalism that distinguished it from the other NIs. First, the definition of what constitutes 'institutions' is considerably broader than in the other approaches, so that it includes not only formal rules, but also 'symbol systems, cognitive scripts, and moral templates that provide the "frames of meaning" guiding human action'. This definition blurred the lines traditionally separating the notions of 'institutions' and 'culture'.

Second, sociological institutionalism takes a distinct position on the relationship between institutions and individual action that flows from the 'cultural' approach. In particular, it suggests that institutions do not simply influence the 'strategic calculation' of actors, but have a deeper effect on their preferences and very identity. As Hall and Taylor (1996: 948) put it:

> The self images and identities of social actors are said to be constituted from the institutional forms, images and signs provided by social life.

This does not mean that actors are not 'rational' in the pursuit of the goals and objectives; rather, it means that these goals and objectives are constituted differently (that is, socially) and are more broadly defined than rationalist theory would suggest.

Finally, sociological institutionalism contrasts with rationalist explanations on how institutions are formed and developed. For rational choice institutionalists, institutions are developed by rational actors to meet particular ends efficiently, such as reducing transaction costs. For sociological institutionalists, institutions are often created and developed because they contribute to social legitimacy rather than efficiency. In some cases, this may mean that the formal goals of an organization are overridden by these broader social goals. Here, a distinction is made between the rationalist 'logic of instrumentality' with the sociological 'logic of appropriateness'. Thus, in the case of delegation to supranational institutions discussed above, it may not be in the instrumental interests of national governments to enhance the EP's powers, but the need to enhance the democratic legitimacy of the EU provides a powerful logic of appropriateness.

Rosamond (2003) suggested that the application of sociological institutionalism may be particularly useful in understanding why the Commission's Directorates General operate in very distinct ways. It may also provide insights into whether 'formally intergovernmental processes . . . conform to established patterns of interstate interaction, or whether they bring about new norms of exchange between the envoys of member states' (Rosamond 2003: 117). Another application relates to the persistence of different national varieties of capitalism despite the centripetal forces or convergent effects of the EU single market and monetary union. Nationally rooted cultural characteristics help explain the persistence of different patterns of capitalism across the eurozone, and these in turn explain the difficulties of following a single set of rules in the eurozone: one of the underlying problems that led to the eurozone crisis (see Chapter 11, 'The Unfolding Eurozone Crisis'; Chapter 20, 'The Eurozone Crisis').

Where change takes place, sociological institutionalists place emphasis on the role of 'norm entrepreneurs': key politicians or member states that may be able to change the existing policy norms. For example, attention might be focused on the role of Germany in reinforcing 'sound money' principles into eurozone governance during the crisis in the early 2010s (Matthijs and McNamara 2016). In other words, the German government acted as a norm entrepreneur.

New Institutionalism Assessed

Put concisely, NI in its three variants reveals that, respectively, formal rules matter to rational action (rational choice institutionalism), time matters to policy and institutional evolution (historical institutionalism), and social context matters to political behaviour within institutions (sociological institutionalism).

For Hall and Taylor (1996: 95), none of the NIs is particularly 'wrong-headed' or 'substantially untrue'; rather, 'each seems to be providing a partial account of the forces at work in a given situation or capturing different dimensions of the human action and institutional impact present there'. The three approaches rest on different assumptions about the world that led them to focus on different questions. This is illustrated in relation to EU enlargement (see Chapter 26, 'Explaining Enlargement'), where sociological institutionalists have placed more emphasis on why the EU decided to enlarge and how we can account for the subsequent negotiations, while rational choice institutionalists have devoted greater attention to the impact of enlargement on the EU's institutional arrangements and historical institutionalists on the process of reform in central and eastern Europe (Pollack 2004: 151).

The various strands of NI have been refined over time, through both empirical research and through engagement with the other strands and with other conceptual approaches to the EU. Other variants of NI have emerged that space prevents us from outlining, such as discursive institutionalism (e.g. Schmidt 2014). New institutionalism has made a significant contribution to the literature on Europeanization (see Chapter 3, 'Europeanization and the New Institutionalisms') by providing sensitivity to how domestic institutions (formal and informal) mediate EU pressures. The NIs also link up with research on governance and network approaches, to which we now turn.

Governance

The practice and study of governance developed in the 1990s and the similar timing to that of the development of NI was not just chance. What was distinctive about governance was a move away from government: a development that reflected new 'softer' forms of rule in domestic politics and the engagement of a wider range of actors in these processes, as well as the growth of the EU itself and other global organizations internationally. New institutionalism's analytical shift away from formal institutions thus reflected trends in the practice of politics and policy making.

Definitions of governance abound (for different perspectives, see Pierre 2000). A particularly useful definition was offered by Kohler-Koch and Rittberger (2006: 28), identifying governance as:

> a process and a state whereby public and private actors engage in the intentional regulation of societal relationships and conflicts. Governance is thus different from government, the latter stressing hierarchical decision making structures and the centrality of public actors, while the former denotes the participation of public and private actors, as well as non-hierarchical forms of decision making.

The term 'governance' therefore recognized that public policy making was increasingly being characterized by wide participation of public, private, and voluntary-sector actors. In the context of the EU, the multi-level governance framework (see ' Multi-Level Governance' below) brought together this increased 'horizontal' mix of societal actors from different sectors with increased 'vertical' interactions between actors organized at different territorial levels (supranational, national, and sub-national).

Some of the literature on governance entailed a normative dimension, termed 'good governance'. The EU itself promoted the notion of good governance and published a White Paper (European Commission 2001) entitled 'European Governance'. The Commission's work entailed exchanges with academics working on governance and the European Commission seeking to improve its own processes.

Arguably the main 'takeaway' from the governance literature is the recognition that governing is not just achieved by the traditional hierarchical means of 'command and control', backed up by legal means (see Börzel 2019). Governance and policy making can still be undertaken by this traditional route—governance by hierarchy—but also through two other methods: governance by markets or by networks (see Table 2.1).

Governance by hierarchy typically takes place in the most centralized policy areas, where the European Commission and Court of Justice have strongest powers and can rely on European law as a means of enforcing policy. The European Central Bank (ECB) exercises equivalent power in the eurozone. Governance by markets applies where member states have competing rules within a loose EU framework, such as with corporate tax policy. Ireland, for instance, seeks to attract technology firms like Google and Apple to invest there, helped by low corporate taxation rates, while the EU's control over such policy detail is constrained. The cornerstone of the EU—the single market (see Chapter 19)—is a hybrid policy. Barriers to trade have been removed and policy discriminating against EU-wide trade are prohibited (hierarchy). In general, however, it is down to companies to compete following market dynamics. Economic behaviour is driven by competition: a familiar situation in national politics as well, for

Table 2.1 Forms of Governance in the EU

Form of governance	Hierarchy	Markets	Networks
Method of governance	Command and control: authoritative decision backed by law	Competition amongst rules	Negotiation, learning
Policy examples	Competition policy, monetary policy in the eurozone Single market	Corporate taxation	Open method of co-ordination (OMC), Common Foreign and Security Policy (CFSP)

instance with the opening up of sectors such as mobile and landline telephony to competing providers. Governance by networks, finally, entails negotiation. This typically takes place in policy areas where the supranational institutions' power is weak. Bargaining or the exchange of ideas between governments and other actors is what drives governance in this third case.

Three particular applications of the governance literature are worth exploring because of their significance to how EU policy making takes place: multi-level governance, regulatory governance, and new methods of governance.

Multi-Level Governance

Multi-level governance (MLG) has assumed considerable value in exploring policy areas that bring together actors from different levels of political authority. In fact, MLG was first developed from a study of EU structural policy and was later developed and applied more widely. An early definition by Gary Marks (1993: 392) referred to:

> the emergence of *multi-level governance*, a system of continuous negotiation among nested governments at several territorial tiers—supranational, national, regional and local.

While accepting that integration involved intergovernmental bargains, MLG theorists reasserted the neofunctionalist critique of realism that individual governments were not as firmly in control as suggested.

Marks et al. (1996) were writing at a time when LI had just become dominant in theorizing integration (see Chapter 1, 'Liberal Intergovernmentalism'). Accordingly, they chose to contrast the claims of MLG against those of LI. They therefore made three key points against the intergovernmental view, as follows (Marks et al. 1996):

1. Collective decision making involves loss of control for the governments of individual states.

2. Decision making competencies in the EU are shared by actors at different levels, not monopolized by the governments of states.

31

3. The political systems of member states are not separate from each other, as Moravcsik assumed (see Chapter 1, 'Theories of European Integration'), but are connected in various ways.

While Marks et al. accepted the central role of the Council of Ministers in EU decision making, they pointed to a number of constraints on the ability of individual governments to control the outcomes of such collective decision making. The use of QMV in the Council was an obvious constraint: any individual government might be outvoted. So, while it was true that governments might be able to attain desired objectives by pooling their sovereignty, this was not the same as arguing that their control of decision making remained intact.

Supranational institutions might be created by member governments to assist them, as Moravcsik argued, but these did not remain under close national government control. For intergovernmentalists, national governments could ultimately choose to rein in the power of these institutions. For MLG theorists, this was difficult in practice because changes to the role of supranational institutions required unanimous agreement, which was difficult to secure with so many member states.

Marks et al. also criticized Moravcsik's argument that national interests were determined purely through the interplay of domestic actors (see Chapter 1, 'Theories of European Integration'). Instead, they argued that component parts of national governments, and also non-state actors, could form alliances with their counterparts in other member states, which influenced national governments' negotiating positions on EU matters. These alliances would not be under the control of the core institutions of the central government, such as the Foreign Office or the Prime Minister's Office, and the Commission in particular would be able to exploit the existence of these **transgovernmental and transnational networks** of actors to promote its policy preferences within the 'domestic' politics of member states.

What this attempt to achieve MLG's 'brand differentiation' from LI rather skated over in relation to the specific case of cohesion policy was the fact that they might both be correct. The seven-yearly revision of cohesion policy tends to be intensely intergovernmental in character and to be focused around negotiation in the Council of Ministers. LI could be helpful in explaining these negotiations. Thereafter, the policy had to be implemented. At this stage it was possible for the European Commission and subnational authorities to work together—perhaps bypassing national governments—in the manner identified by the MLG literature.

Rather than a coherent theory, MLG was initially an amalgamation of perspectives that were primarily directed at what its advocates saw as the misrepresentation of the nature of the EU by the intergovernmental theorists. It did contain some elements of an explanation for the development of the EU, but it was primarily concerned with the analysis of the *nature* of the EU. In fact, it was to be later that Hooghe and Marks (2009) incorporated the insights of MLG as part of the foundations of postfunctionalism (see Chapter 1, 'Postfunctionalism').

In an elaboration of their approach, Hooghe and Marks (2003, 2004) developed a twofold typology of MLG to capture the EU (see Table 2.2). Type I MLG effectively describes the formal institutions of government at various territorial levels (supranational, national, sub-national), which have multiple tasks and responsibilities and have jurisdictions that are clearly distinct from each other. In other words, Type I MLG describes the system-wide governing architecture. Co-existing with Type I MLG, Type II describes the many smaller bodies of governance that are generally set up with a specific purpose, sometimes for a limited time period, and which are deliberately flexible in membership and organization to deal with specific public policy challenges.

Type II MLG was arguably the variant with greatest value for understanding EU policy areas such as the European Structural and Investment Funds that require task-specific cooperation across levels of government. Type I MLG was not too distant from the established literature on federalism, which is itself interested in tiers of government and the distribution of power between them. Federalism, it will be recalled. had acted as a motivating force behind integration itself (see Chapter 1, 'Spinelli and Federalism'). In those early years, advocates of a new form of European international relations to transcend the nation state advocated a federal Europe, and sought a political strategy to achieve it. Federalism is also an analytical literature, and we take the opportunity to point it out in passing. It is a body of work that some analysts use to highlight weaknesses in the EU as a political system or to compare it to the federal system in the United States and others (e.g. McKay 2001; Nicolaïdis and Howse 2001; Fabbrini 2005, 2010; Menon and Schain 2006). Comparison of the EU with American federalism is a popular way of teaching the former in the United States.

The MLG literature has sparked different theoretical debates. For example, Peters and Pierre (2004) suggested that MLG's flexible and informal modes of co-ordination might bring dangers. In particular, the purported advantages of MLG in terms of functional efficiency might be traded for core democratic values as authority seeps away from the formal institutions in which democratic accountability is exercised, or as political actors use these informal and opaque processes to escape accountability for their decisions (see also Chapter 3, 'Democracy and Legitimacy'). To meet this challenge, Jan Olsson (2003) suggested both abolishing the institutions of MLG (multi-level and cross-sectoral partnerships) and allocating their functions to elected institutions, or, more realistically, allowing elected institutions to play a greater role in regulating partnerships.

Building on Olsson's work, Bache and Chapman (2008) put forward three models of democracy—electoral, **pluralist**, and elite-democratic—through which to evaluate the democratic credentials of MLG. Their case study of the structural funds in South

Table 2.2 Types of Multi-Level Governance

Type I	Type II
General-purpose jurisdictions	Task-specific jurisdictions
Non-intersecting memberships	Intersecting memberships
Jurisdictions at a limited number of levels	No limit to the number of jurisdictional levels
System-wide architecture	Flexible design

Source: Hooghe and Marks (2004: 17). Reprinted with the permission of Oxford University Press.

Yorkshire (UK) illustrated that, among the expected complexity and technocracy at this stage of policy making, there were also experiments in local democracy that had not previously been identified in the academic literature. As such, in the context of deep MLG, there is evidence that, while traditional mechanisms of accountability may be undermined, other mechanisms may provide a valuable alternative.

MLG sparked a lot of debate (see Jordan 2001; George 2004). Critical questions were posed. Was it descriptive of the EU rather than a theory? Did it only help explain governance in the cohesion policy area? Did it overestimate the role of subnational authorities?

In summarizing the state of the debate, Bache and Flinders (2004: 197) identified four common strands in the literature on MLG that raised hypotheses for future research:

1. that decision making at various territorial levels is characterized by the increased participation of non-state actors;

2. that the identification of discrete or nested territorial levels of decision making is becoming more difficult in the context of complex overlapping networks;

3. that, in this changing context, the role of the state is being transformed as state actors develop new strategies of co-ordination, steering, and networking to protect, and in some cases to enhance state autonomy;

4. that, in this changing context, the nature of democratic accountability has been challenged.

Regulatory Governance

The literature on regulatory governance in the EU arose from two developments (Insight 2.1). First, changing patterns of state involvement in economic policy resulted in the state playing a more arm's-length role as a regulator. This trend was global in nature, influenced by the policy agendas of the Reagan presidency in the USA (1981–89) or of Mrs Thatcher's privatization and deregulation policies in the UK (1979–90). The second origin came from creating the single European market in the late 1980s (see Chapter 19) and its consequences for EU governance (Majone 1991, 1996). The original laborious efforts to harmonize thousands of European regulations regarding multiple products was set aside in favour of a pattern of mutual recognition of standards at member state level, provided they met broad safety standards. In addition, setting product standards in some new technologies was outsourced to private-sector bodies or EU regulatory agencies. The number of these agencies proliferated with the single market (see Chapter 13, Box 13.1, 'Independent Agencies'). The European Medicines Agency, for instance, monitors the safety of drugs for sale in the EU (www.ema.europa.eu). The emphasis in this proliferation of agencies was upon policy expertise and policy efficiency. In most cases, committees of national regulators oversaw policy implementation. Indeed, EU and member-state regulators began to build issue-specific networks.

There is, it should be pointed out, a downside to delegating power to expert bodies, and that is that it all adds up to reducing political choice. This situation creates specific problems (see the example of the ECB's accountability in Insight 2.1) but cumulatively it is a contribution to the EU's democratic deficit (see Chapter 3, 'The Democratic Deficit').

> ### Insight 2.1 The EU as a Regulatory System
>
> The idea of the EU as a regulatory system is most closely associated with the work of Giandomenico Majone (1996). Rather than a single analytical approach, it offers a terrain of study focusing on the EU's increased use of regulatory instruments and agencies to secure policy objectives. This focus accompanied the changing character of the EU from the late 1980s, with the extensive regulatory activity aimed at completing the single market, and it continues to be important for a polity with limited budgetary policy instruments (see also Chapter 19, 'Evaluating the Single Market').

Like MLG, regulatory agencies threw up some governance problems; specifically concerning democratic accountability. The public might not be so interested in the technicalities of medicine regulation but other agencies had much greater political salience. Arguably, the most significant body of this kind is the ECB, which sets interest rates for the eurozone (see Chapter 20). At the time of the Maastricht Treaty (1992), when the provisions for the ECB were agreed, keeping interest rate and money supply decisions away from politicians was deemed a good thing. It was seen as a way of keeping short-term political thinking out of these decisions. It was an approach to policy that was strongly influenced by German practice. In the 2010s, by contrast, with the ECB setting negative interest rates and selling government bonds to boost the eurozone economy, its policies have faced significant criticism. Paradoxically, the greatest criticism has come from inside Germany because of the unorthodox nature of these policy measures by German standards. Specifically, they are eroding the value of savings and consequently providing fuel for populist criticism of the EU in Germany. However, by design the process for holding the ECB to account is very indirect.

New Methods of Governance

From the 2000s, there was political momentum behind coordinating policy in several policy fields, such as employment policy, or in seeking to enhance the global competitiveness of the EU. However, because the EU did not have clear authority over such matters it could not proceed by passing legislation. Instead, the EU set guidelines, encouraging member governments and societal actors to develop their own action plans. These plans were to involve other stakeholders from the member states. The policy dynamic was to be one of policy learning through exchange of good practice between member states and other 'softer' methods (governance by network) by contrast with the 'command-and-control' route of legislation (governance by hierarchy). This approach became termed the open method of co-ordination (OMC). It was most closely associated with the Lisbon Strategy (Chapter 10, 'The Lisbon Strategy') and the successor programme, Europe 2020 (Chapter 11, 'Europe 2020').

For some analysts these new methods of governance, with their emphasis on benchmarking, peer review, and league tables as ways of evaluating policy success, seemed to offer new opportunities for the EU to help member states enhance their domestic policies through cooperation at EU level. Sabel and Zeitlin (2010; Zeitlin 2015) advanced the OMC as part of a new form of 'experimentalist governance' that was characterized by less interventionist forms of governance. Yet, at the same time the process of learning between member states offered the prospect of benefits.

This form of governance has also been susceptible to criticism, however. Policy performance in relation to the Lisbon Strategy, for instance, was very mixed (Copeland 2012). Furthermore, the European Parliament was distant from the processes and it was not clear that national parliaments were closely involved either, thus raising questions of democratic accountability (Parker 2018).

Governance Assessed

The governance turn was important in revealing how patterns of rule were changing in the EU, just as they were in national politics. The governance literature therefore introduced new ways of exploring the EU as a political system. Multi-level governance, regulatory governance, and new methods of (or experimentalist) governance are by no means confined to the EU alone. However, they offer important insights into the EU's evolution as a political system, supplementing the original hierarchical approach of policy making through the institutions and law (see also Chapter 18).

Policy Networks

In the same way that some analysts advocated treating the EU from a comparative politics perspective, such as Simon Hix (see 'A Shift of Focus', above), those working in public policy analysis also sought to shine a light on EU governance. Richardson (1996) advocated organizing analysis of EU governance around the concepts that he and others had been using for some time to study the policy-making process within member states. He argued in particular for the application of two concepts: policy networks and epistemic communities. The policy network concept was originally developed in studies of public policy making in the United States and later became prominent in Britain, particularly through the work of Rhodes (1981, 1988). It is a mid-range or 'meso-level' concept, aimed at explanation of particular policy sectors or issues, rather than the characteristics of the political system as a whole (the 'macro level').

According to the 'Rhodes model', a policy network is a set of resource-dependent organizations, meaning that each of the groups that makes up the policy network needs something that the others have in order to fulfil its own objectives (Rhodes 1988). The types of resources that organizations bring to a policy network to exchange in the process of bargaining include constitutional-legal, organizational, financial, political, and informational resources. These 'resource dependencies'—the extent to which organizations depend on each other for resources—are the key variable in shaping policy outcomes. As Peterson and Bomberg (1993: 28) put it: 'They set the "chessboard" where private and public interests manoeuvre for advantage.' However, interdependence between network participants is 'almost always asymmetrical' and in some cases it is possible to talk of 'unilateral leadership' within networks (Rhodes 1986: 5).

The policy-networks approach does not constitute a predictive theory of policy making, but contributes to explaining policy outputs. It is actor-centred and therefore contrasts with the institution-focused approaches considered in new institutionalism above. For Peterson and Bomberg (1993: 31):

> Policy networks are essentially descriptive theoretical tools which simply help order facts and evidence in novel ways. However, policy networks can be used to anticipate and explain policy outputs by providing insights into how and why decisions were taken which produced them.

Policy Networks and the Study of the EU

There are two very useful contributions made by the policy network literature to the study of the EU. The first is to propose that the structure of the policy network may impact on the resultant policy. The second is to identify the different scales of decision making in the EU: from the grand bargains reached by member governments on Treaty reform to the much more specific agreements reached in a group of policy specialists on an EU issue such as the total allowable catch of fish in the Baltic Sea. We take each of these insights in turn.

In outlining the importance of different structural characteristics of different types of network, Rhodes (1988) distinguished between different types of network, ranging from highly integrated policy communities to loosely integrated issue networks (see Insight 2.2). These different 'structural characteristics' of networks have different effects on both the internal dynamics of the networks and on the ability of networks to resist external pressures for change. However, policy outputs are generally not just a function of internal network characteristics, but are shaped also by changes in the broader political and economic environment (Rhodes et al. 1996). As such, the approach is often at its strongest when used in conjunction with a macro-level theory of politics or policy making that seeks to explain the broader political context within which the network is situated.

One basic contention evident in the policy network literature is that the more integrated a policy network—i.e. a policy community (Insight 2.2)—the more likely it is that major policy change may be obstructed. A close policy community might also mean that interest groups have quite a degree of influence over the policy decision. The automobile and pharmaceutical sectors were identified as having policy communities (Peterson and Bomberg 2003). By contrast, issue networks are looser and sectoral interests more difficult to enforce. Consequently, the EU institutions have more ability to develop policy solutions without obstruction by interest groups. Hence issue networks are more likely in social and consumer policy (Peterson 1995*b*).

The applicability of the policy-networks framework to the analysis of the EU was questioned by Kassim (1994). He argued that the multinational character and institutional complexity of the EU made it difficult to delimit policy networks, and particularly to identify the relevant public sector actor. Sometimes national agencies would be key; sometimes the Commission; sometimes other EU-level institutions. The institutions themselves often acted as lobbyists in the EU in pursuit of their own objectives. Peterson (1995*a*) responded that while some sectors remained fluid, others had settled into more stable patterns. Indeed, he argued that the Commission was so under-resourced that it had to try to enter into stable relationships with partners that it could trust, which had information that it could use. While he accepted that the delineation

---

Insight 2.2 Policy Communities and Issue Networks

A *policy community* is marked by:

- limited membership;
- stable membership over long periods of time;
- a high level of interaction between the members;
- shared values between members;
- some degree of equality in the distribution of resources;
- a relative balance of power and influence between members.

An *issue network*, in contrast, is marked by:

- large and diffuse membership;
- frequent shifts in the membership;
- fluctuating frequency of contact between members;
- lack of shared values;
- marked inequality in the distribution of resources;
- marked inequality in power and influence within the network.

---

of policy networks at the EU level was a difficult task, Peterson insisted that this did not make it a less important one.

The second major contribution of the policy-networks literature related to the need to be clear about the level (or scale) of the policy-making process that was being analysed. Peterson argued that the policy-networks model was best able to explain what he called 'the policy-shaping decisions', when proposals were being formulated and before a political decision was taken that 'set' the policy (Peterson 1995a: 400). In a subsequent article, he expanded on this argument (Peterson 1995b). He identified three 'levels' of analysis in EU decision making. The highest level he termed the 'super-systemic' or 'history-making' decisions. These were mainly decisions taken by national governments in the European Council or at intergovernmental conferences (IGCs), and were most fruitfully analysed using intergovernmental ideas. The second level he termed the 'systemic' or 'policy-setting' stage. At this level, a combination of intergovernmental and inter-institutional analysis was needed to understand outcomes. The third level he called the 'sub-systemic' or 'policy-shaping' stage. At this level, policy networks were a useful concept for understanding how policy options were formulated in bargaining between the Commission Directorates General, national civil servants, and private actors (see Table 2.3). Levels here are not meant in the (territorial) sense used in MLG (see 'Multi-Level Governance' above). Rather, they are about the scope of the decision and political salience.

Subsequently, Peterson (2009: 109) put his case more strongly, suggesting that 'policy network analysis is never more powerful an analytical tool than when it is deployed at the EU level'. He set out a three-pronged argument for the applicability of the policy-networks approach to the study of the EU: first, that there is considerable variation in how different EU policy sectors operate; second, that much of the EU's policy

Table 2.3 Levels of Analysis in EU Decision Making

Level	Type of decision	Dominant actors	Rationality
Super-systemic	History making	European Council, national governments in IGCs, Court of Justice	Political, legalistic
Systemic	Policy setting	Council of Ministers, Committee of Permanent Representatives (COREPER)	Political, technocratic, administrative
Sub-systemic/ meso-level	Policy shaping	Commission, committees, Council groups	Technocratic, consensual, administrative

Source: Reproduced from *Journal of European Public Policy*, 2 (1995): 71. Reprinted with the permission of the Taylor & Francis Group.

making is highly technical; and, third, that EU policy making is 'underpinned by an extraordinarily complex labyrinth of committees that shape policy options before policies are "set" by overtly political decision makers such as the college of Commissioners, Council of Ministers, or European Parliament' (Peterson 2009: 118).

Jachtenfuchs (2001: 254) made a complementary case for the advantages of network analysis:

> It appears that, on the whole, the fragmented and fluid institutional structure of the EU and the lack of a strong power centre lead to an increase of channels of access and a larger variation of participants in the policy-making process as compared to governance systems in territorial states.

Related Literatures

Parallel to the Anglo-American policy-networks literature exemplified by the work of Rhodes is a related strand of conceptual and empirical literature on network governance that is most strongly associated with German scholars—especially Beate Kohler-Koch and her associates (see Kohler-Koch 1996; Kohler-Koch and Eising 1999). The key difference is that, while the British approach is primarily an analytical model seeking to understand state–society relations in a given policy area, the German approach treats networks as an alternative form of governance to states and hierarchies (Börzel 1998). It is therefore directly linked to the governance literature (see 'Governance' above), and specifically to governance by networks (Table 2.1).

Another literature used in EU policy analysis—this time drawn from IR—is that of epistemic communities. These are epistemic communities, defined by Peter Haas (1992: 3) as:

> a network of professionals with recognised expertise and competence in a particular domain and an authoritative claim to policy-relevant knowledge within that domain or issue-area.

The members of an epistemic community share expertise and knowledge: that is, they hold a common set of understandings about what is right and desirable on that basis,

39

and a common set of assumptions about how to achieve those goals. Epistemic communities are likely to exercise particular influence over policy when policy makers face conditions of uncertainty about the likely consequences of policy choice. Epistemic communities might therefore be used by supranational actors such as the European Commission as a means of furthering the integration of policy. The expert analysis that they provide, and the policy prescriptions that they advocate, if they point in the desired direction, could form a powerful lever for supranational actors to move states in the direction of common European solutions to problems that confronted them.

While developed separately from the Rhodes model of policy networks, the notion of epistemic communities is a compatible approach that provides a way of understanding how professionals can come to dominate policy making. Sabatier's advocacy coalition framework, which offers an explanation for how policy change is brought about by coalitions within networks bound together by a shared belief system, has similar potential (Sabatier 1988, 1998). Moreover, Peterson (2004: 121) suggested that alliances of epistemic communities and advocacy coalitions may form to influence policy making and provides the example of the EU's 'quite radical liberalization of its agricultural sector during the Uruguay Round which gave birth to the World Trade Organization in the early 1990s'.

Policy Networks Assessed

Policy network analysis provides a valuable tool in understanding decision making at the policy-shaping level. The policy community–issue network distinction provides a good way to understand the different character of relations between the EU institutions and lobbyists and other actors across different policy areas. Like the epistemic community literature, that on policy networks is best in explaining technocratic policy making. However, the bigger-scale issues such as how the EU was given authority over the policy in the first place, or how policy goals were set, requires a different set of analytical tools.

EU Governance Approaches

When Hix made the plea to turn to comparative politics approaches, he was concerned to treat the EU like other political systems. There are, however, three approaches to understanding EU governance that do not comply. They have been developed to understand the specificities of EU governance. They are: supranational governance, which was developed in the 1990s; new intergovernmentalism, developed in the 2010s; and differentiated integration, a further analytical approach of the 2010s.

Supranational Governance

Starting from the intergovernmentalism versus supranationalism debate (Chapter 1), a team of scholars claimed to offer an alternative that cut through the dichotomy (Stone Sweet and Sandholtz 1997; Sandholtz and Stone Sweet 1998; Stone Sweet et al. 2001). Supranational governance was an approach that drew on the transactionalism of Karl Deutsch (Deutsch 1953; Deutsch et al. 1957) and on NI as applied to the EU (see

'New Institutionalism' above), although the authors themselves located the origins of their approach in neofunctionalism. Following Deutsch and working with the trend of globalization, Stone Sweet and Sandholtz (1997) argued that transactions across national boundaries were increasing. As they increased, so a supranational society of relevant actors would emerge. These actors would favour the construction of rules to govern their interactions at the supranational level because nationally based rules would be a hindrance to them.

Although with aspirations to be an integration theory, supranational governance's strength was in understanding the EU as a series of regimes for different policy sectors. The authors therefore sought to explain the different extents of supranationalism that existed in different policy sectors. In two edited volumes (Sandholtz and Stone Sweet 1998; Stone Sweet et al. 2001) contributors explored the development of supranational governance in sectors such as air transport, telecommunications, the environment, gender equality, and monetary policy at a time when European integration was developing strongly, with the single market and moves to monetary union.

Supranational governance offered valuable insights into the specific dynamics of supranational rule making in individual policy areas. However, it was criticized for giving a privileged role to transnational business actors, to supranational actors, and to the operation of supranational rules of governance (Branch and Øhrgaard 1999). Indeed, supranational governance is susceptible to the same kind of critique that postfunctionalism has made of neofunctionalism and LI; particularly with respect to its excessive emphasis on the interests and influence of elite actors to the detriment of broader processes of politicization (see Chapter 1, 'Postfunctionalism').

New Intergovernmentalism

New intergovernmentalism, by contrast, has developed explicitly to capture the character of the EU in the period since the Maastricht Treaty of 1992. As its title indicates, the emphasis is on the enduring importance of national governments. New intergovernmentalism is based on six assumptions (Bickerton et al. 2015*b*, 2015*c*: 29–39):

- that deliberation and consensus are the guiding norms of EU decision making;
- that supranational institutions are not 'hard-wired' to seek ever closer union;
- that delegation of new powers is now tending towards 'de novo' institutions (i.e. agencies) rather than traditional supranational ones, i.e. the European Commission;
- that domestic preference formation has taken on a wider significance to the European integration process, extending out to include populism (and Euroscepticism);
- that the difference between high politics and low politics has become blurred (contrasting with Hoffmann's formulation of intergovernmentalism: see Chapter 1, 'Intergovernmentalism'); and
- that the EU is in a state of disequilibrium, reflecting both contemporary socio-economic problems and heightened political contestation around the EU itself.

New intergovernmentalism argues that co-operation has occurred in certain policy areas but without a clear reduction in national authority or a clear increase in supranational authority. The result has been that governance has been based on the institutionalization of intergovernmental exchanges and mutual oversight at the EU level, such as through new methods of government (see 'New Methods of Governance' above).

New intergovernmentalism has enabled insightful analysis of governance (institutional and policy aspects) in the more contested political environment of the 2010s (Bickerton et al. 2015*b*). Its assumptions contrast with those of supranational governance and highlight the way in which the changing political environment within which the EU is operating can impact on its governance.

Differentiated Integration

Differentiated integration has developed in European integration since the UK's non-participation in the exchange rate mechanism of the European monetary system in March 1979. It set a trend that became more explicit with the UK's opt-outs from monetary union and the social chapter of the Maastricht Treaty (Chapter 9, 'Towards Maastricht'). It has now become an established pattern of integration where a member state cannot sign up to a Treaty reform or does not meet the conditions for joining a policy: a situation applying to various member states absent from the eurozone or the Schengen passport-free zone.

Leuffen et al. (2013) have taken differentiated integration one step further and used it as the basis to analyse governance in the EU. Instead of using the term just to highlight the way that in some policy areas not all member states are full participants—termed by them 'horizontal differentiation'—they also look at the different extent of integration across policy areas (termed by them 'vertical differentiation'). In this way, they develop differentiated integration as an analytical tool for comparing governance across different policies of the EU. Of course, they are not the first to conduct a comparison of policy making across sectors—see Wallace et al. (2020), the latest edition of a book first published in 1977. However, in today's EU with its diverse membership, differentiation has become an important way of understanding varying patterns of integration and how they impact on EU governance and policy making (see Chapter 18, 'The European Union's Policy Agenda').

EU Governance Approaches Assessed

The three literatures considered in this section of the chapter depart from the principle of utilizing theories that have applicability in other political systems. Instead, they provide frameworks based around the EU political system itself. They flirt with the risks that arise from being based around one set of circumstances, the EU: for instance, that they may lose relevance if circumstances in the EU change. Nevertheless, they constitute an important part of the theoretical literature on EU governance.

CONCLUSION

If theories of EU governance were relative latecomers to the study of the EU, their proliferation has more than made up for lost time. There are a number of overlapping and related approaches competing for the same space in analysing the operation of the EU system. We have distinguished between NI, governance, policy networks, and EU governance approaches. However, the reality is less clear-cut, not only between these categories, but also within them.

What brings together the approaches and theories discussed in this chapter is that they are primarily mid-range: they seek to explain developments at a sub-system or sectoral level and are not attempts at theorizing the EU system more broadly. As the EU has become more complex, there has been greater application of mid-range theories. Governance theories broadly defined have become more prominent with the increased practice of regulatory and new methods of governance.

After seven decades of governance in the EU and the European Communities, it is scarcely surprising that this chapter contains a diversity of approaches. EU governance has changed over that time frame, as have comparative and EU-specific theories. These theories certainly help the understanding of how EU governance works (see Table I.1)

However, this body of literature is subject to a broad critique; they have failed to address the questions addressed in Chapters 3 and 4 (see Table I.1). Thus, in joining the mainstream of EU studies—like integration theory before it—governance approaches have failed sufficiently to explore the political contestation within the EU. They have failed to understand some of the 'givens' in EU studies, such as underlying questions about power that have become more evident during the crises in the EU during the 2010s. They can be considered to be too descriptive, not asking enough normative/critical questions. In that sense it is also important to consider the consequences of the EU for member states and democracy: covered in Chapter 3. Whitman and Manners (2016: 14) go further and advocate alternative 'dissident' voices that:

> do more than simply critique the existing discourses and practices of EU studies; they raise the possibility of speaking a different language of Europe, one that is critically aware that socio-economic power structures, systems of difference and narratives of exclusion are potentially embodied in all politics.

We explore some of these 'dissident' approaches in Chapter 4.

KEY POINTS

A Shift of Focus

- Approaches from the study of domestic and comparative politics turn away from the focus of IR theories on the process of European integration, and instead treat the EU as a political system, and try to explore 'the nature of the beast'.

New Institutionalism

- New institutionalism argues that analysts have lost sight of the importance of institutions in structuring political action.
- Three varieties of NI can be distinguished: rational choice institutionalism, historical institutionalism, and sociological institutionalism.
- *Rational choice institutionalism* emphasizes the argument that the behaviour of political actors is shaped by the specific framework of formal rules within which they operate.
- *Historical institutionalism* emphasizes the argument that political relationships have to be viewed over time and that decisions are shaped by the nature of pre-existing institutional relationships.
- *Sociological institutionalism* emphasizes the argument that the behaviour of political actors is shaped by informal norms and values.

Governance

- Definitions of governance commonly emphasize the proliferation of non-state actors in the policy process.

- Analytically it is possible to distinguish between governance by hierarchy, markets, and networks.

- Multi-level governance, regulatory governance, and new methods of governance offer important concepts for understanding EU practice.

- Multi-level governance argues that national governments have lost some control over policy to the supranational level, and is particularly useful for understanding terrritorially organized policies such as cohesion policy.

- Regulatory governance captures the arm's-length pattern of rule in the single market and related policy areas.

- New methods of governance have been utilized in policy areas such as the Lisbon Strategy and Europe 2020, where the EU lacks clear Treaty powers.

Policy Networks

- Policy networks offer a 'meso-level' approach that can offer insights into different policy outcomes, contrasting the pattern of relations between actors and institutions in policy communities with that of issue networks.

- Policy networks are concerned with more specific policy issues. The origins of a policy and its main objectives require the use of other theories reflecting the level or scale of what is at stake.

- The literatures on network governance and epistemic communities are complementary to the policy-networks approach.

EU Governance Approaches

- Supranational governance helps understand the accumulation of governance responsibilities at EU level in the late 1980s and 1990s, but seemed less apposite by the 2010s.

- New intergovernmentalism has been developed around the more contested character of EU governance in the 2010s, where national governments and domestic politics have re-asserted themselves.

- Differentiated integration helps understand the complexity of EU governance: the different balance of powers across policy areas; and the pattern whereby not all states are full participants in all EU policies such as the eurozone.

 For additional material and resources, please visit the online resources www.oup.com/uk/bache5e.

QUESTIONS

1. Why did analysts turn to comparative politics approaches to explain developments in the EU?

2. How, and in what ways, do institutions matter in the EU?

3. Explain the 'governance turn' in the analysis of the EU.

4. How useful are policy networks in explaining EU politics?

5. Are 'EU governance approaches' helped or hindered by being based solely on the experience of the EU?

FURTHER READING

The call for a shift of focus to comparative politics approaches was set out in **S. Hix**, 'The Study of the European Community: The Challenge to Comparative Politics', *West European Politics*, 17 (1994): 1–30. His call has been implemented in book form as **S. Hix and B. Høyland**, *The Political System of the European Union*, 3rd edn (4th in preparation) (Basingstoke: Palgrave Macmillan, 2011).

Useful reviews of the new institutionalist research agenda in EU studies are offered by **M. Aspinwall and G. Schneider**, 'Same Menu, Separate Tables: The Institutionalist Turn in Political Science and the Study of European Integration', *European Journal of Political Research*, 38 (2000): 1–36 and **M. Pollack**, 'Rational Choice and Historical Institutionalism', in **A. Wiener, T. Börzel, and T. Risse (eds)**, *European Integration Theory*, 3rd edn (Oxford: Oxford University Press, 2019), 108–27. The three institutionalisms are applied to cases in **G. Schneider and M. Aspinwall (eds)**, *The Rules of Integration* (Manchester: Manchester University Press, 2001), 73–96. Useful for an overview of institutionalist and governance approaches is **S. Saurugger**, *Theoretical Approaches to European Integration* (Basingstoke: Palgrave Macmillan, 2013), Chapters 4 and 5.

In relation to the adoption of governance approaches in EU studies, see **B. Kohler-Koch and B. Rittberger**, 'The "Governance Turn" in EU Studies', *Journal of Common Market Studies*, Annual Review, 44 (2006): 27–49, and **T. Börzel**, 'Governance Approaches to European Integration', in **A. Wiener, T. Börzel, and T. Risse (eds)**, *European Integration Theory*, 3rd edn (Oxford: Oxford University Press, 2019), 87–107. Also recommended is **F. Scharpf**, *Governing in Europe: Effective and Democratic?* (Oxford: Oxford University Press, 1998).

On MLG, the most complete statement of the approach is contained in **L. Hooghe and G. Marks**, *Multi-Level Governance and European Integration* (London: Rowman and Littlefield, 2004). The collection by **I. Bache and M. Flinders (eds)**, *Multi-Level Governance* (Oxford: Oxford University Press, 2004) undertakes a critical assessment of both the potentialities and limitations of MLG, drawing both on theoretical contributions by scholars from different academic traditions and fields, and on different policy studies. On regulatory governance, see **G. Majone (ed.)**, *Regulating Europe* (London; Routledge, 1996). On new methods of governance, see **C. Sabel and J. Zeitlin (eds)**, *Experimentalist Governance in the European Union: Towards a New Architecture* (Oxford: Oxford University Press, 2010).

For an overview of the policy networks approach and its application to the EU, see **J. Peterson**, 'Policy Networks', in **A. Wiener and T. Diez (eds)**, *European Integration Theory*, 2nd edn (Oxford: Oxford University Press, 2009), 105–24. The approach is applied at greater length in **J. Peterson and E. Bomberg**, *Decision Making in the European Union* (Basingstoke: Palgrave Macmillan, 1999).

Supranational governance is outlined in **A. Stone Sweet and W. Sandholtz**, 'European Integration and Supranational Governance', *Journal of European Public Policy*, 4 (1997): 297–317. It is developed in **W. Sandholtz and A. Stone Sweet (eds)**, *European Integration and Supranational Governance* (Oxford: Oxford University Press, 1998). New intergovernmentalism is outlined in **C. Bickerton, D. Hodson, and U. Puetter**, 'The New Intergovernmentalism: European Integration in the Post-Maastricht Era', *Journal of Common Market Studies*, 53 (2015): 703–22, and developed at greater length in **C. Bickerton, D. Hodson, and U. Puetter (eds),** *The New Intergovernmentalism: States and Supranational Actors in the Post Maastricht Period* (Oxford: Oxford University Press, 2015). On the theory and analysis of differentiated integration, see **D. Leuffen, B. Rittberger, and F. Schimmelfennig (eds)**, *Differentiated Integration: Explaining Variation in the European Union* (Basingstoke: Palgrave Macmillan, 2013).

Chapter 3
Theorizing Consequences

Chapter Overview

As the European Union (EU) has increasingly been understood as a political system in its own right, so academic attention has shifted to understanding the implications of this development. This chapter brings together what have usually been presented as separate 'consequences' of European integration. These 'consequences' have become more complex in the 2010s and are interrelated. First, we examine Europeanization: the process through which domestic politics and polities are changed by their engagement with the EU. Second, we consider challenges to integration. During the 2010s the politicization of EU politics during the eurozone crisis and with the 2016 UK referendum—to take two prominent examples—witnessed some rising opposition to the EU. This has taken three forms: a new domestic politicization of the EU; the rise of Euroscepticism; and a questioning of whether the EU is experiencing disintegration. Third, a continuing challenge for the EU has been its democratic legitimacy, and rising Euroscepticism is linked to questions regarding the legitimacy of the EU amongst the public. Hence this chapter deals with these interrelated phenomena. Or, put differently, it is about the EU's impact on the member states, and the issues arising.

Europeanization

The concept of Europeanization became a key theme in studies of the EU from the 1990s. However, it has been defined and applied differently in different studies. Europeanization need not be an EU-related phenomenon, it can arise from other European organizations, such as the Council of Europe. Here, we outline the range of meanings before focusing on the development of Europeanization studies that relate specifically to the EU. We focus on the forms and mechanisms of Europeanization, and how it has tended to use new institutionalism (NI) for its operationalization. We give a brief overview of the areas to which the literature has been applied, before taking stock of its contributions and limitations.

Meanings of 'Europeanization'

Europeanization became a key theme in studies of the EU in the 1990s and 2000s. Its importance grew as a result of two developments. First, with the single market, the proposals for monetary union, and the integration of other EU policy areas,

Europeanization was a prominent real-world phenomenon. An increasing number of policy areas were impacted by European integration, and, as a result of eastern enlargement, so were more states. Thus, and second, an analytical literature sought to give more precise meaning to Europeanization as a term referring to these developments. Buller and Gamble (2002), Olsen (2002), and Bache and Jordan (2006a) each identified five uses of Europeanization, some of which overlap. Drawing on these contributions, we summarize the ways in which various scholars have used the term 'Europeanization' in Table 3.1.

The Development of the Field

An early and influential contribution was Robert Ladrech's study of the EU and France, in which Europeanization was defined as, 'an incremental process reorienting the direction and shape of politics to the degree that EC [European Community] political and economic dynamics become part of the organizational logic of national

Table 3.1 Uses of Europeanization: EU-Specific

Usage	Focus on
A top-down process of change deriving from the EU	The effects of EU membership on domestic politics, policies, and polities (Héritier et al. 2001; Buller and Gamble 2002). Later research highlighted issues of culture, discourse, identity, and norms as 'carriers' of Europeanization (Bulmer and Radaelli 2013).
The creation of new EU powers	The development of EU structures of governance and the accumulation of EU competences (Risse et al. 2001). This usage is similar to the notion of European integration.
The creation of a European lodestar of domestic politics	The idea of the EU as an increasingly important reference point for the political activities of domestic actors, such as sub-national governments and interest groups (Hanf and Soetendorp 1998; Fairbrass 2003).
An increasingly two-way interaction between states and the EU	States seeking to anticipate and ameliorate the effects of top-down Europeanization ('downloading') pressures by 'uploading' their preferences to the EU level. As such, the EU both affects and is affected by domestic processes (Bomberg and Peterson 2000; Börzel 2002).
Changes in external boundaries	The expansion of Europe as a political space, particularly through the process of enlargement (Grabbe 2001, 2003; Olsen 2002, 2003; Schimmelfennig and Sedelmeier 2004, 2005) but also foreign and neighbourhood policy (Börzel 2010; see also Chapters 24 and 25).
A 'smokescreen' for domestic manoeuvres	A process in which domestic actors 'hide behind' the EU to legitimize domestic action (or inaction) that may be unpopular (Dyson and Featherstone 1999; Buller and Gamble 2002; Radaelli 2004; Woll and Jacquot 2010).

politics and policy-making' (Ladrech 1994: 69). In other words, domestic politics was being changed by the response of domestic organizations to the changing context brought about by EU membership.

Yet, while Ladrech observed Europeanization effects in France, he did not suggest that the effects of the EU would be the same across all member states. Thus, fears of harmonization or homogenization were unfounded. Instead, domestic factors played an important role in shaping the nature of the Europeanization effects in France, and would do so elsewhere. There would be 'national-specific adaptation to cross national inputs' (Ladrech 1994: 84). Ladrech's arguments about the importance of domestic mediating factors were borne out in subsequent studies.

In their study of Britain, Bulmer and Burch looked at the effects of EU membership on the machinery of central government and argued that 'while change has been substantial, it has been more or less wholly in keeping with British traditions' (Bulmer and Burch 1998: 603, 2009). At key points in Britain's relationship with the EU, the administrative response had been shaped by the way in which important political actors had perceived the integration process. So, 'the construction of the issue of integration interacts with the prevailing characteristics of national governmental machinery to explain the different starting points for national adaptation' (Bulmer and Burch 1998: 606).

Uploading, Downloading, and Crossloading

While early studies focused on the downward flow of pressures from the EU to the national level, later studies increasingly highlighted the interactive two-way relationship between member states and the EU. As well as being 'downloaded' by the member states from the EU level, ideas and practices are also 'uploaded' from member states to the EU level. The focus on uploading had antecedents in the 'domestic politics' approach developed by Bulmer (1983), while downloading resonated with the even earlier work by Puchala (1975) on post-decisional politics: the processes and politics involved in implementing European decisions. Both emphasized the importance of domestic politics in understanding the dynamics of European integration, which is central to Europeanization research.

Europeanization is similar to another process addressed in comparative public policy, namely policy transfer. Policy transfer refers to the process whereby policies or practices are transferred from one political system to another political system (Dolowitz and Marsh 1996; Bulmer and Padgett 2005). Such policy transfer can take a range of different forms, and is similar in many respects to that evident in Europeanization (see Figure 3.1).

If we concentrate on Europeanization (or policy transfer) within the EU 'box' in the first instance (see Figure 3.1), member states *download* policy agreed at the supranational level. This is the standard understanding of Europeanization. However, as many scholars have pointed out (e.g. Börzel 2002), some member governments may seek to take the lead on a policy, such as Germany did at the outset of EC environmental policy, and *upload* their policy preferences to the supranational level. This means that they they will have less trouble adapting to EU policy when it comes into force. Also possible is a situation where member states learn from each other ('crossloading'). In the EU context, it reflects the way in which new methods of governance are supposed to work.

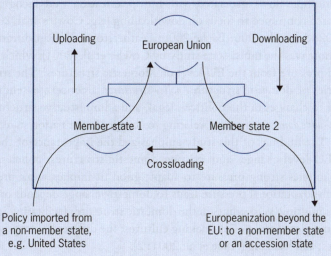

Figure 3.1 Europeanization as policy transfer: directions of flow

Uploading

European Union

Downloading

Member state 1

Member state 2

Crossloading

Policy imported from a non-member state, e.g. United States

Europeanization beyond the EU: to a non-member state or an accession state

EU states exchange good practice and learn ways to improve their policy, facilitated by the EU (see Chapter 2, 'New Methods of Governance'). Other instances of crossloading may occur through the EU-funded 'twinning exercises' to promote learning between policy makers in different states (Papadimitriou and Phinnemore 2004).

At the same time, it is important to note that the processes of Europeanization do not take place in isolation from global policy developments. This can be one of the weaknesses of the Europeanization literature: to only consider the processes contained within the box in Figure 3.1. For instance, in 1978 the US Administration of President Jimmy Carter introduced airline deregulation. In the late 1980s the EC—with the UK and the Netherlands in the lead—took these American ideas and uploaded them to the supranational level. The creation of a single air transport market took over a decade, but at the end of it the member states had transferred all salient powers to the supranational level (Bulmer et al. 2007: 97–113). The result was to open markets for new market entrants such as easyjet and Ryanair and increase competition by weakening the previous arrangements that had given the likes of Air France, British Airways, and Lufthansa protection from lower-cost competition. Member states had to download policy from the EU. The risk of studies focused on the Europeanization framework is that they omit where the liberalization ideas originated from because it was outside the EU.

During subsequent enlargement rounds these aviation rules had to be adopted by the airlines of central and eastern Europe: a form of Europeanization and policy transfer (Europeanization beyond the EU—see Table 3.1). Thus, EU rules are not just downloaded to member states; Europeanization also takes place when policy is transferred out to non-member states. This form of Europeanization applies in particular to accession states, for they are required to adopt the entire EU rule-book before becoming a member state. It can also apply to states agreeing a partnership with the EU, for instance through the European Neighbourhood Policy (Chapter 24, 'The European Neighbourhood Policy'). Through foreign policy, trade, or development aid policy,

49

for instance, Europeanization can also have impacts that go well beyond the EU's neighbourhood (for more, see Schimmelfennig 2015).

While the multiple flows associated with Europeanization were recognized, much empirical research continued to focus on downloading (e.g. Cowles et al. 2001; Dyson and Goetz 2002; Schmidt 2006; Bache 2008; Featherstone and Papadimitriou 2008). Of particular note was the multi-state study by Cowles et al. (2001), which focused on the downward pressure from the EU level on 'domestic structures'. The study looked at two categories of domestic structure: *policy structures*, a concern extending beyond policy content to changes in the political, legal, and administrative structures of policy; and *system-wide domestic structures*, relating to changes in the nation state, its society, and economy. The findings of this study emphasized the importance of the degree of 'fit' between EU-level changes and existing domestic structures, policies, and practices. Poor fit implies strong pressure to adapt; good fit implies weak pressure. The extent to which adaptational pressure leads to domestic change depends on five intervening factors: multiple veto points in the domestic structure; facilitating institutions; domestic organizational and policy-making cultures; the differential empowerment of domestic actors; and learning (Risse et al. 2001: 2).

This theme of domestic adaptation was developed further by Olsen (2002: 932), who, drawing on the new-institutionalist arguments of March and Olsen (1989), argued that:

> the most standard institutional response to novelty is to find a routine in the existing repertoire of routines that can be used. External changes are interpreted and responded to through existing institutional frameworks, including existing causal and normative beliefs about legitimate institutions and the appropriate distribution, exercise and control of power.

Olsen provided two broad explanations for different patterns of Europeanization across member states. The first related to the nature of the pressures 'coming down' from the EU—specifically, that EU pressures are more likely to have an impact in the domestic arena under the following circumstances:

> the more precise their legal foundation; when they are based on hard law rather than soft law; when the affected parties (constituent units) have been involved in developing the arrangement; the greater the independence of their secretariat; if the secretariat is single-headed rather than multiple-headed; and the greater the financial autonomy of the institution or regime.
>
> (Olsen 2002: 933)

The second explanation pointed to differentiated responses to adaptive pressures across member states because 'the (West) European political order is characterized by long, strong and varied institutional histories, with different trajectories of state- and nation-building, resources and capabilities' (Olsen 2002: 934).

The studies summarized above employed different definitions of Europeanization (see Insight 3.1), but common findings emerged. Most obviously, these studies illustrated divergence in the domestic effects of EU membership across different dimensions (e.g. institutions and policies). This was explained by variations in the nature of the EU initiative or decision, and in the degree of fit between this and domestic preferences and practices. Despite the focus on downward causation, there is agreement that

> **Insight 3.1 Definitions of Europeanization**
>
> There are many definitions of Europeanization. The most concise is that of Vink and Graziano (2007: 7):
>
> > the domestic adaptation to European regional integration.
>
> Perhaps the most comprehensive definition of Europeanization comes from Radaelli (2003: 30), who defined it as:
>
> > . . . processes of a) construction, b) diffusion, and c) institutionalization of formal and informal rules, procedures, policy paradigms, styles, 'ways of doing things', and shared beliefs and norms which are first defined and then consolidated in making of EU public policy and politics and then incorporated in the logic of domestic discourse, identities, political structures and public policies.
>
> > (Radaelli 2003: 30)
>
> For framing empirical research with primarily a top-down focus, Bache and Jordan (2006*a*: 30) defined Europeanization as:
>
> > the reorientation or reshaping of politics in the domestic arena in ways that reflect policies, practices and preferences advanced through the EU system of governance.
>
> > (Bache and Jordan 2006a: 30)

Europeanization is a two-way process in which states also seek to upload their preferences to the EU level.

Dyson and Goetz (2002) distinguished between first-generation and second-generation Europeanization studies to illustrate differences between those studies that emphasized the more formal, observable consequences of EU membership and those that focused on less formal and less observable changes (see Table 3.2). Thus, in second-generation studies, Europeanization is not limited to changes in political–administrative structures and policy content, but also focuses on the effects on ideas, discourses, and identities. The second-generation studies therefore reflected the governance turn (see Chapter 2, 'Governance'), NI (Chapter 2, 'New Institutionalism'), and the constructivist research agenda (Chapter 4, 'Social Constructivism'). Researchers' attention was therefore not just on the EU's impact upon formal institutions, but on interests, institutions, and ideas (Anderson 2003).

Europeanization and the New Institutionalisms

As Europeanization research became more fine-grained, it came to be characterized by an NI agenda, including the various sub-branches of that theoretical literature (see Chapter 2, 'New Institutionalism'). The main reason for this development was that Europeanization is just a concept, and not a theory (Bulmer 2007: 47). The three new institutionalisms offered ways to explore the mechanisms of Europeanization. In particular, the contrast between the logic of consequences (a rationalist interpretation) and the logic of appropriateness (a more sociological, 'norm-based' interpretation) was frequently posited to explore research questions (Börzel and Risse 2003). In the

Table 3.2 Summary of Dyson and Goetz (2002) on the 'Two Generations of Europeanization Research'

First generation	Second generation
• Generally top-down approaches, seeking to explain domestic change from EU 'pressures'	• Emphasizes more complex interactions (top-down, bottom-up, and horizontal)
• Assumed 'misfit' between European and domestic levels—particularly formal institutional	• Greater emphasis on the 'political' dynamics of fit: interests, beliefs, values, and ideas
• Emphasis on reactive and involuntary nature of adaptation	• Greater emphasis on voluntary adaptation through policy transfer and learning
• Focus on policy and polity dimensions	• Greater emphasis on politics, e.g. identities, electoral behaviour, parties, and party systems
• Expected increasing cross-national convergence	• Emphasizes differential impact of Europe
• Defined Europeanization in substantive terms—focus on the 'end state' effects	• Emphasizes impact of Europeanization on domestic political, institutional, and policy dynamics

Note: An earlier version of this table appeared in Bache and Marshall (2004).

former case, incentives and resources might facilitate adjustment to the EU at the domestic level, but with the possibility of 'veto points', such as domestic institutional characteristics serving as obstacles to adjustment. In the latter case, socialization and learning or the intervention of 'norm entrepreneurs', who could facilitate domestic absorption of EU-led change, provided accounts of how Europeanization developed (Exadaktylos et al. 2020).

One deployment of these contrasting approaches has been in relation to EU enlargement (see also Chapter 26). Here the question concerned what it was that motivated central and eastern European countries (CEECs) to adapt to the EU's substantial policy rule-book in order to have strong prospects for joining the EU (Schimmelfennig and Sedelmeier 2006: 108–9). Was it a matter of incentives, such as gaining access to EU structural and investment funds and the EU single market that spurred them on? Did these incentives trump the costs of adapting to membership and meeting the all-important conditionality requirements set by the EU, namely the acceptance and assimilation of the formal *acquis communautaire* by accession states? Or was it a matter of the CEE states wanting to establish a European identity, by leaving behind the former influence of the Soviet Union, so that Europeanization was therefore norm-driven? The answer to the overall question—i.e. whether incentives or norms explain candidate states' adaptation—remains disputed (Börzel and Schimmelfennig 2017).

While conditionality may have been important in the short term, recent concerns emerged regarding 'democratic backsliding' in Hungary and Poland (see Chapter 11, 'The Populist Challenge'): the situation whereby these states seemed less committed to the principles of good democratic governance than when they were applicant states. These and similar concerns about prospective member states (see, for instance,

Chapter 26, 'Turkey')—raised questions about the depth of adjustment to the EU's norms. Such concerns also had implications for the EU's enlargement policy in the 2010s (see Chapter 26, 'Enlargement Fatigue?').

Europeanization Applied

Interest in the concept of Europeanization led to a wide range of studies, such as:

- individual member states across politics, polity, and policy dimensions (e.g. Dyson and Goetz (2003) on Germany; Bache and Jordan (2006b) on Britain; and Featherstone and Papadimitriou (2008) on Greece); also see Bulmer and Lequesne (2020);

- specific policy areas in a number of states (e.g. Jordan and Liefferink (2004) on the environment; Faist and Ette (2007) on immigration; and Bache (2008) on cohesion policy);

- institutional effects across different states (e.g. Knill (2001) on national administrations; Hughes et al. (2004) on regionalization) or within a single state (e.g. Bulmer and Burch (2009) on Britain).

Other studies focus on particular parts of Europe (e.g. Schimmelfennig and Sedelmeier (2005) on accession of the CEECs; O'Brennan (2008) on the western Balkans), and some studies cover a range of states and topics (e.g. Cowles et al. (2001); Featherstone and Radaelli (2003)).

Radaelli (2006) suggested that, while it was difficult to map and summarize the diverse range of empirical studies to date, a number of results stood out. In particular, the evidence for the Europeanization of public policies was more robust than the evidence for the effect of Europeanization on political competition, state structures, or the polity. Moreover, while Radaelli was clear that Europeanization did not lead to uniform convergence across Europe, there was evidence of 'clustered convergence' as states with similar characteristics or preferences in a given domain responded in similar ways to particular pressures or opportunities.

Europeanization Assessed

Most recent contributions to the literature have diversified the theoretical frames and raised issues in relation to the scope and methodology of Europeanization research.

Drawing on historical sociology, Trine Flockhart (2010) argued that Europeanization should be understood in terms of a longer time frame. She identified five phases of Europeanization, starting with 'European Self-Realization' in the period up to 1450. Only her fifth phase covered the period since 1945. Her research highlighted that what we typically call Europeanization is really 'EU-ization'. Drawing on critical theoretical frames, notably constructivism (see Chapter 4, 'Social Constructivism'), Woll and Jacquot (2010) looked at 'usages of Europe'—how the EU is something that domestic actors appropriate and exploit for strategic purposes in their own debates.

A key issue in the methodological debate has been the extent to which research design in this area has adequately allowed scholars to assess whether Europeanization—as opposed to other possible factors, domestic or international—is the cause of domestic change. This issue of *causality* was emphasized by Haverland (2005) and subsequently picked up by Exadaktylos and Radaelli (2009), who identified a lack of consistency in research designs and later brought together a number of scholars to look at this issue (Exadaktylos and Radaelli 2012). A central aim of this work was to respond to the criticism that Europeanization research privileges Europe (or the EU) as the explanation for domestic change. In this regard, the policy transfer literature can be instructive (see 'Uploading, Downloading and Crossloading' above).

This methodological reflection on Europeanization research raised fundamental issues relating to underlying theoretical assumptions. Bache et al. (2012) suggested that there had been little explicit reflection on such issues in Europeanization research and argued for a more critical approach, including in research methods. Their argument pressed the claims for critical perspectives (see Chapter 4) to be deployed in Europeanization research.

Europeanization remains a useful concept, but the slackening of the long-standing 'twin dynamics' of deepening (integration) and widening (enlargement) that lay behind the burgeoning of Europeanization research has produced an underlying reversal of the flow of interest: from top-down to bottom-up. Indeed, there are some early analyses of what 'Europeanization in reverse gear' might look like (Gravey and Jordan 2016; Radaelli 2020). This development arises from the growing opposition to European integration.

Analysing Bottom-Up Pressures on the EU

Controversy about European integration has grown significantly during the 2010s. This controversy has arisen from a number of developments. There have always been pockets of opposition to integration, although the UK has arguably been the most prominent in this regard; hence its reputation as an 'awkward partner' (George 1998). For instance, the UK's accession in 1973 was controversial, splitting both major parties, just as Brexit has done in the aftermath of the 2016 referendum. The issue was only settled at that time by a referendum on continued membership in June 1975. The controversy did not disappear; it simply became less consistently salient. In the 2010s, the controversies became more systemic. The eurozone and migration crises brought issues on to the EU's agenda that provoked or exacerbated controversy over the EU in domestic politics.

This increased controversy over EU policies and powers led to a number of significant analytical developments. These included the revival of the so-called domestic politics approach and the emergence of politicization literature as a way to explore that phenomenon; the continued rise of Euroscepticism as a research issue; and the emergence of disintegration as a framework for interrogating the contested status of the EU during the 2010s.

Domestic Politics and Politicization

The domestic politics approach to understanding the EU had been advocated in the 1980s by Bulmer (1983). In essence, it was a level-of-analysis argument. It underlined the importance of understanding political and policy dynamics at member state level in order to understand policy making in the then EC. Up to that point, domestic politics largely had been neglected by neofunctionalists and intergovernmentalists. Moravcsik (1993) incorporated domestic politics analysis into liberal intergovernmentalism (LI) (Chapter 1, 'Liberal Intergovernmentalism'). However, the domestic politics approach had not argued for the rationalist analysis deployed by Moravcsik. Indeed, in applications of the domestic politics approach to Germany and the UK (George 1992; Bulmer and Paterson 2015[1987]) particular attention was devoted to domestic institutional arrangements: something Moravcsik neglected in favour of the role of economic and geopolitical interests in preference formation.

In the 2010s, domestic politics have come under renewed examination in explaining responses to the eurozone and migration crisis and the 2016 British referendum vote on the EU. In fact, some trace the politicization of the EU back to the time of the Maastricht Treaty in that it became clear that there was a breakdown in the '**permissive consensus**' (Lindberg and Scheingold 1970: 41) in public opinion about European integration. Previously, public levels of support for, or toleration of, integration had given quite a lot of independence to political elites. The end of the permissive consensus indicated that the public was no longer going to permit elites to pursue European integration unchecked, as the first Danish referendum revealed in June 1992, when its voters rejected the Maastricht Treaty (Chapter 9, 'After Maastricht'). That the Maastricht Treaty was the turning point is the argument made in new intergovernmentalism (Bickerton et al. 2015a) (see Chapter 2, 'New Intergovernmentalism'). Genschel and Jachtenfuchs (2015: 43) specifically attribute the engagement of mass publics to the EU's intervention in 'core state powers', such as 'money and fiscal affairs, defence and foreign policy, migration, citizenship and internal security'.

The full implications of the end of the permissive consensus came with political contestation around the eurozone and migration crises in the 2010s. While integration theories have some purchase on these developments (Insight 1.2 'Integration Theory and the Refugee Crisis'), other analytical toolkits, such as **politicization**, have offered important insights.

Politicization is one of the component parts of postfunctionalism (Chapter 1, 'Postfunctionalism'). However, it has also emerged as a literature in its own right (De Wilde 2011; Statham and Trenz 2013, 2015; Bellamy and Kröger 2016; De Wilde et al. 2016a). Politicization is not an integration theory but, rather, sets out propositions that are then explored in case studies using a variety of analytical tools. In this sense, politicization is rather like Europeanization: it is a concept that needs another analytical framework to operationalize it. Nevertheless, these propositions are very salient to the political climate of integration in the 2010s, namely that: EU issues have become more salient to domestic politics; EU issues have become more contested, with increasing divergence of preferences; and a wider set of actors and audiences are following EU issues (De Wilde et al. 2016b: 4).

Politicization invites the application of comparative politics analytical frameworks to explore these four propositions. Comparative case studies (e.g. in De Wilde et al. 2016a) reveal the specific circumstances of politicization across member states. The literature has another similarity to Europeanization: the specific form that politicization takes is very much influenced by a distinctive set of characteristics in individual member states.

For example, Statham and Trenz (2013) carried out a monograph-length study of politicization in the context of the protracted negotiations leading to the Constitutional

Treaty and its subsequent rejection by voters in France and the Netherlands in referenda in 2005 (Chapter 10, 'The Constitutional Treaty'). As they noted, one of the motivations of the process leading to the Constitutional Treaty was to improve democracy in the EU. Yet the unintended outcome was the rejection of the proposals (Statham and Trenz 2013: 145–6). Although they find evidence of 'Europeanized public debates' on the Constitutional Treaty, ultimately the politicization of the Constitutional Treaty in France was shaped (or 'mediated') nationally. They were critical of postfunctionalism as developed by Hooghe and Marks (2009) for 'the absence of mass media, communication and a public in their model' (Statham and Trenz 2013: 158). This missing element was of decisive importance for their analysis of the form that politicization took (on the media 'framing' in the EU, see De Wilde 2019).

Euroscepticism

Another way in which bottom-up pressures have been analysed is through the literature on Euroscepticism. The term 'Euroscepticism' originated in the UK context in the mid-1980s (Leruth et al. 2017: 5). It was used to refer to Conservative MPs who were opposed to the direction of integration following agreement on creating the single European market and on the 1986 Single European Act. Gradually, it became a term with EU-wide application.

An important distinction made by Taggart (1998) was between 'soft' and 'hard' Europscepticism (Insight 3.2).

It is important to note that the early work of Taggart (1998) on the concept, and of Szczerbiak and Taggart (2008) in assessing the scale of the phenomenon, focused on political parties. Parties are a kind of touchstone of Euroscepticism: both a cause—through some parties' strategies—and consequence of the phenomenon in wider public opinion. However, research has also been undertaken on Euroscepticism in public opinion in its own right, typically highlighting the link between economic factors and attitudes towards integration (Eichenberg and Dalton 2007; Hobolt and De Vries 2016).

Taggart and Szczerbiak (2018: 1206–11) have charted how the crises of the 2010s have impacted on party-based Euroscepticism across the EU. Their findings revealed that the eurozone crisis had a particularly strong effect on the party systems in debtor states, such as Greece and Ireland, but also in Germany; a creditor state that was central in tackling the crisis. The migration crisis had its main impact in Poland, Hungary, Slovakia,

---

Insight 3.2 Defining Euroscepticism

Hard Euroscepticism: 'principled opposition to the project of European integration as embodied in the EU, in other words, based on the ceding or transfer of powers to a supra-national institution such as the EU'.

Soft Euroscepticism: 'when there was not a principled objection to the European integration project of transferring powers to a supranational body such as the EU, but there was opposition to the EU's current or future planned trajectory based on the further extension of competencies that the EU was planning to make'.

Source: Szczerbiak and Taggart (2017: 13).

and the Czech Republic: states where the level of migration was low but clearly the perception of the issue was higher. Taggart and Szczerbiak (2018: 1206–11) also considered the impact of Brexit on party systems across the EU, but found that difficult to assess. However, one study of its impact on public opinion (De Vries 2017) produced evidence that in the short term Brexit had reinforced *pro*-EU attitudes elsewhere.

'Euroscepticism' has become not only a term more frequently used in EU studies, but one that also offers a conceptual tool that can reveal the form that bottom-up opposition to integration is taking across the member states.

Disintegration

The third literature that has emerged during the 2010s is a consideration of whether the crises, including Brexit, are symptomatic of the EU's *disintegration*. First, we should inject a note of caution. Amidst all the coverage of EU crises, it can be overlooked that the eurozone crisis did actually lead to increased integration through reinforced fiscal surveillance and the creation of a Banking Union. Furthermore, it would be going too far to suggest that disintegration has assumed a significance comparable with integration theory. Nevertheless, the concept of disintegration is way of capturing the accumulation of responses and opposition to integration: the focus of this chapter. Hence it is certainly valid to investigate what disintegration looks like, under what conditions it could arise, and consider whether it is happening. This is the task that has been undertaken by Vollaard (2014, 2018) and Webber (2014, 2019a, 2019b).

A first step is to identify what form disintegration could take. Webber (2019a: 14) identifies three:

- if the EU's sectoral policy coverage were to be reduced;
- if the authority of supranational institutions were to be reduced to the benefit of intergovernmental ones; and
- if a member state were to withdraw—wholly or partially—from the EU.

These indicators of disintegration are developed by turning on their head the indicators used for identifying integration. In his analysis of 'EU disintegration?'—his study's title includes the question-mark—Webber explored the different crises and found evidence of integration and disintegration, depending on the particular crisis (2019a: 210–14). He argued that Germany's continuing commitment to integration would be decisive to the avoidance of disintegration more broadly. Rising politicization alone was identified as a necessary but insufficient condition for disintegration. In this sense, the development of Euroscepticism within Germany has taken on particular significance.

Vollaard's approach was different. He argued that disintegration was not simply integration in reverse. Instead, he drew on the work on political system-building by Bartolini (2005), and considered how that would work in reverse, arriving at the following proposal:

> the process of European disintegration means that actors and resources cannot be locked in as well by the EU, and that the subsequent (partial) exits weaken political structuring within the EU, and the EU's capacity to enforce boundaries and behavioural conformity, to foster loyalty and to allocate goods and values

(Vollaard 2014: 1149).

Vollaard's approach is especially significant in the context of Brexit. If the EU found it difficult to maintain its external boundary, he argued that this might erode compliance, the commitment of other states, and the erosion of public loyalty. Vollaard therefore gave one view of what was at stake for the EU with Brexit, although testing what happens as a result of Britain's exit from the EU at the end of January 2020 will require a longer-term perspective.

Disintegration, whether assessed along the three parameters identified by Webber or around the important issue of boundaries identified by Vollaard, is a potential development arising from bottom-up resistance to integration. However, it is important to recall the insights of historical institutionalist analysis of the EU (Chapter 2, 'Historical Institutionalism') or indeed of the persistent dynamic of spillover in neo-functionalism (Chapter 1, 'Neofunctionalism'). In other words, the EU is like a super-tanker: it can take a long time to turn due to path dependence in its development, and the sunk costs of member states. Politicization and Euroscepticism will need to take on greater significance beyond Brexit if disintegration of the EU is to become a serious possibility. Indeed, Laffan (2019) has demonstrated how the Brexit negotiations brought together the remaining member states (the EU27).

Democracy and Legitimacy

For a long time, European integration proceeded with relatively little public or political debate on the implications for democracy and legitimacy. Decisions were taken by elites in the context of a 'permissive consensus'. The absence of public debate and protest on developments was taken as evidence of consent. European integration appeared to have low salience for most people. Economic integration was relatively uncontroversial in the context of a globalizing marketplace, and unanimous voting procedures were in place to protect perceived national interests.

These circumstances broke down after the 1992 Maastricht Treaty and clearly no longer applied by the 2010s, with rising politicization and Euroscepticism, as we have seen (see 'Analyzing Bottom-Up Pressures on the EU' above). These new circumstances gave renewed salience to two long-standing questions concerning the EU (and the EC before it): 'Is it democratic?' and 'Is it legitimate?' We look at each of these in turn.

The central point concerning democracy—whether in the EU or in a nation state—is whether procedures are in place to ensure the participation of 'the governed' in the political system (see Insight 3.3). Legitimacy, by contrast, has a wider meaning. It concerns whether the public feel a sense of trust towards a political system. This trust derives from three elements: input legitimacy, output legitimacy, and throughput legitimacy (see Insight 3.4). Input legitimacy has a strong overlap with democracy, as defined in Insight 3.3.

Legitimacy therefore encompasses a wider remit than democracy. It can be summarized thus: input legitimacy focuses on the *who* of decision making, output legitimacy on the *what*, and throughput legitimacy focuses on the *how* (Schmidt, 2013: 2). There is a tension between these dimensions, however; by increasing democratic input it may become more difficult to deliver effective policy outcomes. Equally, the public may be

Insight 3.3 Democracy

Christopher Lord (2001: 166–7) suggested that democracy, defined as 'a system of government in which the people rule themselves', can be reduced to two core attributes: 'The first is that the public must be able to control those who make decisions on its behalf, even where it does not directly assume the reins of government; and, second, citizens should exercise such control as equals, since a condition in which some decide on behalf of others is paternalism, not democracy . . . '.

Albert Weale (1999a: 14) defined democracy as a condition in which 'important public decisions on questions of law and policy depend, directly or indirectly, upon public opinion formally expressed by citizens of the community, the vast bulk of whom have equal political rights'.

Insight 3.4 Dimensions of Legitimacy

Input Legitimacy

Input legitimacy concerns whether the EU has legitimacy through *participation*. Are decisions made in a way that involves those being governed: whether through elections, referenda, citizens' assemblies or other means?

Output Legitimacy

Output legitimacy concerns the legitimacy of the *outcomes*, or of the performance of the political system. Does the EU provide policy solutions that address the public's concerns? The more people a policy benefits, the more it is legitimate.

Throughput Legitimacy

Throughput legitimacy is concerned with the political *processes* that define how decisions are made. 'Throughput consists of governance processes with the people, analyzed in terms of their efficacy, accountability, transparency, inclusiveness and openness to interest consultation' (Schmidt 2013: 2; see also Schmidt and Wood 2019).

willing to set aside concerns about a democratic deficit, provided that the EU is seen to be delivering desired policy outputs. This was the case in earlier decades, when the permissive consensus applied, but during the 2010s it has been replaced by what Hooghe and Marks (2009) have termed a 'constraining dissensus'. The controversial nature of the crises experienced by the EU during the 2010s explains why European voters are more willing to vote for Eurosceptic parties to express their frustration.

Whilst democracy and legitimacy are different concepts, their proximity—and the fact that they are sometimes conflated into 'democratic legitimacy'—make it important to be clear about usage and definitions. In the EU, much of the focus both in the analytical literature (Beetham and Lord 1998; Scharpf 1998; Moravcsik 2002; Hix 2008) and in public debate has been around the EU's 'democratic deficit'.

The Democratic Deficit

The notion of the democratic deficit has been defined in a number of ways, but is essentially concerned with the degree to which the EU adequately represents and is accountable to European citizens (see Insight 3.5). However, there is a broader problem across the western world relating to democracy. This phenomenon was charted by Mair (2013) in his book, *Ruling the Void*. He highlighted phenomena such as declining party membership, declining turnout in some elections, and voters' increased willingness to change their allegiance. At the same time, a growing pattern of governance was to delegate some policy functions, such as central banking and competition policy, to experts, thereby making them less directly part of the political arena and creating problems of accountability (e.g. on Britain, see Flinders 2008). The objective of this pattern of governance was to de-politicize policy.

Mair devoted a whole chapter to the EU in *Ruling the Void* (2013: 99–142), and was hard-hitting in his analysis:

> the EU should not be seen as particularly exceptional or sui generis, but rather as a political system that has been constructed by national political leaders as a protected sphere in which policy-making can evade the constraints imposed by representative democracy.

(Mair 2013: 99).

Mair linked this pattern directly to Europeanization. He went beyond conventional diagnoses of the democratic deficit and argued that Europeanization had indirectly hollowed out *national* democracy because EU membership limited the policy space (or policy options) and the policy instruments available at the member state level. In other words, it limited democratic choice at the domestic level (Mair 2013: 115–16). Furthermore, Europeanization had created the difficulty for voters of how to identify policy origin: from the EU or the member state? These criticisms echoed those of Schmidt (2006: 22), who described the situation as characterized by 'politics without policy' at the national level and 'policy without politics' at the EU level. Thus, the policy space was reduced at the member state level, where party politics was more vibrant, but wider at the EU level, where political contestation was more difficult to organize. As noted in Chapter 2, the EU's pre-disposition to regulatory governance by experts has contributed to these problems (Chapter 2, 'Regulatory Governance').

Mair's important contribution was therefore to argue that Europeanization had had an adverse impact on democracy, including at the member state level (see also Mair 2007). Europeanization had contributed to the 'void' mentioned in the title of his

---

Insight 3.5 The Democratic Deficit

- This refers to the idea that EU decisions are 'in some ways insufficiently representative of, or accountable to, the nations and the people of Europe' (Lord 2001: 165).

- It is said that the EU suffers from 'deficiencies in representation, representativeness, accountability and support' (Eriksen and Fossum 2002: 401).

book. Reworking a paradox that Mair notes (2013: 139), it is interesting to contrast the title of one of the first papers on theorizing Europeanization (Börzel and Risse 2000)—'when Europe hits home'—with the bottom-up pressures of domestic politics, expressed through politicization and Euroscepticism. These are when the public 'hits Europe'.

Mair's understanding of the EU's impact on democracy was presented on a very broad canvas. An approach more focused on the democratic deficit—and with a clear 'charge sheet'—was that of Hix (2008: 68–71), who identified five common claims made about the democratic deficit:

- that national parliaments have lost power to national executives in relation to EU policy;
- that the European Parliament (EP) lacked sufficient powers despite increases through successive EU reforms;
- that the voters in EP elections did not see their choice as part of a contest for high office in the EU;
- that the EU was too remote and different from national politics for EU citizens to comprehend; and
- that, largely as a result, the policies that citizens want is not what they in fact get.

In his analysis of these claims, Hix argued that four of the claims did not stack up strongly, but the need to make EP elections about choosing candidates for high office needed to be addressed. In fact, political practice changed with the 2014 elections to the EP—the first after the implementation of the Lisbon Treaty—resulting in the main parties having a lead-candidate (given the German name *Spitzenkandidat*). The assumption was that whichever party won the election would nominate their lead-candidate to be Commission president. This duly happened when Jean-Claude Juncker, the *Spitzenkandidat* of the European People's Party, was nominated and then became President of the Commission in autumn 2014. However, the process was not followed in 2019, undermining one of Hix's proposals for rectifying the democratic deficit (see Chapter 15, 'The EP and the Commission').

Hix's general objective (2008: 163–5) in his proposals was to create 'identifiable EU politics'; in other words, to create a clearly recognizable political contest, with clearer consequences. His wish to 'fill the existing constitutional shell with some democratic political content' (Hix: 2008: 165) was well-intentioned. This development has certainly occurred, and the rise in Euroscepticism in the EP has been notable over the past decade.

In broad terms, there are two ways in which the EU can respond to the concerns about the democratic deficit: through institutional means, or by other means of securing citizens' engagement with the EU. The former found expression in the significant increase in EP powers over the period from the 1986 Single European Act to the 2007 Lisbon Treaty. The latter was concerned with seeking to enhance the sense of a European identity (or of a European 'demos'—the notion of a people that is the root of the word 'democracy'). Such steps included, for instance, the creation of European citizenship in the 1992 Maastricht Treaty or efforts to establish a Charter of Fundamental Rights. Both were efforts to encourage citizens to identify more with the EU and mobilize them into engagement in its democratic process.

Democracy and Legitimacy in the EU Assessed

Debates about the EU's democratic legitimacy have been ongoing for at least five decades (for a comprehensive history, see Sternberg 2013). The introduction of direct elections to the EP in 1979, replacing the previous system of delegates selected from national parliaments, was an early corrective step. The last major reform of the EU—the Lisbon Treaty—also sought to address the issue (amongst many others). It strengthened the powers of the EP, enshrined the principle of democratic equality between EU citizens, gave the national parliaments new control powers, boosted the powers of EU-level parties, and introduced a new form of participatory democracy, the 'citizens' initiative' (whereby EU citizens can initiate legislative action with a petition requiring a million supporters from at least one-quarter of the member states).

Weighed against these steps, however, the 2010s have witnessed a number of developments that have damaged the EU's democratic legitimacy. The EU's difficulties in tackling the eurozone and migration crises damaged its legitimacy and gave fuel to Eurosceptic parties (Kratochvíl and Sychra 2019). The imposition of austerity policies on debtor states such as Greece overrode domestic democratic principles, with little involvement from the EP in the process either. Euroscepticism's populist approach to politics is nationally focused and directly damaging to the idea of creating a European identity or 'demos'. This was most obviously the case with the UK vote in 2016 to leave the EU: the ultimate step to reverse Europeanization.

Finally, several CEECs have taken political steps that seem to call into question the Europeanization undertaken in conjunction with EU accession. These steps have called into question judicial independence (Hungary and Poland), and respect for constitutional court rulings (Romania). In Hungary, there have also been measures purging the administration in favour of party cronies, censorship of the media, and a crackdown on civil society organizations (Magen 2016: 1057). Collectively, these steps are known as 'democratic backsliding'. These developments have compounded the democratic challenges facing the EU, as well as making it more difficult for the EU to promote democracy in its foreign policy.

CONCLUSION

This chapter has brought together several separate 'consequences' of European integration: Europeanization effects; bottom-up responses to Europeanization, such as politicization and Euroscepticism; and continuing questions about democracy and legitimacy in the EU. However, as noted throughout, there are clear links between them. Europeanization as a process has changed domestic politics, policies, and political systems. Most obviously, the process of Europeanization has obscured lines of political accountability, so that citizens are unsure whom to hold to account on particular issues. Political elites may use 'Europeanization' as a smokescreen that conceals their own activities and deliberately misleads voters if it is expedient for them to do so. Equally, political elites may themselves be unclear about where responsibility, and thus accountability, should lie.

On a more positive note, Europeanization effects may enhance output democracy through its strong reliance on expertise in regulatory governance. Common action at the level of the EU may bring 'performance' benefits to citizens: for example, through more efficient management of environmental policy or through the economic benefits arising from the single market. However, for this to enhance legitimacy, it is necessary that the increased efficiency is recognized and that it is recognized as an effect of membership of the EU. It is perhaps a problem that some of the main benefits of European integration are relatively intangible or unrecognized, while some of its failings are not. Moreover, the EU's supporters have the problem of proving the counterfactual: how do we know that member states and their citizens would not have fared as well—if not better—without EU membership? Such questions become even more pertinent at times of political and economic crisis, such as in the context of the eurozone crisis (see Chapters 11 and 20).

KEY POINTS

Europeanization

- The concept of Europeanization has been defined and employed in a variety of ways. For some, Europeanization is a phenomenon that is broader than or separate from the EU but is generally used to conceptualize the changing relationship between the EU and its member (and accession) states.

- Europeanization became increasingly understood as a two-way relationship between the EU and its member states, involving both the *uploading* of ideas and practices from member states to the EU level, and the *downloading* of ideas and practices from the EU level to member states. However, the focus of most research has been on the downloading effects.

- The notion of *crossloading* refers to the transfer of ideas or practices from one state to another: a process in which the EU may or may not play a role.

- *First-generation* studies tended to focus on observable changes through Europeanization, typically focused on the degree of fit or misfit between EU decisions and domestic practices and preferences. *Second-generation* studies placed greater emphasis on the changes in ideas, values, and identities.

- As Europeanization research became more fine-grained, it was increasingly characterized by an NI agenda.

- Most recent contributions to the literature have diversified the theoretical frames, raised issues in relation to the scope and methodology of Europeanization research, and have even explored Europeanization in reverse.

Analysing Bottom-Up Pressures on the EU

- Controversy surrounding the EU during the 2010s led to renewed focus on bottom-up approaches to understanding the EU.

- One way of understanding the increased importance of domestic politics is through the politicization literature. It has explored the greater salience of EU issues in domestic politics, the greater contestation surrounding them, and the widening of interest in them.

- The literature on Euroscepticism has become more central to EU studies. A distinction is made between 'hard Euroscepticism' (principled opposition to integration/the EU) and soft Euroscepticism (opposition to further powers being assumed by the EU).

- The eurozone crisis has impacted on party-based Euroscepticism in debtor states, but also in Germany. The impact of the migration crisis has been significant on party-based Euroscepticism in Poland, Hungary, Slovakia, and the Czech Republic.

- The EU crises during the 2010s have raised questions about whether there is evidence of the EU's disintegration.

63

- Webber identified a reduction in policy range, in supranational institutions' authority, and the withdrawal of a member state as indicators of disintegration, whereas Vollaard placed emphasis on maintenance of the EU's external boundaries.

Democracy and Legitimacy

- For a long time, European integration proceeded with little public debate about the democratic dimension. This changed as the EU's competencies expanded and was given particular impetus through the controversial ratification processes of various Treaties.
- Democracy and legitimacy are contested concepts and their relationship is not always clear in the EU literature. In essence, democracy is concerned with public control over the exercise of power, while legitimacy can be understood in terms of input, throughput, and output.
- The notion of the democratic deficit has been central to much scholarly work in the area, focusing on the lack of accountability of the EU's institutions and the relatively weak position of the EP as the only directly elected body.
- Mair (2013) considered the EU to have been built to avoid political control and that the consequence of Europeanization at member state level has been to limit political debate and to blur lines of accountability.
- Hix's assessment (2008) of the democratic deficit led him to propose a direct link between elections to the EP and selecting EU political leaders, but this only occurred so far in 2014.
- Problems of legitimacy and democracy remain in the 2010s, and democratic backsliding in some CEECs has created new challenges.

 For additional material and resources, please visit the online resources www.oup.com/uk/bache5e.

QUESTIONS

1. Is Europeanization best understood as explaining top-down pressures from the EU that impact on domestic politics and policy?
2. Why is increasing attention being paid to the importance of domestic politics and politicization for developments at the EU level?
3. What is Euroscepticism, and why is it so important to understanding today's EU?
4. Does the concept of disintegration offer insights into recent developments in the EU?
5. Why has the democratic deficit been such a long-standing problem for the EU?

FURTHER READING

Europeanization

A useful introductory article is **J. Olsen**, 'The Many Faces of Europeanization', *Journal of Common Market Studies*, 40 (2002): 921–52. **S. Bulmer and C. Lequesne (eds)**, *The Member States of the European Union*, 3rd edn (Oxford: Oxford University Press, 2020) explore Europeanization as a concept and how the EU impacts on a selection of member states, with a final thematic section of the book that examines the impact of Europeanization on institutions, politics, policy, and political economy. **P. Graziano and M. Vink (eds)**, *Europeanization: New Research Agendas* (Basingstoke: Palgrave Macmillan, 2007) provide a comprehensive collection on Europeanization, with twenty-five thematic contributions from experts in their respective fields, covering theory, methods, politics, polity, and policies.

M. G. Cowles, J. Caporaso, and T. Risse (eds), *Transforming Europe: Europeanization and Domestic Change* (Ithaca, NY: Cornell University Press, 2001) and **K. Featherstone and C. Radaelli (eds)**, *The Politics of Europeanization* (Oxford: Oxford University Press, 2003) remain valuable resources on Europeanization. **F. Schimmelfennig and U. Sedelmeier (eds)**, *The Europeanization of Central and Eastern Europe* (Ithaca, NY: Cornell University Press, 2005) is a useful first stop for the subject of Europeanization and EU accession.

Analysing Bottom-Up Pressures on the EU

The starting point for the literature on politicization is **P. De Wilde, A. Leupold, and H. Schmidtke**, 'Introduction: The Differentiated Politicisation of European Governance', *West European Politics*, 39 (2016): 3–22. The rest of the special issue gives valuable applications of politicization to case studies. **B. Leruth, N. Startin, and S. Usherwood (eds)**, *The Routledge Handbook of Euroscepticism* (London: Routledge, 2017) offers extensive coverage to the Euroscepticism literature. Also recommended is **C. de Vries**, *Euroscepticism and the Future of European Integration* (Oxford: Oxford University Press, 2018). On disintegration, useful starting points are **D. Webber**, 'How Likely is It that the European Union Will Disintegrate? A Critical Analysis of Competing Theoretical Perspectives', *European Journal of International Relations*, 20 (2014): 341–65 and **H. Vollaard**, 'Explaining European Disintegration', *Journal of Common Market Studies*, 52 (2014): 1142–59.

Democracy and Legitimacy

Useful studies on democracy in the EU are the following: **S. Kröger and D. Friedrich (eds)**, *The Challenge of Democratic Representation in the European Union* (Basingstoke: Palgrave Macmillan, 2012); **S. Piattoni (ed.)**, *The European Union: Democratic Principles and Institutional Architecture in Times of Crisis* (Oxford: Oxford University Press, 2015), which includes coverage in the context of the eurozone crisis, and **S. Hix**, *What's Wrong with the European Union and How to Fix it* (Cambridge: Polity Press, 2008). Also of enduring relevance is **F. Scharpf**, *Governing in Europe: Effective and Democratic?* (Oxford: Oxford University Press, 1998). Valuable for exploring the interaction between the eurozone crisis and EU democracy is: **P. Kratochvíl, P. and Z. Sychra**, 'The End of Democracy in the EU? The Eurozone Crisis and the EU's Democratic Deficit', *Journal of European Integration*, 41 (2019): 169–85.

On legitimacy, a good starting point is **V. Schmidt**, 'Democracy and Legitimacy in the European Union Revisited: Input, Output and "Throughput"', *Political Studies*, 61 (2013): 2–22. For a more detailed dissection, see **C. S. Sternberg**, *The Struggle for EU Legitimacy: Public Contestation, 1950–2005* (Basingstoke: Palgrave Macmillan, 2013).

Chapter 4
Critical Perspectives

Chapter Overview

If the 'governance turn' of the 1990s heralded the arrival of significant new voices in the European Union (EU) debate (see Chapter 2), there is now an even wider chorus. The perspectives and theories covered in this chapter are long established in the study of politics, but have only relatively recently become visible in the mainstream study of the EU. Critical perspectives, although very different from each other, are united in challenging key assumptions about how the EU should be studied, and what we can hope to know. They are generally concerned with exposing which actors and ideas are dominant in the EU and highlighting the less obvious manifestations of power that pervade the interrelated worlds of political action and political theorizing (see Part One, 'Theory', Table I.1). They tend to concur with the assertion of critical political economist Robert Cox (1981: 128), who said that, 'Theory is always for someone and for some purpose.' Given the key questions of power and politicization that have been more exposed during the 2010s, 'dissident theory' has come to challenge the more mainstream approaches discussed in Chapters 1 and 2 in a more vigorous way than before (Whitman and Manners 2016).

The range of critical perspectives now applied to the EU is too great to cover in a single chapter. Here we focus on five perspectives which provide a flavour of the variety of critical approaches that have been used to study aspects of the EU. *Social constructivism* offers a critique of rationalist approaches that have dominated much of the study of the EU (see Chapters 1 and 2). *Critical political economy* considers the EU in the context of broader dynamics of global capitalism, often building on earlier Marxist scholarship. *Critical social theory* emphasizes the ways in which the EU has transformed European society and politics in ways that are often unrecognized. *Critical feminism* points to the ways in which the issue of gender has been marginalized in the EU and in mainstream approaches to the study of the EU. Finally, *post-structuralist perspectives* seek to question the prevailing wisdom associated with the EU and its ideals. Several of these approaches engage, at least implicitly, with academia's recent interest in 'decolonizing the curriculum' by looking at some of the biases in the mainstream literature that, for instance, exclude issues of gender and socioeconomic inequality from EU studies. Central to all the approaches covered is an attempt to think critically about assumptions in mainstream EU studies: something that we consider indispensable to understanding the 'nature of the beast' (Parker 2016).

Critical of What?

All of the theories considered in Chapters 1–3 are in their own ways critical of something, often a competing theoretical perspective. However, the 'critical' perspectives considered in this chapter are united in their critique of mainstream 'rationalist' or 'positivist' approaches to the study of the social and political world. 'Positivist' approaches are those that assume a fixed social reality (**ontology**) and understand knowledge of that social reality to be obtained via the neutral observation of an objective scholar (**epistemology**). Many of the approaches considered in the previous chapters fall within this positivist mainstream. Thus, for example, intergovernmental approaches assume that states remain key actors in driving integration (ontology) and that scholars can acquire knowledge about integration by objectively studying the actions of states (epistemology).

In contrast, the critical—often termed 'post-positivist'—approaches discussed in this chapter emphasize the constructed and changeable nature of the social and political world. Many such approaches consider that social reality cannot be objectively observed and believe that various agents, including policy actors and scholars themselves, are involved in its construction. Critical scholarship often seeks to highlight which actors, ideas, or theories are either dominant or excluded in the politics of the EU at particular historical junctures or in particular policy areas. In so doing, they point to the less obvious manifestations of power that pervade the interrelated worlds of political action and political theorizing (for the sorts of questions posed by such approaches see Part One, 'Theory', Table I.1). Implicitly or explicitly, critical work of this kind suggests that 'another Europe is possible' (Manners 2007; Whitman and Manners 2016).

That said, the extent to which 'mainstream' theories are tied to a fixed ontology is itself debatable. For instance, neofunctionalist texts (see Chapter 1, 'Neofunctionalism') refer to interest groups' 'loyalties' *moving* to the EU (or its antecedents) as a new location of power, in a manner that we might associate with processes of 'learning' within social constructivism (see 'Social Constructivism' below). Indeed, the father of neofunctionalism, Ernst Haas (2001: 22), stated that '[a] case can easily be made' that neofunctionalism is a precursor to constructivism. It could be argued that several other theories considered in the foregoing chapters, such as historical and sociological institutionalism (see Chapter 2, 'New Institutionalism'), also sit somewhere between positivist mainstream and post-positivist critical approaches. Moreover, social constructivism, discussed in this chapter, in certain guises explicitly seeks to offer a middle way between these positions. Risse and Wiener (1999: 776) have noted, for instance, that certain strands of social constructivism concur with the positivist epistemology of an objectively observable world even as they reject a fixed ontology.

Positivist and post-positivist positions are consequently best visualized as ideal types on a continuum, with individual scholarly contributions lying somewhere along this continuum. Table 4.1 represents an attempt to map a selection of the theories considered in this, and previous chapters, onto this continuum, although it is important to note that it is a matter for significant debate as to where these are most appropriately placed. Moreover, individual scholars identifying with any given approach may consider their own work to be positioned differently and have a far more nuanced understanding of their ontology and epistemology than the table suggests. Critical approaches that lie towards the post-positivist end of this continuum (those in bold on the table) are the focus of this chapter. These have become increasingly prominent in the study of the EU in recent decades, both due to developments in political theorizing more broadly and due to events in EU politics (Rosamond 2007; Whitman and Manners 2016).

Social Constructivism

Social constructivism entered the debate on the EU not to dispute either the intergovernmental or supranational interpretation of integration, but rather to challenge the (rationalist) assumptions on which the dominant integration theories were built. As such, it should be understood as an 'ontological approach to social inquiry' (Cowles 2003: 110), which regards social and political reality as socially constructed. As Risse underlines (2019: 129), 'social constructivism does not constitute a substantive theory of European integration' . . . 'it does not make particular substantive claims about European integration'. While critical of rationalist approaches, constructivists in both international relations (IR) and EU studies tend to situate themselves at different points on the positivist/post-positivist continuum. Many who would associate with the constructivist label would see their approach as an attempt to bridge the divide, taking seriously social construction while maintaining a commitment to scientific positivism and objectivity.

The social constructivist approach is closely related to sociological institutionalism (Chapter 2, 'Sociological Institutionalism'). Both approaches emphasize that actors' behaviour is influenced by the 'logic of appropriate behaviour' or norms, which Katzenstein (1996: 5) defined as 'collective expectations for the proper behaviour of actors with a given identity'. In this view, political actors internalize social norms, which shape their identities and thus their interests. This is what constructivists refer to as the 'constitutive effects' of norms.

The constructivist view that the actions of individuals cannot be understood in isolation from their social environment contrasts with the rationalists' emphasis on 'methodological individualism', in which the central focus is on 'individual human

Table 4.1 Mapping Approaches on a Positivist/Post-Positivist Continuum

	ONTOLOGY Nature of (social) reality	EPISTEMOLOGY How knowledge is acquired	CONTINUUM (from positivist to post-positivist)
Positivism	FIXED	Objective observation Separation of object and observer	Liberal intergovernmentalism Rational choice institutionalism
Between positivism and post-positivism	(SOMEWHAT) CONSTRUCTED	Objective observation possible Some interest in discourse/ideas	Neofunctionalism Historical institutionalism Sociological institutionalism
Post-positivism	CONSTRUCTED	Focus on shifting discourse/ideas Subjective/normative observation Observer likely to impact upon object of study	**Social constructivism Critical political economy (neo-Gramscian) Critical social theory Critical feminism Post-structuralism**

action' (Risse 2009: 145). However, while constructivists emphasize that individuals' interests and identities are shaped by the social environment in which they exist, equally they argue that the social environment is shaped over time by the actions of individuals. This relationship—sometimes described in terms of **structure and agency** (Hay 2002: 81–134)—is one of two-way interaction and thus, in the words of constructivists, 'mutually constitutive'.

The essential constructivist critique of rationalist approaches is that a focus on material interests (such as economic interests or security) alone offers an inadequate explanation of key developments in European integration. Such an explanation ignores the role played by deeply embedded cultures that shape national positions, and the role of ideas and values that connect political leaders or other actors. As such, a constructivist history of the EU would:

> focus on the ongoing struggles, contestations, and discourses on how 'to build Europe' over the years and, thus, reject an imagery of actors including governments as calculating machines who always know what they want and are never uncertain about the future and even their own stakes and interests.

(Risse 2009: 147)

Constructivist Work on the EU

As noted, constructivism is not a theory as such and constructivist scholars differ significantly in terms of the focus and purpose of their analysis. Drawing on Saurugger (2013: 152), we focus here on two interrelated constructivist research themes: socialization and learning and the social construction of European identity.

Many constructivist scholars have studied how identities evolve through learning and socialization, often with a focus on such processes within European institutions. Socialization refers to the process by which actors develop common understandings and internalize common norms in response. For example, many scholars have considered socialization in relation to relatively new EU governance processes such as the 'open method(s) of co-ordination' (OMC) that are explicitly based on the exchange of best practice between member states and thus learning (see Chapter 2, 'New Methods of Governance'). For instance, Radaelli (2008) has noted that three forms of learning can take place in this context: 'learning at the top' between EU civil servants; 'hierarchical learning' from EU to domestic level; and 'bottom up learning' whereby non-state actors and local actors diffuse their knowledge.

Several constructivists have considered the ways in which ideas about Europe or the EU have been constructed and with what consequence. Such analyses often highlight the ways in which ideas produce outcomes, which a consideration of material factors (alone) cannot easily explain. For instance, Risse argued that the EU's decision to enlarge to twenty-five members in 2004 was largely a function of the member states' socialization into a particular conception of 'Europe'. Commission officials acted as 'norm entrepreneurs' to promote a sense of shared community values (democracy, human rights, and market economics) between the fifteen, which generated a normative obligation towards the applicant states who shared these values. In this way, '[r]hetorical commitment to community values entrapped EU member states into offering accession negotiations to the CEE [central and eastern Europe] and other Eastern European countries despite the initial preferences against enlargement' (Risse 2009: 157) (see also Chapter 26, 'Explanations of the "Eastern" Enlargement'). It was noted, however, that once negotiations began, rationalist accounts provided a more fitting explanation of the strategic bargaining by national governments. This acceptance of the differential appropriateness of forms of explanation is evidence that certain strands of constructivism do not seek to displace rationalist theories entirely, but to contribute to a more complete picture of how the EU works.

Rosamond (2002) has similarly discussed the ways in which concepts such as the 'European economy' and related concepts such as 'European firms' or 'European competitiveness' have been socially constructed. While they may seem like common-sense notions, Rosamond draws attention to the ways in which the Commission, along with networks of interest and advisory groups, was instrumental in constructing them over time and the ways in which significant economic actors came to identify with them (note some similarities here with neofunctionalist ideas about spillover, see Chapter 1, 'Neofunctionalism'). Just as with the case of enlargement highlighted above, such use of discourse was important in determining particular possible policy responses and excluding others. In the case of 'European competitiveness', the concept worked alongside others such as 'globalization' to present the EU within a global context that required a particular, rather narrow, set of 'neoliberal' policy responses (Rosamond 2002: 172). We have arguably seen such responses in the adoption of strategies such as the Lisbon Agenda, in 2000, and Europe 2020, in 2010 (see Chapter 10, 'The Lisbon Strategy' and Chapter 11, 'Europe 2020'; also see 'Critical Political Economy'). There are important affinities between aspects of Rosamond's argument and the work of the critical political economists discussed below.

Ideas about the EU may also be purposefully deployed for strategic reasons in national politics (see also Chapter 3, 'Europeanization'). Hay and Rosamond (2002) highlighted how *ideas associated with* either European integration or globalization may, even in the absence of solid evidence, be presented by political actors as external imperatives to justify unpopular domestic reform measures, particularly to the political economy. As they note (2002: 148):

> In a number of contemporary European contexts, it is the process of European integration (often in the immediate form of the Maastricht convergence criteria) which is (or has been) invoked as the proximate cause of often painful social and economic reforms elsewhere legitimated in terms of globalization.

Whether political actors invoke European integration as the reason for such reforms has depended on the extent to which the EU is popular in a given national polity and likely to aid in legitimating unpopular reforms. Hence it is important to note that, with the EU's increased politicization in the 2010s, critical views of EU policies—for example in debtor states during the eurozone crisis, or of the EU generally in connection with Brexit—have been used to legitimate domestic electoral campaigns by Eurosceptic parties or the Leave campaigns in the 2016 British referendum.

Constructivism Assessed

Risse (2004: 151) usefully highlighted three main ways in which social constructivism contributes to our understanding of the EU:

1. By highlighting the mutually constitutive nature of agency and structure, it allows for a deeper understanding of the impact of the EU on its member states, and particularly on statehood.

2. By emphasizing the constitutive effects of EU rules and policies, it facilitates study of the ways in which EU membership shapes the interests and identities of actors.

3. By focusing on communicative practices, it highlights both how the EU is constructed discursively and how actors come to understand the meaning of European integration.

Conversely, Cowles (2003: 110–11) identified three criticisms of constructivism:

1. that it lacks a theory of agency and shows a tendency to overemphasize the role of structures rather than the actors who help to shape those structures;

2. that much of the early constructivist literature tended to focus its analysis on public actors to the relative neglect of important non-state actors;

3. that there is a tendency amongst some constructivists to identify the good things that have been socially constructed rather than the bad.

The last of these points is of particular concern to the critical approaches considered in the following sections.

Critical Political Economy

In this section, we focus on the work of a group of largely neo-Marxist scholars who have engaged with the EU. Before considering them, it is important to issue two disclaimers. First, not all approaches that are critical of the EU political economy are explicitly critical of mainstream theoretical approaches to the study of the EU covered in Chapters 1–3 of this book. Second, a number of scholars interested in critically reflecting on political economy issues may not associate themselves explicitly with a Marxist or neo-Marxist tradition. Scholars have, for instance, deployed broadly constructivist and post-structuralist approaches in order to make claims that are in some respects similar to those made by authors considered in this section (the work of Rosamond and Hay in 'Constructivist Work on the EU' above and the work of Parker considered in 'Critical Social Theory Work on the EU' below are examples). Thus, while this section focuses on neo-Marxist scholars, it is important to highlight that they are not representative of all those who have said something 'critical' in relation to the EU political economy.

Exponents of neo-Marxist critical political economy (CPE) are united in its emphasis on the role of capitalism and material factors in shaping the social world in terms of distinct classes. However, there are many disagreements among scholars influenced by the work of Marx. A key disagreement can be understood in terms of the aforementioned debate on **structure and agency**: the extent to which capitalism and the relations of production are fixed, unchangeable structures or potentially shaped and influenced in important ways by mediating agents such as states, institutions, or labour movements (for more on this debate, see Bieler et al. 2006).

Those neo-Marxists—notably the 'neo-Gramscian' scholars discussed in 'Critical Political Economy Work on the EU'—who do see some role for agents in shaping political economy have been particularly active in their engagement with the EU as an object of study and will constitute the main focus of this section. This sub-set of neo-Marxist scholars tends to concur with the constructivist assertion that the political and social world is constructed and that ideas and discourses therefore matter in shaping that world. However, they are critical of what they term 'liberal constructivist approaches', asserting that we ought to take more seriously material or capitalist structures and emphasize that EU social and political reality is constructed in ways which favour particular interests or classes (van Apeldoorn et al. 2003; van Apeldoorn and Horn 2019). The work of such scholars thus seeks to expose the ways in which particular elite or capitalist interests are constructed and have prevailed in the context of European integration and constituted a 'neoliberal' order. At the same time, they are critical of an 'orthodoxy' in mainstream studies of integration that has failed to critique such an order and been complicit in its constitution (Ryner 2012; Ryner and Cafruny 2017).

Critical Political Economy Work on the EU

Critical political economists view the EU and its historical evolution in the context of broader developments in the capitalist world economy. They argue that dominant theories of integration serve to obscure deeper underlying explanations and purposes of the EU. Neo-Marxists, such as Peter Cocks and Stuart Holland, were making such arguments in the 1980s. As Cocks (1980: 39) put it:

> Regional integration was a mechanism for accommodating and reinforcing the expansion of European capital while simultaneously protecting it from the possibly excessive rigours of international competition. Ideologically, supranational ideas such as federalism and functionalism provided moral and intellectual justifications at the elite level for European regional organization.

Holland (1980: 89) emphasized the importance of social class and political power to the integration process, suggesting that mainstream accounts excluded these phenomena from their analyses:

> Class analysis has Marxist connotations which raise issues of exploitation and power which are inconveniently disturbing to many of the élites engaged in integration itself. Lifting the lid on class relations opens a Pandora's box of the kind which key exponents and advocates of international integration have been trying to close and bury for some time.

From this perspective, the neofunctionalist theory dominant at the time rested on problematic pluralist assumptions regarding the wide dispersal of power within society, namely that no single group would be able to dominate the integration process (contemporary theories such as liberal intergovernmentalism (LI) could be criticized for similar assumptions). In other words, although neofunctionalism identified the role of elites and interest groups in advancing integration, it did not link the interests of these groups to broader class structures in society and politics. Their dominance in advancing integration was simply put down to the fact that they were better organized than labour interests. Holland accepted that capitalist interests were more effectively organized than labour ones but suggested that this argument obscured a more important explanation for capitalist influence over the process. What was important was not an observable process of business leaders influencing state actors, but a shared world view—or, as Holland (1980: 91–2) put it, 'the combination of governmental élites and the self-electing élites of private capital, bound on a common venture in fulfilment of a common ideology'.

A later generation of scholars built on the work of these neo-Marxists, but believed their predecessors had overestimated the existence of crisis tendencies within capitalism and had not accounted for the considerable variations in types of capitalism over time and space (Cafruny and Ryner 2009: 229). Yet, the starting point for contemporary neo-Marxist scholars of the EU was essentially the same as that of Cocks and Holland, that the dominant theories of integration have basic flaws which obscure understanding of the nature of power in the EU:

> by their very design they are unable to conceptualize adequately power relations that are constitutive of capitalist market structures. In other words, these mainstream theories fail to account for the structural power that determines the particular trajectory of European integration.

(van Apeldoorn et al. 2003: 17)

In particular, 'mainstream theories' make assumptions about the inherent rationality of market forces that leave no room for alternative organizing principles. Specifically, they 'assume either explicitly or implicitly that market forces are expressions of an inner rationality of universal human nature that is held to be the essence of the realm of freedom in political affairs' (van Apeldoorn et al. 2003: 18). Critical political economists dispute the assumption that the market is a reflection of human nature and that its operation equates with freedom in political affairs, and they suggest instead that this starting point obscures the uneven distribution of power inherent in the operation of markets. The consequence is that mainstream theories define power narrowly in relation to control by political authorities and thus the empirical focus is on how this power is organized. In the CPE perspective, this view needs to be supplemented with a view of power derived from social forces (generally, class relations) that underpin market relations and shape formal political authority.

To understand the true nature of power in the EU, van Apeldoorn et al. (2003) proposed a neo-Marxist approach, drawing on the work of Antonio Gramsci. As noted at the start of this section, there are affinities here with social constructivism, with the role of ideas being central to the understanding of Gramsci's concept of 'hegemony'. Unlike most constructivists, though, ideas here are firmly embedded in a particular (historical materialist) conception of social relations. Gramsci argued that the capitalist class does not rule by force, either exclusively or primarily, but through consent generated by the diffusion of its ideas (via state institutions and organizations in civil society). In this way, the specific interests of the capitalist class become internalized by all as the general interest and thus states only need to use force to govern as a last resort. This notion of hegemony owes something to the Marxist idea of 'false consciousness', which suggests that people are unaware of what is in their true interest. From this perspective, it is argued that mainstream theories of the EU not only fail to expose the underlying nature of class power that shapes its emergent political structures, but also in doing so serve to reproduce the consent that legitimizes and thus sustains this state of affairs.

Later analyses from this perspective focused on core aspects of the EU political economy, the single market, and economic and monetary union (EMU). Van Apeldoorn (2002), for instance, focused on the ways in which preference shifts within the European Roundtable of Industrialists—a lobbying group of corporate actors— contributed to the single market agenda in the 1980s. He charted the ways in which actors, who may have once favoured European-level protectionism, gradually came to favour a conception of competition that was global in scope. Horn (2012) discussed how such processes relate to broader shifts in corporate governance in the context of ever-more-liberalized EU capital markets. Such shifts were the result of EU regulatory reforms which, according to Mügge's (2010) analysis, reflected the interests of banks and finance actors. Approaches from this perspective highlight the ways in which the single market project has privileged the interests of certain elites at the expense of citizens and of national democracy (see also Chapter 3, 'Democracy and Legitimacy' and Chapter 19, 'Evaluating the Single Market').

In a similar vein, Gill (1998) considered the ways in which EMU placed constraints on member states and required them to implement a set of neoliberal policy responses. He perceived EU economic and monetary policy as part of a broader trend towards legally embedding or 'constitutionalizing' neoliberal preferences. In the context of the eurozone crisis, such processes of constitutionalization are ongoing according to this perspective, and can be associated with the ideas of a particular strand of neoliberal thought, a German **ordo-liberalism** (Brunnermeier et al. 2016: 65–7).

The implications of these broader neoliberal trends for traditional conceptions of the European welfare state are made apparent by such scholars in analyses of EU strategies such as the Lisbon Agenda of 2000 and Europe 2020 of 2010 (see Chapter 10, 'The Lisbon Strategy' and Chapter 11, 'Europe 2020'). While these strategies appeal to the importance of social cohesion and a European 'social model', critical political economists have drawn attention to the emphasis on increasingly flexible labour markets and the associated retrenchment of traditional models of welfare (often couched in terms of 'modernization') (Hager 2008; Nousios and Tsolakis 2012).

Other scholars working in this tradition explored the possibilities for resistance by 'counter-hegemonic' movements that might challenge the neoliberal direction of travel. Bieler (2011), for instance, assessed the possibility for transnational labour and social movements to resist these trends.

From a rather different starting point, but engaging with the CPE literature, Bulmer and Joseph (2016) sought to highlight the political struggles at the heart of European integration. Drawing on work from German neo-Marxists (Buckel 2011), they highlighted how fundamental political struggles in the EU could be understood in terms of several competing 'hegemonic projects', each of which was seeking to prevail. Of particular significance is that these projects are seen as rooted in domestic politics, with their differing profiles across EU states. Thus, whilst the neoliberal project may indeed prevail, as is the predominant finding across the CPE literature, it is in contestation with several others:

• a national-social project that seeks to achieve socialism at the domestic level (a position perhaps best illustrated by the UK Labour Party under Jeremy Corbyn's leadership);

• a pro-European social-democratic hegemonic project that was influential especially during the Delors presidency of the European Commission, when attempts were made to strengthen social legislation at EU level (Chapter 18, 'Employment, Social Affairs and Inclusion');

- a national-conservative hegemonic project that found increasing expression in the 2010s and reflects the growth of an identity cleavage across European politics, where some voters—typically the 'losers' from globalization—have taken refuge in supporting Euroscepticism (also a factor in the Leave vote in the 2016 UK referendum on EU membership); and

- a left-liberal project that focuses on human rights, women's rights, cosmopolitanism, and ecological issues and is associated with reformist and environmentalist parties.

In their article, Bulmer and Joseph sought to use this clash of domestically grounded projects for hegemony as a way to explain the state of integration in the EU, thereby linking the CPE agenda with wider issues of integration theory. In applying the clash of competing projects to the eurozone crisis, they identified that the power asymmetries between creditor and debtor states enabled Germany's ordo-liberal project to assume a hegemonic position (Bulmer and Joseph 2016: 741–2).

Critical Political Economy Assessed

Contributions from this perspective raise important questions for mainstream theorists, in particular about the assumptions that underpin dominant theories both of European integration and of the operation of the EU as a political system. In addition to highlighting the role of ideas, CPE contributions raise questions about the nature of power in the EU that have often been ignored entirely by mainstream theorists, or dealt with in a cursory manner. In particular, 'critical political economy relates developments in the EU to the constraints and opportunities of capitalism' (Cafruny and Ryner 2009: 237). The eurozone crisis—in many ways a crisis of capitalism manifest in the EU context—has certainly increased the pertinence of such an approach.

Notwithstanding its usefulness, criticisms of the CPE approach are possible. The most obvious one is that these neo-Marxist or Gramscian debates have been self-referential, discouraging engagement with mainstream EU theorists (although many CPE scholars would argue that the lack of engagement is the other way around!). Other critical perspectives covered in this chapter might argue that the CPE approach is too pre-occupied with economic (capitalist) forces to the detriment of other important ones, such as gender, race, culture, and nation. Even those sympathetic to the CPE approach may argue that, while the attempt to alter 'macro'-level structures such as global capitalism is a worthy endeavour, it is quite idealistic. Conversely, those CPE scholars who acknowledge the difficulty of altering capitalist structures could be critiqued for an excessively defeatist assessment of the prospects of the EU/Europe.

Critical Social Theory

Critical social theory perspectives have become increasingly important in studying the EU. They overlap in many ways with the approaches that we have already considered. They support the critique of rationalism and the social constructivist notion that political and social reality is constructed rather than fixed. They generally concur with the idea that language and communication are central to the constitution of social realities. Many critical social theorists also support the notion that mainstream theories are complicit in constituting the EU in a particular way, and some concur to a large extent with the CPE critique of the neoliberal bias of the contemporary EU.

However, critical social theory approaches differ from the other critical perspectives discussed in two principal respects. First, while their object of study is inclusive of the EU, it encompasses broader dynamics in contemporary European society (Delanty and Rumford 2005). In particular, they frequently point to a so-called 'cosmopolitan' reality in Europe, highlighting the ways in which society has become increasingly complex and has transcended national frames of reference and ways of thinking about the world (Beck and Grande 2007). Second, they often explicitly promote a particular normative vision. They do not simply describe a cosmopolitan reality, but also champion it in the face of what they regard as less positive tendencies within European society and mainstream scholarship. In short, they combine a descriptive social theory with normative prescription, although there are differences between scholars within this tradition, both in terms of which attributes of the EU are celebrated and in terms of what a 'better' or 'cosmopolitan' Europe should look like.

Critical Social Theory Work on the EU

Beck and Grande (2007) highlighted the way in which social processes fostered what they called a 'cosmopolitan outlook' in Europe. Such processes include the exchange of social, cultural, and linguistic practices, and a 'cross-fertilization' of identities. These have been facilitated by the EU through integration and enlargement and have broken down traditional boundaries among Europeans, particularly those rooted in nationalism. That is not to say that all is well in contemporary Europe. Beck and Grande recognized that a cosmopolitan outlook is only a partial reality that remains endangered by, in particular, nationalist outlooks. They highlighted the ways in which what they term a 'methodological nationalism' *'blinds us to Europe'* (2007: 18) or, in other words, undermines the cosmopolitan outlook that they identified and advocated. As Delanty and Rumford (2005: 188) put it:

> A cosmopolitan perspective holds many attractions, not least of them being that a major problem in the way Europe is studied, perhaps *the* problem, is that the political and social science associated with the nation-state still pervades EU studies.

These social theory perspectives argue that a particular way of understanding and viewing society and politics that draws for inspiration on the model of the nation state still dominates mainstream scholarship. For instance, many mainstream analyses of European integration view it as a process which erodes the sovereignty of prevailing nation states while tending towards a Europe which increasingly resembles a nation state (see Chapter 1). More recent scholarship has treated the EU as a political system using comparative politics methods modelled on the nation state (see Chapter 2). A methodological cosmopolitanism, by contrast, advocates a 'both–and' Europe (Beck and Grande 2007: 18) where *both* loyalty to nation *and* loyalty to Europe (and, indeed, globally) is possible.

Beck and Grande cited, as realities within the EU that concur with this 'both–and' position, the 'Open Method of Co-ordination' (see Chapter 2, 'New Methods of

Governance') and forms of 'enhanced co-operation' (whereby certain sub-sets of states may co-operate in a policy area—see Chapter 2, 'Differentiated Integration'). For them, these are contexts which make possible *both* co-operation *and* the preservation of some differences (2007: 246). Favell (2008) identified some evidence of this cosmopolitan ethos at the level of individual European identity via his ethnography of the lives of certain mobile EU citizens.

Manners (2002) similarly argued that it was the EU's cosmopolitan—or, as he sometimes put it, 'post-Westphalian'—characteristics that actors (including scholars and European policy makers) should both emphasize and promote. 'Post-Westphalian' refers to the way in which the EU as an entity has overcome nationalism without reproducing it in the form of a new, European state. He was critical of efforts to promote the EU as primarily a military or economic power. Instead, he emphasized the importance of promoting the EU as what he called a 'normative power'. A significant body of scholarship on EU external relations has engaged with this concept (see Chapter 25, 'EU Power in World Politics').

Habermas's work on the EU (2001*a*) shared the idea that the EU can be conceived as an emerging or 'immanent' cosmopolitan entity and similarly encouraged this process. Like these social theorists, he was also concerned with the history of nationalism in the EU and promoted the idea of a 'constitutional patriotism' at the European level. This is a patriotism not based on national or ethnic roots, but on a shared belief in constitutional values such as human rights and democracy. However, he departed from the social theorists discussed in this section in terms of his more explicit critique of processes of neoliberal globalization. Like many critical political economists, he was concerned with these processes and also with the role that the EU had played in reinforcing and promoting them. In particular, he was critical of the detrimental effect that such processes had on the European welfare state and on democracy within the EU (in this sense, Habermas has also been an important contributor to debates on the democratic deficit—see Chapter 3, 'Democracy and Legitimacy').

Habermas nevertheless sought to promote the EU as the agent that might realistically challenge such trends and thus support the preservation of certain features of European social democracy. As he said, 'the challenge before us is not to invent anything but to conserve the great democratic achievements of the European nation-state, beyond its own limits' (Habermas 2001*b*: 6). Habermas's vision of a cosmopolitan EU is closer to a federalist vision of the EU (see Chapter 1) than certain of the social theorists mentioned above would be likely to support (Parker 2009*a*).

Critical Social Theory Assessed

Critical social theory makes an important contribution to the study of the EU in as much as it considers the impact of the EU on European society and culture more generally. It highlights some of the important ways in which the EU has contributed to the constitution of an emerging 'cosmopolitan Europe'; in other words, a European society that has to some extent transcended a one-dimensional nationalist parochialism and shares a set of common values such as human rights, democracy, and rule of law.

Not only are there important differences within critical social theory, but critical political economists would argue that cosmopolitan assumptions may not take seriously enough the economic foundations of the European project. Moreover, other critical perspectives covered in this chapter have detected in certain celebrations of a cosmopolitan Europe a problematic moral superiority or eurocentrism which potentially blinds us to ethically questionable aspects of the contemporary EU (Parker 2009a; see also 'Post-Structuralism' below).

However, it is arguably the rise in the EU of Euroscepticism and populism in the 2010s that presents the strongest threat to this cosmopolitanism. The new identity cleavage identified by Hooghe and Marks (2018) reveals that there is considerable resistance, expressed in Eurosceptic politics, against what politicians from this quarter would regard as patronizing, elitist cosmopolitan positions that are seeking to undermine traditional identities (see Chapter 1, 'Postfunctionalism'). That said, as Recchi et al. (2019) have pointed out, this increasing political division paradoxically coexists with the intensifying 'everyday' cross-border interconnections of Europeans.

Critical Feminism

While CPE might be described as occupying the margins of EU scholarship until the past decade or so, feminist perspectives were even less present. Hoskyns (2004: 33) argued that 'both the core of EU policy making and many of the key concepts of theorizing European integration remain virtually untouched' by feminist and gender analysis. However, feminist scholarship on the EU has grown and diversified in the past decade, most obviously to move beyond a focus on the EU's gender equality policies to analyse the EU in relation to questions of gender more generally.

We briefly cover some of the work that has been done on the EU's gender equality policy, but focus here on the critical strand in the feminist literature, which shares the broad critique of rationalist approaches. Like CPE and social theory, these perspectives combine a critique of the mainstream with a particular normative perspective—in this case, a perspective that emphasizes the importance of accounting for gender both in policy making and in theorizing about the social and political world.

Feminist Work on the EU

Research on gender equality policies is well established in the EU literature. These policies had their origins in Article 119 of the Treaty of Rome (Hoskyns 1996) and developed through subsequent Treaty provisions, directives, Court rulings, and soft-law instruments relating to a range of policy areas, including part-time work, parental leave, sexual harassment, childcare, and violence against women (see Hantrais 2000; Ellina 2003). Locher and Prügl (2009: 183–4), who described the EU gender equality regime as 'one of the more astonishing aspects of European integration', identified a three-stage development in the area: from a focus on equal rights, to positive action, to gender mainstreaming, which means taking into account the gender dimension in all areas and at all stages of EU policy making. Roth (2008: 4) highlighted the ways in which different enlargements led to opportunities and challenges for the development of EU gender equality policies. She cited evidence of the 'uploading' of policies from certain member states to the EU level (particularly from 'Nordic' countries such as Sweden and Finland) and 'downloading' of policy to member states from EU level in cases such as Spain and

Ireland. In a comprehensive discussion of the EU and gender issues, Kantola (2010) considered, among other things, the Europeanization of gender policies, focusing on the impact of the 'downloading' of policies in different member state contexts and their impact beyond the EU (on these concepts, see Chapter 3, 'Europeanization').

While the EU is often seen as progressive in this area, Hoskyns argued that, despite the growth in scope of gender equality measures over time, major EU decisions continued to be taken without reference to gender or without adequate representation of women (Hoskyns 2004: 223). Thus, the Commission's 2001 Governance White Paper was an important document reflecting on EU political good practice, but did not mention the word 'gender'.

Kronsell (2005) extended this critique to integration theories themselves, which she argued had done little to encompass gender dynamics. She critiqued six approaches that she saw as representing the 'state of the art' in EU studies: liberal intergovernmentalism (LI); domestic politics approaches; neofunctionalism; multi-level governance (MLG); supranationalism; and constructivism (Insight 4.1).

Insight 4.1 Feminist Critiques of Selected EU Studies Theories

Liberal Intergovernmentalism

The focus on states as the dominant actors rests upon a narrow conception of the relevant political space and excludes consideration of gender dynamics.

> Moravcsik's idea that states relate to each other and interact in the process of integration—in intergovernmental negotiations—does not take note of the fact that it is and has been almost exclusively men speaking for the state.
> (Kronsell 2005: 1035)

The Domestic Politics Approach

It offers more scope for incorporating gender dynamics by opening up the 'black box of the state' to consider the complex processes at play. However, Kronsell (2005: 1027) suggested that this approach had been 'less prone to include gender and women's interest organizations within the overall assessment of EU integration'.

Neofunctionalism

It has the potential for understanding the contribution of organized interests representing women. However, it does not draw attention to the distinct disadvantage of feminist groups in comparison to more powerful lobbies that shape a range of policies with significant gender implications (Kronsell 2005: 1028).

Multi-Level Governance

It is seen as complementary to feminist analysis because it emphasizes complex interactions involving multiple actors in which power takes multiple forms. However, it overlooks the fact that the policy networks central to the notion of MLG tend to be male-dominated and difficult for women to enter. Thus, for MLG to deliver on its promise, more empirical research is required on the composition and dynamics of relevant policy networks (Kronsell 2005: 1031–2).

Kantola (2019) took this discussion of theories further, notably by considering disintegration in the light of the economic crisis, the rise of populism, and Brexit, and by adopting a wider understanding of gender derived from feminist political analysis. She noted how the economic crisis and populism (including democratic backsliding in some of the CEECs) had impacted adversely on the different aspects of gender equality policy. She noted that aspects of Brexit have been highly gendered in emotional terms, with women's concerns marginalized (see also Guerrina et al. 2018). With evidence from the crises of the 2010s, Kantola (2019) revealed advances in the feminist analysis of the EU as well as empirical evidence of how integration and disintegration impacted on gender issues. As she put it (2019: 73):

> Gender equality is at the heart of integration and disintegration and subtle and overt attacks on it, including scaling down of gender equality policies, commitments and priorities, are key signals of the difficulties the European integration project faces.

In summarizing her critique of dominant EU studies theories, Kronsell (2005: 1035–6) highlighted two points: that they ignore the 'male-as-norm' problem, and that they are based on a simplistic view of power. As Hoskyns (2004: 224) put it, a more gender-sensitive analysis of European integration 'brings the imbalance between the social and the economic in EU policy making into focus, puts the emphasis on democratic legitimacy and forms of participation, and prioritizes the analysis of power relations'. In these senses, there are clear overlaps with the concerns of a 'post-positivist' or critical feminism and those of a number of the other approaches considered in this chapter.

Critical Feminism Assessed

Critical feminist perspectives draw attention to particular policy developments, and raise questions that are not addressed by mainstream theories of the EU. In policy terms, they reveal an EU that is, on the one hand, relatively progressive in relation to gender equality issues, but, on the other, perpetuates gender inequalities and limits the participation of women in key forums. In theory terms, gender perspectives seek to reveal hidden aspects of the EU: most particularly in this case relating to the gendered effects of EU policy making and the mechanisms through which patriarchal domination is reproduced (Locher and Prügl 2009: 181). While feminists have been critiqued for overstating the importance of gender relative to other issues that determine social relations, many feminist scholars would emphasize the complementarities between gender perspectives and some of the other critical perspectives covered in this chapter.

Post-Structuralism

A variety of post-structural (sometimes called 'post-modern') approaches have engaged with the EU as object of study. Drawing on such thinkers as Michel Foucault, Pierre Bourdieu, and Jacques Derrida, they are particularly attuned to the interactions of knowledge, language, and power in the construction of social and political reality. Post-structural accounts overlap considerably with the foregoing approaches but they are distinct in certain respects.

Like social constructivists, post-structuralists reject positivist ontologies, but are sceptical of the attempts of some such approaches to reconcile themselves with a positivist epistemology (see Table 4.1). Like CPE and feminist approaches, they are acutely aware of power relations, but are often cautious about giving undue import to any one key structural factor, such as social class or gender, in determining such relations. Like critical social theory, they are critical of methodological nationalism, but may equally point to the ethical problems inherent in their 'cosmopolitan outlook'.

From a post-structural perspective, 'critique is not that which seeks out resolution, reconciliation or the smoothing out of difficulty, but rather that which discomforts and unsettles one's sense of certainty' (Amoore 2008: 274). In other words, 'post-structural scholars are seeking to "denaturalize" stories about European integration which are spoken as common sense' (Manners 2007: 87). The attempt to unsettle a sense of certainty or 'common sense' in relation to the EU has been the uniting theme of post-structural analysis. Its contribution is focused on highlighting the often-concealed work that is done by discourse, language, knowledge, and power in constituting a variety of 'European' or EU realities and identities.

Post-Structuralist Work on the EU

Post-structuralist work has not been limited to a particular facet of the EU, but has been deployed to consider broad themes of identity, governance, and political economy. However, much post-structural work on the EU emanates from the field of IR and reflects an increasing critical interest in the EU as an actor or presence in world politics and as an ostensible 'area of freedom, security and justice' (see, respectively, Chapters 25 and 23).

Among the first to draw on the work of post-structural thought in EU studies, Diez (1999) appealed to the mainstream to account for the ways in which discourses on the EU shape or constitute the EU's reality. He pointed to the 'performativity' of language in relation to the EU. By way of illustration he noted how, in a relatively Eurosceptic Britain of the 1960s, the European Economic Community (EEC) was often referred to as the 'common market', whereas in relatively pro-European Germany it was referred to as the 'Community'. His point is that the language used in these different contexts was not simply the consequence of different pre-existing feelings towards Europe; rather, it was also constitutive of those very feelings.

Subsequently, Diez (2005) developed a critique of the notion that the EU is a cosmopolitan 'normative power' (Manners—see 'Critical Social Theory' above), highlighting the ways in which such a portrayal of the EU might in some respects cast the EU as superior to various 'others' in world politics and blind us to some of its less virtuous policies (see also Merlingen 2007). Parker and Rosamond (2013) have also offered a critique of this concept, arguing in particular that the 'post-Westphalian' or cosmopolitan reality that was celebrated by Manners might have overcome certain exclusionary effects of nationalism, but the EU's manifestation as a 'market' project might have had other exclusionary consequences (see also 'Critical Political Economy' above). Such work can be situated within a post-structural critique of critical social theory, particularly its celebration of a cosmopolitan Europe/EU (Parker 2009a).

Several post-structural scholars in the sub-field of critical security studies have problematized the relationship between the 'European' ideals of liberty and security, highlighting the paradoxes, even hypocrisies, at the heart of many EU practices and policies (see also Chapter 23, 'Critiquing the AFSJ'). Among other things (with reference to post-9/11 policy on terrorism (De Goede 2008) and immigration policy (Huysmans 2006; Van Munster 2009), they have drawn attention to the ways in which security, enacted with the stated purpose of preserving liberty, has paradoxically undermined that liberty in certain respects for both EU 'insiders' and 'outsiders'. The concept of 'the border' is frequently unsettled in such accounts. A range of scholars have articulated the ways in which the EU's practices and policies—in relation, for instance, to free movement, counterterrorism, and immigration control—have 'multiplied' borders within and beyond EU space (Vaughan-Williams 2008). Recently, scholars have also deployed post-structural philosophy to consider the broader ethical implications of EU responses to the so-called migration crisis (Vaughan-Williams 2015; see also Chapter 11).

Drawing together some of the themes discussed above, Walters and Haahr (2005) deployed Foucault's notion of 'governmentality'—an interest in the particular rationalities that lie behind governmental practices—to explore the ways in which various ideas and practices have constituted Europe as an entity in very particular ways and its forms of government. In so doing, they, among other things, challenged histories of integration that suggested a linear progress, pointing to the alternatives that did not become part of the historical legacy of European integration. For example, with reference to the early days of integration, they noted how proposals to place under public ownership the coal and steel industries—which were central to the early steps in European integration—were ultimately not pursued and, instead, Monnet and Schuman's particular ideas prevailed (see Chapter 5) (Walters and Haahr 2005: 15).

Parker (2012a, 2013) deployed Foucault's work on liberalism to point to some important tensions or ambiguities within EU governance. Considering which identities the EU as governing actor seeks either to promote or to exclude, and drawing together some of the themes of interest to both a CPE and a critical security studies, he highlighted the ways in which the EU has, through its governing logics, discourses, and collective knowledge, attempted to constitute individuals as variously post-national market actors or 'entrepreneurs' and post-national political actors or 'citizens'. This work points to the potentially exclusionary effects of both of these agendas. However, in line with Foucault's interest in political resistance, Parker (2012a, 2013) noted that the ambiguous co-existence of these two governing logics in the EU might open the possibility for practical acts of resistance and re-politicization by those excluded and marginalized by either agenda.

Post-Structuralism Assessed

Post-structural accounts have added a new dimension to scholarship on the EU by drawing attention to the important role of language and discourse in constituting the EU in particular ways. This work highlights a range of difficult questions in relation to the common-sense ideals that the EU professes to embody, such as peace, freedom, and justice. It also contributes to the broader critique of mainstream approaches and extends this to a critical engagement with some of the other critical approaches, and particularly a normative critical social theory. However, those approaches have themselves critiqued post-structural analyses for offering no positive normative vision or agenda (for the EU or more generally) (see Parker 2013: 172–4).

CONCLUSION

This chapter has summarized contributions that can be broadly categorized as 'critical perspectives'. As the discussion shows, these perspectives are not only critical of mainstream theories, but, in many cases, also of each other. Importantly, though, they share an emphasis on the limits of rationalist or positivist approaches.

Several approaches discussed are normative in their intent, seeking to highlight problems with the status quo but also to suggest that 'another Europe' is possible. They are not interested primarily in explaining how integration has taken place or how the EU works. Instead, their purpose is to critically assess these things, pointing in various ways to the often-overlooked dynamics of power within the EU, considering both elite and marginalized voices (see Part One, 'Theory', Table I.1).

To adopt a critical approach is not necessarily to reject a mainstream approach, or vice versa. There may be important overlaps between these positions (see Table 4.1). Moreover, they can be understood in terms of the quite different functions that they perform. Robert Cox (1981) usefully characterized what we have here termed the mainstream as 'problem solving theory'. Such theory views the broad structures of the social and political world as a given, in order to focus on specific problems or issues within that pre-defined world. In contrast, 'critical theory' challenges the fixed nature of that broader social and political world in an attempt to contemplate more fundamental changes. If we accept the importance of both of these functions, then students of the EU do not necessarily need to place themselves definitively within one or other camp.

It is, however, important to consider why these more critical perspectives have been absent for so long within mainstream studies of the EU. Both their exclusion and their gradual (re-)admittance to the mainstream can be accounted for by factors internal to political studies scholarship—a disciplinary politics—and factors related to the politics of European integration and the EU (Rosamond 2007; Whitman and Manners 2016). Recent political crises in the EU, and the increased openness of EU studies to alternative perspectives, are therefore interrelated and likely to foster continued interest in critical approaches.

KEY POINTS

Critical of What?

- Critical perspectives have received increasing attention in the study of EU politics in the past decade or so. Collectively, they challenge mainstream 'positivist' approaches to the study of the EU.

Social Constructivism

- Social constructivism entered the debate on the EU to challenge the positivist (rationalist and materialist) assumptions on which the dominant integration theories were built.
- In relation to the EU, social constructivism puts particular emphasis on how national positions and perceived national interests are shaped through the socialization of national actors within and with EU levels of government.

- Social constructivist work on the EU has analysed the ways in which 'European' identities and ideas are constructed and shifting over time, and with what consequences.

Critical Political Economy

- A broadly neo-Marxist CPE analyses the EU in the context of broader capitalist social relations, often emphasizing the role of elites in driving particular sorts of integration at the expense of subordinate classes. It is critical of a 'liberal' bias in much mainstream theorizing on the EU.
- Scholars working in this tradition have drawn on Gramsci's concept of hegemony to elucidate the ways in which economic elites have been able to push their 'neoliberal' agendas in the EU, often at the expense of the interests of particular classes or rival hegemonic projects.
- Academics working in this tradition have focused their critique on 'economic' areas of EU policy making, such as the single market and monetary union.

Critical Social Theory

- The critical social theory considered in this chapter can be traced to the 'Frankfurt School' of 'Critical Theory' and in particular the work of Jürgen Habermas, who is himself a frequent commentator on EU politics.
- Critical social theory emphasizes the ways in which the EU has facilitated the emergence of a cosmopolitan European society and views this as a positive development worthy of scholarly and political support. But critical social theory is not uncritical of the status quo within the EU.
- Theorists such as Beck and Grande have been critical of a residual 'methodological nationalism' within EU politics and EU scholarship. They oppose both member state nationalism and the attempt to re-invent the EU as a unified state, and advocate a 'both–and' EU of plural identities.
- Habermas emphasizes the 'neoliberal' bias in the EU status quo in his vision of a cosmopolitan EU that resembles a federal Europe built on a social democratic constitution.

Critical Feminism

- There is no single 'gender theory' or 'feminist theory' of the EU, but rather a broad range of perspectives. Such perspectives have often focused on the emergence of gender equality policies at EU level.
- Critical feminists argue that dominant integration theories have done little to develop understanding of gender dynamics in the EU. They are seen to ignore the 'male-as-norm' problem and to be based on a simplistic view of power.
- These concerns have acquired new significance in the context of the economic crisis, the rise of populism, and Brexit.

Post-Structuralism

- Post-structural approaches draw on the insights of a range of (often French) thinkers, including Michel Foucault, Pierre Bourdieu, and Jacques Derrida
- Post-structural work on the EU is diverse in terms of its focus, and includes work on questions of European identity, borders, security, and political economy. There are significant overlaps between post-structuralism and the other critical approaches considered.
- The attempt to unsettle a sense of certainty or 'common sense' in relation to both the EU and strands of EU scholarship has been the uniting theme of post-structural analysis.

For additional material and resources, please visit the online resources www.oup.com/uk/bache5e.

QUESTIONS

1. How does social constructivism shed light on ideas and identities, and their importance to European integration?

2. How do critical political economy approaches redirect concerns about power in the EU in contrast to mainstream theories?

3. Has the EU fostered a cosmopolitan outlook in European society?

4. What insights into the EU are offered by feminist analysis?

5. What contributions have the different critical approaches added to understanding the EU?

FURTHER READING

For a wide-ranging review of critical perspectives on the study of the EU, see **R. Whitman and I. Manners**, 'Another Theory is Possible: Dissident Voices in Theorising Europe', *Journal of Common Market Studies*, 54 (2016): 3–18, which is the lead article in a special issue that is useful to complement this chapter, as well as covering other perspectives, such as neocolonialism in the EU. On teaching critial perspectives, see **O. Parker**, 'Teaching (Dissident) Theory in Crisis European Union', *Journal of Common Market*, 54 (2016): 37–52.

On social constructivism, see the influential collection in the special issue of the *Journal of European Public Policy,* 6(4) (1999), edited by **T. Christiansen, K. Jørgensen, and A. Wiener**. Other helpful contributions are: **J. Checkel and A. Moravcsik**, 'A Constructivist Research Programme in EU Studies?', *European Union Politics*, 2 (2001): 219–49 and **T. Risse**, 'Social Constructivism and European Integration', in **A. Wiener, T. Börzel, and T. Risse (eds)**, *European Integration Theory*, 3rd edn (Oxford: Oxford University Press, 2019), 128–47.

A useful overview of CPE perspectives is offered by **B. van Apeldoorn and L. Horn**, 'Critical Political Economy', in **A. Wiener, T. Börzel, and T. Risse (eds)**, *European Integration Theory*, 3rd edn (Oxford: Oxford University Press, 2019), 195–215. An accessible book-length CPE analysis is offered by **M. Ryner and A. Cafruny**, *The European Union and Global Capitalism* (Basingstoke: Palgrave, 2017). On critical integration theory, see **S. Bulmer and J. Joseph**, 'European Integration in Crisis? Of Supranational Integration, Hegemonic Projects and Domestic Politics', *European Journal of International Relations*, 22 (2016): 725–48.

Key works in the area of critical social theory include **J. Habermas**, *The Postnational Constellation* (Cambridge: Polity Press, 2001); **U. Beck and E. Grande**, *Cosmopolitan Europe* (Cambridge: Polity Press, 2007); and **G. Delanty and C. Rumford**, *Rethinking Europe: Social Theory and the Implications of Europeanization* (Abingdon and New York: Routledge, 2005). For a critical discussion of critical social theory work on the EU, see **O. Parker**, 'Why EU, Which EU? Habermas and the Ethics of Postnational Politics in Europe', *Constellations: An International Journal of Critical and Democratic Theory*, 16 (2009): 392–409.

On feminist/gender approaches, there are several helpful overview pieces, including: **Y. Galligan's** 'European Integration and Gender', in **A. Wiener, T. Börzel, and T. Risse (eds)**, *European Integration Theory*, 3rd edn (Oxford: Oxford University Press, 2019), 174–94; and **E. Prügl**, 'Gender and European Union Politics', in **K. E. Jørgensen, M. Pollack, and B. Rosamond**

(eds), *Handbook of European Union Politics* (London: SAGE Publications, 2007), 433–48. For a comprehensive overview of the EU's impact on gender policies, see **J. Kantola**, *Gender and the European Union* (Basingstoke: Palgrave Macmillan, 2010). For a particular focus on gender and theories of European integration, see **A. Kronsell**, 'Gender, Power and European Integration Theory', *Journal of European Public Policy*, 12 (2005): 1022–40, complemented by the more recent **J. Kantola**, 'European Integration and Disintegration: Feminist Perspectives on Inequalities and Social Justice', *Journal of Common Market Studies*, 57 (Annual Review) (2019): 62–76.

Key works from a post-structuralist perspective include **O. Parker**, *Cosmopolitan Government in Europe: Citizens and Entrepreneurs in Postnational Politics* (Abingdon and New York: Routledge, 2013) or 'Towards an Ambiguous "Cosmopolitics": Citizens and Entrepreneurs in the European Project', *International Theory*, 4 (2012): 198–232; and **W. Walters and J. H. Haahr**, *Governing Europe: Discourse, Governmentality and European Integration* (London: Routledge, 2005).

Part Two
History

Deciding where to begin a history is often difficult, but not really in this case. While there were attempts to integrate Europe before the twentieth century, the end of the Second World War in 1945 provided the catalyst for the phase of European integration with which we are familiar today. There is little dispute among historians that 1945 is the most appropriate starting point for discussing the events leading to the creation of what is today the European Union (EU). Thus, while we reflect briefly on previous attempts to integrate Europe, our point of departure here is the end of the Second World War.

The history we present is largely a familiar account of developments in European integration in the second half of the twentieth century. The history of European integration often told is one that emphasizes individuals, perhaps at the expense of broader social, economic, and political forces that shape events. Our account here generally reflects this dominant approach, not least because it is the function of a textbook to cover the most recognized contributions on the field of study. However, we have sought to add to the dominant narrative in the conclusions to the chapters in this section by drawing on the themes and perspectives discussed in Part One of the book.

We encourage a critical approach to the reading of history. In this respect, readers would be well served by reading Mark Gilbert's (2008) article, which questions many of the assumptions of the way in which the EU's history is often told as the 'progressive story of European integration'. For example, Gilbert (2008: 645) highlights rhetorical devices that are used to present this as a progressive story:

> Choice of terms: construction metaphors abound. References to Europe's 'path', 'march', 'advance', 'progress', are [. . .] commonplace. Moments of relative inactivity are described as 'stagnation'—the 1970s, for instance, are frequently referred to in this way. The process is always 're-launched' or 'revived' after moments of difficulty.
>
> Authorial judgements: the standard used to measure whether major decisions were successes or failures is almost always whether they augmented or reduced the overall degree of supranationality within the Community.

Whether we write the history in this way and, if so, how it might be written differently is something for the readers of this book to reflect upon with reference to the various theoretical perspectives enunciated in Part One.

Chapter 5

From the End of the War to the Schuman Plan (the Late 1940s to the Early 1950s)

Chapter Overview

In 1945, the European continent emerged exhausted from the Second World War. It was soon to be divided between the capitalist West and the communist East. Yet, in the west of the continent something happened that was without historical precedent: some of the states took the first steps towards surrendering their sovereignty in pursuit of European integration. Although there had been many previous plans and movements for a united Europe, they had foundered on the unwillingness of the governments of states to surrender their control over important political decisions. This time, though, practicalities suggested to some political leaders that there were more advantages in pooling the sovereignty of their several states than in trying to meet the challenges of the post-war world alone.

This chapter looks briefly at the long history of plans for European unity that came to nothing, before turning to the period immediately after the end of the Second World War, and the ideas of the European federalists. Their vision of a federal Europe did not appeal to the new governments of the post-war period, but there were practical reasons why some moves to European unity found favour with those governments: the threat of communism and the emergence of the Cold War; the problem of what to do about Germany; and the need to ensure adequate supplies of coal for the post-war economic reconstruction. As a solution to these intersecting problems, the French civil servant, Jean Monnet, came up with a proposal for a European coal and steel community. The proposal, national reactions to it, and the negotiations that led to the setting up of the first of the European communities are all reviewed in this chapter.

Background: The Ideal of European Unity

Our starting point for this discussion of European integration is the end of the Second World War, but the idea of European integration is not unique to this era. Politicians and intellectuals alike aspired to European unity over two centuries. Plans for achieving perpetual peace in Europe by overcoming the division into nation states can be traced back at least to the early eighteenth century, and the *Project for Perpetual Peace* of the Abbé de Saint Pierre (Forsyth et al. 1970: 128). At a practical level, though, moves for European unity took the form of attempts by one nation or another to dominate Europe through conquest. Both France under Napoleon and Germany under Hitler could be accused of trying to forge European unity in this way.

Whereas attempts at enforced European *political* integration foundered, the potential benefits of *economic* integration proved attractive to European political elites. Yet, nineteenth-century experiments with **free trade areas** across nation states were short-lived, while early **customs unions** were specific to regions within nation states. Ultimately, these experiments in economic integration suffered the same fate as attempts at political unity.

Movements in favour of peaceful integration emerged in Europe after the First World War, but the political settlement after the war was based on the peaceful co-existence of nation states rather than integration. The failure of the League of Nations (see Insight 5.1) to sustain peace was rapid and complete, with the resurgence of nationalism in the 1920s and 1930s. The pro-integration groups emerging in Europe after 1918 were unable to offer any practical solutions to this, and the outbreak of the Second World War destroyed hopes of European unity. The aftermath of the war, though, provided the origins for the modern movement for European integration.

Emerging from the war physically devastated, Europe began a process of both economic and political reconstruction. The idea of European unity was present in this process from the outset, as the ideology of federalism had attracted a great deal of support during the war. However, the story cannot be told simply in terms of ideals. Although influential figures showed some degree of attachment to the concept of federalism, the steps that were taken were informed by hard-headed realism about what was necessary for reconstruction to succeed. They were also taken in the context of an emerging Cold War that divided the continent on ideological lines.

Insight 5.1 The League of Nations

- The League of Nations was inspired by the vision of US President Woodrow Wilson. Its Covenant was drawn up at the Paris Peace Conference in 1919, but the US Congress refused to ratify the Treaty so the United States never became a member of the League.

- The League Covenant committed the states that signed to respect the sovereignty and territorial integrity of other states and not to resort to force to resolve disputes, but to submit them to arbitration by the League.

- The League's institutional structure consisted of a General Assembly, in which all member states were represented, and a Council. The Council had four, then later six, permanent members—Britain, France, Italy, Japan; then Germany, from 1926, and the USSR, from 1934.

- Between 1931 and 1939 the League failed to deal effectively with aggression by Japan, Italy, Germany, and the USSR. In 1935, Japan and Germany withdrew from membership.

- Although it failed to prevent war, the League did successfully establish a number of special agencies working at a functional level to deal with matters such as health and the protection of labour. The success of these bodies may have influenced the thinking of David Mitrany (see Chapter 1, 'The Intellectual Background').

The End of the War, Federalism, and The Hague Congress

The war in Europe had extensively destroyed physical infrastructure, disrupted economic production, and caused severe social dislocation. Roads, railways, and bridges had been destroyed by Allied bombing or by the retreating German army in its attempt to slow the advance of the Allied forces. According to Laqueur (1972: 17–18) coal production at the end of the war was only 42 per cent of its pre-war level; pig iron output in 1946 was less than one-third of that in 1938; and crude steel output was about one-third of what it had been before the war. There were millions of refugees wandering around Europe trying to return to their homes, or without any homes to return to.

Accompanying the economic and social dislocation, there was political dislocation as governments that had collaborated with the Nazis were displaced. Germany and Austria remained occupied, and divided between the occupation zones of the Allies. Elsewhere, there was a mood in favour of change; a feeling that there should be no return to the pre-war elites and the pre-war ways.

This mood particularly benefited parties of the left. In Britain, a Labour government was elected in 1945 with a massive majority, despite the Conservatives being led by the wartime hero, Winston Churchill. In France, the provisional government that was set up in 1945 was presided over by General Charles de Gaulle, the conservative leader of the Free French forces, which had fought on from outside of the occupied country; but the first elections favoured the parties of the internal Resistance, particularly the communists but also the socialists and the centre-left Christian party, the *Mouvement Républicain Populaire* (MRP). In Italy, although the Catholic south ensured the emergence of a large conservative Christian Democratic Party, the communists dominated in the industrial north.

The mood for change also fed a strong popular sentiment in the countries that had suffered from fascism, in favour of a decisive move away from nationalism in the post-war reconstruction. Ideas favouring European federalism gained support, particularly in Italy, but also in France, Germany, and elsewhere in continental Europe, although not in Britain or the Scandinavian countries.

The European Union of Federalists (EUF) was formed in 1946 from the wartime Resistance movements. It attempted to exploit the disruption caused to existing political structures by the war to make a new start on a basis radically different from the Europe of nation states, and to create a federal constitution for Europe as part of a more distant plan for global unity. However, it took until 1947 to organize the conference that was supposed to pave the way to the new constitution, by which time national governments had already been restored to office everywhere. The conference, the European Congress, eventually took place in The Hague in May 1948.

The Congress attracted considerable attention at the time. It was attended by representatives of most of the political parties of the non-communist states of Europe, and its Honorary President was Winston Churchill, who had used a speech in Zurich in 1946 to call for a united Europe. Churchill had implied in the Zurich speech that Britain, with its Commonwealth of Nations, would remain separate from the 'United States of Europe' to which he referred. Britain, along with the United States, and possibly the Union of Soviet Socialist Republics (USSR), would be 'friends and sponsors of the new Europe'. The vital development in this project would be a 'partnership' between France and Germany. Beyond this, and the 'first step' of forming a Council of Europe (see Insight 5.2), Churchill did not detail how the process towards European unity should proceed.

The Hague Congress was an occasion for fine speeches, but it gradually became apparent that the British were not interested in being part of a **supranational organization** that would compromise their national sovereignty. While the Congress did lead to the creation of the Council of Europe, this was so dominated by national governments that there was little realistic prospect of it developing in the federal direction that the EUF hoped.

The Council of Europe still exists today, and it has many solid achievements to its credit. In particular, it was responsible for adopting the European Convention on

---

Insight 5.2 **The Council of Europe**

Founded in 1949 as a result of the 1948 Congress of Europe in The Hague, the Council of Europe is not connected to the EU and should not be confused with the European Council, which is the name of the institutionalized summit meetings of the EU heads of state and government.

The Council of Europe is an intergovernmental organization based in the French city of Strasbourg. It originally had ten members, and by 2014 had forty-seven, including twenty-two countries from central and eastern Europe. Its main institutions are:

- the Committee of (Foreign) Ministers;
- the Parliamentary Assembly, consisting of 321 members of national parliaments, with 321 substitutes;
- the Congress of Local and Regional Authorities of Europe;
- the Secretariat;
- the European Commissioner for Human Rights;
- the European Court of Human Rights.

The Council was set up to:

- defend human rights, parliamentary democracy, and the rule of law;
- develop continent-wide agreements to standardize member countries' social and legal practices;
- promote awareness of a European identity based on shared values and cutting across different cultures.

Since 1989, its main job has become:

- to act as a political anchor and human rights watchdog for Europe's post-communist democracies;
- to assist the countries of central and eastern Europe in carrying out and consolidating political, legal, and constitutional reform in parallel with economic reform;
- to provide know-how in areas such as human rights, local democracy, education, culture, and the environment.

Source: http://www.coe.int.

Human Rights in 1950, and it maintained both a Commission on Human Rights (replaced by a Commissioner in 1999) and a Court of Human Rights: the former to investigate alleged breaches of such rights by governments, and the latter to rule definitively on whether a violation of rights has occurred. It also serves useful functions as a meeting place for parliamentarians from the diverse member states and promotes Europe-wide cultural activities. This all falls far short of the hopes of the EUF.

European integration was not to be achieved in one great act of political will, because the will was not there. Some blamed the failure of the Council of Europe to develop in a federal direction on the attitude of the British; but the truth is that no national government, once installed, was willing to surrender much of its power. In 1947, the attention of governments was still focused on national economic reconstruction, not on superseding the nation state. Yet, there were soon more insistent pressures on the governments to move away from national sovereignty than those that the federalists could muster.

The Cold War

To understand the origins of the European Communities, which led to the European Union, it is essential to see them in the context of the emerging Cold War between the capitalist West and the communist Soviet Union. Before the Second World War, advocates of a European union had assumed it would stretch to the borders of the USSR. But as relations between the former Allies deteriorated throughout 1946 and into 1947, it became clear this would be a project confined to the western part of the continent.

Agreement was reached at an Allied summit meeting in Yalta in 1945 to divide Europe at the end of the war into 'spheres of influence'. This was intended by the western Allies to be only a temporary arrangement, but the Soviet Union soon started to make it permanent. Regimes friendly to the USSR were installed in those countries of central and eastern Europe that had been assigned to the Soviet sphere at Yalta. This led Churchill to make a speech in Fulton, Missouri, in March 1946, in which he talked about an 'iron curtain' descending across Europe. The speech did not receive a sympathetic hearing in Washington, where the prevailing mood was still in favour of cooperation with the USSR; but this mood changed in the course of 1946.

In September 1946, communist insurgents restarted a civil war in Greece. This was a decision that could not have been taken without the agreement of the Soviet Union. In 1945, Stalin had ordered the Greek communists, who controlled large areas of the country, not to continue with an armed insurrection against the government that the British had installed in Athens. Greece was in the British sphere of influence according to the Yalta agreement, and it seemed that whatever unwelcome moves Stalin might be making in the Soviet sphere, he was at least intent on respecting the limits set at Yalta. The recommencement of hostilities in Greece threw that interpretation into doubt. During 1946, too, the Soviet Union refused to withdraw its troops from Persia, which was also outside its sphere, and made territorial demands on Turkey.

The weather in the European winter of 1946–47 was particularly severe, and put considerable strain on the economic recovery that was under way. This had direct consequences for the emergence of the Cold War. In February 1947, London informed

Washington that it could not afford to continue economic and military aid to Greece and Turkey. In response, in March 1947, President Truman asked Congress for $400 million of economic and military aid for Greece and Turkey. To dramatize the situation, he spoke of the duty of the United States to assist 'free peoples who are resisting attempted subjugation by armed minorities or by outside pressures'. This became known as the Truman Doctrine, and it marked a clear statement of intent by the US Administration to remain involved in the affairs of Europe and the wider world, and not to allow isolationist sentiments within the country and within Congress to force a withdrawal from an international role.

Perhaps even more significant in converting the US Administration to Churchill's view was the collapse of the Four-Power Council of Foreign Ministers, a standing conference to discuss the administration and future of Germany. Soviet intransigence in that forum, and the eventual walk-out of the Soviet representative in April 1947, convinced those who were trying to negotiate on behalf of Washington that it was not possible to work with the USSR. From that point on, the emergence of separate West and East German states became gradually inevitable.

A second direct consequence of the bad winter and economic setback of early 1947 was that waves of strikes spread across France and Italy. In both cases, the strikes were supported by communists, who engaged in revolutionary anti-capitalist rhetoric. In the light of events in Greece, this was interpreted as further evidence of the Soviet Union attempting to undermine stability outside its sphere of influence, although in both cases it may have been an incorrect interpretation. Certainly, in France, where the Communist Party was part of the coalition government, the strikes appeared to take them by surprise. However, it was very difficult for the French communists not to support their core electorate, and indeed not to interpret the strikes as evidence of the imminent collapse of capitalism. The other parties in the French coalition responded by expelling the communists from the government; the Truman Administration responded with the Marshall Plan.

On 5 June 1947, George Marshall, the US Secretary of State, announced that the US Administration proposed to offer financial and food aid to Europe to assist in its economic recovery (see Insight 5.3). Suspicious of US motives, the USSR and its allies rejected the offer. There were some grounds for this suspicion: the American gesture went far beyond simple altruism to a concern with economic self-interest.

Insight 5.3 The Marshall Plan

- The European Recovery Programme (ERP) was announced by US Secretary of State George C. Marshall in a speech at Harvard University on 5 June 1947.

- It involved the United States giving a total of $13 billion in financial aid to the states of western Europe. The assistance was offered to the states of eastern Europe, but they declined under pressure from the Soviet Union.

- The European states that accepted held a conference in July 1947 in Paris, and set up the Organization for European Economic Co-operation (OEEC) to facilitate the unified response that the United States required.

Marshall presented the American people with a vision of Europe in crisis in 1947. People were starving. The economy had broken down. Milward (1984: 3–4) contested this orthodox view. He denied there was a crisis, although he accepted that there was a serious problem about the ability of the west European states to build and sustain international trade because of a lack of convertible currencies to finance it. In his view, the Marshall Plan was entirely political in its conception and objectives, although its means were entirely economic. The misleading representation of the economic position in Europe was designed to get the agreement of the US Congress to the reconstruction programme.

Marshall Aid offered an injection of dollars into the European economy, which would finance trade between the European states and the United States, and trade between the European states themselves. This was a policy much favoured by those sections of US industry that were involved in exporting. It was less favoured by those sections of US industry that were oriented towards the domestic market, and that suspected that they would pay the bill for European reconstruction without gaining the benefits. This section of domestic opinion was strongly represented within Congress, and so it was by no means a foregone conclusion that the Administration would get its plans through Congress. Following the Soviet Union's rejection of aid, Truman and Marshall were able to justify the Plan as part of the same response to the threat of communism as was the Truman Doctrine. Marshall argued that economic conditions in western Europe in 1947 were so serious that they provided a breeding ground for communism. The struggle had to be waged by economic as well as military means.

Whether it was motivated by genuine concern for the condition of western Europe, or by economic considerations that had more to do with lobbying by the larger US corporations, Marshall Aid came with strings attached. The US Administration was committed to the idea of free trade. It was concerned to see what it described as 'European integration', meaning that national economic barriers to trade should be broken down. Both of the motives discussed above would support this position. Given that the Administration genuinely believed that free trade would strengthen the west European economies, integration was compatible with the stated aim of strengthening western Europe against communist expansion. However, it was also compatible with the aim of creating a large and exploitable market for US exports and for investments by US multinational corporations.

The United States insisted that decisions on the distribution and use of Marshall Aid be taken by the European states jointly. To implement this, a body known as the Committee for European Economic Co-operation (CEEC) was set up. Despite the professed aim of allowing the Europeans to make their own decisions on the use of the aid, the United States was represented on this committee, and because it was contributing all the funds, it clearly had economic and political leverage.

The CEEC was transformed in April 1948 into a more permanent body, the Organization for European Economic Co-operation (OEEC). The OEEC initially had fifteen members, but was soon joined by the newly independent Federal Republic of Germany (1949), while the United States and Canada became associate members in 1950.

For Marshall, and other members of the US Administration, the OEEC was to be the basis for the future supranational economic management of Europe. Nobody was quite clear what 'supranational' meant in this context, but it certainly meant breaking down national sovereignty in economic affairs. In particular, the US view was that western Europe should become a free-trade area as the first step towards global free trade.

This was not a vision that appealed to the governments of the European states involved. The British did not particularly want to be tied into any arrangement with the continental European states. The French had already embarked on their own recovery programme, which was based on a much more restrictive view of the role of free trade and the free market. Other governments shared some of the French concern to keep as much control as possible over their own economies, giving away sovereignty neither to a supranational organization nor to the workings of the international free market.

Crucial to the economic and political stance of the European states was the position of Germany. Whether the German economy and state would be reconstituted was still an open question when CEEC began operations. The United States wanted the decisions to be made by the OEEC. Germany's neighbours were simply not prepared to see that happen. In particular, they were nervous about the extent of political leverage the United States was able to exercise within the OEEC because of its economic influence as the sole contributor to the reconstruction funds. However, despite its economic leverage, the United States simply did not have sufficient political weight to overcome the combined opposition of Britain, France, and the smaller European states to allowing the OEEC to develop as a powerful supranational organization (Milward, 1984: 168–211).

The body within the OEEC controlling policy and administration was the Council of Ministers, which consisted of one representative from each member state. Decisions taken by the Council were binding on members but each member state retained the right of veto. While effective within its limited remit, the OEEC promised little in terms of further integration.

Despite its limitations, the OEEC continued its work for twelve years and, according to Urwin (1995: 22), 'played a major role in driving home the realization that European economies were mutually dependent, and that they prospered or failed together'. In 1961, the OEEC was superseded by the Organization for Economic Co-operation and Development (OECD), which had a broader remit, concerned with issues of economic development both in Europe and globally, and included the United States and Canada as full members.

The German Problem

The German problem came increasingly to dominate the debate about the future of Europe. For the United States and Britain, the future of Germany was inevitably linked to the emerging Cold War. For France and Germany's smaller neighbours, it was still a question of how to prevent the re-emergence of a threat to their sovereign independence from Germany itself.

Initially, Germany's neighbours tried to protect themselves through a traditional military alliance, in which British participation was seen as crucial. This approach produced the Treaty of Dunkirk between Britain and France in March 1947, and the Treaty of Brussels between Britain, France, and the **Benelux** states in March 1948. Both alliances were directed more at forestalling German aggression than they were at the Soviet Union.

The French government also tried to prevent the emergence of any German state. Ideally, the French Foreign Office would have liked to have kept Germany under Allied occupation. Failing that, it wanted the former German state to be divided into a large number of small, separate states. By 1949, it had become apparent that this was not going to happen. Again, the crucial dynamic was the rapidly emerging Cold War. In 1948, the Soviet Union walked out of Allied talks on the future of Germany. The United States and Britain responded by starting to prepare the Anglo-American zones for independence. The French were left in no doubt that they were expected to merge their occupation zone into the new West German state, which would be created under the plans for independence. Once the Federal Republic of Germany came into existence in 1949, the French policy had to be rethought.

The Schuman Plan for Coal and Steel

In May 1950, the French Foreign Minister, Robert Schuman, proposed a scheme for pooling the coal and steel supplies of France and Germany, and invited other European states who wished to participate to express an interest. The idea involved a surrender of sovereignty over the coal and steel industries. It was devised by Jean Monnet, a French civil servant (see Insight 5.4 and Chapter 1, 'Monnet and Functional-Federalism'), and addressed practical problems for France that arose from the establishment of the Federal Republic of Germany. The first problem was how to avert the threat of future conflict between France and Germany; the second was how to ensure continuing supplies of coal for the French

---

Insight 5.4 Jean Monnet

Jean Monnet (1888–1979) was born into a small brandy-producing family in Cognac. He left school at sixteen and, after a period gaining experience of financial affairs in London, he worked for the family business, travelling widely.

In 1915, he was declared unfit for military service, and spent the war in the civil service instead. He rose rapidly to the position of representative of the French government in London.

After the war he was appointed Deputy Secretary General of the League of Nations, but he returned to private life when the family firm got into difficulties in 1922. He subsequently became an investment banker and financier.

In the Second World War he worked first for the British government in Washington, then for de Gaulle in Algiers. He was instrumental in preventing the British and Americans from replacing de Gaulle, who, in 1946, appointed him as head of the French Economic Planning Commission, CdP.

He devised both the Schuman Plan and the Pleven Plan for a European Defence Community (EDC).

He was the first President of the High Authority of the ECSC between 1952 and 1955. Following the defeat of the proposed EDC in the French National Assembly, he resigned from the High Authority to be free to promote further schemes for European integration, setting up the Action Committee for the United States of Europe.

steel industry once the Ruhr region reverted to German sovereign control. The plan was welcomed by the German Chancellor, Konrad Adenauer, and the Benelux states and Italy indicated that they would wish to participate. The British government declined an invitation to take part. The negotiations between the six states that did wish to participate were marked by hard bargaining in defence of national interests, but eventually agreement was reached on what became the European Coal and Steel Community (ECSC). The Six signed the Treaty of Paris in April 1952, and the ECSC came into operation in July 1952.

National Positions and the Origins of the ECSC

The plan for the ECSC was known as the Schuman Plan because it was made public by the French Foreign Minister, Robert Schuman. He was born in Luxembourg, lived in Lorraine when it was part of the German empire, was conscripted into the German army in the First World War, and only became a French citizen after the war, when Alsace and Lorraine reverted to French sovereignty. Thus, he had a particular reason for wanting to reconcile the historic conflict between the two countries.

Milward (1984: 395–6) argued that the Foreign Ministry must have played a role in devising the plan, but the more generally accepted view is that it was drawn up within the French Economic Planning Commission (*Commissariat du Plan*—CdP), which was headed by Jean Monnet. It was the task of the CdP to guide the post-war reconstruction and modernization of the French economy, and it was through his experiences in this task that Monnet came to appreciate the economic inadequacy of the European nation state in the modern world. As he himself put it:

> For five years the whole French nation had been making efforts to recreate the bases of production, but it became evident that to go beyond recovery towards steady expansion and higher standards of life for all, the resources of a single nation were not sufficient. It was necessary to transcend the national framework.

(Monnet 1962: 205)

The wider framework that Monnet had in mind was an economically united western Europe. He saw the need to create a 'large and dynamic common market', 'a huge continental market on the European scale' (Monnet 1962: 205). But he aimed to create more than just a common market. Monnet was a planner: he showed no great confidence in the free-market system, which had served France badly in the past. He placed his faith in the development of supranational institutions as the basis for building a genuine economic community that would adopt common economic policies and rational planning procedures.

Coal and steel were only intended as starting points. The aim was to extend integration to all aspects of the west European economy; but such a scheme would have been too ambitious to gain acceptance all at once.

> Europe will not be made all at once, or according to a single plan. It will be built through concrete achievements which first create a *de facto* solidarity.

(Schuman Declaration 1950)

There had been a clear indication of this need for incrementalism in the failure of various post-war efforts to integrate the economies of France, Italy, the Netherlands, Belgium, and Luxembourg. Although negotiations for an organization to be known as 'Finebel' had proceeded for some time, they were on the verge of collapse in 1950. Besides, the new factor in the equation, and the key factor prompting Monnet's plan, was the emergence in April 1949 of a sovereign West German state.

For Monnet, the existence of the Federal Republic of Germany posed two problems in addition to that of how to create an integrated west European economy. The first was how to organize Franco–German relations in such a way that another war between the two states would become impossible. To a French mind, this meant how to control Germany. The pooling of coal and steel production would provide the basis for economic development as a first step towards a 'federation of Europe', and would change the future of those regions devoted to producing munitions, which had also been 'the most constant victims' of war.

> The solidarity in production thus established will make it plain that any war between France and Germany becomes not merely unthinkable, but materially impossible.

(Schuman Declaration 1950)

The problem of how to control Germany remained at the heart of the process of European integration throughout the early post-war period.

The second problem facing Monnet was the very practical one of how to ensure continuing adequate supplies of coking coal from the Ruhr for the French steel industry. The idea of pooling Franco–German supplies of coal and steel was not new: similar schemes had been proposed on many occasions previously (Gillingham 1991*b*: 135; Duchêne 1994: 202). In fact, the idea of pooling coal and steel supplies had featured in two recent publications, one from the Assembly of the Council of Europe and the other from the UN Economic Commission for Europe (Urwin 1995: 44). These reports were concerned with the very practical problems affecting the coal and steel industries of Europe. There was excess capacity in steel, and a shortage of coal. This combination was of particular concern to Monnet, whose recovery plan for France involved expanding steel-producing capacity. The French steel industry was heavily dependent on supplies of coking coal from the Ruhr.

At the end of the war, the Ruhr region of Germany had been placed under joint Allied control. Its supplies of coal had been allocated between the various competing users by the International Authority for the Ruhr (IAR), which had been established in April 1945. It seemed unlikely that this arrangement could be long continued once the Federal Republic was constituted, which raised the question of how France could ensure that it continued to get access to the supply of scarce Ruhr coal which its steel industry needed. The coal and steel pool had the potential to achieve this.

In summary, Monnet's reasons for proposing the plan to pool Franco–German supplies of coal and steel were a combination of taking a first step on the road to complete integration of the west European economy, finding a way to organize Franco–German relations which would eliminate the prospect of a further war between the two states, and solving the problem of how to ensure continued access for the French steel industry to supplies of coking coal from the Ruhr. That Schuman essentially accepted this thinking, informs the standard explanation for France's participation in the Schuman Plan.

For the Federal Republic of Germany, Chancellor Adenauer accepted the Schuman Plan with alacrity. Yet, if the proposal had been made to serve French interests, why was the German Chancellor so keen on it? As with Schuman, one of the factors was a commitment on the part of Adenauer to the ideal of European integration. Like Schuman, Adenauer came from a border region, in his case the Rhineland. Like Schuman, he was a Roman Catholic and a Christian Democrat. In accepting the Schuman Plan, Adenauer committed himself to Franco–German reconciliation and to European integration. This does not mean, though, that he acted only for idealistic reasons. There were also very practical reasons for Adenauer's acceptance of the Schuman Plan. The Federal Republic needed to gain international acceptance; Adenauer wanted to make a strong commitment to the capitalist West; and the new German government was looking for a way of getting rid of the IAR.

The legacy of the Nazi era and of the war had left Germany a pariah nation. It had also left it divided into two separate states, the Federal Republic in the West and the Democratic Republic in the East. Adenauer wanted to establish the Federal Republic as the legitimate successor to the pre-war German state, but also as a peace-loving state that would be accepted as a full participant in European and international affairs. He also wanted to establish the western and capitalist orientation of the Federal Republic beyond question or reversal. This was important to Adenauer because the Social Democratic Party (*Sozialdemokratische Partei Deutschlands*—SPD) was arguing for the Federal Republic to declare itself neutral in the emerging Cold War in the hope that this would facilitate re-unification of the country. As well as being strongly anti-communist, Adenauer believed that the Democratic Republic was dominated by the Soviet Union, and he feared that the cultural influence of Russia would be damaging to the vitality of German culture and to the process of moral renewal in the aftermath of Nazism, which, as a devout Catholic, he believed to be essential (Milward 1992: 329–30).

The importance for Adenauer of getting rid of the IAR was both political and economic. Politically, it was important to him that the region be integrated into the Federal Republic. Economically, the Ruhr had always been one of the powerhouses of the German industrial economy, so it was important to the prospects of economic recovery that it be unchained from the restrictions that the IAR placed on its industrialists. There was a risk that, in accepting the Schuman Plan, Adenauer would commit his country to a relationship from which French industry would gain at the expense of German industry. However, Adenauer was confident that German industrialists could stand up for their interests within a coal and steel pool (Gillingham 1991a: 233).

The reason why the Benelux states agreed to enter the negotiations for the ECSC was the same in each case: they could not afford to stay out of any agreement between France and Germany on coal and steel. These commodities were essential to the economies of the three states, and there was a high degree of interdependence between the industries in the border regions of France and Germany, and those in Belgium and Luxembourg particularly. There was also support in all three states for any moves that promised to reduce the risk of war between their two larger neighbours.

Italian reasons for joining in the negotiations require a little more explanation than the reasons for Benelux participation. Italy is not geographically part of the same industrial region as the other participants, so there was not the same inevitability about its involvement. In many ways, the reasons for Italian participation in the negotiations resembled those of Germany more closely than those of the Benelux states.

Like Germany, Italy was governed by Christian Democrats; and, as in the case of Adenauer (and of Schuman), the individual who dominated the government was a Roman Catholic and someone who originated in a border region. Alcide de Gasperi came from the Alto Adige region of Italy, which had been part of the Austro-Hungarian empire before the First World War. Like Germany, Italy had to rebuild its international reputation after the war. Mussolini had been Hitler's ally and had ended up as his puppet. Like Germany, Italy was on the front line in the emerging Cold War. Geographically, it had a land frontier with the communist state of Yugoslavia, and only the Adriatic Sea separated it from Albania. At the end of the war there had been a serious risk that the Italian Communist Party would take over the country in democratic elections, and it remained the largest single party in terms of support. De Gasperi therefore had a similar need to that of Adenauer in Germany to enmesh his country in a complex of institutional interdependencies with the capitalist West, to establish its western and capitalist identity politically, economically, and in the minds of its own people.

The other state that was invited to participate in the conference that followed the Schuman Plan was Britain. The negative attitude of the British government has been extensively analysed (J. W. Young 1993: 28–35; Dell 1995; George 1998: 19–22; H. Young 1998).

All accounts accept that there were certain peculiarities of the British position that made it highly unlikely that its government would welcome the proposal. Whereas, in continental Europe, nationalism had been discredited through its association with fascism, in Britain fascism had never succeeded, and the war had been fought as a national war. Unlike the other states, Britain had neither been defeated nor occupied in the war. There was not the same sense in Britain of discontinuity with the past. The attitude of the British governing elite was that Britain was not just another European state; it was a world power with global responsibilities. Although this attitude has been described as a 'delusion of grandeur' (Porter 1987), it had some basis in reality: Britain still had a considerable empire, British companies had interests in all parts of the world, and British armed forces were globally deployed in keeping the peace, or acting as a bulwark against communist encroachment.

The perception at the time was that Britain was economically far stronger than the other western European states, and that tying the future of the British economy to that of the German and French economies was dangerous. Britain had adequate indigenous supplies of coal, and the Labour government had just completed the nationalization of the coal and steel industries. Having campaigned over many years for nationalization, the Labour Party was unlikely to surrender control once it had been achieved. Also, European integration was at this time particularly associated with the leader of the Conservative Party, Winston Churchill. Although there were some Labour Party members who participated in The Hague Congress and remained supporters of a united Europe, the idea was associated with the opposition, not the government.

To add to these general factors, Ernest Bevin, the Foreign Secretary, was personally upset that he had no forewarning of Schuman's announcement. Dean Acheson, the US Secretary of State, was told about the Plan in advance by the French Prime Minister, Georges Bidault, and Acheson subsequently met Bevin, but did not mention the Plan. As Acheson had been given the information in confidence, this was reasonable enough; but it led Bevin to see a Franco–American plot to seize the initiative away from Britain in the formulation of plans for western Europe (Young 1998: 52). Bevin's annoyance was increased when the French government insisted that all those who wished to participate in the scheme must accept the principle of supranationalism. This condition was pressed by Monnet, who was concerned that otherwise the outcome would be another intergovernmental organization. He must have known that it would be an impossible condition for the British government to accept, given the strong attachment of the Labour Party to national sovereignty, and perhaps he did not really want British participation at the outset. It was, after all, the British who had been primarily responsible for the watering down of the commitment to supranational institutions in the Council of Europe.

The British government did not immediately reject the demand for a commitment to supranationalism. Instead, the French were asked to specify exactly what they meant by the phrase, to spell out the full extent of the surrender of sovereignty that was envisaged, and its effects. After some three weeks of inconclusive discussions of the implications of supranationalism, Schuman announced on 1 June 1950 that the principle was non-negotiable, and that any state that wanted to be involved in the negotiations must accept it by 8.00 p.m. on 2 June. The British Cabinet immediately rejected this condition.

From the Schuman Plan to the Treaty of Paris

Negotiations between the 'Six' began on 20 June, with all delegations supposedly committed to the principle of supranationalism. However, both the Belgians and the Dutch had reservations, as became apparent once the opening session was completed and the substantive negotiations began on 22 June (Duchêne 1994: 209).

Monnet insisted that the French delegation should be hand-picked by himself, and he rigorously excluded representatives of the French coal and steel industries from influence in the process. This was not the case with the other delegations, which consisted of diplomats and officials from the national energy ministries, who were open to influence from the affected industries.

There followed months of hard bargaining, during which various departures were made from the original principles set out in Monnet's working document (see Insight 5.5). These concessions were necessary to make a success of the negotiations. That they had to be made reinforces the view that most participants were concerned to use the ECSC to further their own national interests. The biggest concessions were made by the German government, for whom the main potential advantage of the Schuman Plan was the opportunity it offered to get the removal of the constraints imposed by the IAR.

At the end of the war, the Allies had forced the deconcentration of the coal and steel industries in Germany, and the break-up of the cartels that had restricted competition. From the German point of view, this only served to give an artificial advantage to their French competitors. The IAR acted to prevent reconcentration and re-emergence of cartels, so the German industrialists wanted to get rid of it. But they did not want the High Authority of the ECSC to take over those functions from the IAR, whereas Monnet was determined that the High Authority would do exactly that.

From the French point of view, concentration was dangerous because it gave too much political influence to the large industrial concerns. The support of the Ruhr

> **Insight 5.5 Bargaining Concessions in the ECSC Negotiations**
>
> • At the insistence of the Dutch, and supported by the Germans, a Council of Ministers, consisting of representatives of national governments, was added to the institutional structure to curtail the supranationalism of the High Authority.
>
> • At the insistence of the Belgians, a special 'equalization tax' on efficient coal producers was agreed, which would be used to subsidize the modernization of inefficient mines. In practice, this amounted to a subsidy from Germany to Belgium.
>
> • At the insistence of the Italians, the Italian steel industry was allowed to maintain tariffs against the rest of the participants for five years, and to continue to import cheap coking coal and scrap metal from outside the ECSC. As with the Belgian coal mines, there was to be an equalization fund to finance the modernization of inefficient Italian steel plants, although this was much smaller than the coal equalization tax.

industrialists for Hitler had contributed to the Nazis coming to power. Cartelization was a device that, in Monnet's eyes, acted as a restraint on competition. In this view, he was strongly supported by the United States.

The role of the US Administration in the negotiations was vital. Not officially represented at the talks, the United States nevertheless exerted a tremendous influence behind the scenes. A special committee was set up in the US Embassy in Paris to monitor progress, and it acted as a sort of additional secretariat for Monnet. For the United States, the cartel arrangements were an outrageous interference with the operation of market forces and could not be tolerated. There was initially less concern about the concentration issue because the size of the units involved would still be much smaller than those in the United States. However, after the outbreak of the Korean War in June 1950, the US Administration came to the reluctant conclusion that Germany would have to be rearmed. In this context, the issue of not allowing the emergence of the industrial conglomerates that had supported the previous militaristic German regime became more significant in US minds.

After months of hard negotiation, the United States cut through the arguments and forced a settlement. On 3 March 1951, Adenauer was summoned to see John J. McCloy, the US High Commissioner in Bonn, who told him that the delays caused by the Germans were unacceptable, and that 'France and the United States had no choice but to impose their own decartelization scheme' (Gillingham 1991a: 280). Despite vigorous protests from the Ruhr producers, Adenauer accepted the ultimatum because, for him, the political gains of the ECSC were paramount and he could not afford to allow the process to collapse.

It appeared, then, that although Monnet's concept had been severely modified, the essential purpose had been achieved of creating a supranational body that could exercise some control over the coal and steel producers in the interests of promoting efficiency and competition.

The High Authority was funded through a direct levy on Europe's coal and steel firms and had a wide brief on taxes, production, and restrictive practices. Alongside it were established a Council of Ministers consisting of national government representatives, and a Common Assembly. In addition, a Consultative Committee to the High

Authority was established to represent producers, employers, and consumers. More significantly in terms of future integration, a Court of Justice was set up with judges drawn from the national judiciaries to rule on the legality of the High Authority's actions. These institutional arrangements provided in embryonic form the core of the institutional framework of the European Union as it exists today.

CONCLUSION

The history of European integration can be told as a story of ideas, or it can be told as a story of heroic individuals who led their states into closer unity. Both factors had a role in the rapid movement from the end of the war to the start of the first of the European communities, but circumstances were also crucially important in giving the ideas practical relevance and in inspiring the national leaders to push the project forward.

Like previous attempts at political unity in Europe, the attempts made immediately after the war were initially driven by idealism. As with previous attempts, this would not have been enough to overcome the vested interests of national governments in maintaining the status quo, had there not also been strong practical arguments in favour of closer co-operation between states. Such practical arguments were provided by the circumstances in which post-war European leaders found themselves.

The fear of communism taking over the whole of Europe if the western states could not provide economic recovery quickly put political urgency behind the arguments for closer collaboration. The need for reconstruction to be carried out on a rational basis in the European coal, iron, and steel industries was one of the pressing economic necessities. In the longer term, the need for Europe to compete economically with the much larger economies of the United States and the Soviet Union may also have played a part in the thinking of some of the more far-seeing founders of the experiment in European unity, but the immediate practical problems were in the forefront of minds.

KEY POINTS

Background: The Ideal of European Unity

- Plans for European unity have a long pedigree, but prior to the 1950s none had succeeded.

The End of the War, Federalism, and The Hague Congress

- Federalist groups put the idea of European unity on the immediate post-war agenda and attracted a lot of public support in several European states.
- By the time that the Hague Congress was held, in 1948, new national governments were in control of the states of western Europe and were reluctant to surrender any sovereignty.

The Cold War

- A growing rift between the Soviet Union and its former western allies led to the emergence of fears in western Europe of a communist takeover inspired by Moscow.
- The severe winter of 1946–47 led to unrest in several west European states that was exploited by indigenous communist parties, and prompted the United States to propose the Marshall Plan to feed economic recovery.
- The United States favoured European unity and pressed for movement in that direction.

The German Problem

- Germany's neighbours, particularly France, were concerned to guard against a resurgence of German militarism and initially opposed the re-formation of a German state. After the German Federal Republic was set up in 1949, a new approach was needed.

The Schuman Plan for Coal and Steel

- Proposed by Robert Schuman, but devised by Jean Monnet, the plan proposed the pooling of the coal and steel resources of the European states.
- Monnet was trying to solve two problems with one plan: the problem of containing Germany and the problem of ensuring supplies of coal to French industry.
- Six states took part in the negotiations that led to the ECSC.

National Positions and the Origins of the ECSC

- France: Monnet saw the need for a European common market with coal and steel as the start.
- Germany: Adenauer saw the ECSC as a way to restore Germany's international position, establish the Federal Republic as the legitimate successor to the pre-war German state, and consolidate the western and capitalist orientation of the new state.
- The Benelux States could not afford to be left out of a community that pooled the coal and steel supplies of France and Germany.
- In Italy, Alcide de Gasperi had very similar motives to Adenauer in Germany: he wanted to restore Italy's international respectability and confirm its western and capitalist identity.
- Britain was not interested in participating in a coal and steel pool as it had its own supplies of coal, the new Labour government had just nationalized these industries, and it saw itself as a global power with a strong economy.

From the Schuman Plan to the Treaty of Paris

- Months of bargaining led to modification of Monnet's original ambitious plan.
- There was a struggle between France and Germany over the powers of the High Authority of the ECSC and over the attitude to cartels.
- The United States played a vital role behind the scenes.
- The institutional arrangements established for the ECSC provided, in embryonic form, the basic institutional framework of the European Union as it exists today.

 For additional material and resources, please visit the online resources www.oup.com/uk/bache5e.

FURTHER READING

D. W. Urwin, *The Community of Europe: A History of European Integration since 1945* (London and New York: Longman, 2nd edn, 1994) and **Urwin**, *Western Europe Since 1945: A Short Political History* (London and New York: Longman, 4th edn, 1985) should be treated as standard reference sources. A particularly controversial account of the early post-war origins of European integration is given by **A. S. Milward**, *The Reconstruction of Western Europe, 1945–51* (London: Routledge, 1984).

For more information on European federalism, see **M. Burgess (ed.)**, *Federalism and Federation in Western Europe* (London: Croom Helm, 1986) and *Federalism in the European Union: Political Ideas, Influences and Strategies* (London and New York: Routledge, 1989).

There is a considerable literature on the Schuman Plan. For a detailed insight into the process, the account given by **F. Duchêne**, *Jean Monnet: The First Statesman of Interdependence* (New York and London: W. W. Norton and Co., 1994) is indispensable and also provides invaluable insights into the origins of the Pleven Plan. Most of **J. Gillingham**, *Coal, Steel, and the Rebirth of Europe, 1945–1955* (Cambridge: Cambridge University Press, 1991) is devoted to the build-up to the negotiations and the negotiations themselves, and **E. B. Haas**, *The Uniting of Europe: Political, Social and Economic Forces, 1950–1957* (Stanford, CA: Stanford University Press, 1968) contains information on the positions of all the main actors, scattered through a book that is organized thematically, rather than chronologically. The British failure to take seriously the Schuman Plan is recounted in **E. Dell**, *The Schuman Plan and the British Abdication of Leadership in Europe* (Oxford: Clarendon Press, 1995).

For access to various primary sources, the website www.cvce.eu/en is very useful.

Chapter 6

The 'Other' European Communities and the Origins of the European Economic Community (the Early 1950s to the 1960s)

Chapter Overview

In this next period, the post-war ferment continued, and plans for both practical and less practical moves to closer European unity were generated. As in the earlier period, there were broadly three positions contending: that of the federalists, who were committed to a supranational vision for Europe that would supersede the nation states; that of the defenders of national sovereignty, represented by the governments of the states; and that of the pragmatic problem solvers, the epitome of which was Jean Monnet.

The creation of the European Coal and Steel Community (ECSC) was analysed in Chapter 5, 'The Schuman Plan for Coal and Steel'. Negotiations over a plan for a European Defence Community (EDC) ran parallel to those over the ECSC. Connected with the European Defence Community (EDC) was a proposal to create a European Political Community (EPC) to provide democratic European structures for co-ordinating foreign policies. This chapter looks at the development of the EDC/EPC plan and the ultimate failure to reach agreement in 1954. It then examines the experience of the ECSC up to the merger of the High Authority with the Commission of the European Economic Community (EEC) in July 1967, before turning to the Messina negotiations and the road to the Rome Treaties. It also looks briefly at the experience of the other organization that was created at the same time as the EEC, the European Atomic Energy Community (Euratom), which, like the ECSC, was institutionally merged with the EEC in 1967.

The Pleven Plan

While the development of the ECSC set much of the tone and framework for future developments in European integration, it was largely overshadowed at the time by parallel negotiations on another plan devised by Monnet, the Pleven Plan for an EDC. This gave federalists another opportunity to pursue their strategy of 'the constitutional break', moving directly from a Europe of nation states to a federal constitution for Europe. However, the feasibility of doing this was no greater in 1953 than it had been in 1948, and for the same reason: governments were not prepared to surrender their sovereignty.

Following the collapse of the four-power administration of Germany (see Chapter 5, 'The Cold War'), the Cold War developed rapidly. In April 1949, a mutual defence pact, the North Atlantic Treaty, was signed in Washington between the United States, Canada, and ten west European states (Britain, France, the **Benelux** states, Iceland, Italy, Norway, Denmark, and Portugal). This set up the North Atlantic Treaty Organization (NATO). In the same month, the Federal Republic of Germany came into existence. In June 1950, communist North Korea invaded capitalist South Korea. The ensuing civil war involved the United States, acting under the auspices of the United Nations, on the side of the South, and the Soviet Union and communist China on the side of the North. It had a profound impact on western thinking about security.

Like Korea, Germany was divided into capitalist and communist states. While Korea was at that time geographically peripheral to the main global balance of power, Germany was not. The fear in the West was that the Korean invasion was a precursor to an invasion of West Germany from East Germany. In this context, and because the United States was committing troops to the Korean conflict, the US Administration decided that the Europeans had to make a bigger contribution to their own defence. In particular, they reluctantly decided that there was no alternative to reconstituting a German army.

This idea alarmed the French. For them it was unthinkable that a German army should come back into existence. Monnet tried to solve the problem with a proposal based on the same principles as his plan for the ECSC. Under his scheme for an EDC, instead of having a German army, he proposed to pool the military resources of France and Germany into a European army. There would be German soldiers, but they would not wear German uniforms, and they would not be under German command. The corollary, of course, was that the French army would at least partially disappear into the same European force. Monnet's proposal did, however, allow France and the other participants, except Germany, to have their own national armies alongside the European army.

The plan proposed the creation of a European army consisting of fourteen French divisions, twelve German, eleven Italian, and three from the Benelux states. The command of the army would be integrated, but there would be no divisions of mixed nationality. The EDC would have had a similar institutional structure to the ECSC: a Council representing the member states, with votes weighted according to each state's contribution to the European army, alongside a Commission and an Assembly.

As with the pooling of coal and steel, a European army was not a new idea. A similar proposal had been made by the French representatives in the Consultative Assembly of the Council of Europe in August 1950, and had received the support of the Assembly, but had been blocked in the Council of Ministers. Monnet now formalized the idea, making an explicit link to the ECSC. The plan was publicly launched by the French Prime Minister, René Pleven, an old collaborator of Monnet, on 24 October 1950.

Despite the election in Britain, in October 1951, of a Conservative government under Churchill, who professed to be a supporter of European integration, the British were unwilling to become involved in plans for the EDC. The US Administration was initially cautious, but Monnet persuaded the new NATO Supreme Allied Commander in Europe, Dwight D. Eisenhower, and his support swung the Administration behind the scheme (Duchêne 1994: 231). Adenauer welcomed the idea, seeing in it a way of finally ending the Allied occupation of West Germany. The other four states that had joined in the Schuman Plan signed up to talks for essentially the same reasons as they had joined ECSC: the Benelux states did not feel that they could stand aside from such an initiative between their two larger neighbours, and Italy continued to seek acceptance into the European states system.

At Monnet's prompting, Pleven made it a condition of progress on the EDC that the ECSC Treaty be signed first. This was particularly resented in Germany because Monnet had accompanied preparation of the Pleven Plan with a hardening of his attitude towards the position of the German steel cartels in the talks on the Schuman Plan. This had stalled the talks: Adenauer and the German negotiator, Hallstein, felt that they were being railroaded into accepting an unfavourable agreement on the ECSC in order to secure negotiations on the EDC. They were not mistaken. Gillingham (1991b: 146) was clear that these two developments were linked in Monnet's mind. Indeed, the same author (1991a: 264) went so far as to suggest that the Pleven Plan 'saved the Schuman Plan'. This sort of cross-bargaining worked both ways, however. Duchêne (1994: 250) believed that one explanation for Monnet's failure to press home the Treaty provisions against the Ruhr cartels, when he became President of the ECSC High Authority, was that Adenauer warned him that any premature action on this front would jeopardize the ratification of the EDC Treaty in the German parliament.

A problem with the proposed EDC was the plan for a common European army without a common foreign policy. The proposed institutions of the EDC would not be able to provide this. At the insistence of Italy, a clause was inserted into the draft Treaty linking the EDC with the creation of an EPC to provide a democratic dimension to the project. Plans were to be drawn up by the Common Assembly of the EDC, but as delays in ratifying the Treaty stretched out the process, Paul-Henri Spaak, the Belgian Premier, suggested that the Common Assembly of the ECSC, enlarged in membership so as to resemble the proposed EDC Assembly, should prepare the EPC proposal.

The opportunity to draft a Treaty for the EPC was seized on by federalists within the Assembly. In the course of its work, the ECSC Assembly was supplemented by members of the Parliamentary Assembly of the Council of Europe. The draft Treaty was adopted by this ad hoc Assembly on 10 March 1953. It proposed: a two-chamber European Parliament, consisting of a People's Chamber that would be directly elected every five years and a Senate of indirectly elected members from national parliaments; a European Executive Council that would have to be approved by both chambers of the parliament, but, once in office, would have the power to dissolve the People's Chamber and call new elections; a Council of National Ministers; and a Court of Justice. The EPC would not be just a third community, 'but nothing less than the beginning of a comprehensive federation to which the ECSC and EDC would be subordinated' (Urwin 1995: 64).

The fate of the EPC was inevitably linked to the fate of the EDC. The EDC Treaty had been signed in May 1952, but it had not been ratified by any of the signatories when the EPC proposals emerged. In fact, the EDC Treaty was 'rotting before the ink was dry' (Duchêne 1994: 233). Its prospects were crucially dependent on French support, but the French government only signed it on the 'tacit condition that no immediate attempt should be made to ratify it' (Duchêne 1994: 233). German rearmament, even as part of a European army, was unpopular in France. Pleven only managed to get approval for his proposal from the National Assembly by 343 votes to 220. By the time that the intergovernmental negotiations were completed, there had been elections in France and the parliamentary arithmetic did not indicate a clear majority for ratification. In consequence, successive prime ministers refused to bring the Treaty to the Assembly for ratification, fearing that its failure would bring down their government.

This prevarication, which went on for almost two years, caused exasperation in the United States, and, in December 1953, led Secretary of State John Foster Dulles to threaten an 'agonizing reappraisal' of policy. Eventually the Treaty was submitted to the National Assembly by the government of Pierre Mendès-France at the end of August 1954, but the government gave it no support, and indicated that it would not resign if the Assembly voted against ratification. The EDC Treaty was not ratified and the demise of the EDC was accompanied by the collapse of the EPC.

The issue of European defence was eventually solved according to a formula proposed by the British government. The Brussels Treaty of 1948 was extended to Germany and Italy; a loose organization called the Western European Union (WEU) was set up to co-ordinate the alliance; an organic link was made with NATO, to which Germany and Italy were admitted. Adenauer achieved his aim of securing an Allied withdrawal from the whole of West Germany (although not Berlin), and a German army was formed, although it was hedged around with legal restrictions on operating beyond the borders of the Federal Republic. The WEU appeared to contemporary observers to be an organization of no particular importance because it was overshadowed by NATO. However, like other organizations that were set up in the post-war period, it was later to acquire functions that had not been envisaged at the time when it was formed (see Insight 6.1).

The other practical significance of the EDC episode, or rather of the related EPC initiative, was that it kept the federalist idea alive. As Gillingham (1991*a*: 349) put it, it 'kept the cadres in being, dialogue moving, and served as a learning experience'. The importance of this became clear with the 'relaunching of Europe' that followed the collapse of EDC.

Defence was not an obvious next step after coal and steel in the process of building mutual trust through practical co-operation. It was not an issue with a low political profile, but a sensitive issue that struck to the heart of national sovereignty. Had it not been for the international crisis of the Korean War, it would surely not have surfaced at this stage. Monnet himself may have been of this view. Duchêne (1994: 229) reports that several people who were working close to Monnet at the time had the impression that he regarded the EDC scheme as premature. After winning over Eisenhower, Monnet took no further part in the negotiations on the plan, suggesting a lack of further commitment to the project.

With the collapse of the EDC and EPC, the radical federalist strategy of a direct attack on the system of nation states disappeared from this story. The struggle over European integration at this stage became one between nation states who tried to keep control of the process in their own hands, and supranational bureaucracies that tried to push forward the process using means that were later theorized by the neofunctionalists (see Chapter 1, 'Theories of European Integration'). This strategy was particularly

Insight 6.1 The Western European Union

Following the collapse of the EDC, the British government proposed an alternative security structure for western Europe. This involved Italy and Germany becoming signatories to the Brussels Treaty of 1948, by which Britain, France, and the Benelux states had committed themselves to treat any act of aggression against one as an act of aggression against all.

The result was the WEU, which began work on 6 May 1955. Its headquarters were in London. Its institutions consisted of:

- a Council of Foreign and Defence Ministers;
- a Secretariat, headed by a Secretary-General;
- an Assembly (based in Paris), made up of the member states' representatives in the Parliamentary Assembly of the Council of Europe.

In the 1980s, the WEU took on a new role as a bridge between the EC and NATO in the context of efforts to forge a European security and defence identity (see also Insight 25.1). The Treaty on European Union (signed in February 1992) contained, as an annex, a declaration on WEU which read: 'WEU will be developed as the defence component of the European Union and as a means to strengthen the European pillar of the Atlantic Alliance.' The WEU's operational activities were transferred to the EU in 2000. The Lisbon Treaty took over the WEU's mutual defence clause. The WEU Treaty was terminated in March 2010, and the organization was wound up over the following year.

associated with the Commission of the EEC, but it drew on lessons from the experiences of the two other European Communities that did come into existence, the ECSC and Euratom.

The European Coal and Steel Community

The ECSC survived the EDC debacle and began operation in July 1952 under the presidency of Jean Monnet. Although it had considerable powers at its disposal (see Insight 6.2), it proceeded cautiously in using them, but still found itself in conflict with national governments.

In the original plan for the ECSC there was only one central institution, the High Authority. During the negotiations, a Council of Ministers and a European Parliamentary Assembly (EPA) were added to the institutional structure. This reflected concern about the power and possible **dirigiste** nature of the High Authority, but did not allay that concern.

While coal producers were ambiguous about supranational *dirigisme*, most of them hoping for some degree of support for their troubled industry, steel producers were generally hostile to this aspect of the Schuman Plan. German industrialists in particular opposed the *dirigiste* element to the Plan, and the Federal German government supported them. The governments of the Benelux countries also had severe doubts about the role of the High Authority. At the insistence of these governments, a Council of

Insight 6.2 The High Authority

The High Authority of the ECSC had nine members, two each from France and Germany and one from each of the other member states, the ninth member to be co-opted by the other eight. Its seat was in Luxembourg. It had five presidents:

- Jean Monnet (1952–5);
- René Mayer (1955–7);
- Paul Finet (1958–9);
- Piero Malvestiti (1959–63); and
- Rinaldo Del Bo (1963–7).

It had the power under the Treaty of Paris to obtain from firms in the coal and steel sectors the information that it required to oversee the industries, and to fine firms that would not provide the information or evaded their obligations (Article 47).

It could impose levies on production, and contract loans to raise finance to back investment projects of which it approved (Articles 49–51), and it could guarantee loans to coal and steel concerns from independent sources of finance (Article 54). It could also require undertakings to inform it in advance of investment programmes, and, if it disapproved of the plans, could prevent the concern from using resources other than its own funds to carry out the programme (Article 54).

Ministers was included in the institutional structure of the ECSC, alongside the High Authority.

Although its independence was reduced from Monnet's original proposal, the High Authority was still given considerable formal powers. Diebold (1959: 78–9) considered that:

> It was truly to be an imperium in imperio, wielding powers previously held by national governments and having some functions not previously exercised by governments.

Despite these powers, in practice the High Authority proceeded very cautiously. It was in a constant state of tension with member state governments, who did not take easily to having their sovereignty circumscribed by a supranational body. The Council regularly rejected proposals of the High Authority that conflicted with national interests. For this reason, the High Authority needed a strong president who could impose his authority. In their comprehensive history of the ECSC, Spierenburg and Poidevin (1994: 649) argued that the first two presidents, Monnet and René Mayer, fitted this description, as did the last president, Del Bo, although by the time he took office in 1963 the High Authority was already in its twilight years. The two intervening presidents, Finet and Malvestiti, did not carry the same weight (see Insight 6.2).

Even taking account of this difficult relationship with the Council, Haas (1968: 459) considered that, 'in all matters relating to the routine regulation of the Common Market, the High Authority is independent of member governments'. Because of this independence, those governments that were concerned about the possible *dirigisme* of the High Authority took care to nominate as their members people who were not themselves committed to this outlook. For Milward (1992: 105) the most notable feature of the members of the High Authority was that they never liberated themselves from their national governments. Monnet became the first president of the High Authority, but found himself at the head of a group of people who were not in sympathy with his own view on its role. Haas (1968: 459) argued that in 'the ideology of the High Authority, the free enterprise and anti-*dirigiste* viewpoint . . . definitely carried the day'.

This way of presenting the issue is perhaps a little misleading. It suggests that Monnet was in favour of intrusive public-sector intervention and was opposed by other members who favoured free competition. In fact, one of the things that Monnet wanted the High Authority to do was to prevent the reformation of the coal and steel cartels—organizations of producers that regulated the industries through their collaboration on prices and output. Monnet wanted such regulation as there was to be carried out by the High Authority; but he was also committed to preserving competition between producers. The other members of the High Authority were committed to preventing it from interfering with self-regulation of the markets, not to competition. Perhaps this is what Haas meant by a 'free-enterprise' viewpoint, but the terminology tends to suggest that less-regulated markets were the objective. In any case, Monnet was frustrated in his policy objectives for the High Authority.

He was also frustrated in his organizational objectives. Mazey (1992: 40–1) argued that Monnet wanted a small, supranational, non-hierarchical, and informal organization; but that internal divisions, bureaucratization, and pressures from corporatist and national interests foiled him in this. Internal divisions between members of the High Authority itself were reproduced within the administration, and when combined with the non-hierarchical structure that Monnet adopted, this led to increasing problems of administrative co-ordination, delays, and duplication of effort because of overlapping competence.

However, as the demands for administering the common market for coal and steel grew, so did the bureaucratic nature of the High Authority. Problems of co-ordination increased as the different Directorates of the ECSC developed different links with interests and producers in the member states. The consequence was that in the first three years of its operation, 'the administrative services of the High Authority were . . . transformed from an informal grouping of sympathetic individuals into a professional bureaucracy which, in terms of its structure and "technocratic" character, resembled the French administration' (Mazey 1992: 43).

When the ECSC was proposed, coal was in short supply; but by 1959 the increasing use of oil had led to overcapacity in the industry. This became a crisis in 1958, when a mild winter and an economic downturn produced a serious fall in demand. Although economic growth picked up in the second quarter of 1959, stocks of coal at the pithead continued to accumulate because of a second mild winter, low transatlantic freight costs that allowed cheap imports of US coal, and an acceleration of the switch from coal to oil. The High Authority diagnosed a manifest crisis, and in March 1959 asked the Council of Ministers for emergency powers under Article 58 of the Treaty. However, this request failed to achieve the qualified majority necessary, primarily because neither France nor Germany was prepared to grant the extra powers to the High Authority that it requested.

This was one of a series of crises in the history of the European Communities that shook the collective morale of the central bureaucratic actors. The immediate effect was to make it very difficult for the High Authority to respond to the crisis. It had to resort to palliative measures such as social assistance, and a restructuring plan for the Belgian industry, which was hardest hit by the crisis. More fundamentally:

> The High Authority's powerlessness revealed the inadequacy of sectoral integration for which it was responsible and which did not cover competing energy sources—oil and nuclear energy.

(Spierenburg and Poidevin 1994: 652)

The realization that the attempt to integrate in one sector could not be successful unless integration were extended to other sectors might have led to an increase in the competence of the High Authority. The Council of Ministers did ask the High Authority to undertake the co-ordination of energy supplies and to draw up plans for a common energy policy; but by this time the Treaties of Rome had come into effect, creating the two new communities, the EEC and Euratom, each with its own Commission.

The decision to make a new start with new institutions, rather than extending the competence of the High Authority, inevitably produced a conflict between the established bureaucratic actor and the newcomers. Although the High Authority helped the two Commissions to get started by seconding many of its experienced staff, 'there were undeniable jealousies that precluded closer union between the three executive bodies' (Spierenburg and Poidevin 1994: 652).

Finet complained about the 'poaching' of High Authority staff by the Commissions of Euratom and the EEC (Spierenburg and Poidevin 1994: 381) and there were tensions both over issues of responsibility and budgetary matters. The Commissions, one headed by a Frenchman and the other by a German, had the support of the French and German Governments on these matters. More generally, governments were content to see responsibilities of the High Authority transferred to the less supranational new Commissions.

Yet, the ECSC could claim partial success for its activities, for example in limiting restrictive practices in the coal and steel sectors. More importantly, for Monnet, the creation of the ECSC laid vital foundations for further European integration:

> It proved decisive in persuading businessmen, civil servants, politicians and trade unionists that such an approach could work and that the economic and political advantages of unity over division were immense. Once they were convinced, they were ready to take further steps forward.

(Monnet 1962: 208)

While the supranational instincts of the High Authority were kept under control by national governments, it was significant for future developments in European integration that both the Assembly and the Court of Justice were supportive of its supranational efforts. The Court in particular 'stamped its imprint on the ECSC, and in doing so built up a body of case law, an authority, and legitimacy that could serve as foundations for the future' (Urwin 1995: 56).

Six years after signing the Treaty of Paris establishing the ECSC, the six parliaments ratified the Treaty of Rome establishing the Economic Community, taking the major step towards the creation of a common market for all goods and services. Monnet (1962: 211) spoke of a 'new method of action' in Europe, replacing the efforts at domination by the nation states 'by a constant process of collective adaptation to new conditions, a chain reaction, a ferment where one change induces another'. (In 2002, the Treaty of Paris expired. The strategic importance of these two sectors had declined, and the rationale for the ECSC had disappeared.)

Messina

In November 1954, Monnet announced that when his first term as President of the High Authority of the ECSC ended in February 1955, he would not seek a second term. Citing the collapse of the EDC, he said that he wanted to free his hands to work for European unity. He then formed an organization called the Action Committee for the United States of Europe, consisting of leading political and trade union figures from the member states of the ECSC, but also from Britain and other states.

The main proposal to come from the Action Committee was for a European Atomic Energy Community (Euratom). It was accompanied by a plan to extend the sectoral responsibilities of the ECSC to cover all forms of energy and transport. Nothing came of these latter proposals, although transport was given a special place in the Treaty of Rome (EEC). The member governments were simply not interested in extending the remit of the ECSC.

Also accompanying the proposals from the Action Committee was a proposal from Beyen, the Dutch Foreign Minister, for a general **common market**. Richard Mayne (1991: 115) maintained that this scheme also originated with Monnet, but he offered no evidence for this, and it is a view that is flatly rejected by other writers. Duchêne (1994: 269–72) provided evidence that Monnet actually rejected the idea of a general common market, believing that it was too ambitious, and might produce another EDC debacle.

There was no great enthusiasm for further sectoral integration. In so far as business interests expressed support for further integration, it was for an extension of the market aspect of the ECSC, not for the centralized regulatory functions of the High Authority. The lesson that was learned from ECSC was the limitations of sectoral integration. As *The Economist* (11 August 1956) reported:

> In the last four years the Coal and Steel Community has proved that the common market is not only feasible but, on balance, advantageous for all concerned. But it has also shown that 'integration by sector' raises its own problems of distortion and discrimination. The Six have therefore chosen to create a common market for all products rather than continuing to experiment with the sector approach.

On 4 April 1955, Spaak circulated a memorandum to the governments of the six states of the ECSC proposing that negotiations begin on the extension of sectoral integration to other forms of energy than coal, particularly to nuclear energy, and to transport. The proposal met with a cool response; only the French government supported it. Beyen then pressed the case for a relaunch, based on the idea of a general common market.

The Federal German government reacted very positively to Beyen's proposal, but in France the idea of a general common market was strongly rejected by industry, which argued that it would not be able to compete with German industry. French politicians had generally accepted this argument, but there was a growing belief that the excuse could not be used forever, and that French industry would never be competitive until it had to compete. At this stage, though, the mood in France was not conducive to taking such a step, which may explain why Monnet was reluctant to advocate it.

Spaak subsequently met with the Prime Minister of Luxembourg, Joseph Bech, and as a result of that meeting, a formal Benelux initiative was launched combining Monnet's ideas for further sectoral integration with Beyen's idea of a general common market. This proposal was circulated in late April 1955, and was discussed at the beginning of June in Messina in Italy at a meeting of the heads of government of the six, which had originally been called to decide on a successor to Monnet as President of the High Authority of the ECSC.

Agreement was reached at Messina to set up a committee under the chairmanship of Spaak to study the ideas in the Benelux memorandum. The French government was not enthusiastic, and appeared not to expect anything to come of the talks, but it was difficult for France to block them so soon after its rejection of the EDC. Because the agreement to hold talks was reached in Messina, the negotiations took that name. In fact, most of the meetings were held in Brussels. Their success was unexpected, except perhaps by optimistic partisans of integration like Spaak. In fact, the success of the Spaak Committee, which met in Brussels between July 1955 and March 1956, owed a great deal to his energetic and skilful chairing of the proceedings. Also very important, though, were the changed circumstances between the original Messina meeting and the actual negotiations.

One very important change was in the government of France: Guy Mollet, the leader of the Socialist Party, became Prime Minister in 1956. Having originally been sceptical about European integration, Mollet had become convinced that French industry needed to be opened up to competition if it was ever to achieve the sort of productivity gains that lay behind the remarkable German economic recovery. He had also become a member of Monnet's Action Committee, and Duchêne (1994: 287) maintained that a relationship developed between Monnet and Mollet similar to the earlier relationship between Monnet and Schuman.

Mollet was brought to office by the deteriorating situation in Algeria, where French settlers were under attack by the National Liberation Front (FLN) of Algeria. The war that developed there was traumatic for the French, and dominated the nation's attention so that the negotiations in Brussels were able to proceed without attracting much notice from critics. But Algeria was only one of the international events of 1956 that had an effect on the outcome of the Messina negotiations. In October, the Soviet Union invaded Hungary to suppress an anti-communist national movement that had the sympathy of the Hungarian army. Hungary brought home to western Europeans once again the reality of the Cold War that divided their continent. More directly, the Suez Canal crisis also blew up in October.

The nationalization of the Suez Canal by Egyptian President Gamal Abdel Nasser not only caused outrage in France, as it did in Britain; it also offered the French a possible excuse to topple Nasser, whose pan-Arab rhetoric inflamed the situation in Algeria, and whose regime was suspected of sheltering and arming the Algerian rebels. However, once the nationalization had been effected, Nasser gave no further cause for outside intervention. The canal was kept open to international shipping; it was business as usual under new ownership. To foment an excuse to invade, the French government colluded with the Israeli government and hatched a scheme that was subsequently sold to the British government of Anthony Eden. Israel would invade the canal zone; the French and British governments would demand an immediate withdrawal from the canal by the armed forces of both sides. Egypt would certainly refuse, and the combined Franco–British force would then move in to occupy the canal zone and reclaim the canal. The fall of Nasser was confidently expected to follow.

However, the invasion failed because, in the face of opposition from the Soviet Union and, more significantly, from the United States, the British government decided to pull out. France could not carry through the operation alone. The episode was perceived in France as a national humiliation at the hands of the Americans, but also as a betrayal by the British, who were believed to be too subservient to US wishes. It fed support for the nationalist position of Charles de Gaulle, who subsequently came to office as the first president of the new Fifth Republic in May 1958. It also fed into the Messina negotiations, helping them to reach a speedy and successful conclusion.

Directly, Suez underlined much more than events in Hungary the impotence of France in the post-war world of superpowers. It gave support to the concept of France acting with other European states. Indirectly, the clear signs that this episode marked the beginning of the end for the government of Mollet, and the strong indications that he would be succeeded by de Gaulle, who had always opposed European integration, accelerated the efforts to reach agreement. A 'rush to Rome' began in an effort to get the Treaties signed before de Gaulle came to office and aborted the whole experiment.

The Road to the Rome Treaties

The agreements reached in the Spaak Committee were a series of compromises between different national positions, particularly those of France and Germany. Central to the agreement detailed in the Spaak Report of March 1956 was the creation of the general common market favoured by the German government. Although Mollet believed that this step would be good for France as well as for Germany, he had to negotiate concessions that would allow him to get the Treaty ratified in the French National Assembly. There were three main areas where the French government extracted concessions: Euratom, agriculture, and relations with France's overseas territories and dependencies.

Euratom was attractive for many French politicians because they saw it as a means of obtaining a subsidy from Germany for the expensive process of developing nuclear energy, which in turn was linked to the development of nuclear weapons. Although Mollet personally believed that France should confine itself to the peaceful use of nuclear energy, the sentiment in the National Assembly in the aftermath of Hungary and Suez was very much in favour of an independent French nuclear deterrent. Euratom offered the opportunity to devote more national resources to the weapons programme, while depriving Germany of a national nuclear capability, and guaranteeing French access to uranium from the Belgian Congo.

Agriculture was given a separate chapter in the EEC Treaty (see also Chapter 21). Its inclusion, not as part of the general common market, but as, in effect, a further extension of sectoral integration, was another factor that was important in ensuring French ratification of the Treaty. For the French governments of the Fourth Republic, agriculture was both politically and economically important. Politically, small farmers had a

117

disproportionate electoral importance under the voting system that was used in the Fourth Republic. The small farmers were inefficient producers, but were determined to retain their independence, which in effect meant that they had to be subsidized by the state through a national system of price support. By transferring this cost to the common EEC budget, the French state again obtained a subsidy from the more prosperous Germans. Economically, France also had an efficient agricultural sector, and actually produced a considerable surplus of food, so the guarantee of a protected market for French agricultural exports was another concession that helped to sell the EEC Treaty within France.

In the context of decolonization and the war in Algeria, it was very important for all French governments to ensure that the special links with the former colonies were maintained. There were considerable French economic interests that were dependent on trade with these overseas dependencies and territories, and there was a general sentiment in France in favour of the link. The continuation of this special relationship, by guaranteeing preferential access to the common market for the products of the former colonies, was the third important factor to allow the Treaty to obtain ratification in France (see also Chapter 24).

On each of these points, the German government made considerable concessions. There was no sympathy for Euratom in German industrial or government circles; the Germans would have preferred to leave agriculture to national management, and to continue to allow food to be imported as cheaply as possible from the rest of the world; and there was no enthusiasm for supporting the last vestiges of French colonialism. However, in order to obtain the considerable prize of the common market in industrial goods, the German government was prepared to make these concessions to France.

The other major bargaining concession was made to Italy in the form of the inclusion in the Treaty of a commitment to reducing the differences between prosperous and poor regions. This was the Italian government's attempt to claim a subsidy from Germany, given that the problems of the south of Italy represented the main regional disparity within the original six member states.

The Spaak Report was agreed by the governments of the six member states in May 1956. The Spaak Committee was transformed into a conference with responsibility for drafting the necessary Treaties. In March 1957, two Treaties emerged: one for the EEC; the other for Euratom. The Treaties were signed by national governments in Rome in the same month, prior to being passed on for domestic ratification. If the failure of the EDC had meant several steps backwards in the process of integration, the Treaties of Rome promised a major leap forward.

Euratom

The Euratom Commission had similar powers and responsibilities to those of its sister institution, the EEC Commission (see Insight 6.3). While the EEC Commission made skilful use of these powers during its first decade to push forward the process of integration, the Euratom Commission failed to make any significant progress. Illness forced the resignation of its first president, Louis Armand, in the first year. Armand was replaced in February 1959 by Etienne Hirsch, a former colleague of Monnet's at the CdP (see Chapter 5, 'National Positions and the Origins of the ECSC'). Delays over recruitment and establishing priorities meant that, by the time the Euratom

---

Insight 6.3 The Euratom Commission

The Euratom Commission consisted of five members, one from each member state except Luxembourg, which had no national nuclear power programme. During its time it had three presidents:

- Louis Armand (1958–9);
- Etienne Hirsch (1959–62); and
- Michel Chatenet (1963–7).

It was charged to ensure that the member states fulfilled the terms of the Treaty:

- it had the sole right to propose measures to this end to the Council of Ministers;
- it had a duty to oversee the implementation of agreements;
- it represented the Community in the negotiation of agreements with the outside world;
- it was answerable to the EPA for the activities of the Community.

Commission really began work in 1960, the context in which it had been created had changed. In particular, the easing of the coal shortage and reduced concern about dependence on oil from the Middle East in the post-Suez period removed some of the urgency on the development of nuclear energy.

The delay in the start of Euratom operations also allowed national rivalries to become embedded. France, with the largest nuclear research programme had expected the bulk of the subsidies available, but Italy and West Germany rapidly developed their programmes following agreement on Euratom. After 1959, France, which was then under the leadership of de Gaulle, was less enthusiastic about Euratom than it had been. The Hirsch Euratom Commission clashed with the French government over both the right of the Commission to inspect French plutonium facilities and the Commission's decision to divert funds to a joint programme of reactor development with the United States. On the first, Hirsch found no support in the Council of Ministers. On the second, however, the Commission won a majority vote in the Council. Yet, even this victory was hollow, as the French government subsequently insisted that budgetary decisions be taken on the basis of unanimity. Thus, in both instances of conflict with the French government, the Commission's position was ultimately weakened. Further, de Gaulle refused to re-nominate Hirsch as president and his successor, Michel Chatenet, was less assertive in his leadership of the Commission.

From 1962 onwards, Euratom drifted into deeper crisis. In 1964, there was deadlock over the size of the budget, which was eventually resolved only at the cost of the Commission having to make massive cut-backs in the already modest remaining research programme. A second crisis in 1966 meant that Euratom went into the merger year of 1967 having to survive on the system of 'provisional twelfths', which allowed no more than one-twelfth of the previous year's budget to be spent each month until agreement was reached on the new budget.

A number of explanations have been offered for the failure of Euratom (Scheinman 1967). First, because it dealt with a single functional sector, the Commission was unable to offer national governments trade-offs in other policy areas to secure deals on nuclear power. Second, the external environment that favoured the creation of Euratom had changed by the time it became operative. Moreover, internal rivalry between member states increased and was consolidated with the election of de Gaulle. France was particularly important here because the development of nuclear power was a key issue for the French government and was closely linked to the highly political issue of nuclear weapons. Perhaps the key weakness of the Euratom Commission was that it failed to develop a **transnational network** of interests around the nuclear energy issue, which could create a momentum that would overcome national rivalries. In sum, while the Euratom Commission faced inevitable constraints, it also failed to deploy tactics that were important to the relative success of the EEC Commission.

CONCLUSION

Several persistent themes of the book emerge in this chapter: the influence of the Cold War; the difficulties of any direct attack on national sovereignty; spillover from the initial integrative steps to further steps; the tension between *dirigisme* and free-market approaches to integration; the use of European integration as a vehicle to introduce unpopular policies; and the struggle between supranationalism and national interests.

The influence of the Cold War on the whole EDC episode is clear, as is the role of the United States in the affairs of western Europe during this period of its hegemony of the capitalist world. However, the fate of the EDC is vindication of the functionalist analysis that a head-on attack on sovereignty would be resisted, whereas gradual steps to tie states together might succeed.

It is contestable whether the opening of negotiations on the EEC is vindication of the neofunctionalist argument that spillover would operate to move integration forward once the first steps had been taken (see Chapter 1, 'Theories of European Integration'). The line of spillover from ECSC to Euratom is clearer, and was the line of progression favoured by Monnet. However, the proposal for Euratom was countered, rather than complemented, by the proposal from the Benelux states for a general common market. In this can be seen the tension between *dirigisme* and free-market approaches to integration. The general common market was designed to open national markets by removing tariffs, at that time the main barrier to free trade. It stood in marked distinction to the Euratom proposal to extend the system of planning of the 'commanding heights' of the economy from coal and steel to what was expected to be the new main source of energy.

Monnet's scheme also reflected the need to gain the acceptance of the French political elite. France was developing nuclear energy as a priority project, so it could be expected to support Euratom, which offered France the prospect of a subsidy from the other member states for its research-and-development costs. A free market in industrial goods was less likely to find favour in a country where there was less industrial efficiency than in West Germany. However, things were changing in France. There was a growing awareness among the political elite that if France were to keep up with its German neighbour, it had to modernize its economy. Euratom, and concessions on agriculture and overseas territories, were necessary sweeteners to sell the package to the French National Assembly; but the assertion, often made, that the EEC was a deal between German industry and French agriculture hides the truth that, for certain sections of the French political elite, the common market was a useful tool to sweep away the protectionism that was stifling French economic growth. Another theme that reappears later in the story emerges here: this is the argument that 'Europe' is used as a smokescreen by governments to hide behind when pursuing domestically unpopular measures (see Chapter 3, 'Democracy and Legitimacy').

There is no strong evidence that a commitment to maintaining the momentum of integration was a motive for the acceptance of the EEC by the political elite in any of the member states.

Events in Algeria, Suez, and Hungary did, though, bring home to them the weakness of European states in an era of superpowers, and made clinging together more attractive. These dramatic incidents also had an effect on public opinion, and reinforced a general sentiment in favour of federalist ideas. Suez and Algeria in particular caused a crisis of identity among the French public that allowed their government to push through the Treaties of Rome behind a rhetoric of maintaining the momentum of integration. At the same time, the account given here shows that the Messina negotiations were no exception to the rule that national interests will be strongly defended in all moves in the direction of integration.

Finally, the assertion of national control over the supranationalism of the High Authority and the Euratom Commission is clear. If we were to focus only on these forerunners of the EC Commission, the lesson to be drawn would have to be that the member states were suspicious of supranational tendencies in the institutions they had created, and were capable of restraining them. But the first stirrings of a supranational Court of Justice offered a different lesson for the future. The body of case law that the Court began to build up was not particularly controversial, and was not widely noted at the time. It was, however, laying the basis for an independent supranational institution of the future (see Chapter 16).

KEY POINTS

The Pleven Plan

- The outbreak of the Korean War led to concern about the future defence of West Germany.
- Monnet proposed the EDC in an attempt to avert the formation of a German army.
- West Germany supported the proposal as a way of ending Allied occupation.
- The EDC was linked to the EPC by federalists in the Assembly of the ECSC.
- The EDC collapsed when France failed to ratify the Treaty.
- European defence was channelled through the intergovernmental WEU.

The European Coal and Steel Community

- The High Authority was not as powerful as originally planned, but still had considerable formal independence.
- There was considerable suspicion of Monnet's *dirigiste* tendencies among national governments, who consequently nominated members to the High Authority who were mostly not sympathetic to Monnet's aims.
- Monnet tried to run the High Authority on informal lines, but it became internally divided and increasingly bureaucratized.
- Excess supply of coal led to a crisis in 1959. The Council of Ministers refused the High Authority emergency powers to deal with the crisis. This precipitated a collapse of morale in the High Authority.
- Despite its shortcomings, Monnet believed that the ECSC pioneered the development of a community method of working.

Messina

- Monnet served one term as President of the High Authority of the ECSC then resigned and formed the Action Committee for the United States of Europe.
- The Action Committee proposed Euratom.

- The Dutch and Belgian governments proposed a general common market, a proposal that West Germany seized upon as potentially beneficial to German industry.
- The common market met with strong opposition in France.
- Negotiations were carried out against the background of the Soviet invasion of Hungary and the Franco–British Suez expedition, both in 1956.

The Road to the Rome Treaties

- Negotiations were accelerated when it became obvious that the nationalist de Gaulle was likely soon to come to office in France.
- In return for the common market for industrial goods, France extracted concessions on Euratom, agriculture, and its overseas territories, while Italy got a commitment to reduce regional disparities.

Euratom

- By the time that Euratom began operation, the energy crisis that existed when it was negotiated had disappeared. Instead of a shortage of coal, there was a glut of it.
- Whereas France had the only developed programme of research on nuclear energy in the mid-1950s, by the end of the decade Germany and Italy also had independent programmes in competition with that of France.
- The French government did not fully co-operate with the Euratom Commission, and the Commission never managed to build a supportive network of industry groups or technical experts to help it counter French obstructionism.

 For additional material and resources, please visit the online resources www.oup.com/uk/bache5e.

FURTHER READING

On all of the material covered in this chapter, valuable information is contained in **F. Duchêne**, *Jean Monnet: The First Statesman of Interdependence* (New York and London: W. W. Norton and Co., 1994).

The Pleven Plan and the abortive attempt to create an EDC is less written about than the Schuman Plan, but it is the subject of **E. Fursdon**, *The European Defence Community: A History* (London: Macmillan, 1980). Several books are devoted to, or contain extensive sections on, the experience of the early communities: **W. Diebold, Jr**, *The Schuman Plan: A Study in Economic Cooperation: 1950–1959* (New York: Praeger, 1959); **J. Gillingham**, *Coal, Steel, and the Rebirth of Europe, 1945–1955* (Cambridge: Cambridge University Press, 1991); **E. B. Haas**, *The Uniting of Europe: Political, Social and Economic Forces, 1950–1957* (Stanford, CA: Stanford University Press, 1968).

There is one indispensable work on the ECSC: **D. Spierenburg and R. Poidevin**, *The History of the High Authority of the European Coal and Steel Community: Supranationality in Action* (London: Weidenfeld, 1994).

On the Euratom, there is less. The most revealing piece is **L. Scheinman**, 'Euratom: Nuclear Integration in Europe', *International Conciliation*, no. 563 (1967). There is also a discussion of the adoption of Euratom in **A. Milward**, *The European Rescue of the Nation State* (London: Routledge, 1992), 200–11.

For access to various primary sources, the website www.cvce.eu/en is very useful.

Chapter 7

The First Years of the European Economic Community (the 1960s and into the 1970s)

Chapter Overview

The early 1960s was a period of apparent success for the supranational elements within the European Economic Community (EEC). Rapid progress was made towards the creation of both a common market and a common agricultural policy. The only setback during this period was a crisis in 1963 when President de Gaulle vetoed a British application for membership; but in the middle of the decade there was a more serious crisis, when France boycotted meetings of the Council of Ministers in response to proposals for a more supranational method of funding the EEC budget. This crisis and its aftermath took much of the momentum out of the process of European integration for the remainder of the decade, when changes in political leadership in France and West Germany led to a summit meeting in The Hague that gave a renewed mandate for progress. As a direct result of the renewed mandate, the EEC expanded its membership at the start of the 1970s, and made the first moves towards an economic and monetary union and a common foreign and security policy.

The Early Years: 1958–63

It was not obvious in 1957 which of the two new communities, the EEC or the European Atomic Energy Community (Euratom), would become the more important. Within a few years, though, Euratom had lost all momentum. Driven by the vigorous leadership of Commission President Walter Hallstein, the EEC made a successful start and achieved most of its objectives over most of the first decade of its existence.

The institutional arrangements of the EEC followed those of the European Coal and Steel Community (ECSC), with a supranational Commission as the equivalent of the High Authority, a Council of Ministers, and a Parliamentary Assembly. In addition, an Economic and Social Committee played an advisory role. Finally, the Court of Justice was established to interpret the provisions of the Treaty of Rome and to act as arbiter in disputes on Community decisions (see Insight 7.1).

Insight 7.1 The Institutional Arrangements of the EEC

The Commission consisted of nine Commissioners appointed by national governments: two each from France, Germany, and Italy, one each for Belgium, Luxembourg, and the Netherlands. While they were national appointees, Commissioners were not supposed to advocate national interests but to protect the European ideal. The Commission's primary tasks were to make proposals to the Council of Ministers and to implement the Treaty of Rome. (On the Commission, see Chapter 13.)

The Council of Ministers consisted of one representative from each member state. Provision was made for it to vote on proposals from the Commission by qualified majority vote (QMV). For these purposes, seventeen votes were allocated among the six member states: four each to France, Germany, and Italy; two each for Belgium and the Netherlands; and one vote for Luxembourg; a qualified majority required twelve votes, ensuring that a decision required the support of at least four states. However, in the first stage, prior to the completion of the common market, it was agreed that all decisions would be taken by unanimity. (On the Council, see Chapter 14.)

The European Parliamentary Assembly (EPA) of 142 members was a purely consultative body. Although provision was made in the Treaty for direct election, initially the members were nominated by national parliaments from among their own members. (On the contemporary European Parliament, see Chapter 15.)

The Court was made up of seven judges: one from each member state, plus one appointed by the Council. (On the contemporary Court, see Chapter 16.)

For the whole of its separate existence, the Commission of the EEC had only one President. Walter Hallstein had been the State Secretary in the Foreign Office of the Federal Republic of Germany, and had been in charge of the German team during the negotiation of the EEC. Hallstein's appointment was accepted unanimously, a remarkable development only twelve years after the war.

The very lack of a sense of drama in the choice of a German for the most important of the new posts was not only a tribute to Hallstein's achievements and reputation, but also proof of giant progress since the Schuman Plan (Duchêne 1994: 309).

Close to Chancellor Adenauer in his views on west European integration, Hallstein was in no doubt about the political nature of the Commission. In a book published in 1962, he made clear that, in his view, the logic of economic integration not only leads on towards political unity, it involves political action itself.

We are not integrating economics, we are integrating policies. 'Political integration' is not too bold and too grandiose a term to describe this process.

(Hallstein 1962: 66–7)

Hallstein was backed in this view of the role of the Commission by the energetic Dutch Vice-President and Commissioner for Agriculture, Sicco Mansholt. Between them, Hallstein and Mansholt gave vigorous leadership to the Commission, which, according to one observer, constituted 'a relatively united, committed partisan organisation' (Coombes 1970: 259).

The morale of the Commission was increased by its success in getting the Council of Ministers to agree to an acceleration of the timetable for the achievement of a customs union in 1962. It went on to broker agreement on the level of the common external tariff (CET), and at the same time to negotiate acceptance of a common agricultural policy (CAP).

The EEC Treaty (Article 14; now removed) specified a precise timetable for the progressive reduction of internal tariffs. On the original schedule, it would have taken at least eight years to get rid of all such tariffs. This rather leisurely rate of progress reflected the concerns of specific industrial groups about the problems of adjustment involved in the ending of national protection. However, once the Treaty was signed and it became obvious that the common market was to become a reality, those same industrial interests responded to the changed situation facing them. Even before the Treaty came into operation, on 1 January 1958, companies had begun to conclude cross-border agreements on co-operation, or to acquire franchized retail outlets for their products in other member states. Just as the neofunctionalists had predicted, changing circumstances led to changed behaviour.

So rapid was the adjustment of corporate behaviour to the prospect of the common market that impatience to see the benefits of the deals that were being concluded and of the new investments that were being made soon led to pressure on national governments to accelerate the timetable. Remarkably, the strongest pressure came from French industrial interests, which had opposed the original scheme for a common market.

On 12 May 1960, the Council of Ministers agreed to a proposal from the Commission to accelerate progress on the removal of internal barriers to trade and the erection of a CET, and on the creation of the CAP. Pressure had come only for the first of these to be accelerated. Progress was slow on agriculture, the negotiations having been dogged by disagreements over the level of support that ought to be given to farmers for different commodities. But the issues were clearly linked: progress on the CAP to accompany progress on the industrial common market had been part of the original deal embodied in the EEC Treaty.

It seemed that in keeping the linkage between the two issues in the forefront of all their proposals to the Council of Ministers, the Commission had played a manipulative role that coincided with the view of neofunctionalism about the importance of central leadership. Indeed, it is possibly from the performance of the Commission in this period that the importance of leadership from the centre was first theorized and added to the emerging corpus of neofunctionalist concepts. As described by Lindberg (1963: 167–205), the progress of the EEC between 1958 and 1965 involved the Commission utilizing a favourable situation to promote integration. Governments found themselves trapped between the growing demand from national interest groups that they carry through as rapidly as possible their commitment to create a common market, and the insistence of the Commission that this could only happen if the governments were prepared to reach agreement on the setting of common minimum prices for agricultural products.

These agreements were engineered by the skilful use of the 'package deal': linking the two issues together, and not allowing progress on one without commensurate progress on the other. In that way, each member state would agree to things in which it was less interested in order to get those things in which it was more interested. It was just such a package deal that the French President, Charles de Gaulle, was to reject in spectacular fashion in 1965, plunging the EEC into crisis. However, before that, in 1963, there was a warning of the problems that lay ahead.

The 1963 Crisis

As Urwin (1995: 103) noted:

> To some extent, the Commission could be so active because the national governments, through the Council of Ministers had been content to allow it to be so. Even President de Gaulle had on the whole been quite circumspect about the Commission.

However, the Commission's influence and the apparent smooth progress of the EEC received a setback in January 1963 when President de Gaulle unilaterally vetoed the British government's application for membership. The most comprehensive history of this episode is Ludlow (1997), on which the following account is largely based.

Having declined the invitation to be present at the creation, Harold Macmillan announced in the House of Commons in July 1961 that the British government had decided to apply for membership of the EEC. The development was not welcomed by Walter Hallstein, who saw it as potentially disruptive to the smooth progress of integration among the Six. It was also not welcomed by de Gaulle, who had ambitions to use the EEC as a platform for the reassertion of French greatness in international affairs.

To this end, de Gaulle tried to get agreement between the Six on co-operation in foreign policy, which he believed that France would be able to dominate. From 1960, it was agreed that the foreign ministers of the member states would meet four times yearly. De Gaulle also developed a special relationship with the German Chancellor, Konrad Adenauer. This relationship was important in securing support for de Gaulle's plans to extend political co-operation between the Six. The matter was subsequently considered by a committee chaired by the French official, Christian Fouchet (see Insight 7.2). The Fouchet negotiations on political co-operation were taking place in 1961 when the British application was lodged, but they had already run into some difficulties over proposals for foreign and defence policy.

British entry did not fit de Gaulle's plans: it would have provided an alternative leadership for the four other member states, whose governments were suspicious of

---

Insight 7.2 The Fouchet Plan

In 1961, President de Gaulle proposed to the other members of the Communities that they consider forming what he called a Union of States. This would be an intergovernmental organization in which the institutions of the existing three Communities would play no role. It would involve the member states in pursuing closer co-operation on cultural, scientific, and educational matters, and, most significantly, in the co-ordination of their foreign and defence policies.

At summit meetings in 1961, it was agreed to set up a committee under the chairmanship of the French Ambassador to Denmark, Christian Fouchet, and subsequently to ask the committee to prepare a detailed plan for such co-operation.

This 'Fouchet Plan' proposed a confederation of states with a Council of Ministers, a Consultative Assembly of seconded national parliamentarians, and a Commission. However, unlike the Commissions of the EEC and Euratom, this Commission would not be a supranational body with independent powers, but would consist of officials from national foreign ministries.

---

him and wished to resist French domination. Technically, de Gaulle could have vetoed the application, but politically he was in no position to do so. In addition to Fouchet, there were negotiations proceeding in 1961 on two issues that were of crucial importance to France: the CAP, and new association terms for Africa. Also, de Gaulle did not want to make it more difficult for the pro-French position of his ally Adenauer to prevail in Bonn.

The approach that de Gaulle chose to adopt was to allow negotiations on enlargement to open, but to instruct the French delegation to set the price high in the hope that the terms would prove unacceptable to the British government. The French position was presented as defending the Treaty of Rome and the *acquis communautaire*. Both had been so strongly influenced by French demands that their defence was almost the same as the defence of the French national interest. Because the French demands were couched in *communautaire* language, it was very difficult for the other member states to resist them. They were torn between support for British membership and a desire not to dilute the achievements of the EEC to date.

The negotiations did not collapse, but they went on so long that de Gaulle was eventually presented with the excuse that he needed to issue his unilateral veto: the deal on nuclear weapons that was reached between Macmillan and US President John Kennedy at Nassau in December 1962. Macmillan persuaded Kennedy to sell Britain Polaris missiles to carry Britain's independent nuclear weapons. This was presented by de Gaulle as clear evidence that the British were not yet ready to accept 'a European vocation', and used as justification for ending negotiations that had stalled in late 1962 anyway.

The other member states reacted angrily to the veto. Given that the negotiations had run into difficulties, the anger was directed less at their enforced ending than at the way in which de Gaulle had undermined the system of collaborative working that had emerged in the Six, and within which the others had operated throughout the negotiations.

The 1965 Crisis

A more fundamental, and considerably more serious, crisis began in July 1965, when de Gaulle withdrew France from participation in the work of the Council of Ministers in protest at a proposal from the Commission concerning the financing of the Community's budget.

Once agreement had been reached on the details of the CAP, the question arose of how the policy would be funded. For the first time, the EEC would have a budget that went beyond the salaries and administrative costs of the central institutions. The Commission proposed that, instead of the cumbersome method of annual contributions negotiated between the member states, the Community should have its 'own resources'. These would be the revenue from the CET on industrial goods and the levies on agricultural goods entering the Community from outside, which would be collected by national customs officials at their point of entry into the EEC and then handed over to Brussels, after the deduction of 10 per cent as a service charge. The justification was that the goods might be intended for consumption in any part of the Community, and it was therefore unreasonable that the revenue should accrue to the state through which the goods happened to enter the common market.

However, the French President questioned another aspect of the proposal. Using the method of the package deal, the Commission linked the idea of having its own resources with a proposal for an increase in the powers of the EPA, giving it the right to approve the budget. The argument for this was that if the revenues passed directly to the EEC without having to be approved by national parliaments, there would be a lack of democratic scrutiny, which could only be corrected by giving that right to the EPA.

President de Gaulle objected to this increase in the powers of a supranational institution, and when discussion became deadlocked, he showed how important he held the issue to be by imposing a French boycott of all meetings of the Council of Ministers from June 1965. This action was subsequently termed the 'empty chair crisis'. In essence, the dispute was about the very nature of the Europe that the Six were hoping to build. For de Gaulle, primacy had to be given to the interests of national governments.

The Luxembourg Compromise

After six months, an agreement was reached between France and the other five member states in Luxembourg. The so-called 'Luxembourg Compromise' of January 1966 represented a considerable blow to the process of European integration. First, there was agreement not to proceed with the Commission's proposals: funding of the budget would continue to be by national contributions. Second, France demanded that there be no transition to majority voting in the Council of Ministers. This move had been envisaged in the original Treaties once the customs union was complete, and completion was on schedule for January 1966. Under the terms of the Luxembourg Compromise, governments would retain their right to veto proposals where they deemed a vital national interest to be at stake. This agreement was a serious blow to the hope of the Commission that brokering agreement on further integrative moves would be easier in the future.

Third, France made four other demands: that the President of the Commission should no longer receive the credentials of ambassadors to the EEC; that the information services be taken out of the hands of the Commission; that members of the Commission should be debarred from making political attacks on the attitudes of member states; and that the Commission should not reveal its proposals to the EPA before they were presented to the Council of Ministers, as it had with the controversial package on the budget.

The terms of the deal precipitated a collapse of morale in the Commission. In particular, the authority of Hallstein and Mansholt was undermined by the episode. Some Commissioners had warned against a confrontation with de Gaulle on supranationality, but Hallstein and Mansholt had overruled them (Camps 1967: 47). Neither was to regain the air of invincibility that he had acquired in the past. Hallstein withdrew his name from the list of nominations for the presidency of the new combined Commission of the ECSC, EEC, and Euratom that was due to take office on 1 July 1967, and simply served out the remainder of his term. Mansholt stayed on as a Commissioner, but did not put his name forward for the presidency.

Into the 1970s

Whereas the 1960s had been an era of high rates of economic growth within a reasonably stable (if militarily threatening) international environment, the 1970s were times of turbulence and flux in the international economic system.

Under these circumstances, it was very difficult for the Commission to inject new momentum into the process of European integration. Also, although the Hallstein Commission was initially given tremendous credit for promoting integration in the period following the signing of the Treaties of Rome, subsequent reassessments suggested that, in fact, it had done little beyond fill out the details of agreements that had been made between the member states in the EEC Treaty. If this view is correct, then for the Commission to play an active role in the 1970s required a new mandate from the member states.

Between 1967 and 1977 the Commission had four presidents (see Box 7.1). Neither Jean Rey nor Franco Malfatti had a new mandate, and besides they were both preoccupied with the difficult issues involved in combining the three executive bodies of the ECSC, the EEC, and Euratom into a single Commission. When a new mandate *was* given, at a summit meeting in The Hague in December 1969, it involved completion of the financing arrangements for the EC budget, enlargement to take in Britain and the other applicant states, progress to economic and monetary union, and trying to develop a common foreign policy. The first of these was easily accomplished. The second was successfully carried through for three of the four applicants, but at considerable cost in terms of time and resources for the Commission. Economic and monetary union might have been the mandate that the Commission needed to produce a new impetus to integration, but as Tsoukalis (1977) argued, this decision was more akin to the decision to negotiate on the EEC than it was to the Treaty of Rome itself. As we shall see, this proved to be an intractable issue. Progress on co-ordination of foreign policy was made in a purely intergovernmental framework.

Not only were these issues more difficult in themselves: the overall context of the period was unfavourable to further integration. The Luxembourg agreement that ended the French boycott in January 1966 effectively meant that the national veto was retained on all matters that came before the Council of Ministers. Although the Commission had operated with a veto system in the 1960s, the further integration progressed, the more likely it was that particular vested interests would come under challenge, and that individual states would try to block measures.

These tendencies were made more acute by changed economic circumstances. Whereas the early progress of the EEC had taken place against a background of

---

Box 7.1 Presidents of the Commission, 1967–77

1967–70 Jean Rey (Belgium)
1970–72 Franco Maria Malfatti (Italy)
1972 Sicco Mansholt (the Netherlands)
1973–77 François-Xavier Ortoli (France).

sustained economic growth, a recession started in 1971 which really began to bite after the December 1973 decision of the **Organization of the Petroleum Exporting Countries (OPEC)** to force a quadrupling in the price of oil. This context made governments more defensive and less inclined to agree to integrative measures that would weaken their ability to preserve domestic markets for domestic producers. As the economic context changed, the pace of European economic integration slowed and there was no advance towards political union. Uncertainty within member states restricted the scope for Commission activism.

The problems were exacerbated by enlargement, which brought into membership two more states, Britain and Denmark, that were opposed to supranationalism. The cumulative effect of these developments was to ensure that the second decade of the EEC was not marked by the rapid progress on integration that had marked the first decade.

The Hague Summit

The resignation of President de Gaulle in April 1969 appeared to free the way to further integration. De Gaulle was succeeded by his former Prime Minister, Georges Pompidou, who soon let it be known that he did not object in principle to British membership.

Also, in 1969 there was a change of government in Germany. The Social Democratic Party (SPD), which had been the junior coalition partner to the Christian Democrats for the previous three years, became the larger partner in a coalition with the Free Democrat Party (FDP). Willy Brandt, the new Chancellor, intended to pursue an active policy of improving relations with the communist bloc, but was anxious to demonstrate that this *Ostpolitik* did not imply any weakening of German commitment to the EC.

As a result of these two changes, a summit meeting of heads of government was convened in The Hague in December 1969 with the explicit aim of relaunching European integration. This Hague Summit declared the objectives of completion, widening, and deepening. Completion meant tidying up the outstanding business from the 1965 crisis: moving the EC budget from dependence on national contributions to a system of financing from its own resources. Widening meant opening accession negotiations with Britain and other likely applicants. Deepening meant taking the next steps in the process of European integration, specifically in the direction of economic and monetary union and closer political co-operation.

Completion was achieved relatively easily. A system was agreed for the EC to have as its own resources the levies on agricultural products entering the EC under the CAP, and the revenues from the common customs tariff on imports of non-agricultural products from outside of the EC. There were the usual compromises, but France did accept some budgetary role for the European Parliament (EP)—as the EPA became— giving it the right to propose amendments to those parts of the budget that were not classified as 'compulsory expenditure' under the Treaties, and to propose modifications to the items of 'compulsory' expenditure. The Council of Ministers, acting by qualified majority, could amend the amendments, and could refuse to agree to the modifications, so, in effect, it retained the final say on the budget. The distinction between compulsory and non-compulsory expenditure defined expenditure under the CAP as compulsory, so making the bulk of the budget difficult for the EP to amend. Nevertheless, there was an acknowledgement that the EP should have some role in scrutinizing the budget, and there was the prospect that deepening would lead to a larger budget in which agriculture was not so dominant, so there would be more areas of non-compulsory expenditure.

Widening was also achieved within a few years. Negotiations with four applicant states—Britain, Ireland, Denmark, and Norway—opened in June 1970, and were successfully completed by January 1972. Referendums were then held on membership in Ireland, Denmark, and Norway. The first two produced clear majorities in favour of entry, but in September 1972 the Norwegian people, not for the last time, rejected membership. In Britain, the Conservative government of Edward Heath refused to hold a referendum, which it argued was not a British constitutional instrument; but parliamentary ratification was successfully completed. So, on 1 January 1973, the Six became nine.

While enlargement achieved the objective of widening the membership of the EC, it was to cause problems as well. The new member states entered at a time when the economic growth of the 1960s had already started to slow and was about to receive a further setback when OPEC quadrupled the price of oil in December 1973. Not having experienced the positive benefits of membership, neither the governments nor the peoples of these new member states had the same degree of psychological commitment to the idea of European integration as had those of the original six members. In addition, in Britain in particular there was considerable scepticism about the merits of the EC. Edward Heath was personally strongly committed to membership, but he never managed entirely to convince his own Conservative Party; and Heath was soon displaced as Prime Minister when he lost the general election early in 1974, and Harold Wilson once again formed a Labour government.

While in opposition, the Labour Party had been riven with dissension, and membership of the EC had been a central issue. Several of Wilson's cabinet ministers from 1964–70 were committed to British membership. Wilson himself was also convinced of the necessity of membership. But a majority in the party was still opposed, and the pressure from this majority meant that Wilson could not give unqualified approval to entry when Heath negotiated it. On the other hand, his own certainty that membership was necessary, and the importance of the pro-membership minority within the leadership of the party, made it impossible for him to oppose entry. The result was an ingenious compromise of opposition to entry on the terms negotiated by the Conservative government. Labour went into the 1974 election committed to a full renegotiation of the terms of entry with a threat (or promise) of withdrawal if 'satisfactory' terms could not be agreed.

The renegotiation involved serious disruption to other business in the EC, at a time when there were several important issues on the agenda. It also involved a great deal of posturing and nationalist rhetoric from the British government. What it did not involve was any fundamental change in the terms of entry. Nevertheless, the renegotiated terms were put to the British people in a referendum in June 1975, with a recommendation from the government that they be accepted, which they were.

The two-to-one vote in the referendum in favour of Community membership was a passing moment of public favour (which can be contrasted with the 2016 referendum—see the online Brexit Supplement to the textbook). Soon the opinion polls were again showing majorities against membership. Britain had joined at a bad time, and the continuing economic difficulties of the country could conveniently be blamed on the EC. Although the Labour opponents of membership had to accept, for the time being, the verdict of the referendum, they lost no opportunity to attack the EC, and Wilson was prepared to accept this if it diverted attention away from his failure to solve the country's economic difficulties. He himself continued to take a strongly nationalistic line in EC negotiations, as did his Foreign Secretary, James Callaghan, who succeeded him as Prime Minister in March 1976.

By succeeding in widening its membership, the EC placed another barrier in the way of further integration. Yet, it is a mistake to blame Britain alone for blocking further integration. Certainly, Britain became an awkward partner; but as Buller (1995: 36) argued: 'everybody consciously attempts to be obstructive every now and again in European negotiations. It is all part and parcel of politics in this kind of environment.' The degree of awkwardness of all member states increased during this period of economic problems.

While the objectives of completion and widening were achieved, attempts at deepening co-operation between member states met with limited success. The two main objectives agreed at The Hague were 'economic and monetary union by 1980' and the creation of a common foreign policy.

Economic and monetary union (EMU) was the logical next step in the building of the EC. **Economic union** meant that the member states would, at most, cease to follow independent economic policies, and at least would follow co-ordinated policies. This would remove distortions to free competition and would help to make a reality of the common market. Monetary union meant, at most, the adoption of a single Community currency, at least the maintenance of fixed exchange rates between the currencies of the member states.

In 1969, there were the first major realignments of member states' currencies since the EC had started, and the prospect of monetary instability threatened to hinder trade within the common market by introducing an element of uncertainty into import and export deals. In this context, monetary union was seen as a means of making the common market effective.

Following the Hague Summit, a committee was set up under the chairmanship of Pierre Werner, the Prime Minister of Luxembourg, to produce concrete proposals on EMU. It reported within a few months, and in February 1971 the Council of Ministers adopted a programme for the achievement of EMU in stages between 1971 and 1980. The institutional centrepiece of the scheme was the 'snake-in-the-tunnel', an arrangement for approximating the exchange rates of member currencies one to another, while holding their value jointly in relation to the US dollar (see also Chapter 20, 'The "Snake"'). It was to be accompanied by more determined efforts to bring national economic policies into line, with Finance Ministers meeting at least three times per year to try to co-ordinate policies. Thus, there would be progress on both monetary and economic union, the two running in parallel.

The 'snake' did not last long in its original form. It was destroyed by the international monetary crisis that followed the ending of the convertibility of the dollar in August 1971 (see Insight 7.3). Only after the **Smithsonian agreements** of late 1971 had restored some semblance of order to the world monetary system was it possible to attempt once again a joint Community currency arrangement, this time with the participation of the four states that had just completed the negotiation of their entry to

Insight 7.3 The Collapse of the International Monetary System

The key aspects of the international monetary system were agreed at a conference at **Bretton Woods** in New Hampshire in 1944. These were the **International Monetary Fund (IMF)** and the International Bank for Reconstruction and Development (the '**World Bank**'). The **General Agreement on Tariffs and Trade (GATT)** was added later. The system worked, with the United States playing a leading and directive role, and provided a stability that was central to the prosperity of west European economies. However, the gradual erosion of US economic dominance in this period, culminating with the ending of the convertibility of US dollars to gold in 1971, marked the collapse of the Bretton Woods international system and a less secure international economic context.

the EC. That was in April 1972; but it took under two months for this second snake to break apart. In June, the British government had to remove sterling from the system and float it on the international monetary markets. Italy was forced to leave in February 1973. France followed in January 1974, re-joined in July 1975, but was forced to leave again in the spring of 1976. In every case, the currency had come under so much speculative pressure that it had proved impossible to maintain its value against the other currencies in the system.

By 1977, the snake had become a very different creature from that which had been envisaged. Of the nine members of the EC, only West Germany, the Benelux states, and Denmark were still members (Ireland had left with Britain, the Irish punt being tied to the pound sterling at that time). In addition, two non-member states, Norway and Sweden, had joined. Yet, during 1977 even this snake was under strain, and Sweden was forced to withdraw the krona.

European Political Co-operation (EPC) was the more successful attempt at deepening, ironically, since it was only included in The Hague objectives as a concession to France (see also Chapter 25, 'European Political Co-operation (EPC)'). President Pompidou was dependent for his majority in the French National Assembly on the votes of the Gaullist Party of which he was himself a member. De Gaulle had opposed giving budgetary powers to the EP, and Pompidou agreed to this at The Hague. De Gaulle had also opposed British entry to the EC. He had made it clear when a second British application was tabled in May 1967 that there was no point in entering into negotiations, because he would veto British membership. Pompidou had made it equally clear that he was prepared to enter into negotiations, and perhaps even to accept British membership if satisfactory terms could be agreed. Both of these departures from Gaullist orthodoxy were controversial in his own party, and he needed concessions at The Hague in order to be able to sell the package to this domestic constituency.

One of de Gaulle's pet projects had been to set up a system of intergovernmental political co-operation between the member states of the EC. This was the basis of the Fouchet Plan (Insight 7.2), which had been under discussion at the same time as the first British application, and had finally collapsed as a result of the French veto on British entry. It was therefore unsurprising that Pompidou should look for a commitment to revive this project as part of the price for his co-operation on completion and widening. It was agreed at The Hague to set up a committee under the chairmanship of Viscount Etienne Davignon, a senior official in the Belgian Foreign Ministry, to devise machinery for co-operation between the member states on foreign policy issues. This committee reported in October 1970, and the system that it recommended became the basis for some successful diplomatic initiatives. Indeed, EPC came to be seen as one of the few achievements in the 1970s.

One of the successes was the formulation of a common position on the Middle East, which allowed the EC to pursue its clear interest in improving trade with the Arab OPEC states in the 1970s, through the Euro–Arab dialogue. In 1980, this common policy culminated in the Venice Declaration, which went further than the United States was prepared to go in recognizing the right of the Palestinians to a homeland. The nine member states were also extremely successful in formulating a common position at the Conference on Security and Co-operation in Europe (CSCE) in Helsinki in 1975, and at the follow-up conferences in Belgrade in 1977, and Madrid in 1982–83. Again, the common position adopted by the EC ran somewhat contrary to the position of the United States, which regarded the Helsinki process with some suspicion as running the risk of legitimating communist rule in eastern Europe. The Community states also achieved a high degree of unity in the United Nations, voting together on a majority of resolutions in the General Assembly, and developing a reputation for being the most cohesive group there at a time when group-diplomacy was becoming much more common.

Admittedly, there were also failures for the policy of European political co-operation. On balance, though, there were more substantive successes than there were failures. However, all of this remained officially intergovernmental, rather than being rolled up into the more supranational procedures of the EC, so there was a question mark over whether it could be considered to be an advance for the process of European integration. On the other hand, the actual working of the system was less strictly intergovernmental than the formal procedures, a point that is explored further in Chapter 25, 'Theoretical Explanations of Political Co-operation'.

CONCLUSION

The struggle between supranationalism and intergovernmentalism is the clear theme of this chapter. The neofunctionalist interpretation of the history of European integration seems to get both its strongest support and its greatest challenge from the period under consideration. The support comes from the story of the acceleration agreement as told by neofunctionalists (see Chapter 1, 'Theories of European Integration'). The setback came from the actions of de Gaulle in vetoing British entry in 1963 and in boycotting the Council of Ministers in 1965.

Lindberg (1963) took the role of the Commission in the success of the EEC in the 1960s as clear evidence of its centrality to the process. However, this interpretation was strongly contradicted in the intergovernmentalist tradition, notably by Andrew Moravcsik (1998: 159–237; see Chapter 1). Moravcsik's research indicated that the deals were not cut by the Commission but by the governments of other member states. He argued that 'the Commission was ineffective and repeatedly sidelined' (Moravcsik 1998: 233).

The 1965 dispute over the funding of the budget illustrated the continued ability of national governments, even of a single national government, to stop the process of European integration in its tracks.

In the 1970s, when US hegemony began to falter, the EC had to deal with an increasingly turbulent international environment. The theme of the impact of the wider system on developments within the EC is clearly illustrated here, particularly trends in international political economy (see Chapter 4, 'Critical Political Economy'). The retreat into covert national protectionism, to preserve jobs for nationals, was a direct consequence of the shadow that recession cast over the process of European integration.

There seemed little in the period onto which the neofunctionalists could cling as evidence of their theory being vindicated, and the decade from 1966 through to the mid-1970s is often presented as the 'dark ages' of European integration.

Later, though, alternative analyses emerged of the so-called 'dark ages' of integration, which emphasized the importance of work behind the scenes, including significant rulings of the Court of Justice that paved the way for subsequent advances in integration (see Chapter 16, 'CJEU Rulings on the Nature of EU Law').

KEY POINTS

The Early Years: 1958–63

- The EEC Commission under the presidency of Walter Hallstein was very proactive in promoting integration.
- Its apparent successes included getting agreement from the member states to accelerate progress on creating the common market and the CAP.

The 1963 Crisis

- In 1961, President de Gaulle proposed intergovernmental political co-operation.
- Negotiations on the 'Fouchet Plan' were ongoing when Britain applied for EC membership.
- De Gaulle did not want to see Britain become a member, but, rather than risk collapsing the Fouchet negotiations, he allowed negotiations on membership to begin, while trying to ensure that French demands would make the terms of entry unacceptable to Britain.
- When the Fouchet negotiations came near to collapse, and the entry negotiations did not, de Gaulle unilaterally vetoed British entry.

The 1965 Crisis

- In 1965, the Commission proposed a system of financing the CAP that would have given the EEC its own financial resources. This was linked to a proposal to increase the budgetary powers of the EPA.
- De Gaulle rejected the increase in the powers of the EPA, and, when agreement could not be reached, he withdrew France from participation in the work of the Council of Ministers.

The Luxembourg Compromise

- In January 1966, France resumed its place in the Council in exchange for the planned move to QMV being abandoned.
- The terms of the 'compromise' caused a collapse of morale in the Commission.

Into the 1970s

- For the Commission to play an active role in the 1970s it required a new mandate from the member states.
- The context was less favourable to integration in the 1970s than it had been in the 1960s.
- Problems were made worse by enlargement.

The Hague Summit

- Changes of leadership in France and Germany in 1969 appeared to free the way for further European integration. The result was the Hague Summit, which declared the objectives of completion, deepening, and widening.

- *Completion* was achieved through allowing the EC to have its own resources for the first time. The EP was also given some budgetary powers.

- *Widening* was achieved through the entry of Britain, Denmark, and Ireland into the EC in 1973.

- *Deepening* of co-operation on foreign policy through EPC had some success; less so co-operation on monetary union.

For additional material and resources, please visit the online resources www.oup.com/uk/bache5e.

FURTHER READING

When we get to the establishment of the EEC, the range of reading extends considerably. For studies by historians, see **A. Milward**, *The European Rescue of the Nation State* (London: Routledge, 1992) and **A. Milward and A. Deighton (eds)**, *Widening, Deepening and Acceleration: The European Economic Community 1957–1963* (Baden-Baden: Nomos, 1999). Also useful is the official history by **M. Dumoulin and M.-T. Bitsch**, *The European Commission, 1958–1972: History and Memories* (Luxembourg: Office for Official Publications of the European Communities, 2007).

The standard political science account of the early years of the EEC is **L. Lindberg**, *The Political Dynamics of European Economic Integration* (Stanford, CA: Stanford University Press; London: Oxford University Press, 1963); but this is rejected from a liberal intergovernmentalist perspective by **A. Moravcsik**, *The Choice for Europe* (London: UCL Press, 1998), 158–237.

On the British application in 1961, see **P. Ludlow**, *Dealing with Britain: The Six and the First UK Application to the EEC* (Cambridge: Cambridge University Press, 1997). The official history of British negotiations for entry is available in **C. O'Neill**, *Britain's Entry into the European Community: Report by Sir Con O'Neill on the Negotiations of 1970–1972* (London: Frank Cass, 2000). For the 1973 enlargement in broader context, see **W. Kaiser and J. Elvert (eds)**, *European Union Enlargement: A Comparative History* (London: Routledge, 2004).

For access to various primary sources, the website www.cvce.eu/en is very useful.

Chapter 8

The Revival of European Integration (the Mid-1970s to the Late 1980s)

Chapter Overview

Despite some progress following the Hague Summit in 1969, European integration was still at quite a low point in the early 1970s; but signs emerged in the late 1970s of the European Community (EC) turning a corner. A revived Commission, led by Roy Jenkins, secured agreement to be involved in international economic summits; the European Monetary System (EMS) was set up; and membership applications from Greece, Portugal, and Spain reflected positively on the external reputation of the EC. The renewed momentum gathered pace under the Commission presidency of Gaston Thorn, when the basis was laid for an initiative to free the internal market of non-tariff barriers to free trade. That initiative was taken up by Thorn's successor, Jacques Delors, and led to the Single European Act (SEA), which was widely seen as the big breakthrough in the revival of European integration.

Leadership Changes: 1974

Mid-way through the 1970s, there were again coinciding changes of government in both France and Germany, which strengthened the Franco–German relationship. Georges Pompidou died in office in 1974, and was succeeded by Valéry Giscard d'Estaing, who was not a Gaullist, although he was dependent on the Gaullist Party for a majority in the National Assembly. In Germany, Brandt resigned following the discovery that an East German spy had been part of his personal staff, and was succeeded by his former Finance Minister, Helmut Schmidt.

These changes brought to office two strong national leaders who had an excellent *rapport*, and who dominated the EC for the next six years. They were not, though, particularly committed to reviving the process of supranational integration. Their approach was pragmatic rather than ideological, and they were prepared to use any instruments that presented themselves to deal with the problems that their countries faced.

The European Council

In 1974, Giscard d'Estaing called a meeting of the heads of government of the member states to discuss his proposal that the EC should institutionalize such summit meetings. The smaller member states were suspicious of this proposal, which sounded very Gaullist, but Giscard d'Estaing got strong backing from Schmidt, and it was agreed to hold meetings of the heads of state and government three times every year under the title the 'European Council'. At the same time, as a concession to the fears of those governments who saw in this a weakening of the supranational element of the EC, agreement was reached to hold direct elections to the European Parliament (EP) in 1978. The British government was reconciled to this by concessions on the renegotiation of its terms of entry that was taking place at the same time.

Direct elections were not actually held until 1979 because the British government was unable to pass the necessary domestic legislation in time to hold the election in 1978. In the long run, the decision to hold direct elections was far from insignificant (see Chapter 15). In the short-to-medium term, though, the creation of the European Council was much the more significant outcome of Paris, 1974.

The European Council was from the outset an intergovernmental body. It had no basis in the Treaties until the SEA came into force in July 1987. It became the overarching institution of the EU in the 1992 Maastricht Treaty. In the 1970s, it was symbolic of a profoundly intergovernmental era in the history of the EU. However, it later presided over a set of major Treaty reforms and policy initiatives (see Chapter 14).

Other Institutional Developments

The authority of the European Commission was strengthened by the presidency of Roy Jenkins between 1977 and 1981. Jenkins was an established political figure with considerable experience in government. He had held all the major posts in the British cabinet other than Prime Minister. As such, his appointment raised great expectations among those who regretted the decline in the authority of the Commission. Perhaps not all of those expectations were fulfilled. However, Jenkins did enhance the position of the president, and therefore of the Commission, by securing agreement from the heads of state and government that he should be present at meetings of the international economic summits, which had previously been restricted to the leaders of the major industrial nations. This development was strongly resisted by French President Giscard d'Estaing, but was strongly supported by the smaller member states, who felt excluded from an important economic decision making forum, and who therefore wished to see the President of the Commission present to act as a spokesperson for the EC as a whole (Jenkins 1989: 20–2).

Jenkins also undertook a fundamental reform of the internal structure of the Commission, attempting, against considerable opposition from vested interests, to remove some of the causes of the bureaucratization that had been identified as one of the reasons for its decline in influence (Jenkins 1989: 310, 376). Although he was not completely successful, he did have some impact, and the strong leadership he demonstrated in tackling this problem was probably responsible for earning him the nickname 'Roi Jean Quinze', although this was also suggestive of his grand manner.

The other significant institutional development in this period was the introduction of direct elections to the EP in 1979. Until this point, the demands of the EP for greater powers had always been countered by the argument that it lacked democratic legitimacy because it was only an indirectly elected body. After it became directly elected, the EP was in a much stronger position to extract new powers from the member states. The decision to move to direct elections was made at the Rome European Council in December 1975 (see Chapter 15, 'The Struggle for Power'). Further controversy had followed when the first elections were delayed for a year because of the failure of the British Parliament to pass the necessary enabling legislation in time for the May/June 1978 date agreed at Rome. However, the elections in June 1979 were relatively low-key affairs within the member states, with national parties taking a prominent role in the selection of candidates and campaign organization.

The European Monetary System

In the policy field, there was one very significant development in the late 1970s. The decision taken at the Brussels European Council in December 1978 to create the EMS did not exactly constitute a revival of economic and monetary union (EMU), but it did provide a basis for a future step in that direction.

By 1977, the 'snake in the tunnel' had become a system that embraced only five member states of the EC, together with two non-members. During 1977, even this truncated snake was under pressure from international speculation, and Sweden was forced to withdraw. In this far-from-promising context, Jenkins launched an initiative that met with a certain amount of scepticism about its feasibility, even from colleagues within the Commission. In a lecture at the European University Institute in Florence, in October 1977, he called for a new attempt to start the EMU experiment (Jenkins 1977).

The following year, Schmidt and Giscard d'Estaing came up with a joint proposal for what became the EMS. In July 1978, the European Council meeting in Bremen agreed to pursue the idea, and in December 1978, meeting in Brussels, agreed to create what looked remarkably like another snake. It would be more flexible than its predecessor, allowing wider margins of fluctuation for individual currencies, and it would be accompanied by the creation of a new European currency unit (ecu), which would take its value from a basket of the national currencies of the member states, and would be used in transactions within the EMS.

In addition to France and West Germany, the Benelux states and Denmark supported the EMS. After initial hesitation, Italy and Ireland agreed to become full participants. But Britain declined to put sterling into the joint float against the dollar, although it was included in the basket from which the value of the ecu was calculated. Despite the scepticism that had greeted Jenkins's initiative, the EMS did get off the ground, and this time the system did hold together, so that the scheme must be judged a relative success in the context of the overall history of attempts to move towards EMU (see Chapter 20, 'History').

The Southern Enlargements

In 1974, two significant events took place in the Mediterranean: Turkey invaded Cyprus, and a revolution in Portugal overthrew the right-wing Caetano government. Each led to an application for membership of the EC. Subsequently, political developments in Spain led to a Spanish application (see also Chapter 26, 'The Southern Enlargements').

Greece had concluded an Association Agreement with the EC in 1964. This had envisaged eventual membership, but in 1967 Greece entered a period of military dictatorship that precluded an application. The inability of the Greek military to prevent the Turkish occupation of Cyprus precipitated the collapse of the dictatorship, and in June 1975 the new democratic Greek government sought membership of the EC as a means of consolidating democracy. In January 1976, the Commission issued a very cautious Opinion on the ability of Greece to adapt to membership, but political and strategic considerations led the Council of Ministers to accept the application and order the opening of negotiations. Democracy had to be shored up, but also Greece had to be prevented from swinging to the far left and reorienting itself towards the communist bloc. The negotiation of terms of entry for Greece was not easy, and it took up a great deal of the time of the Commission between July 1976 and May 1979, when the Accession Treaty was signed (membership began in January 1981). Nevertheless, the launching of the negotiations gave a new role to the Commission and put it back at the centre of the EC.

An application from Portugal followed the Greek application in March 1977. Again, there were political and strategic reasons for accepting it. The Portuguese revolution threatened to run out of the control of the pro-capitalist forces and to fall into the hands of extreme left-wing groups that would have emphasized relations with the Third World. The Socialist International, with the German Social Democratic Party (SPD) taking a lead, provided support to the Portuguese Socialist Party (PSP), and so when the PSP was elected to government in 1976 there was not much doubt that it would apply for EC membership, nor that the application would be accepted.

Similar political and strategic considerations applied in July 1977 to the acceptance of an application from Spain following the death of the dictator Franco and the restoration of democracy there. In the Spanish case, membership of the EC was held out as a bonus if it decided also to join the NATO alliance. Given Spain's strategic position in the Mediterranean, this was a vital interest of the western alliance.

Whereas the first of these applications stimulated a revival of the role of the Commission, handling three sets of difficult negotiations became a problem, and the Portuguese and Spanish Accession Treaties were not signed until 1985 (membership began in January 1986).

The British Budget Rebate

Another issue that caused problems for the EC in the 1980s was the British budgetary rebate. Although budget contributions had been central to the renegotiation, already by 1976, while transitional arrangements still limited the extent of its contributions,

Britain was the third biggest net contributor to the EC budget, behind Germany and Belgium. In 1977, still under transitional arrangements, the British net contribution was the second highest to that of Germany. By mid-1978, it was becoming apparent that once the transitional period of membership ended in 1980, Britain would become the largest net contributor to the budget.

This situation arose because:

1. Britain imported more goods, especially foodstuffs, from outside the EC than did other member states, and therefore paid more in import levies.

2. Low direct taxes meant that British consumers spent more in proportion to the relative wealth of the country, and Britain therefore contributed more to the budget in value-added tax (VAT) receipts.

3. Payments out of the budget were dominated by the common agricultural policy (CAP), and Britain had a small and efficient farming sector that meant that it received less than states with larger agricultural economies.

The developing position was unacceptable to the Labour government. The Foreign Secretary, David Owen, told the House of Commons that the situation whereby 'the United Kingdom has the third lowest per capita gross domestic product in the Community' yet was already the second highest net contributor to the budget, 'cannot be good for the Community any more than it is for the United Kingdom', and promised that the government would 'be working to achieve a better balance, especially in relation to agricultural expenditure, to curb the excessive United Kingdom contribution' (*Hansard*, 14 November 1978, col. 214).

In fact, the Labour government never had the opportunity to work for a better balance because it lost office in the May 1979 election to the Conservatives under Margaret Thatcher. The new government soon took up the same theme concerning the budget. Shortly after coming into office, Sir Geoffrey Howe, the Chancellor of the Exchequer, announced that the size of the problem was far greater than the Conservatives had realized while in opposition, and something would have to be done about it urgently.

Margaret Thatcher raised the issue at her first European Council in Strasbourg in June 1979, soon after her election victory. Her presentation there was moderate and reasonable, and the complaint was offset by an announcement on the first day of the meeting that Britain would deposit its share of gold and foreign currency reserves with the European Monetary Co-operation Fund that had been set up to administer the EMS. The move was widely interpreted as a sign that sterling would soon join the exchange rate mechanism of the EMS. Discussion of the budgetary issue at Strasbourg was brief and limited to agreeing a procedure for analysing the problem. The Commission was asked to prepare a report by September; this would be discussed by Finance Ministers, and then revised in time for the next European Council in Dublin in late November.

At that November 1979 Dublin European Council, Thatcher adopted an entirely different tone. She insisted that the Commission proposal of a rebate of £350 million was unacceptable, and that she would not accept less than £1 billion. The French said that they would not agree to more than £350 million, which the British would have to accept as full and final settlement of their claim. This provoked an argument that lasted ten hours, during the course of which Thatcher upset her partners by her uncompromising demands for what she insensitively described as Britain's 'own money back'.

This was the tone that Thatcher persistently adopted in negotiations for the next four-and-a-half years. During that time, several temporary abatements of the British contributions were agreed, but a permanent settlement eluded all efforts to bridge the gap between what the British Prime Minister demanded and what the other member states were prepared to pay. British tactics became increasingly obstructionist on other issues, and relations with the other states became increasingly strained.

Relations reached their nadir in May 1982. Britain was blocking agreement on agricultural price increases for 1982–83, linking agreement to a permanent settlement of the budgetary dispute. Finally, the Belgian presidency called a majority vote on the agricultural prices. Britain protested that this breached the Luxembourg Compromise, but the vote went ahead and was passed. Several of the other states, though, appeared shocked at their own behaviour. It seemed apparent that a settlement of the British dispute was necessary before progress could be made in other areas.

Leadership Changes: 1981–82

The confluence of challenges facing the EC at the beginning of the 1980s coincided with the appointment of Gaston Thorn to the Commission presidency in 1981. Member states generally welcomed Thorn's appointment. Although he took over at a difficult time, there was a feeling that he was uniquely well qualified for the job, as few people had a wider experience of the EC. He had served as a member of the EP, and as both Foreign Minister and Prime Minister of Luxembourg, and while in these posts had chaired the Council of Foreign Ministers and the European Council. Early in his presidency, there were two significant changes among the national leaderships with which Thorn would have to work.

In May 1981, François Mitterrand defeated Giscard d'Estaing in the French presidential election. This result was consolidated a month later by a victory for Mitterrand's Socialist Party in elections to the National Assembly. The change broke apart the Franco–German axis because Helmut Schmidt had less in common with the Socialist president than he had with the conservative Giscard d'Estaing. In particular, the Socialist government came into office committed to tackling unemployment, rather than emphasizing low inflation as its predecessor had. However, a U-turn in economic policy in 1983 brought France more into line with the neoliberal and deregulationist tendencies already evident in West Germany and Britain.

The second change in political leadership came in West Germany itself. Although the SPD/Free Democrat Party (FDP) won the 1980 Federal election, dissension within the coalition was increasing in the face of the economic problems facing the country. Within the SPD, the left-wing and the trade unionist membership were demanding some measures of reflation to relieve unemployment, which in 1981 stood at 1.25 million. But, at the same time, the FDP was returning to its basic principles of economic liberalism, represented most strikingly by the Economics Minister, Count Otto Lambsdorff. The clash between the two parties over economic affairs led to the eventual breakdown of the coalition. In 1982, the FDP changed partners and allowed the Christian Democratic Union (CDU)/Christian Social Union (CSU) into office, with Helmut Kohl, the CDU leader, as Chancellor.

Moves to Revive the EC

By the start of the 1980s, there was an acceptance within both national governments and the Commission that the response to challenges facing the EC required, in part at least, institutional reform to facilitate easier and more effective decision making.

The first response came in September 1981 from the foreign ministers of Germany and Italy, and was known as the Genscher–Colombo Plan. This plan called for a new European charter that would supersede the Treaties of Paris and Rome as the basic constitutional document of the Communities, and would bring European political co-operation, together with the EC, under the joint direction of the European Council. This would only be a formalization of the existing situation, although Genscher and Colombo also wished to improve the decision making ability of the Council of Ministers by increasing the use of majority voting, to expand the functions of the EP, and to intensify foreign policy co-operation in security matters.

The Plan received a cool response in the Council, as had an earlier proposal led by Altiero Spinelli—now a senior figure in the EP—that sought to diminish the institutional position of the Council in favour of the Parliament and Commission. Yet, while these two sets of proposals made no immediate impact on integration, they contributed to the European Council beginning a new round of negotiations on the question of political union and possible revision of the Treaties.

On the economic front, attempts by Thorn and his Vice-President and Commissioner for the Internal Market, Karl-Heinz Narjes, to highlight the problems faced by industrialists in trading across national borders within the EC met with little response from national governments. Governments were determined to reserve jobs for their own nationals (read 'voters') by tolerating, or even themselves erecting, non-tariff barriers to trade, and by giving public contracts exclusively to national companies. Yet, Thorn, Narjes, and, particularly, Vice-President Etienne Davignon, the Commissioner for Industrial Policy, laid the groundwork for the agreement that was concluded under the following Delors presidency to free the internal market of all these obstacles by the end of 1992 (see also Chapter 19).

Thorn and Narjes maintained a constant propaganda campaign against barriers to a genuine internal market. This campaign had an effect in raising awareness of the issue, especially when it was taken up by a group of members of the EP (MEPs) who called themselves the Kangaroo Group because they wanted to facilitate trade that would 'hop over' national boundaries. The work of Davignon was less public, but possibly more influential in persuading governments to accept change. He called into existence a network of leading industrialists involved in the European electrical and electronics industries to discuss their common problems in the face of US and Japanese competition. Out of these discussions came the Esprit programme of collaborative research in advanced technologies; but, more significantly, there also arose the European Round Table of Industrialists, which was to become an influential pressure group pushing governments into taking measures to liberalize the internal market of the EC.

Fontainebleau

The European Council meeting at Fontainebleau in June 1984 marked a turning point in European integration. First of all, the summit resolved the British budgetary question, in the context of an agreement to cut back on agricultural expenditure and to increase the Community's own resources through an increase in VAT contributions by member states. The agreement settled five years of dispute and opened the door for reform of the CAP.

The meeting also agreed to set up an ad hoc committee on institutional affairs, which came to be known by the name of its Chair, James Dooge of Ireland. The report of this committee became the basis for the institutional changes that were later to be made, alongside the fundamental policy commitment to completion of the internal market.

When a new Commission assumed office in 1985, under the presidency of Jacques Delors (see Insight 8.1), it offered a visible symbol of a new start under dynamic leadership. Delors proposed that the EC should set itself the target of removing a whole series of barriers to free trade and free movement of capital and labour that had grown up during the 1970s. This project would be pursued with a target date for completion of the end of 1992, and became known as the '1992 programme'. The economic project was linked to a programme of institutional reform that would have far-reaching implications for the way in which the EC made decisions, although those implications were not all immediately apparent.

The most important institutional reform was the introduction of qualified majority voting (QMV) into the proceedings of the Council of Ministers, thus overcoming the blockage to progress imposed by the system that allowed individual governments to veto proposals. It was also intended to revive the momentum of integration, because Delors believed that the freeing of the internal market would lead to spillover into other policy

---

Insight 8.1 Jacques Delors

Jacques Delors was born in Paris in 1925. His father was a middle-ranking employee of the Bank of France, and Jacques went to work for the Bank straight from school. The young Delors was active in Catholic social movements, and became a devotee of the doctrine of 'personalism', a form of Christian socialism associated with the philosopher Emmanuel Mounier. Delors was also an active trade unionist. In the 1960s, he moved from the Bank to a senior position in the French Planning Commission, which had been created by Jean Monnet. Although he was an adviser to the Gaullist Prime Minister Jacques Chaban-Delmas at the end of the 1960s and in the early 1970s, he subsequently joined the reformed Socialist party of François Mitterrand, and was elected to the EP in 1979 as a Socialist. When Mitterrand became President of France in 1981, Delors became Finance Minister in the Socialist government. He was instrumental in moving the government away from policies of economic expansion that were not working and were undermining the value of the currency. He played a crucial role in the negotiation of the 1983 realignment of currencies within the exchange rate mechanism of the EMS, and won the respect of the German government in the process. In 1985, with strong support from Chancellor Kohl of Germany, as well as from Mitterrand, he became President of the European Commission, a post that he retained for ten years.

sectors. In particular, he believed that it would not be feasible to have the single market without strengthening the degree of social protection available to workers at the EC level; and that the single market would set up a momentum towards monetary union.

Despite British reluctance to see these related aspects, the Thatcher government wanted to see the realization of the single market programme. Subsequently, the British Prime Minister tried to block the institutional aspects, but in the meantime the success of Delors's initiative revived the self-confidence of the Commission, which had already begun to recover under Jenkins and Thorn. It also led to a revival of theoretical interpretations of the EC that emphasized the role of the Commission and other supranational actors, thus rekindling the supranational vs intergovernmental debate about the nature of the EC, which had lain dormant during the 'doldrums years' of the 1970s and early 1980s (see Chapter 19, 'Explaining the Single Market').

1985: A Watershed Year

Delors had been Finance Minister in the 1981–83 French Socialist governments, which had tried to tackle the problem of unemployment in France by reflating the economy. The result had been a serious balance-of-payments crisis as the reflation did little to restore full employment, but did suck in imports. There had been two views on how to respond to this. One had been to withdraw from the EMS, and to impose import controls, in contravention of France's EC obligations. The other, of which Delors had been the strongest advocate, had been to revert to national policies of balancing the budget by cutting public expenditure, and to develop a European solution to the problem of unemployment. That view had prevailed, and Delors's advocacy of it made him acceptable to both Germany and Britain as a nominee for the Commission presidency. It had been tacitly accepted that the presidency of the Commission would be given to a German candidate if the Federal Government wished to take it up; but Kohl chose to throw his weight behind Delors.

The Brussels European Council of February 1985 instructed the Commission to draw up a timetable for the completion of the single market. Within a few months of taking office, the British Commissioner for Trade and Industry, Lord Cockfield, produced a White Paper listing the barriers that needed to be removed for there to be a genuine single market inside the EC. This listed some 300 separate measures, later reduced to 279, covering the harmonization of technical standards, opening up public procurement to intra-EC competition, freeing capital movements, removing barriers to free trade in services, harmonizing rates of indirect taxation and excise duties, and removing physical frontier controls between member states. The list was accompanied by a timetable for completion, with a final target date of the end of 1992.

At the Milan European Council, in June 1985, heads of government agreed the objectives of the White Paper and the timetable for its completion by the end of 1992. A massive publicity campaign would be organized to promote the project. It was also agreed, against the protests of the British Prime Minister, to set up an intergovernmental conference (IGC) to consider what changes were necessary to the original Treaties in order to achieve the single market, and to consider other changes to the institutional structure that had been recommended by the ad hoc committee under

James Dooge that had been set up at the Fontainebleau European Council a year earlier. This IGC drew up what became the SEA, which was agreed by the heads of government at the Luxembourg European Council in December 1985, and eventually ratified by national parliaments to come into effect in July 1987. Thus was born the '1992 programme', which did more than any initiative since the Treaties of Rome to revitalize the process of European integration.

The Single European Act

Although modest in the changes that it introduced in comparison with the hopes of federalists in the EP and within some member states (particularly Italy), the SEA rejuvenated the process of European integration. The intention of the SEA appeared relatively modest, seeking to complete the objective of a common market set out in the Treaty of Rome. By the early 1980s, the need for member states to compete in world markets, especially against the United States and Japan, was an overriding concern. A single European market would increase the specialization of production at company level and allow greater economies of scale, leading to more competitive firms. The issue of monetary union as an accompaniment to the single market was not addressed at this stage of developments.

While ostensibly an economic project, the SEA had implications for a range of policy areas such as social protection (see Chapter 18) and the environment (see Chapter 22). More broadly, in its proposals for institutional change, the SEA:

> had potential for revolution, suggesting a shift in the existing balance of power away from the member states towards the Community institutions. The radical political implications of the economic target of a common market—the single internal market—were there for all to read in the document. . . . while the issues of political and economic integration are closely interlinked, the parallel debates tended to muddy the waters of each.
>
> (Urwin 1995: 231)

In retrospect at least, the political implications of the SEA are clear (see Insight 8.2). At the time, though, the SEA was largely seen as a mechanism for implementing the commitment made at Milan to achieve the single market. This goal was not contested by member states. Moreover, the Commission was concerned with emphasizing the practical rather than the political implications of aspects of the reform. Only in the final section of the White Paper did the Commission refer to the wider implications of the internal market project, acknowledging that 'Just as the Customs Union had to precede Economic Integration, so Economic Integration has to precede European Unity' (European Commission 1985: 55). Despite the political implications of the single market being deliberately understated by the Commission, the proposed institutional reforms proved the most controversial aspect of the project.

Institutional Reforms

While the SEA was ostensibly a project to complete the single market, the institutional reforms that it introduced were to be of lasting significance for European integration,

> **Insight 8.2 The Political Provisions of the SEA**
>
> - It introduced QMV for single market measures.
> - It increased the legislative powers of the EP in areas where QMV applied.
> - It incorporated European political co-operation (EPC) into a Treaty text for the first time.
> - It incorporated in the Preamble a reiteration of the objective of an economic and monetary union.
> - It incorporated in the Preamble a commitment by the member states to 'transform relations as a whole among their States into a European Union'.

in particular the introduction of QMV in the Council of Ministers (see Chapter 12, 'The Council of the EU (the Council)'. Qualified majority voting was designed to speed up decision making by reducing substantially the number of areas in which individual states could reject progress by use of their veto. Qualified majority voting would apply to measures related to the freeing of the internal market, although certain measures, including the harmonization of indirect taxes and the removal of physical controls at borders, were excluded at British insistence. Without the extension of QMV, the internal market project was likely to be delayed, and possibly lost, through intergovernmental disputes.

The codification of the commitment to QMV as a formal amendment of the founding Treaties, and as part of a potentially wider reform of the institutional procedures for making decisions, was resisted strongly by Prime Minister Thatcher. The whole issue of institutional reform was one of several where the British government differed from most of its continental European partners. Mrs Thatcher insisted at Milan that no institutional reform, and so no IGC, was necessary. However, it seems that she was persuaded by her Foreign Secretary, Sir Geoffrey Howe, and her adviser on European affairs, David Williamson, that, unless a legally binding commitment were made to an element of majority voting in the Council of Ministers, the measures necessary to implement the Cockfield White Paper would never be agreed.

The Internal Market

The freeing of the internal market was supported by all the member states, and it coincided with the belief of the British Prime Minister in universal free trade. On the other hand, it was also an excellent issue for the new Commission to make into the centrepiece of its programme. As Helen Wallace (1986: 590) explained:

> The internal market is important not only for its own sake, but because it is the first core Community issue for over a decade . . . which has caught the imagination of British policy-makers and which is echoed by their counterparts elsewhere . . . The pursuit of a thoroughly liberalized domestic European market has several great advantages: it fits Community philosophy, it suits the doctrinal preferences of the current British Conservative government, and it would draw in its train a mass of interconnections with other fields of action.

Whereas doctrinal preferences may be sufficient explanation for British support of the internal market project, the support of other member states needs further explanation.

One important factor was the support given to the freeing of the market by European business leaders, some of whom formed the European Round Table of Industrialists in 1983 to press for the removal of the barriers to trade that had developed. This pressure occurred in the context of a generalized concern among governments about the sluggish recovery of the European economies from the post-1979 recession in comparison with the vigorous growth of the US and Japanese economies. In particular, the turning of the tide of foreign direct investment, so that by the mid-1980s there was a net flow of investment funds from western Europe to the United States, augured badly both for the employment situation in Europe in the future, and for the ability of European industry to keep abreast of the technological developments that were revolutionizing production processes.

It was in response to the worry that Europe would become permanently technologically dependent on the United States and Japan that President Mitterrand proposed his Eureka initiative for promoting pan-European research and development in the advanced technology industries. This concern also lay behind the promotion by the new Commission of 'framework programmes' for research and development in such fields as information technology, bio-technology, and telecommunications (Sharp and Shearman 1987). But when European industrialists were asked what would encourage them to invest in Europe, they replied that the most important factor for them would be the creation of a genuine continental market such as they experienced in the United States.

It was therefore in an attempt to revive investment and economic growth that governments other than Britain embraced the free-market programme. The pressure to break out of the short-termism that had prevented the EC from making progress in the 1970s and early 1980s came partly from interest groups, but also from the economic situation that faced governments. The EC, as only one part of the global capitalist economy, was seeing investment flow away from it to other parts of the global economy, and was already being left behind in rates of economic growth and in technological advance by rival core areas within the system. It was a calculation of the common national interests of the member states that led them to agree a new contract, in the form of a White Paper and the SEA.

Beyond these economic interests, other member states were happy to see the SEA's introduction of institutional reforms, and the strengthening of other Treaty provisions, notably on social policy, the environment, the structural funds, research and technology policy, and economic and social cohesion. The SEA therefore created a much wider package deal beyond the immediate confines of the single market programme (for more detail see Chapter 19, 'Explaining the Single Market').

The Role of the Delors Commission

The emphasis that Delors put on the single market was part of a carefully considered strategy. During the autumn of 1984, he considered a variety of candidates for the role of the 'Big Idea' that would relaunch European integration (Grant 1994: 66). Initially attracted to completion of EMU, following the relative success of the EMS, Delors ultimately decided that the idea of completing the internal market was the best starting point. This project was firmly within the boundaries of integration established by the Treaty of Rome. Even more important, perhaps, with policies of market liberalization adopted by key member states, the single market project stood the best chance of winning the support of even the most Eurosceptic governments, Britain's in particular. Moreover, successful completion of the 1992 project had implications for a wide range of Community policies. Most notably, the project would inevitably prompt reconsideration of the advantages of monetary union as a complement to the single market and would also lead to demands for strengthening EC social and regional policies from the member states most likely to be adversely affected by the internal market.

Few dispute that the Delors Commission played a pivotal role in developing and pushing forward the single market programme as a means to the end of ever closer union. The emergence of the programme and eventually the drive towards full monetary union and the adoption of a social charter, all bore the hallmarks of a plan devised in Paris in the light of the failures of the 1981–84 French economic experiment. Delors and the British Commissioner Cockfield worked together closely on developing and promoting the project. Cockfield faced accusations from the British Prime Minister that he had 'gone native' in his support for wide-ranging European integration, and it was no great surprise when Thatcher chose not to renominate him to the Commission in 1988.

Under Delors, the Commission regained the high profile it had under Hallstein, and, irrespective of whether the Hallstein Commission had been the genuine motor of integration, the Delors Commission certainly appeared to play that role by the 1980s. But it was only able to play that role because of the support Delors received from Mitterrand, and because of the diplomatic skill of Mitterrand himself in ensuring that other member states, Germany above all, were carried along with the plan.

Implementing the SEA

While national governments were initially slow to implement the measures detailed in the SEA, businesses began to take advantage of the emerging opportunities offered by the 1992 project. Company mergers accelerated to take advantage of EC-wide economies of scale. In 1988, the business publication *The Economist* noted that in 1987 there were 300 major mergers, compared with only sixty-eight in the previous year. In comparison, by November 1987 the Council of Ministers had adopted only sixty-four of the measures set out in the White Paper (Dinan 1994: 150) (see also Chapter 19, 'Transposition and Enforcement').

The core problem of implementation related to accompanying measures to the SEA; in particular, the demands of southern member states for adequate compensatory mechanisms to balance the adverse effects of market liberalization. While a number of member states were reluctant to commit greater resources to Community regional aid, ultimately these demands had to be satisfied to protect the 1992 programme. Subsequently, at the Brussels European Council of February 1988, the heads of government agreed to a doubling in the allocations to the structural funds to promote greater cohesion as a complement to the internal market.

Overall, though, the 1992 project was a tremendous success for the EC. It led to a revival of investment in Europe, which had been stagnating. The EC experienced a wave of business euphoria, which ensured that the work of public officials in actually agreeing the necessary measures did not waver. By the target date of the end of 1992, 260 out of the consolidated list of 279 measures that had been identified in the White Paper had been agreed in the Council of Ministers, a staggering 95 per cent success rate (Pelkmans 1994: 103).

However, the freeing of the market was not the end of the project as far as Delors was concerned. He saw it as a first step that implied further extensions of integration. In particular, he argued for a social dimension to the project, and for its completion by agreement on monetary union. On both of these issues, he had the support of a majority of the governments of the other member states, but was implacably opposed by the British Prime Minister, Margaret Thatcher.

CONCLUSION

The story told in this chapter is of a gradual recovery of momentum for the EC from the middle of the 1970s through to the success of the SEA and the single market programme. In seeking explanations for these developments, two of the themes of this book are evident: responses to the changing international environment and the revival of some of the neofunctionalist dynamics.

Developments early in the period were primarily responses to problems posed for the west European states by the decline of US hegemony in the context of the continuing Cold War. The EMS, which has been interpreted with hindsight as the start of a process that led to monetary union, was seen at the time more as a response to the chaos in the international monetary system caused by the refusal of the United States to allow the dollar to continue to be used as the cornerstone of the international monetary system. The southern enlargement was primarily a response to the need to stabilize the southern European states as they emerged from right-wing dictatorship so that they did not become subject to communist influence.

Similarly, there is general agreement that global economic developments were the catalyst for the acceptance of the single market. The remarkable economic recovery of the United States and Japan from the second oil crisis contrasted starkly with the sluggishness of the west European economies. Not only was there a marked difference in performance; the success of the United States and Japan was based on the adoption of new technologies into their production processes that threatened to leave western Europe with an obsolete industrial base unless investment could be revived.

At the same time, some of the analyses of neofunctionalists seemed to be vindicated by the single market programme. Interpretations of the relevant importance of different factors certainly vary (on which see Chapter 19, 'Explaining the Single Market'), but there is a considerable body of analysis that attributes a central role to the European Commission under Jacques Delors, and to the European Round Table of Industrialists. Two of the actors whom neofunctionalists had predicted would be influential appeared to be influential in this landmark decision: the Commission and transnational business interests.

Elements of the neofunctionalist analysis also received support from another development: the speed with which businesses responded to the announcement of the 1992 programme to conclude mergers and announce new investment plans vindicated the argument that changed circumstances would lead to changed attitudes and behaviour.

KEY POINTS

Leadership Changes: 1974

- Valéry Giscard d'Estaing became French President and Helmut Schmidt became German Chancellor. They had a good relationship and were able to work well together.

The European Council

- In 1974, Giscard d'Estaing called for the institutionalization of summit meetings of EC heads of state and government. He received support for this from Helmut Schmidt.
- It was agreed that these meetings be institutionalized under the auspices of the European Council and would be held three times each year.
- The creation of the European Council symbolized a profoundly intergovernmental period in the history of European integration.

Other Institutional Developments

- As Commission President, Roy Jenkins managed to secure a place at international economic summits for the Commission for the first time.
- Direct elections to the EP were agreed and the first elections were held in 1979.

The European Monetary System

- Following a call from Jenkins to renew attempts at monetary union, the European Council passed a proposal by Schmidt and Giscard d'Estaing for an EMS in 1978.
- The new EMS would be more flexible than its predecessor, but Britain declined to put sterling in the exchange rate mechanism and play a full role.

The Southern Enlargements

- Following a difficult period of negotiations, the accession of Greece to the Community was agreed in 1979. Portugal and Spain, who applied later, were eventually accepted into the EC in 1985.

The British Budget Rebate

- Britain was set to be the largest net contributor to the Community budget by 1980. The tactics of the Thatcher government over the issue jeopardized progress in other areas until a satisfactory solution was found in 1984.

Leadership Changes: 1981–82

- The appointment of Gaston Thorn to the Commission presidency in 1981 coincided with important leadership changes in France and Germany.

Moves to Revive the EC

- The Genscher–Colombo Plan proposed institutional reforms that received a cool reaction from the Council. However, Commission plans for freeing the internal market began to win over national governments.

Fontainebleau

- The resolution of the British budgetary question at Fontainebleau allowed for progress on both the internal market and institutional reform.

1985: A Watershed Year

- In June 1985, the Council agreed the 1992 timetable for completion of the single market.
- An IGC on institutional reform drew up what became the SEA.

The Single European Act

- For Delors, the single market programme was the 'Big Idea' that would relaunch European integration. On the whole, governments were persuaded of the need for the SEA by the desire to compete with Japan and the United States.
- Companies were quick to take advantage of the opportunities provided by the single market project, but implementation of SEA measures varied across member states.
- The SEA introduced QMV into the Council of Ministers for measures related to the freeing of the internal market, with some exceptions where there were important national sensitivities.
- The freeing of the internal market was an issue with a lot of spillover potential.
- It received strong support from the European Round Table of Industrialists.
- The Commission played a pivotal role in developing and promoting the single market programme.
- It was only possible for the Commission to play its part successfully because of the backing given to Delors by French President Mitterrand.
- Implementation of the single market agreement was delayed by demands from the southern member states for compensatory mechanisms.
- Businesses were quick to prepare for the single market, and became a strong pressure for progress from governments.
- Delors saw it as only the first step, with a social dimension and monetary union to follow. In this, he was opposed by Margaret Thatcher.

 For additional material and resources, please visit the online resources www.oup.com/uk/bache5e.

FURTHER READING

On the 1970s, **K. Middlemass**, *Orchestrating Europe: The Informal Politics of European Union, 1973–1995* (London: Fontana, 1995), 73–110 calls the years between 1973 and 1983 'The Stagnant Decade'. **A. Moravcsik**, *The Choice for Europe: Social Purpose and State Power from Messina to Maastricht* (London: UCL Press, 1998), 238–313 focuses on monetary co-operation and the EMS. For an insider account of part of this period, see **R. Jenkins**, *European Diary, 1977–1981* (London: Collins, 1989). The British budget rebate issue is explained more fully in **S. George**, *An Awkward Partner: Britain in the European Community*, 3rd edn (Oxford: Oxford University Press, 1998), 137–65. For general accounts, see **D. W. Urwin**, *The Community of*

Europe: A History of European Integration since 1945, 3rd edn (London and New York: Longman, 1995) and **M. Dedman**, *The Origins and Development of the European Union 1945–2008: A History of European Integration*, 2nd edn (Abingdon: Routledge, 2010).

C. Grant, *Delors: Inside the House that Jacques Built* (London: Nicolas Brealey Publishing, 1994) and **G. Ross**, *Jacques Delors and European Integration* (Cambridge: Polity Press, 1995) both give accounts of what went on within the Delors Commission. For the analysis of the Single European Act, begin with **D. R. Cameron**, 'The 1992 Initiative: Causes and Consequences', in A. Sbragia (ed.), *Euro-Politics: Institutions and Policymaking in the 'New' European Community* (Washington, DC: Brookings Institution, 1992), 23–74; continue with **W. Sandholtz and J. Zysman**, '1992: Recasting the European Bargain', *World Politics*, 45 (1989): 95–128; and then read **A. Moravcsik**, *The Choice for Europe: Social Purpose and State Power from Messina to Maastricht* (London: UCL Press, 1998), 314–78 or his article 'Negotiating the Single European Act: National Interests and Conventional Statecraft in the European Community', in *International Organization, 45 (1991): 19–56*. For an institutionalist account, read **K. Armstrong and S. Bulmer**, *The Governance of the Single European Market* (Manchester: Manchester University Press, 1998), Chapter 1.

For access to various primary sources, the website www.cvce.eu/en is very useful.

Chapter 9

Maastricht and Amsterdam (the Late 1980s to the Late 1990s)

Chapter Overview

Once the single market programme was under way, Jacques Delors set about trying to exploit its spillover potential to push forward towards monetary union. At the same time, the collapse of communism in central and eastern Europe opened up the prospect of the reunification of Germany, and fears that the larger German state would either dominate the European Community (EC) or turn away from its western European commitments to forge a new central European identity in partnership with the central European states that had formed Germany's traditional economic hinterland in the early twentieth century. To address both issues, the governments of the member states signed another Treaty in Maastricht at the end of 1991. The reaction to the Treaty within member states was worryingly negative; yet, despite that, further Treaty reform was deemed necessary if the former communist states were to be offered a prospect of membership of the EC.

Whereas the start of the Cold War had caused a ferment in western Europe out of which emerged the European communities, its end threw things into as much turmoil. The controlled process that Delors had envisaged, pushing forward from the single market to monetary union and beyond was overtaken by the need to consolidate democracy in the successor states to the failed Soviet bloc, and that meant the EC having to accommodate a whole new group of prospective members. The fallout from this shock gave the initiative back to intergovernmentalism. It also produced a backlash against the pace of change from within the existing member states.

Towards Maastricht

Monetary policy had been largely absent from the Single European Act (SEA), but the logic of the internal market suggested at least some harmonization of taxation policies. Following the SEA there had been growing support for a single currency controlled by a European central bank, but the British government rejected this concept. Despite British opposition, the heads of government agreed in Hanover in June 1988 to set up a committee of central bankers and technical experts, under the chairmanship of Delors, to prepare a report on the steps that needed to be taken to strengthen monetary co-operation. The subsequent 'Delors Report' proposed a three-stage process to monetary union, leading to a single currency by 1999. The report was presented to the June 1989 meeting of the European Council in Madrid, which on a majority vote of eleven to one—Thatcher voting against—agreed to convene an intergovernmental conference (IGC) to prepare proposals for changes to the Treaties to allow movement to a monetary union.

The dramatic collapse of communism in the Soviet Union and other central and eastern European countries in the course of 1989 and 1990 added to the complexity of the situation. This forced a serious reconsideration of the political aspects of the EC. The immediate impact was the destabilization of the geographical area immediately to the east of the EC and, more positively for the EC, the opening up of potential new markets and new sites for investment for west European capital. In addition, the collapse of communism raised the prospect of German reunification.

This 'acceleration of history', as Delors called it, had an impact on the EC and on Delors's plans for its development. In particular, the prospect of a reunified Germany caused alarm in the neighbouring states, particularly over a possible resurgence of German nationalism. A more immediate concern was that the new Germany would turn its attention more to the East and become less concerned with its obligations to western Europe.

Chancellor Kohl of Germany shared these concerns. Kohl had not hitherto been noted for providing strong or dynamic leadership, but he seized the opportunity to go down in the history books as the person who reunified his country. At the same time, however, he did not want to be remembered as the Frankenstein who created a new monster in the centre of Europe. Such concerns led directly to the convening of a second IGC on political union to run alongside the one that had already been called on monetary union. Although Delors supported the move, it was not part of his plan. The IGC on political union, together with that on monetary union, meant that the Maastricht Treaty became a very high-profile issue: 'a treaty too far' as Lady Thatcher later described it.

The two IGCs met throughout 1991, and their proposals were incorporated into the Treaty on European Union (TEU), which was agreed in Maastricht in December of that year, and which created the European Union (EU). Britain, under the new premiership of John Major, agreed to the TEU only when a chapter on social policy had been removed from the main text, and only when it was agreed that Britain could opt out of the final stage of monetary union if its Parliament so decided.

The Treaty on European Union

Intergovernmental negotiations leading up to the Maastricht Summit of December 1991 were tough and much of what was agreed reflected the lowest-common-denominator bargaining position of governments. The TEU was signed in February 1992 and entered into force in November 1993. It marked a further big step on the road to European integration, with important implications for both internal and external activities (see Insight 9.1). (The TEU was revised subsequently, but the Insights in this chapter utilize the original 'Maastricht' text.)

The name of the 'European Economic Community' was officially changed to the 'European Community' and there were important new areas of co-operation in the fields of Common Foreign and Security Policy (CFSP) (see Insight 9.2) and Justice and

Insight 9.1 Extract from Treaty on European Union: Common Provisions, Article B

The Union shall set itself the following objectives:

- to promote economic and social progress which is balanced and sustainable, in particular through the creation of an area without internal frontiers, through the strengthening of economic and social cohesion and through the establishment of economic and monetary union, ultimately including a single currency in accordance with the provisions of this Treaty;
- to assert its identity on the international scene, in particular through the implementation of a common foreign and security policy including the eventual framing of a common defence policy, which might in time lead to a common defence;
- to strengthen the protection of the rights and interests of the nationals of its Member States through the introduction of a citizenship of the Union;
- to develop close co-operation on justice and home affairs;
- to maintain in full the acquis communautaire and build on it with a view to considering, through the procedure referred to in Article N(2), to what extent the policies and forms of co-operation introduced by this Treaty may need to be revised with the aim of ensuring the effectiveness of the mechanisms and the institutions of the Community.

The objectives of the Union shall be achieved as provided in this Treaty and in accordance with the conditions and the timetable set out therein while respecting the principle of subsidiarity as defined in Article 3b of the Treaty establishing the EC.

Insight 9.2 Extract from Treaty on European Union: Provisions on a Common Foreign and Security Policy, Article J.1

1. The Union and its Member States shall define and implement a common foreign and security policy, governed by the provisions of this Title and covering all areas of foreign and security policy.

2. The objectives of the common foreign and security policy shall be:
   - to safeguard the common values, fundamental interests and independence of the Union;
   - to strengthen the security of the Union and its Member States in all ways;
   - to preserve peace and strengthen international security, in accordance with the principles of the United Nations Charter as well as the principles of the Helsinki Final Act and the objectives of the Paris Charter;
   - to promote international co-operation;
   - to develop and consolidate democracy and the rule of law, and respect for human rights and fundamental freedoms.

3. The Union shall pursue these objectives:
   - by establishing systematic co-operation between Member States in the conduct of policy, in accordance with Article J.2;

- by gradually implementing, in accordance with Article J.3, joint action in the areas in which the Member States have important interests in common.

4. The Member States shall support the Union's external and security policy actively and unreservedly in a spirit of loyalty and mutual solidarity. They shall refrain from any action which is contrary to the interests of the Union or likely to impair its effectiveness as a cohesive force in international relations. The Council shall ensure that these principles are complied with.

Insight 9.3 Extract from Treaty on European Union: Provisions on Co-operation in the Fields of Justice and Home Affairs, Article K.1

For the purposes of achieving the objectives of the Union, in particular the free movement of persons, and without prejudice to the powers of the European Community, Member States shall regard the following areas as matters of common interest:

- asylum policy;
- rules governing the crossing by persons of the external borders of the Member States and the exercise of controls thereon;
- immigration policy and policy regarding nationals of third countries:

  — conditions of entry and movement by nationals of third countries on the territory of Member States;

  — conditions of residence by nationals of third countries on the territory of Member States, including family reunion and access to employment;

  — combating unauthorized immigration, residence and work by nationals of third countries on the territory of Member States;

  — combating drug addiction in so far as this is not covered by (7) to (9);

  — combating fraud on an international scale in so far as this is not covered by (7) to (9);

  — judicial co-operation in civil matters;

  — judicial co-operation in criminal matters;

  — customs co-operation;

  — police co-operation for the purposes of preventing and combating terrorism, unlawful drug-trafficking and other serious forms of international crime, including if necessary certain aspects of customs co-operation, in connection with the organization of a Union-wide system for exchanging information within a European Police Office (Europol).

Home Affairs (JHA) (see Insight 9.3). The EC, CFSP, and JHA became part of a three-pillar structure known as the European Union (see Chapter 12, Figure 12.1). While the first pillar remained an area of pooled sovereignty in which the community method of decision making would continue to predominate, the second and third pillars were explicitly areas of intergovernmental co-operation depending largely on unanimous decisions taken by the member governments.

157

Monetary union was the biggest single policy initiative in the TEU (see Chapter 20, 'Origins of EMU'), but, in addition, the Treaty contained a number of other important provisions. In institutional terms, it strengthened the power of the European Parliament (EP) through the extension of the co-decision procedure, which gave Parliament greater legislative power in a range of policy areas (see Chapter 12, 'Decision Making Procedures'); and it created a Committee of the Regions and Local Authorities, in recognition of the growing role of sub-national government in EC affairs, and in line with the principle of subsidiarity (see Chapter 12, 'The Decision Making Institutions (the Union Method)'). The principle of subsidiarity was itself established as a general rule of the Community by the Treaty, having only applied to the field of environmental policy in the SEA (see Insight 16.2 for the current Treaty text).

The Treaty also introduced the concept of European citizenship, and gave the European citizen the following rights: to circulate and reside freely in the Community; to vote and stand as a candidate for European and municipal elections in the state in which he or she resides; to receive protection while in a non-EU country from diplomatic or consular authorities of a member state other than that of his or her state of origin; and to petition the EP or submit a complaint to the Ombudsman (European Union 2005).

In sum, these measures provided a strong political dimension to the economic imperatives that had dominated the integration process to date. More generally, EC competence was established or extended in a number of areas, including education and training, environment, health, and industry. Built on compromise, the TEU included something positive for the EC institutions and for each of the member states involved.

After Maastricht

Although agreed by the heads of governments, the decision to move to a single currency raised concerns within member states. Notably, this decision caused a collapse of support for the EU in Germany itself, where the Deutschmark was held in high regard as the factor that had facilitated post-war prosperity. Problems were made worse when the internal German currency union took effect, following the decision to convert East German Ostmarks at an artificially high rate into Deutschmarks. This led to inflationary tendencies in the unified Germany, which were suppressed by the Bundesbank (the German Central Bank) raising interest rates. This in turn solidified resistance within Germany to European monetary union, and therefore to Maastricht. It also pushed the buoyant European economies into recession, which made it more difficult to sell Maastricht to European citizens, who were already rather alarmed by the pace of change that was being proposed.

It was against this background that the Danish referendum in June 1992 rejected the Treaty by 50.7 per cent to 49.3 per cent. In Denmark, farmers and fishermen had usually been strong supporters of the EC. Danish opposition to membership had been concentrated in Copenhagen and the other urban areas. In 1992, concern about the reforms of the Common Agricultural Policy (CAP) (see Chapter 21) and the Common Fisheries Policy reduced the 'Yes' vote in rural areas, and may have been sufficient to make the difference between a narrow 'Yes' and a narrow 'No'. It was only when concessions were made on monetary union—giving Denmark similar opt-out rights to those of Britain—and on some other issues of concern, that it was narrowly accepted in a second referendum in May 1993.

Perhaps even more significantly, the Treaty was only accepted by the French public by the narrowest of margins (50.3 to 49.7 per cent) in September 1992. Guyomarch et al. (1998: 97–8) identified six factors that shaped this outcome: high unemployment and the argument of the 'No' campaign that, under the TEU, the government would no longer be able to take effective action to create jobs; concern that further integration would lead to a weakening of the level of social security; hostility to the MacSharry reforms of the CAP (see Chapter 21, 'Agricultural Reform'); concern at the effects on previously protected sectors of the economy of the opening of the domestic market; concern at what was seen as interference by Brussels with aspects of the traditional French way of life, including the right to produce and eat unpasteurized cheese, and to shoot migrating birds; and splits in all the main parties on their attitude to the TEU, which deprived the electorate of clear leadership. The same authors pointed to the fact that the controversy generated by the referendum led to an increase in interest in the EU. This meant that in the 1994 elections to the EP, the turnout in France increased against the EU-wide trend, from 50.4 per cent in 1989 to 55 per cent (Guyomarch et al. 1998: 101).

In Germany, there was no referendum, but the strength of public concern about monetary union was such that the Bundestag secured the right to vote on the issue again before any automatic abandonment of the Deutschmark in favour of a common European currency. There was clear evidence of serious public discontent with the Treaty in other member states, not least in Britain.

The Commission after Maastricht

The Commission became caught in this wave of popular discontent about the pace of integration. Delors was personally associated with the proposals on monetary union, which were what caused the greatest concern in Britain and Germany. He had also adopted a very high profile in the run-up to the ratification debacles. In particular, his ill-timed statement shortly before the Danish referendum, to the effect that small states might have to surrender their right to hold the presidency of the Council of Ministers in a future, enlarged EC, was seen as a contributory factor in the negative vote in Denmark.

Delors's comments about small states were actually made in the context of an entirely different debate about enlargement of the EC. The success of the 1992 programme had led to concern among the members of the European Free Trade Association (EFTA) that they were not sharing in the investment boom that 1992 precipitated. Led by Sweden, these states began to broach the question of membership of the EC. Delors was against this because he believed that further enlargement would dilute the degree of unity that could be achieved, and he proposed instead a way in which the EFTA states could become part of the single market without becoming full members of the EC. Membership of the European Economic Area (EEA) would involve the EFTA states adopting all the relevant commercial legislation of the EC, without having any say in its formulation. It was never likely to be a satisfactory agreement for the governments of those states, who would thereby be surrendering sovereignty over large areas of their economies; more significantly, it did not convince the businesses that were already diverting their investments from EFTA to inside the EC. In addition, these states had also pursued foreign policies of neutrality, but the end of the Cold War meant their policies were no longer incompatible with full membership. Consequently, a group of EFTA states decided to press ahead with membership applications, but Switzerland withdrew its application after the Swiss people rejected the EEA in a referendum in December 1992; and the Norwegians again rejected membership in a referendum in November 1994.

Sweden, Finland, and Austria became members of the EU on 1 January 1995 (see Chapter 26, 'History'). The EU that they joined was not the self-confident one that they had applied to join. As well as disagreement about the future direction, and signs of public disaffection with the whole exercise, the European Monetary System (EMS) had effectively collapsed during the ratification problems. Britain had withdrawn and floated sterling, and other states had only been able to remain inside because the bands of permitted fluctuation had been widened from 2.25 per cent either side of parity to 15 per cent.

Delors had started his long period as President of the Commission with a considerable triumph in the single market programme. He ended it with that achievement somewhat overshadowed by the hostile reaction of public opinion in much of the EU to the Maastricht Treaty. Yet, whether it was reasonable to blame the Commission for this debacle is very doubtful. Delors had been upset at the extent to which the Commission had been ignored during the IGCs that prepared the TEU, and had opposed several of the provisions of the Treaty. However, he had adopted such a high profile during his period as president that it was easy for the governments of the member states to pass the blame onto him personally and the institution of which he had been president for ten years.

Political Change

Significant domestic political developments in the mid-to-late 1990s affected the position of key member states on the EU. In Germany, the government of Chancellor Kohl continued uninterrupted, but the authority of the Chancellor was called into question by a number of difficulties on policy and a number of electoral setbacks. In Britain, the Conservative government of John Major experienced a series of defeats in parliamentary by-elections, which reduced its majority. This, combined with the increasingly militant anti-EU position of a significant number of its own MPs, left the government with little room for manoeuvre, and its discourse on the EU became increasingly negative. Just prior to the Amsterdam European Council in June 1997, at which the Treaty of Amsterdam was agreed, the Conservative government lost office in a general election and was replaced by a Labour government under Tony Blair.

In France, there were two changes of government. In May 1995, the Gaullist Jacques Chirac was elected president in succession to the Socialist François Mitterrand.

There was already a conservative majority in the National Assembly, from which Chirac nominated Alain Juppé as his Prime Minister. However, when the two rounds of parliamentary elections were held in May/June 1997, the Socialist Party won the largest share of seats, and formed a coalition with the communists.

Chirac's initial actions as president were viewed with some concern in Germany. His decision to permit the testing of nuclear weapons in the Pacific met with protests throughout the EU, including in Germany. Only the British government supported Chirac on this. Together with the common experience of working together in Bosnia, this incident led to a measure of agreement between France and Britain. Chirac at one stage suggested that France might learn something from the British approach to the EU. However, he gradually came back into line with the position of his predecessor.

Midway through this decade, Jacques Delors stepped down as president of the European Commission after serving three full terms, more than any previous president. He was widely attributed with having turned around the fortunes of the EC following the 'doldrum years', and presided over the acceptance of the single market programme and the blueprint for monetary union. He operated as a '**policy entrepreneur**', initially through the vehicle of the Commission, thereby enhancing its status, then latterly in a more independent role as the confidant and ally of the French President, François Mitterrand, and especially the German Chancellor, Helmut Kohl (Lord 2002: 329–30).

Delors was succeeded by Jacques Santer, who was a very different type of president, and is generally considered to have been a weaker one. He did not get off to a good start. He was not the first choice of the heads of state or government. They had agreed that following Delors, who was a socialist from a large member state, the nominee had to be from the centre-right and from a small member state. This meant that the field was limited. Santer, the Prime Minister of Luxembourg, only got the nomination after John Major had rejected Jean-Luc Dehaene, the Prime Minister of Belgium and the first choice of most of his colleagues, and Helmut Kohl had rejected Ruud Lubbers, the Dutch Prime Minister. Santer's nomination was approved in the EP by a majority of only twenty-one (Lord 2002: 336). At the end of the decade, in 1999, the Santer Commission was forced to resign amidst allegations of financial mismanagement, seriously damaging the Commission's reputation after its achievements under Delors (Chapter 13, 'Financial Management').

Monetary Union

The agreement on monetary union that had been reached at Maastricht represented a compromise between the positions of states with very different perspectives on the issue. Those compromises had to be sorted out in order for the programme for a single currency to go ahead. During 1995, the decisions on the detail of the monetary union began to be settled, generally in favour of German views. These included agreement that the location of the European Central Bank (ECB) would be in Frankfurt, and that the new currency would be called the euro, not the ecu as the French wished, because that name was not liked by the German public. More significantly, during 1996 it was agreed that the convergence criteria set out in the TEU (see Chapter 20, 'Origins of

EMU') would have to be met precisely, with no fudging of the issue, and that there would continue to be a stability pact after the single currency came into existence. French hopes for more political control over the monetary policy of the ECB were also dashed (see Chapter 20, 'Putting Maastricht into Operation (1992–2002)').

Continuing economic recession in Europe hindered the efforts to meet the convergence criteria of those member states that wished to participate in the single currency. During 1995, it was decided to abandon the earlier of the two possible starting dates for the single currency, i.e. 1997, because it was obvious that not enough states, if any, would fully meet the convergence criteria by then. There was also doubt about how many would achieve the targets by 1999, the second of the two possible starting dates. In France and Belgium, the efforts of the governments to reduce the level of their budget deficits to the target of 3 per cent led to strikes and disruption. The imposition of lower public spending on economies that already had high levels of unemployment was a sure recipe for political problems.

However, during the course of 1996 and 1997, a surprising number of states did manage either to achieve or to approach the targets. This caused concern in Germany, because the idea that Italy in particular could possibly observe the conditions of the stability pact in perpetuity was not considered credible. There was a fear that the German public might reject a euro of which Italy was a part. As the trend in the Italian economy moved in the direction of the targets, so the insistence of the Germans that the targets be treated as absolutes grew. On the budget deficit, which was treated as the most important criterion, the German Finance Minister, Theo Waigel, and the President of the Bundesbank, Hans Tietmeyer, insisted that 3 per cent meant exactly 3 per cent or less, not even 3.1 per cent. This was clearly an attempt to set the target at a level that Italy would not be able to reach. The irony was that Germany missed the deficit target of 3 per cent in 1996, and looked like missing it again in 1997. A single currency without German participation was inconceivable, yet the continuing problems posed for the German economy by the absorption of East Germany threatened to disqualify it from membership on its own criteria.

All of this caused some glee within the British Conservative government, which found the whole project of monetary union extremely difficult. For domestic political reasons the government could not join the single currency, even if it met the convergence criteria; but if the project went ahead without it there was a risk that British economic interests would be damaged, and that British political influence within the EU would be permanently diminished. So, it was with a certain air of wishing rather than predicting that Prime Minister John Major said in an article in 1993 that 'economic and monetary union is not realisable in present circumstances' (*The Economist*, 25 September 1993). While there might have been some justification for this view in 1993, by the end of 1997 it was apparent that the single currency would start on schedule in 1999, and although it was not clear which states would be members, it began to look as though all those that wished to join, except Greece, would be in a position to do so.

In January 1999, the euro came into operation for eleven member states—Austria, Belgium, Finland, France, Germany, Ireland, Italy, Luxembourg, the Netherlands, Portugal, and Spain. This meant that the euro became the official currency of these states, although national notes and coins continued in circulation until 2002. Greece was initially excluded from the eurozone by failing to meet the convergence criteria, while Britain, Denmark, and Sweden chose not to join the single currency. Britain and Denmark had negotiated opt-outs, while Sweden excluded itself on the technicality that it had not been a member of the exchange rate mechanism for two years and as such was not eligible. There were concerns over Italy's use of a one-off 'Euro-tax' to ensure it met the budget deficit criterion in the qualifying financial year; and both Belgium and Italy had debt ratios that appeared to go beyond the criteria (see Chapter 20, 'Putting Maastricht into Operation (1992–2002)'). Despite all of this, the completion of monetary union, almost thirty years after the Hague Summit had made it an explicit objective, was a considerable achievement.

Although the single currency came into existence more smoothly than many economists predicted, it soon ran into difficulties. The external value of the euro fell steadily against the US dollar, and the eurozone itself began to exhibit some of the problems of having a single interest rate for such a diverse economic area. National economies on the fringes of the zone, particularly those of Spain and Ireland, began to experience the symptoms of repressed inflation, with rapidly rising property prices and shortages of labour. At the same time, the core economies of Germany and France were experiencing sluggish growth.

It was in this context that, as soon as the new currency came into existence, Oskar Lafontaine and Dominique Strauss-Kahn, Finance Ministers of Germany and France respectively, pressed the ECB to lower interest rates to stimulate growth (see Chapter 20, 'The Single Currency in Operation'). The ECB and its President Wim Duisenberg vigorously resisted such interference, though, and the pressure was reduced after Lafontaine resigned in March 1999.

Enlargement

All member states paid lip-service to the principle of enlargement of the EU to the East, but some states were keener than others. For Germany, the enlargement was an absolute priority; it was also strongly supported by Britain and the Scandinavian countries. However, France, Italy, and Spain had reservations. When the shift was made from the general issue of supporting enlargement to the discussion of the detailed steps that were needed to make a reality of the aspiration, even the strongest supporters were not necessarily prepared to accept the full implications.

Germany's commitment to enlargement was based largely on security considerations. Following reunification, Germany was once again a central European state, having borders with Poland and the Czech Republic. Instability in the region would be right on Germany's doorstep, and admitting its nearest neighbours to the EU was seen as a way of guaranteeing their stability. There were also economic considerations. Before the First World War, German companies and banks had been the leading foreign investors in central Europe, and soon after the collapse of communism German investment began to flow into the area. Guaranteeing the security of those investments was another reason for the German government's support of membership for the central European states.

British motives for welcoming enlargement were less immediately obvious, but reflected a combination of security, economic, and political considerations. In terms of security, British governments since the war had continued to support the principle of global stabilization, even where British investments were not immediately involved. This was a habit of statecraft that dated back to the period before the First World War when Britain was the hegemonic power in the world and shouldered responsibility for policing the international capitalist system. That responsibility had largely passed to the United States in the period since the Second World War, but British governments had consistently supported such efforts at global stabilization. In the situation after the end of the Cold War, the US administrations of both Bush and Clinton made it clear that they expected the EU states to play a leading role in stabilizing central and eastern Europe, and membership of the EU was specifically pressed by the Clinton Administration as a means of achieving this.

In economic terms, British support for further enlargement reflected the hope that British business would be able to profit from access to a larger market. Politically, however, this enlargement would also imply a looser EU, less likely to move in a federal direction. Thus, in both economic and political terms, eastern enlargement suited the Conservative government of John Major.

While the governments of France and the Mediterranean member states could see the arguments for enlargement to the East, and even accepted them, they were apprehensive about the effect that such an enlargement would have on the EU. First, they were concerned that an eastern enlargement would shift the balance of power in the EU decisively to the North, especially coming immediately after the accession of Austria, Finland, and Sweden. Second, and related to the first point, they were concerned that the problems of the Mediterranean, which affected them more than instability in the East, would be relegated to a secondary issue. Instability in North Africa, particularly civil war in Algeria, was already having an impact on them in the form of refugees and threats to their companies' investments in the region. Third, they feared that EU funds that came to them through the CAP and the structural funds would be diverted to central and eastern European economies.

The concern that attention would be diverted from the problems of the Mediterranean was recognized by the German government when it held the presidency of the EU in the second half of 1994. Agreement was reached at the Essen European Council in December 1994 to launch an initiative on North Africa and the Middle East. This assumed more tangible form during 1995, under the successive French and Spanish presidencies, culminating in a major conference in Barcelona from 23–29 November 1995 involving the EU member states, the Maghreb states (Algeria, Morocco, and Tunisia), Israel, Jordan, Lebanon, Syria, Turkey, Cyprus, and Malta. The central and eastern European states were also represented. The conference agreed on a stability pact for the Middle East on the model of the Conference on Security and Co-operation in Europe (CSCE) and the EU agreed to contribute $6 billion in aid and $6 billion in **European Investment Bank (EIB)** loans to the economic development of the region.

The problem of accepting the implications of a commitment to enlargement to the East were apparent in November 1995, when the Commission proposed that agricultural imports from six central and east European states (Bulgaria, the Czech Republic, Hungary, Poland, Romania, and Slovakia) be increased by 10 per cent a year. Britain, Denmark, the Netherlands, and Sweden supported the proposal. France and the Mediterranean member states opposed it, indicating that they would only be prepared to accept an increase of 5 per cent a year. Germany, which was ostensibly the strongest supporter of enlargement, joined the Mediterranean states in opposing the Commission's proposal. This indicated the strength of the farming lobby in Germany, and the fragmented nature of decision making in the country, which allowed the Agriculture Ministry to adopt a line so clearly incompatible with the official policy as enunciated by the Chancellor's office.

The same contradiction in policy emerged after July 1997, when the Commission published its *Agenda 2000* report on the future direction of the EU in the likely context of enlargement. The German Farm Minister, Ignaz Kiechle, publicly stated that the proposed reforms of the CAP were unnecessary. He received no reprimand for this from Chancellor Kohl. In addition to the reform of key policies, the eastern enlargement had implications for the decision making procedures of the EU. This came to be one of the key issues in the IGC that led up to the Treaty of Amsterdam. (On enlargement, see also Chapter 26.)

The 1996 IGC

Originally, the 1996 IGC was intended to review the working of the TEU. Provision for such a review was written into the agreements that were reached at Maastricht in December 1991. However, nobody expected the ratification of the TEU to take as long as it did, with the result that the review started after only two-and-a-half years of experience of the new arrangements. The difficulties in ratifying the TEU also meant that there was little appetite for further fundamental change. Increasingly, the IGC came to be seen as primarily about preparing the ground for the eastern enlargement. There were several institutional issues that needed to be addressed if the EU were to enlarge to over twenty members: the size of the Commission and the EP; the rotation of the presidency of the Council; the extent of qualified majority voting (QMV); and the weighting of votes under QMV (see Part Three: Institutions).

The Commission had twenty members in 1995, and that was already too many for the number of portfolios available, as Jacques Santer found out when he tried to allocate responsibilities without upsetting either national sensibilities or the *amour propre* of his colleagues in the College of Commissioners. Enlargement threatened to produce an unwieldy organization. The British government offered to relinquish its second Commissioner if the other large states would agree to do so, but this was not an easy concession for the others. For Italy and Spain in particular, having two Commissioners was a matter of national pride, singling out their countries as larger member states on a par with Germany, France, and Britain. Even if there had been unanimous agreement to dispense with the second Commissioners, the problem of too many Commissioners would have remained.

The EP would also become unwieldy if the same rough formula that had been used up to the 1995 enlargement were applied to further member states. Clearly, there had to be some limit put on the numbers; but that had implications for the existing distribution of seats.

With twelve member states, and with the presidency of the Council changing every six months, there were six years between presidencies for any one state (see Chapter 14, 'The Council Presidency'). This meant that all the expertise that had been acquired for one presidency was lost by the time the next one came around. There was also concern that the next enlargement would involve mostly small states, as had the 1995 enlargement. Small states often had problems with servicing the presidency. The problems had been eased since the Troika system had come into operation, whereby the present, previous, and immediate future presidents co-operated (see Chapter 14, 'The Council Presidency'). However, the impending enlargement heralded a situation in which there might not be a large state in the Troika for much of the time.

On QMV, the German and French governments wanted to see an extension to cover areas under the JHA pillar of the TEU, but the British Conservative government was adamantly opposed to any extension of QMV. The British government was also, along with Spain, one of the strongest advocates of a re-weighting of the votes under QMV.

Because the number of votes allocated to a state was not directly proportional to its population, the increase in the number of small member states had produced a situation in which measures could be passed under QMV with the support of the representatives of a decreasing proportion of the total population of the EU. In the original EC of six states, votes representing 70 per cent of the population were needed to pass a measure. By 1995, this had been reduced to 58.3 per cent and, on the basis of some reasonable assumptions about the allocation of votes to future members, the proportion required could be as low as 50.3 per cent with an EU of twenty-six states. The French government supported the idea of a re-weighting of votes, but the German Chancellor was hesitant because of the concern expressed by the smaller member states that this would be yet another step towards downgrading their role (on current QMV weightings see Chapter 12, 'The Council of the EU (the Council)').

Beyond these specific institutional issues, each member state went to the IGC with particular issues that it wished to push. Sweden, Denmark, and the Netherlands were concerned to increase the accountability and transparency of Council business, and proposed that a freedom-of-information clause be written into the Treaty. Sweden was also a leading mover in pressing for a chapter on employment policy to be added to the Treaty. Britain wanted reform to the working of the European Court of Justice (ECJ), having suffered several adverse judgments at its hands (see Chapter 16, 'CJEU Rulings on the Nature of EU Law'). Britain and France both pressed for an enhanced role for national parliaments in the policy-making process. France and Germany pressed for more flexible arrangements that would allow some states to proceed faster than others with integration; they also co-operated in putting forward proposals to move towards incorporating the Western European Union (WEU) (see Insight 6.1, 'The Western European Union') into the EU, something that was strongly opposed by the neutral member states (Austria, Ireland, and Sweden) and by Britain.

The IGC was preceded by a 'Reflection Group', which met in the second half of 1995 under the Spanish presidency. This consisted of representatives of the Foreign Ministers and two members of the EP. It had a remit to seek the views of other institutions on progress towards European union, and possible amendments to the TEU, and to prepare a report on the issues that should form the agenda of the IGC.

When he reported on the work of the Group in December 1995, the Spanish Foreign Minister Carlos Westendorp said that there was agreement that the IGC should not aim at fundamental reform, but be about necessary changes; in particular, it should be seen as one part of the process of eastern enlargement. Werner Hoyer, the German representative on the Reflection Group, indicated publicly that the work of the Group had soon deteriorated into an exchange of national positions, and warned that there was a risk of the IGC turning into a confrontation between integrationists and intergovernmentalists.

The IGC opened officially in Turin on 29 March 1996. The special European Council that was called to inaugurate it was dominated, though, by the ban on exports of British beef. This had been imposed in the aftermath of the announcement that bovine spongiform encephalopathy (BSE) in cattle, with which British herds were particularly infected, could be the cause of Creutzfeldt–Jakob disease (CJD) in humans. As British efforts to get the ban lifted made little progress over the coming weeks, John Major threatened to block progress in the IGC, and to refuse to sign any Treaty that emerged from it until the ban was lifted. His government did in fact veto just about every item of EU business over which it could exercise a veto until an agreement was reached on a phased lifting of the ban.

This incident marked a new low in relations between the British Conservative government and the rest of the EU. Patience was already exhausted before Major threatened to block agreement on a new Treaty unless two changes were made to the existing one. First, he demanded agreement to allow the reversal of a decision of the Court of Justice that a directive on a forty-eight-hour maximum working week must apply to Britain, despite the British government's opt-out from the social protocol, because it was a health-and-safety issue and so covered by the SEA. Second, he demanded that changes were made to the Common Fisheries Policy, to prevent fishing boats from other member states buying quotas from British fishermen.

There were some indications that the IGC was deliberately prolonged into 1997 in the hope that the British general election would produce a change of government, which it did. The Labour government under Tony Blair indicated immediately that, while its priorities would remain largely those of its predecessor, it would not block a Treaty over any issue other than that Britain must be allowed to retain its border controls. The way was thus cleared for agreement on the text of a new Treaty at the European Council in Amsterdam in June 1997.

The Treaty of Amsterdam

Agreement was reached at Amsterdam on a rather modest Treaty. In particular, no agreement could be reached on the institutional reforms that were believed to be essential to pave the way for enlargement. Also, there was little extension of QMV because Chancellor Kohl retreated from his earlier advocacy of the principle, and actually blocked its extension to cover industrial policy, social policy, and certain aspects of the free movement of labour.

As a result of what may have been an oversight, the failure to extend QMV to these three areas did not lead to withdrawal of the linked proposal to increase the powers of the EP in the same areas. So, when the EP was given the right to amend or reject proposed legislation in two dozen areas that were brought under co-decision for the first time, these areas were still included.

Dutch plans to extend QMV into eleven policy areas, ranging from cultural activities to industrial policy, ran into German resistance. Kohl insisted that these extensions would undermine the position of the German Länder. The only two extensions of

167

QMV that were agreed were for research programmes and compensatory aid for imports of raw materials. In addition, new areas were agreed in which QMV would apply from the start; namely, countering fraud, encouraging customs co-operation, collating statistics, and laying down rules for the free movement of personal data.

On the number of Commissioners, a compromise was reached that if more than two and fewer than six new members joined the EU, the Commission would continue to have one representative from each member state. However, Spain insisted that it would only surrender its second Commissioner in return for changes in the weighting of votes in the Council, which could not be agreed.

Rules on allowing flexible integration were agreed. In the first (EC) pillar, if a group of member states wanted to proceed with closer integration in a sector, but others did not, those who wanted to go ahead could do so provided that the Council of Ministers agreed to such a proposal by QMV. However, if any member state insisted that the development would jeopardize its vital national interests, it could veto the move.

In the second (CFSP) pillar, the system would be 'constructive abstention'. This would allow a group of member states to undertake a joint action in the name of the EU, if those member states that did not feel they could take part were prepared not to vote against but to abstain, on the understanding that they would not then be required to contribute to the action (see Chapter 25, 'The Common Foreign and Security Policy (CFSP) and Common Security and Defence Policy (CSDP)').

In the third (JHA) pillar, complete freedom of movement was pledged for all individuals within the EU, but the UK and Ireland were allowed to retain border controls. Decisions on immigration, visas, and asylum were to be subject to unanimity for at least five years, and then reviewed, with a view to introducing more flexible arrangements, but with any member state being allowed to apply a veto on changing the procedure.

On CFSP, it was agreed that the Council Secretary General would represent the EU to the outside world. Qualified majority voting would be used on implementing foreign policy measures, but any state that believed its vital national interests were at stake could exercise a veto. The WEU might be incorporated into the EU in the future, but the North Atlantic Treaty Organization (NATO) was reaffirmed as central to Europe's defence. The Amsterdam Treaty also amended the TEU to distinguish between, on the one hand, deciding the principles and general guidelines of the CFSP, and common strategies in pursuit of these, and, on the other, the adoption of joint actions, common positions, and implementing decisions.

Finally, it was agreed that a zone of freedom, security, and justice for EU citizens would come into force within five years of ratification. This was the big policy idea of the Amsterdam Treaty and 'communitarized' some of the EU's JHA policies (see Chapter 23, 'History').

CONCLUSION

Where Chapter 8 told a story of movement from a relatively low point in European integration to a new high point with the SEA, this chapter tells a reverse story. The period started from the new high point reached at the end of the 1980s, but finished with the new EU in something of a crisis once again.

With the very important exception of the agreement on monetary union, the TEU was predominantly an intergovernmental Treaty. Its most significant innovations were the second and third pillars, both of which were intergovernmental in nature. In part, the problems that it was designed to solve were a consequence of spillover from the SEA: for example, pressures to develop more systematic ways of dealing with effects of greater flows of people across borders caused by the single market programme. In part, though, the problems arose from the international context within which the member states were operating, which is why the CFSP was so central to the TEU.

Enlargement of the EU to the states of central and eastern Europe, which was the biggest item on the post-Maastricht agenda, also received its impetus from the changing international context. The collapse of the Soviet Union posed the threat of instability in the former communist states of Europe. As with the EC and the Mediterranean enlargements in the 1970s, eastern enlargement in the forthcoming twenty-first century was part of the enhanced security role for the EU in the world after the decline of US hegemony.

A definite tension developed, though, between the will of all EU member states to consolidate democracy and capitalism in eastern and central Europe and the willingness of any particular member state to accept economic sacrifices to allow that enlargement to happen. Willing the end did not appear to mean necessarily willing the means. Domestic politics often assumed priority when it came to agreeing the details of reforms to the common policies and to the central institutions that everyone agreed were necessary to facilitate the enlargement.

Concern to prevent further slippage of powers from the national or subnational level to the supranational level was apparent throughout the EU by the time of Amsterdam, indicating an increasing emphasis on intergovernmentalism. There were the first indications that a new form of co-operation was emerging, one that cast the Commission in a different role as an impartial arbiter and referee of agreements for co-ordinated national action rather than as enforcer of legally binding commitments, a development that would also have implications for the role of the European Court of Justice.

Yet, despite the intergovernmental emphasis of the new Treaties, developments after Maastricht illustrate a theme that had been largely neglected by governments and analysts until then: the importance of legitimacy for the process of European integration. In a majority of member states, the EC had an independent legitimacy of its own because it represented European integration, which was perceived as a 'good thing'. The aftermath of Maastricht raised questions about whether this was still the case, questions that would become more urgent in the light of subsequent developments, as explained in the following chapters.

KEY POINTS

Towards Maastricht

- In June 1989, the European Council agreed to Delors's three-stage plan for monetary union by 1999, despite British opposition.
- The collapse of communism in central and eastern Europe and the prospect of a reunified Germany focused minds on the political aspects of European integration.
- In 1991, IGCs were held on both monetary union and political union. The proposals of these IGCs were incorporated into the TEU, agreed at Maastricht in December 1991.

The Treaty on European Union

- The TEU marked a major step on the road to European integration. It committed most of the member states to adopting a single currency, extended EC competence in a range of areas, strengthened the powers of the EP, created a Committee of the Regions, and introduced the concept of European citizenship.

- The Treaty created a three-pillar structure known as the EU, consisting of the EC pillar and the intergovernmental pillars of the CFSP and JHA.

After Maastricht

- The decision to move to a single currency caused concern within member states, not least Germany, which had a strong attachment to the Deutschmark.
- The TEU was rejected by a majority of the Danish people in a referendum in 1992, and was only accepted in 1993, following major concessions. A referendum in France (1992) was only narrowly in favour.
- By the time Austria, Finland, and Sweden became members in 1995, the EU was not the confident one they had applied to join.

The Commission after Maastricht

- The Commission became caught up in the wave of unpopularity affecting the EU. Delors's high-profile presidency ensured that he was the focal point of much of the criticism.

Political Change

- Significant domestic political developments during this period affected the position of key member states on the EU and shaped the prospects for flexible integration.
- In 1995, Delors was succeeded by Jacques Santer as president of the Commission.

Monetary Union

- In 1995, details of monetary union began to emerge. The ECB would be located in Frankfurt and the single currency would be called the 'euro'.
- In 1999, the euro came into operation in eleven member states, although national currencies continued in circulation until 2002.

Enlargement

- While member states were generally supportive of further enlargement to include countries of central and eastern Europe, there were a number of concerns over the impact this would have on key policies, and on decision making procedures.

The 1996 IGC

- The 1996 IGC focused on the institutional changes necessary to prepare for further enlargement. This IGC was also marked by conflict over the British 'beef' crisis, which resulted in the Major government blocking agreement on a range of issues.

The Treaty of Amsterdam

- Resulting from the 1996 IGC, this Treaty was relatively modest in scope. In particular, it did not contain the decision making reforms most thought necessary for incorporating several new member states.

 For additional material and resources, please visit the online resources www.oup.com/uk/bache5e.

FURTHER READING

The negotiation of the Maastricht Treaty is analysed by **M. Baun**, 'The Maastricht Treaty as High Politics: Germany, France and European Integration', *Political Science Quarterly*, 110 (1996): 605–24, and **A. Moravcsik**, *The Choice for Europe: Social Purpose and State Power from Messina to Maastricht* (London: UCL Press, 1998), 379–471. Also see **M. Baun**, *An Imperfect Union: The Maastricht Treaty and the New Politics of European Integration* (Boulder, CO: Westview, 1996).

The aftermath of the signing of the Treaty is analysed in: **B. Criddle**, 'The French Referendum on the Maastricht Treaty, September 1992', *Parliamentary Affairs*, 46 (1993) 228–38; **D. Baker**, **A. Gamble, and S. Ludlam**, '1846–1906–1996? Conservative Splits and European Integration', *Political Quarterly*, 64 (1993): 420–34, and 'The Parliamentary Siege of Maastricht 1993: Conservative Divisions and British Ratification of the Treaty of European Union', *Parliamentary Affairs*, 47 (1994): 37–60; **H. Rattinger**, 'Public Attitudes towards European Integration in Germany and Maastricht: Inventory and Typology', *Journal of Common Market Studies*, 32 (1994): 525–40.

On the politics that led up to the Amsterdam Treaty, see **G. Edwards and A. Pijpers**, *The Politics of European Treaty Reform: The 1996 Intergovernmental Conference and Beyond* (London, and Washington, DC: Pinter, 1997). Useful guides to the Treaty are **European Commission**, *The Amsterdam Treaty: A Comprehensive Guide* (Brussels and Luxembourg: European Communities, 1999) and **A. Duff**, *The Treaty of Amsterdam: Text and Commentary* (London: Federal Trust/Sweet and Maxwell, 1997).

A reaction to Amsterdam from an intergovernmentalist perspective is given in **A. Moravcsik and K. Nicolaïdis**, 'Explaining the Treaty of Amsterdam: Interests, Influences, Institutions', *Journal of Common Market Studies*, 37 (1999): 59–85. Other analyses are offered by **E. Philippart and G. Edwards**, 'The Provisions on Closer Co-operation in the Treaty of Amsterdam', *Journal of Common Market Studies*, 37 (1999): 87–108, and **Y. Devuyst**, 'The Community-Method after Amsterdam', *Journal of Common Market Studies*, 37 (1999): 109–20.

For access to various primary sources, the website www.cvce.eu/en is very useful.

Chapter 10

From Amsterdam to Lisbon (2000–09)

Chapter Overview

The same themes as emerged in Chapter 9 continued to dominate the European Union (EU) throughout the first decade of the new century. Enlargement became the main issue, driving forward repeated reforms of the Treaties, and national electorates showed themselves increasingly discontented with the pace of change and their sense that they were being taken for granted by the political elites.

Far from the Amsterdam Treaty marking the end of a phase of institutional and constitutional revision in the EU, it had scarcely entered into force before further Treaty reform was on the agenda. Throughout the year 2000, a new intergovernmental conference (IGC) met to discuss outstanding institutional issues that had not been settled at Amsterdam. It concluded in December 2000 with the longest European Council in history, which led to the Treaty of Nice. That was followed by the setting up of a Constitutional Convention at the end of 2001, which produced a blueprint for a Constitutional Treaty in 2003 that was signed in October 2004. The Constitutional Treaty was intended to replace the existing Treaties, but it was rejected in key national referendums in the course of 2005, precipitating a crisis within the EU that was papered over rather than resolved by the adoption of a less far-reaching Treaty at Lisbon at the end of 2009. This appears to be a story of growing problems for the further extension of European integration, but in between the Treaty episodes, progress was made in some important areas of common policy.

The Nice Treaty

The Treaty of Amsterdam made institutional reform a precondition of enlargement and contained a protocol anticipating further discussions on reform. The Cologne European Council of 1999 referred to this protocol in agreeing to set up an IGC to discuss the outstanding institutional issues that had not been resolved at Amsterdam, particularly in relation to the weighting of votes in the Council, the size and composition of the Commission, and the possible extension of qualified majority voting (QMV).

The IGC opened in February 2000, under the Portuguese presidency, and continued into the French presidency in the second half of the year, but there were major disagreements on all of the outstanding issues identified above, and these had not been resolved by the time the heads of government met at Nice at the end of 2000 to try to agree the final text of the new Treaty.

Nice turned out to be the longest European Council in the history of the European Community (EC)/EU. For four days, the heads of government haggled over the areas that would become subject to QMV, and over the weighting of votes. Membership of the Commission proved less difficult, although really tough decisions were deferred by allowing the size of the College of Commissioners to grow to twenty-seven before there would be a move to having fewer than one commissioner per member state; but in return for giving up their second commissioner the large member states fought even harder on the weighting of votes in the Council. In the end, an agreement was reached that just about opened up the prospect of the EU being ready for enlargement. The Treaty strengthened the powers of the President of the Commission and provided for one commissioner per member state from 2005, with the proviso that the maximum number in future should be twenty-six, and from that point onwards a rotation system would ensure parity among states. In relation to the European Parliament (EP), the Treaty extended the co-decision procedure and also changed the allocation of seats between states and set a maximum of 732 Members of the European Parliament (MEPs) (a number that would increase again: see Chapter 15, 'Composition and Functions').

The veto was removed from twenty-nine of the seventy Treaty articles where it still applied, but in important areas national interests prevented movement. Britain would not agree to the removal of the veto on tax or social security harmonization. Although QMV for trade negotiations was extended to services, exceptions were made at French insistence for audio-visual services, education, and health. Maritime transport was exempted from QMV at the insistence of Denmark and Greece. At German and French insistence, many aspects of immigration and asylum policy were not trans-ferred to QMV. Perhaps most significantly, though, Spain, with the support of Portugal and Greece, retained the right to veto changes to the cohesion funds until after the conclusion of the negotiations on the 2007–12 Financial Perspective. This cast further doubt on the possibility of keeping the cost of enlargement to the com-mon budget within limits acceptable to the net contributors.

On the weighting of votes under QMV, the large member states seemed to gain an advantage over the small. The re-weighting, which would apply from 1 January 2005, left the small and medium-sized states with a smaller percentage of the total vote relative to the larger states than under the previous system. There was also the insertion of a clause requir-ing any measure agreed by QMV to comprise the votes of governments representing at least 62 per cent of the population of the EU. The effect was to put Germany, France, and Britain—or any two of these three plus Italy—in a position where they could effectively block progress on any measure on which they agreed to co-operate. In compensation, the small states were allowed a clause that a measure agreed under QMV would also have to have the support of a majority of the member states. The cumulative effect of these two concessions to different coalitions of 'bigs' and 'smalls' was to make the decision making system much more complex, and also to make it more difficult than previously to achieve a qualified majority, which now required a 'triple majority'—a majority of weighted votes, a majority of member states, and a 62 per cent or higher majority of the population (on cur-rent QMV rules and weightings see Chapter 12, 'The Council of the EU (the Council)').

The Treaty of Nice was formally signed in the following February, following eleven months of negotiation. Existing concerns over the low level of public support for the

EU were raised further when the Irish people rejected the Treaty by a vote of 53.87 per cent to 46.13 per cent in a referendum in June 2001, with a turn out of only 32.9 per cent. Although this decision was reversed in a second referendum in October 2001, and the Treaty of Nice entered into force in February 2003, the Irish episode reflected the serious challenges facing the EU on the road to further deepening and widening.

The Lisbon Strategy

In March 2000, a special European Council held in Lisbon agreed to a new EU strategy on employment, economic reform, and social cohesion, with the goal of making the EU 'the most competitive and dynamic knowledge-based economy in the world' by 2010. Its adoption was justified with reference to the challenge of globalization:

> The European Union is confronted with a quantum shift resulting from globalization and the challenges of a new knowledge-driven economy. These challenges are affecting every aspect of people's lives and require a radical transformation of the European economy.

(Presidential Conclusions, Lisbon Special European Council, 23–24 March, para. 1)

The outcome subsequently became known variously as the Lisbon Strategy, the Lisbon Process, or the Lisbon Agenda. Success of the Strategy depended on strengthening investment in research and development, reducing bureaucracy to stimulate innovation and entrepreneurship, and improving the employment rate to 70 per cent overall, including a minimum of 60 per cent for women.

Two features of the Strategy were particularly significant. First, economic competitiveness and social cohesion were placed side by side as objectives. Critics of the Strategy from the left maintained that the economic competitiveness elements represented a victory for the advocates of an Anglo-Saxon model of capitalism, while critics from the right argued that the social cohesion elements represented a victory for the advocates of a 'social Europe'. It seems more likely that the new approach represented less the victory of one model of capitalism over the other than a political compromise between the positions of the left and right.

Second, the Lisbon Strategy was to be pursued through what the Presidency Conclusions to the summit described as the 'Open Method of Co-ordination' (OMC) (for more detail see Chapter 18, 'The European Union's Policy Agenda'). Its main features, as delineated at Lisbon, were common guidelines to be translated into national policies, combined with periodic monitoring, evaluation, and peer review organized as mutual learning processes and accompanied by indicators and benchmarks as means of comparing best practice. In essence, this was an extension of the approach already adopted 'in the procedures for co-ordinating national economic policies under the EMU established in the Maastricht Treaty, and in the employment chapter of the Amsterdam Treaty' (Borras and Jacobsson 2004: 187–8). As such, it was a departure from the 'community method' of decision making, whereby the Commission makes proposals for legislation and the Council of Ministers (increasingly in conjunction with the EP) adopts the legislation, which then supersedes national legislation. Most significantly, it was a departure in the direction of a more intergovernmental process, where policy competence would not be transferred to the EU, but would be retained at the national level, the Commission would play a less prominent role as the facilitator of intergovernmental co-ordination, and the EP and European Court of Justice would have no real role at all (see Chapter 2, 'New Intergovernmentalism'). To strengthen this impression of firm national control over the process, it was agreed that one European Council out of three each year—the spring meeting—would be devoted to reviewing progress.

In March 2004, the European Council appointed the former Dutch Prime Minister, Wim Kok, to convene a committee of experts who would carry out a mid-term review of progress towards the commitment made in Lisbon. The Kok report, *Facing the Challenge*, was presented to the European Commission on 3 November 2004, and to the European Council the following day. It confirmed what everyone knew already: that delivery on the process of reform had been 'disappointing'.

Although it was already too late to meet some of the targets that had been set for 2010, the report argued that the date should not be abandoned, as there was a need to instil a sense of urgency into the process, and the embarrassment of reaching 2010 with results that were so bad that Lisbon would become 'a synonym for missed objectives and failed promises' might impart some momentum.

Beyond that, the report pointed to the need to focus on core objectives and to allocate responsibilities more precisely. So long as the Lisbon Agenda remained so broad, it ran the risk of being about everything, and therefore about nothing. The number of key indicators should be reduced from over 100 to just fourteen; and the emphasis should be placed clearly on growth and employment, because they were essential to underpin the social and environmental objectives. While the governments of the member states had to accept the main responsibility for the relative failure to date, the Commission ought to be made the unambiguous co-ordinator of the process. It needed to be prepared to name and shame those member states that were simply not doing enough. To be able to do this without fear, it needed to monitor the process closely, and the report recommended that the next President of the Commission should make driving the Lisbon Agenda forward the main mandate for his period in office.

European Security and Defence Policy

Up to September 2001, steady progress was being made on security and defence policy. The smooth progress ran into choppy waters, though, following the terrorist attacks in the United States on 11 September of that year (see also Chapter 23, 'History', on the implications for EU co-operation on internal security matters; and Chapter 25, 'CFSP and CSDP in Action', on external security and defence).

The initial response from the EU was to declare solidarity with the United States, and this support was maintained during the subsequent US campaign in Afghanistan to unseat the Taliban government, which had harboured and supported the Al-Qaeda terrorists. Nevertheless, the effect of the united EU response was somewhat spoiled by Britain, France, and Germany trying to act independently of the EU as a whole. In October 2001, their respective leaders—Blair, Chirac, and Schröder—met outside of the EU forum to discuss their responses to 'September 11', and intended to do so again in London in early November. However, on the second occasion vigorous protests by other member states led to the invitation to participate being thrown open to other states and to the EU High Representative, Javier Solana (see Chapter 25, 'CFSP and CSDP in Action').

The most serious problems for the EU resulted from the determination of the Bush Administration to make Iraq the next target after Afghanistan. There was no evidence that the secular Ba'ath regime of Saddam Hussein supported Islamic terrorism, or had any involvement in the September terrorist attacks. Similarly, there was no more than circumstantial evidence, which subsequently proved to be totally inaccurate, that Iraq possessed weapons of mass destruction with which it could attack the United States or its allies. In the build-up to the eventual invasion of Iraq, the EU split over how to react to the US initiative.

In January 2003, in response to French and German statements implying that the EU was opposed to the US attitude towards Iraq, eight European states signed a letter indicating their support for the United States. Five of the eight were existing members of the EU—Britain, Denmark, Italy, Portugal, and Spain—while the other three were prospective members—the Czech Republic, Hungary, and Poland. Then ten former communist states, seven of them EU applicants, jointly expressed their support for the US position in February, which infuriated the French government. President Chirac publicly rebuked the ten, saying that they had shown bad manners, and had 'missed a good opportunity to keep quiet'. He pointedly went on to remind the prospective members who had already negotiated entry that the decision to admit them to the EU on 1 May 2004 had yet to be ratified by national parliaments; and he indicated that Bulgaria and Romania, who were still in the early stages of negotiating membership, had been particularly foolish to associate themselves with the statement.

In March 2003, France publicly declared that it would veto any resolution in support of military action against Iraq that might be presented by the United States and Britain to the United Nations Security Council. This caused a serious division between the two member states that had been in the forefront of efforts to create the European Security and Defence Policy (ESDP). On 18 March, Tony Blair made a strong attack in the House of Commons on the French position.

Following the invasion of Iraq in March 2003, Franco–British relations were at a very low ebb, and the prospects for an ESDP looked poor. Yet, by the end of the year there were signs of improvement, particularly following Blair's agreement in principle that the EU should have the joint planning capacity to conduct operations without the involvement of NATO, a concession that appeared to alarm the United States. So, the signs were that the British wanted to facilitate the relaunch of the ESDP.

The Constitutional Treaty

In December 2001, the heads of government, meeting in Laeken (Belgium), agreed to move beyond the modest institutional changes agreed in the Nice Treaty. The adoption of the *Declaration on the Future of the European Union* committed the EU to transforming its decision making procedures to make them more democratic and transparent and to prepare the ground for a European Constitution. The vehicle for moving forward reform was a Constitutional Convention, which brought together representatives of national governments and parliaments from both the member and accession states with representatives of the EU institutions (see Insight 10.1), and which was chaired by the former French President, Valéry Giscard d'Estaing. It would be a unique forum in both its role and composition, designed to secure legitimacy for the reforms by incorporating the views of a broad range of actors. In addition to the formal members of the Convention and observers, various business representatives, non-governmental organizations, academics, and other interested parties would be consulted on specific topics. The Convention's Chair would report on progress at each European Council meeting and receive the views of the heads of government, and the Convention's final report would provide the starting point for discussions and decisions at an IGC scheduled for 2004.

The proposals of the Convention for a Constitution for Europe were submitted by Giscard d'Estaing to the Thessaloniki European Council in June 2003. There followed a formal IGC, at which some of the proposals were amended, but the Treaty establishing a Constitution for Europe was signed by the heads of government and the EU Foreign Ministers in October 2004. Once ratified within member states, it would replace the existing Treaties.

The Treaty that was agreed had implications for the founding principles of the EU, the institutions, the decision making process, and its policies. It also specified for the first time the areas that would be the exclusive competence of the EU, and those areas that would be shared between the EU and the member states. Both of these were long-standing federalist demands, although national governments had become increasingly

---

Insight 10.1 Composition of the Constitutional Convention

In addition to its Chairman (Valéry Giscard d'Estaing) and two Vice-Chairmen (Giuliano Amato and Jean-Luc Dehaene), the Convention comprised:

- fifteen representatives of the heads of state or government of the member states (one from each member state);
- thirteen representatives of the heads of state or government of the candidate states (one per candidate state);
- thirty representatives of the national parliaments of the member states (two from each member state);
- twenty-six representatives of the national parliaments of the candidate states (two from each candidate state);
- sixteen members of the EP;
- two representatives of the European Commission.

There were alternates for each full member.

Observers were invited to attend from the Economic and Social Committee (three representatives), the Committee of the Regions (six representatives), the social partners (three representatives), and the European Ombudsman.

The Laeken Declaration provided for the candidate states to take a full part in the proceedings without, however, being able to prevent any consensus emerging among the member states.

Source: http://european-convention.europa.eu.

aware of the possible protection that a clear demarcation of spheres of competence would offer against the creeping extension of competence that had sometimes occurred as a result of the Commission's **policy entrepreneurship**.

At the time, there was divergent opinion on the significance of the Treaty. On content, some viewed it as a little more than a 'Nice II' or a 'tidying-up' exercise that mainly brought together existing rules and agreements into a single, more comprehensible Treaty. More sceptical observers viewed it as a major step away from the sovereignty of nation states and towards the creation of a European super-state.

As with the earlier Treaties, the Constitutional Treaty had to be ratified by the member states before entering into force. Some states chose to ratify through parliament, others by referendum. The ratification process was expected to last for two years and the Constitution expected to come into force on 1 November 2006, but in May 2005 the French referendum returned a 55 per cent vote against. This was followed shortly afterwards by a negative vote in the Netherlands of almost 62 per cent.

The French vote almost certainly let the British government of Tony Blair off the hook, faced as it had been with holding a referendum that most commentators believed it could not win. Although there had been a clear prior agreement by the heads of government that *all* member states would attempt to ratify the Treaty before the position was re-assessed, the British government maintained that there was no point in it proceeding to a referendum after the French and Dutch 'No' votes, and unilaterally announced an indefinite postponement.

Enlargement

In October 2002, the Commission declared that the applicant states—Cyprus, the Czech Republic, Estonia, Hungary, Latvia, Lithuania, Malta, Poland, the Slovak Republic, and Slovenia—were in a position to conclude negotiations successfully by the end of that year and would be ready for membership in 2004. In April 2003, the EP gave its assent to the accession of these states. On 1 May 2004, the EU's biggest enlargement brought in ten new member states and over 100 million more citizens, taking the size of the Union to twenty-five states and increasing its population by 75 million to 450 million.

Two applications from central and east European countries remained outstanding in 2004: Bulgaria and Romania, neither of which was deemed ready for membership. However, both states joined in 2007.

Negotiations opened with Croatia in 2004, and an application was accepted from the Former Yugoslav Republic of Macedonia (FYROM, now North Macedonia—see Chapter 26, 'Further Applications'). Other Yugoslav successor states were expected to apply, and several Soviet successor states expressed an interest in joining, but were ruled out by the EU (see Chapter 26, 'History'). However, the major outstanding issue at this stage was the question of Turkey.

Turkey had had an association agreement envisaging membership since 1963. It was excluded from the enlargement process in 1997, largely through opposition from Greece and Germany. However, it was offered the prospect of future negotiations in 1999 following a change of government in Germany in 1998 and a dramatic improvement in Greek–Turkish relations in 1999. Further, a decision by the EU in 1999 to allow states to negotiate entry at their own pace made it easier to open negotiations with Turkey, and more difficult not to do so. A change of government in Turkey in 2002 produced rapid progress to meeting the Copenhagen criteria. Moreover, the international climate meant that geo-strategic factors were increasingly in Turkey's favour, although opposition to its accession remained strong in some states in 2004, particularly in France (see Chapter 26, 'Turkey').

The European Parliament and the New Commission

In June 2004, in the run-up to the national votes on ratification of the Constitutional Treaty, there were elections to the EP. The date for the enlargement had been set to allow the new member states to take part in the elections. This in turn was the first stage in a new constitutional timetable, which had applied for the first time in 1995, whereby the election of the new EP was followed by the nomination of the new Commission. There was hope among EU leaders that the publicity that enlargement had generated would result in an increased turn out for the elections in June 2004. In fact, turn out, which had fallen in every election since 1979, declined further to a record low of 45.7 per cent. As noted above, in the new member states it was much lower. It was unclear at this stage what conclusions should be drawn from this. Pat Cox, the President of the EP, expressed the view that the low turn outs in the new member states reflected the fact that the citizens felt they had already shown their support for the EU in the referendums on accession in 2003.

In line with the new constitutional timetable, the EP elections were followed by the nomination of the new Commission. In June 2004, the European Council nominated Portuguese Prime Minister José Manuel Durao Barroso as the next Commission President. The conservative Barroso was appointed after some dispute within the Council over Romano Prodi's successor. The French and German governments had sought to install the Belgian Prime Minister Guy Verhofstadt, while Britain had backed Barroso. In the end, Barroso's appointment was not only seen as a compromise between federalists and Atlanticists, but also reassured the concerns of smaller states. It was also in line with the expectation of the EP that the nominee would be drawn from the same political 'family' as the majority that had been returned in the elections. This, combined with Barroso's competent and convincing manner in his own confirmation hearing before the EP, resulted in a comfortable majority in favour of his nomination, but the MEPs were highly critical of some of the other nominations and of Barroso's allocation of portfolios to individuals, resulting in the withdrawal of one nominee and some reallocation of responsibilities.

The Lisbon Treaty

In the wake of the French and Dutch votes, the European Council of June 2005 called for a period of reflection. The passage of time would allow for the depoliticization of some of the more sensitive issues raised in the referendum campaigns and held the prospect of a change of government in some key states, France and the Netherlands in particular (Christiansen 2010: 24).

For a while, the Treaty fell from public view. Indeed, at one point, Commission President Barroso declared that the Treaty would not come back for several years (Church and Phinnemore 2010: 61). However, in June 2006, the European Council asked the incoming German presidency to present a report on how to end the constitutional impasse.

In short, the task facing the German presidency was one of reconciling the demands of the maximalist eighteen states who had ratified the Constitutional Treaty and wanted to retain as much of it as possible, with those of the minimalists, who wanted simply to amend the EU's rules (Dedman 2010: 176). EU leaders meeting in Berlin in March 2007 used the opportunity of the fiftieth anniversary of the Treaties of Rome to emphasize the symbolic aspects of European integration in a less controversial manner—the non-binding Berlin Declaration on the Union's aims and values—while also calling for a new Treaty to be in place by 2009. A new IGC was called for the summer of that year.

Reflection brought the conclusion that what was needed was separation of the more controversial symbolic (constitutional) aspects of the Treaty from the practical requirements of institutional reform. In January 2007, the new German presidency announced plans to revive the Constitution and began a series of bilateral and multilateral meetings with national leaders to discuss ways forward. The tone of domestic politics revealed in these meetings signalled to the German negotiators that the EU needed to step back from its initial ambitions (Carbone 2010: 222).

On 19 June, the German presidency presented its 'draft mandate'. It proposed that instead of consolidating and replacing the existing Treaties—the Treaty on European Union (TEU) and the Treaty establishing the European Community (TEC)—these should be amended to incorporate most of the provisions of the Constitutional Treaty. However, the more controversial aspects of the Constitutional Treaty would be dropped: the term 'constitution', an article referring to symbols of the Union (including the EU anthem and flag) and references to an 'EU Minister' for foreign affairs. The EU's legal instruments would remain as regulations, directives, and decisions and not be replaced by the terms 'law' and 'framework law'. In short, the text would be 'changed significantly in order to remove the kind of language that could be seen as an indication of statist aspirations' (Christiansen 2010: 25–6).

The mandate for the IGC to finalize a 'reform treaty' was soon agreed by the European Council and subsequently by the EP, the Commission, and the European Central Bank (ECB). The IGC was launched on 23 July 2007, and negotiations over the content of the new Treaty continued into the autumn. Sticking points included the Polish government's position over various institutional changes (in particular relating to blocking minorities in the Council of Ministers) and UK and Irish opt-outs in justice and home affairs (JHA). The text of the new Treaty was finally agreed in Lisbon in October 2007 and signed by heads of state and government in the same city in December. While some of the more controversial aspects of the Constitutional Treaty were removed, the vast majority of its provisions were retained in the Lisbon Treaty. Over sixty revisions were made to the TEU and nearly 300 changes were made to the TEC (or Treaty on the Functioning of the European Union (TFEU) as it would be renamed). The terms of the Treaty are reviewed in detail in Chapter 12, 'The Treaties'. Dedman (2010: 177) commented that:

> Lisbon contained 95 per cent of what was in the Constitutional Treaty as its Chief Architect, Valéry Giscard d'Estaing was keen to announce in successive interviews, undermining governments' cases against referendums that they had originally promised but now insisted were not necessary.

Ultimately though, re-badging the Treaty as a more technical 'reform treaty' allowed a number of governments—such as France, the Netherlands, and the UK—to avoid ratification via referendum (Sedelmeier and Young 2008: 2). Only Ireland was committed to a popular vote.

Despite the revisions that the Treaty contained, on 12 June 2008 the Irish people rejected it with a vote of 53.4 per cent against (from a turn out of 53.1 per cent). The vote shook EU leaders, while giving succour to those who had viewed the revised Treaty as simply a cynical attempt to repackage a Treaty once rejected. As Copsey and Haughton (2009: 2) noted:

> The very fact that Ireland was the only Member State to ask its citizens to pass judgement on the treaty only fuelled the fires of critics of the EU such as Czech President Vaclav Klaus, for example, who could not contain his glee when the result was announced, claiming he could write a better treaty from his hospital bed.

Opinions varied on the reasons for the vote against. Those disappointed by the outcome spoke of misinformation being spread about the purposes of the Treaty in relation to issues such as abortion, euthanasia, and defence policy. Domestic politics also played a role, not least the unpopularity of Irish Prime Minister Bertie Ahern, who was in favour of a 'Yes' vote. There was also wide recognition that the 'Yes' campaign had been lacklustre. The Irish people were clearly not persuaded of the case for the Treaty, despite the fact that the EU remained broadly popular in Ireland: a Eurobarometer poll taken soon after the referendum showed that 87 per cent of Irish people thought Ireland benefited from EU membership, a higher percentage than for any other state (Dedman 2010: 178).

Despite the Irish vote, and the soul searching this caused, EU leaders urged other member states to continue with the ratification process: eighteen had already done so and these were joined by another five by the end of 2008. The four countries that had not ratified by this point were Ireland, the Czech Republic, Germany, and Poland.

At the European Council of December 2008, Ireland was given reassurances in relation to areas of concern raised in the referendum campaign, including taxation policy, family and social issues, and foreign policy. In exchange, the Irish government agreed to hold a new referendum by the end of 2009 (Carbone 2010: 224–5). The European Council also reversed its decision on reducing the number of Commissioners, so that all states retained one each. While some claimed this had been an issue in the Irish referendum—not least the Irish Commissioner Charlie McCreevy and former Commissioner Ray MacSharry—there was general recognition among EU leaders that this move was neither necessary nor desirable, particularly for smaller states.

That there were not referendums in other member states did not mean the absence of controversy. In Germany, the Federal Constitutional Court had been asked to rule on the compatibility of the Lisbon Treaty with the German constitution (the Basic Law). Its 2009 judgment ruled that the Treaty was compatible, but placed domestic conditions on further transfers of power, conditions that have been interpreted as likely to contribute to a decline in Germany's support for integration in the future (Bulmer and Paterson 2010). The presidents of both the Czech Republic and Poland refused to sign the ratification instruments and there were splits between political elites in a number of member states.

However, the fate of the Treaty ultimately rested on a positive vote in the second Irish referendum. That this was secured in October 2009 with a clear majority in favour (67.13 per cent of a 59 per cent turn out) was largely explained by deteriorating economic circumstances, although this time the 'Yes' campaign was far more effective and the negative consequences for Ireland of a 'No' vote emphasized more (van der Veen 2010). The second Irish referendum cleared the way for the Treaty to come into effect on 1 December 2009.

CONCLUSION

Why did national governments keep proposing reforms to the Treaties when national electorates were so reluctant to accept them? And why did national electorates reject the proposals?

One of the main reasons for the repeated efforts to revise the Treaties was enlargement (see Chapter 26). Arrangements that had worked tolerably well for fifteen member states were less viable for twenty-seven or more. At the same time, the new members were predominantly medium-sized states, and the straight application of the existing rules on voting and allocation of seats in the central institutions would have significantly reduced the influence of the larger member states.

Intergovernmental bargaining made it difficult to get agreements on new arrangements that would suit everyone, which is why the first attempts to resolve the problems resulted in inadequate solutions in the Amsterdam and Nice Treaties.

There was also growing concern during the late 1990s and into the 2000s about the inability of the EU states to act in concert in matters of external security and defence. The inability of the European states to take effective concerted action in response to the tragedy in former Yugoslavia in the late 1990s (see Chapter 25, 'History') was compounded by the new sense of urgency to ensure security co-operation in the wake of the terrorist attacks on the United States in September 2001 (Chapter 25, 'CFSP and CSDP in Action').

Enlargement was also one of the factors in the rejection of the proposals by national electorates. Enlargement caused concern in existing member states about the dilution of the benefits that they derived from the budget of the EU, and following the successful admission of the new member states in 2004 there was growing concern about the employment implications of the free movement of workers from the new east European member states to the older member states. Although nearly all of the older member states had imposed restrictions in the short term on free movement, these controls were limited to a maximum of five years, or seven if it could be proved that the free movement would seriously disrupt the economies of the old member states. The concerns for the future were compounded by the effects of the monetary union, which led to a weakening of economic performance in some participant states.

Our primary analytical theme here is that of legitimacy—a recurring theme since the Maastricht Treaty (see Chapter 9, 'Conclusion' and Chapter 3, 'Democracy and Legitimacy'). Scholars have identified a gap between elites and public opinion in relation to integration, and domestic political audiences have become more difficult to ignore.

The decision to create a Constitutional Convention to make proposals for a Constitutional Treaty was in part a response to existing concerns over the EU's legitimacy and the Convention model itself was seen as a step in the direction of more open and inclusive decision making at the EU level. However, the operation of the Convention was subject to contrasting interpretations. Intergovernmentalists emphasized the dominance of national governments and the hard-bargaining approach to negotiations, while others emphasized the supranational dimension and a process characterized largely by problem-solving rationality (see Chapter 2, 'Rational Choice Institutionalism'), rather than bargaining.

The draft Treaty that emerged was viewed differently in different member states. For example, the right in Britain saw the Treaty as a major step towards a federal Europe and the loss of national sovereignty. By contrast, many on the left in France saw the Treaty as dominated by the Anglo-Saxon model of capitalism and a threat to French models of social welfare. The Constitutional Treaty was in large part an attempt to bring the EU closer to its citizens, but it was seen to have the opposite effect. At the same time, it did galvanize a widespread public debate on the EU in those states where a referendum took place.

The EU's action in re-packaging many of the proposals from the rejected Constitutional Treaty in the Lisbon Treaty, and then pushing it through as a 'reform treaty' without a popular vote in any of the member states except Ireland, was viewed as high-handed elitism by those who had voted against the earlier Treaty. The demand of the EU for a second referendum in Ireland was also viewed with cynicism in many quarters. Dedman (2010: 175) claimed that the first vote was treated by EU leaders as a 'mistake' and that '… this contempt for popular opinion actually confirms Eurosceptics' charge that the EU is elitist and undemocratic'. The whole episode further undermined the legitimacy of the EU.

KEY POINTS

The Nice Treaty

- Nice became the longest European Council in the history of the EC/EU as leaders negotiated over institutional changes in preparation for enlargement. There was particular tension between large and small states over voting weights under QMV, and more widespread disagreement about the extension of QMV to new areas of policy.

- Reform of voting weights led to a complex 'triple majority' system, which seemed to advantage the larger member states against the smaller.

- QMV was extended into around thirty new areas, but the veto remained in others.

- In a parallel initiative, also confirmed at Nice in December 2000, the EU set out its commitment to citizens' rights in the Charter of Fundamental Rights of the European Union.

The Lisbon Strategy

- In March 2000, a special European Council in Lisbon agreed to pursue a new strategy to make the EU more competitive.

- The strategy was to be pursued through the OMC.

- In November 2004, the Kok Report described progress as disappointing, despite some achievements.

- Commission President Barroso made the strategy a priority of his term in office.

European Security and Defence Policy

- Progress on the ESDP was stalled by the 2001 terrorist attacks on the United States, with splits emerging between key member states on how to respond to the subsequent US decision to take military action against Iraq.

The Constitutional Treaty

- The Constitutional Convention prepared the ground for a European Constitution. It was unique in its composition and purpose.
- The Convention's proposals were presented in June 2003 and, following some amendments, the Treaty establishing a Constitution for Europe was signed by the EU heads of government and their Foreign Ministers in October 2004.
- The worst fears of the Treaty's supporters were realized in May 2005 when the French referendum returned a 55 per cent vote against. The vote prompted arguably the biggest crisis in the EU's history.

Enlargement

- In 2004, ten states—Cyprus, the Czech Republic, Estonia, Hungary, Latvia, Lithuania, Malta, Poland, Slovakia, and Slovenia—became members of the EU and Romania and Bulgaria joined in 2007 (for details, see Chapter 26, 'The Eastern Enlargement').
- Negotiations with Croatia opened in 2004.

The European Parliament and the New Commission

- Turn out at EP elections fell to a record low in 2004, and national issues remained prominent in the election campaigns in most member states.
- Barroso's appointment was a compromise between federalists and Atlanticists, and also appeased smaller member states.
- The proposed Commission hit problems over a number of nominees, and the changes that were made were seen as a victory for the EP.

The Lisbon Treaty

- The rejection of the Constitutional Treaty in France and the Netherlands in 2005 increased uncertainty over the EU's legitimacy and future trajectory.
- After a period of reflection, some of the more controversial aspects of the Treaty were removed. References to 'constitution' and key symbols were dropped.
- The revised 'Lisbon Treaty' was signed in the Portuguese capital in December 2009.
- For some, the Lisbon Treaty was a serious dilution of the intentions of the Constitutional Treaty; for others the substance of the original remained and the revisions were seen as mainly cosmetic.
- In Ireland, the only state to hold a referendum, 53.4 per cent of the public voted against ratifying the Treaty in June 2008.
- Although there were no other referendums, ratification proved controversial in other member states, most notably Poland and the Czech Republic.
- Following assurances in relation to areas of concern, including taxation policy, family and social issues, and foreign policy, a second Irish referendum in October 2009 produced a vote of 67.13 per cent in favour of ratifying the Treaty.

For additional material and resources, please visit the online resources www.oup.com/uk/bache5e.

FURTHER READING

On the Treaty of Nice, see **M. Gray and A. Stubb**, 'Keynote Article: The Treaty of Nice—Negotiating a Poisoned Chalice?' in **G. Edwards and G. Wiessala (eds)**, *The European Union: Annual Review of the EU 2000/2001* (Oxford: Blackwell, 2001), 5–24; and **K. Feus (ed.)**, *The Treaty of Nice Explained* (London: Federal Trust for Education and Research, 2001).

Detailed analysis of the Constitutional Convention's process, and of the emergence of the resultant Treaty, is available in **P. Norman**, *The Accidental Constitution: The Making of Europe's Constitutional Treaty* (Brussels: EuroComment, 2003). For analyses of the European Constitution, see **C. Church and D. Phinnemore**, *Understanding the European Constitution: An Introduction to the EU Constitutional Treaty* (London: Routledge, 2006), and **G. Amato and J. Ziller (eds)**, *The European Constitution: Cases and Materials in EU Member States' Law* (Cheltenham: Edward Elgar, 2007).

Assessments of the 2004 European elections are contained in **J. Lodge (ed.)**, *The 2004 Elections to the European Parliament* (Basingstoke: Palgrave Macmillan, 2005).

M. Carbone (ed.), *National Politics and European Integration: From the Constitution to the Lisbon Treaty* (Cheltenham, UK; Northampton, MA: Edward Elgar, 2010) covers the domestic politics of Treaty reform. The period before the second Irish referendum is covered by both **M. Dedman**, *The Origins and Development of the European Union, 2nd edition, 1945–2008* (London: Routledge, 2010) and **R. McAllister**, *European Union: An Historical and Political Survey*, 2nd edn (London: Routledge, 2010). Further reflections on the Lisbon Treaty can be found in *EUSA Review*, 23, 1 (European Union Studies Association, USA) Winter 2010.

For access to various primary sources, the website www.cvce.eu/en is very useful, while the European Convention's work is archived at: http://european-convention.europa.eu/.

Chapter 11

The EU in Crisis (2009–19)

Chapter Overview

The decade after the Lisbon Treaty was adopted in 2009 can be characterized as one of crisis for the EU. First, the eurozone crisis posed severe challenges for the often-unwieldy European institutions, which were forced to act and implement reforms quickly in order to safeguard the viability of the single currency. Second, in 2015 a significant spike in the number of refugees fleeing war in Syria and attempting perilous crossings of the Mediterranean Sea to the EU presented a governance challenge for certain member states and a test for the EU's mechanisms for managing migration and asylum. Third, in 2016 the UK, one of the largest EU member states, held a referendum on its future membership of the EU, leading to a vote narrowly in favour of leaving the EU. As of that date, no other state looked likely to follow the UK's lead, but the populist politics that had, according to many analysts, been an important driver of Brexit, was thriving in a number of other EU states—including in Poland, Hungary, and Italy. Taken together, these crises amounted to a veritable existential crisis for the EU as it approached the third decade of the twenty-first century.

The Unfolding Eurozone Crisis

The euro at first appeared to be relatively unaffected by the financial crisis that hit the global economy in 2007, even as certain European economies felt its force (see Insight 11.1).

Then, in October 2009, a new Socialist government took office in Greece and revealed that the fiscal position of the state was far worse than the previous government had admitted. It soon became apparent that Greek government statistics had concealed the true extent of the national budget deficit, which was far in excess of the 3 per cent of GDP allowed under the rules of the eurozone. In December 2009, two of the leading agencies that rate national creditworthiness downgraded Greece, and financial markets became reluctant to buy Greek government debt. This was despite a show of intent by the Greek government to tighten government finances by cutting expenditure and increasing taxes, a move that provoked street demonstrations and strikes (for an overview, see Chakrabortty 2011).

In February 2010, EU leaders met to consider whether Greece should be given assistance to allow it to cover its existing debts. As the cost of borrowing money on the international markets became steadily higher for the Greek government, there was a risk of it having to default on some of its debts, which could have led to a serious

Insight 11.1 From 'Global Financial Crisis' to 'Eurozone Crisis'

The causes of the global financial crisis (GFC), which began in 2007, were widely debated, but excessive indebtedness in the banking sector is central to many accounts. Of particular significance was mortgage securitization in the US: the process whereby large volumes of 'sub-prime' mortgage debt—mortgages sold to individuals in the US with low levels of credit-worthiness—were effectively sold on to domestic and international financial intermediaries such as investment banks, often with 'triple-A' credit ratings. This process spread the risks associated with highly risky loans to the global financial system, while reducing or eliminating the risk to the originator of the loan, who was thereby incentivized to issue further loans. When interest rates rose in many economies in the mid-2000s in response to, inter alia, inflation induced by rising oil prices, many individuals, including many with 'sub-prime' mortgages, defaulted on their loans and the waves were felt throughout the global economy. While the proximate cause was the US housing sector, it is important to note that this was a transatlantic crisis; many European banks were invested in sub-prime and a similar dynamic was ongoing within housing markets in the EU itself. For instance, countries such as the UK, Ireland, Spain, Hungary, and the Baltic states had particularly high and rapidly increasing levels of mortgage debt in the 2000s. These circumstances prompted government bailouts of various sorts, which, coupled with the frailties of the euro as a currency area (see Chapter 20), led to the protracted crisis in the eurozone. (For an excellent and comprehensive overview of the crisis see Tooze 2018*a*.)

collapse in the value of the euro. Yet there was strong resistance in Germany to what was seen as a bail out for a country that had been profligate in its fiscal management.

By April, though, it was apparent that the markets had decided Greece was incapable of rescuing itself, and belatedly the other members of the eurozone agreed a €30 billion rescue package. This turned out to be too little too late, even after the International Monetary Fund (IMF) offered to put up another €15 billion. Spreads between the interest rates on Greek and German government bonds (the difference in the cost of borrowing) reached 4.69 per cent after the package was agreed, and one credit agency slashed Greece's rating even further.

At the beginning of May 2010, a €110 billion package was agreed by eurozone finance ministers, comprising €80 billion from the other fifteen euro states at 5 per cent interest, well below what Greece would have to pay on financial markets, with the rest being provided by the IMF. Greece had to accept a €30 billion package of spending cuts and tax increases to reduce its budget deficit by five percentage points in 2010 and a further four percentage points in 2011. As it became increasingly likely that the crisis would spread beyond Greece, agreement was also reached on a general facility of €750 billion (supported by the EU and the IMF) available to all eurozone states that might find themselves under pressure (see also Chapter 20, 'Crisis Management').

At the end of September 2010, the Irish government announced that the cost of rescuing its ailing banking sector would be much higher than anticipated, leading to a downgrading of Ireland's sovereign debt by credit ratings agencies. Following Ireland's request in November 2010, the EU/IMF granted the country an assistance package worth €85 billion. In accord with what was by now 'a drearily familiar script' (Cohen 2012), in April 2011 Portugal requested financial assistance following downgrades in its own sovereign debt, and in May a package worth €78 billion over three years was agreed.

Throughout the second half of 2011, the crisis continued and European leaders agreed in October on a second package of support for Greece, which faced continuing pressure from the financial markets despite the initial support packages. Notably, this package included 'private sector involvement'; in other words, private holders of Greek debt were required to take losses. Given the level of social upheaval in Greece—a consequence of the austerity being implemented in accordance with EU/IMF conditionality—Prime Minister George Papandreou announced a referendum on the new deal. But under significant pressure from European governments the referendum was called off, leading to Papandreou's resignation in November. His replacement as head of an interim coalition government was the economist and former vice-president of the European Central Bank (ECB), Lucas Papademos. In 2012, a second bail-out package was finally agreed.

During the same period, Spain and Italy were hit by a wave of ratings downgrades, and the cost of borrowing was becoming particularly acute in Italy. This led to the resignation of Silvio Berlusconi as Prime Minister in November and his replacement by Mario Monti—an economist by training and a former EU Commissioner—who, until mid-2013, headed an interim government tasked with implementing a series of austerity measures and liberalizing the Italian economy. The appointment of two une-lected and ostensibly 'market friendly technocrats' in Greece and Italy could be inter-preted as evidence of the way in which the crisis had exacerbated a 'democratic deficit' in the EU (see Chapter 3, 'Democracy and Legitimacy'). That said, following drawn-out election processes in both countries—in 2012 in Greece and 2013 in Italy—new coalition governments were formed, headed by new prime ministers. Although they did not garner enough votes to govern, in both countries new radical political parties made important electoral breakthroughs: in Greece the left-wing anti-austerity party, Syriza, led by Alexis Tsipras, and in Italy, the populist Five Star Movement (M5S) (see 'The Populist Challenge' below).

In late 2011 and 2012, the crisis continued, with the title feature of *The Economist* asking in November 2011: 'Is This Really the End?' A number of further downgrades of eurozone countries' sovereign debts occurred during this period, including that of France, which was stripped of its triple-A status. Throughout 2012, the situation in Spain grew increasingly critical, with further downgrades of sovereign debt, the con-sequence in large part of downgrades to a number of Spanish banks that had signifi-cant exposure to its severely ailing housing and construction sectors. In May 2012, Bankia, a conglomerate of several Spanish regional banks, was nationalized, and in June Spain became the first country to request financial assistance in order to recapital-ize its banking sector. This was the first assistance package to be managed via the European Stability Mechanism (ESM) (see below and Chapter 20, 'Long-Term Reforms'). It was accompanied by policy conditionality, which focused in particular on reform and regulation of the banking sector.

In June 2012, Cyprus became the fifth eurozone member state formally to request financial assistance from the EU/IMF. It had previously been loaned €2.5 billion by Russia (with whom it had close relations due to the large number of Russians who reside and bank in Cyprus), but this had proved to be insufficient. Like the other cases discussed, Cyprus had faced a series of downgrades (and was downgraded to 'junk' status in March) and, like Ireland and Spain, its banking sector was under particular pressure owing to its exposure to a burst property bubble, and in this case also its inter-dependence with the ailing Greek economy. Following prolonged wrangling over the conditions of the deal, in March 2013 a €10 billion loan was agreed that included the usual range of EU/IMF conditions, but also a controversial levy on all personal bank deposits over a certain amount. After protests and vociferous criticism from both within and beyond Cyprus (including a rejection of the deal by the Cypriot parliament), this latter condition was ultimately removed.

In 2013, Ireland exited its programme with the EU/IMF, followed by Spain and Portugal in 2014 and Cyprus in 2016. However, Greece's travails continued into the second half of the decade in a context of intensifying social hardship and political upheaval. Breaking four decades of two-party rule, Syriza won a resounding electoral victory in January 2015 on a platform of renegotiating the country's bail-out terms with the EU/IMF. In the following months, Greece came close to crashing out of the single currency: in June, it failed to meet an IMF repayment and imposed capital controls limiting bank withdrawals; and in July, it held a referendum on the terms of a third bail-out deal, which the Greek people overwhelmingly (60 per cent) rejected. Despite the referendum result, Tsipras was effectively forced to accept EU demands for a new round of austerity (another event that raised questions about the EU's impact on national democracy). This paved the way to a third bail-out programme for Greece, worth 86 billion euros. Greece exited this programme in 2018, but remained heavily indebted. Moreover, like all the other countries that exited their programmes, Greece remained subject to EU economic governance rules and oversight via the so-called 'European semester' (see Chapter 20, 'Long-Term Reforms').

As discussed in Chapter 20, these short-term bail outs operated through institutional mechanisms that were initially designed to be temporary, but later became permanent. Long-term reforms to economic governance focused on establishing stricter EU-level rules governing the economies and fiscal positions of eurozone member states. These included the establishment of the 'Fiscal Compact' contained in the Treaty on Stability Co-ordination and Governance (TSCG) (see Insight 11.2) and a series of reform packages aimed at ensuring closer oversight by the EU of member state economies (see Chapter 20, 'Long-Term Reforms' for more details on various other reform packages).

The ECB was increasingly active throughout the crisis. In 2012, its president, Mario Draghi, declared that 'the ECB is ready to do whatever it takes to preserve the euro. And believe me, it will be enough' (Wilson 2012). With this declaration, the ECB was able to narrow bond-yield spreads within the eurozone (see also Chapter 20, 'Crisis Management'). Some voices, particularly in Germany, argued that these interventions exceeded the ECB's Treaty mandate. But such interventions were arguably fundamental to the survival of the euro.

However, the ECB and the EU were arguably not active enough in regulating a highly leveraged financial sector in the years preceding the crisis. Indeed, many in Europe were initially keen to portray the GFC, incorrectly, as a uniquely Anglo–American phenomenon (Insight 11.1). When they did acknowledge a need to deal with the crisis in relation to Greece, they placed the emphasis on sovereign or public debt rather than a build-up of private debt in the banking and finance sectors, and hence pushed an austerity agenda (see Insight 11.2).

From around 2011, the EU started to recognize more fundamental flaws in the European financial and monetary system and sought to implement a number of reforms geared towards greater regulatory oversight and the prevention of another crisis. However, progress was slow in this area and the EU's financial system remained fragile at the end of 2019: Italian banks were a particular but not a unique point of fragility, and many experts were concerned that the system remained insufficiently robust to endure a further crisis.

The election of Emmanuel Macron as President of France in 2017 looked like it might galvanize efforts towards further substantive reforms. However, it was apparent in 2018 that important differences remained with an increasingly constrained German Chancellor Merkel. Moreover, the emphasis on fiscal discipline remained central to the EU's economic-governance agenda (see Chapter 20, 'Long-Term Reforms'). In October 2018, the European Commission issued an unprecedented rebuke to the Italian government for its deviation from the fiscal rules. Its 'populist' government (see Insight 11.3) had refused to comply with the Commission's demands. While the acute crisis phase may have ended, the eurozone continued to face significant challenges.

The Refugee Crisis

The refugee crisis—or, perhaps more accurately, the crisis of refugee governance in the EU—unfolded against the backdrop of the fallout from the 2011 'Arab Spring' uprisings in the Middle East (see Chapter 25, 'CFSP and CSDP in Action'). Political

---

Insight 11.3 Populism

There is significant debate in the academic literature on the definition of the term 'populism'. One common definition understands it as a 'thin ideology' that makes appeal to 'the people' in contrast to 'the elite' or 'the establishment'. Populists usually present the former as under threat in some way from the latter. By this definition, populism (given its 'thinness' as substantive ideology) can be appropriated as a strategy by the political right or the political left and it can include very different understandings of who constitute 'the people' and 'the establishment' (for a good introduction, see Mudde and Kaltwasser 2017). Populist parties are more often than not 'anti-system' parties, inasmuch as they reject or seek explicitly to overhaul those aspects of the status quo that, they argue, have produced negative outcomes for 'the people'. This becomes an issue for the EU when its core values—or even its very existence—are portrayed as a problematic aspect of that status quo or 'system' by such parties, especially when those parties are in government (see also Chapter 1, 'Postfunctionalism'; Chapter 3, 'Democracy and Legitimacy').

---

turbulence led to increased migration from these parts of the world into the EU, particularly from around 2013, with a significant spike in refugee numbers in 2015 as the Syrian civil war intensified. In particular, growing numbers of people were trying to reach the EU by embarking on treacherous crossings of the Mediterranean Sea, particularly between Turkey and the Greek islands (eastern Mediterranean route), but also between North Africa (particularly Libya) and Italy (central Mediterranean route). This led to both increased arrivals by sea (Table 11.1) and significant fatalities (Table 11.2).

These movements of people presented a significant governance challenge for the EU and its member states. The Schengen system permitting passport-free and effectively borderless travel across much of the EU (Chapter 23, 'The Refugee Crisis') meant that refugees were able to move from Greece or Italy to other member states of the EU. Many sought to reach, and claim asylum in, Germany, Sweden, and other prosperous member states with relatively permissive attitudes towards migration and already significant migrant populations. But this possibility of cross-border mobility worked against a key pillar of the EU's asylum governance, namely the so-called

---

Table 11.1 Migrant Arrivals by Sea

Year	Greece	Italy
2014	77 163	170 100
2015	853 650	153 842
2016	173 614	181 436
2017	29 501	119 370
2018	32 742	23 370
2019	62 445	11 469

Source: IOM's Missing Migrants Project.

Table 11.2 Deaths by Route

Year	Eastern Mediterranean	Central Mediterranean	Western Mediterranean
2014	59	3165	59
2015	804	3149	102
2016	434	4581	128
2017	62	2853	224
2018	174	1314	811
2019	71	770	477

Source: IOM's Missing Migrants Project.

Dublin Regulation, which specifies that an application for asylum should be made and processed at the point of arrival in the EU (Chapter 23, 'The Refugee Crisis'). As the number of asylum seekers increased rapidly in 2015, this Regulation put disproportionate pressure on the governance capacities of arrival states such as Greece and Italy—both countries that, notably, had been at the sharp end of the eurozone crisis—and in practice it became impossible to implement.

The crisis exposed not only significant problems with the EU's governance regime for migration and asylum, but also a lack of consensus with respect to its reform. In the midst of the unfolding crisis, the Commission acknowledged the limits of the Dublin Regulation and proposed in May 2015 the establishment of a quota scheme, whereby states would share the costs (and benefits) of processing and welcoming refugees. However, this was controversial and split the member states, with Hungary staunchly opposed. A voluntary scheme for the relocation of 40,000 migrants from Italy and Greece was all that the states were able to agree in June 2015, but this was woefully insufficient to deal with the scale of the flows.

Consequently, the human and political crisis intensified throughout the summer and autumn of 2015. Hungary, under a populist leadership (see 'The Populist Challenge' below), controversially began to build a barrier along its border with Serbia in July. The following month, and in a sign of growing tensions between Hungary and Germany on the issue, Germany's Chancellor Merkel unilaterally suspended the Dublin Regulation, permitting Syrian asylum seekers to enter and remain in Germany regardless of their point of entry to the EU. In defiance of Merkel's position, at the start of September Hungary's Prime Minister, Viktor Orban, sought to prevent migrants transiting through Budapest from travelling onwards to Austria and Germany, arguing that they should seek asylum at their point of entry to the EU (in accordance with Dublin).

Later that month, a harrowing photo of the drowned Alan Kurdi—a young Syrian boy whose body was washed up on a Turkish beach—was published in media throughout Europe and, at least temporarily, this seemed to trigger a wave of sympathy for the plight of refugees and vindicate Merkel. However, Germany suspended its own permissive policy later in September as it struggled to cope with the number of arrivals and this had knock-on effects for transition states such as Austria, Hungary, and Croatia, where border restrictions multiplied throughout the autumn.

Against this chaotic backdrop, and despite significant opposition, a mandatory relocation scheme was agreed in late September, unusually and controversially, using a qualified majority vote in the Council (see Chapter 16, 'The Council of the EU (the Council)'). This scheme sought to relocate 160,000 refugees from Greece and Italy over the following two years. However, in November, following terrorist attacks in Paris perpetrated by a group that included some Iraqi migrants, the public and political mood towards migrants, including refugees, hardened significantly. The European Commission and certain member states—including receiving states such as Italy, Greece, and Germany—continued to press for collective responses throughout 2016, including reform of the Dublin Regulation and the implementation of ambitious refugee quotas (see Chapter 23, 'The Refugee Crisis'). But when the mandatory relocation scheme closed at the end of September 2016, under 20,000 of the 160,000 target number of refugees has been relocated, with Hungary and Poland notably refusing to take any. Moreover, the Schengen system remained vulnerable in light of the moves by many member states to impose ostensibly 'temporary' border controls.

The EU was ultimately able to limit the number of refugees entering via the eastern Mediterranean route through the adoption of a controversial agreement with Turkey in late March 2016, under the terms of which Greece would be able to return migrants to Turkey. In exchange, the EU undertook: to give financial aid in support of refugees (€6 billion); to grant access to the Schengen travel area for Turkish nationals; and to resettle some refugees from camps in Turkey to the EU (for each Syrian returned to Turkey, one refugee would be resettled). As of 2019, the EU had relocated over 20,000 refugees from Turkey to certain member states. However, Turkey expressed concern in 2018 that the EU had been slow in offering the financial aid, and failed to finalize the arrangements vis-a-vis the Schengen travel area. Moreover, the process for returning migrants from the Greek islands to Turkey was slow in practice and the future for the approximately three million Syrian refugees in a politically unstable and relatively poor Turkey was uncertain. The long-term prospects of the deal were still in doubt at the end of 2019, given the poor state of Turkey–EU relations, which took a turn for the worse when Turkey—following the withdrawal of US troops—began a military operation in Kurdish Northern Syria that was condemned by the EU.

As regards the central Mediterranean route, in February 2017, Italy, backed by the EU, signed a controversial Memorandum of Understanding with Libya, which required the Libyan authorities to stem the flow of migrants. Consistent with a broader EU approach aimed at externalizing the management of migration (see Chapter 23, 'AFSJ Policy Measures'), the policy did lead to a fall in arrivals via this route and in the number of deaths at sea (see Table 11.2), but left many migrants trapped in appalling detention conditions in a highly unstable Libya. Following the establishment of a populist government in 2018 (see Insight 11.3), Italy adopted an even more hard-line position; that summer Matteo Salvini, Italy's far-right Interior Minister, twice refused to allow boats from Libya with migrants on board to disembark at Italian ports and threatened to do a deal with Libya that would permit the return of migrants. Partly as a consequence of these policies, the number of migrants taking the western Mediterranean route to Spain increased sharply in 2018, and this was reflected in a spike in the number of deaths at sea on this route.

The crisis was primarily one of EU collective governance and solidarity, and was closely related to the rise of populist and nationalist political parties in many member states. The economic stagnation resulting from the GFC and eurozone crisis, as well as a spate of terrorist attacks from 2015 (see Chapter 25, 'CFSP and CSDP Action'), certainly provided fertile territory for such parties to exploit and politicize increased migration, as discussed in greater detail below ('The Populist Challenge').

Brexit

On Thursday 23 June 2016, Britain decided in a national referendum to leave the EU. With a turnout of 72.2 per cent of eligible voters, 51.89 per cent voted to leave, against 48.11 per cent who voted to remain. While the vote was, formally speaking, 'advisory', the government quickly committed to leaving, and notified the EU in March 2017 of its intention to do so. This set the clock ticking on a two-year period during which the UK would negotiate the terms of its withdrawal. Towards the end of this period the British government, led by Prime Minister Theresa May, managed to reach a 'Withdrawal Agreement' with the rest of the EU, only for it to be rejected by the British Parliament in 2019. This led to May's replacement as Prime Minister by Boris Johnson in July 2019. It also precipitated repeated extensions to the UK's date of departure. At the end of 2019, the UK held a general election that delivered a significant majority for the Conservative Party. This allowed Johnson to get his slightly revised Withdrawal Agreement through Parliament, which paved the way for the UK's departure from the EU on 31 January 2020. A transition period, during which the UK would remain aligned with the EU while it negotiated a future trading relationship, was due to last until December 2020.

Our online Brexit Supplement offers an updated and a far more detailed analysis of Brexit. It describes in detail the background to the vote, the difficult process through which the UK negotiated its departure from the EU, and the impact of the vote on domestic politics in the UK. It also offers an analysis of the likely impact on the EU, including the impact on the institutions of the EU (see also Chapters 12–17); and it considers whether Brexit is likely to be a unique phenomenon or one that is reflective of a broader anti-system, anti-EU, and populist politics in the EU. As discussed in 'The Populist Challenge' below, this kind of politics is certainly apparent elsewhere, although in most cases it does not take on the 'hard' Eurosceptic form (see Chapter 3, 'Euroscepticism') that it does in the UK.

 Visit the online resources for access to a Supplement including coverage of Brexit www.oup.com/uk/bache5e.

The Populist Challenge

The crises discussed up to now collectively amounted to an existential crisis for the EU. The eurozone crisis threatened the very survival of the euro, the unravelling of which would lead to substantial economic turmoil for the EU and quite possibly trigger further disintegration. The refugee crisis threatened the survival of the Schengen free-travel area (see Insight 23.2), which is a central pillar of the EU's single market. Finally, Brexit, was a precedent that the EU and pro-EU leaders did not wish to see repeated. As noted, the last of these crises was, at least to some extent, driven by a 'populist' or 'anti-system' politics (see Insight 11.3): the UK Independence Party (UKIP) had, along with increasingly emboldened Eurosceptics in the Conservative Party, long sought to politicize and criticize the EU, and especially its rules on the free movement of people.

The broader emergence of such a politics across the EU was arguably a consequence of a long-term crisis of market liberalism (dating back to the 1980s and 1990s), associated with increasing inequality, 'depoliticization', and the erosion of democracy (Hopkin 2020; see also Chapter 3, 'Democracy and Legitimacy'). But the EU's multiple crises in the 2010s—particularly the eurozone and refugee crises—certainly fuelled the populist turn, with political actors and parties that could be described as anti-system growing in stature, and in some member states forming governments (as well as establishing themselves in the European Parliament (EP)—see 'Other Developments' below). Whatever prompted their rise, these anti-system parties represented a further crisis for the EU, particularly when they led national governments that challenged some of the very principles upon which the EU was founded.

Democratic Backsliding in Hungary and Poland

In pursuit of their accession to the EU, Hungary and Poland embarked on a process of 'Europeanization' (Chapter 3, 'Europeanization') that led to them becoming members in 2004 (see Chapter 26, 'The Eastern Enlargement'). However, populist parties established themselves in government in both countries during the 2010s: in Hungary, Fidesz, under the leadership of Viktor Orban, achieved a landslide electoral victory in 2010, and retained its sizeable majority in 2014 and 2018; and in Poland, the Law and Justice Party (PiS), under the leadership of Jaroslaw Kaczynski, won the 2015 elections with an outright majority, and was re-elected in 2019. Fidesz's initial electoral success was closely linked to the significant impact of the GFC in Hungary (Insight 11.1), which precipitated a widespread disillusionment in democracy. This rendered Orban's critique of liberal markets and liberal democracy and his support for an economic nationalism (often blurred with an ethnic nationalism) particularly compelling. Later, his tough line in the context of the refugee crisis served to galvanize his support (see 'The Refugee Crisis' above).

Poland weathered the GFC far better than Hungary; indeed, it continued to grow economically throughout the crisis. However, the spoils of this growth were not shared evenly, and the transition to a market economy left many people vulnerable. In 2015, PiS stood on a successful platform that promised to expand significantly the welfare state. As in Hungary, however, this economic interventionism was accompanied by a conservative and illiberal nationalism, hostile to migration and minorities.

The EU has long been concerned about the illiberal drift in these states. Particular concerns relate to reforms to the judiciary (the rule of law) and the media that have undermined their independence in both states. Hungary also controversially sought to control the activities of foreign universities, effectively forcing the US-accredited Central European University to leave Budapest in 2019. The EU was initially criticized for its passivity in the face of this illiberal drift in Hungary. That said, following cases brought by the Commission, the Court of Justice of the European Union (CJEU) did rule against some moves in these areas in relation to both countries, and such rulings led to the reversal of some controversial policies (for instance, the reinstatement of judges in Poland) (Shotter 2018). More dramatically, the EU deployed its so-called 'Article 7 procedure' in relation to both states; the Commission launched the procedure against Poland in 2017 and the EP against Hungary in 2018. This procedure allows member states to determine, by a majority of four-fifths, whether there is a clear risk of a serious breach of EU values. Member states are thereafter able to issue recommendations and, by unanimous agreement, sanctions, such as a restriction on voting rights or limits on receipt of EU funds (see Chapter 12, 'Legislative Procedures'). In late 2019, this process was stalled, with both states pledging to block in the Council the imposition of sanctions on the other. That said, the Commission continued to refer these states to the CJEU in relation to reforms to the rule of law; for instance, in October 2019, it made a referral in relation to a Polish policy that permitted the sanctioning of judges for their court rulings. Significant domestic public support remained for the governments in both states, but at the same time those publics overwhelmingly backed continued EU membership. That reality made it tricky for both the EU and these populist governments to calculate the potential political risks of further confrontation.

Populism in Italy

Italian politics was driven by the fallout from the eurozone and migration crises (see 'The Unfolding Eurozone Crisis' and 'The Refugee Crisis' above), which paved the way for the emergence of populist parties. The turn to technocratic government under Monti in 2011 was endorsed by the mainstream centre in Italian parties, leaving populist parties the Five Star Movement (M5S) and Northern League to offer the only meaningful opposition. The emergence and success of the former—a vocally anti-establishment party co-founded by the former comedian Beppe Grillo in 2009—was, in part at least, a consequence of the eurozone crisis. M5S's mix of anti-austerity policies and Italian nationalism appealed to many of the victims of that crisis. The latter was originally established in the early 1990s to make the case for the secession of Northern Italy. It was transformed from 2013, under the leadership of Matteo Salvini, into a party with a far wider audience—and rebranded as the League ('Lega')—embracing Italian nationalism, Euroscepticism, and particularly opposition to migration. Its anti-migration message was particularly popular during the refugee crisis and led to electoral success in 2018. Indeed, Lega became the largest party in the centre-right coalition that, along with M5S, formed the Italian government in 2018. Due to the complexities of the Italian political system of coalition, this effectively made Salvini, who became Interior Minister, and M5S leader, Luigi Di Maio, who became Labour and Economic Development Minister, the most powerful figures in Italian politics between 2018 and 2019.

On taking office, both leaders denounced EU economic governance, particularly restrictions on government spending, and, as noted above, early in his tenure as Interior Minister Salvini controversially refused port access to migrant boats (see 'The Refugee Crisis' above). In the summer of 2019, the EU expressed concerns in relation to Italy's public debt and threatened its defiant governing coalition with sanctions (see 'The Unfolding Eurozone Crisis' above). That coalition broke down in August 2019 as a result of disagreements between the two parties, and a more progressive, centrist, and pro-EU government was formed in September. While an unpredictable M5S remained in the governing coalition, support for the party declined significantly. However, despite being pushed out of government, Salvini's Lega remained the most popular party in Italian politics at the end of 2019. Given Italy's size and importance within the eurozone, its fragile banking sector, and its role as a key receiving state for migrants, the state of Italian politics looked likely to remain a major preoccupation for the EU at the start of 2020.

Other Developments

Elections and Appointments

In the decade under consideration in this chapter, three elections to the European Parliament took place: in June 2009, May 2014, and May 2019.

Because of the delay with the ratification of the Lisbon Treaty, the 2009 elections took place under the existing rules, meaning that 736 Members of the European Parliament (MEPs) were elected, rather than the 750 provided for in the new Treaty. The main feature of these elections was that turn out was again down—from 45.6 per cent in 2004 to 43.2 per cent in 2009. This was the lowest turn out since direct elections began thirty years earlier, and added further weight to concerns about the contribution of the EP to the Union's democratic legitimacy. In 2010, José Manuel Barroso secured a second five-year term as President of the Commission. His reappointment had faced some opposition within the EP, most notably from the Greens and some MEPs on the left, but his case was helped by a strengthening of centre-right parties in the EP elections of June 2009. The new Commission as a whole was approved by a vote in the EP on 9 February 2010.

In May 2014, for the first time 751 MEPs were elected to the EP (750 plus a president), in accordance with the Lisbon Treaty's rules. Turn out was similar to the 2009 elections, at around 43 per cent. Populist and Eurosceptic political parties enjoyed electoral success in a number of member states. Of particular note, the right-wing *Front National* (FN) won the largest share of the vote in France (25 per cent), as did UKIP in Britain (27 per cent). Notwithstanding these significant advances for Eurosceptic parties, in terms of overall numbers of seats the large party groups remained the dominant forces in the EP. For the first time in 2014, the so-called '*Spitzenkandidat*' (German for 'lead candidate') process was used to elect a Commission President, which linked the outcome of the EP elections to the appointment of the Commission President (see Chapters 13 and 15 for further details). This led to the appointment of the EP's lead candidate, Jean-Claude Juncker.

The next EP elections were held in May 2019. Turn out was higher than in 2014, at just over 50 per cent. Again, populist and Eurosceptic parties increased their share of seats in the EP and the two dominant political groups lost their overall majority (for results, see Chapter 15, 'Composition and Functions'). Ursula von der Leyen became the first female President of the Commission in December 2019. In a departure from the process in 2014, she was, notably, not the *Spitzenkandidat* (see Chapter 13, 'Composition and Appointment').

External Relations and Enlargement

On 1 July 2013, Croatia became the twenty-eighth member of the EU (see Chapter 26, 'Croatia'). Twelve Croatian MEPs were elected in spring 2013 and joined the EP from July. The membership prospects of other western Balkan states improved throughout the period, although a combination of slow reform processes and 'enlargement fatigue' meant that no other states had joined by the end of 2019 (see Chapter 26, 'Enlargement Fatigue?' for details). Negotiations with Turkey, which had begun in 2005, slowed during the period and were frozen at the end of 2019 (see Chapter 26, 'Turkey'). The EU was active in other areas of external relations throughout the decade, although its power in world politics was, in important respects, arguably waning (see Chapter 25, 'The CFSP and CSDP in Action'; 'EU Power in World Politics').

Europe 2020

In 2010, the EU launched its 'Europe 2020' strategy as the successor to the Lisbon Strategy/Agenda (see Chapter 10, 'The Lisbon Strategy'). Like its predecessor, it focused on promoting jobs and growth. Framed in the context of the then-emerging eurozone crisis, the Europe 2020 strategy (European Commission 2010a) claimed to provide the vision required for member states to 'exit from the exceptional support measures adopted to combat the crisis'. It supported the moves towards budgetary consolidation (austerity), while emphasizing that this should be 'growth-friendly'. The strategy referred to the EU as embodying a 'social market economy' and promoted such an economy in a similar fashion to the Lisbon Strategy. The new strategy established specific targets for governments in the areas of employment, education, research and innovation, social inclusion, and poverty reduction; and it put in place a series of programmes aimed at achieving these targets. Progress monitoring was incorporated into the European semester process of socio-economic governance of member states (see Chapter 20, 'Long-Term Reforms').

Nobel Peace Prize

In 2012, the EU was the recipient of the Nobel Prize for Peace in recognition of its role in advancing peace, reconciliation, democracy, and human rights in Europe. This was a controversial decision for many, given the ongoing eurozone crisis and the diminishing public support for the EU. Indeed, the award prompted protests from an awkward coalition of anti-EU, left wing, and peace campaigners; a group of peace prize laureates wrote a letter criticizing the award of the prize to the EU; and a number of EU leaders opted to snub the award ceremony (Higgins 2012). For others, it served as an important reminder of the EU's achievements in the service of peace in Europe, which, as the Nobel Committee President Thorbjørn Jagland said, 'should not be taken for granted'. This was the line adopted by the European leaders who collected the award. For instance, Commission President Barroso stated in his acceptance speech that, 'our quest for European unity . . . is not an end in itself, but a means to higher ends. In many ways, it attests to the quest for a cosmopolitan order . . . in which abiding by common norms serves universal values.' And 'this federalist and cosmopolitan vision is one of the most important contributions that the European Union can bring to a global order in the making' (for more on cosmopolitan thinking in relation to the EU, see Chapter 4, 'Critical Social Theory').

The Budget

In December 2013, EU leaders reached an agreement on a €960 billion budget for the seven-year period 2014–20. In the context of austerity within the EU, discussions over the budget were heated. While a number of net-contributor member states, including the UK, argued for a reduction in the budget, EU institutions and some net-recipient member states opposed significant cuts. The budget that was eventually agreed represented a 3 per cent reduction on the previous multi-annual budget. It was the first time that the budget had been reduced. The most notable cuts were to cohesion policy and the Common Agricultural Policy (CAP), while investment in research and competitiveness-related activities was increased. In late 2019, discussions were ongoing with respect to a multi-annual budget for the period 2021–27.

CONCLUSION

The period following the start of the economic crisis threw up major challenges for the EU, in particular: the eurozone crisis; the refugee crisis; Brexit; and a rising populism in many member states.

In response to the eurozone crisis, following a period of 'firefighting', a long-term bail-out mechanism was established and a number of reforms geared towards greater fiscal discipline and EU oversight were passed, including an agreement among the majority of member states on an intergovernmental Treaty outside of EU law (see Insight 11.2). However, the effects of the crisis prompted widespread political and social upheaval and public dissatisfaction. Various tensions emerged between member states, particularly between 'creditor' and 'debtor' eurozone states. The crisis prompted the posing of fundamental questions about the nature of European political economy, such as what were the key ideas and agendas that dominated economic and monetary union prior to and during the crisis, and who were the winners and losers from such agendas (see Chapter 4, 'Critical Political Economy'; Chapter 20, 'Critical Voices'). Responses to the crisis also raised questions in relation to democratic legitimacy: in particular, to what extent the EU's socio-economic governance potentially undermines national democracy and self-determination (see Chapter 3, 'Democracy and Legitimacy').

The refugee crisis, which intensified from 2015 following upheaval in the Middle East, represented a further significant challenge for EU governance. With increasing numbers of asylum seekers entering EU territory, particularly via Greece and Italy and, to a lesser extent, Spain, the EU's system for processing asylum applications broke down and national borders that had effectively been removed between mainland European EU states (due to 'Schengen'—see Chapter 23, Insight 23.2) were, in a number of instances, effectively re-imposed. This crisis further compounded divisions between member states: in this case, between those states pushing for a more permissive approach and associated reforms to the governance of migration and asylum, and those states advocating a more restrictive approach and the maintenance of the governance status quo. Populist and Eurosceptic political parties and groups were able both to foster and to exploit fears related to migration. Indeed, this crisis (along with the eurozone crisis) was a major factor in their electoral success in a number of EU member states.

The starkest manifestation of growing Euroscepticism in the EU was Brexit. Britain's decision to leave was a shock to the EU and pro-EU groups throughout the continent (see the online Brexit Supplement). While the 'hard' Euroscepticism that had led to the victory of the 'Leave' vote in 2016 in Britain was not clearly apparent in other member states, populist parties with views that were at odds with EU policies and principles were elected to govern, or to participate in governing coalitions, in a number of member states. This was the case in, among other states, Hungary, Poland, and Italy. The governing parties of the first of these two states dramatically clashed with the EU over domestic reforms to the judiciary and media that appeared to undermine the independence of those institutions. In Italy, two anti-system parties formed part of a governing coalition in the period 2018–19. The popularity of these and other populist parties and movements throughout the EU had increased dramatically as a consequence—in part at least—of the eurozone and refugee crises. This rising popularity was evidenced in the results of the 2014 and 2019 EP elections.

These multiple crises meant that at the end of the second decade of the twenty-first century, the EU was grappling with fundamental questions relating to its purpose and its future. With good reason, scholars began seriously to consider the factors that might lead to the disintegration of the EU or certain EU policies (see also Chapter 3, 'Disintegration'; Chapter 1, 'Postfunctionalism'). However, it should be clear to readers of these history chapters that 'crises' of various sorts have accompanied the process of integration from its inception. Indeed, crises have, in some cases—including over the past decade—acted as important drivers of further integration in the manner that Monnet (see Chapter 1, 'The Intellectual Background') might have anticipated. Moreover, the EU institutions, and the interdependencies that they create, are not easily or quickly dismantled. At the end of 2019, it was, therefore, still far too early to ascertain fully the consequences of the various crises that had beset the EU in the 2010s.

 Visit the online resources for access to a Supplement including coverage of Brexit www.oup.com/uk/bache5e.

KEY POINTS

The Unfolding Eurozone Crisis

- The eurozone crisis dominated EU business after 2010. Its effects were acutely felt in several 'debtor' member states in the eurozone. These states were the recipients of a series of bail outs from other EU member states and the IMF. The bail outs required 'debtor' states to make significant budgetary cuts and pursue policies of austerity.

- The crisis created tension between 'debtor' and 'creditor' states in the EU.

- The ECB carved an important role for itself in crisis management, pledging to 'do whatever it takes to preserve the euro'.

- The EU introduced a series of long-term reforms to its economic governance aimed at stabilizing the economic situation in the eurozone (see also Chapter 20, 'The Eurozone Crisis').

The Refugee Crisis

- Following political turbulence in the Middle East, the number of asylum seekers travelling to the EU increased dramatically in 2015. They mostly travelled to the EU via the Mediterranean, entering primarily through Greece, but also Italy and Spain.

- These movements placed pressure on the EU's system for collectively governing migration and internal borders (see also Chapter 23, 'The Refugee Crisis').

- Divisions emerged between member states keen to maintain the governance status quo and those pushing for reform. As a result, Commission proposals for reforms to migration governance were constrained.

- Populist political parties used anti-migrant and nationalist rhetoric to stoke fears, and this proved a successful strategy in a number of member states.

Brexit

- The British people narrowly voted to leave the EU in a 2016 referendum on membership. The outcome represented a significant shock to the EU and to pro-EU movements and leaders in the UK and beyond.

- After a difficult process, the UK finally left the EU in early 2020, although many aspects of its future relationship with the EU remained to be resolved (see the online Brexit Supplement to this textbook).

The Populist Challenge

- Populist and anti-system parties became increasingly popular in a number of member states throughout the 2010s, partly by exploiting the social, economic, and political fallout from the eurozone and refugee crises.

- Populist parties were elected to govern in Hungary and Poland. These parties clashed with the EU on its so-called 'fundamental values', particularly relating to the rule of law.

- Populist parties also established a foothold in government in Italy in 2018–19. Given its size and importance within the eurozone, and its significant role in relation to migration governance, the country was a major preoccupation for the EU at the end of the 2010s.

Other Developments

- Despite the crises, other 'business as usual' continued in the period, with EP elections in 2009, 2014, and 2019.

- A further enlargement to include Croatia took place in 2013.

- In 2010, the EU launched its replacement to the Lisbon Strategy; 'Europe 2020', aimed, in particular, at reforming the European model of growth.

- In 2012, the EU was awarded the Nobel Peace Prize.

 For additional material and resources, please visit the online resources www.oup.com/uk/bache5e.

FURTHER READING

For reading relating to the crises discussed in this chapter, see further reading suggestions in Chapter 20 (on the eurozone crisis); Chapter 23 (on the refugee crisis); and in the online Brexit Supplement (on Brexit). For more detailed analysis of each of the crises discussed in this chapter, see **D. Dinan, N. Nugent, and W. Paterson (eds)**, *The European Union in Crisis* (London, Palgrave Macmillan, 2017).

Part Three
Institutions

Theories derived both from international relations (IR) and from the analysis of domestic policy making include positions that emphasize the importance of institutions. In the IR literature on international regimes, there is an emphasis on institutions as 'persistent and connected sets of rules (formal and informal) that prescribe behavioural roles, constrain states, and shape expectations' (Keohane 1989: 3). In the 'new institutionalist' approaches to the study of domestic policy making, there is a similar emphasis on the importance of institutions, broadly defined. In short, *institutions matter*, although not only institutions matter, nor is it only formal institutions that matter. However, to understand the politics of the European Union (EU) it is necessary to know something about the nature of the formal institutions and the relationships between them. The long-standing debate between intergovernmentalist and neofunctionalist accounts of integration is reflected in assessments concerning which of the institutions are most influential.

There are six chapters in this part of the book. The opening chapter on 'The Institutional Architecture' provides essential introductory information on the institutions, the Treaties, the legislative and budgetary processes, and other broad features. It presents the context within which the institutions operate, and provides background to understanding the debates that are presented in later chapters.

For most of the rest of this part of the book, the choice of which subjects to include was straightforward. Traditionally, the EU has had four 'main' institutions: the Commission, the Council of the EU, the European Parliament (EP), and the Court of Justice of the European Union (CJEU). The Lisbon Treaty gave the *European Council* separate status from the *Council of Ministers*, which was renamed the *Council of the EU*. The European Council is now considered more fully, but, because of the similarities in its make-up, it is considered within the same chapter as the Council of the EU. All five of the main institutions are therefore treated in detail. The final chapter in this part deals with 'Organized Interests', the interaction of which with the formal institutions is a central component of the EU's decision making process.

Chapter 12

The Institutional Architecture

Chapter Overview

Up to now, this book has introduced the institutions of the European Union (EU) as part of the history of European integration, and their powers have only been briefly outlined. To understand the debates that surround the institutions themselves, though, it is necessary to understand in more detail their powers and their roles in relationship to one another. The same material is needed to understand the debates around the various policies of the EU, which are the subject of Part Four of the book.

This chapter examines the pattern of institutions and the formal rules that govern them. It also gives information on the composition of the less-important institutions, although for the main ones—the Commission, the Council of the EU (or 'Council') and the European Council, the European Parliament (EP), and the Court of Justice of the European Union (CJEU)—that information is provided in the separate chapters devoted to them.

The chapter starts with a review of the Treaties that form the founding 'constitutional' documents of the EU. The main institutions involved in the processes of decision making are then introduced. Decision making is examined, covering both the budgetary and legislative procedures. Brief consideration is also given to the different decision making processes on foreign and security policy. The chapter then looks at the implementation of decisions once they have been made. Finally, the chapter returns to some broader considerations relating to the post-Lisbon institutional architecture.

The Treaties

The EU is governed by treaty. Specifically, since the implementation of the Lisbon Treaty in December 2009, it has been governed by two Treaties: the Treaty on European Union (TEU) and the Treaty on the Functioning of the European Union (TFEU). In order to understand the current arrangements, it is necessary to look at the evolution of Treaty provisions.

There were three 'founding Treaties'—the Treaty of Paris (1951) and the two Treaties of Rome (1957) (see Chapter 6, 'The European Coal and Steel Community' and 'The Road to the Rome Treaties'). They were supplemented in ways that affected the powers of the institutions by three further Treaties in the 1960s and early 1970s. One merged the Councils and the Commissions of the three Communities, while the other two were concerned with budgetary provisions. After the last of these, in 1975, there were no further major revisions of the Treaties for another decade, but then there were four new Treaties in the next fifteen years: the Single European Act (SEA); the Maastricht Treaty; the Amsterdam Treaty; and the Nice Treaty (see Box 12.1). Leaving aside the Treaty of Paris, which expired in 2002, and the Euratom Treaty, which maintains its separate status, by 1997 the Treaties had been consolidated into two: the TEU, and the Treaty establishing the European Community (TEC). The Constitutional Treaty, agreed at the Brussels European Council on 18 June 2004, was designed to consolidate the existing Treaties into one. However, following its abandonment in 2005, the somewhat more modest Lisbon Treaty made revisions to the existing Treaties (see Chapter 10, 'The Lisbon Treaty'). However, it also renamed the TEC the TFEU. Although more modest than the Constitutional Treaty that was originally planned, the Lisbon Treaty was very important. First of all, it changed the general organization (or architecture) of the EU in a way comparable with the earlier Maastricht Treaty. Second, it included many amendments to the existing Treaties.

The Maastricht Treaty had introduced a structure consisting of three 'pillars': the EC pillar, governed by the TEC; and two intergovernmental pillars, covering the Common Foreign and Security Policy (CFSP) and Justice and Home Affairs (JHA) (see Figure 12.1), governed by the TEU. Subsequent amendments, made by the Treaties of Amsterdam and Nice, scaled back the policies covered by the JHA pillar by moving some to the EC pillar. However, the CFSP remained distinctively intergovernmental. This three-pillar structure was an important part of the EU's functioning from 1993 to 2009. However, it was abolished as of December 2009. The CFSP remains distinctively intergovernmental, but all other policies are consolidated into a single order governed by the TFEU.

Box 12.1 The Treaties

- The Treaty of Paris (signed 1951; took effect 1952) created the European Coal and Steel Community (ECSC)

- The two Treaties of Rome (signed 1957; took effect 1958): the first created the European Atomic Energy Community (Euratom); the second created the European Economic Community (EEC)

- The Treaty Establishing a Single Council and a Single Commission of the European Communities, also known as the Merger Treaty (signed 1965; took effect 1967)

- The Treaty Amending Certain Budgetary Provisions of the Treaties (1970)

- The Treaty Amending Certain Financial Provisions of the Treaty (1975)

- The Single European Act (signed 1986; took effect July 1987)

- The Maastricht Treaty (signed 1992; took effect November 1993), which introduced the Treaty on European Union (TEU)

- The Treaty of Amsterdam (signed 1997; took effect 1999)

- The Treaty of Nice (signed 2001; took effect 2003)

- The Lisbon Treaty (signed 2007; took effect December 2009)

- The Treaty on Stability, Co-ordination and Governance in EMU (signed 2012; took effect January 2013)

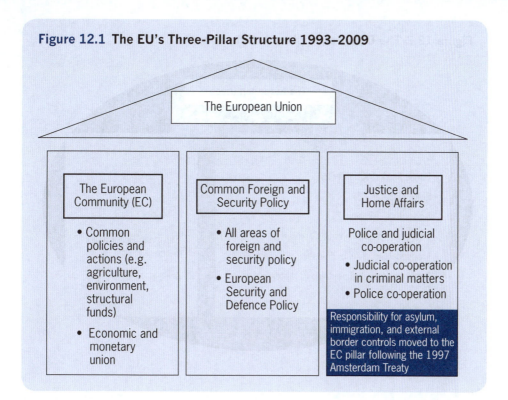

Figure 12.1 The EU's Three-Pillar Structure 1993–2009

The European Union

The European Community (EC)	Common Foreign and Security Policy	Justice and Home Affairs
• Common policies and actions (e.g. agriculture, environment, structural funds) • Economic and monetary union	• All areas of foreign and security policy • European Security and Defence Policy	Police and judicial co-operation • Judicial co-operation in criminal matters • Police co-operation Responsibility for asylum, immigration, and external border controls moved to the EC pillar following the 1997 Amsterdam Treaty

The staff of the EU institutions constantly refer to the Treaties. They are always careful to check the Treaty base of any action that they take. In the Preamble of any legislative proposal, the Commission is formally obliged to state under which Article of the Treaties it is making the proposal. This incessant engagement with the text of the Treaties has led to the internal discourse of the institutions being peppered with references to Articles of the Treaties, usually just citing them by number.

However, as the founding Treaties were amended and added to by the later ones, the numbering grew more and more complex, with letters having to be used in addition to numbers. Finally, at Amsterdam in June 1997, the heads of government agreed to renumber the Articles and consolidate all revisions to the original Rome Treaty on the European Economic Community (EEC) in the TEC. The other Treaties, including the TEU, were kept separate. The Lisbon Treaty repeated this renumbering exercise. In this book, we use the Treaty Article numbers following the Lisbon Treaty revisions, occasionally followed by the old one in brackets where it is relevant. Where the reference is purely historical, the numbering prevailing at the time is given first, followed by the current, 'post-Lisbon' numbering in brackets. In all cases, the reference is to what is now called the TFEU (previously the TEC), unless it is indicated that it is to the TEU.

The key distinction between these two Treaties is as follows. The TEU sets out:

- the broad principles governing the EU, such as its commitment to democracy;
- the general role of the institutions;
- the principles governing who may apply to join the EU;
- how a member state may leave the EU (a provision that was introduced by the Lisbon Treaty).

207

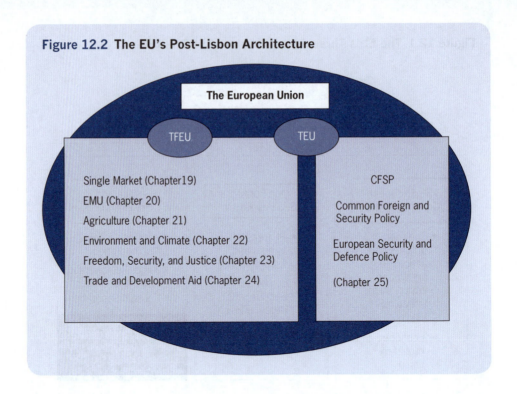

Figure 12.2 The EU's Post-Lisbon Architecture

The European Union

TFEU

TEU

Single Market (Chapter19)

EMU (Chapter 20)

Agriculture (Chapter 21)

Environment and Climate (Chapter 22)

Freedom, Security, and Justice (Chapter 23)

Trade and Development Aid (Chapter 24)

CFSP

Common Foreign and
Security Policy

European Security and
Defence Policy

(Chapter 25)

The TEU also sets out the details of the operation of the CFSP, making clear that it is not subject to the full authority of the Court of Justice. The TFEU, by contrast, sets out the detailed operation of the institutions and of all other policy areas. In what follows, the arrangements covered by the TFEU will be termed the **Union method**. As an indication of the scale of the revisions made by the Lisbon Treaty, over sixty changes were made to the TEU and nearly 300 were made to the TEC, in addition to renaming it the TFEU (see Figure 12.2).

The Decision Making Institutions (the Union Method)

This section considers the Union method. Later in the chapter (in 'The Decision making Institutions (CFSP below), we discuss the arrangements for CFSP. The main decision making institutions of the EU that are central to the Union method are, with one exception, those that were set up in the Treaty of Rome (EEC):

- the Commission;
- the Council of the EU;
- the EP.

The exception is the European Council. This body was set up in 1974 and has grown in importance, but the Treaties did not spell out its operation in detail until the Lisbon Treaty.

In addition to the main institutions there are also two consultative committees:

1. the Economic and Social Committee, which was in the original Treaty of Rome (EEC), and which in 2002 became the European Economic and Social Committee (EESC) following the incorporation within it of the formerly independent Consultative Committee of the European Coal and Steel Community (ECSC);

2. the Committee of the Regions (CoR), which was established in 1994 under provisions in the Maastricht Treaty.

Under the Union method, just as in CFSP, the European Council should be seen as the main agenda setter of the EU. Either through overseeing Treaty reform or through identifying policy strategy, it steers the broad direction of integration and of individual policies. However, it does not legislate. In legislation, it is the European Commission that plays the initial role. It is the proposer of legislation, and the Council of the EU and the EP are the joint legislative decision makers. The EESC and the CoR also have a right to be consulted on legislative proposals. Implementation of legislation once it has been passed is partly a responsibility of the Commission, but mostly it is the responsibility of the member states. The Commission and the CJEU act as watchdogs to ensure that the member states fulfil their obligations.

A similar division of functions exists for budgetary decision making. The European Council agrees the multi-annual financial perspectives, setting the EU's financial envelope for a seven-year period. The Commission proposes the annual budget; the Council of the EU and EP jointly decide on the annual budget. The CJEU and the Court of Auditors perform a watchdog role.

The European Council

As discussed above, the European Council plays an important agenda-setting role, and has oversight of all EU activity including CFSP. Article 15 TEU states:

> The European Council shall provide the Union with the necessary impetus for its development and shall define the general political directions and priorities thereof. It shall not exercise legislative functions.

This latter sentence is important, since it makes a clear delineation of responsibilities between the European Council and the Council of the EU. While this is a functional distinction—the European Council plays a political role, while the Council of the EU plays a legislative one—the other essential difference is of composition. The European Council comprises the EU's top political figures: the heads of state and government of the member states, the President of the European Council, the President of the European Commission, and the EU's High Representative of the Union for Foreign Affairs and Security Policy (HRUFASP). By contrast, the Council of the EU comprises ministers with a specific policy responsibility. Fuller discussion of the membership of both bodies is undertaken in Chapter 14, but the key point here is that the European Council represents the EU's summit of member-government power and has the political clout to drive forward the EU's agenda. The European Council has effectively positioned itself at the apex of the EU, guiding the direction of all EU policies. In practical terms, this situation means that legislation and other decision making typically takes place in a context that the European Council may already have shaped.

The Commission

In the formal decision making system of the EU, the Commission has two important roles (see Figure 12.3). It submits legislative proposals to the Council of the EU, and it draws up the draft annual EU budget for agreement by the Council of the EU and the EP.

The Commission is formally the sole institution with the right to propose legislation. In the view of the Commission, it is only its monopoly of the right of initiative that allows a coherent agenda to emerge for the EU as a whole. However, even leaving aside its limited authority in CFSP, there are several qualifications to its exclusive right to initiate proposals. First, as noted, the European Council—the EU summit meetings—sets out the EU's strategy and *may* therefore set the agenda that the Commission then follows in terms of specific legislation. Second, as a legacy of the situation relating to JHA under the three-pillar EU structure from 1993 to 2009, the Commission shares the right of initiative in measures relating to police and judicial co-operation (see Chapter 23).

The Commission's exclusive right to initiate legislation was also somewhat undermined by an amendment made under the Maastricht Treaty. Under Article 225 TFEU, the EP 'may, acting by a majority of its component Members, request the Commission to submit any appropriate proposal on matters on which it considers that a Union act is required for the purpose of implementing the Treaties'. Given that the democratic legitimacy of the EP has been increasingly emphasized, it would be difficult for the Commission to ignore such a request. Mirroring this power, the 'Council acting by a simple majority may request the Commission to undertake any studies the Council considers desirable for the attainment of the common objectives, and to submit to it any appropriate proposals' (Article 241 TFEU). Finally, even in the areas in which it retains the full right of initiative, to say that the Commission is the sole proposer of legislation should not be taken to imply that it works on legislative proposals in isolation. In practice, it has always consulted widely with interest groups, committees of technical experts, and civil servants from the member states. Nevertheless, despite the qualifications to its right of initiative, the standard practice is that the Commission initiates legislation and therefore plays a powerful role in the legislative process.

The Commission's legislative proposals can only be amended by the Council of the EU if the latter acts unanimously, and the Commission may withdraw or amend its own proposals at any stage as long as the Council has not acted on them. However, where the EP has the right of co-decision with the Council, and where the Council and the EP cannot agree on the text presented by the Commission, they may agree an alternative in a Conciliation Committee that can be passed without unanimity in the Council (see 'Decision Making Procedures' below). The alternative does not have to be proposed by the Commission.

Figure 12.3 Decision Making Institutions of the EU (Post-Lisbon Powers)

EUROPEAN COMMISSION

Initiates legislation
Drafts annual budget

COUNCIL OF THE EU

Decision-making powers
Joint budgetary authority

EUROPEAN PARLIAMENT

Co-decision powers
Consent powers
Consultation
Joint budgetary authority

CoR and EESC

Consulted
Issue Opinions

The Council of the EU (the Council)

The Council of the EU consists of representatives of the member states. Most meetings in the Council structure are not of Ministers themselves, but of various committees of member state officials (see Chapter 14, 'COREPER and other Preparatory Bodies'). Nearly all business for the meetings of Ministers is filtered through such committees, and then through the Committee of Permanent Representatives (COREPER), which consists of the ambassadors from the member states to the EU (see Chapter 14, 'COREPER and other Preparatory Bodies').

The Council makes decisions on proposals from the Commission either unanimously or through qualified majority voting (QMV) depending on the Treaty provision. As was explained in Chapter 7 ('The 1965 Crisis'), in 1965 de Gaulle blocked the formal transition to QMV, but the SEA introduced it for legislative acts related to the single market programme, and it has been extended at every subsequent Treaty reform to cover a range of other policies. The TEU's Article 16(3), as revised by the Lisbon Treaty, presented QMV as the default provision for decision making: 'The Council shall act by a qualified majority except where the Treaties provide otherwise.' There was quite a large number of new provisions for QMV in the Lisbon Treaty, but many of them were limited in scope. The key moves to QMV were on energy security, emergency humanitarian aid, intellectual property, social security for migrant workers, and judicial co-operation (the last after a five-year transition period that expired in 2014) (see Box 12.2). The key areas that remain subject to unanimity are: tax; social security; foreign policy; common defence; operational police co-operation; language rules; and the location of the EU's institutions.

Two additional points are worth noting about the extension of QMV in the Lisbon Treaty. First, the Treaty provided for some institutional matters to be decided by QMV in the European Council—for instance, when deciding its own president or in proposing to the EP a candidate for the President of the European Commission. These changes were an important innovation for the summit meetings, which had traditionally reached decisions by unanimous consent. Second, the Lisbon Treaty introduced potentially significant provisions for further moves to QMV without the need for Treaty revision. By including so-called passerelle clauses, it is possible to move some policy areas to QMV, notably on CFSP (but not defence-related matters), the multi-annual financial framework, employment law, environmental taxation, and judicial co-operation on family law. In each case, the European Council has to agree to the step by unanimity, and then in most cases has to get agreement from all national parliaments (Dougan 2008: 642). By early 2019, these clauses had not been used, despite pressure from the Juncker Commission to unlock decision making on matters of environmental taxation and CFSP. Indeed, many of the issues subject to unanimity seem unlikely to change under a *passerelle* clause—such as taxation, social security, citizens' rights, the location of the EU institutions, and languages.

Box 12.2 Policy Areas Covered by Qualified Majority Voting

The Maastricht Treaty extended QMV to:

- environment;
- development co-operation;
- the free movement of workers.

In the Treaty of Amsterdam, QMV was extended to:

- freedom of establishment;
- equal pay and treatment of men and women;
- mutual recognition of qualifications;
- the framework programmes for research and development;
- the internal market;
- public health;
- access to official documents;
- consumer protection;
- combating fraud;
- co-ordination of national provisions on the treatment of foreign nationals;
- customs co-operation.

The Lisbon Treaty extended QMV to:

- energy security;
- emergency humanitarian aid;
- social security for migrant workers;
- intellectual property;
- specific areas of judicial and police co-operation (with effect from 2014).

QMV also applies to the implementation of a range of policy areas.

The voting arrangements in the Council have been disputed over the history of European integration. The scheduled move to QMV was one of the triggers of the 1965 'empty chair' crisis (see Chapter 7, 'The 1965 Crisis'). At each round of Treaty reform from the SEA onwards there have been disagreements over which policy issues should be moved from unanimous voting to QMV. Thus, it might come as something of a surprise that despite widespread provision for QMV, the Council tends to practice consensual decision making (Häge 2013), although recent research suggests that national governments often issue public statements to express their dissatisfaction even where they have voted in favour (Hagemann et al. 2019). Here it appears that states use public statements to distance themselves from decisions, whilst maintaining the norm of consensual decision making.

A new voting system was provided for in the Lisbon Treaty under Article 16 (TEU) to operate from November 2014. Although one of the thorniest issues in negotiations leading to the Lisbon Treaty, on the face of it the provisions under Article 16 are very straightforward. Under the new rules, a double qualified majority is introduced that requires:

- support from 55 per cent of the members of the Council comprising at least fifteen member states where voting on proposals tabled by the Commission;
- support from at least 65 per cent of the population of the EU.

A blocking minority has to include at least four member states, thereby limiting the ability of the biggest states to block measures. The figures are different for votes on proposals that were not tabled by the Commission. In that case, the qualified majority must be 72 per cent of the member states, representing at least 65 per cent of the population of the EU.

The weighting of votes for twenty-seven states is indicated in Table 12.1.

The European Parliament (EP)

In the original blueprint for the ECSC, Jean Monnet did not include any parliamentary body—but in an attempt to make the new community more democratic, a European Parliamentary Assembly was added to the Treaty of Paris (Diebold 1959: 62). This body was carried over into the Treaties of Rome.

The EP has consistently tried to insert itself more effectively into the decision making process of the EU, especially since 1979 when it became a directly elected body. Under the original process, the Council of the EU was obliged to consult the EP before deciding on legislative proposals made by the Commission, but it could ignore the EP's opinion if it wished. This remains the case in only a very few policy areas following a series of reforms from the SEA to the Lisbon Treaty. In most policy areas, the so-called **ordinary legislative procedure (OLP)** applies. Under the OLP, the EP, taking its decision by simple majority, co-legislates with the Council, which may decide by QMV. The EP is able to block legislation altogether, an ultimate power that makes it difficult for the Council to ignore amendments proposed by the EP, lest the legislation as a whole be lost. These powers are outlined under the heading 'Decision Making Procedures' below.

The EP formally co-decides with the Council on the annual budget, and its approval is necessary for the budget to be given effect (see 'Decision Making Procedures' below).

Table 12.1 Qualified Majority Voting Percentage of Total EU Population by State EU27

Austria	1.97	Greece	2.40	Romania	4.37
Belgium	2.55	Hungary	2.19	Slovakia	1.2
Bulgaria	1.58	Ireland	1.08	Slovenia	0.46
Croatia	0.92	Italy	13.68	Spain	10.44
Cyprus	0.19	Latvia	0.43	Sweden	2.27
Czech Republic	2.35	Lithuania	0.63		
Denmark	1.29	Luxembourg	0.13		
Estonia	0.30	Malta	0.11		
Finland	1.23	Netherlands	3.87		
France	15.04	Poland	8.50		
Germany	18.50	Portugal	2.30		

Source: European Parliament (2019*a*: 28).

The other areas in which the EP has gained influence are in holding the Commission and the Council of the EU to account, and these powers are examined in Chapter 15, 'Composition and Functions'.

The European Economic and Social Committee (EESC)

The EESC consists of representatives of producers, farmers, workers, professionals, and of the general public. It is divided into three groups representing employers, workers, and 'various interests', although members are not obliged to join any of the groups. The 'various interests' group includes farmers, the professions, the self-employed, consumers, and environmental groups. Its 329 members are proposed by national governments and formally appointed by the Council of the EU. They sit on the EESC in a personal capacity and formally may not be bound by any mandate or instructions from their organizations.

The main work of the EESC is carried out by its six sections, which are the equivalent of the committees in the EP. They are:

1. Agriculture, Rural Development, and the Environment;
2. Economic and Monetary Union and Economic and Social Cohesion;
3. Employment, Social Affairs, and Citizenship;
4. External Relations;
5. Single Market, Production, and Consumption;
6. Transport, Energy, Infrastructure, and the Information Society.

A secretariat general is responsible for the EESC's administration.

The EESC is consulted on a range of issues, including agricultural matters, freedom of movement for workers, the right of establishment of companies, social policy, internal market issues, measures of economic and social cohesion, and environmental policy. In addition, the Commission may consult it on any matter that it thinks appropriate; the EESC has the right to issue Opinions on any matter on its own initiative.

In practice, the EESC is not particularly influential. It has become overshadowed by the EP, which has increased its legitimacy and powers significantly over the past decades as a result of direct elections and, more recently, with the growth of legislative powers. By contrast, the EESC's powers have remained consultative and its influence has declined in comparative terms. Under the Lisbon Treaty, the EESC's term of office was extended from four to five years.

The Committee of the Regions (CoR)

The CoR was created by the Maastricht Treaty, and was given the right to be consulted on proposals that affected regional and local interests, and the right to issue Opinions on its own initiative. Its members are chosen by the member states and officially appointed by the Council of the EU. As with the EESC, they moved to a five-year, renewable term with implementation of the Lisbon Treaty. Like the EESC, the CoR has 350 members and with the same breakdown of membership (see Table 12.2).

The members, collectively known as the Assembly, participate in the work of seven specialized commissions that are responsible for drafting the CoR's Opinions. The Bureau, which organizes the work of the Committee and its commissions, includes the chair, a first vice chair, plus one vice chair from each of the member states, elected by the members of the Assembly. They also include the chairs of the political groups. A secretariat general is responsible for the Committee's administration. In 2019, the CoR Bureau adopted a strategy to secure gender balance amongst its members. However, whilst there was gender parity in the Chairs of the Commission in 2019, the wider membership of the Committee remained disproportionately male. The CoR has called upon nominating organizations in the member states to address the imbalance in membership by nominating more women in future.

At first sight, the CoR appears to be another incarnation of the EESC, with which it originally shared a meeting chamber and support staff. However, there is an important difference: the CoR is strongly backed by political actors of considerable influence. The CoR was created at the insistence of the German Federal government under pressure from the Länder, the regional states that make up the German federation. With the political weight and the resources of these significant political actors behind it, the CoR acquired influence on those policies of the EU that have a regional focus. The Commission therefore has every incentive to work closely with the Committee, particularly because the Commission itself has tended to favour the emergence of a 'Europe of the regions' that would break down the domination of all decision making by the central governments of the member states. So, as well as being another constraint on the freedom of action of the Commission, the CoR provides it with a potential ally against national governments.

In 2009, and linked to the momentum associated with the Lisbon Treaty, the Committee proposed a political project to 'build Europe in partnership' through its

Table 12.2 Membership of the European Economic and Social Committee and Committee of the Regions

Austria	12	Latvia	7
Belgium	12	Lithuania	9
Bulgaria	12	Luxembourg	6
Croatia	9	Malta	5
Cyprus	6	Netherlands	12
Czech Republic	12	Poland	21
Denmark	9	Portugal	12
Estonia	7	Romania	15
Finland	9	Slovakia	9
France	24	Slovenia	7
Germany	24	Spain	21
Greece	12	Sweden	12
Hungary	12		
Ireland	9		
Italy	24	**TOTAL**	**329**

White Paper on multi-level governance (MLG) (Committee of the Regions 2009). The Committee explicitly took on the role of advocate of MLG and undertook consultation on how to embed it more strongly in its programme of work. This step bears some resemblance to the way in which the European Commission has been seen to encourage more integration through cultivated spillover (see Chapter 1, 'Theories of European Integration'). In this case, the CoR has explicitly embraced and sought to promote the body of academic work on MLG (see Chapter 2, 'Multi-Level Governance').

Decision Making Procedures

There are two categories of decision making procedure within the Union method: that for adopting the annual budget of the EU—the budgetary procedure—and those used to adopt legislation, i.e. the legislative procedures. The precise workings of these procedures are usually facilitated by inter-institutional agreements.

The Budgetary Procedure

The budget demonstrates the importance of the European Council as agenda setter. The annual budget negotiations take place within a multi-annual financial framework (MFF), which is proposed by the Commission, but the focus of the political bargaining is in the European Council. Under the Lisbon Treaty, the MFF must also then be formally signed off by the Council of the EU, deciding—like the European Council—by unanimity. The EP's involvement is limited to giving its consent to the Council's agreement. The current financial framework runs from 2014–20 and was agreed in 2013. Within the European Council, the United Kingdom, with support from the Netherlands and Sweden, wanted to scale back the budget proposed by the Commission and a settlement that showed real spending cuts compared to the previous period. Discussed at several European Council summits, agreement was reached in June 2013, with German Chancellor Angela Merkel acting as a broker between budget 'hawks' and those governments that were concerned about cuts to support for agricultural policy and the structural funds. The proposals still needed the consent of the EP, however, and it was keen to deploy its new powers under the Lisbon Treaty. In bargaining with the Council of the EU, it managed to secure some detailed changes under different budget headings and some concessions on flexibility within the budget, as well as a top-up to the 2013 annual budget in order to ensure it remained in balance. The MFF for the period 2014–20 amounted to some €960 billion (in 2011 prices; and €1,083 billion in 2019 prices), which budget 'hawks' could present as a reduction in real terms, compared to the previous financial framework.

The annual budgetary negotiations thus take place within limits strongly influenced by the European Council, which plays no formal role in the annual process. The annual budgetary procedure was amended by the Lisbon Treaty and is now set down in Article 314 TFEU. Happily, this change arising from the Lisbon Treaty brought simplification, abolishing a previous distinction between different categories of spending (see Bache and George 2006: 238–40 for the pre-Lisbon process).

The budgetary procedure begins with the Commission drawing up a preliminary draft budget, which it has to do under the Treaty by 1 September of each year, but which it normally completes by June (see Figure 12.4). The work is performed by the Budget Directorate General in consultation with the other services of the Commission and under the supervision of the Budget Commissioner. In preparing this document, the Commission is constrained by the multi-annual budgetary framework agreements.

Once the preliminary draft budget is prepared, and agreed by the Commissioners as a whole, it is sent to the Council of the EU, which formally has until 1 October to adopt a draft budget. Often, however, the draft budget has been adopted earlier than this. Most of the detailed work at this stage is done by the Budget Committee, a specialist body responsible to the Council. The Budget Committee is 'composed of senior officials (the "tough guys") from the national finance ministries' (Hayes-Renshaw and Wallace 2006: 43). The Council acts by QMV to adopt its position.

The draft budget is then sent to the EP, which has forty-two days either to approve the Council's position (or to take no decision), in which case the budget is approved, or to amend the Council's position, for which an absolute majority of members of the European Parliament (MEPs) is required. The Budgetary Committee of the EP takes the lead, co-ordinating with the other specialized committees as necessary, and then reports to the plenary for the vote. Typically, in the past, the EP has proposed a lot of amendments to the preliminary draft budget, most of which increase expenditure to the maximum permissible level. If this occurs, the draft budget goes back to the Council. The Council then has ten days to consider its response to the amendments proposed by the EP. It either then accepts the EP's amendments (by QMV), thereby

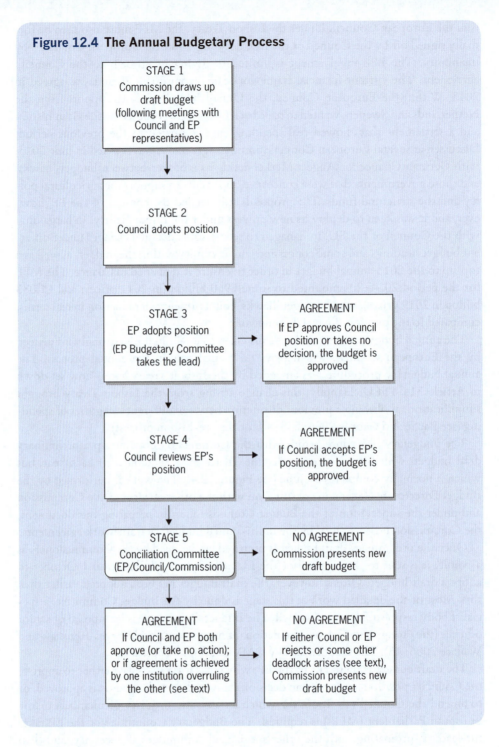

Figure 12.4 The Annual Budgetary Process

STAGE 1
Commission draws up draft budget (following meetings with Council and EP representatives)

STAGE 2
Council adopts position

STAGE 3
EP adopts position
(EP Budgetary Committee takes the lead)

AGREEMENT
If EP approves Council position or takes no decision, the budget is approved

STAGE 4
Council reviews EP's position

AGREEMENT
If Council accepts EP's position, the budget is approved

STAGE 5
Conciliation Committee (EP/Council/Commission)

NO AGREEMENT
Commission presents new draft budget

AGREEMENT
If Council and EP both approve (or take no action); or if agreement is achieved by one institution overruling the other (see text)

NO AGREEMENT
If either Council or EP rejects or some other deadlock arises (see text), Commission presents new draft budget

adopting the budget, or rejects them, which would lead to the convening of the Conciliation Committee.

The Conciliation Committee comprises an equal number of representatives of the Council and of the EP. The Commission is also present and attempts to broker an agreement. The Committee has twenty-one days to reach an agreement by a qualified majority of the Council and a majority of the EP. If no agreement is reached, the Commission has to present a new budget. However, if agreement is reached in the Conciliation Committee, the draft budget as amended is set for the final stage of the process.

This stage is arguably the most complex and this section should be read in conjunction with Figure 12.4. There are fourteen days for the EP and Council to act. If they both approve (or fail to act), the budget law is approved. If the EP adopts the budget but the Council rejects it (by QMV), the EP may decide to restore some or all of its amendments. If it can secure an absolute majority and three-fifths of the votes, the amendments are restored and the budget law is approved. If the three-fifths threshold is not met, the amendments fall and the 'conciliated' budget is passed. Symbolically, the President of the EP declares the budget to be adopted when that stage is reached. In all other circumstances, which includes the Council adopting the budget by QMV but the EP rejecting by absolute majority, the budget falls and the Commission has to present a new proposal.

If no budget has been agreed by the 1 January start of the financial year, the EU has to operate on a system known as 'provisional twelfths'. This means that, each month, one-twelfth of the previous year's budget total is released to cover expenditure. This will obviously prove cumulatively more restrictive as the year progresses, and in particular it will mean that new programmes, which had no budget line the previous year, will not be able to begin operation. Although there was the possibility of the 'provisional twelfths' regime being used for the 2011 budget, agreement was eventually reached after brinksmanship over the first use of new Lisbon Treaty provisions.

As revised in the Lisbon Treaty, the budget process has given more powers to the EP. In addition, detailed parts of the process were revised, including the functioning of the Conciliation Committee. The new arrangements draw on experience with adopting legislation under the ordinary legislative procedure (see 'Legislative Procedures' below). The annual process has also depended on some ground rules. These have taken the form of an inter-institutional agreement (IIA). The latest budgetary IIA was adopted in 2013, but a new draft IIA was issued by the Commission in 2019 as part of the process of laying the groundwork for the 2021–27 multi-annual financial framework. These agreements govern how the three institutions (Commission, Council, and EP) work together, as well as detailing technical issues to enable the decision making process to run smoothly. The pattern of EU budgetary expenditure can be seen in Figure 12.5, which shows the budget for 2018.

There is one other part to the budgetary process. Every year, the Commission is required to submit to the Council and the EP the accounts of the previous financial year. These are considered by both institutions in the light of the annual report from the Court of Auditors. The EP receives a recommendation from the Council, and in the light of this and its own deliberations, gives discharge to the Commission in respect to implementation of the budget (see Chapter 15, 'The Struggle for Power'). This means that the EP formally acknowledges that the Commission has implemented the budget properly and efficiently.

Legislative Procedures

The Lisbon Treaty provided some significant simplification of previous legislative procedures. It reduced the number from four to three. It also created the OLP as a default

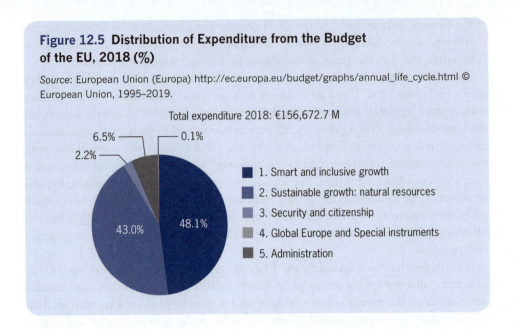

Figure 12.5 Distribution of Expenditure from the Budget of the EU, 2018 (%)

Source: European Union (Europa) http://ec.europa.eu/budget/graphs/annual_life_cycle.html © European Union, 1995–2019.

Total expenditure 2018: €156,672.7 M

- 1. Smart and inclusive growth
- 2. Sustainable growth: natural resources
- 3. Security and citizenship
- 4. Global Europe and Special instruments
- 5. Administration

pattern. All other arrangements are termed 'special legislative procedures' but there is quite some variation between them, so the term is not of much use in this outline. The process becomes 'special' if the Council decides by unanimity and/or the EP uses the consultation or consent procedures.

The three main procedures are:

1. the ordinary legislative procedure (or co-decision) (see Figure 12.6);
2. consultation (see Figure 12.7);
3. consent.

The Ordinary Legislative Procedure (Co-decision)

Until the reforms introduced by the 1986 SEA, the EP had not really functioned as a legislative body. In other words, it had not gone through a process of scrutinizing legislation and then tabling amendments, which the Council in turn had to consider and take into account. Previously, the EP's role was restricted to giving Opinions, which the Council could simply ignore (see 'The Consultation Procedure' below). The first step away from this, introduced in the SEA, was the co-operation procedure. It entailed two readings of legislation, each followed by the Council taking a decision. The second step, one of the key changes introduced by the Maastricht Treaty into the EU's legislative process, was the co-decision procedure. Unlike the co-operation procedure, co-decision did not leave the Council with the last word, but introduced a Conciliation Committee to try to reconcile differences at the end of the process. The co-operation procedure had more or less disappeared as a result of amendments in the Amsterdam Treaty, but was formally abandoned by the Lisbon Treaty, and so is not considered in detail here. However, the Lisbon Treaty made a further change by using the terminology the 'ordinary legislative procedure' to designate what is now the norm in EU law making: namely, the provision for QMV in the Council combined with co-decision between the Council and the EP.

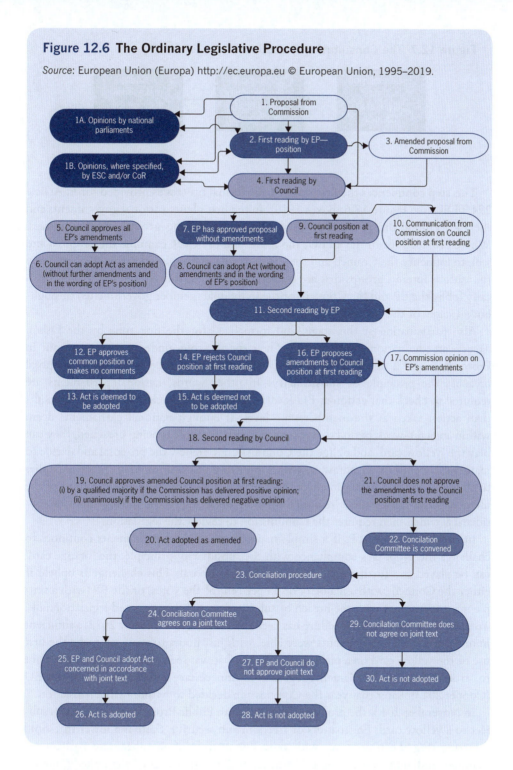

Figure 12.6 The Ordinary Legislative Procedure

Source: European Union (Europa) http://ec.europa.eu © European Union, 1995–2019.

The OLP is based on the principle of parity between the EP and the Council: neither institution may adopt legislation without the other's agreement. The procedure starts informally with the Commission consulting interest groups, civil servants from the member states, and MEPs in order to gather expertise and gain feedback on its initial ideas. The Commission then formally publishes a proposal after securing internal agreement.

Figure 12.7 The Consultation Procedure

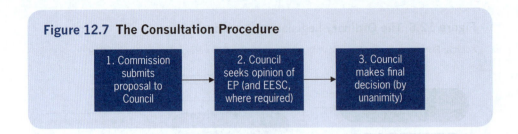

This step commences the first stage of the formal process as provided for in Article 294 TFEU (see Figure 12.6: boxes 1–10). In the first phase, national governments and the EP examine the proposal in their respective working groups and committees. Where provided for in the TFEU, the EESC and the CoR examine the proposal and seek to influence the Council and the EP. This role is also played through lobbying by the various interest groups that are potentially affected. Indeed, interest groups typically lobby the EP and the Council (or the individual member governments) throughout all stages of this process.

Also participating at this stage, and formalized for the first time by the Lisbon Treaty, are the national parliaments. Their specific role, under a process set out in Protocols 1 and 2 of the TEU, is to scrutinize whether the Commission's proposal breaches the principle of **subsidiarity**. In other words, national parliaments are required to check that action at EU level is appropriate and can better achieve results than action taken at the member-state level. If enough national parliaments deem within an eight-week period that the subsidiarity principle is being breached, they can play the 'yellow card' and oblige the Commission to review the proposal and decide to maintain, amend, or withdraw it, with supporting justification. This practice applies to all legislation and means in effect that the parliamentary chambers of a third of the member states must issue a 'reasoned opinion' objecting to the infringement of subsidiarity, which then requires the Commission to review the legislation.

In the case of the OLP, if a simple majority of national parliaments continues to challenge the proposal's compliance with the subsidiarity principle, the 'orange card' can be played as a further challenge against the proposal. This challenge is upheld if either the Council (with a majority of 55 per cent of the votes) or the EP (with a simple majority) agrees with the breach of subsidiarity, and the proposed legislation falls. To date, the yellow card procedure has been used three times. In May 2012, a sufficient number of national parliaments were able, with just hours to spare, to make the first use of the yellow card on a piece of legislation that was seen as impacting on the right to strike, which the parliaments regarded as unnecessary interference from the EU (Cooper 2013). Later that year the Commission decided to withdraw the legislation.

In November 2013, the proposal for a European Public Prosecutor's Office was subject to a yellow card. For matters of freedom and security, there is a lower threshold for triggering the procedure, with only one-quarter of member-state parliaments required; and, on this occasion, parliaments in eleven states issued a reasoned Opinion on the grounds of interference in their judicial systems. In this instance, the Commission reviewed the proposal and found it to be appropriate. However, the Commission subsequently adopted the directive using powers of enhanced co-operation (see Insight 12.2 below) so that it applied to only twenty-two member states.

In 2016, fourteen parliamentary chambers from eleven states objected to a directive on the posting of workers (i.e. workers being sent by their company to work in another EU country) on the grounds that the directive interfered with states' competence to decide remuneration laws for themselves. The Commission undertook a review and found no case to answer, so the legislation was adopted. The posting workers directive was, however, held up as an example of an East–West divide, with East European states worried about the potential negative implications of the increased regulation of posting workers for their nationals who relocate to other states for work (Barbière 2018). To date, the orange card procedure has not been used, and it seems difficult to envisage the circumstances under which it might be.

Leaving aside the (very rare) intervention of the national parliaments through the 'card' procedures, the first stage of the OLP is characterized by the EP holding its first reading, and deciding to approve the proposal or suggest amendments. In the latter case, the Commission may choose to adopt the EP amendments. If the Commission reissues the proposal, the Council may decide by QMV when it holds its first reading. If the Commission has not revised its proposal, the EP's amendments are only passed if unanimity is secured in the Council. If the EP and Council are of the same view, the legislation is adopted, and this has become the predominant pattern (see Chapter 15, 'Debates and Research'). Where no agreement has been reached, the Commission is given the opportunity to offer its Opinion, including whether it supports the Council's common position.

This Opinion commences the second phase (see Figure 12.6: boxes 11–20) comprising scrutiny by first the EP and then the Council, working on the basis of the Council's common position. Once again, it is quite likely that legislation will be agreed at this stage. However, if the EP rejects the common position, or the Council does not approve the EP's amendments, then the third phase is triggered and a Conciliation Committee is convened (Figure 12.6: boxes 22–28). The Committee consists of representatives of the member states in the Council and an equal number of representatives of the EP.

With the help of the Commission, which acts in the role of a facilitator, the Conciliation Committee tries to negotiate a mutually acceptable compromise text, which can then be recommended to both institutions. The Committee has six weeks in which to do so, operating on the basis of QMV for the Council members and simple majority voting for the EP members. Provided that they can agree a joint text, the legislation goes back to the Council and EP for final adoption, for which a six-week period is available. The Council is likely to adopt the legislation, since its delegation will have comprised a representative of each member state. However, it is more difficult to ensure that the EP delegation to the Conciliation Committee represents the whole of the EP. Hence a very small number of instances have arisen in which the EP has not approved the Committee's joint text. Along with a different scenario—namely, the failure on the part of the Committee to reach an agreement—these two sets of circumstances result in no legislation being adopted. The introduction of the conciliation process marked an important change in inter-institutional relations through empowering the EP. However, conciliation is now rarely used: between 2014 and 2016 no Conciliation Committee was convened and 97 per cent of OLP legislation was adopted via early reading agreement at first or second reading (European Parliament 2017).

The Lisbon Treaty brought in three changes, which are worth reiterating here. First, national parliaments have been given powers in the early stages of the process. Second, the use of the ordinary legislative procedure has become the norm. Third, it is important to note the very close alignment of the ordinary legislative procedure with the provisions of QMV in the Council. The second and third changes suggest a more supranational legislative process, while the first change offers the opportunity for national parliaments to intervene in the process and in rare cases (in which the requirements of the orange card can be met) to stop more legislation at EU level.

The Consultation Procedure

The original 'consultation procedure' for deciding on EU legislation involved the Commission submitting a proposal to the Council of Ministers, which was then obliged to seek the opinion of the EP, and, where required by the Treaty, of the EESC. In the *Isoglucose* case (1980), the CJEU ruled that the Council could not act legally in deciding on a proposal from the Commission without receiving the opinion of the EP. However, having received that opinion, the Council could, if it so wished, simply ignore it and agree to the proposal, or reject it. Amendments could only be made by unanimity in the Council. This procedure still exists (see Figure 12.7), but the Lisbon Treaty has further reduced the circumstances under which it can be used to about twenty. For example, agricultural policy, transport, the structural funds, and asylum and immigration were among the prominent policy areas in which consultation was replaced by OLP through the revisions, thereby strengthening the EP's powers.

Consent

Prior to the Lisbon Treaty, the EP was able to block decisions under what was then known as the assent procedure. This was originally introduced for agreements with non-member states, but was extended to other policy areas through different Treaty reforms. Some policy areas assigned to the assent procedure were subsequently re-allocated to co-decision; for instance, the structural funds (as a result of the Lisbon Treaty), and citizens' rights (as a result of the Amsterdam Treaty).

The Lisbon Treaty introduced the renamed consent procedure. Its main area of application is agreements with non-member states (including the accession of new members). New areas added include some aspects of judicial co-operation as well as the multi-annual financial framework for the EU budget. Consent requires the EP's agreement for a measure to be adopted. There is no provision for the EP to amend proposals. However, the fact that its consent is required does give it considerable influence at the stage when proposals are being prepared.

Implementation

The policy process does not end once agreement has been reached on a legislative proposal. The agreement still has to be implemented before the policy has any real existence. In other words, implementation is an integral part of the policy process. For many types of legislation, the primary implementers are the governments and administrations of the member states. The Commission itself has a central role in the case of other types of legislation, and is charged by Article 17 TEU to 'ensure the application of the Treaties, and of measures adopted by the institutions pursuant to them'. In performing this latter task, the Commission has recourse to judicial authority through the referral of cases to the CJEU. Finally, the implementation of all financial instruments is subject to scrutiny by the Court of Auditors.

National Authorities and Implementation

There are three main types of EU instruments that are legally binding: decisions, directives, and regulations. Alongside these are recommendations and Opinions. They do not have legal status; they are of political significance only. The legal instruments may be legislative or non-legislative: a new distinction introduced by the Lisbon Treaty. Hitherto, attention has focused on legislative instruments as part of an exploration of the role of the institutions in law making through the ordinary and special legislative procedures. However, non-legislative instruments (that is, those that do not go through the whole legislative process) such as European Commission rulings on competition policy, do have legal force, perhaps requiring a company to pay a large fine for anti-competitive behaviour.

Much of this chapter is concerned with decision making in relation to legislative instruments, notably via the OLP (see 'The Decision Making Institutions (the Union Method)'above). However, before examining the specific instruments, it is important to note three areas where the work is political in nature. First, the work of the European Council is concerned with reaching political agreements (or failing to do so) and not with legislating. Second, in CFSP (see 'The Decision Making Institutions (the Union Method)' above), political decisions are predominantly declaratory, making diplomatic pronouncements such as condemning states for breaching democratic principles or for aggression against other states. Legislation is unusual in CFSP, so political decisions are the norm. Finally, on some policy issues where the EU lacks clear authority (see 'The Post-Lisbon Architecture of the EU' below), the member states may meet to exchange good practice with a view to learning from each other but without any commitment to legislate. This pattern of EU member state co-operation is known as the open method of co-ordination (OMC). It has been practised particularly in the period from 2000 on a range of issues, such as combating social exclusion, raising female participation in the workforce, and, in particular, in the context of enhancing the EU's global competitiveness. The EU is thus a very political animal, although much—but by no means all—of its work is underpinned by law. Where its work is political in nature, implementation is normally a matter of 'political will' at the domestic level.

Where its work has legal underpinning, the EU system has clearer rules about implementation, depending on the legal instrument utilized. Decisions are addressed to particular individual legal actors, such as companies or individual states. Directives are the most common form of general legislation agreed in the Council of the EU; it is left to individual member states to decide *how* they are incorporated into national law. Regulations are directly applicable in all member states.

Where directives are concerned, there are two stages of implementation for national authorities. First, the directives have to be transposed into national law through appropriate national legal instruments. Second, they have to be implemented on the ground—that is, they have to be applied by national administrative authorities.

Regulations do not need the extra stage of being transposed into national law through national legal instruments, since they are directly applicable. However, it is still the responsibility of national administrative authorities to ensure that they are applied.

In both aspects of implementation, the record of member states in delivering upon what they have agreed varies considerably. This means that the outcomes of EU decisions do not always reflect the original aim. The Commission monitors the record of member states in implementing EU law in specific areas and the Juncker Commission put emphasis upon better enforcement to accompany its better law-making agenda (European Commission 2017).

The Commission and Implementation

Formally, the Commission has overall responsibility for the implementation of EU decisions. There are several processes of implementation in the EU, in each of which the Commission has a role. First, there is the implementation of common policies that are centrally administered by the Commission itself. These are few, but some of the powers of the Commission—notably competition policy, including the control of large-scale mergers—fall under this heading. A slightly different area is the administration of international policies such as the provision of food aid, where again the Commission is the sole responsible EU body, although it has to work in conjunction with other organizations. Second, there is the implementation of common policies, which takes place partly at the European level and partly at the national level: the administration of the Common Agricultural Policy (CAP) and the structural funds come under this heading. Third, there is the implementation of Council directives, where the Commission has a dual role as guardian of the Treaties: to ensure that directives are promptly and accurately incorporated into national law in the member states, and to ensure that they are actually implemented on the ground.

Under Article 258 TFEU, if the Commission considers that a member state has failed to fulfil its obligations, it is required to deliver a reasoned Opinion on the matter, after giving the government of the member state concerned the opportunity to submit its own observations. If the state does not comply with the reasoned Opinion, the matter may be brought before the CJEU. Another member state may also bring an alleged infringement of obligations to the attention of the Commission, which is required to act on the matter within three months, or the case automatically goes to the CJEU.

The Court of Justice of The European Union (CJEU)

Article 19 TEU charges the CJEU to ensure that European law is observed. It is the final arbiter on the interpretation of the Treaties and the application of EU law. As such, it is a referee in disputes between institutions and member states.

Where the CJEU is asked to rule on whether a member state has fulfilled its obligations under EU law, its decision is final. Originally there was no penalty other than moral pressure if a member state still failed to fulfil its obligations after an adverse ruling by the Court. However, the Maastricht Treaty amended Article 171 EEC (now Article 260 TFEU), to allow the Commission to return to the CJEU if it felt that a state was not complying with a ruling, and to request that a financial penalty be levied against the state.

The Court of Auditors

In 1975, the Treaty Amending Certain Financial Provisions of the EEC created a new institution: the European Court of Auditors. The Treaty confers upon the Court of Auditors the main task of auditing the accounts and the implementation of the budget of the EU, with the dual aim of improving financial management and the reporting to the citizens of Europe on the use made of public funds by the authorities responsible for their management.

The Court of Auditors is based in Luxembourg, and consists of one member from each member state appointed for a renewable six-year period. Members must have belonged to national audit offices, or be especially qualified for the office, and their independence must be beyond doubt. The members of the Court themselves elect a President from among their number for a period of three years. The court has some 850 staff, of whom about two-thirds are auditors.

This Court examines the accounts of all revenue and expenditure of the EU to determine whether the revenue has been received and the expenditure incurred in a lawful and regular manner. It provides the EP and the Council with a statement on the reliability of the accounts, and publishes an annual report. It also prepares special reports on aspects of the audit, either on its own initiative or at the request of another institution, and delivers Opinions on request from the other institutions concerning the financial implications of proposed legislation.

The Decision Making Institutions (CFSP)

The 1992 Maastricht Treaty introduced a three-pillar structure. As already noted, this structure was abolished as a result of the Lisbon Treaty and the 'Union method' became the predominant character. Nevertheless, some EU activity remains subject to different arrangements: namely, the CFSP, which used to be the second pillar of the EU. Reflecting this situation, the CFSP is governed by the TEU, whereas the TFEU addresses those policy areas governed by the Union method.

The CFSP is concerned with a range of activities, such as (see also Chapter 25):

- safeguarding the common values, fundamental interests, independence, and integrity of the Union in conformity with the principles of the United Nations Charter;
- strengthening the security of the Union;
- preserving peace and strengthening international security;
- promoting international co-operation;
- developing and consolidating democracy and the rule of law, and respect for human rights and fundamental freedoms.

With the passage of the Lisbon Treaty, these objectives are now absorbed into a wider set of goals relating to the EU's external action, including trade and aid policy, which are governed by the Union method.

The Lisbon Treaty introduced the new position of HRUFASP, a position which was held by (Baroness) Catherine Ashton from 2010 to 2014 and Federica Mogherini from 2014 to 2019. Josep Borell assumed the post in December 2019. The role of HRUFASP is combined with that of Vice-President of the European Commission. The HRUFASP thus pulls together two strands of external action that are subject to different decision making rules. Here, the concern is with the rules concerning foreign and security policy, but not trade, aid, enlargement, or other provisions covered by the TFEU.

CFSP is almost exclusively intergovernmental in character. In consequence, the CJEU, the Commission, and the EP are either absent or have very limited powers. The principal actors are the European Council, the Council of EU (meeting as the Foreign Affairs Council), and the HRUFASP.

The key characteristics of decision making on the CFSP are as follows:

- The European Council is responsible for the strategic interests and objectives of the Union.
- The European Council acts unanimously on the basis of recommendations from the Council of the EU.
- The HRUFASP may submit proposals to the Foreign Affairs Council on CFSP matters (and chairs this formation of the Council as well).
- The decisions under CFSP are non-legislative in nature. This makes clear that the legislative procedures considered above under the Union method are not applicable.

The CFSP is put into effect by the HRUFASP, who acts as an international envoy and negotiator, and by the member governments, using national and Union resources. These resources refer to the diplomatic networks of the member states, the Commission, and the Council. These networks were brought together following the passage of the Lisbon Treaty to form the European External Action Service (EEAS).

- The work of the Foreign Affairs Council is prepared by a committee of diplomats known as the Political and Security Committee.
- The HRUFASP consults regularly with the EP on policies under the CFSP and shall 'ensure that the views of the European Parliament are duly taken into consideration' (Article 36 TEU).

The character of the CFSP is overwhelmingly intergovernmental, requiring unanimous decisions. Because the member states were not ready to risk any surrender of control over foreign and security policy, CFSP is not subject to the Union method. Nevertheless, there are some departures from this intergovernmental pattern. First, the already-accepted practice of 'constructive abstention' may be utilized. Under this arrangement, a member government may abstain from a decision—as opposed to voting against it—and is consequently not bound by it. However, it is expected that any government in this situation will act in a spirit of solidarity and not work against the interests of the majority (Article 31 TEU). Further, there are some specific circumstances in which decision making may be by QMV. Essentially, these circumstances relate to the operationalization of decisions already reached by unanimity, or to the appointment of special representatives. If this provision sounds like a shift towards supranationalism, it is worth bearing in mind the following safeguard clause:

> If a member of the Council declares that, for vital and stated reasons of national policy, it intends to oppose the adoption of a decision to be taken by qualified majority, a vote shall not be taken. The High Representative will, in close consultation with the Member State involved, search for a solution acceptable to it. If he [sic] does not succeed, the Council may, acting by a qualified majority, request that the matter be referred to the European Council for a decision by unanimity.

(Article 31(2) TEU)

This provision bears some relationship to the Luxembourg Compromise of 1966 (see Chapter 7, 'The Luxembourg Compromise'), except that it only applies to the CFSP. Where QMV *is* used, the voting rules are the same as those outlined for the Union method (see 'The Decision Making Institutions (the Union Method)').

Decision making under CFSP remains largely intergovernmental in character, as national governments are concerned to retain their full authority. However, the creation of the EEAS raised the possibility that diplomats across the EU and the EU institutions would, by virtue of their networked relations, develop shared understandings that may transcend the purely national perspectives that have predominated hitherto. In addition, in 2018 there was a move for some states to work more closely together on Common Security and Defence Policy under the procedure of enhanced co-operation (see Insight 12.2 and Insight 25.2, 'Permanent Structured Cooperation (PESCO)').

The Post-Lisbon Architecture of the EU

This section turns to other architectural considerations that Lisbon introduced that need to be taken into account. The first is the creation of a catalogue of competencies that sets out the balance of authority between the EU and the member states. The second relates to **differentiated integration**: the situation whereby not all member states participate in all of the EU's activities, such as the single currency. The third concerns the somewhat haphazard emergence of a set of 'emergency brake' procedures. The fourth is slightly different, but also relates to scattered provisions across the Lisbon Treaty, known as *passerelle* clauses, which permit future procedural changes to take place on specific matters without the need to go through the whole process of Treaty reform (see 'The Decision Making Institutions (the Union Method)' above). Taken together, they have potentially important implications for the EU's decision making processes.

Catalogue of Competencies

Behind this legal terminology is a rather simple matter: what the EU can or cannot do. This issue was shaped by the debate at the time of the Maastricht Treaty concerning subsidiarity (see 'Decision Making Procedures' above). The basic principle of subsidiarity is that decisions should be taken as closely as possible to citizens. Or put another way, the EU should demonstrate that it can deliver policy more effectively than the member governments (or even sub-national governments). This concern chimed with British governments, which had consistently revealed a concern about the loss of national sovereignty. However, it has also been supported by sub-national governments, notably the German Länder, which became concerned in the run-up to the Maastricht Treaty that their national government was giving up sub-national law-making powers to the EU, thus reshaping the balance of domestic power in the German federation. This concern has never really gone away, and a catalogue of competencies was a German demand in the constitutional debate so that there could be some demarcation of what the EU can or cannot do (Bulmer 2010). Accordingly, the Lisbon Treaty spells out four types of EU competence: exclusive; shared; co-ordination; and supporting, co-ordinating, and supplementary action (see Insight 12.1). The CFSP provisions are not included in the detailed catalogue of competencies in the TFEU because they are outside the Union method and therefore contained in the TEU.

Insight 12.1 The EU's Catalogue of Competencies

Areas of Exclusive Competence
Customs Union

Competition rules for the internal market

Monetary policy for those states in the eurozone

Conservation of marine biological resources under the Common Fisheries Policy

Common commercial policy

Where an international agreement is necessary to enable the Union to exercise its internal competence.

Areas of Shared Competence

Internal market

Aspects of social policy

Economic, social, and territorial cohesion

Agriculture and fisheries (except marine conservation)

Environment

Consumer protection

Transport

Trans-European networks

Energy

Area of freedom, security, and justice

Aspects of public health safety

Research, technological development, and space

Development and humanitarian aid

Areas of Policy Co-ordination

Member states' economic policies

Member states' employment policies

Member states' social policies

Areas of Supporting, Co-ordinating, or Supplementary Action

Protection and improvement of human health

Industry

Culture

Tourism

Education, vocational training, youth, and sport

Civil protection

Administrative co-operation

The Common Foreign and Security Policy

The Union shall have competence . . . to define and implement a common foreign and security policy, including the progressive framing of a common defence policy.

Source: Summarized from Articles 3–6 TFEU. The CFSP provisions derive from Article 2 TEU.

Exclusive competencies represent the core business of the EU or what Duff (2009: 32) terms the 'lynch-pins of the acquis communautaire'. Most of these powers are long-standing. Two innovations were embodied in the Lisbon Treaty. First, marine conservation was made an exclusive competence of the EU, on the basis that preservation of fishing stocks would only be effective if responsibility were to lie at Union level. Second, the Lisbon Treaty slightly strengthened the competencies of the EU in external relations. The wording relating to the external authority of the EU that derives from its internal competencies was strengthened, and intellectual property and foreign direct investment were added to powers in commercial policy.

As regards areas of shared competencies, the list again mainly codifies the existing balance of authority. The main exceptions were the addition of space policy and some shifts within the environmental and energy provisions to include climate change and energy security, respectively. In areas of supporting action, there were some small additions: namely, administrative co-operation, civil protection, tourism, and sport. The catalogue of competencies forms an important component of the EU's post-Lisbon architecture. However, there are possibilities for the EU to promote co-operation between its member states even where it lacks clear authority according to the catalogue of competencies. In these areas, the European Commission may simply facilitate exchanges of views between the member states through the OMC. If a member state decides to change its policy following such exchanges, it acts within the domestic context, since there is no basis in the Treaties for EU legislation.

Differentiated Integration

Differentiated integration allows for permanent or temporary arrangements whereby not all member states proceed at the same pace in all policy areas. Differentiated integration has been practised within the EU since the 1970s, notably in monetary

231

policy. The Maastricht Treaty provided opt-outs for the UK regarding monetary union and the social chapter, although the Labour government of Tony Blair opted into the latter in 1997 at the time of the Amsterdam Treaty. Under the Amsterdam Treaty, the UK and Ireland exercised opt-outs, thereby retaining passport controls and not participating in the practices of the Schengen area (see Chapter 23). By early 2014, only eighteen of the twenty-eight member states had joined the single currency. These examples of differentiated integration developed in an ad hoc manner. However, from the Amsterdam Treaty onwards, member governments started to make general provision for core groups to proceed more quickly with integration, should they wish to do so. The official terminology for this practice is 'enhanced co-operation'.

Enhanced co-operation was introduced in the Amsterdam Treaty largely as a response to the obstructionist European diplomacy of the British Conservative government of John Major, which had a small parliamentary majority during the period 1992–97. German Chancellor Helmut Kohl was concerned at integration having to proceed at the pace of the slowest ship in the convoy. The provisions of the Amsterdam Treaty were designed to circumvent such a situation, but were quite tightly drawn and had negligible practical impact on the EU. Their basic principles were that enhanced co-operation could be used only as a last resort, that it needed a majority of the member states as participants, and that it had to allow other member states to join at a later stage. The safeguards were so tightly drawn that, according to David Phinnemore (2010: 39), it was not until 2008 that the first formal proposal was made to use these provisions.

The Lisbon Treaty has relaxed the requirements for enhanced co-operation in a number of ways. They are now governed by Article 20 TEU and Articles 326–34 TFEU. The basic principles are set out in Insight 12.2. The conditions are less onerous than before, so resort to them can be expected to be greater. In particular, it is possible for the core group to decide that it wishes to take decisions by QMV within enhanced co-operation even in a policy area in which the Treaties provide for unanimous voting for the member states. Potentially, such a decision could then bypass provisions for an emergency brake (see below).

Had they been in existence at the time, these provisions for enhanced co-operation might well have been used in the mid-1990s to bypass the obstructionism of the then British government; it is perhaps worth bearing in mind that a Eurosceptic government—from whichever member state—might in future find itself marginalized, rather than being able to hold up policy making. Enhanced co-operation was used for the financial transaction tax—often known as the Tobin tax—which eleven member states planned to introduce with the agreement of the EP. The UK was among the opponents of the original proposal for an EU-wide tax because of concerns about its impact on the City of London. The British government challenged the legality of the tax before the CJEU. Whilst at the time of writing, the Tobin Tax has yet to be introduced, Brexit may open a window of opportunity for this measure to be adopted. Another case related to judicial co-operation in relation to divorce proceedings, was approved in 2012 by fourteen member states, with Lithuania subsequently joining. The EU patent (a form of legal protection for inventions) is subject to a similar process. The EU patent simplifies the protection of inventions compared to a system where separate approval was needed in each state. Twenty-five member states (excluding Italy and Spain) approved the legislation in 2012 so that, once all the ratification processes were completed, a patent could be obtained with validity across all those states. In 2017, twenty-five states agreed to enhanced co-operation in the field of Common Security and Defence Policy (see Insight 25.2, 'Permanent Structured Co-operation').

A slightly different manifestation of differentiated integration that emerged from the eurozone crisis is the Treaty on Stability, Co-ordination and Governance in the Economic and Monetary Union, usually termed the Fiscal Compact. This Treaty was signed in March 2012 and is designed to bring in stricter, EU-monitored control of public expenditure in the member states. However, it was only signed by twenty-five states, as Britain and the Czech Republic did not wish to be bound by its rules. This is a Treaty version of differentiated integration, although it is not formally part of the

---

Insight 12.2 Enhanced Co-operation in the EU

- Enhanced co-operation may only be practised in the EU's non-exclusive competencies (see Insight 12.1) and must follow detailed provisions in Articles 326–34 TFEU.

- Enhanced co-operation shall aim to advance the EU's objectives, protect its interests, and reinforce its integration process.

- A minimum of nine member states is needed to launch enhanced co-operation.

- Enhanced co-operation shall be open at any time to all member states.

- 'The decision authorising enhanced co-operation shall be adopted by the Council as a last resort, when it has established that the objectives of such co-operation cannot be attained within a reasonable period by the Union as a whole, and provided that at least nine Member States participate in it' (Article 20(1) TEU).

- All members of the Council may participate in its deliberations, but voting is confined to those member states participating in enhanced co-operation following rules set out in Article 330 TFEU.

- Only participating member states are bound by the resultant acts in the framework of enhanced co-operation. These acts do not form part of the *acquis communautaire*, which accession states must accept prior to membership.

- Enhanced co-operation must not undermine the internal market or economic, social, and territorial cohesion.

- Requests to move to enhanced co-operation are addressed to the Commission in the case of the Union method, and to the HRUFASP in the case of CFSP. The Commission and HRUFASP give their Opinion. The decision to proceed is taken by the Council of the EU acting unanimously.

- Procedures are spelt out in the TFEU for any state wishing to join an existing group of states undertaking enhanced co-operation. In the Union method, the Commission takes a decision within four months. In CFSP, unanimous agreement is needed by the Council of Foreign Affairs, but with only the core group voting.

EU's legal framework. Twenty-two states are bound by the Fiscal Compact: the nineteen euro-area states and Bulgaria, Denmark, and Romania. Croatia is also eligible to join the Compact, but had not done so at the time of writing. In short, the Fiscal Compact is a further manifestation of the increasing differentiation that is perhaps an inevitable outcome of the size of the EU and the diversity of interests among the member states.

Emergency Brakes

In a very small number of policy areas, the Lisbon Treaty introduced an emergency brake. The principle is that a member government can suspend the OLP (in which it could be overruled by a QMV decision) and appeal to the European Council (Dougan 2008: 643–4). The details differ between the policy areas, but apply to the co-ordination of social security systems and judicial co-operation. An emergency brake may also be invoked in the CFSP to stop an operational decision being taken by QMV. In short, the emergency brake has emerged as a device that was built into the Lisbon Treaty where one or a small number of governments had concerns about sovereignty, but were prepared to recognize that QMV was likely to make decision making more effective in principle.

Passerelle Clauses

The idea behind a *passerelle* clause is that it offers the opportunity to change the decision making procedure, without the need for Treaty reform. For example, in a range of policy areas, it is possible to move to the OLP from one of the special legislative procedures, thereby adding either QMV in the Council or co-decision with the EP, or both. In all cases, the shift would be towards a more supranational set of decision making rules. Commission President Jean-Claude Juncker described the *passerelle* clauses of the Lisbon Treaty as 'lost treasure' in his 2018 State of the Union address (Juncker 2018). He argued that they could be used to secure EU positions on human rights and the launching civilian missions that had been blocked by individual member states under unanimity rules. However, the *passerelle* clauses require approval by a 'super-majority': namely, the agreement of all member states in the European Council, and approval by the EP under the consent procedure. In addition, in most cases, national parliaments have six months in which to lodge an objection, otherwise the change to QMV is deemed to be approved. There are also some special cases in which a move to QMV in the Council could occur, but not to the OLP because the EP's powers remain under the consent procedure, for instance in connection with the EU's multi-annual financial framework (see Dougan 2008: 642).

The basic principle of these clauses is to enable a more efficient decision making method to be introduced if this is an uncontroversial step, and provided that the super-majority can be achieved. The need for Treaty reform in order to make such changes is side-stepped, although the super-majority offers some comparison to the requirements of Treaty ratification. However, despite Juncker's speech, by early 2019 no use had yet been made of the clauses, although the Commission had published a Communication advocating their use in relation to tax policy (European Commission 2019a).

CONCLUSION

The Lisbon Treaty made some fundamental changes to the EU's architecture. The abolition of the three-pillar system introduced in the Maastricht Treaty provided some simplification. The creation of the default pattern of the OLP under the Union method should also help students to find their way out of what had become a procedural maze. However, the use of enhanced co-operation and the possibility of deploying *passerelle* clauses does risk restoring some complexity.

So, the decision making procedures of the EU are complex, but were tidied up somewhat by the Lisbon Treaty. In theory, this tidying should lead to greater clarity over the legislative procedures to be followed on particular policy issues. In the past, the procedure to be followed was by no means immediately apparent. In such cases, the Commission could exercise some discretion in deciding under which Articles of the Treaties it would bring forward its proposals. Sometimes this was challenged. For example, in 1990, the Commission brought forward proposals on maternity rights under what was then the new Article 118A of the EEC Treaty (now Article 153 TFEU), which the SEA had introduced. This meant that the measure was subject to QMV in the Council, rather than unanimity. The British government objected to the Treaty base, and threatened to refer the matter to the CJEU, before eventually accepting a compromise solution. Nowadays, the predominance of the OLP provides a fair measure of consistency across the legislative process, with the Commission, the Council of EU, and the EP the dominant institutional actors. Behind the scenes of the formal constitutional arrangements, interest groups always exercise a considerable influence on both the content of proposals and the outcome of the decision making process. At the implementation stage, the Commission and the CJEU are particularly important in the Union method, but national governments are often the key to how policies are implemented.

The formal relationships outlined in this chapter are only one part, although an important part, of the analysis of the role of the EU institutions. The informal relationships between the institutions themselves, and between the institutions and the member states, are not covered here. In the chapters that follow, these informal relationships enter the discussion, and attention focuses on the academic debates that have been generated about these relationships and their implications.

KEY POINTS

The Treaties

- The EU was founded by the Treaty of Paris (1951) and the two Treaties of Rome (1957), which were amended and supplemented by later Treaties.

- The Maastricht Treaty (1992) created the three-pillar EU.

- In 1997, the various Treaties were codified into two: the Treaty on the European Community (TEC) and the Treaty on European Union (TEU).

- The Lisbon Treaty, implemented in December 2009, abolished the EU's 'pillar' architecture dating from 1993 and created the 'Union method', which applies to all policy areas except the CFSP. The TEC was renamed the Treaty on the Functioning of the EU (TFEU).

The Decision Making Institutions (the Union Method)

- The European Council sets the EU's broad policy agenda and the general direction of integration.

- The Commission has the sole formal right to initiate legislation, although this has been undermined in practice.
- The Council of the EU has to agree to proposals for them to become law. Originally, it had to agree unanimously, but there has been a steady move towards the adoption of QMV.
- Since it became directly elected in 1979, the powers of the EP have grown, particularly in relation to the legislative process, until today it is effectively a co-legislator with the Council of EU in most policy areas.
- The EP is co-equal decision maker with the Council on the annual budget.
- The EESC consists of representatives of producer and consumer groups, and has to be consulted before certain categories of legislation can be adopted, but its Opinions are not often influential.
- The CoR consists of representatives of regional and local authorities, and is an advocate for MLG in the EU's territorially organized policies.

Decision Making Procedures

- There are two main types of decision making in the Union method: budgetary and legislative.
- The EU annual budget passes through a complex process, which involves the Commission, the Council, and the EP.
- The Lisbon Treaty made the OLP the norm: QMV in the Council and co-decision with the EP. Consultation and consent remain for a reduced set of circumstances.

Implementation

- Implementation is an integral part of the policy-making process.
- Three main types of EU legislative instrument are legally binding: decisions, directives, and regulations.
- While the Commission has formal responsibility for implementation, in practice national authorities play an important role.
- The CJEU has the power to interpret EU law, and its decisions are final.
- The Court of Auditors checks the legality and regularity of EU expenditure.

The Decision Making Institutions (CFSP)

- In CFSP, which is predominantly intergovernmental in character, the Commission, the EP, and the CJEU have less authority than under the EU pillar.
- The HRUFASP plays a key role in CFSP decisions and in co-ordinating the External Action Service.

The Post-Lisbon Architecture of the EU

- The EU's powers are set out in a catalogue of competencies.
- In a small range of policies, the Lisbon Treaty built in a number of 'emergency brakes' to ensure that the member states can appeal if supranationalism threatens their sovereign interests.
- The Lisbon Treaty has increased the prospects for the emergence of further core groups in specific policy areas or 'pioneer' groups on individual items of legislation. It also introduced possibilities to move to more supranational decision making on specific policies under *passerelle* clauses.

For additional material and resources, please visit the online resources www.oup.com/uk/bache5e.

QUESTIONS

1. What is the main purpose and functions of the EU Treaties?

2. What were the main changes introduced by the Lisbon Treaty?

3. What are the advantages and disadvantages of qualified majority voting?

4. What are the main procedures of decision making in the EU and how do they differ?

5. How and why do institutions matter in the EU?

FURTHER READING

In view of the continuing influence of the changes brought about by the Lisbon Treaty, an important reference is **J.-C. Piris**, *The Lisbon Treaty: A Legal and Political Analysis* (Cambridge: Cambridge University Press, 2010). Shorter accounts on the Lisbon Treaty are offered by

A. Duff, *Saving the European Union: The Logic of the Lisbon Treaty* (London: Shoehorn Books, 2009) and, from a more legal perspective, by **M. Dougan**, 'The Treaty of Lisbon 2007: Winning Minds not Hearts', *Common Market Law Review*, 45 (2008): 617–701. For more detail on decision making and implementation, see chapters 4 and 11, respectively, of **H. Lelieveldt and S. Princen**, *The Politics of the European Union* (Cambridge: Cambridge University Press, 2011). Two special issues have explored the implications of Lisbon for the Council and Parliament, respectively: **S. Fabbrini** and **U. Puetter (eds)**, 'Integration without Supranationalisation: The Central Role of the European Council in Post-Lisbon EU Politics', *Journal of European Integration*, 38, special issue (2016); and **E. Bressanelli** and **N. Chelotti (eds)**, (2019). Power without Influence? Explaining the Impact of the European Parliament Post-Lisbon. *Journal of European Integration* 41(3): 265–76.

Chapter 13

The European Commission

Chapter Overview

When the European Economic Community (EEC) was established, the European Commission was expected to be the motor of European integration. Because of this, it attracted considerable academic attention, becoming a focal point for the theoretical disputes between intergovernmentalists and supranationalists (see Chapter 1, 'Theories of European Integration'). This chapter sets out the Commission's functions and its structure, before detailing its role in policy making. It reviews the debate on the extent to which the Commission is an autonomous political actor or simply an agent of the member states. It then turns to the increasing challenges faced by the Commission in securing effective implementation of European Union (EU) policies and its response to concerns over its financial management of EU programmes.

Functions

The Commission has several key functions in the political system of the EU. It is the formal initiator of legislative drafts and of the budget (see Chapter 12, 'Decision Making Procedures'). It may act as a mediator during the legislative process, for instance in helping to find agreement between the member governments, or between the Council of the EU and the European Parliament (EP). It has an important role in managing certain Commission policies, such as competition policy, where executive powers lie at the EU level. It is the 'guardian of the Treaties', in that it is entrusted with ensuring, in those areas in which policy is implemented by member states' authorities, that they are correctly putting EU legislation into effect. It has traditionally held an important role in external economic relations, such as trade negotiations. Finally, it is the 'conscience of the European Union'. Traditionally seen as *the* supranational voice of the collective interest in EU legislation, the Commission has found competitors for this role in recent decades: notably the EP, in which the EU's elected representatives develop their own positions. The European Council, as the institution in which heads of government set the EU's strategic direction, has become the intergovernmental voice of the collective interest. As noted in Chapter 12, 'The Decision Making Institutions (the Union Method)', these Commission functions relate to the Union method and not to Common Foreign and Security Policy (CFSP), in relation to which its functions are very limited.

Composition and Appointment

In an echo of debates between intergovernmentalists and supranationalists, the Commission has been pilloried by Eurosceptics as a bureaucratic monster that is out of control and usurps the rights of the member states. In fact, it is a relatively small organization in comparison not just with national civil services, but even with individual departments of state in national governments.

The European Commission consists of a College of Commissioners and a permanent civil service. On 1 January 2019, the Commission employed 32,399 staff according to its own figures (European Commission 2019b). However, once a host of auxiliary staff, contract agents, and service providers are excluded this figure comes down to roughly 22,000. Of this smaller figure, around 19,000 are permanent or temporary administrators, the rest being employed either in scientific research, as translators and interpreters, or in the Commission delegations around the world. 'The Commission' in fact refers both to the Services of the Commission and to the College of Commissioners. However, these should be clearly distinguished, not least because, as Cram (2001: 776) pointed out, 'the members of each may have very different perspectives and, most importantly, very different interests or preferences'.

The Services are divided into twenty-nine Directorates General (DGs), plus a number of special services. They are listed in Table 13.1. The DGs are the equivalent of national civil service departments of state. Originally, they were known by their number only (e.g. DG IV for the Competition Directorate General), but this system was abolished under Romano Prodi's presidency of the Commission (1999–2004) as part of a reform designed to bring the structure of the DGs more into line with the designation of portfolios within the College of Commissioners. Instead, a set of acronyms is now utilized (see Table 13.1).

The permanent senior administrators (in the so-called AD category) number about 11,500; additionally, about 1,000 'Detached National Experts' are seconded from the member states. Recruitment to the permanent posts is on the basis of merit, although a loose quota system is utilized to ensure an approximate balance of nationalities and gender.

Political direction is given by the College of Commissioners. Since the Maastricht Treaty, Commissioners have been appointed for five-year terms (previously four-year) in order to achieve an alignment with the five-year terms of the EP. The pattern of the appointment process was adjusted in the Lisbon Treaty. Starting with the 2010–14 Commission, the process was as follows.

'Taking into account the elections to the European Parliament', as Article 17 TEU puts what is now recognized to be a politicized process, the European Council proposes a candidate for President of the Commission. He or she must be approved by a majority of members of the European Parliament (MEPs); if not, the European Council must propose a new candidate. In 2014, Jean-Claude Juncker became the first '*Spitzenkandidaten*' whose selection was formally linked to the outcome of the EP elections. Juncker was the candidate for the European Peoples' Party (EPP) group, which secured the most MEPs in 2014 (see Chapter 15, 'Composition and Functions'). Juncker used this platform as a departure point for developing a 'political' mandate (Kassim 2017). Juncker wanted his Commission to be different from its predecessor: it would 'take political responsibility for its actions, respond to the interests of

Table 13.1 The Directorates General and Services of the Commission (June 2019)

Policies	External relations	General	Key services
DG Agriculture and Rural Development (AGRI)	DG International Co-operation and Development (DEVCO)	DG Budget (BUDG)	Secretariat General (SG)
DG Climate Action (CLIMA)	DG European Neighbourhood Policy and Enlargement Negotiations (NEAR)	DG Communication (COMM)	Legal Service (SJ)
DG Communications Networks, Content and Technology (CONNECT)	DG Civil Protection and Humanitarian Aid Operations (ECHO)	DG Human Resources and Security (HR)	European Anti-Fraud Office (OLAF)
DG Competition (COMP)	DG Trade (TRADE)	DG Informatics (DIGIT)	European Personnel Selection Office (EPSO)
DG Economic and Financial Affairs (ECFIN)		DG Interpretation (SCIC)	European Political Strategy Centre (EPSC)
DG Education, Youth, Sport and Culture (EAC)		DG Translation (DGT)	European Statistics (EUROSTAT)
DG Employment, Social Affairs and Inclusion (EMPL)			Infrastructures and Logistics—Brussels (OIB)
DG Energy (ENER)			Infrastructures and Logistics—Luxembourg (OIL)
DG Environment (ENV)			Internal Audit Service (IAS)
DG Financial Stability, Financial Service and Capital Markets Union (FISMA)			Joint Research Centre (JRC) Office for Administration and Payment of Individual Entitlements (PMO)
DG Health and Food Safety (SANTE)			

Table 13.1 (Continued)

Policies	Key services
DG Internal Market, Industry, Entrepreneurship and SMEs (GROW))	Publications Office (OP)
DG Justice and Consumers (JUST)	Service for Foreign Policy Instruments
DG Maritime Affairs and Fisheries (MARE)	Article 50 Taskforce
DG Migration and Home Affairs (HOME)	
DG Mobility and Transport (MOVE)	
DG Regional and Urban Policy (REGIO)	
DG Research and Innovation (RTD)	
DG Taxation and Customs Union (TAXUD)	

Source: http://europa.eu/about-eu/agencies/index_en.htm, December 2019.

Note: In parentheses are the acronyms utilized within the European Commission and elsewhere. Directorates General are denoted DG; others are Services.

citizens, and be prepared to defend the European Union (EU) and itself' (Kassim and Laffan, 2019: 49). The process for 2019 was more problematic as the largest political group (again the EPP) put forward a candidate (Manfred Webber) who failed to secure support from the Council. Instead, the Council proposed Ursula von der Leyen, who was largely unknown outside Germany and was regarded as a close political ally of German Chancellor Angela Merkel. The appointment of the Commission's first female President was consequently mired in controversy due to the unconventional way that she was nominated. This was unfortunate, considering the progress her appointment represents in terms of gender representation in the upper echelons of the EU.

The member states put forward candidates for the post of Commissioners. The President-Elect of the Commission then selects a team and assigns portfolios before submitting the line-up to the Council of the EU for approval by qualified majority vote (QMV). One of the Commissioners is the High Representative of the Union for Foreign Affairs and Security Policy (HRUFASP; see Chapter 14, 'The Council Presidency').

The EP, acting by the consent procedure (see Chapter 12, 'Decision Making Procedures'), must then approve the Commission team, following individual hearings of the candidates. Finally, after this investiture by the EP, the Council of the EU formally appoints the Commissioners (again with QMV available).

The number of Commissioners has increased over the years as a result of enlargements. Until 2005, each state had one Commissioner, and the larger member states (France, Germany, Italy, Britain, and Spain) had two each. In the Treaty of Nice (see Chapter 10, 'The Nice Treaty'), it was agreed that, starting with the Commission that took office on 1 January 2005, the number of Commissioners would be limited to one per member state. The Lisbon Treaty (Article 17 TEU) made provision for the number of Commissioners to be reduced further with effect from November 2014. Its size would correspond to two-thirds of the number of member states, and be selected on the basis of equal rotation between the member states. When the Irish people rejected the Lisbon Treaty in the June 2008 referendum, the possibility of there not being an Irish Commissioner after 2014 was an issue that came to the fore. Consequently, it was decided that one Commissioner would continue to be appointed for each member state, and this was confirmed by the European Council in May 2013. This arrangement satisfied Irish concerns, but means that it is increasingly difficult to find meaningful responsibilities for each Commissioner, especially in the event of future enlargement.

The 2019–24 College comprised twenty-seven Commissioners (see the list, with their portfolios, in Table 13.2). The UK refused to appoint a Commissioner, given its commitment to leave the EU, even though there was a period of two months between the Commission taking office and the UK leaving the EU in January 2020. Commissioners are sworn to abandon all national allegiances during their tenure of office, and they are bound by the principle of collegiality, so all actions are the responsibility of the Commission as a whole.

The term of the Commission President is renewable and José Manuel Barroso's term was renewed in 2009 for five more years (see Chapter 15, 'The Struggle for Power'). Jean-Claude Juncker only served one term from 2014–19. A new College was appointed in December 2019 (see Table 13.2, and see Chapter 15, 'The Struggle for Power' for a discussion of the appointment process). A list of presidents of the Commission is given in Table 13.3. There are also seven vice-presidents, one of whom—as HRUFASP, a joint appointment with the Council of the EU—represents the EU on the world stage. In 2014, a new system of vice-presidents was established. Previously, the role of VP was purely honorary. However, under Juncker the seven vice-presidents were made responsible for co-ordinating cross-cutting horizontal policy areas, to provide political leadership and mitigate policy fragmentation across the Commission.

Each Commissioner has a team of policy advisers, typically six or seven. Collectively, the advisers are known by the French word *cabinet* (pronounced 'cab-ee-nay'). The President's *cabinet* is larger, approximately double the size of the others. The members of the *cabinet* act as the eyes and ears of the Commissioner within the organization, and perform a valuable co-ordination function—particularly valuable because the structure of the Commission tends to produce fragmentation of the policy-making process between the DGs. It is widely accepted that the dynamism of Jacques Delors's presidencies would not have been possible without the sheer energy and effectiveness of the President's *cabinet* under the leadership of Pascal Lamy, who later went

Table 13.2 Commissioners and their Portfolios (2019–24)

Ursula von der Leyen	President	German
Josep Borrell Fontelles	Vice-President; High Representative of the Union for Foreign Affairs and Security Policy	Spanish
Frans Timmermans	Executive Vice-President; European Green Deal	Dutch
Margrethe Vestager	Executive Vice-President: A Europe Fit for the Digital Age	Danish
Valdis Dombrovskis	Executive Vice-President: An Economy that Works for People	Latvian
Maroš Šefčovič	Vice-President; Inter-Institutional Relations and Foresight	Slovakian
Věra Jourová	Vice-President; Values and Transparency	Czech
Dubravka Šuica	Vice-President; Democracy and Demography	Croat
Margaritis Schinas	Vice-President; Promoting our European Way of Life	Greek
Johannes Hahn	Budget and Administration	Austrian
Phil Hogan	Trade	Irish
Mariya Gabriel	Innovation, Research, Culture, Education and Youth	Bulgarian
Nicolas Schmit	Jobs and Social Rights	Luxembourgish
Paolo Gentiloni	Economy	Italian
Janusz Wojciechowski	Agriculture	Polish
Thierry Breton	Internal Market	French
Elisa Ferreira	Cohesion and Reforms	Portuguese
Stella Kyriakides	Heath and Food Safety	Cypriot
Didier Reynders	Justice	Belgian
Helena Dalli	Equality	Maltese
Ylva Johansson	Internal Security	Swedish
Janez Lenarčič	Crisis Management	Slovenian
Adina Vălean	Transport	Romanian
Olivér Várhelyi	Neighbourhood and Enlargement	Hungarian
Jutta Urpilainen	International Partnerships	Finnish
Kadri Simson	Energy	Estonian
Virginijus Sinkevičius	Environment, Oceans, and Fisheries	Lithuanian

on to become a Commissioner himself. Martin Selmayr, head of Jean-Claude Juncker's Cabinet, was also widely regarded as being very influential in driving forward Juncker's agenda (Peterson 2017).

Table 13.3 Presidents of the European Commission

Walter Hallstein (West Germany)	1958–67
Jean Rey (Belgium)	1967–70
Franco Maria Malfatti (Italy)	1970–72
Sicco Mansholt (Netherlands)	1972
François-Xavier Ortoli (France)	1973–76
Roy Jenkins (UK)	1977–80
Gaston Thorn (Luxembourg)	1981–84
Jacques Delors (France)	1985–94
Jacques Santer (Luxembourg)	1995–99
Romano Prodi (Italy)	1999–2004
José Manuel Barroso (Portugal)	2004–14
Jean Claude Juncker	2014–19
Ursula von der Leyen	2019–24

Each member of the *cabinet* has responsibility for monitoring one or more areas of policy, and there are weekly meetings of these specialists, chaired by the relevant member of the President's *cabinet*, to discuss issues that are current and to monitor the progress of draft legislation. The heads of the units—*chefs de cabinet*—also meet weekly, two days prior to the weekly meetings of the College of Commissioners. All draft legislation that has been prepared within the DGs has to go to the College for final approval, in keeping with the principle of collegiality. Before it gets there, it is considered by the *chefs*, and if difficulties that can be resolved are spotted at that stage, the draft will be referred back for amendment or further consideration. Where differences are highly politicized, the matter will be allowed to go through to the College for discussion.

The Commission in the Policy-Making Process

There is considerable academic debate around the role of the European Commission in the policy-making process. There is no doubt about its formal role: it has the sole right to initiate proposals for legislation in all policy areas under the Union method, with the exception of the area of freedom, security, and justice (AFSJ), for which this power is shared (see Chapter 23, 'Freedom, Security, and Justice'). Thus, without a proposal from the Commission, neither the Council of the EU nor the EP can legislate. However, the debate centres on whether the Commission actually determines the direction in which the EU moves, particularly given the European Council's similar aspirations (see Chapter 14, 'The European Council') as well as those of the EP.

In reality, the Commission has come to be seen as the body that puts together the detailed proposals that operationalize the political programme and strategy defined by the European Council. That is not to say that the Commission is a mere secretariat 'following orders', because it retains autonomy on drafting proposals within the broad direction offered by the European Council. In addition, the European Council cannot, given the infrequency of its meetings, offer direction in all policy areas, so has to concentrate on what it sees as its priorities. Finally, as the Commission President is a participant in the European Council, there is scope for the Commission to play a part in shaping the European Council's agenda.

The Commission and the Member States

The changing fortunes of the Commission have been outlined in Chapters 7–11. For instance, its status declined after the empty chair crisis of 1965. Theorizations of the role of the Commission moved from the neofunctionalist view of it as the 'motor of integration' to the intergovernmental view of it as no more than the servant of the member states. This balance of opinion swung back under Jacques Delors's presidency (1985–94) after the launch of the single market programme in the mid-1980s. After this development, it rapidly became a widely accepted view that:

> The renewed drive for market unification can be explained only if theory takes into account the policy leadership of the Commission.

(Sandholtz and Zysman 1989: 96)

This view did not go unchallenged, though (see Chapter 19, 'Explaining the Single Market'). The disagreements over the role of the Commission in the single market programme represented fundamental disagreements about the nature of the Commission in more general terms. Is it simply an agent of the member states, acting at their behest and under their control, or is it an autonomous actor in its own right, capable of playing a leadership role in the EU? Echoes of this debate can be found amidst the eurozone crisis (see Chapter 11). On the one hand, the European Council has been the key institution for agreeing bail outs for the debtor states, new fiscal arrangements, and a changed banking regime in the EU. Equally, however, the fiscal arrangements, under the Fiscal Compact, have empowered the Commission to enforce the new rules.

If the argument that the EU is an intergovernmental organization is to hold, then those who defend the position have to confront the assertion that the Commission is the prime mover of the process of European integration. This assertion was made from the early days of the EEC by Lindberg (1963) and other neofunctionalists (see Chapter 1, 'Theories of European Integration'). The counterargument is that the Commission is simply an international secretariat like many others that help the member states of international organizations to achieve their collective aims. It simply acts on behalf of the member states and in accordance with their will. This view has been strongly argued by intergovernmentalists, notably Andrew Moravcsik (see Chapter 1, 'Theories of European Integration'). Each argument is now examined in turn.

The Commission as an Agent of the Member States

The intergovernmentalist view of the Commission is that it is only an agent of the member states. Its function is to make it easier for governments to find agreement on the details of co-operation with each other. Where there is agreement on the broad agenda for co-operation, it is convenient for member states to delegate some control over the detailed agenda to the Commission. They see it as a reliable source of independent proposals because it has technical information, and as a neutral arbiter between conflicting national interests. Delegating the making of proposals to the Commission in this way reduces the costs of co-operation by reducing the risk that 'decisions will be delayed by an inconclusive struggle among competing proposals, or that the final decision will be grossly unfair' (Moravcsik 1993: 512). Where there are alternative proposals that might win majority support, the choice is often decided by which proposal is backed by the Commission. Although this delegation of the right to make detailed proposals gives the Commission a certain formal power to set the agenda, in the intergovernmentalist view, the Commission does not determine the direction in which the EU moves. It is only helping the member states to agree on the details of what they have decided that they want to do anyway.

This intergovernmental interpretation also coincides with a principal–agent interpretation of delegation to the Commission that draws on work from comparative politics rather than integration theory (see Chapter 2). Majone (2001) argued that there are two reasons for delegating to agencies such as the Commission: for reasons of efficiency and of credibility. The efficiency argument is that the agency—in this case, the European Commission—is endowed with better information and expertise than the individual member governments or the EP. The credibility argument is that it may be less exposed to being captured by powerful groups, such as the corporate lobby or, indeed, a powerful member state. The Commission's function of 'guardian of the Treaties' is an important aspect of this credibility argument, since member states seeking to undermine EU legislation can ultimately be brought before the Court. These interpretations have generated significant debate and empirical testing (see, for instance, Franchino 2007).

The concern of Eurosceptic politicians and the critique offered by neofunctionalists is that the Commission may use the margin of discretion that the member states have delegated to it to try to manoeuvre the member states towards objectives that they had not anticipated. It is difficult for the states to keep a check on exactly what the Commission is doing because it is in possession of more information than they are. Nevertheless, there are ways in which the member states can keep a check on the Commission (Pollack 1997, 2003). First, they have set up a whole complex of implementation committees of national experts to monitor the actions of the Commission. There are approximately 270 of these committees—collectively known as comitology—but grouped into two broad categories. Advisory Committees give the Commission the greatest discretion; Examination Committees make their decisions subject to being overruled by a QMV decision in the Council of the EU. There is also a set of Regulatory Committees, which are gradually being phased out, and which provide a potential veto point for the Commission's decisions or the proposed measure is referred to the Council of the EU for review. The Lisbon Treaty sought to tidy up this comitology system, which had developed in a rather ad hoc manner, as well as to ensure that the EP has proper oversight of it (Article 291 TFEU). Second, Article 263 of the Treaty on the Functioning of the European Union (TFEU) allows challenges through the Court of Justice of the European Union (CJEU) to the actions of the Commission should any individual member state, or any directly affected individual or company, believe that the Commission has overstepped its mandate. Other EU institutions, such as the EP and the Court of Auditors, also monitor the activities of the Commission, providing member states with the information that they need to keep a check on it.

The Commission as an Autonomous Actor

The alternative to the view that the Commission is no more than an agent of the member states is that it can and does act autonomously to provide policy leadership to the EU. Defenders of this view point to key resources that allow it to do so: its sole right of initiative in the legislative process; its ability to locate allies among influential interest groups; and its powers under the competition clauses of the Treaties to act against monopolies (for a fuller list, see Nugent and Rhinard 2015).

The Commission does not have to wait passively for the member states to ask it to bring forward proposals. It can identify a problem that has already started to concern governments and propose a European solution. It can use its sole right of initiative to package issues in the form least likely to engender opposition in the Council of the EU or the EP. Where there is opposition from member states to the full-blown development of a policy, the Commission may propose instead a limited small-scale programme; where there is resistance to a directive or regulation, the Commission may propose a less threatening recommendation or Opinion. In each case, the limited step establishes a precedent for action in the policy sector and can be followed up later with further steps if and when the environment in the Council of the EU is more conducive (Cram 1997: 162–3).

The Commission can also act to put the Europeanization of a policy sector onto the agenda (cultivated spillover—see Chapter 1, 'Theories of European Integration'). By involving domestic interests at the EU level, through instruments such as advisory committees, the Commission seeks to win converts to the idea that an issue can best be handled at the European level. In the aftermath of the 2007 financial crisis, it actively advocated the strengthening of EU regulation of hedge funds and other financial instruments, aware that it had support in the EP and that the member governments were on relatively weak ground, since the failure of domestic regulation was part of the explanation for the crisis.

Similarly, the Commission can utilize, and, if necessary, create, transnational networks of producers who will be its allies in the private sector and bring pressure to bear on governments to transfer competence in a sector to the EU level. It was most successful at this approach in the 1980s and 1990s: in the cases of technology policy (Sharp and Shearman 1987; Sharp 1989; Peterson 1991), telecommunications (Dang-Nguyen et al. 1993; Fuchs 1994), and energy (Matlary 1993). In each of these last two sectors, it encouraged industrial users to press governments to move away from national monopolies to create a European market under European regulation. It has also supported civil society groups to ensure their voice is heard in policy making in line with its 2001 White Paper on governance (European Commission 2001).

Once governments have become aware of a problem, and faced up to the possibility of a European solution, the Commission can use technical experts to increase the pressure on governments, as it did with the Cecchini report of economists for the single market (see Chapter 19, 'Explaining the Single Market'), or for monetary union, the

Delors Committee, which consisted mainly of central bankers (see Chapter 20, 'Origins of EMU').

Nevertheless, any move to develop a European competence in a policy sector will produce counter-pressures from groups that benefit from the status quo. The Commission can break down this opposition by threatening the use of its existing powers if actors in the sector will not co-operate to find a negotiated way forward. Again, it did this to achieve the opening up of national monopolies in telecommunications and energy supply and liberalizing the air-transport sector (Bulmer et al. 2007). In each case, the Directorate General for Competition threatened to use its powers under what was then Article 90 of the Treaty (now Article 106 TFEU). This Article specifically stated that national public monopolies were subject to the rules prohibiting the prevention of competition within the common market. The vested interests against change were therefore faced with the alternative of either reaching an agreement with the Commission to allow phased and regulated competition, or of facing legal proceedings. In many cases, these Article 90 challenges were linked to proposed legislation on liberalization going through the Council of the EU. In all three cases cited, the alternative of having some say in *how* the transition from national monopoly to European market was carried out proved more attractive than the uncertainty of the alternative of legal proceedings, and the resistance to the Commission's proposals was seriously weakened as a result.

This pattern of Commission activism became less evident from the mid-1990s. Greater concern for subsidiarity, checks on the regulatory burden of Commission action, enlargement to twenty-eight states, and the changed EU agenda have been major contributors. A key emphasis of the Commission from 2005 to 2009 was the competitiveness of the European economy, but the Lisbon Strategy was much more one of policy co-ordination via the open method of co-ordination (OMC) (see Chapter 18, 'The European Union's Policy Agenda') and therefore not amenable to Commission activism. The Commission was not a driver of reforms during the eurozone crisis. The pace of reform was set by the European Council. However, the Commission has been given important new oversight powers to monitor states' fiscal policy to ensure states do not run up unsustainable public debt (see Chapter 20, 'Long Term Reform'). As noted above in 'Composition and Appointment', the Juncker Commission endeavoured to push an explicitly 'political' agenda but was stymied by a series of crises, notably Brexit, the refugee crisis, and a crisis of legitimacy and democracy in Poland and Hungary (Peterson 2017) (see Chapter 11). On refugees, the Commission did manage to push through relocation quotas for member states, which Juncker touted as a key achievement of his presidency. One other notable success of the Juncker presidency, building upon a key theme of the two preceding Barroso Presidencies, was the push to reduce EU regulation, leading to a sustained drop in policy outputs over time from 2004 onwards (Kassim et al. 2017).

The Commission and the European Parliament

While most attention has been paid to the relationship between the Commission and the member states, sympathetic practitioners have expressed concern about the erosion of the autonomy of the Commission resulting from the extension of the powers of the EP (De Gucht 2003). Similarly, some academic observers identified an erosion of the Commission's powers and independence within the decision Making process

(Tsebelis and Garrett 2000, 2001; Majone 2002; Burns 2004). Four main ways in which this has happened are identified:

1. Although the Commission and the EP have traditionally been allies in attempting to wrest powers away from the member states, the Commission resisted suggestions that the EP be given an equal right of legislative initiative. The Commission argued that sharing the right of initiative would weaken its ability to give coherence and strategy to European legislation. Formally, the Commission has maintained its monopoly of initiative. Yet, since Maastricht, the EP has the right to request that the Commission 'submit any appropriate proposal on matters on which it considers that a Community act is required for the purpose of implementing this Treaty' (Article 225 TFEU). Majone (2002: 376) considered that this 'comes close to a true right of legislative initiative'.

2. The introduction of the ordinary legislative procedure (OLP) (see Chapter 12, 'Decision Making Procedures') has made it more difficult for the Commission to play the role of motor of integration because its proposals have to satisfy a larger number of actors. Specifically, OLP requires the Commission to satisfy a majority in the EP as well as in the Council of the EU (hereafter abbreviated to the Council). The more actors that have to be brought into agreement, the more the proposals are likely to become compromises, rather than reflect the autonomous preferences of the Commission.

3. OLP also opens the possibility of the Council and the EP agreeing an entirely different legislative text from that put forward by the Commission. If the Council and the EP cannot reach agreement on an amended version of the original Commission proposal, a Conciliation Committee is convened, in which the representatives of the two legislative institutions seek to reach agreement directly with one another. This may mean agreement on an entirely different text. The compromise text then has to be agreed in the Council by QMV, and by the EP by a simple majority. Thus, the original centrality of the Commission's proposal, which could only be amended by unanimity in the Council, is circumvented, thereby eroding the Commission's autonomy.

4. The changes made in the Treaty of Amsterdam further eroded the Commission's influence. Because the Council and the EP could reach agreement at first reading under the revised procedure, there was an incentive for them to open direct informal contacts at a much earlier stage than under the original version of the OLP. Indeed, the vast majority of legislation adopted via OLP is now agreed at first reading with a full Conciliation Committee rarely convened (see Chapter 12, 'Decision Making Procedures').

The Commission and Managing Implementation

Up to this point, we have focused on the role of the Commission in policy making. However, the Commission also has to be an effective manager of EU business if it is to play its part in putting policy into practice. Concern at its effectiveness initially emerged at the start of the 1990s. In 1991, the then Secretary General of the Commission, David Williamson, admitted to the failings of the Commission when it came to implementing the growing body of EC legislation. This analysis was echoed by Metcalfe (1992) and other academic observers. They had noted that the Commission was better adapted to proposing policies and legislation than to implementing them once they were agreed. Metcalfe went so far as to argue (1992: 118) that: 'The EC has a management deficit at least as significant for its future effectiveness as its more widely recognised democratic deficit.'

It had long been argued that the two functions of initiation and implementation required different types of organizational structure, which Coombes (1970) identified as *organic* and *mechanistic* organizations. He described the Commission as an organic organization, well equipped to generate proposals, but lacking sufficient of the qualities of a classical mechanistic bureaucracy to implement them effectively. Others have seen this bias against implementation as embodied in the culture of the Commission.

During the 1990s, the implementation problems of the Commission increased as a result of several factors:

1. The success of the 1992 Programme and other policy initiatives taken under Delors's presidency left the Commission with a much larger body of legislation to implement.

2. The extension of EU competences into new policy sectors, such as social and environmental policy, raised different problems of implementation (Peters 1997: 191).

3. The question of consistent implementation of single market rules became an issue because of the wide disparities between member states that were shown up by Commission monitoring reports. The states with the better records felt that they were being placed at a competitive disadvantage in comparison with states that were less meticulous about applying the rules.

4. The crisis over the ratification of the Maastricht Treaty (see Chapter 9, 'After Maastricht'), and the subsequent renewed emphasis on the principle of subsidiarity, further complicated the relationship between the Commission and the member states (Laffan 1997b: 425).

5. The internal Commission crisis that culminated in the resignation of the Santer Commission in 1999 (see 'Financial Management' below) revealed poor management and accountability structures within the Commission.

In consequence, the incoming Commission of Romano Prodi initiated a major programme of reform, for which the British Vice-President of the Commission, Neil Kinnock, took responsibility (Metcalfe 2000). It entailed changes to the structure, organization, and management of the Commission, designed not only to improve its implementation capacity, but also to make its operations more efficient. Changes were introduced to terms of appointment of both Commissioners and personnel in the Services. Codes of conduct were introduced relating to their practices. As Metcalfe wrote at the time (2000: 819): 'The management deficit is not just about the inadequacies within the Commission—it is a structural problem that threatens the performance of the whole system.' A decade later, it became possible to evaluate the reforms. Hussein Kassim (2008: 548) offered the following verdict: 'When crisis forced member governments to intervene, the Commission in a case of self-reform under delegation seized the "once-in-a-generation" opportunity to implement an internal reform agenda.'

The Commission as Implementer

The Commission operates in two modes as implementer. First, there are a very few policy sectors in which the Commission has direct implementation powers. The most notable is competition policy, which has been called 'the first supranational policy' (McGowan and Wilks 1995). Others are fisheries and some of the programmes involved in the external relations of the EU, such as the Humanitarian Aid Programme. Second, for most internal policies, the Commission sits at the apex of a multi-level system of implementation that extends down to the central authorities of the member states, then below them to sub-national authorities and agencies. Morten Egeberg has argued that this multi-level EU administration represents a 'transformation of executive politics in Europe' (Egeberg 2006). In this second mode, the Commission acts as the agent of the member states; national and sub-national actors are the agents of the Commission. The problem for the Commission is ensuring that these agents do not pursue their own agendas.

This problem is compounded by two circumstances. First, the Commission has scarce personnel resources and lacks independent information. Second, the number of agents that it has to monitor has been increased by the fragmentation of public administration that has taken place in many member states under the banner of the 'New Public Management' (Peters 1997: 198). In consequence, the Commission has had to operate as the manager of European networks of member-state administrators. The latter may take on a 'double-hatted' role as both domestic policy managers and as part of an EU-centred administration co-ordinated by the Commission (see Egeberg 2006 for examples). The creation of the European External Action Service following the Lisbon Treaty added further complexity because it brought together administrative capacity from both the Commission and the Council of the EU. Unsurprisingly, it experienced 'growing pains' in the immediate aftermath of its launch in 2011 (Allen and Smith 2012: 162–4).

Majone (2002) argued that the transfer of new competences to the EU had not involved increasing the exclusive competences of the EU, but had involved the extension of the number of areas in which the EU and the member states shared competence, or in which competences were dispersed to new institutional actors, such as the European Central Bank (ECB) (Majone 2002: 376). The reluctance of member states to transfer further exclusive competences to EU institutions reflected their concern about the loss of control that earlier transfers had involved. However, it also reflected a realization that the implementation role of the Commission could not be increased further without an increase in its size and resources that the member states were unwilling to sanction (Majone 2002: 382). In the view of Majone (2002: 382–3), this situation obliged the Commission to share responsibility with national administrative authorities, even though it was difficult to do so because of differing national regulatory philosophies and differing levels of national administrative competence.

At the same time, the Commission faced the prospect of becoming increasingly subject to political interference with performance of its implementation function because of the reform measures taken to deal with the democratic deficit. The Lisbon Treaty reinforced this trend by stating in Article 17 TEU that the nomination of the Commission President must take into account the elections to the EP. The danger of such politicization is that it risks adversely affecting the credibility principle that lies behind delegation to the Commission in the first place. Equally, the emergence of a political Commission with an alternative power base in the Parliament suggests that the new intergovernmentalist argument about a resurgent Council may be overstated (Peterson 2017) (see Chapter 1, 'Theories of European Integration').

Majone (2002: 387) argued that there was a case for a 'fourth branch of government' on the model of US federal regulatory agencies. In fact, further independent agencies were created in connection with the transfer of new competences. They were mainly charged to collect and collate information, but some have regulatory powers. The number of these agencies more than doubled between 2003 and 2017 and by 2017 they had a collective budget of some €3.4 billion and employed some 11,000 staff (European Court of Auditors 2017). These figures do not include the Single Resolution Board, which was created to support the Banking Union and has a separate budget of €6.6 billion (Chapter 20, 'Long-Term Reforms'). A key issue with the proliferation of these agencies was that they developed inconsistent sets of management rules and standards, making them more exposed to criticism over conflicts of interest and potential scandals. Consequently, an effort was made to provide standardized arrangements. This momentum was driven by provisions in the Lisbon Treaty to bring agencies under more systematic control, including their accountability to the Court and the EP. A list of these agencies is given in Box 13.1. Three agencies are concerned with CFSP activity. As an illustration of their continued growth, the European Banking Authority was created in 2011 to oversee national banking regulation in the aftermath of the financial and eurozone crises.

Box 13.1 Independent Agencies

EU Agencies

Agency for the Co-operation of Energy Regulators (ACER)
Body of European Regulators for Electronic Communications (BEREC)
Community Plant Variety Office (CPVO)
Euratom Supply Agency (ESA)
European Agency for the operational management of large-scale IT systems in the area of freedom, security, and justice (eu-LISA)
European Agency for Safety and Health at Work (EU-OSHA)
European Asylum Support Office (EASO)
European Aviation Safety Agency (EASA)
European Banking Authority (EBA)
European Border and Coast Guard Agency (FRONTEX)
European Centre for the Development of Vocational Training (Cedefop)
European Centre for Disease Prevention and Control (ECDC)
European Chemicals Agency (ECHA)
European Environment Agency (EEA)

European Fisheries Control Agency (EFCA)

European Food Safety Authority (EFSA)

European Foundation for the Improvement of Living and Working Conditions
   (EUROFOUND)

European Global Navigation Satellite Systems Supervisory Authority (GSA)

European Institute for Gender Equality (EIGE)

European Insurance and Occupational Pensions Authority (EIOPA)

European Maritime Safety Agency (EMSA)

European Medicines Agency (EMEA)

European Monitoring Centre for Drugs and Drug Addiction (EMCDDA)

European Network and Information Security Agency (ENISA)

European Police College (CEPOL)

European Police Office (EUROPOL)

European Railway Agency (ERA)

European Securities and Markets Authority (ESMA)

European Training Foundation (ETF)

European Union Agency for Fundamental Rights (FRA)

Office for Harmonization in the Internal Market (OHIM)

The European Union's Judicial Co-operation Unit (EUROJUST)

Translation Centre for the Bodies of the European Union (CdT)

CFSP Agencies

European Defence Agency (EDA)

European Union Institute for Security Studies (ISS)

European Union Satellite Centre (EUSC)

Note: Excludes Euratom agencies as well as executive agencies established to administer individual EU programmes.

Source: http://europa.eu/about-eu/agencies/index_en.htm, December 2019.

Financial Management

Alongside the Commission's burgeoning implementation problems, concern also grew about effective financial management of EU programmes. As Laffan (1997*b*: 427) noted, for many years, the annual reports of the Court of Auditors highlighted weaknesses in the Commission's financial management. As one response, the Maastricht Treaty upgraded the status of the Court of Auditors to that of a full EU institution, and raised the status of budgetary discipline and sound financial management to central principles (Laffan 1997*b*: 429).

The resignation of the Santer Commission in 1999 was partly due to problems of financial mismanagement, so it came as no surprise that the Commission's reform White Paper of 2000 included, as one of four key components, reform of the system of financial control and management (Kassim 2008: 659). Internal accountability was overhauled, with financial responsibility decentralized to Director Generals, and the creation of an Internal Audit Service (see Table 13.1). More broadly, the Commission has to make sure that fraud is not taking place using EU funds, but in this case including through malpractice at member state level. The main weapon to this end is the European Anti-Fraud Office, known by its French acronym, OLAF (see Table 13.1).

CONCLUSION

The debate over the role of the Commission remains central to explanations about the nature and pace of European integration. It is clearly central to one of the themes of this book: the debate about the nature of the EU itself. If the Commission can be shown to be an autonomous actor, the argument that the EU is an intergovernmental organization is severely weakened. The supranational challenge was greatest under the Delors Commissions (1985–94) and has fallen away in more recent years, although Jean-Claude Juncker endeavoured to create a 'political' Commission, building upon his status as the first *Spitzenkandidaten* with a mandate from the European Parliament (Peterson 2017). However, one element of this political agenda has been to work much more closely with the Council, suggesting that rather than the traditional binary view of the Commission as either the agent of the member states or an autonomous actor, the contemporary reality is more nuanced. The Commission faces a complex range of challenges, a more active European Council, and a powerful European Parliament to which the President, at least between 2014 and 2019, was arguably more accountable. Whilst it is no longer the sole motor of integration, if indeed it ever was, the Commission remains central to driving and supporting the European policy agenda. The Commission has faced a challenge to its autonomy, especially with the growing role of the European Council, but it still nevertheless enjoys a good deal of room for manoeuvre within EU governance process.

The Commission has been fiercely criticized in its role as manager of EU policies and finances. It was forced to put its house in order following the crisis in 1998–99. Oversight of policy implementation remains a concern. While implementation is never straightforward for domestic legislation within member states, it becomes even more difficult in a union of twenty-seven member states, in which the Commission is dependent on national and sub-national tiers of government for effective compliance. Added to this, the proliferation of actors involved in the policy process and the increased role of 'agency government' has made the Commission's task even more difficult, since it is now managing complex networks of implementing bodies. Such developments have been central to the increased interest in the application of the concepts of governance and policy networks to the EU and of multi-level administration (see Chapter 2, 'Governance' and 'Policy Networks'). While governance in the EU has become increasingly complex as the integration process has developed over the decades, the Commission has proved to be very resilient in maintaining a central role in administering EU policy, as well as in its formulation.

KEY POINTS

Functions

- The Commission initiates legislation, may act as a mediator, manages some policy areas, is guardian of the Treaties, is a key actor in international relations, and the 'conscience of the EU'.

Composition and Appointment

- The Commission consists of a College of Commissioners and the Services.

- The Services are the permanent civil service of the EU.

- The Commission President is a particularly influential figure, and is nominated by the European Council and then approved by the EP.

- The Commissioners are appointed by the European Council, subject to approval by the EP.

- There is one Commissioner per member state. They are sworn to abandon national allegiances.

The Commission in the Policy-Making Process

- Formally, the Commission has the sole right to propose EU legislation.

- There is debate about how much autonomy it actually has.

- The intergovernmentalist view is that the Commission is merely the agent of the member states; the supranationalist view is that the Commission can and does achieve a degree of autonomy from the member states to pursue its own agenda.

- Treaty changes designed to deal with the democratic deficit have reduced the autonomy of the Commission by increasing the control over it by the EP.

The Commission and Managing Implementation

- The Commission was originally more active as a proposer than as an implementer of legislation, although the balance has shifted in more recent times.

- In most areas, the Commission has to work alongside the national administrations of the member states, leading to suggestions that it should evolve as a manager of European networks of implementation agents.

- Increasing politicization of the Commission because of its subjection to closer control by the EP threatens its perceived independence, and also points to the need for the emergence of transnational regulatory networks.

Financial Management

- The 1999 Commission crisis triggered a root-and-branch reform of the Commission's financial management.

 For additional material and resources, please visit the online resources www.oup.com/uk/bache5e.

QUESTIONS

1. What is the primary role of the European Commission and how has that role changed over time?

2. Who holds the Commission to account and how effective are those processes?

3. Jean-Claude Juncker wanted a 'political commission'—what do you think this means and do you agree with his ambition?

4. Is the Commission simply the agent of the Member States?

5. What are the main challenges facing the Commission and how well equipped is the Commission to meet those challenges?

FURTHER READING

Three useful publications cover different aspects of the Commission's role. The first is by **H. Kassim et al.**, *The European Commission of the Twenty-First Century* (Oxford: Oxford University Press, 2013). It relies on extensive survey and interview data within the institution. The second is by **Anchrit Wille**, *The Normalization of the European Commission* (Oxford: Oxford University Press, 2013). The third is **A. Ellinas and E. Suleiman**, *The European Commission and Bureaucratic Autonomy* (Cambridge: Cambridge University Press, 2012). **N. Nugent and M. Rhinard** provide an updated and comprehensive overview in their textbook, *The European Commission* (Basingstoke: Palgrave Macmillan, 2015). There are a number of assessments of the Juncker Commission, including **H. Kassim and B. Laffan's** assessment 'The Juncker Presidency: The "Political Commission" in Practice' in *Journal of Common Market Studies*, 57 (2019): 49–61 and **J. Peterson's** analysis of how the Juncker tried to navigate the era of crisis in 'Juncker's Political European Commission and an EU in Crisis', *Journal of Common Market Studies,* 55 (2017): 349–67.

Chapter 14

The European Council and the Council of the European Union (EU)

Chapter Overview

This chapter examines those institutions principally composed of government representatives. The European Council is the name for the periodic summit meetings of heads of state and government that are largely responsible for determining the direction of the integration process. The Council of the European Union (EU) (often still referred to as the 'Council of Ministers' and in shorthand as the 'Council') is a multi-faceted and multi-tiered institution that does not have a constant membership, but involves different ministers, depending on the policy under consideration. Even that, though, is not the full extent of the complexity of the Council. The work of the meetings of ministers is prepared by a myriad of committees, consisting primarily of national officials that are brought together by the Committee of Permanent Representatives (COREPER) and a large number of preparatory committees at technical level. Each of these is considered in what follows.

Definitions and Distinctions

It is important at the outset of this chapter to be clear about terminology. The subject matter of the chapter is the hierarchy of EU institutions composed of representatives of national governments, which are important in different ways. The European Council is at the top of this hierarchy and is the institution that brings together the EU's heads of government (or, in the French case, the head of state). The European Council was established in 1974, and has been a formal EU institution since the implementation of the Lisbon Treaty (in December 2009). It is not to be confused with the Council of Europe (see Insight 5.2), which is a completely separate international organization from the EU. The other institution to be considered in this chapter is the Council of the EU or, as it is often termed, the Council of Ministers. It is the Council of the EU that is referred to with the shorthand term 'the Council'. The so-called Council hierarchy comprises the European Council and the Council of the EU, as well as other preparatory bodies arranged beneath it (see Insight 14.1).

Insight 14.1 The EU's Intergovernmental Institutions

The European Council

The European Council holds summit meetings of the heads of state and government a minimum of four times per year, with provision for additional meetings. Since 2014 the number of European Council meetings has increased from an average of six to approximately ten per annum, which have included meetings to discuss Article 50 negotiations on the UK's exit from the EU. Further informal sessions also take place.

The Council of the EU

This consists of a representative of each member state 'at ministerial level', authorized to commit the government of the member state. It meets in ten different formations, depending on the subject matter under consideration (see Box 14.1).

The Committee of Permanent Representatives (COREPER)

The Permanent Representatives are the ambassadors of the member states to the EU. Their deputies meet as COREPER I and the Representatives themselves as COREPER II. They prepare business for the meetings of ministers.

High-Level Preparatory Bodies and the Working Parties

COREPER itself is prepared by a small number of specialized committees, such as on agriculture or trade policy. At the lowest level are Council working parties, which deal with most specialist policy issues. There are more than 150 such committees and working groups.

The Presidency

Prior to the Lisbon Treaty, the presidency was held for six months by one member state as determined by a rota. A representative of this state chaired all meetings of the Council and, indeed, of meetings in the Council hierarchy. The Lisbon Treaty ended the simplicity of this set-up by turning the presidency into a 'trio' of three states playing the above role across an eighteen-month period. Separate arrangements were introduced for the President of the European Council, who is elected by a qualified majority of the Council for a two-and-a-half-year term of office. The High Representative of the Union for Foreign Affairs and Security Policy chairs the Council of Foreign Affairs, except when commercial policy is discussed, under which circumstances the state holding the rotating Council presidency chairs. The Euro Group, which meets to deal with Single Currency matters has a President who is elected for two-and-a-half years by a simple majority of Euro Group members, and who chairs meetings and sets the group's agenda.

The Secretariat

The state holding the presidency is assisted by a Council Secretariat of over 3,000 staff.

The Council of the EU was first set up as part of the European Coal and Steel Community (see Chapter 5, 'The Schuman Plan for Coal and Steel'). Nearly seven decades later, its activities span the full range of public policy. Two things have remained constant, however. First, it enshrines the importance of member governments in the EU. Second, it remains the focal point of the making of EU legislation;

although it has been joined increasingly over recent years by the European Parliament as a co-legislator (See Chapter 12, 'Decision Making Procedures'). Its principal functions are decision making and legislating. The European Council was created in 1974 as part of an effort to re-energize the integration process in a more intergovernmental way, given the setback suffered by the supranational method in the aftermath of the 1965 crisis (see Chapter 7, 'The 1965 Crisis'). The European Council has become the motor of European integration in the subsequent period.

These two institutions may grab the headlines, but a large majority of decisions are made before they reach them: at the level of COREPER or the preparatory technical committees.

Intergovernmental and Supranational Interpretations

As with Chapter 13, a key theme in this one is the relationship between the intergovernmental and supranational interpretations. On the face of it, both the European Council and the Council of the EU, comprised as they are of member governments and their officials, represent intergovernmentalism 'writ large'. The top layers of the hierarchy bring together 'the core executive' of the EU member states: the prime ministers, foreign ministers, and other departmental ministers, together with their officials. However, in their seminal study of the Council of Ministers, Hayes-Renshaw and Wallace (2006: 321) put paid to this simplistic analysis:

> to view the importance of the Council as the victory of intergovernmentalism over supranationalism, or to expect the Council to be able to 'run' the EU, is to misunderstand the institutional constellation of the EU. The Council shares and diffuses power between countries, between different kinds of interests and constituencies, and between national and EU levels of governance. The Council cannot act alone but is dependent on intricate relationships with other EU institutions.

The supranational argument is less easy to present, but revolves around several points of departure from intergovernmentalism:

- that ministers and officials from the member states are partners who may work together frequently and will have regard to collective solutions as well as the national interest;
- that the provision for qualified majority voting (QMV) changes the calculation of ministers away from 'hard bargaining' based exclusively on the national interest, even if they prefer not to vote but to decide by consensus;
- that the Council increasingly needs to work with the European Parliament (EP) in the 'ordinary legislative procedure'(See Chapter 12, 'Decision Making Procedures' and Chapter 15, 'The Struggle for Power');
- that there is some evidence of socialization into shared values among participants at all levels in the hierarchy of intergovernmental institutions.

259

The European Council

Over the years, the European Council has held meetings at least twice a year and generally three or four times although, as noted in Insight 14.1, since 2014 it has met far more regularly. The Lisbon Treaty states that it shall meet 'twice every six months' (Article 15(3), TEU). Additional informal meetings are also called in response to urgent matters. The origins of the European Council were in the summit meetings that started with the 'relaunching of Europe' at The Hague in 1969 (see Chapter 7, 'The Hague Summit'). The first formal meeting of the European Council was in Dublin in March 1975.

The Rationale for the European Council

After de Gaulle's resignation in 1969, there was a wish by national governments to restart the development of the European Community (EC), but in the direction that they, not the Commission, decided; hence the Hague Summit of that year. The 1965 crisis had led to a loss of confidence inside the Commission. If the Commission was not going to drive the EC forward, another motor would be needed. The agreement to formalize summits in the form of the European Council was an indication that the governments were determined to play a continuing role. Despite the European Council taking on a fundamental role in steering the course of integration from the mid-1970s, its elusive and under-institutionalized nature led to its neglect in the academic literature.

The origins of the European Council stemmed from the French President, Valéry Giscard d'Estaing, and the German Chancellor, Helmut Schmidt, who both came to office in 1974. Both had been Finance Ministers and had participated in numerous meetings on the international monetary system. They both strongly valued the opportunity to sit with their counterparts and hold informal discussions in confidence without the requirement to take formal decisions (Bulmer and Wessels 1987: 76). This 'Library Group' approach, which was quite informal, was important at the outset, but the Lisbon Treaty can be seen as its abandonment. Characteristic of the earlier 'Library Group' approach was a strong effort to keep the European Council outside of the Treaties in order to allow it as much flexibility as possible in its political actions. This informality eventually became unsustainable, as the EU grew to encompass twenty-eight (now post-Brexit twenty-seven) states.

The existence of the European Council was first acknowledged formally in the 1986 Single European Act (SEA), albeit in just three sentences. The Maastricht Treaty (1992) formalized the European Council but did not cite it as being one of the EU's institutions. It gave the European Council a very small number of specific tasks: notably in economic and monetary policy, and in setting the direction of the Common Foreign and Security Policy (CFSP). However, the Lisbon Treaty set out much more explicitly the role of the European Council and unambiguously refers to it as an institution of the EU (see Insight 14.2).

A further explanation for the establishment of the European Council was to 'orchestrate' the activities of the Union. The 1969 Hague Summit had demonstrated that the heads of government could set the direction of integration: both broadly through

Insight 14.2 The European Council's Post-Lisbon Functions

1. **General political guidance and momentum**
   - 'The European Council shall provide the Union with the necessary impetus for its development and shall define the general political directions and priorities thereof. It shall not exercise legislative functions' (Article 15 TEU).

2. **Oversight of Treaty reform and enlargement**
   - Any proposals to revise the Treaties through the 'ordinary revision procedure' will be decided on by the European Council, which will consult the EP and the Commission and may decide by a simple majority to either convene a Convention or an intergovernmental conference (IGC) to consider the proposals (Article 48 TEU).
   - Under 'simplified revision procedures', the European Council can agree less significant changes that nevertheless affect the character of the EU: for instance, to change decision making rules to the ordinary legislative procedure (QMV in the Council and co-decision with the EP). (See Chapter 12, 'The Post-Lisbon Architecture of the EU' on the *passerelle* clauses).
   - The European Council sets the eligibility conditions for accession states (Article 49 TEU).
   - The European Council sets the guidelines for the process should a member state wish to withdraw from the EU (Article 50 TEU).

3. **Foreign policy making**
   - The 'European Council shall identify the strategic interests and objectives of the Union ... [in relation] ... to the common foreign and security policy and to other areas of the external action of the Union' (Article 22 TEU).
   - 'If international developments so require, the President of the European Council shall convene an extraordinary meeting of the European Council in order to define the strategic lines of the Union's policy in the face of such developments' (Article 26 TEU).

4. **Decision maker of last resort**
   - Nominates the Commission President and appoints the Commission after the EP's consent (Article 17 TEU).
   - Appoints the High Representative (HRUFASP) (Article 18 TEU).
   - Decides on Council formations and presidency rota (Article 236 TFEU).
   - Decides on number of Commissioners (Article 127 TEU and 244 TFEU).
   - Decides on size of the EP (Article 14 TEU).
   - Acts as court of appeal if a member state invokes the 'emergency brake' arrangements (scattered across the TFEU, but see Articles 48, 82, and 83 as examples).

5. **Policy monitoring**
   - 'The European Council shall define the strategic guidelines for legislative and operational planning within the area of freedom, security and justice' (Article 68 TFEU).
   - The European Council 'shall, acting on the basis of the report from the Council, discuss a conclusion on the broad guidelines of the economic policies of the Member States and of the Union' (Article 121 TFEU).

authorizing enlargement negotiations and specifically through triggering particular policy initiatives, such as foreign policy co-operation. The European Council could also overcome the risk of policy segmentation, which arose because no single body could take an overview of policy. The General Affairs Council (see 'The Council of the EU' below) was supposed to act as policy co-ordinator, but the heads of government had more authority to play that role. Finally, the European Council was also an attempt to present a united front to the outside world and its role in this respect has expanded, to some extent usurping the role of the Council of Foreign Ministers.

Composition and Organization

Although the European Council comprises the heads of government or state, they are not the only participants. Traditionally, the foreign ministers of the member states have also participated, as has the Commission President and one Vice-President. Membership was redefined under the Lisbon Treaty as follows (Article 15 TEU):

- the heads of state or government of the member states, together with the President of the European Council and the President of the Commission;
- the High Representative of the Union for Foreign Affairs and Security Policy (HRUFASP);
- as necessitated by its agenda, heads of government may each be assisted by a minister and, in the case of the President of the Commission, by a member of the Commission.

As noted in Insight 14.1, the Presidency of the European Council became a separate appointment for two-and-a-half years. Herman Van Rompuy, the former Belgian Prime Minister, held the post for five years (2009–14) before being replaced by Donald Tusk, former Polish Prime Minister, who also held the post for five years (2014–19). Tusk was replaced in 2019 by another former Belgian Prime Minister, Charles Michel. The presidency no longer follows the previous system whereby meetings were chaired by the head of government from the presidency country. This change was introduced to ensure continuity in the European Council's work and to give an external face to the institution, for instance in reporting to the EP on its work. The HRUFASP is now closely involved in the European Council's work: a step that reflects the importance of foreign and security policy. Finally, the Treaty of Lisbon amended the previous default situation whereby heads of government were accompanied by their foreign ministers. In reality, some changes had already occurred before the Lisbon Treaty, notably with economic or finance ministers attending the annual spring European Council meeting on the European economy.

Whilst the European Council had studiously avoided any internal regulation of its activities under the 'Library Group' model, it took the radical step via the Lisbon Treaty of agreeing new rules of procedure (European Council 2009), something that was already well established for the other institutions. The Treaty provides for qualified or simple majority voting in the European Council, for instance in appointing its President, although the standard practice is decision making by consensus. In any event, neither the President nor the Commission President may vote. Herman Van Rompuy's selection as the first President of the European Council was widely interpreted as an attempt to ensure the office did not have too high a profile and did not challenge the authority of national leaders in the way that a better-known politician might. That trend continued with the appointment of Tusk and Michel.

The President's functions are to: convene meetings; prepare sessions; maintain continuity of work; represent the European Council in inter-institutional discussions (for instance, reporting to the EP); and draw up conclusions from its meetings.

One consequence of the new position was a possible confusion of roles with those of the Commission President, the HRUFASP, not to mention the country chairing ministerial discussions in the Council of the EU. Another consequence of the new position was an anticipated expansion of the European Council's activities. Kietz and von Ondarza (2010: 4) reported Van Rompuy as planning smaller, more frequent (six to eight per annum), and thematically organized sessions of the European Council, building on the pattern established by the annual spring session on the European economy. Another development worthy of note was that the government heads from the eurozone states held meetings during the financial and eurozone crises from 2008.

Functions and Dysfunctions

The European Council has five main functions (see also Insight 14.2), as follows:

- *General political guidance and momentum* To this end, the European Council is like a 'board of directors' giving general guidance to the EU on its future direction. Although the details have to be filled out by interaction between the Commission, the Council of the EU, and the EP, if the European Council gives a lead, the presumption is that the Commission will make proposals and the Council and EP will try to reach agreement on policy.

- *Oversight of Treaty reform and enlargement* The European Council has been closely involved in authorizing and then finalizing all Treaty reforms from the 1986 SEA through to the 2012 Fiscal Compact. Of course, the European Council does not tie up twenty-seven government heads in detailed negotiations; those are conducted by officials and ministers. But without its initial agreement to start the process, and its consent at the end of it, Treaty reform would not be possible. Ever since the Hague Summit in 1969, summit meetings have taken key decisions on enlargement. For instance, the Copenhagen criteria of 1993 specified the requirements expected of all accession states and were defined at a European Council meeting in the Danish capital.

- *Foreign policy making* Over the years, the European Council has issued many foreign policy declarations. These range from the 1980 Venice Declaration, in which it set out key principles on the Middle East, such as recognizing the Palestinian right to self-determination and to a homeland, to its December 2003 approval of a European Security Strategy. These powers were further developed by the Lisbon Treaty.

- *Decision maker of last resort* From its very first meeting, the European Council has been called on to tackle problems that could not be resolved lower down the system. For many sessions from 1979 to 1984, the British Conservative government's efforts to secure a rebate on its budgetary contributions were on the European Council's agenda. However, it is not just a court of appeal, but is also brought in where decisions require its authority. It has had to thrash out agreement on the multi-annual financial perspectives (see Chapter 12, 'Decision Making Procedures'). The Lisbon Treaty added specific provisions for the European Council to act as court of appeal if a member state wishes to use the 'emergency brake' because an exceptionally important interest is at risk of being overruled in the Council by a QMV decision (see Dougan 2008: 643–4). Similarly, on Brexit, although the Commission took the lead in negotiating with the UK, it was the European Council that acted as the final decision maker on the extension of the Article 50 process to 31 January 2020. Finally, the European Council makes a number of key appointments, as well as being able to take decisions on the size of some of the institutions (see Insight 14.2).

- *Policy monitoring* Increasingly, the heads of government have sought to monitor the subsequent development of their own policy initiatives, in part to ensure policy delivery. For instance, the Lisbon Strategy on enhancing European competitiveness and the successor programme, known as Europe 2020, resulted in monitoring at the annual spring session of the European Council. Starting with the Tampere Programme of 2000, the European Council agreed a series of five-year programmes for developing the area of freedom, security, and justice (AFSJ). This role has become firmly established through five-yearly programmes, typically with the Commission providing a mid-term review on progress (see Chapter 23, 'The Area of Freedom, Security, and Justice').

The European Council can still function as a forum for personal contact between heads of government. While the meetings have become more formal as the number of member states has increased, opportunities for informal conversations still exist—for instance, during meals.

In carrying out these functions, the European Council faces some serious problems. These can be considered the *dysfunctions* of the European Council. They can be summarized as problems of overload, over-optimism, over-cautiousness, and over-expectation.

- *Overload* During the late 1970s and into the 1980s, there was a tendency for more and more problems to be referred up from the Council of the EU to the European Council, so that it often found itself considering quite detailed and technical issues. However, since the introduction in the SEA and the Treaty on European Union (TEU) of QMV into the work of the Council of the EU, the tendency for matters to be referred up has receded.

- *Over-optimism* Sometimes, the atmosphere of mutual co-operation that can be generated, together with the expectation that something will come out of every European Council, can lead to commitments being made that subsequently prove difficult to honour. When they go home after the meeting, heads of government may not be able to get the agreement of their own political parties or their cabinets/councils of ministers to carry through the commitment.

- *Over-cautiousness* The publicity can make it more difficult for heads of government to make concessions that might be made in a less exposed bargaining context.

- *Over-expectation* If the meetings do not produce dramatic results, this can cause disillusionment among the European public because the media has built up expectations.

Intergovernmentalism and Informality in the European Council

Although the European Council 'is the body universally recognized as the ultimate intergovernmental protectorate in the EU', it is also 'one which has paradoxically increased the supranational character of the EU over its three decades of operation' (Lewis 2003a: 1006). It has increased the supranational character of the EU because it provides the political framework for supranational legislation and other agreements. Although the heads of government do not themselves formally agree legislation, if they say that something should happen, it will be acted upon by the Commission and the Council of the EU. Thus, the European Council gives legitimacy to supranational actions that might otherwise be contested at the level of the Council of the EU. There is an inherent tension here between the intergovernmental and supranational characteristics of the European Council that is reflected in the debates that have emerged around 'new inter-governmentalism' (see Chapter 2, ' New Intergovernmentalism'). A key claim of proponents of this approach (Bickerton et al. 2015a, 2015b) is that the European Council has seen a remarkable degree of ideational convergence, at least in the areas of economic governance, and justice and home affairs (JHA), amongst heads of state and government. This convergence has been matched by a desire to take control of these areas and develop new policies without delegating responsibility to other supranational organizations such as the Commission. This behaviour is simultaneously intergovernmental, as it is the European Council acting, but results in the development of new supranational policies—reflecting the hybrid nature of the institutions comprising the Council.

Although its functions are now more specified, the European Council is still a forum for informal contact between heads of government, and this can increase the degree of collegiality of the institution. In the past, it was particularly important where French and German leaders had a close relationship—Giscard d'Estaing and Schmidt in the second half of the 1970s; Kohl and Mitterrand in the 1980s—since the Franco–German relationship had in some senses become the motor of integration. If leading members of the European Council remain in post for several years, they can become socialized into more co-operative working with the other heads of government. This effect is never likely to work as strongly for the heads of government as it does for other levels of the Council hierarchy, because the frequency of interaction is lower and the level of politicization of the heads of government is higher—but in reading the analyses of the Council and its committees as supranational phenomena, it should be borne in mind that some of the same effects may operate even at the highest level of the European Council.

The Council of the EU

The Council of the EU is not an institution with a constant membership. It meets in a variety of formations, depending on the subject under discussion (see Box 14.1). It should be noted that all formations act in the name of 'the Council of the EU' and may decide on any business. Formally, there is no hierarchy between different

Councils. However, the General Affairs Council (GAC), normally attended by Foreign Ministers, has a co-ordination function between the various technical councils and a relationship to the European Council, which implies that it has additional authority over the technical expertise possessed by the other formations.

The GAC was re-established as a separate formation after passage of the Lisbon Treaty, having previously been known as the General Affairs and External Relations Council (GAERC). GAERC was by far the busiest Council formation and a very important one as well, meeting on twenty-two occasions in 2006. However, following the Lisbon Treaty, the GAERC was split into the GAC and the Foreign Affairs Council. The latter is chaired by the HRUFASP.

Apart from the GAC and the Foreign Affairs Council, the other key formations are: the Council of Economic and Finance Ministers (ECOFIN), which normally meets every month, and the Agriculture and Fisheries Council (Agfish), which also normally meets monthly. In the past, other formations have been important: for instance, the then Council of Internal Market Ministers (now the Competitiveness Council) during the single market programme in the late 1980s and early 1990s (see Chapter 19, 'Project 1992: Freeing the Internal Market').

ECOFIN meetings are important in the Council's informal 'pecking order' because of the importance and centrality of their subject matter. This position was enhanced in the late 1990s because the issue of monetary union dominated the agenda of the EU. The start of the single currency (the euro) on 1 January 1999 complicated the institutional position because, since then, the finance ministers from those member states that are also members of the eurozone have met prior to the full meetings of ECOFIN to discuss single currency matters (see Chapter 20). The existence of this Euro Group was

Box 14.1 Formations of the Council of the EU

- Agriculture and Fisheries: production of food, rural development and management of fisheries
- Competitiveness: internal market, industry, and research
- Economic and Financial Affairs: economic policy co-ordination, monitoring of member states' budgetary policy and public finances, financial markets and capital movements, and economic relations with third countries
- Environment: environmental protection, resource use, protection of human health and international environmental issues such as climate change
- Employment, Social Policy, Health, and Consumer Affairs: also includes equal opportunities
- Education, Youth, Culture, and Sport
- Foreign Affairs: CFSP and ESDP, trade policy, development co-operation
- General Affairs: cross-cutting issues such as enlargement and multi-annual financing, plus preparation for, and follow-up of, European Council meetings
- Justice and Home Affairs: the area of freedom, security, and justice (AFSJ)
- Transport, Telecommunications, and Energy.

formally recognized in a Protocol attached to the Lisbon Treaty. It is chaired by its own President, elected for a two-and-a-half-year term from among the national economic and finance ministers. Meetings of ECOFIN are prepared by three specialist groups, the Economic and Financial Committee; the Economic Policy Committee; and the Budget Committee, depending on the agenda issues.

The Agfish Council also has a privileged status because of the importance of agriculture to the EU, although this position has been scaled back in relative terms due to the rise of other policy areas. Agfish business is prepared by the Special Committee on Agriculture (SCA), the work of which becomes especially intensive at the time of the annual fixing of agricultural prices in the first half of each year.

The importance of the other Councils can be regarded as a function of two factors: first, the extent of EU competence (see Insight 12.1); and, second, the intensity of policy activity. Thus, a Council formation such as Education, Youth, and Culture, in which the EU has only supporting competences, does not carry the 'clout' of the Competitiveness Council, which covers important economic issues over which the EU has greater authority. The frequency of meetings varies considerably, although most of the sectoral councils meet between twice and four or five times a year (Hayes-Renshaw and Wallace 2006: 38–9; Bulmer and Burch 2009: 55–6).

The functions of the Council are characterized by Hayes-Renshaw and Wallace (2006: 323–7) as being legislature, executive, setter of guidelines, and forum. The Council's role as legislature was set out in Chapter 12, 'Decision Making Procedures'. The Council meets in public when voting on a legislative act (Article 15 TFEU). The executive function relates to where the Council takes decisions that are not legislative in character. This is most obviously the case in CFSP, but is also applicable, for instance, in some of the work of ECOFIN and the Euro Group. Although the European Council has tended to set policy guidelines, there are some policy areas in which the Council steers the course of policy, such as overseeing the details of enlargement negotiations. This function is particularly associated with the GAC. Finally, the Council serves as a forum in those policy areas in which member state policy is being co-ordinated. The growth of this pattern of governance—known as the open method of co-ordination (OMC)—since the late 1990s has increased this 'forum' function for the Council (see Chapter 18, 'The European Union's Policy Agenda').

Voting rules were discussed in Chapter 12, 'The Council of the EU (the Council)'. It was noted that there is a norm of consensus, so whilst QMV can be used in Council, even in an EU of twenty-seven states there is an ongoing norm that decisions will be taken without voting (Häge 2013). Novak (2013) suggests that this decision to behave consensually is at least for some states informed by a desire to avoid blame domestically for failing to secure national preferences. Hence the norm of consensus can mask underlying disagreement. For instance, in a situation where only one state makes its opposition known, the chair is able to decide that a formal vote is unnecessary. States may also make a formal statement registering reservations, typically for the benefit of domestic public opinion, but again without a formal vote being called. Hagemann et al. (2019) found that national governments have adopted this strategy of issuing public statements to distance themselves from measures they have chosen not to block.

A Purely Intergovernmental Institution?

Fritz Scharpf (1989) contrasted 'problem solving' and 'bargaining' as modes of negotiation within the EC. His distinction at least partly corresponds to the differences between theorists about how to understand the operation of the Council. For intergovernmentalists, the Council is simply 'a forum for hard bargaining' (Lewis 1998: 479, 2000: 261). For those who adopt a more supranational perspective, combined with a social constructivist theoretical position (see Chapter 4, 'Social Constructivism'), bargaining takes place between actors whose positions are influenced, at least partially, by their social interaction with their ministerial colleagues from other member states; 'communicative rationality' is at least as important as 'instrumental rationality', which means that the discussion is about how to find a solution to common problems, rather than just about playing a negotiating game to win, and there is an instinct to proceed consensually (Lewis 1998: 480–1).

The hypotheses that these theories generate are fairly clear. If the supranational theorists are correct, one would expect to find more collegiality, and a discourse more oriented to joint problem solving, in Councils that meet more frequently than in those that meet less frequently, and also in the more technical Councils rather than in the more political Councils (although deciding what is technical and what is political is notoriously difficult).

The extent to which ministers meeting in the different Councils engage in hardheaded intergovernmental bargaining, or adopt a more supranational approach, is difficult to research. Perhaps the requirement for legislative decisions to be taken in public will enable observation of ministers' behaviour, but much of the Council's work—not to mention the work of its preparatory bodies—continues to be held in private.

One particularly interesting research finding in this respect is that very few issues are actually decided by the ministers themselves. Hayes-Renshaw (2017: 89) suggests that approximately two-thirds of Council decisions are A-points: that is, where ministers rubber-stamp decisions taken lower down the Council hierarchy. B-points are those in which ministers themselves need to reach political agreement, but which issue may then be referred back to the preparatory bodies for the details to be negotiated.

COREPER and other Preparatory Bodies

There are three levels of committee considered in this section: COREPER, which is the formal filter beneath the Council; a group of high-level preparatory bodies, such as the Political and Security Committee (PSC), which is responsible for CFSP and European Security and Defence Policy (ESDP) co-ordination; and, beneath them, over 150 Council working parties, some with sub-committees (see Council of the EU 2018*a*).

Although it formally only prepares the agenda and meetings of the Council, COREPER has a great deal of discretion about what it classifies as A-points or B-points on the agenda. So, although COREPER and the working groups formally prepare the meetings of the ministers, in one sense the ministers can be said to set the agenda for the meetings of the committees. This is the case where an issue has been discussed at ministerial level, and broad consensus has been reached, but the issue is then referred back down the hierarchy for the detail to be filled in.

COREPER

The Permanent Representatives are the ambassadors from the member states to the EU. Each heads up what is officially an embassy to the EU. They perform some formal functions in Brussels, but their main task is to co-ordinate the work of the various committees that meet under the banner of the Council of the EU. Where possible, they negotiate an agreement arising from the work undertaken by the committees ahead of a meeting of the Council of the EU. This they do in the context of COREPER.

COREPER meets at least weekly at ambassador level as COREPER II, and at deputy level as COREPER I. Both prepare the agendas of meetings of the Councils of the EU. COREPER II is responsible for the agendas for meetings of the GAC, the Foreign Affairs Council, and ECOFIN. COREPER I is responsible for the agendas of all other Councils. It is worth noting that two bodies, the Special Committee on Agriculture and the PSC, more or less substitute for the role of COREPER in the specific domains of agriculture and CFSP/ESDP, respectively. The Antici Group of officials, named after the Italian official who was the chair of the first such group, assists COREPER and the GAC in preparing the European Council.

Several early studies of COREPER indicated that its members considered themselves to have a dual role. According to Hayes-Renshaw et al. (1989: 136), while the Permanent Representatives 'are the trustworthy executors of the instructions from their respective capitals', they also have strong ties of solidarity with their colleagues in COREPER. These ties were thought to develop as a result of intensive social interaction in Brussels. Committee members eat, drink, and breathe EU issues seven days a week. Lewis (1998: 487) argued that this constant interaction between the same individuals built up a considerable legacy of 'social capital', meaning that the individuals concerned trust one another, and understand and have sympathy for each other's points of view.

The ties are also the result of all of the Permanent Representatives being in the same position vis-à-vis their national governments. All of them will have sympathy with one of their number who is bound by a tight mandate on a particular issue, because they are sometimes placed in that position themselves. In such a situation, they will try to help each other out, perhaps by persuading their own government to make concessions if they feel that the issue is not so important for them. The attitude of the Permanent Representatives to a negotiation is ambivalent: they all want their government's position to prevail; they also want to reach agreement, even at the cost of not achieving all of their own government's objectives in the negotiation (Hayes-Renshaw et al. 1989: 136).

One explanation of this approach is based on rational choice and game theory. It is also compatible with an intergovernmental bargaining image of the committee. On this view, when Permanent Representatives make concessions, or urge their governments to make concessions, it is not just because they feel a sense of social solidarity with their counterparts from other member states. It is also indicative of the strong sense that they have of being involved in a continuous process of bargaining with the same partners. In the language of game theory, they are involved in *iterated* games (that is, the same game is repeated several times with the same participants). This changes the calculation of what is rational as compared with isolated games. In a one-off game, it is rational to take any step to damage your opponent's position and to further your own, even so far as cheating on the rules if you can get away with it. In iterated games, the use of such tactics is likely to backfire during a subsequent round. If you have reneged on a deal in one round of negotiations, it will be difficult to get anyone to conclude a deal with you in subsequent rounds.

This logic of iterated games in EU bargaining is more apparent to Permanent Representatives than it sometimes is to ministers, who have many other concerns, such as accounting for their Brussels diplomacy to their national parliaments and cabinet colleagues, and who are less intensively socialized into the Union method of bargaining. It means that Permanent Representatives are often involved in trying to educate their governments about the nature of the EU bargaining process. It would be a foolish government that did not listen seriously to the advice of the Permanent Representative when deciding on its national negotiating position. This could be taken as evidence that the intergovernmentalist view, that national preferences are formulated independently of influence from the EU level, is partial at best.

Another explanation of the approach of COREPER, which also challenges the intergovernmentalist view, is based on social constructivism. Lewis (2000) identified five main features of the operation of COREPER that resulted from the circumstances and socialization processes identified above. He labelled these: diffuse reciprocity; thick trust; mutual responsiveness; a consensus reflex; and a culture of compromise.

- *Diffuse reciprocity* means that the Permanent Representatives will support one of their number on an issue that is important to that individual's member state but less important to their own, and in return will expect to receive such support when they themselves have a problem. This is not the same as the sort of formal agreement that is allowed for in rational-choice bargains, in which deals are done that A will support B on issue C in return for the support of B on issue D. The reciprocity is diffuse, not specific. It relates to the collectivity of COREPER across the whole range of issues.

- *Thick trust*—as opposed to 'thin trust'—means that the Permanent Representatives feel that they can be honest and open with one another without anything that they say being reported back to other governments. In restricted sessions, they feel that they speak freely, knowing that what they say will not be shared beyond the meeting.

- *Mutual responsiveness* means that the Permanent Representatives, because they work together so closely, come to understand one another's perspectives and problems, and will try not to approach an issue in a way that they know will cause problems for other members of COREPER.

- The *consensus reflex* is deeply embedded in the culture of COREPER. Although there is provision for QMV where the Treaty specifies, it is not used extensively, and is always the last resort. COREPER will continue to seek a consensus long after it is apparent that a qualified majority could be mustered if a vote were called.

- The *culture of compromise* arises from a spirit of accommodation that brings together the previous features. Lewis (2000: 271) refers to the Permanent Representatives spending extra time to 'bring everyone on board', even if one member state is being inflexible in its position.

In short, the regular, 'face-to-face encounters between Council members produces trustworthy relationships that foster mutual responsiveness and understanding' (Lewis 2017).

High-Level Preparatory Bodies

There are several of these high-level preparatory bodies. Some have been mentioned already: the three that prepare ECOFIN; the SCA in agricultural policy; and the PSC as one of the preparatory bodies for the Foreign Affairs Council. Two other bodies prepare the Foreign Affairs Council: the Trade Policy Committee, which deals with the common commercial policy, and the EU Military Committee, which is responsible for ESDP and which may be attended by the chiefs of military staff of the member states, but is more likely to be attended by Brussels-based military attachés.

Lewis (2000) went on to ask whether the pattern of socialization applied to these bodies as with COREPER. He surveyed six of these preparatory bodies, which correspond to the present-day SCA, the Trade Policy Committee, the Budget Committee, the Economic and Finance Committee (EFC), the PSC, and the K-4 Committee (a co-ordinating body for JHA that was later split up). The conclusion of this investigation (Lewis 2000: 282) was that only the EFC came close to exhibiting the five features to anything like the same extent as COREPER. This somewhat weakened the thrust of the supranationalist argument, but not the validity of the social constructivist approach, because the empirical findings underlined the need to investigate the 'sociality and normative environment in which interests are defined and defended' (Lewis 2003*b*: 262).

Lewis's research was pioneering in highlighting the socialization effects operating in the Council, but recent studies (Naurin 2018) suggest that upon closer inspection the EU's famed socialization effects have in fact had limited effect, as the outcomes of Council voting tend to reflect domestic national preferences. However, it is worth noting that Naurin uses a different (more quantitative) approach from Lewis, which fails to unpack whether domestic preferences may have themselves been shaped by officials working in Brussels.

The Working Parties

Moving further down the hierarchy, the working parties that prepare recommendations for the Permanent Representatives involve intensive interaction between national and Commission officials. The processes of socialization that Lewis and others argued apply to COREPER also apply here. Although the people who sit on these committees are national representatives, early research by Beyers and Dierickx (1998: 307–8) showed that members of working groups soon started to judge other members on the basis of the level of expertise that they showed in the committee rather than on nationality.

Ludlow (1991: 103) went further, arguing that 'Commission officials act as thirteenth members of the Council machinery', implying that the distinction between national and Commission representatives was almost meaningless in the work of these groups. More recent analyses concur, suggesting that the Council operates as a forum in which transnational epistemic communities come together to solve problems (Lewis 2017).

The thrust of all of these arguments is that the members of the working parties develop a sense of collegiality and engagement in a joint enterprise that makes it more sensible to see them as individuals participating in a team effort than as representatives of individual states. They are operating very much at the 'problem-solving' end of Scharpf's spectrum of types of negotiation. Agreements are reached largely on the basis of convincing arguments, not political weight or bargaining skill.

The Council Presidency

Under the original Treaty provisions, a different member state assumed the presidency of the Council every six months. During its period of office, that member state had responsibility for preparing and chairing meetings of the European Council, the Council of the EU and its various committees, and also for some functions of representing the EU externally. In the course of its six months in charge, the presidency arranged and chaired between seventy and ninety meetings of ministers, and many more times that of committees. In addition, at least one European Council meeting fell during the six months' presidency. Although assisted in this considerable task by the Council Secretariat (see Insight 14.3), the civil service of the state holding the presidency carried much of the burden of this work. Some authors, for instance Tallberg (2003), argued that states holding the presidency were able to advance their interests during their term in charge of the EU's agenda.

This system was subject to two main criticisms: that six months was too brief a period for the tenure of the presidency; and that the scale of demands on the country holding the presidency had outstripped the capacity of all but the largest member states to cope (for analysis of the old system, see Hayes-Renshaw and Wallace 2006: 154–7). The increasing range of policy areas from the 1980s simply added additional activities for the presidency to prepare. Moreover, with twenty-seven member states, holding the presidency is infrequent: once every fourteen years.

The Lisbon Treaty aimed to tackle these issues. The new system comprises four different presidencies:

- the European Council—an appointment for two-and-a-half years, this arrangement is consistent with the European Council being designated a separate institution;
- the Council of Foreign Affairs, chaired by the HRUFASP for Foreign Affairs and Security Policy (a five-year appointment) (see Chapter 26);
- the Euro Group, which comprises only states in the eurozone and elects its own president to a two-and-a-half-year term (see Chapter 21);
- a 'trio presidency' of three member states, which spans an eighteen-month period, and is responsible for other sectoral Councils and their preparatory bodies.

Insight 14.3 The Council General Secretariat

- The Council Secretariat employs about 3,000 people. It is the 'institutional memory' of the Council of the EU and assists with the organization of meetings, and can help with mediating between national delegations. It is based in Brussels in the Justus Lipsius building.

- The two most senior positions were, until the Lisbon Treaty, the post of Secretary General and High Representative and the Deputy Secretary General. The former position was held by Javier Solana between 1999 and 2009. The appointment of Catherine Ashton (2009–14) to an enhanced position that straddles both the Commission and the Council resulted in change at the top of the Council Secretariat. Federica Mogherini held the role from 2014 to 2019 and was replaced by Josep Borell of Spain in 2019.

- The Council Secretariat has a Legal Service, as well as over 1,000 translators. Interpreters are drawn from the European Commission's staff. There are currently seven Directorates General (DGs).

The trio system had, in fact, commenced in 2007 after reform to the Council's rules of procedure. The Lisbon Treaty merely formalized this change. The basic principle is that the state holding the presidency for six months has an agreed programme with the states preceding and succeeding its term in office. Thus, at the start of 2020, Croatia (January–June) held the six-month presidency, and the trio presidency consisted of its two predecessors, Finland (July–December 2019), and Romania (January–June 2019). Their trio programme was presented to the Council in November 2018 (Council of the EU 2018*b*). The current sequence of presidencies, agreed in 2016, is set out in Table 14.1.

Table 14.1 List of Council Presidencies, 2020–25

Member state	Time period
Croatia	January–June 2020
Germany	July–December 2020
Portugal	January–June 2021
Slovenia	July–December 2021
France	January–June 2022
Czech Republic	July–December 2022
Sweden	January–June 2023
Spain	July–December 2023
Belgium	January–June 2024
Hungary	July–December 2024
Poland	January–June 2025
Denmark	July–December 2025

Council presidencies, even in their scaled-back role after the Lisbon Treaty reforms, continue to entail a lot of organizational responsibilities. For instance, the Irish presidency (January–July 2013) was reported to have entailed 2,477 meetings at all levels of the Council hierarchy, 374 three-way meetings of the EP and Council as part of inter-institutional decision making, and fifty-four ministerial Councils (Laffan 2014: 91). The preceding presidency had been held by Cyprus, and the number of meetings placed a significant burden on a state with a small diplomatic service.

CONCLUSION

The European Council and the Council of the EU are quite different institutions, with different paths of development. The European Council is of central importance to the 'high politics' of the EU, while the Council of the EU is central to decision making and legislation. The European Council has moved from the informality of the 'Library Group' to an institution in its own right. The Council of the EU has gradually become more of a co-legislator as the powers of the EP have increased (see Chapter 15, 'The Struggle for Power'). Like the Council of the EU, the European Council holds occasional informal sessions to try to attain some of the advantages of the less-structured organization of the past. Formal sessions of the Council of the EU have to take place with camera and screen facilities so that the speakers can be identified in a chamber comprising the member state delegations (plus the presidency, the Commission, the Council Secretariat, and interpreters), each being permitted a minister and at least one official. In other words, meetings are typically attended by over a hundred participants.

The increased size of the Council may reduce the socialization effects reported in earlier research. The ongoing tensions between Poland and Hungary and other EU states, along with the increasing willingness of the so-called Visegrad States of central and eastern Europe to work together (See Chapter 22, 'History') may challenge the norm of consensus. It may also be that the Lisbon Treaty's strengthened provisions for enhanced co-operation will lead to greater use of pioneer groups of like-minded states (see Chapter 12, 'The Post-Lisbon Architecture of the EU').

At first sight, it would appear obvious that the Council of the EU is an intergovernmental organization. However, this is a simplification of a complex situation. First, it is clear that the Council of the EU as a collective entity may also be regarded as a supranational institution, because it can and does agree to legislation that is then binding on all of the member states. Second, it is not clear that the Council of the EU, in all of its manifestations, operates simply as an intergovernmental bargaining forum. Lewis (2017) describes it as a hybrid that fuses intergovernmentalism with transnational expertise to form a set of consensus-generating epistemic communities.

To try to analyse the role of the Council of the EU as a whole would be a mistake. It is important to disaggregate its component parts in order to understand at exactly which point in the machinery issues are dealt with. Only with this knowledge can an informed judgement be made concerning the key actors involved and their motivations. Even then, the task is complicated by the secrecy that surrounds the activity of the Council in virtually all of its manifestations. The holding of open sessions when passing legislative acts—as formalized in the Lisbon Treaty—may simply transfer the secrecy to other venues or to other parts of Council sessions. Here it is worth noting the provisions in Article 16 TEU, that 'each Council meeting shall be divided into two parts, dealing respectively with deliberations on Union legislative acts and non-legislative activities'.

The most informed research suggests that a high proportion of Council of the EU's decisions are taken relatively low down in the decisional hierarchy. It is here, within COREPER and the preparatory bodies, that observers have found the greatest departure from intergovernmentalism in

Council activities. At the ministerial level, decisions tend to be more politicized and national positions less open to negotiation. However, to complicate matters further, evidence suggests that, even at the ministerial level, some formations of the Council are more collegial than others (Beyers 2010). Studies also suggest that there is considerable variation in the degree of collegiality exhibited by the different manifestations of the Council (Lewis 2000, 2017). The conclusion must be, therefore, that the argument between intergovernmental and supranational theorists cannot be settled finally so far as the Council is concerned: context is important. There is a strong case for making nuanced judgements about the extent to which the Council is intergovernmental. The increasing provision for decision making in the Council of the EU by QMV is a further dimension to any departure from pure intergovernmentalism, since even the provision—if not the practice—can result in a shift in the calculation of national interests.

The other theoretical debate around the Council of the EU concerns whether to approach it using the techniques of rational choice institutionalism and game theory, or whether to understand it as a case study in social constructivism. To some extent, this division corresponds with the division between intergovernmental and supranational theories of the nature of the Council of the EU. Intergovernmentalists tend to favour rationalist approaches to understanding its workings because they see it as a forum for hard bargaining around national interests, and it is in understanding the operation of such forums that rational choice and game theory have made some of their biggest contributions. Supranationalists tend to rest their arguments on evidence that the representatives of the member states on the various committees and Council of the EU formations become socialized into a different construction of what they are trying to achieve from a simple defence of national interests, and into informally institutionalized procedures that emphasize consensus and co-operation, rather than instrumental bargaining. However, it is possible to accept a social constructivist epistemology and still come to the conclusion on the basis of empirical evidence that the socialization process does not operate very effectively in some of the committees and some of the manifestations of the Council.

KEY POINTS

Definitions and Distinctions

- There is a hierarchy of EU institutions that comprise representatives of national governments.
- At the top of the hierarchy is the European Council, which consists of regular summit meetings of the heads of government of the EU member states.
- Below the European Council is the Council of the EU, which consists of several Councils of national Ministers for different areas of policy, together with their preparatory bodies of officials.

Intergovernmental and Supranational Interpretations

- At first sight the Council is a purely intergovernmental body.
- A deeper analysis reveals a more complex picture, with elements of supranationalism.

The European Council

- The European Council was established in the 1970s to provide a collective response to the challenges of economic interdependence, to allow national governments collectively to control the direction of the EC, to avoid policy segmentation, and to present a united front to the outside world.

- The functions of the European Council now include: to provide general direction to the EU; to oversee Treaty reform and enlargement; to make key foreign policy decisions; to act as policy maker of last resort; and to monitor the development of certain policies.

- The European Council faces problems of overload, over-optimism, over-cautiousness, and over-expectation.

- The European Council's work has arguably resulted in it increasing the supranational character of the EU.

The Council of the EU

- The Council of the EU meets in a variety of formations, depending on the subject under consideration.

- Although there is no formal hierarchy of Council meetings, informally the GAC and those sectoral Councils concerning foreign affairs, finance, and agriculture have the highest status.

- The frequency with which ministers meet in sectoral Councils can lead to the emergence of a sense of collective enterprise, marked by communicative rationality rather than instrumental rationality.

- Because of the large measure of secrecy in which the Council of the EU meets, it is difficult to research the degree to which individual Councils engage in problem solving rather than bargaining around national interests.

COREPER and other Preparatory Bodies

- A large proportion of 'Council' decisions are actually taken lower down the decisional hierarchy. Arguments that the Council is a supranational entity are strongest at this level.

- The Permanent Representatives of member governments interact regularly and develop trust and solidarity, which makes agreement between them easier than between politicians who are less regularly engaged and who have broader concerns.

- The operation of COREPER can be explained either from a rational-choice bargaining perspective as the behaviour appropriate to actors involved in iterated games, or from a social-constructivist perspective as the building of a new sense of identity among the Permanent Representatives.

- Other senior preparatory bodies have not achieved the same degree of trust and solidarity as COREPER, with the exception of the Economic and Financial Committee.

- National representatives on working parties also undergo a process of socialization that produces a problem-solving approach, in which decisions are taken more on the strength of evidence than of political considerations.

The Council Presidency

- Originally, the Council presidency applied to all levels of the hierarchy and rotated between member states every six months. This system was criticized on the grounds of brevity of tenure and for the scale of the demands that it placed on smaller member states.

- Following the Lisbon Treaty's implementation, the European Council has its own President, as does the Council of Foreign Affairs and the Euro Group. All other business is run by 'trio presidencies' comprising three states over a period of eighteen months.

 For additional material and resources, please visit the online resources www.oup.com/uk/bache5e.

QUESTIONS

1. What is the difference between the European Council and the Council of the EU?

2. To what extent does new intergovernmentalism offer new insights into Council behaviour?

3. How consensual is decision making in the Council of the EU?

4. Is the Council of the EU a supranational or an intergovernmental institution?

5. What are the advantages and disadvantages of making Council decision making more transparent?

FURTHER READING

The most recent detailed interpretation of both institutions is by **U. Puetter**, *The European Council and the Council. New Intergovernmentalism and Institutional Change* (Oxford: Oxford University Press, 2014). **Puetter** has also authored an interpretive article on the European Council: 'Europe's Deliberative Intergovernmentalism: The Role of the Council and European Council in EU Economic Governance', *Journal of European Public Policy*, 19 (2012): 161–78. **D. Naurin** has written two key pieces that test the assumptions of Council socialization: 'Generosity in Inter-Governmental Relations: The Impact of State Power, Pooling and Socialisation in the Council of the European Union', *European Journal of Political Research*, 54 (2015): 726–44, and 'Liberal Intergovernmentalism in the Councils: A Baseline Theory?', *Journal of Common Market Studies*, 56 (2018): 1526–43. **S. Hagemann et al**. in 'Signals to their Parliaments? Governments' Use of Votes and Policy Statements in the EU Council', *Journal of Common Market Studies*, 57 (2019): 634– 50 and **S. Novak**, in 'The Silence of Ministers: Consensus and Blame Avoidance in the Council of the European Union', *Journal of Common Market Studies*, 51 (2013): 1091–107, both analyse the impact of domestic factors on Council behaviour. **W. Wessels** provides a comprehensive textbook treatment of the European Council in *The European Council* (Basingstoke: Palgrave Macmillan, 2015). Finally, 'The European Council: A Formidible Locus of Power' (by **P. de Schoutheete**) and 'The Council of Ministers: Conflict, Consensus and Continuity' (by **F. Hayes-Renshaw**) are each given chapter-length consideration in **D. Hodson and J. Peterson (eds)**, *The Institutions of the European Union*, 4th edn (Oxford: Oxford University Press, 2017).

Chapter 15

The European Parliament

Chapter Overview

The European Parliament (EP) is the one directly elected institution of the European Union (EU). The members of the EP (MEPs) are elected once every five years, and since the first direct elections in 1979, the EP has campaigned for more power and influence. Over the subsequent period, there has been a considerable increase in its powers, including through the Lisbon Treaty. The struggle for increased powers is discussed in more detail in 'The Struggle for Power' below, after the basic structure and functions of the EP have been summarized. The chapter then turns to look at debates and research on the EP. One theme of the academic debate is the extent to which the EP has become an effective independent actor in the affairs of the EU, and how far it will continue to move in that direction in the future. This clearly parallels the discussion in Chapter 13, on the Commission and Chapter 14, on the Council.

Composition and Functions

The EP, elected in June 2019 consisted of 751 MEPs, divided between the member states in a manner approximately proportionate to size of population, although the small countries were somewhat over-represented to strengthen their voice. The UK left the EU on 31 January 2020, at which point the number of MEPs was reduced to 705. The distribution of those seats post-Brexit is shown in Table 15.1.

The EP meets in plenary session in Strasbourg for three or four days every month except August, and additional plenaries are held in Brussels. However, most of its work is channelled through standing committees, which may change designation following elections (see Box 15.1 for those in the 2019–24 Parliament). It can also establish temporary committees, either as special committees or committees of inquiry. Special committees normally sit for a year and investigate topical issues. For example, a Special Committee on the Financial, Economic, and Social Crisis was established in 2009, and one on Tax and Corporations in 2015. Committees of inquiry normally investigate suspected maladministration or breaches of EU law. For example, the EP set up a committee to investigate the 'dieselgate' scandal on emissions measurements in the automotive sector in 2016 (European Parliament 2015; see Insight 17.3). Committee meetings are normally held in Brussels.

The EP has a President, a Bureau, a Conference of Presidents, and a Secretariat. The President is elected by the MEPs from among their number for a two-and-a-half-year renewable term. The President represents the EP on official occasions and in relations with other institutions, presides over debates during plenary sessions, and chairs meetings of the Bureau and the Conference of Presidents. The Bureau consists of the President, the fourteen Vice-Presidents, and five 'quaestors' who deal with administrative and financial matters relating to MEPs. The members are elected by the MEPs for a term of two-and-a-half years. The Conference of Presidents consists of the President and the Chairs of the Political Groups. It draws up the agenda for plenary sessions, fixes the timetable for the work of parliamentary bodies, and establishes the terms of reference and size of parliamentary committees and delegations. The Secretariat consists of over 7,500 administrative and clerical staff, working for the EP and its political groups. Around one-third of the staff are in the language service, concerned with translation and interpretation.

The political composition of the EP is determined by the elections, which are held every five years. Historically, the three largest political blocs in the EP have been the European People's Party (EPP) (largely Christian democrats), Social Democrats (currently called the Progressive Alliance of Socialists and Democrats) and the Liberals (currently called Renew Europe). The Parliament elected in 2019 (see also Table 15.2) was distinctive because for the first time in the EP's history the two largest groups failed to secure enough seats between them to command an absolute majority. This outcome means that a wider coalition of parties is needed to secure the majorities that are required for legislation to be adopted. The 2019 elections saw a further increase in the representation of Eurosceptic and far-right parties, which had done particularly well in 2014 (see Table 15.2). There were two further noteworthy elements of the 2019 elections. First was the participation of the UK. Brexit had been anticipated by 31 March 2019, but following an extension of the Brexit deadline to 31 October 2019, the UK was required to participate in the European elections. The Eurosceptic Brexit Party secured twenty-nine of the seventy-three UK seats, to become the largest

Table 15.1 Distribution of Seats in the European Parliament Post-Brexit (2020)

Austria	19	Germany	96	Poland	52
Belgium	21	Greece	21	Portugal	21
Bulgaria	17	Hungary	21	Romania	33
Croatia	12	Ireland	13	Slovakia	14
Cyprus	6	Italy	76	Slovenia	8
Czech Republic	21	Latvia	8	Spain	59
Denmark	14	Lithuania	11	Sweden	21
Estonia	7	Luxembourg	6		
Finland	14	Malta	6		
France	79	Netherlands	29	**TOTAL**	**705**

Source: https://www.europarl.europa.eu/news/en/faq/12/how-many-meps.

Box 15.1 Committees of the European Parliament (as of August 2019)

- Agriculture and Rural Development Committee
- Budgets Committee
- Budgetary Control Committee
- Civil Liberties, Justice, and Home Affairs Committee
- Constitutional Affairs Committee
- Culture and Education Committee
- Development Committee
- Economic and Monetary Affairs Committee
- Employment and Social Affairs Committee
- Environment, Public Health, and Food Safety Committee
- Fisheries Committee
- Foreign Affairs Committee
  - Security and Defence Sub-Committee
  - Human Rights Sub-Committee
- Industry, Research, and Energy Committee
- Internal Market and Consumer Protection Committee
- International Trade Committee
- Legal Affairs Committee
- Petitions Committee
- Regional Development Committee
- Transport and Tourism Committee
- Women's Rights and Gender Equality Committee.

national delegation within the EP, although these MEPs did not affiliate themselves with a larger cross-national political group and the UK's exit on 31 January 2020 saw them leave the Parliament. Second was the 'green surge', which saw the Green Group increase its size from fifty to seventy-four MEPs, although this was adjusted down to sixty-seven MEPs following Brexit.

The powers of the EP are summarized in Insight 15.1. It has legislative, budgetary, and supervisory functions. In the legislative field, it has emerged as a co-legislator with the Council of the EU in most areas of EU legislation, primarily via the ordinary legislative procedure (OLP) (co-decision), which applies to over eighty specific provisions in the Treaty on the Functioning of the European Union (TFEU). The various legislative procedures, and the powers of the EP in each of them, are discussed in Chapter 12, 'Decision Making Procedures'. The EP and the Council of the EU are the joint budgetary authorities of the EU. The budgetary procedure, and the role of the EP in it, is again described in Chapter 12, 'Decision Making Procedures'.

The supervisory functions of the EP relate to the Commission and the Council. Under the Maastricht Treaty, the EP was given the right to approve the appointment of the President and members of the Commission. The Treaty of Amsterdam strengthened the power relating to the President, who needed specific approval by the EP. Under the Lisbon Treaty, the candidate for the presidency has to be chosen taking into account the results of the most recent EP elections: a provision that led to parties entering the 2014 and 2019 elections with candidates nominated to become Commission President (See Chapter 13, 'Composition and Appointment'). The EP has the power to dismiss the whole of the Commission on a vote of censure—but it cannot target individual Commissioners. A motion of censure requires a positive vote from an absolute majority of MEPs and two-thirds of the votes cast. The EP also has the right to ask the Commission written and oral questions.

In respect of the European Council and the Council of the EU, the powers of the EP are more limited. It can table written and oral questions about the activities of the Council of the EU, and the Foreign Minister of the state holding the presidency of the Council reports to the EP at the beginning and end of the presidency. For the European Council, the Lisbon Treaty (Article 15 TEU) formalized the practice whereby the EP is given a report following each European Council meeting. The President of the EP is invited to the start of European Council sessions 'to be heard' (Article 235 TFEU), but does not participate in its meetings after this opening opportunity to make a contribution.

Outside the 'Union method', the EP is to be kept informed of developments relating to Common Foreign and Security Policy (CFSP) and the Parliament's views are to be taken into consideration. The High Representative of the Union for Foreign Affairs and Security Policy (HRUFASP) is responsible for maintaining relations with the EP.

Insight 15.1 The Powers of the European Parliament

Legislative

- Under the OLP, the EP shares the final decision on most proposals with the Council (co-decision).
- Consent is required for the enlargement of the EU, agreements with third countries, and a range of other decisions.
- It delivers opinions on Commission proposals under the consultation procedure in a limited number of policy areas.

Budgetary

- Its approval is required for the annual budget.
- Its Budgetary Control Committee checks expenditure (together with the Court of Auditors).

Supervisory

- It approves the appointment of Commission President.
- It approves the appointment of the Commission after public hearings.
- It questions the Council and Commission.
- It can censure and dismiss the whole Commission.

The Struggle for Power

In the original Treaties, the forerunner of the present EP was neither directly elected nor endowed with significant powers. Members of the European Parliamentary Assembly (EPA) were members of national parliaments who were seconded to the EPA. The EPA had the right to be consulted by the Council of Ministers before legislation was agreed, but its opinion could be, and frequently was, ignored; it could dismiss the Commission as a whole on a vote of censure, but only if it could achieve the difficult degree of unity needed to reach the double majority requirement (two-thirds of those voting, constituting an absolute majority of members).

From the outset, though, the EPA set about trying to extract the right to be directly elected, and to have stronger powers. This process of parliamentarization has seen the EP's powers considerably extended to encompass budgetary, supervisory, and legislative domains. Key turning points have included the adoption of the budgetary treaties of 1970 and 1975; the introduction of direct elections by universal suffrage in 1979; the 1980 *Isoglucose* ruling of the Court of Justice of the EU (CJEU), giving Parliament a de facto delaying power; the Single European Act (SEA) of 1987, introducing the co-operation procedure and the assent procedure; the Treaty of Maastricht in 1993, bringing in the co-decision procedure, and giving Parliament the right to allow (or not) the Commission as a whole to take office through a vote of confidence; and the Treaty of Amsterdam, which greatly extended the scope of co-decision, modified it to Parliament's advantage, and gave Parliament the right to confirm or reject a designated President of the Commission. The Lisbon Treaty greatly extended the scope of co-decision renaming it the Ordinary Legislative Procedure (OLP), while renaming assent as the consent procedure (see Chapter 12, 'Decision Making Procedures').

In achieving these gains, the EP has used a number of tactical devices. First, most of its members have lobbied for increased powers for the EP within their national parties. Here, the most significant step forward was the introduction of direct elections. Direct elections 'created a new class of elected representatives in Europe . . . whose career depended on making something of the European dimension' (Corbett et al. 2003: 356). Second, the argument that the powers of the EP needed to be increased in order to close the 'democratic deficit' has been consistently used by the EP. The academic debate about the EU's democratic and legitimacy deficits is reviewed in Chapter 3, 'Democracy and Legitimacy'. Third, it has made the most extensive use possible of its existing powers, and tried to stretch the definition of those powers. In this, the EP sometimes found an ally in the CJEU. A number of CJEU judgments, on cases brought to it by the EP, increased the powers of the EP in the 1980s and 1990s, starting with the 1980 *Isoglucose* judgment. These judgments are examined in Chapter 16, 'CJEU Rulings on the Powers of the Institutions'. Alongside this 'minimalist' approach, the EP has also pursued a 'maximalist' approach. In 1984, the EP, under the leadership of the Italian federalist MEP, Altiero Spinelli, produced its draft Treaty Establishing the European Union (TEU). It had little influence on the shape of the EU at the time, but set out the EP's ambition and provided inspiration for some of the changes introduced by the member states in later Treaty reforms. During the Constitutional Convention of 2002–03, sixteen MEPs participated in the drafting of what became the Constitutional Treaty (see Chapter 10, 'The Constitutional Treaty').

In what follows, the powers of EP and how they were gained are discussed in more or less the order that they were granted. The granting of additional budgetary powers came before direct elections, but so fundamental were direct elections that they are discussed before the budgetary powers. After that, the increased legislative and scrutiny powers are considered.

Direct Elections

Agreement to replace the EPA with a directly elected body was reached at the Rome meeting of the European Council in December 1975. Why was this decision taken— and what were its consequences?

The decision took place in a less-than-transparent deal between the heads of government in the European Council. Germany, Italy, and the Benelux countries had long favoured a directly elected EP. The governments of these states were convinced by the argument that transferring competences to the EC would lead to a democratic deficit unless there were a directly elected parliament at that level that could take over the role of scrutiny that would be lost to national parliaments. The crucial shift was on the part of France under the presidency of Valéry Giscard d'Estaing.

This shift in position placed Britain, which was even more reluctant, in a more isolated position. Having agreed to the elections, the Labour government, which was contending with divisions in its own party and was reliant on support from the Liberal Party to stay in office, delayed the implementation arrangements. Consequently, the first elections were put back a year, until June 1979. The first directly elected Parliament sought to exploit its new democratic credentials by several routes. It challenged the Council over the annual budget. It was also emboldened to demand more powers of decision making and control over the Commission.

Budgetary Powers

The first granting of additional powers to the EP came in the Treaty of Luxembourg in 1970, when it was given the right to amend 'non-compulsory' items of expenditure in the budget. This agreement was the outcome of an intergovernmental negotiation about the settlement of the long-running budgetary dispute that had led to the 1965 crisis (see Chapter 7, 'The 1965 Crisis'). France continued to be reluctant to grant any budgetary powers to the still indirectly elected EPA at that time, but President Pompidou was anxious to get the system of 'own resources' agreed prior to the opening of entry negotiations with Britain. For France, the goal was to set up a budgetary system to fund the Common Agricultural Policy (CAP) in a way that would leave France a large net beneficiary from the system. As Britain would inevitably lose out from such a system, agreement could not be left until after British entry because the British government would block any such settlement. However, the other five member states insisted that the loss of parliamentary control over national budgetary contributions must be redressed by an increase in the control of the EPA. As with all such intergovernmental negotiations, the outcome was a compromise.

A distinction introduced by the French between expenditure items that followed directly from Community legal acts (compulsory expenditure) and expenditure that did not, such as administrative expenses (non-compulsory expenditure), was accepted, albeit grudgingly by some delegations (the Dutch delegation most notably) as it gave the EP a final say over only about 4–5 per cent of the entire Community expenditure (that is, non-compulsory expenditure).

(Rittberger 2003: 217)

Subsequently, in the 1975 Budget Treaty, the EP was granted the formal right to reject the budget as a whole. Working with these limited powers, the EP pushed its budgetary role to the maximum, especially after the first direct elections in 1979, so that '[i]n the early 1980s the annual budgetary cycle was punctuated with unending disputes between the institutions on what were relatively small amounts of money' (Laffan 1997a: 77).

In December 1979, the first directly elected EP blocked the passing of the budget for 1980 in a test of strength against the Council. For several months, the European Community (EC) had to survive on the system of 'provisional twelfths', whereby it is allowed to spend each month an amount equivalent to one-twelfth of the previous year's budget. Eventually, the MEPs came under tremendous pressure from their national parties to lift their veto, which they did without winning any further concessions on the substance of the budget from the Council—but a marker had been put down that the Council should not treat the directly elected EP with disdain. An informal agreement was reached on resolving such disputes should they arise in the future, although this did not prevent another crisis the following year, when the EP passed a budget that exceeded the maximum rate of increase. The EP was taken to the CJEU by the Council, but an out-of-court agreement was reached in June 1982. Again, the EP gave way on the substance of the dispute, but in return got agreement on a joint declaration on the definitions of compulsory and non-compulsory expenditure, and on the respective roles of the two institutions in the budgetary process (Laffan 1997a: 82).

After further acrimonious exchanges in each of the next two years, in 1985 another serious crisis erupted. The EP was becoming increasingly agitated at the failure of the member states to provide adequate funds for new common policies that had been agreed. The main reason for this failure was an inability to bring under control expenditure on the CAP, over which the EP did not have the power of amendment. At first reading on the 1986 budget, the EP inserted amendments to reduce agricultural expenditure, which it had no right to do. The Council removed the amendments, but the EP restored them, and declared the budget passed. The case went to the Court again, where the budget was declared illegal, but the CJEU intervened decisively, telling the Council and the EP that they were joint budgetary authorities, that neither could act unilaterally, and that they had to find means of reaching agreement (Laffan 1997a: 82; Corbett et al. 2003: 360–2).

It was clear that the disputes and delays in agreeing the annual budgets could not go on indefinitely. Out of this awareness arose the 1988 Inter-Institutional Agreement on Budgetary Discipline. After this, the budget ceased to be at the forefront of the EP's struggle for power. Finally, as a result of reforms in the Lisbon Treaty, the distinction between compulsory and non-compulsory expenditure was abolished. The EP also secured the right to approve the seven-year multi-annual budget. Consequently, the EP and the Council are co-equal budgetary authorities and follow the procedures set out in Chapter 12, 'The Budgetary Procedure'.

Influence in the Legislative Process

The EP has long been committed to being a co-legislator with the Council of the EU. This goal was gradually achieved, first through the now-abolished co-operation procedure, and then through the co-decision procedure (see Chapter 12, 'Decision Making Procedures'). The crucial breakthrough was the introduction of the co-operation procedure in the SEA. This legislative innovation was insisted upon by the governments of those states—especially Germany and Italy—that were most convinced by the federalist arguments and concerns regarding the democratic deficit (Rittberger 2003: 220). Consensus gradually emerged between the governments that, for the single market to be created, they would have to accept qualified majority voting (QMV), otherwise every individual measure would be vetoed by the government of the state that stood to be most adversely affected. This implied, though, that national parliaments would no longer be able to reject a proposed measure by instructing their government's representative to veto it in the Council. The democratic deficit argument implied that the loss of control by the national parliaments should be made up by an increase in the role of the EP.

Once the principle of a larger role for the EP in the legislative process had been established, the extension of that role followed, along with reform of the cooperation procedure. Subsequent Treaty reform increased the number of policy issues to which the OLP applies and the co-operation procedure was abolished by the Lisbon Treaty. The move to the OLP provoked an academic debate as to whether and how the EP is able to exercise legislative influence (see 'The EP and Inter-Institutional Bargaining' below).

The EP and the Commission

There are two main aspects of the ability of the EP to exercise control over the Commission. The first is in its powers over the appointment of the College of Commissioners. The second is in its power to dismiss the College if it disapproves of their conduct.

The power of the EP in the appointment of a new Commission was originally zero. This is an area, however, in which the maximalist strategy (formal rule change) produced results: Treaty amendments gave the EP limited powers that were then exploited fully under the minimalist strategy (informal rule changes). At Maastricht, the heads of government agreed to consult the EP on the choice of the President of the Commission and to give it the right to consent (or not consent) to the appointment of the College of Commissioners as a whole. They also agreed to bring the term of office of the Commissioners into line with that of the EP, so that the newly elected Parliament would be asked, as one of its first acts, to approve the proposed new Commission. In 1994, the EP introduced hearings of Commissioners Designate. In the Amsterdam Treaty, there was a further extension of powers, when the EP was given a formal right of approval of the European Council's nominee for President. These changes were made with an eye on the need to address the democratic deficit. It was hoped that the new powers would persuade voters that the EP was an institution that had the characteristics of a real parliament, and thereby contribute to increased interest in the European parliamentary elections (Smith 1999: 68).

Having gained the right to approve the appointment of the President, and separately of the other Commissioners as a whole, the EP reverted to its minimalist strategy of making the most extensive use possible of its powers. It adapted its internal rules of procedure so that the approval or rejection of the Commission President required only a simple majority, and if the nomination was rejected, the member states would be asked to make a new nomination. It also adopted a rule of procedure that the approval of the Commission as a whole would follow parliamentary hearings in which each of the Commissioners would be subjected to cross-examination *in public* by the members of the relevant specialist committee of the EP (Judge and Earnshaw 2002: 355). These procedural adaptations increased the leverage of the modest extra powers granted in the Maastricht Treaty.

The other aspect of parliamentary control over the Commission is in its power to dismiss Commissioners. Here, the Treaty gives the EP what at first sight is a powerful weapon. If a motion of censure on the Commission is passed by a two-thirds majority of the votes cast, representing a majority of MEPs, then the Commission must resign as a body (Article 234 TFEU). However, this right is less powerful than it seems for at least two reasons. First, the majority required is very difficult to attain. Second, the most likely reason for a censure is because of the behaviour of an individual Commissioner or a small number of Commissioners, yet the censure motion can only target the College as a whole.

Despite these problems, at the end of the 1990s, the EP managed to use this blunt instrument to effect a shift in its influence. In 1998, its Budgetary Affairs Committee postponed a decision on whether to discharge the 1996 budget because it was unhappy with the response of the Commission to certain charges of lax financial administration. Although the Committee subsequently decided by one vote to recommend the grant of discharge, the EP meeting in plenary rejected the recommendation. Jacques Santer, the President of the Commission, then made the issue one of confidence by challenging the EP either to give discharge to the budget or to lay down a motion of censure on the whole Commission. This the EP did, although when it was voted on in January 1999, it failed to get even a majority, let alone the two-thirds majority that was required. However, the vote of 232 for and 293 against was the biggest vote ever for a motion of censure, and prompted the Commission to agree to set up a committee of independent experts to report to the EP on fraud, mismanagement, and nepotism in the Commission. When the report appeared in March 1999, it was so damning of the level of mismanagement by some Commissioners that the whole Commission resigned. Although the EP had not managed to summon the substantial majority needed to censure the Commission formally, by adept use of its limited powers, it achieved a considerable 'informal' victory.

At this point, the powers of the EP to approve the new Commission President and College of Commissioners took centre stage. The new nominee for Commission President was Romano Prodi. He anticipated that the EP would want to seek some assurance that, in future, it would not need to attack the whole Commission if, as had been the case with the Santer Commission, the problem lay with certain individuals. In fact, the Santer Commission probably could have survived had one individual Commissioner (Edith Cresson) agreed to resign, but her refusal to do so left the Commission with no option but to resign as a whole. Prodi therefore told the EP at his own confirmation hearing that he would require every individual Commissioner to promise to resign if asked by the President to do so. The promise was repeated by Prodi's successor, José Manuel Barroso. Although it did not give the EP the right to dismiss individual Commissioners, it did mark a further advance towards that goal. The EP then underlined the importance that it set on this development by requiring each of the proposed new Commissioners to make a public declaration at their confirmation hearing that they would resign if asked by the President to do so. In July 2000, a new Framework Agreement on Relations between the European Parliament and the Commission was adopted by the EP. In it, the commitment of Prodi to hold Commissioners individually responsible was strengthened by a commitment that, if the EP were to express a lack of confidence in an individual Commissioner, the President would consider whether to ask that individual to resign.

Five years later, the EP again flexed its muscles during the confirmation hearings for the incoming Barroso Commission, when the EP expressed an unwillingness to confirm the new Commission in office if the Italian nominee, Rocco Buttiglione, was a member of the team, and expressed doubts about the competence of other nominees. After something of a stand-off, Barroso agreed to rethink the position. Buttiglione's nomination was withdrawn, the Italian government put forward another Italian nominee, and two other changes were made to national nominations. This outcome was achieved because of the impressive degree of independence demonstrated by MEPs in the Socialist and Liberal groups, in the face of intense pressure from national governments to allow the contested nominations.

Ratification of the Lisbon Treaty did not bring about major changes to this status quo. The Treaty itself mainly introduced nuances into the provisions for approval of the Commission President. As noted already, the nomination—once again of Barroso—had to take into account the elections to the EP, as newly provided for under Article 17 TEU. He was then 'elected', as the new terminology described this process. During the hearings, Bulgarian Commissioner Designate Rumiana Jeleva (International Co-operation, Humanitarian Aid, and Crisis Response), a former MEP, performed poorly and failed to allay concerns that she had conflicts of interest. She resigned as Commissioner Designate on 19 January 2010. The Bulgarian Prime Minister then nominated Kristalina Georgieva, and she 'passed' her hearing in early February. Following this change of line-up, the Commission was approved on 9 February 2010 by a 'vote of consent' (as it is now termed) under Article 17 TEU. In January 2013, the (Maltese) Commissioner for Health and Consumer Protection was forced to resign after allegations of corruption in relation to funding from the tobacco industry (European Voice, 2012). This first resignation by an individual Commissioner was facilitated by the EP's attempts to strengthen its controls during the scandal that occurred under the Santer Commission.

The appointment of the von der Leyen Commission in 2019 was a protracted affair. Three nominees were rejected by the Parliament. Romanian socialist Rovana Plumb and Hungarian Fidesz party appointee, László Trócsányi, were rejected by the Legal Affairs Committee over conflicts of interest (Rankin, 2019). France's first nominee, Sylvie Goulard, a liberal, was also rejected, over ethical concerns regarding her use of a European Parliament assistant for domestic political work, which is against the EP's rules. This was the first time a large state like France had seen its nominee rejected. To add to von der Leyen's woes, the UK government, in anticipation of Brexit, refused to nominate a Commissioner. These various problems and delays meant that von der Leyen's Commission was sworn in a month later than expected, on 1 December 2019.

The Lisbon Treaty's requirement that election of the Commission President should take account of the election outcome led to proposals, including from the Commission, for each transnational party group in the EP to nominate a candidate ahead of the 2014 elections, with the assumption being that the candidate from the party group that secured the most seats in the EP would become Commission President. In 2014, Jean-Claude Juncker, former Prime Minister of Luxembourg was selected as Commission President via this 'Spitzenkandidaten' (literally 'lead candidate') process and committed to running a 'political' Commission which, in theory at least, was more accountable to the EP (see Peterson 2017). However, in 2019 the Spitzenkandidaten process was fatally undermined when the European Council refused to endorse the candidate of the largest group (the EPP), the uncharismatic and little know Manfred Weber. The Council went on to reject the other candidates selected by the European party groupings, selecting instead the little-known Ursula von ver Leyen, a German Christian Democrat ally of German Chancellor Angela Merkel. Here we see a reassertion of Council control over appointing to key positions. It remains to be seen how these events will affect the 2019–24 Commission work programme. However, the 'death' of the Spitzenkandidaten process (Gray et al. 2019) suggests that this move to bring voters closer to the EP through appointing the Commission President has failed.

Debates and Research

Debate and research on the EP have been far-reaching and diverse and falls into four broad areas (see Hix et al. 2003; Ripoll Servent and Roederer Rynning 2018):

- work on the general development and functioning of the EP;
- research on political behaviour and EP elections;
- research on the internal politics and organization of the EP;
- examinations of inter-institutional bargaining between the EP, the Council, and the Commission.

The first of these has been dealt with already in this chapter. In this section of the chapter, each of the other three categories of research will be briefly reviewed to indicate the main academic concerns. Related debates on the EU's democracy and legitimacy are considered in Chapter 3, 'Democracy and Legitimacy'.

Political Behaviour and EP Elections

The strongest argument for the direct election of the EP was that it would increase the legitimacy of the institution and thereby of the EU as a whole—yet turnout in European elections fell between 1979 and 2009. Overall turnout declined from 63 per cent (1979) to 49 per cent (1999), to 46 per cent (2004), and 43 per cent (2009). For the 2014 elections, which saw the first attempt to link explicitly the outcome of the elections to the selection of the Commission President, electoral turnout was again 43 per cent, thereby failing to fall for the first time since elections were introduced. In 2019, turnout increased for the first time in the EP's history, to 50 per cent, increasing in twenty-one EU states and by more than 10 per cent in seven of those states (European Parliament 2019*b*). Turnout varies between member states, but is typically much lower than for national elections.

There are two dominant explanations in the literature to account for the turn-out and voting behaviour exhibited at European elections: the second-order election (SOE) and the European salience theses. According to Ripoll-Servent and Roederer-Rynning (2018) the SOE thesis is based on the assumption that citizens are not as interested in EP elections as national elections and so they either 'vote with their heart', by voting for parties they like regardless of their chances of success, or they 'vote with their boot' by punishing parties in national government. The SOE thesis holds that these two tendencies often result in smaller, less mainstream parties getting better results in EP elections. In contrast, the 'European salience' model suggests that these less mainstream parties do better because voters *do* care about Europe, and therefore a party's position as being either pro- or anti-EU can be a determinant of EU electoral outcomes (Hobolt and Spoon 2012; Ripoll Servent and Roederer Rynning 2018).

Generally speaking, EU election campaigns are fought on domestic issues rather than European ones. Most of the campaigning centres on the record of the national government rather than on party positions on European issues. Consequently, the SOE thesis is still regarded as the most persuasive (Ripoll Servent and Roederer Rynning 2018). However, the 2014 elections, which were held against the background of the eurozone crisis (see Chapter 11), brought about a rise in support for Eurosceptic and other protest parties, suggesting that the European salience thesis may apply in some states. The 2019 elections again saw far-right and Eurosceptic parties do well, increasing the number of right-wing MEPs within the EP. However, the performance of the right varied across states. In some countries, such as Italy, Eurosceptic parties did well, but in others where they were expected to do well, such as Germany, overall support fell. The 2019 election results consequently underline the challenges associated with trying to find one explanation for EP election voting behaviour, which varies across time and space.

Internal Politics and Organization of the EP

Research on the EP's internal politics has focused upon the committee work in the EP; party groups; and the independence of MEPs.

Committee Work in the EP

A burgeoning literature has emerged on EP committee work (for a fuller review, see Ripoll Servent 2018: 216–66). This work has built upon research questions and methods that have been applied to committee work in the US Congress (Whitaker 2011; Yordanova 2013) investigating questions such as how party groups have tried to influence the allocation of committee chairs, membership, and the important task of selecting a rapporteur; the MEP charged with producing a committee report on a piece of legislation. Mamadouh and Raunio (2003) showed that the allocation of all of these positions tended to be influenced by national delegations within the EP's transnational party groups. Whitaker (2019) found that MEPs generally secure their preferred committee allocation, particularly if they are incumbents. Other studies have focused upon the behaviour of different committees in seeking to shape policy outcomes (Burns 2013, 2019; Ripoll Servent 2013).

The Party Groups

Just as the EP cannot expect to extend its power and influence unless MEPs show themselves to be competent, so it cannot do so by definition if it lacks independence and autonomy. The main constraint on MEPs acting autonomously is the influence of national political parties. Unless the party groups in the EP can establish their autonomy from national parties, the EP will be constrained.

MEPs do not sit in the EP in national delegations, but in transnational party groups. A party group may be established by twenty-five MEPs from at least one-quarter of the member states. These rules have fluctuated over time in line with the accession of new member states and changes to the size of the EP. The aim has remained constant: to promote groupings that have a truly transnational character. Each party group has its own administrative and support staff, paid for out of the central budget of the EP. Groups are co-ordinated by a Bureau, consisting of a Chair, a Vice-Chair, and a Treasurer as a minimum. The groups play an important role: for instance, in setting the agenda of the EP and allocating speaking time in plenary sessions. A full list of the groups, and their level of representation in the 2019–24 Parliament, is given in Table 15.2.

There are definite advantages to being a member of one of the party groups. The groups receive funding from the EP to cover their administrative costs. Memberships of committees, and their chairs and rapporteurs, are allocated to groups in proportion to their size. (For a list of EP committees, see Box 15.1). It is

Table 15.2 Membership Numbers of Political Groups in the European Parliament February 2020

Group	MEPs
European People's Party	187
Progressive Alliance of Socialists and Democrats	148
Renew Europe	97
Greens/European Free Alliance	67
Identity and Democracy	76
European Conservatives and Reformists	59
European United Left/Nordic Green Left	40
Non-attached	31
Total	**705**

Source: European Parliament (2020).

Note: These figures reflect that post-Brexit the UK's seventy-three MEPs left, and twenty-seven of the UK's seats were redistributed to other member states.

not surprising, therefore, that there are strong incentives for national parties and individual MEPs to form a group. For instance, the Rainbow Group in the 1984–89 Parliament consisted of members of environmentalist parties, regionalist parties, and anti-EC Danish MEPs; the only thing that they had in common was a wish to draw down the funding and other advantages that would be denied them if they did not join a group. As Table 15.2 indicates, a number of MEPs were not located within a political group.

Even the longer-established groups may be subject to change, highlighting the way in which the EP's party system is weak even if its committees are quite powerful: a characteristic that makes it comparable to the US Congress. Following the 2009 election to the EP, the British Conservative Party formed the cornerstone of a new group, the European Conservatives and Reformists. Previously, it had been in a grouping known as the European People's Party and European Democrats (EPP–ED). However, when David Cameron campaigned for the leadership of the Conservative Party, he made a commitment to withdraw from this grouping on the grounds that it was too pro-European, thus tapping into the Euroscepticism of his party's backbenchers in the national parliament. The EPP–ED thus became the EPP from 2009. On the centre left of the political spectrum, the Socialist Group adopted a broader title after the 2009 elections—the Progressive Alliance of Socialists and Democrats—to accommodate the Italian Democratic Party, which had only been established in 2007 as an amalgamation of several parties.

These shifting formations also hint at the fact that cohesion of transnational parties is different from that in national parliaments. Not only can genuine differences of national perspective lead to divergence in voting behaviour in the EP, but, as noted above, the MEPs in the party groups are also subject to pressure from their national parties. In many, although not all member states, the proportional representation (PR) electoral systems that operate make it easier for national party leaders to put pressure on their MEPs, because European elections are held on the basis of closed party lists—that is, the voter is presented with a list of the candidates for that party in the order of preference decided by the party, and is unable to change the order. Thus, the chances of an individual being elected on any particular level of vote for the party depend on where he or she is placed on the list. As the lists are drawn up by the national party organizations, the MEPs face the prospect of being dropped down the list, and of their seats being jeopardized, if they offend the national party leadership too much.

Despite the relative weakness of the transnational party groups, research indicates that their internal cohesion has generally increased over time. For instance, Hix, Kreppel, and Noury (2003; see also Hix et al. 2005) undertook an analysis of **roll-call voting** over the period from 1979 and concluded that the party system in the EP had become more consolidated over time. As the powers of the EP have increased under successive revisions of the Treaties, so the party groups have tended to become more cohesive in order to be more effective.

> Where the parties have similar policies (on EU integration and external trade) they tend to vote together, and where they have differing positions (on environmental, agriculture, economic and social issues) they tend to vote on opposite sides.

(Hix et al. 2003: 327)

One important point provides context to this pattern of growing cohesion: namely, the striking number of near unanimous votes in the EP. For instance, Hix et al. (2003: 318) reviewed roll-call votes over the period 1979–2001 and found that the two largest party groupings, the socialists and the EPP (Christian Democrats), voted together in a minimum of 61–71 per cent of cases depending on the parliamentary term. In national parliaments, party cohesion and competition arise because of the government's wish to secure its legislative programme and the opposition's wish either to obstruct or to modify the legislation. This situation finds no parallel in the EP because there is no EU government based on a majority of MEPs. Instead, co-operation between the two main party groupings is incentivized by the rules of the OLP (Hix and Høyland 2011: 144). Specifically, amendments at the second reading in the EP require an absolute majority of MEPs, and that is most easily achieved if the two largest groups can find common ground. Equally, this requirement for an absolute majority may contribute to the fact that agreement is increasingly found between the EP and the Council at the first reading. In some circumstances, inter-institutional dynamics can encourage the EP to line up in opposition to the Council. Both groups may sometimes share a common interest in increasing the powers of the EP, resulting in a strategic calculation in favour of voting together in the later stages of the legislative process (see Kreppel 2000). However, it is worth noting here that the composition of the 2019–24 EP raises particular challenges, as there is no longer a majority for the two main political groups, which means that stable coalitions may be harder to find (VoteWatch 2019).

What this discussion makes clear is that the party politics of the EP has become a major area of research, strengthened by the growing importance of the EP in the legislative process. In a survey of twenty years of the OLP, independent EU affairs think-tank VoteWatch, found that the participation rate of MEPs in roll-call votes had gone up over the period; that party cohesion had increased in the transnational party groups; that legislation was increasingly adopted at the first reading; and legislation was being adopted by larger majorities (VoteWatch 2013).

Research on the party groups has opened up a debate about whether behaviour in the EP reflects 'party politics as usual' or whether the distinctive character of the EU's institutions prevents the patterns of behaviour that we would recognize from national parliaments (Lindberg et al. 2008). Alongside this, the debate concerning the behaviour of party groups in the EP has advanced considerably and attention has now begun to explore partisan voting in other institutions: notably, the Council of the EU and the European Council (Hagemann and Høyland 2008; Tallberg and Johansson 2008, Hagemann et al. 2019), in which the focus has traditionally been upon governments voting along national lines.

A sign of the maturity of the field is that new research is emerging that moves beyond the confines of debates about how cohesive the political groups are to embrace radical theoretical perspectives. For example, Kantola and Rolandsen Agustín (2019) analyse the role of gender in the EP and its party groups, revealing that although the EP is the most gender equal of the EU's institutions, the practices of its party groups continue to perpetuate gendered roles and divisions of labour.

The Independence of MEPs

A key area of academic interest is the relationship between national parties and their MEPs and the degree of independence MEPs can exercise. The degree of latitude allowed to MEPs by their national parties is strongly linked to the electoral system: those elected via closed lists, where voters simply vote for a party, are more dependent upon their national parties than those elected via open lists, where the voters can select individual candidates (Ripoll Servent 2018: 198). Moreover, MEPs' ability to access positions of power within the Parliament is strongly linked to the willingness of their national party delegation to support them. However, an MEP who frequently defects from the European Party Group line to follow national interests will not be seen as a credible European legislator. Hence, MEPs who want to hold positions of responsibility within the Parliament have to tread a fine line between keeping their national party happy and behaving as a credible policy maker in a transnational legislature. Ringe (2010) suggests that MEPs navigate this potentially treacherous terrain by engaging in a series of negotiations with their national party, European political group, and committee colleagues. Exactly who is involved and how varies depending upon the issue and how salient (important) it is for each of these different legislative stakeholders.

Historically, MEPs were generally perceived as being established politicians seeing out their career, or as young careerists using the EP as a ladder to national positions. However, as the powers and influence of the EP have grown, the prospect for MEPs of developing a political career within the Parliament has become more viable, and a key cohort who seek to pursue an active career within the EP is now discernable (van Geffen 2016).

The EP and Inter-Institutional Bargaining

This is an area that has attracted a lot of academic attention, which has centred on the extent to which the effective influence of the EP over the legislative process has really increased. The general view of the progression from consultation through the now-abolished co-operation procedure to the OLP was that 'the consecutive institutional reforms are moving the EU towards a genuinely bicameral system' (Crombez 2000: 366). On the face of it, each step represented an increase in both the power and influence of the EP. However, some analysts have challenged this automatic growth of power and crucially argued that this increase in power has not necessarily translated in to increased policy influence.

Under its original power—the *consultation* procedure—the EP's opinion could be ignored, whether the voting rule was unanimity or QMV. However, the SEA also introduced the *co-operation* procedure. Under this procedure, the Commission and the EP shared the power to determine the final form of the legislation. If the EP and the Commission could agree on a proposal that was acceptable to a coalition in the Council that constituted a qualified majority, they together had the decisive influence on the form of the legislation. The co-operation procedure was largely replaced by the Amsterdam Treaty and finally abolished by the Lisbon Treaty.

The *co-decision* procedure, introduced by the Maastricht Treaty, changed the inter-institutional balance again. As introduced at that stage it gave the EP:

- three readings of legislation;
- the right to negotiate directly with the Council via a Conciliation Committee on any amendments for which there was an absolute majority in the EP, but with which the Council did not agree;
- an absolute right of veto.

While academics—largely using rational choice or game-theoretical interpretations—argued over the impact of this change, in particular regarding the Commission's powers (see Garrett and Tsebelis 1996; Tsebelis and Garrett 1996; and the counter-arguments by Crombez 1996, 1997, 2000; Moser 1996, 1997; Scully 1997*a*, 1997*b*), others observed that this debate missed the informal aspects of the inter-institutional bargaining process (Burns 2004). This failing is perhaps related to the rational choice framework of analysis that they adopted, which risks over-emphasis on rules and rational behaviour. Scholars whose approach involved intensive research 'in the field' were clear that 'the informal dimensions of inter-institutional relations are of major significance in understanding policy-making in the EC' (Judge et al. 1994: 45).

Initially, the Council attempted to minimize the impact of the changes on the way in which legislation was dealt with. However, the determination of the EP to make the maximum use of its new powers soon convinced the Council that it could not carry on as before. The EP showed itself willing to take even relatively uncontroversial legislation to conciliation unless its positions were taken seriously. As a backlog of legislation began to mount, the Council agreed to institute informal 'trialogues' with the Commission and EP in an attempt to ease the passage of important measures.

Subsequently, the experience of trying to make the co-decision operate effectively led to further changes to the formal rules at Amsterdam, which allowed the Council and EP to conclude the process at first reading if they could reach agreement, and changed the rules of conciliation, so that there was no longer the possibility of legislation that had been rejected by the EP being passed if the Conciliation Committee failed to reach agreement. The decision to allow agreement after the first reading reflected the concern of the Council Secretariat that, with the transfer of even more areas to co-decision, the system needed to be streamlined. However, the new rule implied a further extension of informal discussion, effectively involving the EP in the formulation of legislative proposals at the same early stage as the Commission consulted with the Council.

The change of rule on what happened after an unsuccessful conciliation simply reflected acceptance that the EP would never accept the reinstatement of a Council common position, as it had demonstrated in 1994. According to Shackleton and Raunio (2003: 173), in an assessment that is given authority by the fact that Shackleton was the Head of the Conciliations Secretariat of the EP at the time:

> Co-decision is now seen as an interlinked, continuous procedure where it is essential and normal that there be intensive contacts throughout the procedure from before first reading onwards. Such contacts offer the opportunity of coming to agreements without having recourse to the time-consuming procedure of conciliation.

Since these changes there has been a clear trend towards early agreements, which makes the formal rules of the conciliation stage of less practical relevance. For example, there were no conciliations held in the first half of the 2014–19 parliamentary session (European Parliament 2016). The increased use of informal practices and norms also underlines that the analysis of the EP's power cannot simply rely on interpretation of formal rules: informal rules and conventions are also important factors.

What emerges from practice on the ground and academic analysis is that, through Treaty reform and informal agreements, the EP has become a co-legislator with the Council. However, the extension of the OLP post Lisbon to encompass over eighty-five areas of policy has also revealed that the Parliament faces limitations when it seeks to exercise those powers. The EP has found its room for manoeuvre constrained, especially for policies that touch on areas of core state powers, such as economic governance (Bressanelli and Chelotti 2018).

CONCLUSION

The themes of the book that are brought out in this chapter reflect the way EU studies have developed. Originally, the debate was about whether the EP was a 'toothless tiger', with the Council acting as the main legislative body. After a long struggle, the EP has emerged as a full co-legislator with the Council in almost all areas of EU business; CFSP being the main exception. Academic attention has shifted from the trajectory of the EP's development, reflecting an integrationist frame (Chapter 1), to research agendas that characterize legislative studies in comparative politics (Chapter 2). Rational choice institutionalists investigate the way that MEPs individually, and the EP collectively, respond to the formal institutional rules, especially under the OLP. By contrast, sociological institutionalists or social constructivists focus on the role of norms and culture as an important part of the everyday politics of the EP, and new research has started to bring feminist lenses to study the operation of the EP and its parties (Chapter 4, 'Feminist Work on the EU'). Finally, available roll-call voting databases, notably via VoteWatch Europe, have facilitated the analysis of the evolving party politics within the EP.

Understanding the character of the EU as an organization is clearly affected by the view that is taken of the effective influence of the EP. If it is accepted that the successive changes in the EP's formal role have made it a co-legislator with the Council of the EU, then the view that the EU is no more than an intergovernmental organization cannot be sustained. There is no other such organization internationally in which the member governments have to share decision making with a directly elected institution. With the further extension of its powers that occurred under the Lisbon Treaty, it is no longer tenable to regard the EP as a 'toothless tiger'; it is in fact a very powerful legislature.

The main reason why the powers of the EP were extended is attributable to the argument that this would help to close the democratic deficit, and therefore the legitimacy deficit of the EU. The evidence does not indicate that much has been achieved in that direction, in particular because there are limits to the legitimacy of the EP's democratic mandate that may only be eased with the development of a stronger sense of European identity among EU citizens. The Lisbon Treaty arguably recognized this situation by giving new powers to the national parliaments (see Chapter 12, 'Decision Making Procedures'). Nevertheless, the austere economic circumstances in the aftermath of the financial and eurozone crises have led some commentators to emphasize a 'new intergovernmentalism', in which the member governments have sought to assert their position in the face of the supranational institutions like the EP (Bickerton et al. 2015a). Moreover, the election of an increased number of Eurosceptic MEPs in the 2014 and 2019 elections suggests that fundamental problems remain in relation to voter identification with the EP.

KEY POINTS

Composition and Functions

- The EP elected in May 2019 had 751 seats, which were distributed between the member states approximately in proportion to population. After Brexit, the size of the Parliament was adjusted down to 705 seats.

- It meets monthly in plenary sessions in Strasbourg, but most of its work is done in Committee in Brussels.
- Organizationally, it has a President, a Bureau, a Conference of Presidents, and a Secretariat.

The Struggle for Power

- The forerunner of the EP (the EPA) was not directly elected and had limited powers.
- The EP has steadily increased its powers by putting pressure on national parties and governments, arguing that it needed increased powers to close the EU's democratic deficit.
- The first direct elections to the EP took place in June 1979. Direct election emboldened MEPs to challenge the member states over the budget and to demand more powers.
- In 1970, the power of the EP over the budget was increased when it was given the power to amend 'non-compulsory expenditure', which excluded the CAP. In 1975, it was given the power to reject the budget as a whole. As a result of the Lisbon Treaty, the EP and the Council of the EU are co-equal budgetary authorities.
- The EP can force the Commission as a whole to resign by a motion of censure, but to do so requires a positive vote from an absolute majority of MEPs and two-thirds of the votes cast. It cannot dismiss individual Commissioners.
- Originally, the EP had no say in the appointment of the Commission. Under successive Treaty amendments, it gained the right to elect the governments' nomination for President and subsequently hold a vote of consent for the new College of Commissioners.
- The 2014 election signalled a shift towards choosing competing candidates for the post of Commission President via the *Spitzenkandidaten* process, even though national politics remained the key focus of election campaigns.
- In 2019, the *Spitzenkandidaten* process was fatally undermined when the European Council refused to endorse any of the candidates chosen by the European party groups.

Debates and Research

- The electorates in member states tend to treat European elections as less important than national elections. They are fought primarily on domestic issues, and turn-out is typically lower than for national elections.
- MEPs sit in transnational party groups, which can contain within them a wide variety of ideological positions, but research indicates that the degree of group cohesion has increased as the powers of the EP have increased.
- In the early years, no obvious career path existed, but research has indicated that being an MEP is increasingly seen as a career option in its own right.
- The role of the EP in the legislative process has moved from the weak position in the consultation procedure, through successively stronger positions under co-operation and co-decision.
- Academic debate over the power of the EP in the legislative process has been contested from different perspectives. A concentration on formal rules by some analysts has been criticized by others who hold that informal rules can be as important.

 For additional material and resources, please visit the online resources www.oup.com/uk/bache5e.

QUESTIONS

1. What are the main powers and roles of the European Parliament? How and why have these changed over time?

2. What are the implications of the 'death' of the *Spitzenkandidaten* process for the relationship between the Parliament and the Commission?

3. Why do party groups form coalitions in the Parliament and what effect can this have upon the positions they adopt?

4. Which is the most convincing explanation for turn-out in European elections: the SOE thesis or the European Salience thesis?

5. How independent are MEPs?

FURTHER READING

A. Ripoll Servent and **C. Roederer Rynning** provide a useful and up-to-date review of the literature on the EP in a piece analysing whether it conforms to a model of a 'normal parliament' in 'The European Parliament: A Normal Parliament in a Polity of a Different Kind', *Oxford Research Encyclopaedias, Politics* (New York: Oxford University Press, 2018), DOI: 10.1093/acrefore/9780190228637.013.152. A useful special issue analysing the impact of Lisbon on the EP's power and influence is provided by **E. Bressanelli and N. Chelotti (eds)**, (2019) 'Power without Influence? Explaining the Impact of the European Parliament Post-Lisbon', *Journal of European Integration* 41(3): 265–76. A good review of the emergence of the EP is offered by **B. Rittberger**, *Building Europe's Parliament: Democratic Representation beyond the Nation State* (Oxford: Oxford University Press, 2005). For general guides to the EP, see **R. Corbett, F. Jacobs, and D. Neville**, *The European Parliament*, 9th edn (London: John Harper Publishing, 2016) and **A. Ripoll Servent**, *The European Parliament* (London: Palgrave Macmillan, 2018). For a study of the politics within the EP from a comparative-politics standpoint, see **S. Hix, A. Noury, and G. Roland**, *Democratic Politics in the European Parliament* (Cambridge: Cambridge University Press, 2007). On the EP's Committee system, see **R. Whitaker**, *The European Parliament's Committees: National Party Influence and Legislative Empowerment* (London: Routledge, 2011). Also recommended is the website of VoteWatch Europe: **http://votewatch.eu**.

Chapter 16

The Court of Justice of the European Union

Chapter Overview

Unlike international organizations more broadly, much of the work of the European Union (EU) is undertaken through legislation and other legal acts. It therefore follows that its legal system is an important feature. At the apex of that system sits what is formally known as the 'Court of Justice of the European Union' (CJEU), which comprises two courts: the Court of Justice and the General Court. The first of these, still commonly referred to as the European Court of Justice (ECJ), but discussed here as the CJEU, is most important. It makes binding decisions on disputes over Treaty provisions or secondary legislation. It therefore plays an essential role in developing the EU and providing the legal underpinnings to processes of integration.

This chapter looks first at the structure and functions of the Courts, and then at some of the CJEU's main rulings and their significance. It considers rulings on the powers of the institutions, some key legal judgments made in response to questions referred to the CJEU by national courts, and some illustrations of the impact of CJEU rulings on EU policy. The chapter then turns to look first at the evolving political reactions towards the judgments of the Court, and then at the debate over the ways the CJEU's jurisprudence has had an impact upon the process of European integration and the relationship between member states and the CJEU.

Context

There is consensus on the need for a European judicial order to exist with an authoritative interpreter of both the Treaties and the secondary legislation (directives, regulations) put in place by member states. This task falls to the CJEU. As sometimes occurs with courts more generally, especially constitutional courts such as the US Supreme Court or the German Federal Constitutional Court, the CJEU has been criticized for stepping beyond its legal role into the realm of politics. However, unlike controversies in other political systems, the CJEU not only has to tread the line between law and politics, but it also polices the boundary between EU and national law and politics. This is important because 'there is joint responsibility between national courts and the Union courts for the interpretation and maintenance of EU law' (Chalmers et al. 2010: 142). The CJEU has been accused of ruling in favour of integrationist solutions to disputes. This has provoked hostility from member states that see their powers or sovereignty being undermined by Court rulings. In the 1990s, the CJEU was subjected to increased criticism from member states for its radical jurisprudence, known as judicial activism. It has been suggested that since then the CJEU's activism has waned (Kapsis 2010) and that EU law has become 'decentred' as more responsibility has been passed to lower levels (Cardwell and Hervey 2015). More recently, the jurisprudence of the CJEU has become the focus of debates over the rule of law and the status of democracy in Hungary and Poland, and was a key element of critical Brexiteer discourses in the UK.

Structure and Functions

Structure

The Court of Justice of the EU comprises two courts:

- the Court of Justice (referred to in this chapter as the CJEU);
- and the General Court.

It is the CJEU that is of greatest interest in this chapter, but it is worth briefly discussing the General Court.

The General Court was established in 1989 as the Court of First Instance, but was renamed by the Lisbon Treaty in 2009. It was created to help the CJEU with the sheer volume of business that it had to get through. It comprises at least one judge from each member state. However, due to its workload the decision was taken in December 2015 to increase the number of judges to two per state by 1 September 2019. One reason for the increase in workload was the decision to add the work of the EU civil service tribunal (a specialized court for hearing disputes between employees of the EU's institutions) to the General Court's remit in 2016. The other reasons for increased workload include the enlargement of the EU to encompass new states and the expansion of competences post-Lisbon into new policy areas, thereby expanding the CJEU's jurisdiction. The General Court is effectively the central administrative court of the EU. It can act in a range of circumstances, but plays a particularly important role in hearing 'challenges by private parties adversely affected by EU measures'; notably, in competition law or external trade law (Chalmers et al. 2010: 147). The most important cases, including those of most political significance, are the responsibility of the CJEU.

Like the General Court, the CJEU meets in Luxembourg, which is a legacy of its origins dating from its creation as part of the European Coal and Steel Community when all the institutions were located there (see Chapter 5, 'The Schuman Plan for Coal and Steel'). It comprises one judge per member state and eleven advocates-general, who are appointed by common accord of the governments of the member states and hold office for a renewable term of six years (Article 19 TEU). The judges are chosen from persons whose independence is beyond doubt and who are of recognized competence. Approximately half of the judges and advocates-general are replaced every three years. Candidates for the positions of judge or advocate-general are scrutinized by a panel comprising former EU judges, national Supreme Court judges, and a nominee of the European Parliament (EP). The panel's Opinion is offered to the Council on candidates' suitability, although it is not binding in its effect. Like other EU institutions, the CJEU has struggled to diversify its membership—especially as the senior echelons of the legal profession in EU member states remains dominated by men (Galligan et al. 2017). Hence the current composition of the CJEU is three-quarters male.

The judges select one of their number to be President of the Court for a renewable term of three years, and as yet there has been no female President elected. The President directs the work of the Court and presides at hearings and deliberations. The advocates-general assist the Court in its task. They deliver legal Opinions on cases before the Court at a stage before the CJEU issues its own judgment.

The CJEU's work is primarily conducted in chambers of three or five judges; important matters can, upon request, come before a Grand Chamber of fifteen judges and exceptionally important ones come before the Court as a whole (Chalmers et al. 2010: 145). Like the General Court, the CJEU has problems keeping up with the volume of cases referred to it. The CJEU's authority is confined to 'Union business'. It therefore has no jurisdiction on Common Foreign and Security Policy (CFSP). The CJEU's remit was expanded at the end of 2014 as a result of provisions in the Lisbon Treaty. This arose from the transfer of remaining areas of Justice and Home Affairs (JHA) co-operation to the 'Union method' as part of the Area of Freedom, Security, and Justice (AFSJ), taking effect after a five-year transition period from the Lisbon Treaty coming into effect (see Chapter 23). The Lisbon Treaty also required the EU to seek formal accession to the European Convention on Human Rights (ECHR). The ECHR is administered by the Council of Europe (a non-EU body), which has a court, the European Court of Human Rights (ECtHR), based in Strasbourg. The ECHR applies to all EU member states and a further nineteen Council of Europe members. Whilst the Lisbon Treaty required the EU to seek accession to the ECHR, the CJEU rejected a proposed accession agreement on the grounds that it compromised the autonomy of EU law. At the time of writing, the EU has not acceded to the ECHR but the CJEU does draw upon the jurisprudence of the ECtHR.

Functions

It is the responsibility of the CJEU to ensure that the law is observed in the interpretation and application of the EU Treaties, with the exception of the provisions relating to foreign and security policy. To enable it to carry out that task, the Court has wide jurisdiction to hear various types of action and to give preliminary rulings.

The Court may hear several different categories of proceeding, as follows:

1. *Failure to fulfil an obligation (TFEU Articles 258, 259, and 260).* A member state may be taken to the Court by the Commission or by another member state for failing to act to meet its obligations under the Treaties or EU secondary legislation. If the Court finds against the state so charged, it must comply without delay. If it fails to do so, the Commission may go back to the Court and ask, under Article 260 of the Treaty on the Functioning of the European Union (TFEU), for a fine to be imposed on the state.

2. *Application for annulment (TFEU Articles 263 and 264).* This judicial review power allows a member state, the Council, the Commission, the EP, the Court of Auditors, the European Central Bank (ECB), and the Committee of the Regions (CoR) to apply to the CJEU as plaintiffs for the annulment of EU acts or legislative acts. By way of the national court system, individuals may seek the annulment of a legal measure that is of direct concern to them. The annulment may be sought and granted on grounds of lack of competence, infringement of an essential procedural requirement, infringement of the Treaty, or misuse of powers. Expansion of the scope of Article 263 under the Lisbon Treaty has extended judicial review beyond acts of the Commission, the Council, and the EP to include such acts of the European Council, the ECB, and EU agencies that have legal effects (Dougan 2008: 676).

3. *Failure to act (TFEU Articles 265 and 266).* The Court may review the legality of a failure to act by a Community institution (the EP, the European Council, the Council, the Commission, or the ECB), and penalize silence or inaction.

4. *Actions to establish liability (TFEU Article 268).* In an action for damages, the Court rules on the liability of the EU for damage caused by its institutions or servants in the performance of their duties.

5. *Appeals (TFEU Article 256).* The Court may hear appeals, on points of law only, against judgments given by the General Court in cases within its jurisdiction.

6. *Reference for a preliminary ruling (TFEU Article 267).* Preliminary rulings are judgments by the Court on the interpretation of the Treaties or secondary legislation arising under the Treaties. Under Article 267, national courts that are hearing cases involving EU law may request a ruling from the CJEU on the interpretation of the law, and where the issue is raised before a national court against the judgment of which there is no appeal in domestic law, that court must seek a preliminary ruling from the CJEU. The CJEU cannot deliver a preliminary ruling unless it is asked to do so by a national court.

Although judges are usually thought of as conservative, that cannot be said of the CJEU judges. It has been argued in the past that the CJEU has done more than any other institution to advance European integration (Freestone 1983: 43). Its approach has been heavily criticized by some commentators as stepping beyond the bounds of legal interpretation to become political (Rasmussen 1986). Perhaps this lack of conservatism is because some of the members of the CJEU are not judges by profession. Many of the appointees have been academics rather than professional lawyers. Whatever the reasons, the CJEU pursued a form of judicial activism that created a supranational legal order in the mid-1960s. This development came at the time when the 'empty chair' crisis brought political integration to a halt and entrenched an intergovernmental political order, thus demonstrating why the legal dimension of integration must be kept in view. The Court's judicial activism was to be found both in judgments on the powers of the institutions arising from actions brought under the Articles listed above, and in Article 267 referrals from national courts seeking clarification of points of EU law.

CJEU Rulings on the Powers of the Institutions

The biggest beneficiary of the CJEU's distinctive approach to institutional relations was the EP. In a series of judgments, the CJEU interpreted the powers of the EP in an expansive manner. Key cases, which are considered here, were:

> *Roquette* v. *Council* (1980) (the *Isoglucose* case) Case 138/79;
>
> *Parti Écologiste, 'Les Verts'* v. *Parliament* (1986) Case 294/83;
>
> *European Parliament* v. *Council* (1988) (the *Comitology* case) Case 302/87;
>
> *European Parliament* v. *Council* (1990) (the *Chernobyl* case) Case C-70/88.

The *Isoglucose* Case (1980)

In March 1979, the Commission submitted to the EP a draft regulation on fixing quotas for the production of isoglucose—a food sweetener produced from cereals—to take effect from the beginning of July. The draft regulation went to the EP's Committee on Agriculture, which reported to the May plenary session of the EP. However, the plenary rejected the report of the Committee, containing an Opinion on the regulation. This effectively meant that the quotas could not be introduced at the beginning of July (1979 was an election year for the EP, so there was no June plenary). In the meantime, the Council had considered the draft regulation and agreed to adopt it. Faced with a possible delay of four months or more, the Commission acted on the approval of the Council and published the directive in the Official Journal.

Subsequently, an individual who was directly affected by the directive brought a case to the CJEU under Article 173 of the EEC Treaty (now Article 263 TFEU), claiming that the Council and Commission had acted beyond their powers by adopting the directive without having received the Opinion of the EP. The Court could have decided that the EP had been consulted, and had failed to deliver an Opinion in time. Instead, it upheld the complaint, choosing to interpret 'consult' to mean that the formal Opinion of the EP had to be delivered before the Council could act.

In its judgment, the Court insisted that the EP had a duty to give an Opinion within a reasonable length of time, without defining what would be considered reasonable. Thus, the judgment gave the EP a significant power to delay legislation by holding back on formally delivering its Opinion.

Les Verts v. *European Parliament* (1986)

In 1984, the French Green Party (*Les Verts*) stood candidates for election to the EP for the first time. In doing so, it discovered that those of its opponents that had been represented in the previous Parliament had been funded by the EP to defray their election expenses. Subsequently, the Greens brought a case to the CJEU under Article 173 EEC (now Article 263 TFEU) claiming that the EP had acted beyond its powers in effectively supporting the election of existing parties at the expense of new parties.

The immediate issue here was whether any such case could be brought to the Court. Article 173 explicitly said: 'The Court of Justice shall review the legality of acts of the Council and the Commission.' There was no mention of the CJEU reviewing the legality of acts of the EP. The Court nevertheless accepted the case on the grounds that, although the Treaty did not explicitly make the actions of the EP subject to judicial review, this omission was not in keeping with the spirit of the Treaty.

The Court argued that the EP must have been omitted from Article 173 because when the Treaty was signed the EP had no real powers. Subsequently, it had acquired powers that would normally be subject to judicial review. These included the powers that were contested in this case, and as these *should* be subject to judicial review, the Court would review them.

In this judgment, the CJEU increased its own powers by a unilateral reinterpretation of the Treaty. Although apparently acting in a way that would restrict the powers of the EP, the judgment also took the first step towards giving the EP a legal personality that it had not been granted by the member states when they signed the Treaty. Once it had been decided that the EP could be a defendant in such a hearing, it seemed logical that it should also be accorded the right to be a plaintiff—that is, that it be allowed to bring cases to the Court under the same Article. The Court was given the opportunity to take this step in the next case reviewed below.

European Parliament v. Council (the Comitology Case) (1988)

This case was brought by the EP under Article 175 EEC (now revised as TFEU Article 265), which said:

> Should the Council or the Commission, in infringement of this Treaty, fail to act, the Member States, and the other institutions of the Community may bring an action before the Court of Justice to have the infringement established.

The EP argued successfully that it was allowed to bring a case under this Article because it was one of the 'other institutions of the Community'. But it also argued that it should be allowed to bring a case under Article 173 if the issue was one of another institution acting beyond its powers, rather than of not acting at all. The EP argued that it was illogical for it to be allowed to bring a case under Article 175, but not under Article 173. It also quoted the Court's judgment in *Les Verts* that the EP could be a defendant under Article 173, and argued that if it could be a defendant, it was illogical that it should not be allowed to be a plaintiff.

The Court rejected the EP's arguments. It said that: there was no logical link between the circumstances outlined; the EP could normally rely on the Commission to take up a case under Article 173 on its behalf, and the member states had recently had the specific opportunity to grant this right explicitly to the EP in the Single European Act and had declined to do so. However, within a short period of time, the Court appeared to have a change of heart on the issue.

European Parliament v. Council (the Chernobyl Case) (1990)

In this case, the EP applied to the Court for a review of the procedure adopted for agreeing a public health regulation on the permissible radioactive contamination of food that could be sold for public consumption following the Chernobyl disaster (see Insight 16.1). The Commission proposed the regulation under Article 31 of the Euratom Treaty, which dealt with basic standards for the protection of the health of the general public arising from radiation. Proposed legislation under this Article was

303

Insight 16.1 Chernobyl

On 26 April 1986, a major accident occurred at the Chernobyl nuclear power station in Ukraine. Radioactive pollution extended over a vast geographical area. Contamination was detected in the food chain as far west as Ireland. The EU introduced standardized rules on the permissible levels of radioactive contamination, and provided financial support for the farmers worst affected.

---

subject to the consultation procedure. The EP maintained that the matter was a single market issue, and therefore should have been introduced under (the then) Article 100A of the EEC Treaty (now TFEU Article 114). This would have brought it under the co-operation procedure, and given the EP a second reading. The EP wished to challenge the Treaty base under which the regulation was adopted, but first had to establish that its case was admissible because it was invoking Article 173 EEC (now Article 263 TFEU).

Despite the Court's decision in the *Comitology* case, its decision in this one, coming soon after, was even more surprising. Here, the Court decided that the EP could bring the case after all, despite its reasoning in the *Comitology* judgment, because the CJEU's role was to preserve the institutional balance. In the *Comitology* judgment, the Court had asserted that the Commission could normally be relied upon to protect the prerogatives of the EP where Parliament required an Article 173 case to be brought. However, in this instance, the dispute over the Treaty base pitted the Commission against the EP. Therefore, in these and similarly limited circumstances, the EP had to be granted the right to be a plaintiff in an Article 173 case. The other argument that had appeared in the *Comitology* judgment, that the member states had only recently declined to grant this power explicitly to the EP, now disappeared from view.

CJEU Rulings on the Nature of EU Law

If the jurisprudence of the CJEU has pushed back the limits of the Treaty in judgments based on judicial review cases, it has been even more radical in its judgments on references for preliminary rulings. In a number of judgments, the Court laid out principles that expanded the EU's legal order. The following cases were particularly important:

Van Gend en Loos (1963) Case 26/62;

Costa v. *ENEL* (1964) Case 6/64;

Van Duyn v. *Home Office* (1974) Case 41/74;

R. v. *Secretary of State for Transport, ex parte Factortame* (1990) Case 213/89;

R. v. *Secretary of State for Transport, ex parte Factortame* (1991) Case C-221/89;

Francovich v. *Italy* (1991) Cases C-6 and 9/90.

Van Gend en Loos (1963)

In this early case, the Court first asserted the principle that EU law confers rights on individuals as well as on member states. This was the principle of 'direct effect', which had no explicit authority in the Treaties, and represented a dramatic departure from international law. Under international law, Treaties are held to impose obligations on the states that sign and ratify them, but neither to confer rights nor impose obligations directly on individual citizens.

A Dutch company claimed that its rights had been breached by the Dutch government, which had levied a higher rate of duty on formaldehyde—a chemical used as a disinfectant and preservative, and in the manufacture of synthetic resins—after the date on which it was agreed in the EEC Treaty that there would be no increase in internal tariffs. The Dutch government maintained that the company had no power to claim a right deriving from an international Treaty. The Court disagreed. It maintained that a new legal order had come into existence with the signing of the Treaty, in which citizens could claim rights against their governments. The ruling of the Court contained the following famous phrase:

> the Community constitutes a new legal order of international law for the benefit of which the states have limited their sovereign rights, albeit within limited fields, and the subjects of which comprise not only member states but also their nationals. Community law therefore not only imposes obligations on individuals but is also intended to confer upon them rights that become part of their legal heritage.

(Quoted in Kuper 1998: 5)

As a result of this judgment, 'in individuals and in the national courts, the CJEU found two powerful allies in efforts to force national governments to comply with European law' (Kapsis 2010: 183).

Costa v. ENEL (1964)

In this case, the Court first asserted the supremacy of EU law over national law. Again, there was no explicit authority for this in the Treaty. An Italian court referred the case to the CJEU, asking whether an Act of the Italian Parliament, passed later in time than the Act that embodied an EU directive into Italian law, took precedence. The Court said that it did not, making clear that national law cannot take precedence over EU law. This was a perfectly logical position, but it had particular consequences for those states—in this case Italy, but after its accession in 1973, also the UK—in which Parliament holds sovereignty. In such systems, the principle that prevails is *lex posterior priori derogat*: 'the later law overrides the earlier'. The *Costa v. ENEL* judgment struck at the heart of this principle of parliamentary sovereignty and became a key element of arguments about 'taking back control' in Brexit debates in the UK.

Van Duyn v. Home Office (1974)

A Dutch national who had been debarred from entering Britain because she was a member of the Church of Scientology, which the British Home Office considered to be a socially undesirable organization, brought a case in the English courts challenging the ruling. This case was brought on the grounds that Article 48 of the EEC Treaty (now Article 45 TFEU) committed the member states to allow free movement of workers, and that the British government had accepted Directive 64/221, which implemented this Treaty provision as part of the acquis communautaire when it joined the EC. The Court was asked to decide whether rights could be acquired directly in this way from a directive that had not yet been incorporated into national law.

The Court decided that the directive did, in fact, have direct effect. Although the relevant directive had not yet been explicitly incorporated into English law, the Court maintained that the defendant could still quote it as grounds for her opposition to the British government's position. This ruling had wide implications, since a member state's failure to transpose a directive could not prevent citizens from invoking it in the national courts.

The *Factortame* Cases (1990, 1991)

These cases arose because Spanish fishermen had been purchasing British fishing vessels, and with them the quotas that the boats had been allocated to catch fish under the EU's Common Fisheries Policy. In effect, the Spanish fishermen had been catching fish on the British quota and landing it in Spain. The British government had responded by passing the Merchant Shipping Act 1988, which required 75 per cent of the shareholders and directors of a company to be British in order for the company to be able to register as British. The Spanish fishermen claimed that this was a breach of their rights under European law.

In its 1990 judgment, the CJEU underlined the supremacy of European law, but also empowered the House of Lords to overturn British legislation: the first time that British courts had been allowed to set aside an Act of Parliament. (At the time, the House of Lords was the highest court in the UK: a function now played by the Supreme Court, which was established in 2009.) The ruling had major constitutional implications in Britain. In its 1991 ruling, the CJEU subsequently agreed with the Spanish fishermen that the Merchant Shipping Act was in breach of European law because of its discriminatory nationality rules on ownership. Each of these steps caused a furore in the British Parliament, both because of what was seen as the manifest unfairness of allowing Spanish fishermen to take fish on the British quota, but also because of the domestic constitutional implications. The full impact of the CJEU's judicial activism only really came home to many British parliamentarians with these cases.

Francovich v. *Italy* (1991)

Before this case arose, the Italian government had already been taken to the CJEU by the Commission and charged with not incorporating into Italian law a directive that gave redundant workers the right to compensation, and made such compensation the first claim against the assets of a bankrupt employer. It had still not been incorporated when workers for a bankrupt Italian company took a case to court in Italy because they had received no compensation for redundancy. The Court's ruling established the principle of state liability—that is, that any government that did not properly implement European law was liable to claims for damages by its own citizens.

Subsequently, the Court used the same principle, that a government that did not properly implement EC law was liable to claims for damages, to decide that the Spanish fishermen in the *Factortame* case were eligible for compensation from the British government for loss of earnings during the period when they were prevented from catching fish on the British quota. It also decided, in another case— *Brasserie du Pêcheur* (1996)—that a French brewery could claim damages from the German government for the period when the German government enforced its beer purity laws, which the Court had subsequently ruled to be an illegal barrier to trade. So in these two cases, the liability of a government that had not properly applied a directive to be sued for damages was extended beyond its own citizens to cover other citizens of the EU.

CJEU Rulings and Policy Impact

The CJEU has made many important rulings that have not only defined the shape of the legal order (see 'CJEU Rulings on the Nature of EU Law' above) or, as discussed earlier ('CJEU Rulings on the Powers of the Institutions'), by clarifying the powers of the institutions, its rulings have also been influential for EU policies. The single market will serve as illustration.

The original route to creating a common market was based upon agreeing harmonized regulations. This method proved unwieldy, since it could be highly contentious as to what should be the ingredients of, say, beer. As unanimity was needed in the Council, progress was going to be very slow. However, in 1979, the CJEU made a ruling known as *Cassis de Dijon* (Case 120/78), which centred on Germany's discriminatory alcohol legislation. The CJEU ruled that if cassis (a French blackcurrant liqueur) was acceptable under French legislation, then it should be acceptable in Germany as well, unless some pressing public health argument could be mounted. The *Cassis de Dijon* ruling, which identified no pressing public health argument, set an important principle: namely, that of mutual recognition. In other words, if goods lawfully met the standards of one member state, they should be accepted for sale in another member state. This principle was fundamental to the achievement of the single market, since it made clear that it was not necessary to harmonize legislation for every product. Instead, mutual recognition combined with a much more limited legislative package would accomplish the single market (see Chapter 19).

A second example relates to air transport liberalization. Prior to the 1990s, air transport was highly regulated and dominated by national flag carriers (British Airways, Air France, Lufthansa, and others), which were typically state-owned. Routes across Europe were regulated between pairs of governments and pairs of airlines. Intra-EU competition was very limited, because all routes were duopolies between flag carriers, which shared revenues on individual routes. The European Commission, with support from the British and Dutch governments, was trying to liberalize the market, but progress was slow because of the vested interests of the airlines, the other governments, and other actors. In 1986, the CJEU issued its *Nouvelles Frontières* judgment (Joined Cases 209–213/84). The ruling effectively declared the current bilateral air transport regime to be contrary to the EU's competition rules. With the authority of this ruling behind it, the Commission could apply more pressure to secure the passage of its liberalization legislation, which was later to usher in the era of low-cost air travel associated with easyJet and Ryanair (Armstrong and Bulmer 1998: 177–8).

It is important to point out that many of the CJEU's rulings are not as significant as these cases. Nevertheless, a proper understanding of the dynamics of those policy areas falling under the 'Union method' is usually facilitated by grasping a set of court judgments. Since the EU is distinctively characterized by its legislation and its supranational body of law, these features tend to be integral to policy dynamics. It is also worth underlining that the Commission has an important role in ensuring that agreed legislation is put into effect. Under Articles 258–260 TFEU, it proceeds through a set of stages that may ultimately lead to the CJEU. The ultimate sanction, introduced by the Maastricht Treaty, is for the CJEU to impose a penalty where a state has not complied with an earlier judgment. This power was first used as a result of a ruling by the CJEU in 2000 (*Commission* v. *Greece*, Case C-387/97), when the Greek government was fined for failure to comply with a 1992 CJEU ruling concerning the closure of a toxic waste tip on the island of Crete. The fine was €20,000 for each day of delay beyond the original 1992 ruling. Although a lengthy process, this case showed that a member state could receive a substantial fine for flouting a CJEU ruling.

The Rise of Subsidiarity, the CJEU, and EU Law

After a long period during which the pro-integration stance of the CJEU was tolerated by the governments of the member states, there was something of a backlash against the process of European integration generally, and against the CJEU more particularly, in the 1990s. The difficulties that were encountered in several member states in getting ratification of the Maastricht Treaty reinforced a tendency that had already been apparent in the inclusion in that Treaty of clauses on subsidiarity (see Insight 16.2). The desire to limit the transfer of competences from member states to the EU institutions came from different quarters: John Major's government in Britain; some subnational governments (notably the German *Länder*); and the French government, which pressed for the *acquis communautaire* to be reviewed in the light of subsidiarity.

> The formal introduction by the Maastricht Treaty (TEU) of subsidiarity as a general principle into EC ... law both symbolized and contributed to a gradual change in the political and legal culture of the European Community. If much of the Community's legal activity before the 1990s reflected a self-conscious teleology of integration, the teleology of subsidiarity suggests a rather different future.
>
> (De Búrca 1998: 218)

In more recent years, the CJEU's judicial activism has arguably declined, although intense debates continue among legal scholars (see Kelemen 2012). Several factors may be seen as explanations. The first is the greater attentiveness to subsidiarity in the post-Maastricht period. Equally, the EU's character has diversified from the more 'classical' forms of top-down governance associated most closely with the original form of the

> ### Insight 16.2 Subsidiarity Articles of the TEU and TFEU
>
> #### Article 1 of the TEU
>
> This Treaty marks a new stage in the process of creating an ever closer union among the peoples of Europe, in which decisions are taken as openly as possible and *as closely as possible to the citizen* [Our italics].
>
> #### Article 5 of the TFEU
>
> In areas which do not fall within its exclusive competence, the Community shall take action, in accordance with the principle of subsidiarity, only if and insofar as the objectives of the proposed action cannot be sufficiently achieved by the Member States and can therefore, by reason of the scale or effects of the proposed action, be better achieved by the Community.

Common Agricultural Policy (CAP). The growth of regulation via EU agencies (rather than 'command-and-control' by law) in the aftermath of the single market is one form of diversity and the open method of co-ordination (OMC) is another, since it entailed member state co-operation where the role of law, and thus the CJEU, was minimal.

Another explanation is the maturing of the EU such that the CJEU is less of a player in the transformation of Europe and more of a kind of constitutional court within the EU. The scope for the CJEU to be transformative has become limited because it is shaped by its own prior rulings. Thus, the era of the major rulings on the nature of EU law (see 'CJEU Rulings on the Nature of EU Law' above) has declined. In addition, with the exception of the transfer of fiscal authority to the supranational level as part of rectifying design faults of the eurozone, the willingness of states to pursue deeper integration reached a plateau with the Lisbon Treaty. Moreover, the Treaty on Stability Co-ordination and Governance (see Insight 11.2), often known in shorthand as the Fiscal Compact, was not signed by all member states and is not part of EU law. This development highlights the emergence of a more diverse legal order. Differentiated integration creates its own challenges for the CJEU and the legal order of the EU, since there is no longer one legal system for all member states. Cardwell and Hervey (2015) have argued that the accumulation of these developments has amounted to a 'decentring' of EU law as the European legal order has become diverse.

Court Curbing? The CJEU and the Member States

Kelemen and Schmidt (2012) note that while authors disagree as to the extent of the CJEU's activism, the pro-integrative role of the European court system as a whole is undisputed. Consequently, a key question that has occupied scholars concerns how the Court has been able to get away with its radical jurisprudence, or as Kelemen

(2012) puts it, how has the CJEU been able to avoid 'court curbing' mechanisms by which member states may attempt to restrain its remit of action? In the 1990s, an academic debate emerged on this question that paralleled the intergovernmental vs neofunctionalist debate of the 1960s (see Chapter 1, 'Theories of European Integration'). The intergovernmental case is considered first below, and then the 'legal neofunctionalist' argument.

The Intergovernmental Case

The central proposition of the intergovernmental case was that the CJEU 'helped to facilitate integration, but only to the degree that member state governments desired it'. Although governments did sometimes contest cases brought to the CJEU, they often accepted and applied the judgment after it was handed down. This reflected the fact that governments were under pressure from domestic interests that would be adversely affected by a particular interpretation of EC law, and so argued against it. However, member states all accepted that they would be better off in the long term if the rules of the single market were implemented by everyone, which required an independent and impartial referee to adjudicate on disputed interpretations of the rules, such as the CJEU. To refuse to accept an adverse ruling would weaken the legitimacy of the impartial referee, and that was a cost that member states would be loath to pay.

In some cases, the strength of a domestic interest that was adversely affected by a ruling of the CJEU would be sufficiently great that the government of a member state would attempt to placate it by unilaterally, but covertly, not implementing the ruling (Garrett 1995). In that way, the state could avoid weakening the legitimacy of the independent arbitrator, while possibly avoiding the political costs of not doing so. Whether this course was followed would depend on the relative gains to the member state from the existence of an efficiently functioning internal market when set against the political cost of upsetting a powerful interest group. The states that stood to gain the most from the single market—generally the more northern member states—would be most reluctant to risk damaging the legitimacy of the CJEU even by covert non-compliance. Those that stood to gain less—mainly the southern member states—might be more inclined to engage in unilateral non-compliance to try to evade the political costs of displeasing a powerful domestic vested interest. Even then, the government would try to conceal evasion, and would plead implementation problems if caught.

For its part, the CJEU was very aware that its legitimacy was dependent on the behaviour of the member states. If governments were openly to flout its decisions, its legitimacy would be seriously damaged, and pressure might build for its powers to be weakened by revision of the Treaties. As a result, according to this intergovernmentalist interpretation, the CJEU avoided making decisions that would place powerful governments in a difficult position. It was able to do this because, although the Treaty prohibited restrictions on internal trade, exceptions were allowed if 'justified on grounds of public morality, public policy or public security; the protection of health and life of humans, animals or plants; the protection of national treasures possessing artistic, historic or archaeological value; or the protection of industrial and commercial property' (Article 36 TFEU).

The Neofunctionalist Case

Under the neofunctionalist account, the CJEU was portrayed as the prime mover of European integration, with member state governments passively accepting this lead. The CJEU had used European law as a 'mask' to cover its integrationist agenda, wrapping its promotion of integration in the discourse of legal logic and necessity. It had also used the law as a 'shield' to protect itself from political attack. If the governments of the member states did not like the activism of the CJEU, they had the means available to counter it, either by non-compliance with the rulings or by amendment of the Treaties. Yet, the first had not been done to any significant degree, and the second had not been done at all. Authors Burley and Mattli (1993) used the example of the famous *Cassis de Dijon* case to illustrate this argument, and were subsequently challenged specifically on their interpretation of this case by Garrett (1995).

The 'mask and shield' part of the argument was frequently quoted in later contributions to the debate (Garrett 1995: 171–2; Garrett et al. 1998: 149–50). However, it was never a particularly strong element in the neofunctionalist argument. As Carrubba (2003: 78) pointed out:

> First, to assume that law 'masks' the political ramifications of a decision is to suggest that governments are incapable of evaluating what outcome would serve their purposes best. Since governments make observations on CJEU cases on a regular basis, it seems demonstrably implausible that the governments do not have well-formed preferences over outcomes. Further, to say that the legal venue 'shields' decisions from political interference, owing to the domestic norms of the rule of law, is to assume that governments will obey court rulings because governments have been observed doing so in the past. There are a number of reasons why governments may obey court rulings in one situation and not in another.

The threat of Treaty revisions could also 'be dismissed fairly easily' (Carrubba 2003: 76) because it required the unanimous consent of all member states' governments, which was unlikely to be achievable given the commitment of some states to the enforcement of the single market, and of others to the enhancement of integration.

The second part of the legal neofunctionalist argument was stronger. It started with the observation that, for the legal doctrines of the CJEU to be effective, they had to be accepted by national courts. This seemed to have happened. By making Article 267 references for a preliminary ruling, national courts had been the main accomplices of the CJEU in its 'constitutionalization' of the Treaties. Why had this collaboration taken place? Burley and Mattli (1993) suggested that a legal version of neofunctionalism was at work. Spillover was implicit in the concept of EC law itself, but it was cultivated by the CJEU to give the most integrationist interpretation possible to the existing laws. Other actors—national courts, private individuals—fed the process simply by pursuing their own self-interest in a rational manner within the changed context: for example, individuals did so by bringing cases against their own governments under European law when they felt that their rights had been breached.

Alter (1996, 1998, 2001) went further, arguing that the Article 267 procedure (previously the Article 177 procedure) actually empowered lower national courts. They were used to having their judgments overturned on appeal by higher national courts, but by making Article 267 references, they could directly influence the evolution of national legal principles. Higher courts might be able to overturn the substance of their judgments, but they were unable to challenge the points of European law on which they were based.

The CJEU has also been careful always to get the national courts on its side by proceeding in what another advocate of this theory, Mancini (1991: 185), described as a 'courteously didactic' manner. The judges:

> developed a style that may be drab and repetitive but explains as well as declares the law, and they showed unlimited patience vis-à-vis the national judges, reformulating questions couched in imprecise terms or extracting from the documents concerning the main proceedings the elements of Community law that needed to be interpreted with regard to the subject matter of the dispute.
>
> (Mancini 1991: 185)

In this way, the European judges won the confidence of their national colleagues. Those who presided over even the lowest courts knew that they would receive sympathetic treatment if they were to make an Article 267 referral, and were therefore more inclined to do so.

This co-opting of national courts raised the stakes for national governments that might be inclined to defy the jurisprudence of the CJEU, for it would also be defying the jurisprudence of their own domestic courts. The indirect political costs of undermining the legitimacy of the rule of law in the domestic arena are potentially considerably higher than the costs of undermining the CJEU. Research reported by Carrubba (2003: 95) indicated that European publics would be inclined to support their own government if it were in dispute with the CJEU, but not if it were in dispute with national courts.

A criticism of this analysis is that the alliance forged between the CJEU and lower national courts is not the whole story. The reception of the jurisprudence of the CJEU by national supreme courts has been less enthusiastic. Problems have arisen with the reception of the judgments of the CJEU by the Italian, French, British, and German Supreme Courts (Kuper 1998: 19–27). In no case has a national Supreme Court attempted to negate a decision of the CJEU: were one to do so, it would cause a constitutional crisis. In several cases, though, the national Supreme Court has disagreed with the reasoning of the CJEU, while finding alternative lines of legal reasoning to arrive at the same substantive decision. In particular, the doctrine of the supremacy of EU law over national law has not been universally accepted by member states. However, this is compatible with the argument that lower courts were prepared to collaborate with the CJEU on preliminary rulings because that increased their influence within their national legal hierarchies. The corollary of that argument is that higher courts would see their influence weakened, and so would be expected to resist the jurisprudence of the CJEU.

CONCLUSION

This review of the role of the CJEU particularly raises two of the themes that run through the book. The first is the theme that has been most prominent in the chapters on the institutions: the intergovernmental–supranational debate about the nature of the EU. A second theme is that of legitimacy.

If the role of the CJEU is approached in the same way as was the discussion about the role of the Commission in Chapter 13, 'The Commission in the Policy-Making Process'—that is, whether it is an agent of the member states or an autonomous actor in its own right—there is little doubt that the judgments of the Court have gone beyond what the governments of the member states were expecting. The radical jurisprudence of the Court may represent the logical consequences of the actions of the member states, but it is not a logic that was thought through by their governments, nor was it always welcome to them. In this sense, the CJEU has proved itself to be an autonomous, supranational actor in the process of European integration.

As intergovernmentalists would point out, the member states can rescind those powers that they have given to the Court—but this is not easy, because, without an independent and authoritative interpreter of the law, all of the rules put in place by the Treaties and by EU secondary legislation would be subject to different interpretation by different parties. There has to be an authoritative source of interpretation, and it has to be unquestionably independent. Some parties to any dispute will not like some of the decisions of the independent arbitrator, but they will abide by them rather than see the collapse of the system from which they benefit generally. The result is to make it difficult to recall powers once delegated. Treaty changes require unanimity, and if even one member state is happy with the thrust of the CJEU's decisions, it will not be possible to reduce its powers because its one supporter has a veto on any attempt to do so.

There is no doubt that the CJEU has the formal right to reach the decisions that it does. Whether those decisions are accepted as legitimate is another matter. Most decisions of the Court have not impinged on the consciousness of national politicians or members of the public. They have received legitimacy through being accepted by national courts, especially those lower down the legal hierarchy. When CJEU judgments have come to the attention of national politicians, there has sometimes been a strong negative reaction, suggesting that the legitimacy of the Court's doctrines does not extend beyond the national courts and professional judges. The strength of reaction in Britain to the *Factortame* judgment is indicative of this. As Carrubba (2003: 96–7) noted, 'public perceptions of institutional legitimacy are critical to the EU legal system being able to act as an effective democratic check', but 'the CJEU remains woefully short on public legitimacy today'.

The highest courts in the member states have been less comfortable than have lower courts with the judgments of the CJEU. In consequence, difficult domestic constitutional issues have been raised intermittently. Essentially the CJEU has, in effect, 'constitutionalized' the EU from the raw material of the Treaties (Weiler 1999: 19–29). It has had plenty of scope to impose its own interpretation of what that constitution should look like because Treaties are not carefully crafted legal documents; rather, they are the outcome of diplomatic negotiations and compromises. These far-from-watertight documents leave judges plenty of space to fill in the gaps. In doing so, the CJEU has enunciated principles that conflict with some fundamental national constitutional principles. The legal conflict shows the impossibility of taking several different national constitutions and reconciling them with one overarching European constitution. The political reaction raises again the issue of identity, which appears in the discussion of the legitimacy of the EP in Chapter 3, 'Democracy and Legitimacy'. National politicians and publics find it difficult to accept that decisions made by their democratically elected national institutions can be overruled by an organization that has far less legitimacy in their eyes.

While this debate about the role of the CJEU in European integration has subsided somewhat, attention has shifted to the role of EU law in a more diversified EU in the post-Maastricht period. As the CJEU has matured towards a constitutional court for the EU, attention has shifted from its role in integration to its role in EU governance. This development reflects the 'turn' in EU studies more generally towards governance approaches.

While this chapter has necessarily been selective in the material covered, it should be clear that the CJEU's impact through its rulings has been felt widely: across the EU institutions; across the EU's policies; and across the member states. Integration has not only been economic and political, as charted elsewhere in this book, but it has also had an important legal dimension. Moreover, the legal and political dimensions are often closely intertwined.

KEY POINTS

Context

- The CJEU is the authoritative interpreter of the Treaties and EU secondary legislation.
- It is sometimes accused of making political decisions that favour European integration at the expense of the powers of member states.

Structure and Functions

- The Court consists of one judge per state and eleven advocates-general.
- It is charged to ensure that EU law is observed.
- It has wide-ranging powers to hear various types of action and to give preliminary rulings.

CJEU Rulings on the Powers of the Institutions

- The EP has been a major beneficiary of the Court's radical jurisprudence.
- Although on occasions the Court has found against an extension of the EP's legal position, it also reversed this in subsequent judgments.

CJEU Rulings on the Nature of EU Law

- The CJEU has been most radical in cases referred by national courts under Article 267.
- In early rulings, the Court stated the principles of 'direct effect'—that EU law confers rights on individuals—and the supremacy of EU over national law. Subsequent rulings confirmed these principles.
- A series of later cases also produced rulings that surprised the governments of the member states, because they placed upon them obligations to which they did not think that they had agreed.

CJEU Rulings and Policy Impact

- The CJEU's rulings have had significant impact on policy areas such as the single market.

The Rise of Subsidiarity, the CJEU, and EU Law

- The CJEU has been criticized for stepping beyond its legal role and behaving politically in favouring judgments that advance European integration.
- The CJEU's judicial activism has declined in more recent years.
- Subsidiarity and differentiated integration, along with a maturing of the system, have encouraged diversity in the EU legal system, while the CJEU has matured towards the role of an EU constitutional court.

Court Curbing? The CJEU and the Member States

- Both intergovernmental and neofunctionalist explanations have been offered of why member states have accepted the radical jurisprudence of the CJEU.
- The intergovernmental argument is that member states have tolerated the rulings of the CJEU because it is important to them to have an independent arbitrator that can enforce the single market contract between them, and they do not want to undermine the legitimacy of the arbitrator by defying its rulings.

- The neofunctionalist case is that the CJEU had used the legal system as a 'mask' and a 'shield' to advance integration further than the member states have wanted, and that it has recruited national courts to assist it in this process.

 For additional material and resources, please visit the online resources www.oup.com/uk/bache5e.

QUESTIONS

1. What is the main role of the CJEU and how has it changed over time?
2. What are the fundamental principles of EU law?
3. How and why can the CJEU impact policymaking?
4. How has the CJEU shaped the EU's integration process?
5. Do you think there is a case for curbing for CJEU's activism and what are the obstacles to doing so?

FURTHER READING

For a useful review of scholarship on the EU's judicial system, see **A. Arnull**, 'European Union Law: A Tale of Microscopes and Telescopes', in **M. Egan**, **N. Nugent**, **and W. Paterson (eds)**, *Research Agendas in European Union Studies: Stalking the Elephant* (Basingstoke: Palgrave Macmillan, 2010), 168–88. Useful authoritative textbooks on EU law include **C. Barnard and S. Peers (eds)**, *European Union Law*, 2nd edn (Cambridge: Cambridge University Press, 2017), **D. Chalmers**, **G. Davies**, **and G. Monti**, *European Union Law*, 3rd edn (Cambridge: Cambridge University Press, 2014), **P. Craig and G. De Búrca**, *EU Law: Text, Cases and Materials,* 6th edn (Oxford: Oxford University Press, 2015), **S. Weatherill**, *Cases and Materials on EU Law* (Oxford: Oxford University Press, 2016), or **R Schütze**, *European Constitutional Law* (Cambridge: Cambridge University Press, 2012).

A view of the relationship between the CJEU and both national courts and national governments that is in line with what has here been described as the 'legal neofunctionalism' perspective is presented in **K. J. Alter**, *Establishing the Supremacy of European Law: The Making of an International Rule of Law in Europe* (Oxford: Oxford University Press, 2001). **R. D. Kelemen**, 'The Political Foundations of Judicial Independence in the European Union', in the *Journal of European Public Policy*, 19(1) (2012): 43–58 applies a court-curbing framework to the CJEU to explain its relative independence. **J. Guth and S. Elfving**, *Gender and the Court of Justice of the European Union* (Routledge Research in EU Law, 2018) offer a novel take on CJEU scholarship by using the lens of gender to examine the Court's composition and work.

Chapter 17

Organized Interests

Chapter Overview

The term 'interest group' is used to describe a range of organizations outside of the formal institutions that seek to influence decision making. They provide a link between state actors and the rest of society, sometimes termed 'civil society'. Within the political systems of member states, interest group activity is long established, and it has increased considerably in the European Union (EU) arena since the launch of the single market programme in the mid-1980s.

This chapter looks first at the general growth of interest group activity at the European level, before analysing the types of group that try to influence EU policy making and the forms of representation open to interests. The resources that interest groups bring to the task are considered, as is how these resources enable the groups to gain access to institutional actors. The chapter then looks at the strategies and tactics that groups use to try to influence the different institutions. Finally, it looks at the issue of regulating interest group access to the institutions.

The Growth of Interest Group Activity at the EU Level

Interest group activity aimed at EU decision makers has grown spectacularly, particularly from the launch of the single market programme in the mid-1980s. During the period of market building (Chapter 18, 'The European Union's Policy Agenda'), as the Commission completed the Single European Market (SEM), it was keen to secure the support of business interests. However, as it moved to market regulating by bringing forward rules to ensure that the SEM functioned effectively, the Commission sought to engage with a wider group of actors to ensure balance in the rules that were produced (Dür, Bernhagen, and Marshall, 2015; Greenwood 2017). For example, the Commission has encouraged the creation of advocacy groups of non-governmental organizations for women's rights, the environment, and social protections (Greenwood 2017). These groups perform a dual function: they deliver knowledge and expertise to the Commission and Parliament, but they also legitimate the EU's activities by bringing the wider public interest to the institutions' attention (Bouwen 2009).

Finding precise statistics on the growth of activity over time is challenging, as is identifying the current scale of activity. A first problem is ensuring that the definition of interest groups is clear. If an encompassing approach is to be adopted, corporate lobbying by individual firms should be included, as should the offices of regional and local governments, as well as law firms and public affairs consultants that lobby the EU on behalf of clients. Another important distinction is between these different types of groups and lobbyists; the latter being larger because the category includes the individuals working for the former. The Corporate Europe Observatory, a research and campaign group that tracks corporate behaviour and access to policy making at the European level, estimated in 2017 that there were approximately 25,000 lobbyists in Brussels (Corporate Europe Observatory 2017).

The European Commission and European Parliament (EP) set up a Joint Transparency register in 2011 that covers 'traditional lobbyists' but also law firms, non-governmental organizations (NGOs), think-tanks, and other organizations. As of 28 December 2019, there were 11,892 organizations and individuals included (Joint Transparency Register 2019). Organizations have to sign up to a code of practice to be registered and the growth in those registering since 2011 reflects the growing acceptance of this system (see Figure 17.1). The register takes an inclusive approach to the definition of interest groups; for example, it includes think-tanks and churches. However, it should be noted that the register is not without its flaws. Greenwood and Dreger (2013) found that the quality of data was insufficient, that some registrants allocated to the NGO category could be assigned elsewhere and that the aggregation of statistics could give a misleading picture. It is also not a mandatory system, so it does not constitute a comprehensive register of lobbying organizations and does not cover the Council. These flaws may explain the discrepancy between the Corporate Europe Observatory estimates of lobbyists (25,000) and those officially registered (11,892).

For many organized interests, the development of direct representation at the EU level is in addition to their continuing attempts to influence national governments as part of their overall strategy to shape EU policy. However, the Brussels end of the strategy is increasingly important. Factors that contribute to this include:

- the growing policy competencies of the EU;
- changes in the formal rules of decision making;
- the receptiveness of EU officials to interest-group representations;
- the 'snowballing' effect of groups following the lead of others, so as not to risk being disadvantaged;
- the Commission's support for a wider engagement of European civil society, particularly in the period following its 2001 White Paper on Governance, in which it committed itself to trying to ensure that the policy process was not biased towards certain interests (European Commission 2001).

In line with the maxim that 'where power goes, interest groups follow', the increasing power of EU institutions is an important reason for the rapid growth in interest group activity at the European level. Whereas, in the early years, the coal and steel industries and agriculture were the sectors most affected by the setting up of the European Communities (EC), there are now very few policy sectors that do not have an EU dimension (see Chapter 18, 'Major Policy Areas').

Increased competencies have been accompanied by changes in the rules of decision making (see Chapter 12, 'Decision Making Procedures'). The move within the Council of the EU to qualified majority voting (QMV) for most policy sectors makes it less sensible to lobby only at the national level, because a single state no longer has a veto over legislative proposals where QMV applies. There has also been a shift of power within the policy-making process to the EP, while the Commission's key role as initiator of legislation remains.

The EU provides relatively easy access for those seeking to influence decision making. The importance of organized interests to policy makers, particularly in the complex emerging system of the EU, means that many groups find themselves greeted by an open door when they seek discussions in Brussels. Justin Greenwood (2011: 5) has spelt out the need for interest groups and other lobby organizations from the perspective of the EU institutions:

> Apart from the need for policymaking expertise, and implementation and monitoring capacity, the potential for consolidated collective viewpoint, and the potential to enhance legitimacy, EU institutions also work with organized civil society because the latter has the ability to convey political messages.

Equally, the freedom of access to interest groups has led to pressure to regulate lobbying in order to ensure that groups do not 'capture' a policy area to the detriment of the collective interest. Given that industrial and professional groups predominate, with public interest groups representing a minority, the danger of capture is not insignificant. Although no one can be sure of the benefits of lobbying activities in Brussels, the fear of missing out has become a motivating factor for EU-level activity, and those organizations that do not have an established presence operate at a disadvantage.

Types of Interest Group

There are different ways of classifying interest groups. We have followed the categories used in the EU Transparency Register and offer some illustrations of each type (and their number) from the total of 11,892 registered on 28 December 2019 (Joint Transparency Register 2019).

1. *Professional consultancies, law firms, self-employed consultants (N = 1,070)*. Law firms, many of which have not registered, may help their clients by drafting legislative amendments that they hope members of the European Parliament (MEPs) will be able to utilize during the ordinary legislative procedure.

2. *In-house lobbyists, trade and professional associations (N = 6,192)*. This category includes trade associations like the Chemical Industries Association, as well as big corporations like Microsoft or Shell.

3. *Non-governmental organizations (N = 3,109)*. Examples here would be the European Women's Lobby or Friends of the Earth Europe.

4. *Think-tanks, research, and academic institutions (N = 887)*. There are numerous think-tanks in Brussels, most of which are undertaking analysis rather than directly lobbying, but sometimes the distinction can break down, especially if

the funding is from big corporate players. The Centre for European Policy Studies and Bruegel are major think-tanks. Individual universities may act as lobbyists because they often receive sizeable amounts of research funding from the EU, although they tend to be represented collectively.

5. *Organizations representing churches and religious communities (N = 59).* Churches may act in connection with welfare issues and therefore deem it appropriate to register, as in the case of the Churches' Commission for Migrants in Europe.

6. *Organizations representing local and regional authorities or other public bodies (N = 575).* Reflecting the EU's multi-level governance and its source of funding via the Cohesion Funds, many authorities act as lobbyists, for instance, the German federal states (Länder), or the City of Malmö.

The increase in registrants over time is provided in Figure 17.1.

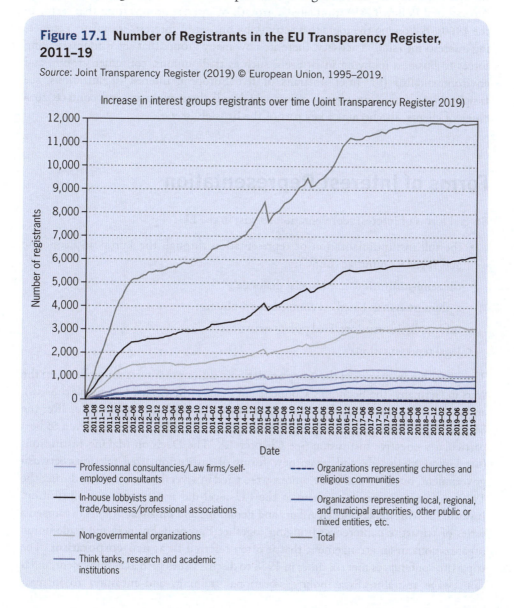

Figure 17.1 Number of Registrants in the EU Transparency Register, 2011–19

Source: Joint Transparency Register (2019) © European Union, 1995–2019.

Different types of organization can represent any given set of interests at the same time. Business interests provide a good example. Business representation in Brussels takes the form of individual companies, collective national organizations (such as the Confederation of British Industry), and collective European organizations. The last category includes BUSINESSEUROPE, which brings together national business associations (and was known until January 2007 as the Union of Industrial and Employers' Confederations, or UNICE), and the European Round Table of Industrialists (ERT), which is made up of chief executives of major firms. The ERT was particularly active in moves to launch the single market programme in the mid-1980s (see Chapter 19, 'Explaining the Single Market'). In addition, firms individually or collectively might employ lobbying consultancy firms to advance their case.

Business interests were represented in Brussels from the establishment of the European Economic Community (EEC) in 1958. The creation of the Common Agricultural Policy (CAP) stimulated a growth of interest groups from that sector in the 1960s. Following the logic that activity by one set of interests stimulates competing interests into similar activity, there are now many groups that act as countervailing forces to business lobbying in Brussels, such as trade unions, consumer groups, and environmentalists (for brief portraits of five European interest organizations, see Insight 17.1). Lobbying consultancies, which sell their expertise and contacts to a range of clients, also became a key part of the Brussels 'scene'.

Forms of Interest Representation

Several forms of interest representation coexist in the EU:

- the full institutionalization of representation through the European Economic and Social Committee (EESC);
- the semi-institutionalized 'social dialogue';
- a pluralist system based on competitive lobbying;
- informally institutionalized policy networks;
- legal representation.

The EESC has its origins in the 'corporatist' institutions that were set up between the wars in Germany (the Economic Council) and France (the *Conseil Economique et Social*), and which were created or recreated in five of the six original member states after the Second World War, Germany being the exception. The EESC has not proven to be a particularly effective institution (see Chapter 12, 'The Decision Making Institutions (the Union Method)'), and when new forms of institutionalized relations between government, business, and trade unions were tried in several member states during the 1970s, attempts to replicate them at the EU level did not involve this institution. Instead, the Ministers of Social Affairs and Economic and Financial Affairs organized a series of tripartite conferences bringing together European business and trade union organizations in an arrangement that is often referred to as **neo-corporatism**. The tripartite conferences met six times in 1978 to discuss issues such as employment, infla-tion, wage restraint, fiscal policy, vocational training, and measures to increase

Insight 17.1 Illustrations of EU-Level Interest Groups

BUSINESSEUROPE can trace its origins back to the establishment in 1958 of the Union of Industrial and Employers' Confederations of the European Community (UNICE). It changed its name in 2007. BUSINESSEUROPE is a 'horizontal' body comprising industrialists' and employers' groups. Specific industries also have their own organizations. It has forty member federations from thirty-five countries, including Turkey and Iceland. It has around forty-five staff in Brussels, and its member organizations have offices nearby. Website: http://businesseurope.eu.

The **European Round Table of Industrialists** was established in April 1983 when a group of leading European business leaders from companies such as Fiat, Philips, and Volvo met to form an organization to promote Europe's industrial competitiveness. It now comprises chief executives and chairs of fifty-five major European multinational companies from eighteen countries. Its principal aim is to promote sustainable growth and prosperity in Europe. It has a small secretariat in Brussels. Website: http://ert.eu.

The **European Trade Union Confederation (ETUC)** styles itself as 'the voice of European workers'. The ETUC can trace its origins back to the 1950s, but only took on its current title in 1973. Owing to competing trade union organizations in some member states (Christian, socialist, communist), it was only by the 1990s that the ETUC took on its broad representative character of today. It comprises ninety national trade union confederations from thirty-eight European countries and ten industry federations (such as the European Metalworkers' Federation). It works for a European social model comprising sustainable economic growth, full employment, and social protection. Its secretariat is in Brussels. Website: http://etuc.org.

The **Committee of Professional Agricultural Organizations (COPA)** and the **General Confederation of Agricultural Co-operatives (COGECA)** are the key interest groups relating to the farming sector. Set up in 1958 and 1959, respectively, they have a shared secretariat based in Brussels. COPA comprises farmers' unions from the member states, while COGECA's membership is of member states' agricultural co-operative associations. COPA–COGECA has a large number of working parties on different agricultural products: from eggs and poultry to wine. Website: http://copa-cogeca.be.

The **European Women's Lobby** was created in 1990. It aims to promote women's rights and equality between women and men in the European Union. It has member organizations in all EU member states and has a small secretariat in Brussels. Website: http://womenlobby.org.

Source: All information is sourced from the respective websites.

productivity. The business groups were reluctant participants, though, and by the end of 1978, the European Trade Union Confederation (ETUC) had withdrawn from the process because of lack of progress.

The idea was revived by Jacques Delors when he became President of the Commission. In 1985, an approach was made to both ETUC and UNICE to open a 'social dialogue' to flank the momentum towards the single market. Delors suggested that, if the idea were accepted, the Commission would refrain from introducing further social legislation and would instead let it emerge out of the dialogue. Initially, two working parties were set up: on employment policies and on new technology and work. They met at the chateau of Val Duchesse outside Brussels, and the dialogue therefore became known as the 'Val Duchesse process'.

From the outset, there were difficulties about the status and functioning of the social dialogue, which was incorporated into the Social Protocol of the Maastricht Treaty. It was agreed that, where the social partners could negotiate agreement on any aspect of social legislation, that agreement would automatically be accepted by the Commission and formulated as a proposal to the Council of the EU, with the expectation that it would become part of the social legislation of the EC—although it would not apply to Britain, which at that time had an opt-out from the Social Protocol. The first piece of legislation to be agreed in this way, in 1995, concerned paid parental leave. However, subsequent progress was limited. The lack of enthusiasm of UNICE and its member organizations for EU-level neo-corporatism reflected the fact that business interests are in a stronger position to get their views heard under the alternative, pluralist system of interest representation.

Separate from this 'social dialogue' approach, many specialized interest groups are able to secure membership of EU advisory committees, assuring themselves of 'semi-institutionalized' status via this route.

A pluralist approach to lobbying suggests that interest groups operate in a more open and competitive political process. This pluralist approach is generally associated with lobbying in the United States. However, there are clear differences between lobbying in the EU and in the United States. As Cornelia Woll puts it (2006: 461): 'According to most studies, lobbying in the US is much more direct and aggressive than in the EU, where lobbyists take a more subtle and consensus-oriented approach.' Pluralism tends to be characterized by the dominance of large firms, putting them in an advantageous position to become core members of any emerging policy networks. In theory, this pluralist system could be just a temporary stage in the evolution of interest representation. In some of the more established policy sectors, such as agriculture, the EU system entails informal institutionalization based on policy networks (see Chapter 2, 'Policy Networks').

Increasingly the lobbying landscape in Brussels is heterogeneous and complex. Hence, the relationship between organized interests and the EU varies according to the area being regulated and the institutional actors involved. Coen and Katsaitis (2013) characterize these diverse patterns of interest representation in the EU as 'chameleon pluralism'. For example, several Commission Directorates General (DGs) have contact groups for 'civil dialogue', including the DGs responsible for Development, Trade, the Environment, and Employment and Social Affairs. However, elsewhere, the Commission has encouraged the establishment of interest groups, such as, in 1990, the European Women's Lobby (Seibicke 2019). It also has financial resources to promote the work of civil society groups, helping to even out differences in power and access (Greenwood 2017).

Finally, although it constitutes a very different activity from lobbying, for certain categories of interest group, targeting the Court of Justice of the EU (CJEU) has been a particularly fruitful activity. Mazey (2012) argues that women groups have secured favourable CJEU decisions to support their advocacy work in advancing gender equality. In the field of environmental policy, NGOs have been key actors in highlighting non-compliance with EU decisions by member states (Hofmann 2019).

Resources

The extent to which groups command resources of varying types is crucial to understanding their relative influence. It is important to note that the term 'resource' does not just refer to money but also to expertise and credibility (Ripoll Servent 2018; see Insight 17.2). Indeed, Coen and Richardson (2009: 7) suggest that trust and credibility are the 'strongest lobbying currency in Brussels'. However, it would be naïve not to acknowledge that access to a large budget helps with being able to develop and deliver evidence and expertise. The control of key resources is an important factor in deciding whether a group will secure 'insider status' with policy makers or remain outside the core process. When it comes to such resources, size matters: larger organizations are generally better resourced than smaller ones. At the level of individual firms, big-business interests possess far more of the resources that are needed to operate effectively than do small-business interests. For example, large firms will often have their own public relations departments, which means that they are better equipped to present their views than smaller firms. Also, the complexity and multi-level nature of EU decision making puts a premium on being able to deploy sufficient personnel to cover all possible access points. Only large individual firms or other particularly well-resourced interest groups are able to pursue their own information gathering and lobbying without joining forces with other actors. To become more effective, smaller organizations have to pool resources. For example, environmental non-governmental organizations have joined forces to become the Green 10—they share office space in Brussels and have a shared website (https://green10.org). However, while there are resource advantages in separate interests coming together, such combinations of interests increase the risk that they will encounter problems of collective action: the interests aggregated within a combined group may find it difficult to agree among themselves about priorities and tactics (Mazey and Richardson 2015).

The disparity in material resources does not necessarily mean that large individual firms have the best access to the policy-making process and even if they do secure access, they may not secure influence. A key debate in the literature has concerned whether and to what extent different types of interest groups can exercise influence. On the one

---

Insight 17.2 Resources Available to Interest Groups

- information and expertise;
- economic muscle;
- status;
- power in implementation;
- the organization of the interest into a non-competitive format;
- coherent organization with representative outlets able to make decisions with ease and alacrity;
- the ability of a group to influence its members;
- reputational capital—trust and credibility.

hand, there is an argument that the EU is biased towards business interests particularly compared to national systems, as there are proportionally more businesses present at the EU level (Berkhout et al. 2018), and they can bring to bear greater resources. For example, it was reported in 2018 that Google had spent over €30 million on lobbying over the EU Copyright Directive, which sought to bring up-to-date rules on ownership rights, for example in relation to music and film, to reflect changed practices in the digital age (i.e. streaming) (Corporate Europe Observatory 2018). However, despite these huge outlays of money, it has also been suggested that business interests are not more influential than other interests and rather that policy outcomes often reflect the preferences of citizen groups (Dür et al. 2019). The overall argument that emerges from a close reading of these different interpretations is that a number of factors shape the success of interest group strategies, and what counts as success depends upon the methods used.

Dür et al. (2019: 5) argue that business interests do often successfully shape EU policies—they are keen to stress that business interests rarely 'suffer all-out defeat'. However, they argue that business interests generally prefer low regulation and have a preference towards the status quo (i.e. keeping things as they are), whereas NGOs often prefer regulations that secure protection for citizens and the environment. Whilst businesses may be successful is securing some derogations (slowing down the implementation of laws or protecting particular sectors) they consistently fail to prevent the adoption of regulations that advance citizen, environmental, or other protections and, which ultimately increase costs to business actors. Dür et al. (2019) suggest a number of conditions that shape the success of interest groups. The first is the level of conflict or issue salience. Where there is high salience—i.e. a controversial issue—then business influence is likely to be lower. Whilst this argument applies to conflict between business and non-business actors, it is worth noting that Rasmussen (2015) finds that where businesses disagree with each other (are internally divided) they are also less likely to achieve their goals. The second key determinant for Dür et al. (2019) is the level of EP involvement—where the EP is involved in policy making, businesses are less likely to achieve their goals. Third, when the policy makers need information and/or the alternative supply of information is low, then businesses also tend to do better in achieving their goals. Finally, in general where policy making is more open and transparent businesses are less likely to achieve their goals. Overall, Dür et al.'s (2019) study reiterates a common message from the literature (see Coen and Katsaitis 2013; Greenwood 2019), which is that the extent to which different institutional actors are involved in policy making is critical in shaping the success of interests groups, an issue we address in the next section.

Organized Interests and the Institutional Actors

The Commission

For a number of reasons, the Commission is an important target for interest groups, in that:

- it has a central role in setting the agenda;
- all proposals have to pass through it;

- it is within the Commission that the detail of proposals is decided;
- it is receptive to approaches from interest groups.

The Commission's agenda-setting role is of particular importance to interest groups. If they want to get particular issues placed on the agenda of the EU, the Commission is a good place to start lobbying. Alternatively, if they want to prevent measures from coming onto or rising up the agenda, influence in the Commission is vital. This means that the Commission is an important channel to monitor. It also means that it is the primary place for influencing the detail of proposals, which is often what concerns interest groups.

The Commission is widely recognized as being receptive to interest-group representations. Mazey and Richardson (2015) suggest that the Commission recognizes the utility of interest groups as sources of information, support, and legitimacy. They also argue that it is in the Commission's interest to build coalitions and networks of support to improve the chances of success for its proposals. Certainly, the Commission's limited human resources make it dependent on the information and expertise that interest groups can offer. However, the nature of the groups that the Commission engages with and how it chooses to do so varies across issue area and DG (Coen and Katsaitis 2013).

Coen and Richardson (2009) argue that for new product and market-regulating policies the Commission is more likely to rely upon technically well-informed interest groups that can enable fast and efficient policy making. However, for redistributive policies the Commission needs to secure wider buy-in and is consequently more likely to engage in wider consultation to gather the views and secure the support of affected actors. Here the CAP provides an interesting example, where, on the one hand, the Commission has long-established relationships with the agricultural lobby, but on the other hand, has also engaged in wide-ranging consultation exercises to bring in other voices, which can legitimate its preferences for reform (see Chapter 21).

It is also important to note that the Commission is not simply a passive recipient of interest group activity but has also played a key role in developing and guiding particular kinds of activities. For example, the Commission has deployed resources over the years to fund those groups that would otherwise be under-represented, such as civil society organizations. However, Commission funding does raise questions for those groups about whether their activities are compromised by accepting such money.

The Council of the EU

The authority of the Council makes it an important target for interest groups. Yet in reality there is little opportunity for them to lobby either the European Council or the Council of the EU directly. These institutions meet behind closed doors and, generally, groups do not have direct access. Currently, the Council is not covered by the EU Transparency Register. The desire to keep meetings confidential was a stumbling block during discussions to widen the Register to include the Council and to make registration mandatory (see ' Regulating Lobbying' below). As Council members are supported by national administrations and permanent officials in Brussels, the Council has less need for the information resources of interest groups than does the Commission, and is thus less receptive to approaches. The consequence is that most lobbying of the Council is indirect, rather than direct.

To influence the Council indirectly, groups seek contact with individual national governments. Initially, of course, they will try to influence their own national government—but as understanding of the EU policy process has grown, interest groups' lobbying techniques have become more sophisticated, and interest groups in one particular member state may now seek to influence governments in other member states. Which governments matter will vary with the issue concerned. For obvious reasons, the member state holding the Council presidency will be a particular target.

Although lobbying national governments is only an indirect way of influencing EU affairs, it is a process that is familiar to most interest groups. It is, as Greenwood (2003: 39) argued, an arena 'where established policy networks and dependency relationships operate which can equally well be used for the purposes of EU representation as for the governance of domestic affairs'. Moreover, for those groups that do not have the necessary resources to lobby EU institutions, the national route may remain the only real option. However, the value of lobbying individual governments has declined with the extension of QMV in the Council. Even where a group has successfully persuaded a government of its case, under QMV it is far from certain that the government will be able to assist, assuming it is persuaded of the lobbyists' case in the first place.

Bouwen (2002: 381) noted that, at the ministerial level, the Council is the most intergovernmental of the institutions—but at the level of the officials involved in the preparation of the ministerial meetings, there is also a considerable degree of supranationalism. Officials are likely to be concerned with the impact of legislation on the European market as a whole, as well as the narrower focus on national interests, so the expert committees might well be open to representations from European associations. Expert knowledge is less needed from outside sources, as there is plenty available from national officials who staff the committees that consider the proposed legislation.

The European Parliament

Despite the fact that the EP traditionally had less influence over decision making than either the Council or the Commission, it has always attracted considerable attention from interest groups (see Dionigi 2017). This is largely because of its long-standing advisory role, which has been viewed as an indirect route to influencing the other institutions. Moreover, MEPs are relatively accessible. In particular, those with a constituency interest in an issue will be the focus of attention. Its post-Lisbon status as co-legislator also makes the EP a very important focus of lobbying. As noted by Rasmussen (2015: 366), 'although the EP is not the only lobbying game in town, it cannot be ignored by interest groups who want to leave their fingerprints on EU legislation'. Whilst historically the EP has been seen as a 'natural ally' for groups lobbying on behalf of consumers, the environment, and a range of human rights including women's and children's rights, the growth in its powers mean that it has also become the target of extensive lobbying from business interests (Dionigi 2017). However, as noted above, Dür et al. (2019) find that when the EP is involved in decision making, legislative outcomes are less likely to reflect the preferences of business actors.

Like the Commission, the EP lacks the national administrative support that is available to the members of the Council. The Parliament has therefore sometimes relied upon interest groups for expertise, although it now has a well-developed research service that can provide reports to support legislators. In general, MEPs will give 'preference to those outside interests that either represent a broad constituency such as trade unions, social movements, or political parties or those that can provide them with an aggregate view on the most efficient ways to deal with the problems and economic consequences' (Lehman 2009: 58).

Broadly speaking then, the Commission and EP are the main site of lobbying activity in Brussels and the EP is seen as being critical in mediating business influence. However, a key challenge for all the EU institutions has been how to remain open to representation without being captured by particular interests. One way in which they address this issue is through regulating lobbying activity.

Regulating Lobbying

The huge growth in lobbying activity at the EU level has raised a range of issues around access and transparency, which have been highlighted by some high-profile cases. In 2011, *Sunday Times* journalists exposed that MEPs were willing to submit amendments to EU legislation in return for cash (Waterfield 2011). In 2012, Maltese Commissioner for Health and Consumer Protection, John Dalli resigned following allegations that he had been involved in improper lobbying relations by the tobacco industry (Henry 2019). In 2015, the dieselgate scandal erupted (see Insight 17.3), which revealed a close relationship between car companies and the German government and the European Commission.

Initial moves to formally regulate lobbying at the EU level dated back to 2005, when Commissioner Siim Kallas launched the European Transparency Initiative as a way of trying to raise trust in the lobbying process (Eising and Lehringer 2010: 195–6). This approach was consistent with the Commission's 2001 White Paper on Governance. It culminated in the Commission establishing the register for lobbyists in 2008. The shared Transparency Register between the Commission and the EP was agreed and launched in 2011. However, as noted, the register is not mandatory and does not cover the Council. Talks on extending the register to include the Council, tighten the rules, and make the Register mandatory collapsed in April 2019. There were a number of key issues upon which the institutions could not agree. The Council argued that COREPER representatives as employees of national governments could not be bound by EU regulations. The Parliament suggested that it did not want MEPs' mandates to be restricted when conducting negotiations. The Commission insisted that Parliament and Council should only meet with interests included in the register, which is a rule by which Commission officials are bound (Nielsen 2019). Whilst the institutions could not agree on these matters, it is worth noting that the European Parliament adopted new rules of Procedure in December 2019, which included the rule that 'Members should adopt the systematic practice of only meeting interest representatives that have registered in the Transparency Register (European Parliament 2019d, Rule 11a). Nevertheless, there are ongoing

> ### Insight 17.3 Dieselgate
>
> In 2015, the dieselgate scandal erupted. In this case it came to light that car companies were routinely and knowingly fitting 'cheat' devices to their vehicles for emissions testing as part of the approval process. Cars were being approved that could not meet emission limits in real-world situations. Moreover, these emissions, primarily of nitrous oxides, are injurious to human health. The scandal was brought to light by the Environmental Protection Agency in the United States and mainly concerned German car manufacturer Volkswagen, although other companies have been implicated over time. Skeete (2017) argues that the EU regulatory regime had been designed to include 'flexibilities' at the request of car companies, which those companies then exploited in order to release vehicles onto the market that could not reach the stipulated emissions limits. The dieselgate scandal shed fresh light on the way in which large national champions (in this case Volkswagen) could lobby effectively at national and European levels to shape legislation in ways that benefited their interests. The case also revealed that the Commission was limited in its ability to secure compliance with emission rules, instead having to reply upon member states. This case suggests that the arguments that the EU system of governance has avoided regulatory capture through the establishment and support of civil society and non-governmental organizations may be overstated.

challenges over access and a continuing lack of transparency, particularly when it comes to lobbying the Council. Organizations such as the Alliance for Lobbying Transparency and Ethics Regulation (ALTER-EU) (http://alter-eu.org) and Corporate Europe Observatory, which campaign for lobbying transparency and seek to limit the predominance of business interests, provide useful data and provide some kind of counterbalance to the business lobby.

CONCLUSION

This chapter raises issues connected with two of the themes identified in the opening section of the book. The first is the theme of supranational versus intergovernmental interpretations of the nature of the EU (Chapter 1, 'Theories of European Integration'). The second is the theme of how best to ensure the EU's legitimacy and combat the democratic deficit (Chapter 3, 'Democracy and Legitimacy').

Interest group activity may provide a litmus test for the degree to which the supranational institutions of the EU exercise independent influence over the policy process. If interest groups transfer their lobbying activities away from national governments to Brussels, this may be taken as an indication that the EU is a supranational organization. However, such a conclusion has to be modified in the light of arguments and evidence presented in this chapter. First, the increased level of interest group activity in Brussels has not replaced activity at the national level, but has generally supplemented it: lobbying tends to follow a multi-level approach. Second, although groups must have some reason to expend financial resources on establishing a presence in Brussels, this does not mean that the reasons are well founded: they may simply be afraid of missing out on something. There is a point at which the sight of other groups swarming to Brussels will lead groups to follow on the assumption that there must be something worth pursuing, even if there is not.

Once located in Brussels, groups will not all be equally effective in influencing the institutions. The extent to which organizations are able to secure their preferences depends upon a number of variables, such as how salient the issue is, and which institutions are involved. Some studies suggest that business interests are more influential than other interests, such as organized labour, consumers, or environmental groups. Within the category of business interests, large firms are more influential than small firms. Whether this relative influence matters, of course, depends on the answer to the question of how much independent influence the supranational institutions have over policy outcomes. If they do have some influence, and if it is true that big-business interests have the most influence over the supranational institutions, then this could provide one explanation for the observation that the policies that emanate from Brussels tend to be pro-business and in line with an Anglo-Saxon model of capitalism. For their parts, and in different ways, the Commission and the EP seek to ensure that a wide range of interests is heard in the policy process.

On the other hand, the domination of the process by big-business interests may not be as clear as several writers suggest. Beyers (2004) showed that interests that feel themselves excluded can make their voice heard by politicizing the process, while the research undertaken by Dür et al. (2019) indicated that while business interests may enjoy privileged access to the institutions, that does not necessarily translate into influence. Indeed Dür et al. suggest that the participation of the EP in decision making and the salience of a policy are critical factors shaping how much influence business can exercise.

The second theme highlighted by the chapter is that engagement with interest groups is an important way for the EU institutions to obtain legitimacy at the input stage of policy making. It is particularly clear that the Commission is dependent on the expertise of interest groups, thereby legitimating its work. There have been attempts to advance this type of interaction as a new form of governance, characterized by the Commission's engagement with civil society. However, it is questionable whether this interaction offers a solution to the EU's democratic deficit. Moreover, if lobbying lacks transparency, its legitimacy is called into question. Attempts to regulate lobbyists' access to the institutions have been the response to this concern, but the ability of corporations to lobby at the national level can undermine such efforts, as the dieselgate scandal illustrates only too well.

KEY POINTS

The Growth of Interest Group Activity at the EU Level

- Interest-group activity in Brussels has increased greatly since the mid-1980s.
- Factors in this growth are: the growing policy competence of the EU; the perception of a shifting balance of institutional power in Brussels, most notably in favour of the EP; the receptiveness of EU officials to interest group representations; and the 'snowballing' effect of groups following the lead of others so as not to risk being disadvantaged.

Types of Interest Group

- There are several different types of interest organization active in Brussels.
- Business interests were the first to locate in Brussels, and still account for the largest number of groups.
- Interest groups representing workers, consumers, environmental interests, and other parts of civil society have become increasingly active.

Forms of Interest Representation

- Five forms of interest representation coexist in the EU: 'corporatist'; 'neo-corporatist'; pluralist; informally institutionalized policy networks; and legal representation.
- Of these five, pluralism and informal institutionalization predominate.

Resources

- The most effective interest groups in a pluralist system are generally those that control key resources such as information and expertise, economic muscle, and status.
- Small organizations can pool resources, but they may then find problems in agreeing on priorities and tactics.
- The three types of information sought by the institutions are expert knowledge, information on the needs and concerns of actors in the relevant sector across Europe, and information on the needs and concerns of national actors in the sector.

Organized Interests and the Institutional Actors

- For some EU actors, interest groups are an important source of information and legitimation and, as such, are enthusiastically consulted.
- The Commission is in need of the expert knowledge that big-business interests can often provide most effectively, but it has also sought to cultivate links with European-level associations and to promote less-represented social interests.
- The Council is less reliant on organized interests than other institutions and, as such, is less open to approaches. Much lobbying of the Council is indirect, through individual national governments.
- The EP is a key target for organized interests, particularly following the growth of its powers since the mid-1990s. MEPs are thought to be particularly sympathetic to representations on issues of broad public interest.

Regulating Lobbying

- Both the Commission and the EP have sought to regulate lobbyists' access.
- The Joint Transparency Register addresses some concerns, but does not cover the Council and is not mandatory.
- The dieselgate scandal underlines the influence of national governments and the challenges of regulating lobbying and access at the national level.

 For additional material and resources, please visit the online resources www.oup.com/uk/bache5e.

QUESTIONS

1. What are the different types of interest group that operate at the European level?
2. Why do interest groups seek to shape EU policy making?
3. What do integration theories suggest about interest group activity? Has reality matched those expectations?
4. What shapes business group's ability to influence EU policy making?
5. Should there be greater regulation of interest groups at EU level?

FURTHER READING

For a thorough and comprehensive review of organized interests in the EU, see **J. Greenwood**, *Interest Representation in the European Union*, 4th edn (Basingstoke: Palgrave Macmillan, 2017). In addition to considering interest group strategies, resources, and channels of influence, this book includes separate chapters on some of the major interests, including business, labour, and territorial interests. For an accessible (though non-academic) guide to '*Lobby Planet Brussels*', see Corporate Europe Observatory (2017).

   M. Dionigi provides an excellent analysis of business mobilization around the European Parliament in *Lobbying the European Parliament, The Battle for Influence* (Basingstoke: Palgrave Macmillan 2017). **A. Dür**, **P. Bernhagen, and D. Marshall** provide a nuanced argument about how businesses can shape policy in *The Political Influence of Business in the European Union* (Ann Arbor, MI: University of Michigan Press 2019). Two valuable collections of essays on interest groups are **D. Coen and J. Richardson (eds)**, *Lobbying the European Union: Institutions, Actors, and Issues* (Oxford: Oxford University Press, 2009), and **J. Beyers**, **R. Eising, and W. Maloney (eds)**, *Interest Group Politics in Europe: Lessons from EU Studies and Comparative Politics* (Abingdon: Routledge, 2009). The latter volume comprises articles published in a special issue of *West European Politics,* 31 (2008): 1103–302.

Part Four
Policies

EU institutions and lobby groups, outlined in Part Three, come together in making EU policy. Chapter 18 forms a bridge between Parts Three and Four of the book. It looks at the EU's policy responsibilities and its patterns of policy making. It also focuses on the so-called policy cycle, examining how institutions and actors become involved from the stages of agenda setting, when policy is quite loosely defined, right through to the implementation of that policy. Chapter 18 also briefly covers some major policy areas to which we cannot devote a full chapter within the confines of a general textbook in which policies comprise just one part.

In this edition of the book, we deploy a system that organizes policies around the functions they play: whether they aim to make markets work more efficiently ('market-building' policies, such as the single market), whether they are concerned with overcoming the deficiencies of market solutions (market-correcting policies, such as payments to weaker economic regions through cohesion policy), whether they are designed to limit the effect of economic activity (market-cushioning policies such as those on the environment or climate change), or whether they are more explicitly political policies, such as foreign, security, and defence policy.

Creating a common market has been a central objective of the process of European integration since the signing of the Treaty of Rome (EEC) in 1957. It represents a classic case of market-building policy. In the mid-1980s, the project to complete the *single market* revived the faltering process of European integration, and attempts to understand the success of the single market programme, and the spillover from it to other common policies, generated a revival of theoretical endeavour.

Arguably the most significant policy spillover was that from the single market to the creation of a single currency. *Economic and monetary union* has been around as an objective since the Hague Summit in 1969 (see Chapter 7, 'The Hague Summit'). It had proved both controversial and elusive. From an economic perspective, a motivating factor following the achievements of the single market was the goal of 'one market, one money', highlighting a market-building view of the policy. Nevertheless, the policy was also political, transferring a major nation-state power to the EU level. Politics partly explains why monetary union was achieved without the participation of all member states.

As with the single market, the explanation for monetary union generated heated academic debate, as rival theories sought to explain this momentous step in integration. Many of the economic and political issues that critics had believed would prevent the creation of the single currency were not resolved once it was created. This became apparent to even the most optimistic of observers with the eurozone crisis, which began in the late 2000s (see Chapter 11, 'The Unfolding Eurozone Crisis'). The result of the crisis was the need for reform to monetary union and enlivened academic debate about the eurozone crisis, deploying the full range of theories outlined in Part One of the book.

Agriculture, along with cohesion policy, accounts for some three-quarters of EU spending. It is a policy area where reliance on markets is deficient, necessitating market-correcting policy. Agriculture was the first common policy of the EC, conceived of at a time when post-war food shortages were still a recent memory. Unlike market-building policies, which are typically concerned with removing barriers, the Common Agricultural Policy (CAP) had to put in place 'market orders' for different products through policy interventions. The CAP has been re-organized through several episodes of reform to control costs and bring it into line with international trade rules, but retains significance within the EU's policy portfolio.

In Chapter 22, we consider environmental and climate change policies, which are market cushioning in nature. Environmental policy originated in trying to limit the side effects of economic activity within the EU. Over time, environmental measures began to come into tension with the economic growth objectives of the single market. More recently, the global challenge of climate change has augmented environmental policy and given that policy a wider, international focus.

Following the end of the Cold War, with the opening of EU borders in the single market and increasing numbers of refugees arriving at the EU's borders, EU co-operation on justice and home affairs (JHA) became a new set of policy concerns. These concerns were explicitly political and brought the EU to addressing key state concerns such as immigration and policing. This policy area was central to the Amsterdam Treaty (see Chapter 9, 'The Treaty of Amsterdam'), and was given the new, aspirational, name of an *area of freedom, security, and justice (AFSJ)*. A key component of this policy, asylum policy, reached major salience in 2015, with the increased flow of refugees into the EU, especially those fleeing the Syrian civil war. The political character of this policy has been underlined by the political controversy over EU migration policy more broadly and the rise of populist parties. This is the last internal policy to be considered, in Chapter 23.

While all EU policies have an external dimension, the two policy sectors mentioned in the previous paragraph operate very close to the interface between the internal and external aspects of policy. External relations proper have two aspects: economic and political. Although not constituting the totality of the EU's external economic relations, *trade and development aid* together form the most important part, and have also been the subject of academic analysis from a wide variety of different theoretical perspectives. The EU's external relations come about as the external face of internal policies. Thus, trade policy is the external aspect of market building within the EU. Development aid originally arose because of former colonial–political relationships, but has economic objectives as well. External political relations in the traditional sense of foreign and security policy come under the general heading of the *Common Foreign and Security Policy* of the EU, considered in Chapter 25.

Finally, the process of *enlargement* is another political policy whereby external relations are transformed into internal relations. In the process, accession states take on the market-building, market-correcting, and market-cushioning policies. This process not only seeks to strengthen political stability in Europe but also has profound implications for the operation and nature of the EU as a whole. The promise of accession is an important incentive, allowing the EU to bring about changes in the politics and governance of neighbouring states. A much lighter-touch version of this externalizing of internal policies comes with the European Neighbourhood Policy (see Chapter 24, 'The European Neighbourhood Policy'). In this case, states to the east and south sign agreements with the EU. They may align some of their policies, for instance on market building, in return for EU funding and a commitment to helping broader goals of security and stability, but without a commitment from Brussels to their eventual membership.

Chapter 18

Policy Making and Policies in the European Union

Chapter Overview

The policy responsibilities of the EU are rather extensive. Starting in 1958, with policies on internal tariffs, agriculture, and overseas development, the EU has gradually acquired competency (i.e. powers) in more and more areas of policy. Although there has been no Treaty reform since the 2009 Lisbon Treaty, and despite the series of crises affecting the EU during the 2010s, integration has not come to a halt. Notably, fixing the eurozone crisis necessitated greater fiscal surveillance and EU regulation of the banking sector. A complex system of policy making has emerged to deal with these responsibilities. This chapter reviews the principal factors affecting the different patterns of policy making, and the main policies that have not been given separate chapters to themselves in the rest of Part Four.

The principal factors affecting the different patterns of policy making are the type of policy, the powers given to the EU's institutions by the Treaties, and the extent of integration of the policy area (including whether all member states fully participate). As noted in Chapter 12, 'The Decision Making Institutions (CFSP)', the most striking difference in policy making relates to the Common Foreign and Security Policy (CFSP) and its defence affiliate, the Common Security and Defence Policy (CSDP). Both of these are governed according to the more intergovernmental pattern of the Treaty on the European Union (TEU) (Chapter 25). The chapter then explores the policy cycle: the passage of policy issues from the agenda-setting stage to the implementation stage. In a final section, it identifies some important policy areas that are worth being aware of but where space precludes chapter-length treatment.

The European Union's Policy Agenda

What are the policy areas of the EU? In July 1988, in a speech to the European Parliament (EP), Jacques Delors predicted that, 'In ten years, 80 per cent of economic legislation—and perhaps tax and social legislation—will be directed from the Community' (European Parliament 1988: 140). It was a prediction that raised the hackles of critics of European integration, while opening an academic debate concerning how to measure the '80 per cent' claim (see Töller 2010). In 2019, the Europa website listed some thirty-six policy responsibilities (see Table 18.1) These responsibilities include some added by the Lisbon Treaty, for example space and sport. However, the

Box 18.1 The EU Member State Balance of Policy Competence

Areas of Exclusive Competence

- Customs union
- Competition rules for the internal market
- Monetary policy for those states in the eurozone
- Conservation of marine biological resources under the common fisheries policy
- Common commercial policy
- Where an international agreement is necessary to enable the Union to exercise its internal competence.

Areas of Shared Competence

- Internal market
- Aspects of social policy
- Economic, social, and territorial cohesion
- Agriculture and fisheries (except marine conservation)
- Environment
- Consumer protection
- Transport
- Trans-European networks
- Energy
- Area of freedom, security, and justice
- Aspects of public health safety
- Technological development and space
- Development and humanitarian aid.

Areas of Policy Co-ordination

- Member states' economic policies
- Member states' employment policies
- Member states' social policies.

Areas of Supporting, Co-ordinating, or Supplementary Action

- Protection and improvement of human health
- Industry
- Culture
- Tourism
- Education, vocational training, youth, and sport
- Civil protection
- Administrative co-operation.

The Common Foreign and Security Policy

- Intergovernmental

Source: summarized from Articles 3–6, Treaty on the Functioning of the European Union (TFEU).

policy areas vary considerably in significance: from an essentially EU-internal issue such as institutional affairs to the global concerns of foreign and security policy. Thus, before looking at the policies in more detail in the chapters that follow, we establish some criteria for comparing the EU's policy areas.

For many years of European integration there was no formal listing of EU policies. This absence led to criticism on the grounds that there were no clear boundaries to the EU's powers. The Lisbon Treaty finally corrected this omission and provided a 'catalogue' of policy competences. The listing (see Box 18.1) is important because it categorizes the balance of policy responsibilities between the EU institutions and the member states. Hence, in 'areas of exclusive competence', such as the customs union, the member states have delegated all power to the EU institutions. At the other end of the spectrum is the CFSP, where member governments are the key players. For completeness, it should also be noted that in areas such as primary and secondary education, or housing, the EU's powers are virtually non-existent. The vast majority of EU policies entail the sharing of powers between the EU and the member states. Thus, a first important way of classifying EU policies is by the extent of authority that is held by the supranational institutions of the EU.

A second way of classifying EU policies is to do so by their purpose (Sbragia 2003). Some policies are *market building* (or *making*) in character. That is, they are designed to make economic markets operate more efficiently. Classic examples would include the single market or the competition policy: both are designed to make the market mechanism work well through a limited degree of policy regulation. However, not all policy can operate in this manner. In policy areas where markets do not function

Table 18.1 Policy Competence of the European Union

Agriculture	Employment and Social Affairs	Institutional Affairs
Audiovisual and Media	Energy	Justice and Home Affairs
Budget	Enlargement	Maritime Affairs & Fisheries
Climate Action	Enterprise	Multilingualism
Competition	Environment	Regional Policy
Consumers	EU Citizenship	Research and Innovation
Culture	Food Safety	Single Market
Customs	Foreign and Security Policy	Space
Development and Co-operation	Fraud Prevention	Sport
Digital Economy and Society	Health	Taxation
Economic and Monetary Affairs	Humanitarian Aid	Trade
Education, Training, and Youth	Human Rights	Transport

Source: http://ec.europa.eu © European Union, 1995–2020.

effectively or where regions are left behind by economic competition, the EU may introduce *market-correcting* policies. This was the character of the original CAP as established in the 1960s, but now much reformed (see Insight 21.1). More recently, cohesion policy was conceived, against a backdrop of new member states joining and bringing wider territorial disparities with them, as a way to help economically weaker regions to build infrastructure and try to get on an even footing with the wealthier parts of the EU. Economic activity can also have adverse consequences that necessitate *market-cushioning* policy. This is particularly the case with the environment and climate change, but also applies to health-and-safety policy. In each case, the objective of the policy is to minimize harm. Finally, there are policies that are explicitly political (or non-market) in nature and that are residual to these categories, such as the CFSP and the Area of Freedom, Security, and Justice (AFSJ). This classification system, it should be noted, works best with EU internal policies. The classification system's emphasis on markets underlines the continuing importance of the economic dimension of European integration.

A third way of classifying policies derives from the instruments that are used (Kassim and Le Galès 2010; Le Galès 2011). It is worth noting that the EU's range of policy instruments is somewhat constrained by its own limitations as an organization. It does not have a large budget of the type possessed by the member states. Furthermore, it has no direct taxation powers over its citizens. With so much of EU policy put into practice within member states, the EU is consequently reliant on their authorities' use of policy instruments.

The classic form of policy instrument is legal/legislative in nature and regulatory in form. The internal market, competition, agriculture, fisheries, and trade are examples of EU policy of this kind, where law making and regulation are key. Budgetary expenditure is a further significant policy instrument that the EU uses, despite its limited budget. It uses this funding in two different ways. In agriculture or research and innovation, it allocates funding to specific policy functions. By contrast, in cohesion policy it disburses money in an explicitly redistributive manner, funded primarily by richer member states and directed at the economically weaker ones. The EU is able to leverage member-state money (through the requirement for 'matched funding') for many of the cohesion-policy projects as well as those in research and innovation, thus extending the impact of the EU's limited budget.

The EU goes beyond the more traditional policy instruments of money and legislation, however, and this development has expanded from the 1980s in line with practice in other political systems. Two types of 'new governance' instrument can be identified. Agreement and incentive-based instruments are used particularly in the cohesion funds (CFs), requiring partnership agreements at local project level in order to maximize local buy-in on EU-funded projects. Another policy method used from the 1980s has been performance standards as a policy instrument. For example, league tables have been used in the single market policy area to compare how member states measure up in putting into operation policy agreed in the EU institutions. League tables can be an important device for monitoring performance where EU legislation through directives needs to be transposed by member states (see Chapter 19, 'Transposition and Enforcement'). Furthermore, the Lisbon Strategy and its successor 'Europe 2020' have included policies designed to increase the EU's competitiveness, often implemented through techniques such as peer review and benchmarking in policy areas where the EU lacks clear legislative authority. Although such techniques predated it, the Lisbon Strategy gave them the name the 'Open Method of Co-ordination' (OMC) (see Chapter 10, 'The Lisbon Strategy'). The broader point, however, is that different policy instruments are suited to different policy areas (see Table 18.2). CFSP is an outlier on policy instruments, since it is largely reliant on co-operation between governments, using declaratory or diplomatic politics and, exceptionally, financial sanctions against third countries. Some powers are delegated to the EU's High Representative of the Union for Foreign Affairs and Security Policy (HRUFASP) and a supporting diplomatic infrastructure, the European External Action Service (EEAS), but the legal basis is intergovernmental in nature.

A final means that discriminates between individual policy areas is the presence or absence of so-called differentiated integration (see also Chapter 12, 'Differentiated Integration'). Some EU policies are regarded as necessarily comprising all member states; the single market (most obviously—the clue is in the name!) and trade policy being clear cases. In some other policy areas, however, issues of national sovereignty, or lack of readiness at member-state level, have resulted in either policy opt-outs or situations where some states proceed with integration at a faster pace. The UK was the 'European champion' at opt-outs, notably in relation to the single currency and the Schengen passport-free zone. By contrast with the UK and Denmark, who negotiated formal opt-outs from the single currency, the states that acceded to the EU from 1995

Table 18.2 Patterns of EU Policy

Policy area	EU competence	Policy purpose	Policy instruments	Differentiated membership?
Single market	Shared	Market making	Legal, regulatory	No
Monetary policy	Exclusive	Market making	Legal, regulatory	Yes (eurozone)
Agriculture	Shared	Market correcting	Legal, regulatory, and budget	No
Environment and climate change	Shared	Market cushioning	Legal, regulatory, and new instruments	No
Freedom, security, and justice	Shared	Political	New instruments; limited legal, regulatory	Yes (Schengen)
Trade	Exclusive	N/A (external)	Regulatory	No
CFSP/CSDP	Intergovernmental	Political	Interstate cooperation and diplomacy	Yes (permanent structured co-operation (PESCO))

onwards were all expected to join the single currency, and have no opt-outs. Many have joined; some treat membership with less urgency. In any case, the EU has to agree their entry on the basis of performance requirements. To take a different case, Bulgaria, Croatia, Cyprus, and Romania are expected to join the Schengen zone—they have no opt-out—but they have not yet been admitted owing to concerns about the performance standards on policing and border controls. In the eurozone and Schengen zone, therefore, integration takes place at different speeds.

Table 18.2 seeks to summarize the variation amongst policies using the classifications discussed above for the policy areas considered in the following eight chapters. Enlargement is excluded, as it is a policy that transfers all EU policies to accession states, and is therefore difficult to accommodate within the framework. What the table reveals is considerable diversity between the policies that will become clearer in succeeding chapters. In particular, Table 18.2 reveals CFSP and CSDP as outliers, reflecting their different Treaty base. The development from 2017 of permanent structured co-operation (PESCO), a provision in the Lisbon Treaty, was a means of intensifying CSDP in the face of concerns about the implications of possible British disengagement from European security after Brexit, and about President Trump's commitment to the North Atlantic Treaty Organization (NATO) (see Chapter 25, 'The CFSP and CSDP in Action'). It has extended differentiated integration to a further policy area.

The European Union's Policy Cycle

All political systems have a policy cycle that represents the different stages of policy making. The key stages of the policy cycle are set out in Figure 18.1. The stages start from agenda setting, when a policy first comes onto the political agenda, progressing through decision making to policy review and feedback.

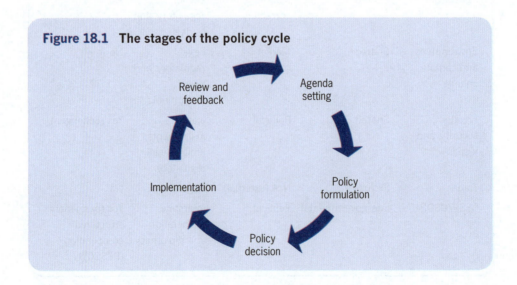

Figure 18.1 The stages of the policy cycle

Agenda Setting

How do policies such as those discussed in the following chapters come onto the EU's policy agenda? What is the typical pattern according to which policy issues flow through the EU's political system? The answers to these questions provide important context to considering the policy areas themselves.

Policies find their way onto the EU agenda, rather than remaining domestic issues, for a variety of reasons. At the outset of integration, with the creation of the European Coal and Steel Community (ECSC), joint control over the heavy industries not only assured member states access to important raw materials, but also assured states neighbouring Germany that there was a new political commitment to constrain the extremes of nationalism that had brought about two world wars. The coal and steel sectors were then not only key to industrial development, but also to the industries of war. The first point to make, therefore, is that many of the policy areas have come on to the EU's agenda not only for economic or other functional reasons, but also because of an underlying political commitment to end the turbulent relations between nation states over the period from 1870 to 1945.

Put in terms of integration theories, sometimes there is an obvious functional logic to trying to solve a policy problem collectively. Sometimes member-state governments have realized the limits of their own capacity, and economic welfare or combatting cross-border problems has necessitated delegating powers to the EU in order to provide policy solutions that could not optimally be provided at the member-state level. This is the motivation that the economic historian Alan Milward outlined in his book, *The European Rescue of the Nation State* (Milward 1992). Or, to give a more recent illustration, cross-border environmental pollution or combating climate change are issues where there are obvious limits to member-state control, and collective action via the EU has developed. It is worth noting that the two motivations—functional and explicitly political ones—are central to debates about European integration. Functional dynamics lie at the heart of neo-functionalism, whereas 'the European rescue of the nation state' is about governments explicitly deciding to delegate new powers to the EU in line with intergovernmentalism.

What has changed over the period since the 1950s is that the dynamics behind the functional logic and the rescue of the nation state have changed significantly. Whereas in the early1950s the challenges were concerns about renascent German military power and the security of a Europe divided by the Cold War, in the contemporary EU it is globalization and the resultant economic challenges, climate change, migration, the more hostile international environment in the era of presidents Trump and Putin, and the rise of Chinese power. Of course, there are other challenges from within the EU: the eurozone crisis, which necessitated greater integration of fiscal and banking-sector surveillance at the EU level to improve monetary stability or the implications of Brexit, to take two examples. Each of these challenges comprises a functional logic of strengthened integration at the EU level, but requires the member governments to agree to it. This is why the debate between neofunctionalism and liberal intergovernmentalism remains so vibrant today.

Even the British government, often hostile to the adoption of European solutions, recognized in the 1980s that the economic problems of Europe, including its competitiveness with Japan and the United States, could only be effectively tackled by joint action to create a genuine single European market (see Chapter 19, 'Project 1992: Freeing the Internal Market').

Sometimes it is because the problem itself arises from *spillover* from other EU policies (see Chapter 1, 'Theories of European Integration'), and therefore demands a European solution. The single European market led to a spate of cross-border business mergers, some of which threatened to create monopolistic enterprises that would prevent the achievement of greater competition, which was the purpose of the single market initiative. This put pressure on national governments to agree to regulation of mergers at European level (see 'Major Policy Areas' below). Sometimes domestic interest groups have pressed governments for the transfer of regulation to the European level, as occurred with the liberalization of national telecommunications (see Insight 19.2, 'The Liberalization of Telecommunications'). Sometimes governments are receptive to a European approach to problems because it allows them to escape political unpopularity for the measures that are necessary. For instance, in the 1990s the wish to join the monetary union planned in the Maastricht Treaty enabled Italian governments to push through domestic reforms that had been blocked by the inefficiencies of its own political system (Dyson and Featherstone 1999: 452–533).

The institution where policy issues are definitively put on the EU policy agenda is the European Council. Indeed, the examples cited in the previous paragraph arose from declarations by the European Council. While the Commission may exploit the circumstances to influence agenda setting, it does not set the agenda in terms of strategy and large-scale initiatives.

Policy Formulation

Once an issue is accepted as a legitimate item on the policy agenda of the EU, a complex political and bureaucratic process is set in motion, which involves a plethora of actors. This process was usually, and still often is, based on the formal institutional procedures outlined in Chapter 12, 'Decision Making Procedures', although other processes are increasingly used, including the OMC (see 'The European Union's Policy Agenda' above).

Although the details of the involvement of different institutional actors vary according to the procedure that is relevant to a particular policy issue, all the formal procedures begin with the Commission formulating a proposal for legislation. In doing this, the Commission normally consults widely. It will usually discuss the range of options with the most obviously relevant interest groups at an early stage. There is no point in coming up with proposals that stand no chance of being accepted by governments due to strong lobbying against them by interest groups at national level.

The Commission will also consult widely with technical experts in the field, either on an ad hoc basis or through its own complex of expert committees. Just as there is no point in formulating proposals that interest groups will work hard to block, there is no benefit in pushing through legislation that will prove to be impossible to implement, a possibility that can be avoided by consulting experts. Finally, the Commission will sound out officials from member governments to discover the parameters within which it might prove possible to get an agreement in the Council of Ministers.

Of course, the Commission will receive conflicting opinions and advice when formulating its proposals, and will have to make judgements of its own between these viewpoints. There is sometimes an element here of the Commission being forced to go for the lowest common denominator in order to ensure that it can get some legislation through. This is most often likely to be the case where the policy area is a new one for the EU, when the premium for the Commission is to make a start on building an *acquis communautaire* that can form the basis for further advance at a later date. Often, though, the Commission will take risks in order to push a certain position. This can backfire if the legislation is not passed, but in many cases the Commission has already ensured that it has allies amongst national governments and MEPs, who will back its proposals against opposition.

In preparing its proposals, the Commission will also often consult those MEPs who have a particular interest in a policy area, especially those who are members of the relevant specialist committee of the EP. It is sometimes assumed that the EP is inevitably an ally of the Commission, because it too is considered to be an institution with a vested interest in further European integration (Garrett and Tsebelis 1996; Tsebelis and Garrett 1996). However, the relationship between the EP and the Commission is much more complicated than that. MEPs have to respond to democratic pressure from their constituents, they face party-political pressures, and they too are subject to lobbying from a wide variety of interest groups. Also, the EP has a vested interest in standing up to the Commission to prove its independence and importance.

Decision Making

Legislative decision making was considered in Chapter 12 and can follow different processes, but here we use the 'default' one, the ordinary legislative procedure (OLP) (see Chapter 12, 'Decision Making Procedures'). The key participants at this stage are the Council of Ministers, the Committee of Permanent Representatives (COREPER), and other preparatory committees composed of member state officials, and the EP. This formal stage is crucial to the fate of the Commission's policy proposals. Reaching agreement depends on the extent of contestation over an issue—how far one or more states feel the legislation will adversely affect their national interests—and on the interplay between the Council and the EP. Buonanno and Nugent (2013: 98) refer to the REACH (Registration, Evaluation, Authorisation and Restriction of Chemicals) Directive, which was designed to regulate some 30,000 substances. This was a contested piece of legislation affecting the chemical sector, environmentalists, and other interest groups, with different balances between them across the member states. It took from October 2003 to December 2006 before the legislation was agreed, having been greatly modified after a complex struggle entailing both the Council and the EP.

Some legislation falls at this stage because agreement cannot be achieved. For example, in 2011 the European Commission proposed a Financial Transaction Tax. It was designed to ensure that transactions by financial institutions contributed to public finances, especially in light of the role those institutions had played in the financial crisis in the previous decade. However, some states with important financial centres, such as the UK, opposed the tax because of fears about its impact, and legislation simply could not be agreed. Unusually, this was not the end of the proposal, as some member governments remained keen on it. The Commission re-introduced the proposal in 2013 using the enhanced co-operation provisions introduced under the Lisbon Treaty (see Insight 12.2), necessitating support from at least nine states before it could be agreed as a measure applicable in those states. Although this was achieved, legal challenges, Estonia's decision to withdraw its support (leaving ten protagonists), and complications arising from Brexit stalled the process, and it had not been agreed by the end of 2019. Decision making, whether of all member states or—very occasionally—under enhanced co-operation, can thus be protracted and complex due to different national and socio-economic interests.

Implementation

Once passed, legislation needs to be implemented, either by the Commission or more usually by member-state authorities (Chapter 12, 'Implementation'). In some cases, the Commission or EU agencies have the powers to put policy into practice themselves; for example, the Commission's key role in executing competition policy. However, in many cases legislation is needed in the member states. The European Commission oversees this step, which is termed transposition, seeking to ensure that legislation is correctly put into effect. However, this is a major task and it is often reliant on others bringing to its attention where implementation is not occurring or is faulty in application. For instance, environmental interest groups may play this role at the local level and inform the Commission where European legislation is not being observed.

In this event, a three-stage process is followed (see Chapter 13, 'The Commission and Managing Implementation'), potentially leading to an authority being taken all the way to the Court of Justice of the EU (CJEU). This occurred in 2008, when the European Commission took Italy to the CJEU over its failure to have adequate waste disposal plans, thus breaching the EU Waste Directive (see Lelieveldt and Princen 2011: 264–5). In 2007, refuse had been building up on the streets of Naples, creating a health hazard and leading residents to set it on fire. Eventually, in December 2014, the CJEU fined the Italian government €40m and threatened a similar fine every six months if the situation was not resolved. This was a striking and unusual case, but it does show what ultimately can happen if implementation is not carried through.

Review and Feedback

The policy loop is completed with the review and feedback stage. In some cases, policy has a review clause. This is sometimes incorporated into legislation where a member state did not get all it hoped in EU negotiations and hopes to strengthen legislation at a future point by inserting a review clause. Sometimes, it becomes necessary to amend legislation. At this stage, interest groups and member-state officials will lobby the Commission. There would be no need for the agenda-setting stage. Instead, the cycle would re-start with the policy formulation stage, led by the Commission.

Overview

The simplified version of the EU policy cycle outlined here is displayed, with the key policy players inserted, in Figure 18.2. It is only a typical policy cycle. Some processes differ; for example, the above-mentioned OMC (see Chapter 11, 'Europe 2020').

As outlined in Chapter 12, 'The Decision Making Institutions (CFSP)', the institutional arrangements for foreign and security policy are quite different. A different treaty (the TEU) governs the process, and the supranational institutions, notably the CJEU and the EP are much weaker. The HRUFASP and the European External Action Service, which provides diplomatic support, are the key players alongside the Foreign Affairs Council (see Figure 18.3). An important additional point is that a lot of

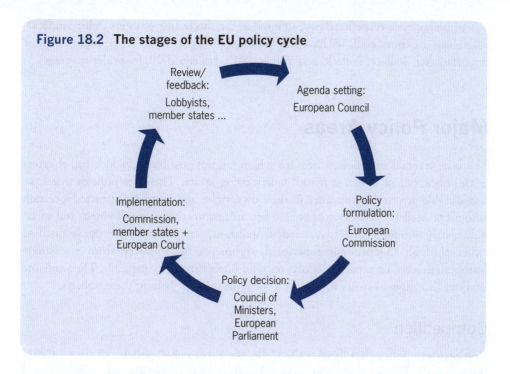

Figure 18.2 The stages of the EU policy cycle

- Agenda setting: European Council
- Policy formulation: European Commission
- Policy decision: Council of Ministers, European Parliament
- Implementation: Commission, member states + European Court
- Review/feedback: Lobbyists, member states ...

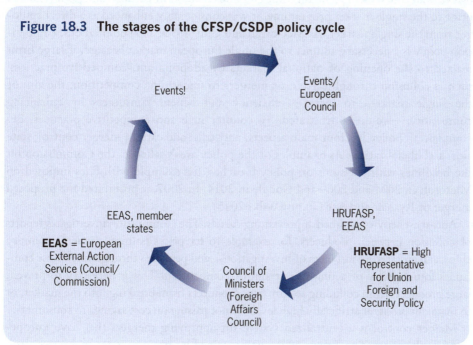

Figure 18.3 The stages of the CFSP/CSDP policy cycle

- Events/European Council
- HRUFASP, EEAS
  HRUFASP = High Representative for Union Foreign and Security Policy
- Council of Ministers (Foreign Affairs Council)
- EEAS, member states
  EEAS = European External Action Service (Council/Commission)
- Events!

CFSP/CSDP action is in response to global affairs, such as the Russian insurgency in eastern Ukraine or political instability in Libya. Not all policy is reactive to external events: some is concerned with development of European capacity and strategy. Nevertheless, Figure 18.3 indicates that agenda setting is in many cases the product of external challenges.

The policy cycle is useful to have in mind in the succeeding chapters, where individual policies are considered. We have selected those policy areas that we consider the most important (see Wallace, Pollack, and Young, 2015, 8th edn 2020, for wider coverage).

Major Policy Areas

There are several major policy areas for which it is not possible to include full chapters in this book but of which it is well worth being aware. These are policies that have considerable practical significance in their own right, and that have attracted a certain amount of academic attention as well. They are: competition, employment and social policy, cohesion policy, energy, research, and transport. Most of these can be justified either through independent functional arguments, as spillover from the single European market, or as part of efforts to build European policy capacity. The academic analyses also allow us to say more about the political logic behind these policies.

Competition

Competition policy has been called the 'first common policy' of the EC/EU (McGowan and Wilks 1995). Yet, though some elements of competition policy existed prior to the single market programme, it was considerably enhanced as a direct spillover from the single market. As McGowan and Cini (1999: 177) pointed out, competition policy is a necessary adjunct to the single European market because, if large firms reacted to the opening of national markets by adopting anti-competitive practices, such as collusion through cartels, or mergers to undermine competition, the aim of the single market—to increase efficiency and benefit consumers by enhancing competition—would be frustrated. To counter such anti-competitive practices, EU competition policy has four main aspects: anti-trust and cartels, merger control, state aids, and liberalization. As examples of the policy area's salience, the Commission hit the headlines with decisions on policy breaches, for example with fines imposed on Microsoft in 2004 and 2009 and Google in 2014. In 2007, it prohibited the proposed merger of Ryanair and Aer Lingus (Wilks 2015).

Anti-trust activity is aimed at preventing cartels. The Commission investigates reports of collusion between producers, for example to fix prices (salmon, cement, memory chips, and air fares are instances of investigations), and penalizes through fines those companies found guilty of acting in restraint of competition. This is necessary to prevent large producers from colluding to stop new producers from breaking into the market, or to maintain profits at artificially high levels by not passing on cost savings to consumers.

Merger control is a centralized system for approving mergers that have Europe-wide implications. The Treaty of Rome contained no provisions for merger control. Various attempts by the Commission to persuade the member states to redress this omission failed, until the single market programme led to a big increase in the number of cross-border mergers (McGowan and Cini 1999: 178–9). Merger control was pushed to the top of the agenda by the ruling of the CJEU in the *Philip Morris* case (1987) that the power to prevent market domination through mergers could be inferred from other Articles of the Treaty. In this case, the Court acted as the EU's *agenda setter*. The ruling introduced a major element of uncertainty into the calculations of industry about how extensive the inferred powers of the Commission might be, and this uncertainty led in turn to demands from big companies for the member states to adopt clear legislation defining those limits. At the *decision making* stage, the Council of Ministers eventually adopted a regulation in December 1989, and it became effective in September 1990 (McGowan and Cini 1999: 180).

The Commission has considerable autonomy in merger control. At the *implementation* stage, a merger task force within the Directorate General (DG) for Competition considers proposed mergers. Merger control is very political because it raises issues such as whether large European companies should be allowed to emerge to act as 'European champions' in global competition with companies from the United States and Japan. This is the position particularly of French governments, and contrasts with the position of liberal governments, such as the Dutch, for whom the preservation of competition in the European market is key. Under the guidance of a series of Commissioners who have shown a strong commitment to the free-market interpretation, the Directorate General has moved in that direction, but all rulings have to be approved by the full College of Commissioners, and here the outcome is not always certain, as political considerations can intervene.

Politics is even more at the forefront of policy on state aids, which involves the Commission investigating instances where the government of a member state grants any of its own companies subsidies, loans, tax breaks, loan guarantees, or preferential purchase deals on goods and services, to ensure that this is not giving those companies an unfair competitive advantage. As Mitchell Smith (1998: 58) pointed out, the difference between merger control and state aids is that in the latter the Commission is confronting governments directly rather than just the firms involved.

Pursuing competition cases has always been a time-consuming process, and the Directorate General for Competition has long felt under-resourced and under pressure with *implementation*. With the prospect of further enlargement of the EU, the DG moved to involve national competition authorities more in the enforcement of EU competition law. This move was formally implemented in 2003 through a Council Regulation known as 'the Modernization Regulation' (1/2003). Since then, the Commission has operated within a formally constituted European Competition Network of national competition authorities, leaving its own expert staff to concentrate on particularly complex cases, especially those that have extensive cross-national implications and those that are most politically sensitive.

Competition policy therefore has a market-building character, is reliant on legal regulation, and applicable to all member states. In the context of the policy cycle, it is worth noting that the amount of competition policy legislation has been quite limited. Rather, much of the policy activity consists of the Commission using its implementing powers to act on anti-trust, cartel, merger, and state-aid matters.

Employment, Social Affairs, and Inclusion

From a focus on workers' rights in the early years of the European Economic Community (EEC), employment and social policy has come to emphasize the liberalization of labour markets in the context of the Lisbon Strategy (see Chapter 10, 'The Lisbon Strategy') to improve the global competitiveness of the EU.

At first, social policy was about the protection of workers' rights. The Treaty of Rome, generally a laissez-faire document, contained mention of the need to achieve social cohesion, to improve health and safety at work, to facilitate the free movement of labour, to promote equality between men and women in the workplace, to harmonize social security provision, and to promote a social dialogue between management and workers. The political reason for this focus was to create a level playing field of competition by imposing on all producers the same levels of protection for employees as applied in the most regulated markets. An example of this is gender equality, which was given its own Article of the Treaty of Rome (originally Article 119, now Article 157 TFEU) because France had extensive domestic legislation on equal pay between men and women before the EEC was set up, and wanted to ensure that the competitiveness of French companies was not damaged by this in comparison with other member states.

After the common market had been established, some of the first pieces of social legislation to be passed concerned the equal rights of women and men in work-related matters. The Equal Pay Directive of 1975 imposed a legal requirement of equal pay for equal work; the Equal Treatment Directive of 1976 made discrimination illegal in access to employment and training and in respect to rights concerning dismissal; and the Social Security Directive of 1978 required equal treatment in access to state benefits. All of these were rights that were already embodied in French domestic legislation, and the other member states came under intense pressure from trade unions and women's groups to adopt them at European level. That pressure was increased by the CJEU with its rulings in equality cases such as *Defrenne* (1978), in which it stated that although Article 119 (EEC) dealt explicitly with equal pay between men and women, the Article clearly established the principle of elimination of discrimination between men and women in the workplace as a fundamental principle of Community law.

Other than in legislation on gender equality, social policy had made little progress by the mid-1980s. European Commission President Jacques Delors tried to revive it by arguing that the single market needed a social dimension if it were to be acceptable to those who would initially lose out. Yet the member states were prepared to make only health and safety in the workplace subject to qualified majority voting (QMV) in the Single European Act (SEA).

Through his agenda setting, Delors laid the foundations for what at one stage looked like a promising approach to extending the social dimension. He instituted a 'social dialogue' with representatives of employers and employees at the European level, mainly involving the Union of Industries in the European Community (UNICE) and the European Trade Union Confederation (ETUC). Fundamental disagreements between the two sides meant that little progress was made in the early rounds of talks, but Delors managed to get the dialogue incorporated into the Social Protocol of the 1992 TEU (Maastricht Treaty), and it became part of the Social Chapter of the Treaty after the British Labour government signed up to the Protocol at Amsterdam in 1997.

Achievements during this phase of the social dialogue included on European Works Councils, enabling consultation between management and workers in European multinational companies, agreed in 1994 (Falkner 2000: 707–8). Subsequent directives were adopted on parental leave (adopted by Council in June 1996), and two on 'atypical work' in 1999—one on the rights of part-time workers and one on the rights of workers on fixed-term contracts (Falkner 2000: 709–11). By 1999, though, policy focus had moved away from protecting the rights of workers towards providing opportunities for work for the unemployed, including increased female participation in the workplace.

Persistent unemployment throughout the EU led to the introduction in the Amsterdam Treaty of a new title on Employment, which called for a 'co-ordinated strategy for employment'. A special 'jobs summit' was held in Luxembourg in November 1997, at which a strategy was agreed that became the model for what the later (2000) Lisbon European Council was to call the open method of co-ordination (OMC, see 'The European Union's Policy Agenda' above). The Luxembourg process involves agreement on a common set of European targets, with member states drawing up what were originally called National Action Plans for Employment (NAPs), which subsequently became National Reform Programmes (NRPs) that were submitted to the Commission and Council for scrutiny, and recommendations in response (Adnett 2001: 353–9). This annual review process was part of the Lisbon Strategy and the emphasis was on labour market liberalization. The Commission's review powers were strengthened in the Lisbon Strategy's successor—Europe 2020—because of the connection between improving the competitiveness of labour and the need to boost economic growth in the context of the eurozone crisis (see Chapter 11, 'The Unfolding Eurozone Crisis').

Although no member state is obliged to adopt a particular approach to achieving its objectives, the emphasis on emulating best practice has led to moves to free labour markets of restrictions and provide training for the unemployed, an approach more in line with the Anglo-Saxon model of capitalism than with the various continental models that have traditionally put more emphasis on protecting the rights of those in work. On the other hand, Adnett (2001: 360) reported that there was little evidence of a convergence of national policies, and that indeed in some areas there was evidence of increasing diversity.

Following the Lisbon European Council (2000), the OMC was also applied to social policy as more traditionally understood in the EU. At Lisbon, member states committed themselves to drawing up NAPs to combat poverty and social exclusion, to devise indicators for assessing progress, and to develop mechanisms for ensuring the achievement of objectives in these fields (Hodson and Maher 2001: 726, Table 1). These areas of policy were followed through the OMC because 'there was simply no political support for the further transfer of legal competencies to the EU in these areas' (Borras and Jacobsson 2004: 190).

In the area of employment and social policy, the OMC produced progress where the traditional method of European legislation was severely hindered by the lack of any consensus over priorities, and where the prospect of more such legislation risked further damaging the legitimacy of the EU. The result was to change the nature of the policy sector, both the content of policy outputs and the process. With regard to the latter the influence of the EP and the CJEU was weakened by their effective and formal exclusion from the OMC, putting the states in control of the design and implementation of EU social policies, marginalizing both the Commission and the social partners (Edquist 2006; Gold et al. 2007). This pattern reflected the trends found in the new intergovernmentalism (see Chapter 1, 'New Intergovernmentalism'). Substantively, the OMC approach changed the nature of policy, for a while sidelining the social dialogue. One effect was to introduce more diversity into policy and policy making.

In 2017, the EU launched an initiative to try and breathe new life into the policy area by strengthening longer-standing processes. The European Pillar of Social Rights was launched by the Commission and proclaimed by the Council and the EP at a meeting in Gothenburg that was attended by social partners. The pillar was concerned with delivering new, more effective rights for citizens in three particular domains: equal opportunities and access to the labour market; fair working conditions; and social protection and inclusion. This initiative was an attempt to respond to the adverse impact on workers and welfare systems of the financial and eurozone crises. As part of strengthening the policy area, in 2019 the Commission introduced a discussion paper (European Commission 2019*g*). In the context of the Commission's 2017 White Paper on the future of the EU, the Commission also considered using the Lisbon Treaty's so-called *passerelle* clauses (see Chapter 12, '*Passerelle* Clauses') to introduce QMV provisions in the few remaining parts of the policy area where the Treaty continues to provide for unanimous voting in the Council.

Over time this policy area, which comprises different issues, has shifted priorities and methods of governance. Responding to the consequences of globalization, the eurozone crisis, and the rise of populism, attempts are now being made to improve labour rights (*market correction*), whereas earlier initiatives over recent decades have emphasized labour market liberalization (*market building*).

Cohesion Policy

Cohesion policy, understood here as being concerned with territorial cohesion, can be traced back to the European Regional Development Fund (ERDF) that was set up in the early 1970s (Bache et al. 2015: Chapter 22). It is an explicitly redistributive, market-correcting policy aimed at correcting disparities between regions of the EU. At several stages of integration, enlargement has spurred on the policy. Similarly, it has been used as side-payments to less-developed member states, helping them to agree to policy developments from which they might not be the main beneficiaries. Cohesion policy is delivered through the European Structural and Investment Funds (ESIF). These currently comprise:

- the ERDF, which promotes balanced development across the EU's different regions;
- the European Social Fund (ESF), which invests in Europe's human capital—its workers, its young people, and jobless, thus linking in a regionally focused manner with the employment and social cohesion initiatives just discussed;
- the Cohesion Fund (CF), which supports transport and environment projects in member states where the gross domestic product (GDP) per capita is less than 90 per cent of the EU average (from 2014–20: Bulgaria, Croatia, Cyprus, the Czech Republic, Estonia, Greece, Hungary, Latvia, Lithuania, Malta, Poland, Portugal, Romania, Slovakia, and Slovenia);
- the European Agricultural Fund for Rural Development (EAFRD), which focuses on the competitiveness, environmental sustainability, and balanced territorial development in rural areas;
- and the European Maritime and Fisheries Fund (EMFF), which supports adaptation of the fisheries sector, including through encouraging diversification and sustainability.

The origins of the ERDF can be traced back to the first EU enlargement in 1973. Amongst the incoming member states, the UK and Ireland were keen on the policy, while Italy as an existing state was also a protagonist. In the case of Ireland and Italy, it was their need to address regional equality that was the primary motivation, while the UK was searching for a tangible benefit flowing from membership, given domestic contestation over membership and the recognition that British agriculture was too small to benefit from the main expenditure policy of the EC, the CAP.

As has been the underlying principle with all these funds, the ERDF relied on co-funding from the member states. This placed the member states in a key position with regard to implementing the policy. As the UK came to realize the increasing levels of its net contributions to the EC budget (Chapter 8, 'The British Budget Rebate'), it sought to undermine the European Commission's efforts to make ERDF money additional to existing domestic resources. The UK government regarded the policy as a way of reimbursing budget contributions (Bache 1998). It took several reforms before this issue could be resolved.

The term 'cohesion policy' came into usage with the coincidence of Spanish and Portuguese accession in 1986 with the commitment to the single market programme. Their accession increased the number of EC regions with a per capita GDP less than 50 per cent of the EC's average. As these regions would be under particular pressure in the heightened competition of the single market, Article 130A SEA 1987 (now Article 187 TFEU) set out the need to strengthen 'economic and social cohesion' within the EC, in particular through 'reducing disparities between the various regions and the backwardness of the least-favoured regions' (European Commission 1989: 11). Consequently, cohesion policies (regional and social) were developed and expanded to limit these effects.

Cohesion policy has undergone periodic reform to update its objectives in light of the wider policy context of the EU, as well as further rounds of enlargement (Bache 2015; Bache et al. 2015: Chapter 22). These reforms occurred in 1988, 1993, 1999, 2006, and 2013, and another is under negotiation for 2020. The 1993 reform was notable for introducing the CF as a side-payment to poorer states at the time when the EU had committed to monetary union. The 1999 reform was made in anticipation of the forthcoming eastern enlargement of the EU. In the 2006 reform, the structural funds were explicitly linked to the Lisbon Strategy for raising the EU's competitiveness (see Chapter 10, 'The Lisbon Strategy'). The 2013 reform was focused around 'investment for jobs and growth' (against the backdrop of the financial and eurozone crises) and 'European territorial co-operation'. By now, cohesion policy was commanding substantial budgetary resources: in 2013, 38.1 per cent of the EU budget (Bache 2015: 259).

At each successive reform, the principles of cohesion policy were reviewed and reformed. Additionality of funding and partnership with member-state authorities have been ever-present commitments. At the same time, the precise focus of the funding has been redefined in light of the challenges perceived at the time. Box 18.2 sets out the scale of the policy commitments during the period 2014–20.

With cohesion policy subject to a seven-year review-and-reform cycle, it has become an integral part of the parallel process of setting the EU's multi-annual financial framework (MFF) (see Chapter 12, 'The Budgetary Procedure'). The debate

> **Box 18.2 Cohesion Policy Funding 2014–20**
>
> Total of up to €325.1 billion:
>
> - 'Investment for growth and jobs': €313.2 billion—€164.3 billion for less developed regions; €31.7 billion for transition regions; €49.5 billion for more developed regions; €66.4 billion for member states supported by the CF;
> - 'European territorial co-operation': €8.9 billion;
> - 'Top-up for youth employment initiative': €3.0 billion.

concerning the forthcoming MFF and reform of cohesion policy has had to take into account the loss of the UK's budgetary contributions in the context of Brexit.

Cohesion policy has offered the clearest evidence of multi-level governance in operation, although there remains considerable analytical contention. Alongside agriculture (see Chapter 21), cohesion has become a key market-correcting policy in the EU.

Energy

Energy is a policy area where objectives have changed as a result of changing circumstances. Prompted by the experience of the single market, from the 1990s the main objective of energy policy for the Commission was the liberalization of national markets, which were dominated by monopolistic national suppliers. This resulted in high energy costs, which damaged the global competitiveness of European manufacturers. The situation came to the fore in the aftermath of the single market programme, with the Commission acting as a policy entrepreneur to cultivate spillover. This story is told in a later chapter (see Insight 19.3).

Once the principle had been established that national energy markets would be opened up to competition from other member states, the potential existed to shift other aspects of energy policy to the EU level. In 2004, the Commission identified problems concerning the high level of dependence of the EU on fossil fuels and on imported sources of energy, such as Russian gas. Fossil fuels are finite, and burning them contributes to global warming. The supply of imported energy is liable to disruption from international crises, which can also increase prices quite dramatically. In consequence, the need arose to develop co-ordinated programmes to save energy, to use it more efficiently, and to develop alternative sources.

In 2005, the European Council approved the development of a comprehensive European energy strategy, and, in 2006, the Commission produced a Green Paper outlining such a strategy (European Commission 2006a). The first Commission proposals to implement this strategy were brought forward in January 2007, including the introduction of binding targets for each member state to switch to the use of renewable energy sources—biomass, hydro, wind, and solar—by 2020. The Council also accepted these proposals.

The Commission used concerns raised by wider global developments, particularly concern about the security implications of an over-reliance on energy from unstable parts of the world and about climate change, to expand its competence beyond those concerned with opening the market to cover these other issues. The Commission also recognized spillover from energy policy into both transport and research policy. Thus, the transfer of energy supply from a national to a European market brought in its train the prospect of whole new areas of competence for the EU. The Lisbon Treaty amended the wording of Title XXI of the TFEU on energy policy to reflect these revised policy objectives, emphasizing security of supply and the need to achieve energy efficiency and energy saving in the context of environmental concerns.

Energy policy came into its own as a *market-building* policy, extending the single market to the liberalization of energy supply within the EU. However, climate change concerns have changed the emphasis to *market cushioning*. Externally, the policy faces a different challenge, namely where member states seek their own energy supply arrangements, risking the principle of solidarity in relation to energy security. This situation is illustrated most graphically by Nordstream 2, a gas pipeline under construction that links Russia with Germany (via the Baltic seabed) and risks diverting trade and transit revenues away from some other member states.

Transport

A common transport policy was one of the Titles of the original Treaty. There is an obvious functional necessity for efficient cross-border transport, to make a reality of the ideal of a common market, and a functional logic to organizing it at the European level. Arising from this, the European Commission has responsibility for the planning and part-financing of trans-European networks (TENs) for different modes of transport. Despite several statements of support for the TENs, though, the member states have never been prepared to provide adequate funding, so that the programme is always lagging behind the aspirations.

Spillover from the single market programme allowed the Commission to push through measures to open national transport markets to competition. The liberalization of air transport contributed to a reduction in fares and a consequent increase in passengers; and the liberalization of rail transport, which began with the implementation of a first package of measures in March 2003, held out the prospect of opening 70–80 per cent of rail freight traffic over main lines to competition. In the road haulage industry, internationally competitive firms had long argued against the principle of cabotage with respect to loads, a principle that had reserved to national transport firms the right to transport national goods. This had meant that lorries carrying goods from their own state to another member state had to return home empty, which was obviously economically inefficient. It was possible to get agreement on the abolition of this principle once the single market was in operation. During this phase, transport policy was about *market-building* measures.

As with other policy sectors, different problems were exacerbated by the opening of the markets, and these provided a continuing agenda for action by the Commission, including a White Paper on Transport in 2001 and another in 2011. The latter is particularly concerned with:

- improving transport and mobility in the EU, while at the same time meeting the target of reducing greenhouse gas (GHG) emissions by 60 per cent;
- completing a single European transport area across all modes of transportation;
- improving technology and infrastructure for transport; and
- making sure these goals are included as necessary in international trade deals.

355

The White Paper (European Commission 2011) included an ambitious set of specific objectives on everything from improved mobility, increased road safety, and transport security to increased transport sustainability and the phasing out of conventionally fuelled cars from cities by 2050. As with energy policy, the inclusion of sustainability goals has added a *market-cushioning* dimension to policy.

Research and Innovation

Although a European technological community had been part of the original vision of Jean Monnet, technological research was not included in the Treaty of Rome. The breakthrough occurred in 1982, after advocacy by the Commission, with the Council of Ministers' approval of the European Strategic Programme in Information Technology (ESPRIT).

The reasons for this breakthrough were similar to those that brought about the even bigger breakthrough of the single market programme (see Chapter 19, 'Explaining the Single Market'). The weak recovery of Europe from the 1979 oil-price shock, in comparison with the vigorous recovery of the United States and Japan, showed that the policy of supporting national champions was clearly not working. It was increasingly apparent that the United States and Japan had a range and scale of research and technological development programmes that no individual European state could afford to match (Peterson 1992: 231).

Those were the structural factors that made the 1982 breakthrough feasible. Agency was provided by Étienne Davignon, the EC's Commissioner for Industry from 1977 to 1985. Davignon responded to the concern about Europe's technological performance in electronics by convening the 'Big 12 Round Table' of leading European electrical and electronics firms. Here, then, was a prime example of the Commission, in the form of Davignon, playing the role of a policy entrepreneur: identifying a problem, suggesting a solution at the European level, and then working with a transnational network of producers as allies in the private sector to bring pressure to bear on governments to adopt a European solution.

Once the principle of centrally funded research was established in the field of electronics and information technology, other industries soon began to demand that they get similar support. Research and technology policy was formally incorporated into the Treaties with the 1986 SEA, thus giving the policy process greater institutional underpinning. A whole series of multi-annual 'Framework Programmes'—the first being 1984–87, before Treaty provision had taken effect—served to put the policy into practice. In the 2000s, these programmes became closely linked to the Lisbon Strategy to boost the EU's competitiveness.

The Eighth Framework Programme, covering the period 2014–20, was given the title *Horizon 2020* (echoing the EU's updated 'Europe 2020' programme for economic competitiveness) and allocated a budget of approximately €70 billion, a big percentage increase over the allocation to its predecessor the Seventh Framework Programme. It was divided into three pillars:

- Pillar 1: Excellent Science, to support cutting-edge scientific projects;
- Pillar 2: Industrial Leadership, to improve Europe's industrial competitiveness;
- Pillar 3: Societal Challenges, to address health and other societal issues.

Instead of funding specific topics, as in the past, *Horizon 2020* aimed to fund horizontal research on tackling challenges such as climate change or demographic change.

A successor programme, called Horizon Europe, covers the period 2021–27. Each new multi-annual programme follows on from a *review* of the performance of its predecessor. One thing looks likely to change with Horizon Europe: it will be without the participation of a big player in science: Britain. The Commission has sought a budget of €100bn across the time period. Horizon Europe sees a re-naming of the pillars:

- Pillar 1: Open Science, to support frontier research;
- Pillar 2: Global Challenges and Industrial Competitiveness, which in many ways combines the goals of pillars 2 and 3 under Europe 2020;
- Pillar 3: Open Innovation, to make the EU a world leader in innovation, supported by a European Innovation Council and a European Institute of Innovation and Technology.

Research and innovation policy is distinctive amongst the policy areas considered in this section. Legislation is limited in nature. Rather, the policy is driven by budgetary resources and in many cases in partnerships between funding agencies or with universities and other bodies. This means that the policy cycle is applicable to each Framework Programme, and linked to approval of the multi-annual financial framework which determines the budget. The bulk of policy relates to approving projects for funding, in a manner that resembles cohesion policy. The policy area is about policy interventions in a *market-correcting* direction.

There are numerous other policies that we cannot consider in the textbook: from consumer protection to humanitarian aid (See Table 18.1). In the chapters that follow, we consider the most important policies, deploying the theories from Part One of the book and the classification of policy set out in 'The European Union's Policy Agenda' above.

CONCLUSION

One of the first conclusions that leaps out from this brief review of the policy process and of various policy sectors is the diversity of EU policy and policy making. As suggested by governance and networks approaches (see Chapter 2, 'Governance' and 'Policy Networks'), different rules and practices are important in different policy areas, and even within them. Making sense of EU policy and policy making therefore requires some way of classifying the differences between them. We offered a classification system based on the competencies possessed by the EU; the economic or political purpose of the policy; the policy instruments used; and the presence/absence of differentiated integration (see Table 18.1). The characteristics of individual policies are not fixed: they may change over time, as policies are reformed or circumstances change.

In reviewing the policy cycle, it becomes apparent that a number of policies have come onto the EU agenda because of spillover from the single market, which highlights the continuing theoretical relevance of neofunctionalism (see Chapter 1, 'Neofunctionalism'). The validity of neofunctionalism is also clear in the role played by the Commission in exploiting the spillover pressures to engineer transfers of competence to the EU, often through forming alliances with interest groups. However, the persistent importance of the European Council, the strongest institutional manifestation of intergovernmentalism, highlights that this theory is also extremely pertinent to the development of the EU's policy portfolio. The resilience of national sovereignty has also been found in the practice of differentiated integration and resort to the OMC in a number of policy areas. Both developments allow member governments to keep a tighter control over developments. They also point to the importance of new forms of policy instrument, beyond legislation and regulation.

KEY POINTS

The European Union's Policy Agenda

- The EU's policies vary according to the competence given to the EU, as set down in the Lisbon Treaty.
- Policies can be classified as market building, market correcting, market cushioning, and political.
- The policy instruments used differ according to policy.
- The growth of differentiated integration has introduced further variation between policy areas.

The European Union's Policy Cycle

- Policy agendas are composed of problems that governments face as a result of domestic political pressure and/or international developments.
- Issues on domestic policy agendas are pushed up to the EU level because of functional logic, arising from spillover from other EU policies
- The European Council is ultimately responsible for adding issues to the European agenda, highlighting the continuing importance of member governments.
- The Commission is key to the policy-formulation stage.
- The Council and Parliament are the key actors in decision making.
- Implementation is in most cases the responsibility of member-state authorities, with supranational oversight by the Commission and the CJEU as adjudicator.
- The CFSP has a policy cycle of its own because of its different legal basis that privileges national governments.

Major Policy Areas

- Competition policy developed largely through spillover from the common market and single market. It is an area in which the Commission has considerable autonomy, but in exercising its powers it is often brought into conflict with individual national governments.
- Employment and social affairs have varied in emphasis over the decades and combine legislative and new governance approaches.
- In the energy sector, spillover from the single market allowed the Commission to mobilize a coalition of industrial users of energy in favour of liberalization of national energy markets. It then became logical to handle security of supply and environmental effects at the EU level.
- A similar process operated for transport: spillover from the single market allowed the Commission to push through liberalization of national markets, and then other issues such as sustainable transport needed to be handled at the European level.
- Research policy started with the ESPRIT programme in the electronics and information technology sectors. Multi-annual programmes have evolved over the subsequent period through to *Horizon 2020* and its successor from 2021, Horizon Europe.

For additional material and resources, please visit the online resources www.oup.com/uk/bache5e.

QUESTIONS

1. How can we distinguish between the characteristics of different EU policy areas?
2. How valuable is the notion of a 'policy cycle' for understanding EU policy making?
3. Which institution do you consider to be the EU's agenda setter?
4. How and why are the characteristics of foreign and security policy making so different from those of policy areas such as the single market or monetary union?
5. In what ways do employment/social policy and cohesion depart from market-making policies such as the single market?

FURTHER READING

A valuable textbook on policy making and the policies is **L. Buonanno and N. Nugent**, *Policies and Policy Processes of the European Union* (Basingstoke: Palgrave Macmillan, 2013). An alternative text with wider policy coverage is **H. Wallace, M. Pollack, Roederer-Rynning, C. and A. Young (eds)**, *Policy-Making in the European Union* (Oxford: Oxford University Press, 8th edn, 2020). There are individual chapters to follow up on several of the 'other policies' included in this chapter—competition, energy, research, and social/employment policy.

Also useful for reading beyond this chapter is **E. Versluis, M. van Keulen, and P. Stephenson**, *Analyzing the European Union Policy Process* (Basingstoke: Palgrave Macmillan, 2011). Chapters 9–11 of **H. Lelieveldt and S. Princen**, *The Politics of the European Union* (Cambridge: Cambridge University Press, 2nd edn, 2015) also offer useful material on EU policy making.

On the OMC, it is worth consulting **S. Borras and K. Jacobsson**, 'The Open Method of Co-ordination and New Governance Patterns in the EU', *Journal of European Public Policy*, 11 (2004): 185–208.

Chapter 19

The Single Market

Chapter Overview

Although the European Union (EU) is much more than just a common market, the economic ideal of a common or single European market lies at the core of its 'market-building' agenda (see Chapter 18, 'The European Union's Policy Agenda'). The aspiration to create a common market was fundamental in the decision in the mid-1950s to set up the European Economic Community (EEC). Thirty years later, the decision to institute a drive to achieve a single internal market by the end of 1992 was fundamental to the revival of European integration.

This chapter looks at the original decision to create a common market, the patchy record of progress from the 1960s through to the 1980s, then at the moves to complete the internal market—what became known as the single market programme—in the 1980s. It reviews the development of internal market policy, the record of implementation beyond 1992, and it outlines recent policy developments in relation to the single market in the context of the eurozone crisis, which began in 2009. Finally, it considers the academic literature on the single market, outlining the main explanations for its development and exploring some key ideological or normative perspectives on its consequences.

History

Article 9 of the Treaty of Rome (EEC) stated, 'The Community shall be based upon a **customs union**.' Also, a substantial section of the Treaty was devoted to the free movement of persons, services, and capital (now Articles 45–66 Treaty on the Functioning of the European Union (TFEU)). Together, these objectives constitute the construction of a common or single European market (SEM). Progress in achieving them has varied over time.

The decision to create a common market reflects two of the main motivations for setting up the EEC: to avoid any return to the national protectionism that had been economically disastrous for Europe between the world wars, and to promote economic expansion by creating a large internal market for European producers that would rival the large US market. The history of the decision is recounted in Chapter 6.

It was clear that the creation of a customs union would result in an uneven distribution of benefits and losses between the member states; although the precise distribution of those benefits and losses could not be predicted in advance, there were reasonable grounds for believing that West German industry might gain more than French industry would. That is why French negotiators were anxious to ensure that other commitments were made in the Treaty of Rome, to develop policies in areas in which their country could be expected to benefit more than West Germany, particularly agriculture (see Chapter 21). But the reason why the plunge was taken to create the EEC was that all six states expected their economies to be better off as a result of creating the internal market, even if some benefited more than others.

In 1960, the Council of Ministers took the decision to accelerate the original time-table for removing internal tariffs and quotas, and erect a common external tariff, so that the common market would be completed by 1968 instead of 1970.

All seemed to be progressing smoothly, until, in July 1965, President de Gaulle withdrew France from all participation in the work of the Council of Ministers, plunging the European Community (EC) into crisis (see Chapter 7, 'The 1965 Crisis'). This crisis was to blame for taking much of the momentum out of the EC. However, de Gaulle did not stop the completion of the customs union, which was complete by July 1968. He did cause a delay, though, in the implementation of the rest of the Treaty. The wait turned out to be much longer than just for the retirement of de Gaulle. By the time that Pompidou became President of France, and adopted a more accommodative attitude to the EC, world economic circumstances had begun to shift away from the high growth of the 1950s and 1960s. By the time that the negotiation of the entry of Britain, Ireland, and Denmark had been completed at the start of 1972, clearing the way for a further deepening of the level of economic integration, the capitalist world was teetering on the brink of recession, and was soon to be pushed over the edge by the Organization of Petroleum Exporting Countries (OPEC) (see Chapter 7, 'Into the 1970s').

Throughout the '**stagflation**' years of the 1970s, further progress on the creation of a genuinely free internal market became almost impossible (Hodges and Wallace 1981; Hu 1981). Given the economic problems that they were experiencing, and the political problems that resulted, governments became particularly prone to short-termism, and sensitive to the protectionist impulses of domestic interest groups and public opinion. This was not a favourable environment for strengthening the internal market. Indeed, throughout the 1970s, there was a marked retreat from the common market by the member states. Unable to raise tariffs or quotas against imports from other members of the EC, governments became adept at finding different ways of reserving domestic markets for domestic producers. Non-tariff barriers (NTBs) proliferated.

These NTBs took a wide variety of forms. Some, such as state aids to industry, were against the competition clauses of the EEC Treaty, and the Commission frequently took member states to the European Court of Justice (later named the Court of Justice of the EU—see Chapter 16—and hereafter, for purposes of clarity and consistency, referred to as the CJEU). However, the compliance of guilty states with the rulings of the CJEU was often tardy, and only effected once an alternative system for supplying the aid had been devised. The long process of investigation by the Commission, issuing of warnings, reporting to the CJEU, and waiting for the case to make its way to the top of the Court's increasingly long agenda, then had to begin all over again.

Other NTBs were more subtle. Particularly prevalent were national specifications on the safety of products, some of which were so restrictive that only nationally produced goods could meet them without modification to their basic design. Differing regulations could prevent a single manufacturer from producing on the same production line for the whole EC market; in effect, the market was fragmented into a series of national markets again. Governments also used border customs formalities to make importing difficult, and only placed public contracts with national companies (Pelkmans and Winters 1988: 16–53).

Project 1992: Freeing the Internal Market

In the mid-1980s, the situation in the EC began to change rapidly, again in response to the changing international economic environment. In June 1984, at the Fontainebleau meeting of the European Council (see also Chapter 8, 'Fontainbleau'), two major steps were taken in breaking out of the *immobilisme* that had been afflicting the EC. First, agreement was reached on the long-running dispute over British contributions to the Community's budget; second, a committee was set up to look into the need for reform of the institutional structure and decision making system of the EC.

At the beginning of 1985, a new Commission took office under the presidency of Jacques Delors, and in June 1985 Lord Cockfield, the British Commissioner for Trade and Industry, produced a White Paper on the freeing of the internal market from NTBs to trade in goods, services, people, and capital (European Commission 1985). This listed some 300 separate measures, later reduced to 279, covering the harmonization of technical standards, opening up **public procurement** to intra-EC competition, freeing capital movements, removing barriers to free trade in services, harmonizing rates of indirect taxation and excise duties, and removing physical frontier controls between member states (see Insight 19.1). The list was accompanied by a timetable for completion.

At the Milan European Council in June 1985, the heads of government accepted the objectives of the White Paper and the timetable for its completion by the end of 1992. It was also agreed, against the protests of the British Prime Minister, Margaret Thatcher, to set up an intergovernmental conference (IGC) to consider what reforms of the decision making process should accompany the initiative to free the market. The outcome of this IGC was the Single European Act (SEA), which was agreed by the heads of government at the Luxembourg European Council in December 1985, and eventually came into force, after ratification by national parliaments, in July 1987. It introduced qualified majority voting (QMV) into the Council of Ministers, but only for measures related to the freeing of the internal market, and even here certain areas—including the harmonization of indirect taxes and the removal of physical controls at borders—were excluded at British insistence.

Beyond 1992

The deadline of the end of 1992 was the target date for the Council of Ministers to agree all the 279 measures in the White Paper. To facilitate meeting the deadline, the Commission drew up a timetable for proposals to be made and to be agreed. As a result of this, over 95 per cent of the measures mentioned in the White Paper had been agreed by the end of 1992 (Calingaert 1999: 157). This remarkable record of success, however, needs to be set against three further considerations, as follows:

- Council agreements have to be implemented; thus, agreement in the Council did not in itself mean that the single market was working. Before that stage was reached, there were two further requirements: transposition and enforcement.

- The 5 per cent of the measures that had not been agreed included some of the most intractable and controversial in the White Paper.

- The White Paper did not cover some areas in which businesses wanted to see liberalization, because they were considered too controversial.

Insight 19.1 The Commission's White Paper on Freeing the Internal Market

The White Paper provided no simple definition of what 'freeing the internal market' constituted, but it dealt with four 'freedoms':

- the free movement of goods;
- the free movement of services;
- the free movement of labour;
- the free movement of capital.

The aim of the White Paper was to remove physical barriers, fiscal barriers, and technical barriers to these four freedoms of movement.

The removal of physical barriers was dealt with by a series of proposed directives to end elaborate border checks on goods crossing from one EC member state to another, which were costly in themselves and caused long delays.

The removal of fiscal barriers was dealt with in a series of proposals to harmonize rates of VAT and excise duties.

'Technical barriers' was a portmanteau term covering a range of different things, including national standards for products, barriers to the free movement of capital, the free movement of labour, and public procurement rules.

National standards were dealt with by the adoption of the so-called 'new approach'. This was based on the principle enunciated by the CJEU in its judgment in the *Cassis de Dijon* case (Case 120/78, 1979). Ruling that the German government had acted illegally in preventing the sale of a French liqueur in Germany because its alcohol content was lower than specified in German law, the CJEU stated that any product that could legally be offered for sale in one member state should also be allowed to be offered for sale in every other member state. The only exceptions permitted to the principle were those imposed on health-and-safety grounds. In order to overcome this potential barrier, the Commission proposed that minimum health-and-safety standards for all products should be laid down by two European standards authorities, each of which is known by the initial letters of its name in French: CEN (the European Committee for Standardization), and CENELEC (the European Committee for Standardization of Electrical Products). If products met these minimum standards, they would be awarded a 'c.e.' mark, and could not legally be prevented from being put on sale in any member state.

Barriers to the free movement of capital had already started to disappear within the EC, and the White Paper simply proposed to complete this process through three directives covering cross-border securities transactions, commercial loans, and access to stock exchanges in other countries.

Barriers to the free movement of labour were to be tackled by directives covering the extension of rights of residence that already existed for workers, to citizens who were not active members of the labour force (students, retired people, the unemployed), and guaranteeing non-discrimination in access to social and welfare benefits. The Commission also undertook to prepare guidance and draft directives on the mutual recognition of professional and educational qualifications.

Public procurement referred to the purchasing policies of public authorities, which in most member states discriminated in favour of national suppliers and contractors. The aim was to open the largest contracts to competitive bidding by firms from across the EC.

These difficulties post-1992 are reviewed below. It must be noted, though, that the single market programme has, overall, been a considerable success, and that the momentum has been maintained despite the problems.

Transposition and Enforcement

Once a directive has been agreed by the Council of Ministers, it has to be transposed into the national laws of the member states (see Chapter 12, 'Implementation'). This process was slower in some states than in others, which meant that there were transposition problems ongoing more than a decade after the 1992 agreement. The Commission kept a running tally of the record of member states on transposition, and published the results annually as a league table. Concern about the low level of transposition overall, and particularly in certain member states, led to agreement in 2003 on an Internal Market Strategy that set the target for every state of keeping its 'implementation deficit' below 1.5 per cent. This meant that, at any one time, no state should have failed to transpose more than 1.5 per cent of all single market directives that had been agreed at EU level. Some member states responded vigorously to the target. For example, Ireland more than halved its implementation deficit between May 2003 and January 2004 to get below 1.5 per cent. Other member states, however, responded less well to the target. Although there was variation in the performance of member states, a small group of persistent offenders emerged, consisting of France, Germany, Greece, Italy, and Luxembourg. At the other end of the spectrum, Denmark, Spain, Finland, and Britain (in approximate order of merit) consistently kept within the target (European Commission 2004a).

Even when the member states have transposed internal market legislation, it still has to be enforced, and the record of national governments on this is very variable. The Commission has had to deal with a constant flow of complaints from member states about infringements of the rules by other member states, although the records of different states vary considerably. Two areas in which the record on enforcement is particularly bad are those products for which there are no harmonized EU standards, and public procurement.

Where there is no uniform EU standard for a product, internal market regulations require national authorities to accept the standards of other member states. However, companies have often found their products being subjected to a battery of national test and certification requirements, especially in France and Germany.

Similar problems of non-recognition in the absence of harmonized standards have arisen in the services field, in which there has been a marked reluctance to recognize the qualifications of individual workers, thus putting limits on the free movement of labour. Barriers have also been placed in the way of service companies operating across frontiers.

On public procurement, despite EU directives obliging public authorities to advertise tenders for large contracts, very few contracts have been awarded to non-national firms, and concerns related to corruption persist.

Problem Areas

Some issues that were included in the White Paper proved particularly difficult for member states to agree on, and this is why only 95 per cent of the programme had been agreed by the end of 1992. Two that stand out are tax harmonization and company law. Arguably, agreement on both is necessary if there is to be a genuine single market in which companies can operate without regard to national boundaries. Without harmonization of taxes and a common company statute, companies that operate in several different states face a complex of regulations and paperwork. Others have argued from a broadly neofunctionalist perspective that the spillover pressures (see Chapter 1, 'Theories of European Integration') of a single market have even more significant implications, creating a logical impetus for integration in a range of politically sensitive areas, including public services of various kinds and monetary policy (see Chapter 20).

While the areas of tax and company law were included in the White Paper but did not lead to integration, other areas were not mentioned, but some integration did take place. Two notable examples were telecommunications and energy. These were identified by businesses in the EU as two of the areas that most raised their costs of production in comparison with the United States. They were omitted from the 1992 Programme because they were sectors that had traditionally been in public ownership in the member states, and they had a public service aspect to them. However, the Corfu European Council in June 1994 recognized that the extension of the internal market to telecommunications and energy was a priority action to raise European competitiveness. The Commission then tried, and to a certain extent succeeded, to liberalize these market sectors (see Insights 19.2 and 19.3), although it was considerably more successful in the case of telecommunications than in the energy sectors, largely because energy was more highly politicized within member states and the pressure for change was not so great. With increased concern in the early twenty-first century about energy supplies and about the need to reduce carbon emissions, though, it became possible to build on the loose agreements reached earlier and a new package was agreed in late 2009.

The Services Directive

Telecommunications and energy supply are specific examples of service industries, which as a whole proved to be much more difficult to liberalize than did trade in goods (see Insights 19.2 and 19.3). By 2005, only 20 per cent of sales of services in the EU were traded across frontiers. This slow progress led the Lisbon European Council in March 2000 to request that the Commission produce an action plan to remove barriers. Liberalizing services was part of the 'Lisbon Agenda' (see Chapter 10, 'The Lisbon

Insight 19.2 The Liberalization of Telecommunications

Telecommunications in Europe was traditionally dominated by national monopoly suppliers— the post, telegraph, and telephone (PTT) public utilities. Attempts by the Commission to involve itself in the sector prior to 1982 proved fruitless. It was a sector dominated by national policy communities, which collaborated with each other at the international level to preserve the status quo.

An opportunity was opened for the Commission by the implications of deregulation of the telecommunications market in the United States in the early 1980s. This led to pressure from the government of the United States for the EC to open its markets for telecommunications equipment. AT&T, which had been forced to open up its domestic operations, was anxious to recoup lost revenue by moving into Europe, and IBM was looking to diversify into what promised to be an increasingly profitable market (Dang-Nguyen et al. 1993: 103).

The Commission responded by commissioning a number of reports on how Europe was losing out to the United States following US deregulation. It also mobilized producer groups that had an interest in seeing an increase in the efficiency and a decrease in the cost of telecommunication services: the Union of Industrial and Employers' Confederations of Europe (UNICE), and the Information Technology User Group (INTUG).

Another element in the strategy was that the Commission tried to ride its project on the back of the single market programme. Its discourse on telecommunications drew heavily on the 1992 Programme. Its approach assumed that a single market required a common infrastructure, of which telecommunications would be a part. Thus, the creation of a European policy for telecommunications gathered momentum by association with the 1992 Programme (Fuchs 1994: 181).

Having established the legitimacy of a European policy for the sector, in 1987 the Commission produced a Green Paper on the *Development of the Common Market for Telecommunications, Services and Equipment*. This discussion document became the basis for the development of a policy in the sector much as the White Paper on the internal market had been the basis for the 1992 Programme. It advocated deregulation and increased competition, proposals that were consistent with developments in those member states that had begun to respond to the problem at national level, of which Britain was the leader.

The Green Paper advocated the separation of regulation of the sector from operation of the system, a reform that had already been introduced in Britain, France, and Germany; and the introduction of open network provision (ONP), so that rival operators could compete using a common infrastructure. A concession to the PTTs was that they would remain in control of the provision of network services.

In 1988, the year after the publication of the Green Paper, the Directorate General for Competition issued an administrative directive on the liberalization of the terminal-equipment market. The Commission argued that it had the right to act without specific approval by the Council of Ministers because it was acting in pursuance of Article 90(3) of the Treaty of Rome (EEC) (now Article 106(3) TFEU), under which the Commission is charged to ensure that special rights conferred on national companies by their governments do not prevent the completion of the common market. Although the Council of Ministers had approved the Green Paper—which listed liberalization of the market among its objectives—France, Belgium, Germany, and Italy took the Commission to the CJEU, alleging that it had exceeded its powers by not seeking the approval of the Council for the directive. In March 1991, the Court found in favour of the Commission.

With backing from the CJEU, and assisted by strong pressure on national governments from the users of telecommunications, the Commission managed to secure the passage of a series of directives between 1992 and 2002, when a telecommunications regulatory package was agreed that came into effect in 2003. This set up a framework for national regulation. In late 2009, agreement was reached on further reform that would create EU-wide regulation of the sector.

Insight 19.3 The Liberalization of Energy Supply

According to Matlary (1997), a similar approach to that used in the case of telecommunications was used to push forward a common energy policy. Like telecommunications, the energy sectors were dominated by national monopolists, which most commonly were publicly owned. An open market in energy was originally part of the White Paper on the single market, but the opposition of national monopoly suppliers led to it being excluded. However, the Commission returned to the issue in 1989, making proposals for a phased dismantling of national monopolies over the electricity grids and gas supply networks. The linking of energy policy to the single market programme was explicit. In April 1991, Sir Leon Brittan, the Commissioner for Competition Policy, said that there were two sectors that were vital to the internal market: telecommunications and energy.

It was unlikely that the national monopolists themselves would support liberalization moves, but the Commission was able to mobilize the support of large industrial users of energy, working through the existing institutionalized networks of UNICE and the European Round Table of Industrialists (ERT).

Negotiations in the Council of Ministers were protracted. The French government in particular was reluctant to end the monopoly of Electricité de France (EdF) over the distribution of electricity in France. It claimed that its primary concern was to protect the access of rural French domestic consumers to electricity at the same price as was available everywhere else in France. This was known as 'the public service argument'. However, it was also bowing to intense pressure from the *Confédération Générale du Travail* (CGT) trade union, which feared that liberalization would mean job losses.

Eventually, in June 1996, agreement was reached on a phased liberalization of electricity supply over six years, but it would only apply to large industrial users. The whole process of negotiation then had to be repeated to secure an agreement on liberalization of the market in gas supply, with the French government fighting as hard to protect the position of Gaz de France as it had to protect EdF. Eventually another compromise deal was reached in December 1997.

Strategy'). Following widespread consultations, in July 2002, the Commission published its *Report on the State of the Internal Market for Services*. This was followed in January 2004 by a proposed Services Directive (see Insight 19.4).

The Services Directive ran into vocal political opposition because it proposed to apply to services the 'country-of-origin principle' that had applied to trade in goods since the *Cassis de Dijon* judgment of the CJEU in 1979 (see Insight 19.1 and Chapter 16, 'CJEU Rulings and Policy Impact'). Under the *Cassis* judgment, if a good could be sold legally in one of the member states, it could be sold legally in any member state. This meant that where there were no EU-level standards for a product, it had only to meet the national standards of the state in which it was produced, for it then to be

Insight 19.4 What is the Scope of the Services Directive?

The Services Directive applies to the provision of a **wide range of services**—to private individuals and businesses—barring a few specific exceptions. For example, it covers:

- **distributive trades** (including retail and wholesale of goods and services);
- the activities of most **regulated professions** (such as legal and tax advisers, architects, engineers, accountants, surveyors);
- **construction** services and **crafts**;
- **business-related services** (such as office maintenance, management consultancy, event organization, debt recovery, advertising, and recruitment services);
- **tourism** services (e.g. travel agents);
- **leisure** services (e.g. sports centres and amusement parks);
- **installation** and **maintenance** of equipment;
- **information society** services (e.g. publishing—print and web, news agencies, computer programming);
- **accommodation** and **food** services (hotels, restaurants, and caterers);
- **training** and **education** services;
- **rentals** and **leasing** services (including car rental);
- **real estate** services;
- **household support** services (e.g. cleaning, gardening, and private nannies).

The Services Directive does not apply to the following services, which are explicitly excluded:

- **financial** services;
- **electronic communications** services with respect to matters covered by other Community instruments;
- **transport** services falling into Title V of the EC Treaty;
- **healthcare** services provided by health professionals to patients to assess, maintain, or restore their state of health where those activities are reserved to a regulated health profession;
- **temporary work** agencies' services;
- **private security** services;
- **audiovisual** services;
- **gambling**;
- certain **social services** provided by the state, by providers mandated by the state, or by charities recognized as such by the state;
- services provided by **notaries** and **bailiffs** (appointed by an official act of government).

In any event, national rules and regulations relating to these excluded services have to comply with other rules of Community law, in particular with the freedom of establishment and the freedom to provide services as guaranteed in the Treaty on the Functioning of the European Union.

Source: Commission website: https://ec.europa.eu/growth/single-market/services/services-directive_en; http://ec.europa.eu © European Union, 1995–2019.

legally exported to any other member state. Although it had caused some protest at the time, this principle had come to be accepted for trade in goods. The application of the same principle to trade in services, though, was not readily accepted.

For services, the country-of-origin principle meant that if the company that provided a service met the legal requirements of the member state in which it was based, it could offer the service in other member states. This implied, for example, that a British building firm could build a house in Germany using British workers whose terms and conditions of employment complied with British law, even if they did not comply with German law. From the outset, this alarmed both employers and trade unions in those member states that had the highest wages and conditions of service. The concern really became focused, though, in the aftermath of the 2004 enlargement. Whereas there might be a small difference in employment standards between Britain and Germany, the differences between the established member states and the new entrants were considerable. Fierce opposition was mounted to the directive in the run-up to the 2004 European Parliament (EP) elections, especially in Germany, France, and Sweden. In France, the directive was given the name 'the Frankenstein directive', a rather poor pun on the name of the Commissioner who introduced it, Frits Bolkestein, suggesting that the directive was a monstrous creation that would destroy jobs and social consensus.

When the new Commission took office in late 2004, the Services Directive became the responsibility of the new Irish Commissioner for the Internal Market, Charlie McCreevy. He quickly indicated that he would listen to the criticisms that had been voiced, and consider amending the directive. Some such action was considered prudent because the directive had become one of the issues around which discontent had crystallized in the French debate and referendum on the EU Constitution (see Chapter 10, 'The Constitutional Treaty'). This did not mean that there were no underlying tensions: the new member states in particular were extremely keen to see the directive adopted in something like its existing form, as they expected to benefit considerably from it.

The directive was finally adopted on 12 December 2006, with a deadline for transposition into national legislation of 28 December 2009. At first reading, the EP removed the Commission's proposed country-of-origin principle. In its final form, the directive explicitly stated that its provisions did not affect national labour laws. The EP also excluded from the directive some of the most controversial services: broadcasting; postal services; audiovisual services; public transport; gambling; healthcare. The EP also successfully provided member states with a series of legally valid excuses for restricting activity by non-national companies, including national security, public health, and environmental protection. Notwithstanding these apparent safeguards, it is notable that, according to some commentators, subsequent CJEU rulings on freedom of establishment and services challenged national social and collective labour rights (Scharpf 2010 and see 'Evaluating the Single Market' below).

The Single Market beyond the Eurozone Crisis

The post-2009 eurozone crisis (see Chapters 11, 'The Unfolding Eurozone Crisis' and 20, 'The Eurozone Crisis') had important repercussions for the functioning of the single market. It led to a substantial decline in intra-EU trade and, as with previous economic crises, raised concern among supporters of the single market that this downturn would prompt a significant upsurge in economic nationalism and protectionism.

369

It was against this crisis backdrop that then Commission President Barroso (2005–14) asked former Commissioner Mario Monti (who was also briefly interim Italian Prime Minister during the crisis—see Chapter 11, 'The Unfolding Eurozone Crisis') to write a report on the future of the single market. Entitled 'A New Strategy for the Single Market' (Monti 2010), the report amounted to a plea to populations and national governments to avoid economic nationalism and adopt further specific measures to promote market integration. Monti's report served as the basis for the two Commission communications, the Single Market Act (2011) and the Single Market Act II (2012). These communications established a set of priorities for single market reforms in a range of areas where further economic benefits might be had, including energy and transport networks, intellectual property, the digital economy, and services.

Under the Juncker Commission presidency (2014–19), three key priorities under the single market agenda were the creation of a 'capital markets union', the pursuit of a so-called 'digital single market', and the 'better regulation' agenda. In line with the single market commitment to the free movement of capital (and building on prior initiatives such as the Financial Services Action Plan (1999)) the former aimed to develop better integrated capital markets (markets in stocks and shares), reflecting a long-term ambition to emulate the US financial system. These integrated markets would, according to the Commission, absorb citzens' savings and facilitate greater investment in European businesses (especially small and medium-sized enterprises, SMEs) and foster much-needed economic growth in a post-crisis EU where the fiscal (tax-and-spend) capacities of member states (especially in the eurozone) were significantly constrained (Braun and Hübner 2018, see also Chapter 20). Such a union requires far-reaching alignment of rules and regulations in areas such as financial accountancy and law. While some steps were taken in this area, at the time of writing in 2019, work was ongoing.

The so-called 'Digital Single Market' agenda sought to remove regulatory and other barriers in relation to online and digital commercial activities. The elimination of mobile phone roaming charges in 2017 was an important achievement in this area. In 2019, work was ongoing in relation to, among other areas, e-commerce and copyright.

Finally, the 'Better Regulation' agenda was applied to all EU regulation from 2015. Its aim was to conduct robust impact assessements to increase the quality of EU rule making, in particular by assessing the efficiency of regulation and ensuring that burdens on business were not excessive.

Explaining the Single Market

There are four episodes in the story of the single market that have attracted attempts at explanation using theoretical perspectives: the original decision; the 1960 acceleration agreement; the successful initiative to complete the internal market by 1992; and the pattern of successes and failures in pursuit of this objective.

The Original Decision

The original commitment to create a common market is best explained using an intergovernmentalist framework. There might, though, be the possibility of constructing an explanation based on neofunctionalism (see Chapter 1, 'Neofunctionalism'), stressing spillover from the European Coal and Steel Community (ECSC) (see Chapter 6, 'The European Coal and Steel Community'). According to neofunctionalism, the success of the ECSC ought to have led other groups of producers to put pressure on their governments to extend the common market to their products so that they too could benefit. Yet there is no evidence that any national group of producers lobbied for the extension of the ECSC. So, the experience of the creation of the EEC does not lend support to the neofunctionalist concept of political spillover.

There is also little evidence of supranational actors playing a key role in the original decision. The proposal for the EEC originated with the Dutch government supported by the Belgian government, and was a revival of a scheme that they had long favoured and had implemented on a more limited scale between themselves in the form of the Benelux economic union. The initiative was taken by the political and administrative elites in small states, in pursuit of what they perceived as their national interest in being part of a larger economic grouping.

The Acceleration Agreement

Although the original decision to create a common market did not lend support to the neofunctionalist idea of spillover, the surprisingly rapid progress that was made in the 1960s towards achieving the common market did seem to do so. In particular, a decision taken by the Council of Ministers in 1960 to accelerate the original timetable for removing internal tariffs and quotas, and erecting a common external tariff, was celebrated by Leon Lindberg (1963: 167–205) as a graphic illustration of political spillover at work.

The EEC Treaty (Article 14) specified a precise timetable for the progressive reduction of internal tariffs. On the original schedule, it would have taken between eight and twelve years to get rid of all internal tariffs. This rather leisurely timetable reflected the concerns of some industrial groups about the problems of adjustment involved in ending national protection. However, once the Treaty was signed and it became obvious that the common market would become a reality, those same industrial interests responded to the changed situation facing them. Even before the Treaty came into operation on 1 January 1958, companies had begun to conclude cross-border agreements on co-operation, or to acquire franchised retail outlets for their products in other member states. They also started to put pressure on national governments to accelerate the timetable. Remarkably, the strongest pressure came from French industrial interests, which had opposed the original scheme for a common market.

According to Lindberg, such groups were supported in this endeavour by the Commission, which helped to 'cultivate' this spillover (see Chapter 1, 'Neofunctionalism'). It should be noted, though, that this neofunctionalist interpretation has been challenged from a liberal intergovernmentalist perspective (Moravcsik 1998: 159–237)

The 1992 Programme

The decision to adopt the 1992 Programme provoked a fierce academic debate about the explanation. All voices in this debate agreed that structural factors favoured the single market. The differences concerned the role of supranational versus national actors.

371

The structural context was the sluggish recovery of the European economies from the post-1979 recession in comparison with the vigorous growth of the US and Japanese economies. In particular, the tide of direct foreign investment turned, so that, by the mid-1980s, there was a net flow of investment funds from western Europe to the United States. This augured badly both for the employment situation in Europe in the future, and for the ability of European industry to keep abreast of the technological developments that were revolutionizing production processes. European industrialists indicated that what would be most likely to encourage them to invest in Europe would be the creation of a genuine continental market such as that which they experienced in the United States. It was therefore in an attempt to revive investment and economic growth that governments embraced the single market programme.

While there was scholarly agreement on this part of the explanation, disagreement arose over which institutions were responsible for turning the concern with the competitiveness of the EC into a positive programme for action. From a position that was close to neofunctionalism, although missing the commitment to the key neofunctionalist concept of spillover, various analysts emphasized the role of the Commission, the CJEU, and of supranational business interests. This analysis, though, was comprehensively contested by Andrew Moravcsik (1991a).

Cowles (1995) made among the strongest cases for the importance of business interests and notably the ERT (see also, for a critical perspective, van Apeldoorn 2002). Sandholtz and Zysman (1989) also noted the importance of the ERT, but emphasized the role of the Commission: 'The renewed drive for market unification can be explained only if theory takes into account the policy leadership of the Commission' (1989: 96). In their explanation, the Commission manipulated a conjunction of international events and domestic circumstances to push forward the process of European integration, much as neofunctionalists had expected it would back in the 1960s. It was seen as providing the essential leadership to exploit the prevailing international and domestic circumstances. In one of the earliest assessments of the single market programme, Stanley Hoffmann (1989), who had been the main advocate of intergovernmentalism in the 1960s (see Chapter 1, 'Intergovernmentalism'), emphasized the particular importance of Commission President, Jacques Delors.

Before assuming office in January 1985, Delors spent much of the autumn of 1984 casting around for a 'big idea' that would provide a focus and an impetus for the incoming Commission (Grant 1994: 70). Institutional reform, monetary union, and defence co-operation were all considered, but eventually the completion of the single market was chosen. There were two main reasons for this decision. First, extensive consultations indicated that each of the other possibilities would be strongly resisted by the governments of some member states, but the opening up of the European market would command general support. Second, Delors believed that market integration would inevitably bring other important issues onto the agenda. For example, it would only be possible to pass all of the laws necessary to complete the single market if there were a reform of the decision making process; in addition, movement towards a more integrated market would raise the question of monetary integration.

So, Delors was instrumental in giving the single market objective a high priority, and he encouraged business interests (notably the ERT) to bring pressure to bear on governments to support the single market programme, so utilizing a transnational network to push forward the issue. He commissioned the Cecchini Report (Cecchini

1988) of leading European economists to put the weight of technical experts behind the project. Delors acted as a policy entrepreneur, recognizing an opportunity to promote a policy that went with the grain of existing thinking, that would increase the level of integration between the member states, and that would put other integrative measures onto the agenda in its wake.

Moravcsik (1991*a*) contested these neofunctionalist or supranational accounts. He considered two broad explanations for developments that furthered European integration: supranational institutionalism and intergovernmental institutionalism. His first category, supranational institutionalism, covered explanatory factors such as pressure from the EC institutions (primarily the EP and the CJEU), lobbying by transnational business interests, and political entrepreneurship by the Commission; it was therefore a model consistent with neofunctionalist theory. Moravcsik tested it against the empirical evidence relating to the SEA and found it wanting. He argued that the EP was largely ignored in the negotiation of the SEA; the transnational business groups came late to the single market, when the process was already well under way as a result of a consensus between governments on the need for reform; and the Commission's White Paper on the single market was 'a response to a mandate from the member states' rather than an independent initiative from a policy entrepreneur (Moravcsik 1991*a*: 45–8).

His second category, intergovernmental institutionalism, stressed bargains between states, marked by lowest-common-denominator bargaining and the protection of sovereignty. It was an example of what Keohane (1984) had described as the 'modified structural realist' explanation of the formation and maintenance of international regimes, but it took more account of domestic politics. Moravcsik (1991*a*) endorsed this explanatory approach, which was in line with the liberal intergovernmental theory (Chapter 1, 'Liberal Intergovernmentalism') that he later elaborated more fully (1993, 1998). He emphasized, in particular, the importance of the convergence of the preferences of key states—particularly France, Germany, and Britain—in support of 1992 project.

Bulmer (1998), summarizing the insights from research conducted and published by Armstrong and Bulmer (1998), argued that both neofunctionalist and intergovernmentalist accounts oversimplified the relationship between the actors. While Moravcsik was formally correct to stress that the Cockfield White Paper was a response to a request from the heads of government, the request came from the European Council. Although the Commission is not a formal member of the European Council, it has 'insider status' at these meetings, and Delors was able to use his position at the table to press the case for the SEM. For Bulmer, this privileged access, and the use made of it by Delors, illustrated the importance of institutional arrangements: an important aspect of the new (historical) institutionalist approach (see Chapter 2, 'New Institutionalism').

The Success of the Programme

Bulmer (1998) also provided an historical institutionalist explanation for the success of the 1992 Programme. Once it was launched, the single market framework changed the context within which the EC operated. A new logic operated on governments holding the presidency; the CJEU became very important in interpreting the new commitments; and new norms were spread throughout the EC.

Once the single market programme was accepted and publicized, governments holding the presidency found themselves under pressure to record a high rate of success on both the passage of directives and the transposition of directives into national legislation. A successful presidency was now judged partly on that record.

In every one of the six case studies looked at by Armstrong and Bulmer (1998), the role of the CJEU in handing down judgments on contested interpretations of the rules was significant. Given the clear and explicit commitment of the member states to the single market programme, these judgments favoured free-market interpretations. For example:

> In air transport, the EC had played next to no regulatory role until the 1980s. The ECJ's [CJEU's] ruling that existing bilateral regulatory arrangements were illegal, combined with the QMV introduced by the SEA, made liberalization inevitable and thus skewed things in favour of states advocating, and with expertise on, such a policy (the UK and the Netherlands).

(Bulmer 1998: 380)

Alongside the intervention of the CJEU, applying the new norms that had been incorporated into interpretation of existing EC law by the adoption of the single market programme, the above quotation makes clear that the move to QMV in the Council of Ministers on single market measures was also important to the success of liberalization in this sector.

From the perspective of historical institutionalism, the success of the single market programme can be explained by the way in which the SEA changed the formal rules, and the adoption of the single market programme changed the normative context within which those rules were operated.

Evaluating the Single Market

Not all scholarly engagement with the single market has been primarily explanatory in nature. As suggested above, both its character and its impact have been politically contested. Normative or ideological contestation of this sort is also present within the academic literature, particularly among political economists (see Table I.1). Unlike a mainstream European integration literature described in 'Explaining the Single Market' above, the focus of such scholarship is not primarily on the extent of market integration or on the question of whether its key drivers have been nation-states or other actors. Rather, it is interested in the impact of such integration on national social settlements and European society at large.

Majone (1996) is among the advocates of the SEM (see also Insight 2.1). For him the single market project has allowed the EU to emerge as a regulatory centre which ensures a credible and efficient European marketplace. His account connects developments in Europe with more general moves towards regulatory modes of governance globally since the 1970s, particularly in the United States. He understands the willingness of member states to delegate regulatory competences to the EU in terms of their desire to overcome the above-mentioned issues of regulatory competition and the strategic use of regulation (e.g. to gain a competitive advantage in a particular area).

This delegation involves a transfer of policy-making responsibilities from the domain of what Majone terms a 'majoritarian' politics to 'non-majoritarian' institutions such as regulatory agencies and judiciaries. 'Majoritarian' politics is the domain of national party and parliamentary politics and interest group lobbying, which may be suitable for making policy with 'redistributive' implications, but for Majone can have a negative impact on market efficiency. From this perspective a 'non-majoritarian' technocracy associated with the EU and particularly the Commission is best equipped to maximize market efficiency, which in turn has widespread 'welfare' benefits for Europeans. In this sense, Majone does not recognize arguments which claim that the EU suffers from a democratic deficit because it is legitimated in terms of its 'output' (see Chapter 3, 'Democracy and Legitimacy').

A number of critiques, explicitly or implicitly rooted in analyses of contemporary European capitalism informed by critical approaches to the political economy (see Chapter 4, 'Critical Political Economy'), are far less sanguine about the effects of the SEM (for a comprehensive review, see Cafruny and Ryner 2017). According to many of these critics, both the single market project and the economic and monetary union (EMU) were informed by and served to embed a broader, US-led, structural turn towards a post-Bretton Woods epoch of finance-driven neoliberalism from the late 1970s (Caffruny and Ryner 2007; Ryner and Caffruny 2017) (see also Chapters 4, 'Critical Political Economy' and 20, 'Critical Voices').

Such scholarship often points to the ways in which a neoliberal regulatory governance has undermined both the 'redistributive' schemes to which Majone refers and the distinct national models of welfare capitalism that are a feature of the broader so-called 'European social model'. While it is acknowledged by some such critics that processes of market integration might have generated positive economic outcomes in the early period of integration in a way that facilitated the creation of welfare states (Milward 1992), it is claimed that more recent policy has had the opposite effect.

In particular, the 1992 project is regarded by many as opening the way for the EU to regulate not only the anti-competitive practices of non-state actors but increasingly the ostensibly anti-competitive activities of states themselves (Scharpf 1998; Buch-Hansen and Wigger 2010). From this perspective, the EU, often at the bidding of corporate interests such as the ERT (van Apeldoorn 2002), became a promoter of 'neoliberal' policies such as privatization, welfare retrenchment, and liberalised corporate governance (Horn 2012).

The aforementioned liberalization of services is a part of such a logic. For instance, Scharpf (2010) has highlighted the ways in which, notwithstanding the 'social safeguards' introduced to the Services Directive, CJEU rulings (notably the 2007 *Laval* and *Viking* rulings) have prioritized the liberalization of services over national social and collective labour rights. More generally, he has suggested that the SEM has been a key factor in constituting a structural asymmetry which prioritizes economic over social and democratic priorities, or 'negative' over 'positive' integration at different governance levels within the EU (Scharpf 1998). More recently, critics of the aforementioned 'capital markets union' have highlighted that such a policy is consistent with the broader neoliberal financialization that was, for many critical political economists, an underlying cause of the eurozone crisis (Braun and Hübner 2018).

However, from a broadly constructivist position (see Chapter 4. 'Social Constructivism'), it can be argued that both these advocates and critics tend to overstate the structural imperatives associated with the SEM. In short, the single market may not be an entirely 'depoliticized' domain: its scope is contestable by a variety of agents and, indeed, it has been politically contested. This was manifest in the above-mentioned debacle over the Services Directive and in a number of CJEU decisions which have, contrary to a generally liberal market bias, protected the social prerogatives of nation-states (Hay and Wincott 2012: 144). More generally, such contestation is apparent in the continued distinctiveness of welfare capitalism among EU member states, many of which have not undertaken wholesale neoliberal reforms (Hay and Wincott 2012).

Since around 2015, debates on the single market of this sort have played out in British left-wing politics in the context of Brexit. So-called 'Lexiteer' arguments have made the case that the EU single market imposes neoliberal policies on Britain and this constitutes an argument for leaving the EU. However, this view has been challenged by many others on the British left (Parker 2016).

CONCLUSION

Whether called the 'common market' or the 'single market', the building of a geographical area free of barriers to economic and commercial activity has always been central to the process of European integration. It has also been central to attempts to theorize the process. Some of the fiercest arguments have raged over the theoretical implications of developments in this policy sector. Such debates have concerned the key explanatory factors for market integration, with intergovernmental and supranational accounts identifying and prioritizing different actors and drivers.

They have also concerned the normative status of different aspects of market integration: whether, for various reasons, they ought to be regarded as a good thing or a bad thing. Despite the apparent victory of pro-market ideas, these normative or ideological debates have been present in Europe since the ECSC and have never been entirely settled. Indeed, the series of economic, social, and political crises that hit the EU after 2009 once again prompted such debate (see also Chapters 11 and 20). This was reflected in the concerns of single market advocates, including the European Commission, who cautioned against a return to national economic protectionism in Europe. On the contrary, pushing the single market agenda further, via such initiatives as a 'capital markets union' and a 'digital single market', was seen by such actors as the way to foster economic growth and address the fallout from the crises.

While well-established regulatory structures may render a significant reversal in single market policies difficult, popular dissatisfaction with the EU may, at the very least, act as a brake on further market integration (in accordance, for instance, with a postfuntionalist theory—see Chapter 1, 'Postfunctionalism'). Moreover, a full or partial break-up of the euro (see Chapter 20, 'The Eurozone Crisis') would have significant repercussions for the single market (Dullien 2012).

KEY POINTS

History

- The original decision to create a common market was one of the pillars on which the EEC was constructed.
- Progress towards this goal varied over time, with agreement to accelerate the timetable in the 1960s. By the 1980s, progress had stalled, and was even going backwards with the proliferation of NTBs.

Project 1992: Freeing the Internal Market

- In the mid-1980s, the governments of the member states adopted proposals from the Commission for the freeing of the internal market from NTBs by 1992, and this was linked to changes in the institutional rules.

Beyond 1992

- Despite a good record on passing directives to implement the 1992 Programme, both transposition of directives into national legislation and enforcement of the new rules were uneven between member states.
- Some policy sectors that were included in the 1992 Programme proved particularly difficult on which to get agreement, especially tax harmonization and company law.
- Other policy sectors were so controversial that they were not included in the original programme at all, especially telecommunications, energy, postal services, and railways.
- The liberalization of services generally proved difficult.

Explaining the Single Market

- Liberal intergovernmentalism effectively explains the original commitment to the common market.
- Agreement to accelerate progress on the common market in the mid-1960s was interpreted by Lindberg (1963) as support for neofunctionalism because of the role of the Commission and industrial interests, but this was later contested by Moravcsik (1998).
- Academic explanations of the acceptance of the 1992 Programme in the mid-1980s agreed on the importance of the global economic environment, but disagreed on the respective role of national governments, the Commission, and supranational interests.
- Historical institutionalism provides an explanation for the continued momentum of the single market, based on the institutionalization of new rules and norms.

Evaluating the Single Market

- The creation of an ever more integrated single market has been accompanied by a normative debate among political economists, with some highlighting its positive economic and social benefits and others pointing to its inherent neoliberal bias and negative consequences.

 For additional material and resources, please visit the online resources www.oup.com/uk/bache5e.

QUESTIONS

1. What explains the initial creation of a 'common market' in Europe?
2. What were the key drivers of the '1992 Single Market Programme'?
3. Why was the liberalization of services particularly controversial?
4. What are the key arguments in favour of the Single European Market?
5. Why do some critics regard the Single European Market as too neoliberal?

FURTHER READING

The great debate between theorists about the single market began with **W. Sandholtz and J. Zysman**, '1992: Recasting the European Bargain', *World Politics*, 42 (1989): 95–128; and continued with **A. Moravcsik**, 'Negotiating the Single European Act: National Interests and Conventional Statecraft in the European Community', *International Organization*, 45 (1991): 19–56. **P. Budden** responded to Moravcsik's arguments from a pluralist perspective in his article, 'Observations on the Single European Act and the "Relaunch of Europe": A Less "Intergovernmental" Reading of the 1985 Intergovernmental Conference', *Journal of European Public Policy*, 9 (2002): 76–97. Another contribution worth reading is that by **M. G. Cowles**, 'Setting the Agenda for a New Europe: The ERT and EC 1992', *Journal of Common Market Studies*, 33 (1995): 501–26. For a new institutionalist account, see **K. Armstrong and S. Bulmer**, *The Governance of the Single European Market* (Manchester: Manchester University Press, 1998).

On the case studies of telecommunications and energy, see **P. Humphreys and S. Padgett**, 'Globalization, the European Union, and Domestic Governance in Telecoms and Electricity', *Governance: An International Journal of Policy, Administration, and Institutions*, 19 (2006): 383–406.

For an excellent critical political economy account, see **M. Ryner and A. Cafruny**, *The European Union and Global Capitalism: Origins, Development, Crisis* (London: Palgrave Macmillam, 2017), especially Chapter 3.

Chapter 20

Economic and Monetary Union

Chapter Overview

Economic and monetary union (EMU) first became an official objective of the European Community (EC) in 1969, but it was not achieved until thirty years later. In some respects, it is the logical corollary of the market-building endeavour associated with the common and single market, although it is also political inasmuch as it involves the transfer of a key sovereign competence (see Chapter 18, 'The European Union's Policy Agenda'). This chapter examines the various attempts at EMU between 1969 and 1992, the launch of the single currency, the euro, and its subsequent progress up to and including the crisis that engulfed the eurozone in the late 2000s. It then looks at some of the explanations for and critiques of EMU that have been offered by various academic commentators.

History

Economic and monetary union first came to the fore as an objective of the EC in 1969 when the Commission produced the Barre Report. In December of the same year, the Hague Summit meeting of the EC heads of government made a commitment to the achievement of EMU 'by 1980'.

To make the commitment to EMU was one thing, but to agree how to do it was another. There were two broad approaches that were represented most clearly by the positions of the French and West German governments. The French government wanted a system for the mutual support of fixed exchange rates between national currencies. It argued that this in itself would produce economic convergence (Dyson 1994: 79–80). The West German government rejected that approach because it believed that it would involve using up West Germany's considerable foreign currency reserves to support the currencies of states that were following what the Germans saw as irresponsibly lax and inflationary economic policies. For West Germany, common economic policies had to come first—and they wanted their preference for monetary stability, rather than the growth-orientated policies of France, to be the basis of the common policies. At the time, the French position was described as 'monetarist', because it advocated monetary union ahead of economic union, while the German position was described as 'economist', because it advocated economic union ahead of monetary union (Tsoukalis 1977; Dyson 1994: 79–80).

The 'Snake'

This fundamental disagreement produced the compromise proposals of the Werner Committee in November 1970 (see Chapter 7, 'The Hague Summit'). Werner proposed that the co-ordination of economic policy and the narrowing of exchange rate fluctuations should proceed in parallel. This arrangement for approximating the exchange rates of member currencies one to another became known as the 'snake in the tunnel' because each currency could move up and down ('snake' up and down) between a minimum and maximum value against other currencies in the system, which formed a floor and a ceiling of fluctuation (the tunnel).

Although the original 'snake' collapsed following the ending of the convertibility of the dollar in August 1971, it was reconstituted in April 1972, only to run into the same problems as its predecessor. Essentially, the problem was that some of the economies of the member states were very much weaker than that of the strongest, West Germany, and the West Germans were not prepared to support the value of the currencies of the weaker economies. For example, in 1972, the German Federal Bank (Bundesbank) refused to intervene in the foreign exchanges to support the pound, with the consequence that speculation forced sterling out of the system.

By 1974, economic divergence was glaringly apparent in the EC, indicating that there were definite structural weaknesses in the economies of the peripheral states, including Britain. France sat delicately balanced on the edge between centre and periphery. These strains caused the complete collapse of the original EMU experiment after 1973.

The European Monetary System (EMS)

In October 1977, the Commission President Roy Jenkins took the initiative to revive EMU (see Chapter 8, 'The European Monetary System'). It was taken up by West German Chancellor Helmut Schmidt and French President Valéry Giscard d'Estaing.

By this time, one of the main factors that had been a barrier to German enthusiasm for the original snake had been removed. Gradually, the governments of the other member states were coming around to accepting the West German economic priority of controlling inflation. Mainly this reassessment of policy was because of the acceleration of inflation following the 1973 oil-price rises (see Chapter 7, 'Into the 1970s'). It was obvious that the economies that were having the least success in controlling inflation were also those with the highest rates of unemployment, and the poorest record on growth.

In December 1978, the Bremen European Council created the EMS. The central element was the exchange rate mechanism (ERM) for holding fluctuations in exchange rates within narrow bands. Accounting within the system was in a notional currency called the 'ecu', the value of which was an average of the values of the member currencies (Britain remained outside of the ERM, but sterling was included in the calculation of the value of the ecu). This system limited fluctuations in the values of the participating currencies for a number of years.

Origins of EMU

Moves to strengthen and extend the EMS were part of the programme of the Delors Commission from the outset. However, the issue really came into the forefront of debate in the aftermath of the decision to free the internal market by the end of 1992.

Insight 20.1 The Delors Report

The 'Delors Report' proposed a three-stage progression to monetary union.

1. The EC currencies that remained outside the ERM of the EMS (those of Britain, Greece, Portugal, and Spain) would join, and the wider band of fluctuation would disappear.

2. Economic policy would be closely co-ordinated, the band of fluctuation of currencies within the EMS would be narrowed, and the governors of central banks would meet as a committee to prepare the ground for the institution of a European Monetary Co-operation Fund (EMCF).

3. National currencies would be irrevocably locked together, and the ecu would become a real currency in its own right, administered by the EMCF.

At the end of 1985, the Luxembourg European Council agreed on the terms of the Single European Act (SEA), including a commitment to monetary union. Further progress had to wait until the June 1988 Hanover European Council, which agreed to set up a committee of central bankers and technical experts, under the chairmanship of the President of the Commission, to prepare a report on the steps that needed to be taken to strengthen monetary co-operation. The report of this committee (see Insight 20.1) was accepted by the June 1989 European Council meeting in Madrid. The momentum was sustained when the December 1989 European Council in Strasbourg agreed to set up an intergovernmental conference (IGC) to consider the institutional changes that would be necessary in order to move towards monetary union.

Monetary Union in the 1990s

The IGC on monetary union took as its negotiating text the report of the Delors Committee, which recommended that movement to monetary union should be to a timetable. This starting point still left plenty of significant details to be negotiated. Before the IGC began to meet in 1991, West Germany was reunified with East Germany in October 1990. Germany entered the negotiations as clearly the largest state, as well as the largest economy in the EC, putting it in a particularly strong negotiating position. Also in 1990, Britain joined the ERM.

Early in the IGC, there was a consensus that a monetary union would only be sustainable if it were underpinned by a considerable degree of economic convergence. The Treaty on European Union (TEU) provided five convergence criteria that would have to be met by any state before it could take part in the monetary union. Prospective members would need to have:

- a budget deficit of not more than 3 per cent of gross domestic product (GDP);
- a public debt of not more than 60 per cent of GDP;
- a level of inflation no more than 1.5 percentage points above the average level achieved by the three states with the lowest levels of inflation;

381

- interest rates that were no more than 2 per cent above the average level of the three states with the lowest levels;
- a record of respecting the normal fluctuation margins of the ERM for two years.

These criteria reflected the policy priorities of the German government in that they were all concerned with monetary stability.

Although the criteria were stringent, the Treaty did appear to leave room for some relaxation if states were moving in the right direction on all of the relevant indicators. At the same time, it was written into the Treaty that any state that did qualify would join the monetary union when it was set up, which would be in 1997 if possible, and not later than 1999. Only Britain was initially allowed to opt out of signing up for the monetary union in advance, although following the rejection of the Maastricht Treaty in the Danish referendum in June 1992, Denmark was granted a similar opt-out clause in a Protocol to the Treaty.

Putting Maastricht into Operation (1992–2002)

On 16 September 1992, Britain was forced out of the ERM by intensive speculation against the pound. The next day, the Italian lira also had to leave the mechanism. Then, in August 1993, the system came under so much pressure that it only survived by allowing the value of each national currency to fluctuate by 15 per cent either side of its notional value within the system. This was a very large margin of fluctuation for a system that was supposed to approximate to fixed rates of exchange.

One interpretation of these developments was that the member states were not ready for a single currency if they could not hold their exchange rates. Another interpretation was that the episode showed how important it was to move to a single currency so that speculators could not push the economies of the members apart. Certainly, the problems deflected neither French President François Mitterrand nor German Chancellor Helmut Kohl from their commitment to monetary union.

It was not entirely clear, though, how much support the President and the Chancellor had in their own countries. In France, high unemployment made the policy of tying the franc closely to the Deutschmark increasingly unpopular, and the country was paralyzed by strikes in the later months of 1995, as the government tried to introduce policies that would allow it to meet the convergence criteria. In Germany, public opinion polls showed growing opposition to abandoning the Deutschmark, despite a consensus among the political elite to insist that the monetary union was the only course for the country. In November 1995, a poll published in *Die Woche* indicated that 61 per cent of the German people were opposed to the single currency (*Financial Times*, 11–12 November 1995).

Public scepticism about the single currency put the German government in an even stronger position in the bargaining about the detail of the arrangements. It could always argue that unless the German public was confident in the arrangements made, there would be no German participation, and therefore no single currency. In this way, Germany won all of the main arguments.

> ### Insight 20.2 The European Central Bank (ECB)
>
> The TEU set up an ECB charged with conducting the monetary policy of the eurozone. Its governing council consists of an Executive Board plus the governors of the national central banks. The Executive Board consists of a President, a Vice-President, plus four other members. They are appointed by common accord of the member states for a non-renewable term of eight years, and must be 'of recognized standing and professional experience in monetary and banking matters' (TEU Article 283(2)). In October 2011, Jean-Claude Trichet completed his term as President of the ECB and, in the midst of the crisis in the eurozone, was replaced by Mario Draghi, a former governor of Banca d'Italia. In November 2019, Christine Lagarde, formerly head of the International Monetary Fund (IMF), was appointed as ECB President.

It was agreed that the European Central Bank (ECB) (see Insight 20.2) would be located in Frankfurt; then, that the name of the new currency would not be the 'ecu', which the French preferred because it was the name of an old French coin, but the 'euro', because the German people did not have confidence in the existing ecu.

France put up a stronger fight on three other issues:

1. the level of political control that would be exerted over the ECB;
2. the rules that would govern budgetary policy after the start of the single currency;
3. the identity of the first president of the ECB.

On the level of political control, the German government insisted that the ECB should be as independent as it was possible to make it. This was the only way that the German people would have confidence that the single currency would be run on a sound basis. The French government never accepted this: it wanted the ECB to be answerable to national governments.

This fundamental philosophical clash also underlay the differences between the two governments on the terms of the budgetary rules that would apply after the start of the single currency. The German government wanted the Maastricht convergence criterion for budget deficits—that budget deficits should not exceed 3 per cent of GDP—to become permanent. It also wanted a system to penalize states that overshot this target, and proposed a fine that would be automatic. The French government argued that the fine should be discretionary, and that the finance ministers should decide the issue in the light of prevailing economic circumstances. The clash between the German preference for 'rules-based' economic governance and the French preference for discretionary governance has long had an impact upon the politics of the single currency, including in the context of the post-2008 crisis (see 'The Eurozone Crisis' below).

The Stability and Growth Pact (SGP), agreed at the Dublin European Council in December 1996, effectively made the Maastricht convergence criteria permanent requirements for the participating states. It was agreed that states that ran a deficit in excess of 3 per cent of GDP would be fined, but the fine would be automatically waived if GDP had fallen by more than 2 per cent in the previous year. If GDP had fallen by less than 2 per cent, but by more than 0.75 per cent, the finance ministers would have discretion to decide whether a fine should be imposed. This compromise allowed everyone to claim that they had won, but the rules-based system was generally in accord with the preferences of the German government.

When a new Socialist government was elected in France in June 1997, it made clear that it was unhappy with the SGP that had been agreed at Dublin. At the Amsterdam European Council in June 1997, it was agreed that the SGP would be supplemented by an employment pact, and this was written into the Treaty (see Chapter 18, 'Employment, Social Affairs, and Inclusion'). Nevertheless, as with Dublin, the outcome at Amsterdam on monetary union has to be seen primarily as a success for the German government. The French government accepted the SGP in return for much less than the employment chapter that it had originally wanted to be written into the Treaty.

Having lost the major arguments on EMU to Germany, the French government made an issue of the identity of the first president of the ECB. In May 1998, at a special European Council meeting in Brussels that had been called to launch the single currency, the French President, Jacques Chirac, refused to accept the nomination of the Dutchman, Wim Duisenberg, as the first president of the ECB. Duisenberg had been President of the forerunner of the ECB, the European Monetary Institute, and was the first choice of the clear majority of member states, including Germany. Eventually, in order to satisfy the French President, Duisenberg reportedly agreed to step down halfway through his term of office to allow the Governor of the Banque de France, Jean-Claude Trichet, to take his place (although this was publicly denied by all parties) (Kaltenthaler 2006: 94–5). Trichet would eventually replace Duisenberg in 2003.

The launch of the single currency was only slightly marred by this political controversy, and the financial markets reacted calmly to the shenanigans. The euro formally came into existence on 1 January 1999 with eleven members. Only Greece, in the end, was excluded by the convergence criteria. Britain, Denmark, and Sweden met the criteria, but excluded themselves. Britain and Denmark were allowed to do this under the terms of their 'opt-outs'. Sweden was able to claim on a technicality that it had not fulfilled the conditions because it had not been a member of the ERM for two years prior to the launch of the euro. Denmark and Greece joined a revised ERM-2 that was set up at the same time as the launch of the single currency, but which retained the wide 15 per cent fluctuation band. Britain and Sweden chose not to join ERM-2.

The ERM-2 continues to operate as, in effect, a training area for future members of the single currency, in which they are obliged to adopt good habits of economic management. The 2004 enlargement committed all of the new member states to becoming members of the single currency, but they were required to fulfil the convergence criteria before being allowed in, and had to be members of the ERM-2 for two years. Slovenia, Cyprus, Malta, Slovakia, Estonia, Latvia, and Lithuania have since joined the euro (see Box 20.1).

The Single Currency in Operation

The Euro Group

Because decisions on matters relating to the monetary union needed to be taken by the governments of the participating states, in 1998 an informal 'Euro Group' was set up consisting of the eurozone finance ministers, each accompanied by one economic official, together with representatives of the ECB and the Economic and Financial

> **Box 20.1 Membership of the EMS and the Single Currency**
>
> | Year | Event |
> |------|-------|
> | 1979 | Start of EMS; joined by Belgium, Denmark, France, Germany, Ireland, Italy, Luxembourg, and the Netherlands (all of them then member states of the EC except Britain) |
> | 1986 | Portugal and Spain joined the EC and the EMS |
> | 1989 | Spain joined the ERM |
> | 1990 | Britain and Portugal joined the ERM |
> | 1992 | Britain and Italy forced out of the ERM |
> | 1996 | Italy re-entered the ERM and Finland joined |
> | 1998 | Greece joined EMS and the ERM |
> | 1999 | Austria, Belgium, Finland, France, Germany, Ireland, Italy, Luxembourg, the Netherlands, Portugal, and Spain formed the eurozone; Denmark and Greece joined a revised ERM-2 |
> | 2001 | Greece joined the euro |
> | 2002 | Introduction of euro notes and coins |
> | 2004 | Estonia, Lithuania, and Slovenia joined ERM-2 |
> | 2005 | Cyprus, Latvia, and Malta joined ERM-2; rules of eurozone SGP revised |
> | 2007 | Slovenia joined the euro |
> | 2008 | Cyprus and Malta joined the euro |
> | 2009 | Slovakia joined the euro |
> | 2011 | Estonia joined the euro |
> | 2014 | Latvia joined the euro |
> | 2015 | Lithuania joined the euro |

Committee of EU officials. It meets ten to twelve times a year, usually on the evening before the formal sessions of the Economic and Financial Affairs Council (ECOFIN) meeting of the Council of Ministers. It elects a president for two years—since 2018, the Portuguese finance minister, Mario Centeno—and it is the presidency that issues the invitations, prepares the agenda, and afterwards circulates an informal memorandum of the most important points discussed and agreed.

A system of 'Euro summits'—regular meetings of the heads of government of eurozone member states—has emerged alongside Euro Group meetings since 2010 and was institutionalized in the Treaty on Stability Co-ordination and Governance which entered into force in 2013 (see Insight 11.1).

Problems of Monetary Union

Although the single currency came into existence more smoothly than many economists predicted, it soon ran into difficulties. The external value of the euro fell steadily against the US dollar, and the eurozone itself began to exhibit some of the problems of having a single interest rate for such a diverse economic area. In particular, macroeconomic imbalances became apparent, with Spain and Ireland experiencing the symptoms of repressed inflation, including rapidly rising property prices and shortages of labour, while the core economies of Germany and France were experiencing sluggish growth. A majority of states within the eurozone experienced lower rates of growth and higher unemployment than the economies of those EU member states—Britain, Denmark, and Sweden—that remained outside the single currency.

Against this background, it was perhaps unsurprising that the Danish people rejected membership of the euro in a referendum in September 2000, that the British government concluded in June 2003 that the time was not right to make an application to join, and that the Swedish people followed the Danish example in September 2003.

Redefining the Stability and Growth Pact

While Britain and Sweden were in the process of deciding that they did not want to be part of the eurozone, serious disputes broke out among the member states that were in the single currency over the application of the SGP. In particular, the requirement to keep budget deficits below 3 per cent of GDP proved very difficult to achieve in the context of low growth, teetering on the brink of recession. Although agreement was reached on making both Portugal and Ireland come into line when they breached the spending limits, by 2003, the states in the dock were the two giants of the eurozone: France and Germany. In November 2003, the eurozone finance ministers discussed a formal proposal from the Commission that sanctions be applied against both France and Germany unless they took steps to reduce their budget deficit for 2004 below the 3 per cent limit. Once it became obvious that there was no majority for the Commission's proposal, the Italian presidency proposed a suspension of the sanctions, and this was accepted by a majority vote. With this decision, the SGP in effect became no more than a set of guidelines on policy to national governments.

Yet, neither Germany nor France ever challenged the principle of the pact, and in an attempt to minimize the damage that their action might cause, both agreed voluntarily to try to reduce spending for 2004. This seemed to make it clear that the principle at stake was not the need for fiscal discipline, but who was in charge: national governments or the European Commission.

That principle was also the reason for the decision of the European Commission, in January 2004, to take the Council to the European Court of Justice (ECJ) under Article 230 (previously 173) of the Treaty. The decision was taken by a majority vote in a badly divided College—but the view prevailed that it was the duty of the Commission in its role as guardian of the Treaty to test the legality of the pact. In July 2004, the ECJ ruled that the Council had acted illegally in suspending the pact's mechanism for sanctioning member states, but affirmed that responsibility for making the member states observe budgetary discipline lay with the Council, not the Commission.

In March 2005, the SGP was revised to relax the conditions under which a 3 per cent deficit would not be considered 'excessive', and the timetable for correcting an excessive deficit was stretched. A member state exceeding the 3 per cent deficit could argue that it was doing so legitimately if it was trying, through its excess expenditure, to achieve European goals or to 'foster international solidarity', both of which are very broad objectives. Conditions for the correction of an excessive deficit were also considerably eased. These reforms to the pact were made possible by an apparent convergence in French and German interests, with the latter accepting (at least temporarily) greater flexibility and discretion in economic governance.

Euro Notes and Coins

The other main development in monetary union after 1999 was the introduction of euro notes and coins on 1 January 2002. Between 1999 and 2002, the euro officially existed as an international currency, but national currencies continued to be used for domestic purposes. The replacement of the national currencies with the euro notes and coins was a significant development because it gave physical form to the new currency for ordinary citizens of the eurozone, and made it a part of their daily lives. The creation of a single currency in physical form provided an important symbol of European integration and for some signalled an important step towards the development of a European identity (Risse 2003).

The Eurozone Crisis

The various causes of the eurozone crisis, which began in 2009, are debatable. It has been connected to the broader financial crisis of the capitalist world that began in 2008, itself the consequence of excessive risk-taking and indebtedness by banks, other financial institutions, and publics in Europe and beyond (see Insight 11.1; also Tooze 2018a). It has been connected to the more specific weaknesses in the governance of the single currency: the failure of states to follow rules, or of European institutions to enforce them, and the failure of the rules themselves to address growing macro-economic imbalances in the eurozone. More generally, it has been connected to a perceived lack of political and economic (particularly fiscal) integration in Europe, which for many is a necessary but missing counterpart to monetary integration.

A flurry of activity from EU institutions and actors in response to the crisis sought to address each of these issues. This was done through a combination of crisis management aimed at bringing short-term respite and substantive reforms aimed at establishing a more robust system of monetary and economic governance (see also Chapter 11, 'The Unfolding Eurozone Crisis'). It also entailed—albeit to a much lesser extent—ensuring proper regulation of banks and financial institutions. Whether all of these reforms had gone far enough to protect against a further crisis was certainly highly questionable at the time of writing in 2019.

Crisis Management

The EU was largely reactive in its response to the unfolding crisis in the eurozone. When the crisis first became manifest in Greece in 2009—following its sovereign debt downgrade and the realization that its budget deficit was far worse than it had reported—EU leaders were relatively slow to appreciate and react to the wider implications. After some procrastination, a €110 billion bail out for Greece was agreed as part of a bilateral agreement with other eurozone member states and the International Monetary Fund (IMF). But as the bond markets and credit rating agencies turned their attention to other eurozone states, and it became clear that Greece would not be a stand-alone case, the EU and IMF put together a larger financial support mechanism worth €750 billion. This had three components: the European Financial Stability

Facility (EFSF), backed by member states, was authorized to raise €440 billion; the European Financial Stabilization Mechanism (EFSM), backed by the EU budget, was able to raise €60 billion; and the IMF was to provide a further €250 billion. In 2010 and 2011, support packages were put in place via these mechanisms for Ireland, Portugal, and Greece (its second 'bail out'). In each case, these packages were operationalized following negotiation with the European Commission and the IMF of domestic reform programmes, which required unanimous approval by the Euro Group and the signature of a memorandum of understanding (MoU) by the relevant state. The implementation of these programmes was to be assessed by the European Commission, IMF, and the ECB (known collectively as 'the troika'). As noted below, these financial support mechanisms were subsequently superseded by a permanent mechanism, meaning that, after 2012, support was no longer channelled from EFSF/EFSM (for a more detailed chronology, see Chapter 11, 'The Unfolding Eurozone Crisis').

In addition to these various support mechanisms, the ECB played an active role in crisis management. In particular, at the end of 2011, the ECB injected money into Europe's struggling banks through so-called Long-Term Refinancing Operations (LTRO). This provided temporary liquidity to a banking sector in which banks were nervous even to lend to each other.

The ECB intensified this interventionism in 2012. In July, President Draghi famously stated that, 'the ECB is ready to do whatever it takes to preserve the euro. And believe me, it will be enough.' This was followed up with a practical commitment to so-called outright monetary transactions (OMTs): a pledge to purchase member states' sovereign debt if required. With these moves, the ECB was able to bring to an end the acute phase of the crisis: it calmed markets, radically narrowing bond–yield spreads within the eurozone, and thereby easing the burden of debt refinancing on struggling member states.

Long-Term Reforms

In addition to these acts of 'fire-fighting', the EU developed long-term reforms aimed at both solving the crisis and preventing its recurrence. Despite clear differences within the EU on both the major causes and potential solutions to the crisis, a programme of substantive reform did emerge, which, as with the initial design of EMU, was generally in line with German preferences.

As the crisis unfolded, EU leaders recognized, in December 2010, that a more permanent financial assistance mechanism than EFSF/EFSM (due to expire in 2013) would be required for dealing with crisis situations in eurozone member states. This permanent institution, the European Stability Mechanism (ESM) was agreed by Treaty and established on 27 September 2012, with a lending capacity of up to €500 billion. To receive assistance from this mechanism ESM member states must—as with previous mechanisms—sign an MoU and must have ratified the 'fiscal compact'. In other words, assistance would once again come with significant conditionality, particularly in terms of so-called fiscal consolidation (economic austerity). In 2012 and 2013, respectively, Spain and Cyprus first received funds through this new mechanism, while Greece, Portugal, and Ireland continued to receive funds from the temporary mechanisms. Greece's third support package in 2015 came from the ESM.

The major reforms to economic governance sought to render meaningful and substantially 'harden' the previously flouted rules associated with the SGP. The 2011 'six-pack' of legislation was aimed at reinforcing both fiscal surveillance mechanisms and enforcement mechanisms of the SGP, while also increasing EU oversight of member states' budgetary and economic policies in order to avoid large macro-economic imbalances. Such oversight was facilitated by reforms to the economic co-ordination timetable, particularly the introduction of the so-called 'European semester' after 2011, which allowed for closer monitoring of national budgets by the Commission. The 2013 'two-pack' of legislative reforms built on the 'six-pack', reinforcing oversight with respect to eurozone member states and particularly those in receipt of financial assistance.

The 'fiscal compact' within the Treaty on Stability Co-ordination and Governance (TSCG) (on the Treaty see Insight 11.2) referred to and built upon these reforms and significantly contributed to this reinforcement of economic governance. It was signed by twenty-five member states (all excluding the UK and Czech Republic) and called for balanced-budget rules to be written into national laws or constitutions. At its heart was the so-called 'golden rule', which limits structural deficits to no more than 0.5 per cent of GDP over the full economic cycle. Along with the above-mentioned legislation, the TSCG also referred to monitoring by the European Commission of national economic and budgetary policies and foresaw costly sanctions for governments that breached the SGP deficit limit of 3 per cent. These sanctions could only be blocked by a 'reversed qualified majority' in the Council: in other words, a qualified majority (see Chapter 12, 'The Council of the EU (the Council)') is needed to reject (rather than approve) the Commission decision.

These long-term reforms initially focused then on the need for greater economic and fiscal discipline in EU member states. However, critics argued that such reforms were based on a misdiagnosis of the crisis as one of public debt, and were potentially counterproductive (see 'Critical Voices' below). From this perspective, it was in fact an excessively indebted and over-leveraged banking and finance sector that lay at the root of the Global Financial and eurozone crises, and it required radical reform (see Chapter 11, 'The Unfolding Eurozone Crisis' and Tooze 2018a).

The EU institutions did belatedly recognize this to some extent. A 2012 report by the Presidents of the Council, Commission, Eurogroup, and ECB entitled 'Towards a Genuine Economic and Monetary Union', called for a range of measures that would essentially lead to a greater regulation of finance and more extensive pooling of economic and financial risk. Following these proposals, the EU worked towards the establishment of a European Banking Union (EBU). The EBU strengthened the role of the ECB in regulating and supervising European banks and established a common mechanism for dealing with banking failures.

However, many of the proposals made by the four Presidents did not come to fruition, including proposals for debt mutualization (a version of what has commonly been called 'eurobonds'). Acknowledging the need for further efforts, in 2015 the four Presidents (plus this time the President of the Parliament) published a 'Five Presidents' report entitled 'Completing Europe's Economic and Monetary Union' (European Commission 2015b). One important proposal in this new report was for a common (European) bank deposit insurance scheme. This was intended to address a key aim of the EBU, which was to break the so-called 'doom loop' between private and sovereign debt (whereby banking debt becomes sovereign debt when the sector is bailed out by national governments). In 2017 and 2018, the Commission issued a series of new proposals, including for the establishment of a European Monetary Fund (EMF) that would encompass and expand upon the role of the EMS.

In summary, the emphasis of post-crisis reforms was, in accord with German and creditor state preferences, on greater fiscal discipline and increased powers of oversight from the EU centre. For Germany, such discipline is regarded as the quid pro quo for the collective commitment to 'bail-out' mechanisms such as the ESM, which might otherwise create a situation of so-called 'moral hazard', whereby states in receipt of financial assistance are able to continue in their profligate ways. Otherwise put, Germany has a strong preference for delegating a risk-management or risk-reduction strategy to individual states rather than adopting a risk-sharing approach. German concerns in this regard are also the key reason why proposals from the EU institutions and the French (supported by many debtor states) which aimed at risk-sharing (including for 'eurobonds' and collective deposit insurance) were not successfully pursued. However, questions were emerging at the time of writing in 2019, as to whether the enforcement of fiscal discipline at a national level was politically sustainable (see Chapter 11, 'The Populist Challenge').

Explaining and Critiquing EMU

Academics have vigorously debated both why the decision to adopt a single currency was finally made, and why the particular form of monetary union was agreed. Supranational and intergovernmental explanations have both been offered in the literature, while international factors form the background to both sets of explanation. Moreover, both before and particularly during the crisis, a range of voices, emerging in particular from a critical political economy literature (see Chapter 4, 'Critical Political Economy'), offered an important critique of EMU.

Spillover

It could be argued, as it was argued by the Commission, that pressure for monetary union came as spillover from the decision to free the internal market. Making a reality of the single market implied eliminating the fluctuations in exchange rates that were a source of interference with trade across national boundaries. However, Sandholtz (1993: 20–2) rejected the argument that there was a clear functional spillover from the single market to a single currency. The reasoning behind it was contentious:

> Among economists, there is no consensus on the desirability of monetary integration, much less on its functional necessity.

(Sandholtz 1993: 21)

However, he argued that there was clearly what others have called 'cultivated spillover'. This occurs when the Commission 'cultivates' pressure on the governments of member states to adopt further measures of integration (see Chapter 1, 'Theories of European Integration').

Others have emphasized the role of central bankers in cultivating spillover. Verdun (1999: 317), for instance, identified central bankers as an important epistemic community in this process (see Chapter 2, 'New Institutionalism'), involved early on, notably through their participation in the Delors Committee, which produced the report on EMU. Later, they played an active role in the drafting of the relevant articles of the Treaty. Central bankers tended to agree that the aim of monetary policy was to achieve price stability and that, to achieve this, monetary policies had to be freed from political influence.

Irrespective of whether the initial moves to EMU can be regarded in terms of functional spillover, some commentators read the crisis from 2009 itself as providing the functional spillover pressures that would lead to further economic and political integration (Niemann and Ioannou 2015). The German journalist, Gabor Steingart, offered an extreme version of such an argument, interpreting the initial responses to the crisis as, 'the birth pangs of a new country ... the United States of Europe' (*The New York Times*, 22 May 2010). At the time of writing, this interpretation was, to say the least, highly questionable. Indeed, for other commentators some kind of 'disintegration' remained possible; in part, as a consequence of this crisis (see, for instance, Webber 2014, 2019a).

Intergovernmental Explanations

Intergovernmentalists have often argued that a government might welcome having its hands tied by commitments to the EC/EU, and this argument can be applied to EMU in particular:

> monetary union would provide price stability for governments that would be unable, for domestic political reasons, to achieve it on their own.

(Sandholtz 1993: 35)

This hypothesis might explain why German preferences prevailed on the issues of the independence of the ECB and the constitutional commitment that the ECB should aim for price stability above other goals. Whatever other governments' public protestations that they found the German preferences too restrictive, in private they perhaps welcomed the opportunity to be tied into policies that they believed to be right, but did not believe that they could persuade their electorates to support. In states in which the general value of the EU was never in doubt, this technique was used without undermining the legitimacy of EU membership itself. Arguably this was due to the concept of 'output legitimation': the notion that the EU can, despite removing certain policy areas from national democratic oversight, maintain its legitimacy—and a 'permissive consensus'—as long as it delivers a set of positive outcomes, particularly economic (see Chapter 3, 'Democracy and Legitimacy'). In the context of the post-2008 crisis, such output legitimacy was, however, significantly undermined (see Chapter 11, 'The Unfolding Eurozone Crisis').

Another explanation for EMU starts from the experience that member states had of the EMS. Sandholtz (1993: 27–30) noted that the EMS was working well, but that there was growing discontent in France and elsewhere with the way in which decisions on interest rates were made by the Bundesbank in the light of conditions only in West Germany, and these were then transmitted throughout the EMS member states because of the need to keep all currencies aligned. Furthermore, Cameron (1997) identified the way in which adjustment costs within the EMS fell particularly heavily on the weak-currency states. If the exchange rate of a weak-currency country threatened to fall below the range of its parity, it was expected to take the necessary action to support its currency. Failure to maintain the parity could lead to a devaluation, which would again place adjustment costs on the weak-currency state by feeding inflationary tendencies. Relatedly, states that had higher levels of inflation would find that their exports were relatively less competitive, while states with lower rates of inflation would find their exports becoming steadily more competitive. This is how West Germany came to run large surpluses with all of its main EC trading partners (although, as noted above, such imbalances were not overcome in the context of EMU). To these factors, Loedel (1998) added a further motivation for France: international monetary influence. It was with West Germany that the United States conducted such dialogue as it held with Europe on international monetary matters, while other members of the EMS had no say in such monetary diplomacy.

It is clear, though, that the asymmetries in the EMS do not explain why West Germany supported the single currency. After all, the EMS was a system that favoured German interests. Here, Sandholtz (1993: 31–4) invoked West German foreign policy aims. EMU can be seen from this perspective as a means of balancing West German policy to the East with a strengthening of its interdependence with the EC. In particular, the issue became linked to German reunification. In late 1989, Kohl produced a ten-point plan for German unification. Shortly afterwards, the EC states agreed to convene the IGC on EMU in 1990. Sandholtz suggested that this decision was precipitated by the concern of France and other neighbours of Germany that the reunified German state would lose interest in the EC, and might even become nationalist again. Such a danger became a theme of speeches given by Helmut Kohl in defence of the single currency. He repeatedly associated the single currency with European integration, and European integration with the avoidance of war in Europe. The single currency was an essential step on the way to political union, which in turn was essential to peace and stability.

In contrast, Moravcsik (1998: 381) was dismissive of the explanation based on German reunification because, he maintained, the timing was wrong. Firm commitments by France and West Germany to move decisively forward with EMU—and opposition by Britain to that goal—predated the fall of the Berlin Wall and remained unchanged after unification was completed in August 1990. He argued that there was a German economic interest in monetary integration. The steady appreciation of the Deutschmark against other currencies was reducing the competitiveness of German exports, and merging it into a wider European currency offered the opportunity to dampen down this trend. Concerns about currency appreciation intensified in the 1990s in the face of the large costs of reunification and the collapse of the ERM in 1992 (Moravcsik 1998: 392).

Kaltenthaler (2002) attempted to cut through the dichotomy between explanations of German policy that stressed geo-political factors and those that stressed economic interests by distinguishing three distinct groups of actors who influenced German policy on monetary union whenever it was proposed. The first group was a 'foreign policy coalition', consisting of the Foreign Ministry and the Chancellor's office. The second group was a 'monetary stability coalition' of state actors with responsibility for financial and monetary policy, consisting primarily of the Finance Ministry and the

Bundesbank. The third group consisted of societal actors, predominantly bankers and industrialists operating through organizations such as the Federation of German Banks (BDB), the Federation of German Industry (BDI), and the German Chambers of Commerce (DIHT). There was always a tension between these actors. The foreign policy coalition had the primary aim of 'embedding Germany in western institutions' (Kaltenthaler 2002: 70), and was particularly concerned to maintain the key diplomatic relationship with France. The monetary stability coalition, as the name implies, was concerned to ensure that domestic monetary stability was maintained. Which of these coalitions had the greater success in influencing policy was largely determined by their ability to attract the support of the third group, the societal actors (Kaltenthaler 2002: 72–3).

When the French government, dissatisfied with the asymmetrical operation of the EMS, first proposed moving to full monetary union in early 1988, the immediate reaction of the West German government was cool. This reaction reflected the combined opposition of the monetary stability coalition and societal interests, which saw the French proposal as a device to gain control of German monetary policy and move it away from its emphasis on price stability. Chancellor Kohl and Foreign Minister Genscher both supported the proposal for geo-strategic reasons, to shore up the alliance with France. The balance of power shifted, though, with the fall of the Berlin Wall and the prospect of reunification. The banking and industrial interests saw tremendous prospects for expansion into East Germany, and therefore very much favoured reunification. France, though, held a veto over reunification, because it was one of the four powers that had occupied Germany after the war (together with Britain, the United States, and the Soviet Union), and the agreement of all four was needed for reunification to proceed.

Kaltenthaler (2002: 80) disagreed with Moravcsik (1998) that reunification was unimportant in explaining the commitment to monetary union, but whereas Sandholtz (1993) emphasized the strategic thinking behind the decision (that Kohl and Genscher wanted to reassure France and the other EU member states that it was still committed to the EU), Kaltenthaler emphasized the politics behind the decision. The foreign policy coalition won the support of the societal interests when it seemed as though monetary union was the price that would have to be paid to get France to agree to reunification. However, in the IGC, the monetary stability coalition was able to dictate the terms of monetary union because, on the principle of monetary stability, it still had the backing of the societal interests.

Intergorvermentalism has also been deployed to understand the response of the EU to the eurozone crisis. Developing his argument from a liberal intergovernmentalist perspective, Schimmelfennig (2015) described the post-crisis bargaining between eurozone states in terms of a 'chicken game' situation. This is a situation wherein all actors have a strong preference for avoiding a costly situation, but all wish to limit their own costs when it comes to ensuring that situation is avoided. Applied to the crisis, it was clear that no member states wanted to see the break-up of the euro given the likely costs, but they had very different preferences with respect to the steps that should be taken to avoid such an outcome. Putting things somewhat crudely, on the one hand, Germany and other creditor states wanted to pursue what we describe in 'Long-Term Reforms' above as a 'risk-management' strategy, which would be implemented nationally but enforced at EU level. On the other hand, France and the debtor states preferred what we describe above as a 'risk-sharing' approach. Schimmelfennig argues that because the costs of break-up were asymmetrical in this case (certainly in the short-term they would have been worse for the debtor states), it was the debtor states that backed down and the German preferences that ultimately prevailed.

Critical Voices

It is not surprising that the crisis in the eurozone—a crisis of EMU and potentially of the EU more generally (see Chapter 11, 'The Unfolding Eurozone Crisis')—provoked a range of critical commentary from both within and beyond academia. It should be noted, however, that a number of scholars, particularly those adopting a critical political economy perspective (see Chapter 4, 'Critical Political Economy'), were long-standing critics of the single currency and its design. Many such scholars critically expounded on the neoliberal (see Gill 1998; Ryner and Cafruny 2017; Parker and Tsarouhas 2018) or German ordo-liberal (see Bonefeld 2012; Berghahn and Young 2013) bias inherent in EMU.

As long ago as the late 1990s, Gill (1998) argued from a neo-Gramscian perspective that EMU's rule-based juridical regime (part of what he termed a neoliberal 'new constitutionalism'), effectively restricting an autonomous national fiscal policy, would significantly circumscribe the possibilities and flexibility available to the governments of member state in terms of economic policy making. Such policies were portrayed as detrimental to distinct varieties of capitalism and welfare and also national democracy. The persistent breaching of the SGP in the first decade of the single currency brought into question Gill's assertions (Parker 2008). But the moves described above, to harden economic and fiscal governance during the crisis, particularly for those countries in receipt of financial assistance, might amount to the realization of Gill's thesis. The crisis certainly served to reinforce claims of a democratic deficit in the EU and can be linked to the rise of populist political movements and parties in certain member states (see also Chapters 3, 'Democracy and Legitimacy' and 11, 'The Populist Challenge').

Many commentators and academics argued, from a 'neo-Keynesian' perspective, that the official reforms, geared towards policies of austerity, not only had socially deleterious effects, but would also undermine aggregate demand (consumption) and therefore economic growth in the European economy. They would therefore extend and prolong the crisis (see, for instance, Blyth 2013; Patomaki 2013). Such 'neo-Keynesian' views were echoed in political debate during the crisis.

Others have argued that the ECB bears a significant responsibility for the escalation of the crisis. Tooze (2018b) has, in particular, suggested that under Trichet in the early period of the global financial crisis and the eurozone crisis (see Insight 11.1), the ECB might have been far more active in defending sovereign states against the bond market. He suggests that it chose not to because Trichet actively used the ECB's power to impose fiscal discipline in line with the abovementioned ordo-liberal and German preferences.

For many of these critics, the roots of the crisis lay, above all, in the financial sector (Tooze 2018a). Any policy reforms should therefore involve radical reforms to finance at various levels of governance. However, as noted in 'Long-Term Reforms' above, neither limited reforms nor a substantive banking union had materialized by 2019.

CONCLUSION

Economic and monetary union raises many of the issues that are consistent themes of this book. The debate between supranational and intergovernmental interpretations of the nature of European integration rages as fiercely here as it does for the single market programme; and the creation of another independent supranational institution, the ECB, feeds the argument between the same positions about the nature of the EU and its institutions. The form of monetary union that was adopted gave rise to a chorus of critiques of EMU, that became all the louder in the context of the post-2008 crisis.

The previous history of attempts to achieve EMU clearly indicated that the attempt at the end of the 1980s would have to face up to the difficult issue of the form that the monetary union would take. French and German views on the matter had long differed. France favoured institutional arrangements that would put the ECB directly under the guidance and ultimate control of the governments of the member states. West Germany favoured an independent central bank, not because the West German government wanted to increase the degree of supranationalism inherent in the EC's institutional architecture, but because the West German post-war tradition was that the value of the currency should not be subject to political interference, but should be determined by an independent bank. The Bundesbank had always been fiercely independent of the federal government in West Germany, and the confidence of the West German people in the new currency would be vitally dependent on similar arrangements applying to the ECB.

In terms of economic governance, a divide between these two countries has also long existed. Germany favoured a strict rules-based system which would promote economic discipline (and convergence) among member states within the eurozone, while France favoured greater flexibility and discretion in national economic management. Ultimately, German preferences prevailed on both the ECB and economic governance. However, persistent breaching of the SGP (including by Germany) created doubts about the effectiveness of economic governance. Such concerns intensified during the eurozone crisis.

In the context of the crisis, the German-inspired rules-based system was significantly hardened. At the same time, however, the crisis precipitated various forms of 'fire-fighting'—notably the deployment of financial assistance to struggling states and an increasingly activist and politicized ECB—which created anxiety in Germany. The conditions attached to financial support served at the same time to exacerbate the sense in heavily affected 'debtor' member states that monetary union (and the EU more generally) had limited the ability of member states' governments to manage their domestic economies and thereby effectively undermined national democracy (Parker and Tsarouhas 2018; see also Chapter 11, 'The Unfolding Eurozone Crisis', and Chapter 3, 'Democracy and Legitimacy').

For many observers, the underlying issue—long recognized but still apparently insoluble—is that monetary union does not amount to political and economic union, but might ultimately require such union (Cohen 2012). The post-2008 crisis, and assaults by the financial markets on the sovereign debt of certain member states, revealed—indeed, it may to some extent have been *caused by*—the weakness of a system which has a single centralized monetary policy but no common fiscal or transfer policy. However, radical reforms in that direction will not be easily achieved given opposition from key member states, as described (see also Marsh 2013). Member states within the eurozone have very different views on what form any deeper integration should take and those outside are unlikely to want to become involved in the project in the near future (see also Chapter 11).

KEY POINTS

History

- In 1969, the Hague Summit committed the EC to achieve 'EMU by 1980'.

- There was tension over EMU between Germany and France. Germany made anti-inflationary policies the priority; France made economic growth the priority, even at the risk of higher inflation.

- This disagreement led to the compromise proposals of the Werner Committee for closer co-ordination of economic policy, accompanied by tying together the exchange rates of member states within narrow margins of fluctuations (the 'snake in the tunnel').

- The snake was ultimately broken by a combination of divergence in the economic performance of the members and the US policy of allowing the dollar to devalue.

- In the period following the 1973 oil crisis, other member states began to follow Germany's lead in supporting a low-inflation policy. This removed a major barrier to greater currency co-operation.

- In October 1977, the Commission President, Roy Jenkins, called for a new attempt at EMU. This initiative was supported by German Chancellor Schmidt and French President Giscard d'Estaing.

- In December 1978, the Bremen European Council created the EMS.

Origins of EMU

- In 1988, the Hanover European Council set up the Delors Committee to report on the steps needed to strengthen monetary co-operation in the light of the single market.

- An IGC in 1991 set a timetable for completion of monetary union, which would be not later than January 1999.

- The Maastricht Treaty (1992) set stringent criteria to ensure the convergence of member state economies prior to participation in monetary union.

Putting Maastricht into Operation (1992–2002)

- Germany won all of the main arguments over the details of the monetary union, including the name of the single currency, the criteria that would guide its operation, the location of the ECB, and the identity of its first governor.

- The euro was launched in January 1999. Only Britain, Denmark, and Sweden declined to take part, while Greece failed to meet the qualifying criteria.

- Denmark and Greece joined a revised ERM-2. Later members of the EU were required to be members of this system for two years before being allowed into the euro.

The Single Currency in Operation

- A Eurogroup was set up by the members of the single currency. It assumed considerable importance, weakening the role of ECOFIN.

- Euro notes and coins were introduced at the start of 2002.

- When France and Germany breached the rules of the SGP in 2002–03, they refused to accept censure from the Commission. In March 2005, the mandatory system for enforcing budgetary discipline was replaced by a more flexible set of guidelines.

The Eurozone Crisis

- The eurozone crisis began in 2009 when it was revealed that Greece had concealed the true state of its public finances and it became increasingly difficult for the Greek government to finance its debt. The crisis soon spread to other eurozone states.

- The EU responded with a series of crisis management 'fire-fighting' exercises, including a 'bail-out' mechanism for struggling member states and a series of interventions by the ECB. These came with tough conditions attached, which effectively imposed austerity programmes on governments in receipt of assistance.

- Germany and other northern 'creditor' member states emphasized lax rules of economic governance in explaining the crisis and their reform preferences were geared towards toughening such rules.

- France and southern 'debtor' member states emphasized the need for greater political management of EMU, and increased solidarity, particularly from Germany.

- The social, political, and economic effects of the crisis led to a sharp decline in the popular legitimacy of the EU and can be linked to the rise of populism in some member states.

Explaining and Critiquing EMU

- Supranationalist explanations have included spillover, the role of the Commission, and the role of central bankers as an epistemic community.

- Intergovernmental explanations have stressed geo-political factors and domestic economic factors.

- Critical perspectives on EMU argue that both its original design and recent 'crisis' reforms contain a neoliberal bias which privileges particular groups and is inherently anti-democratic.

 For additional material and resources, please visit the online resources www.oup.com/uk/bache5e.

QUESTIONS

1. Why did it take so long to achieve the long-standing aspiration to establish a single currency?
2. Which theories of integration are most convincing in explaining the drive towards EMU?
3. What were the main causes of the eurozone crisis?
4. Critically assess the responses of the EU to the eurozone crisis.
5. Has the eurozone crisis driven further integration (and is that likely to continue)?

FURTHER READING

A starting point for further reading that attempts to explain the development of EMU is **D. R. Cameron**, 'Economic and Monetary Union: Underlying Imperatives and Third-Stage Dilemmas', *Journal of European Public Policy*, 4 (1997): 455–85, which examines why the member states perceived EMU to be in their national interest, and considers some of the practical problems involved in operating a single currency. **W. Sandholtz**, 'Choosing Union: Monetary Politics and Maastricht', *International Organization*, 47 (1993): 1–39, reviews the history of the decision on monetary union, and analyses it in the light of theoretical perspectives, including neofunctionalism and intergovernmentalism. The intergovernmental viewpoint is best represented by **A. Moravcsik**, *The Choice for Europe: Social Purpose and State Power from Messina to Maastricht* (London: UCL Press, 1998), 379–471. An excellent, detailed history is provided by **K. Dyson and K. Featherstone**, *The Road to Maastricht: Negotiating Economic and Monetary Union* (Oxford: Oxford University Press, 1999). Slightly more recent books that provide valuable insights are **M. Chang**, *Monetary Integration in the European Union* (Basingstoke: Palgrave Macmillan, 2009), and **D. Marsh**, *The Euro: The Politics of the New Global Currency* (New Haven, CT, and London: Yale University Press, 2009).

Books dealing specifically with the post-2008 crisis include **M. Matthijs and M. Blyth (eds)**, *The Future of the Euro* (New York: Oxford University Press, 2015) (especially Chapter 1), **O. Parker and D. Tsarouhas (eds)**, *Crisis in the Eurozone Periphery: The Political Economies of Greece, Spain, Ireland and Portugal* (London, Palgrave Macmillan, 2018) (especially Chapter 1), and **D. Marsh**, *Europe's Deadlock: How the Euro Crisis Could be Solved—and Why it Won't Happen* (New Haven, CT, and London: Yale University Press, 2013). For a critical political economy perspective that places EMU and the eurozone crisis into a broader context of capitalist development in Europe, see **M. Ryner and A. Cafruny**, *The European Union and Global Capitalism: Origins, Development, Crisis* (London, Palgrave Macmillan, 2017). **A. Tooze**, *Crashed: How a Decade of Financial Crisis Changed the World* (Allen House, 2018) (especially Part III) will be useful for those seeking to contextualize the eurozone crisis in relation to the broader post-2007 global financial crisis.

Chapter 21

Agriculture

Chapter Overview

The Common Agricultural Policy (CAP) was the first redistributive policy of the European Community (EC), and for many years the only one. It was designed as a market-correcting policy that sought to put in place measures to protect the European agriculture sector from international pressure through a combination of price support for EU products and high external tariffs for agricultural imports. The primary purpose of the original CAP was to ensure security of food supplies in the Community. However, the CAP rapidly proved highly expensive and encouraged overproduction. The policy was subject to damaging publicity and extensive criticism for its wine lakes and butter mountains and the dumping of cheap exports on international markets. Yet despite the policy's obvious flaws it proved notoriously difficult to reform. Farmers' groups fiercely resisted change and their importance in the domestic politics of key member states ensured that early reforms were slow and piecemeal. Only in the context of new internal and external pressures from the 1990s was significant change secured.

History

Agriculture was one of only four common policies that had its own title in the Treaty of Rome. The importance given to the sector owed a great deal to food shortages at the end of the Second World War. Governments agreed that it was important to ensure adequate supplies of food at reasonable prices. To achieve this goal, it was necessary to provide an adequate income to farmers, while taking measures to increase their productivity. All of the states involved in the original EEC were in agreement on these objectives.

France had a particular interest in agriculture (see Chapter 6, 'The Road to the Rome Treaties'). Small French farmers were politically important because they had the sympathy of the French people. On the other hand, France also had a lot of large and efficient farms. Part of the price that the French insisted on for their participation in the common market in industrial goods was the subsidization of the cost of maintaining their small farmers, plus the guarantee of a protected market for French agricultural exports.

Had the EC simply abolished restrictions on free trade in foodstuffs, the effect would have been to produce competition between member states to subsidize their own farmers. So free trade was not viable. Yet, it was also recognized that the equalization of food prices was important for fair competition in industrial products. Higher food prices meant that workers demanded higher wages, thus raising industry's costs. To have a level playing field of competition in industrial goods, cost differences arising from the effect of food prices needed to be limited.

Before reform in the 1980s, the CAP was a price support system. Every year national Ministers of Agriculture decided the level of prices for agricultural products that were covered by the CAP. These prices were ensured by the intervention of the Commission in the market to buy up enough of each product to maintain the agreed price. If prices subsequently rose above the agreed level, the produce that the Commission had purchased and placed into storage would be released onto the market to bring the price back down. In practice, though, this did not occur.

Prices were set at the level that would ensure the least efficient farmers in the EC an adequate income, which encouraged the more efficient, large-scale farmers to maximize their output, because the price was more than adequate to guarantee them a return on their investment. In short, farmers had an incentive to overproduce and consequently, surpluses in most products became permanent. The Commission's interventions in the market were all in one direction: to keep up prices by intervention buying. The amounts of produce in storage constantly grew and became an embarrassment, prompting press reports of 'food mountains' and 'wine lakes'. The cost of storage also became a significant burden on the Community budget. In an attempt to address at least this part of the cost, a decision was made in the course of the 1970s to encourage the export of the surpluses instead of storing them. As world market prices for all products covered by the CAP were consistently lower than the guaranteed internal prices, it was necessary for the EC to pay farmers the difference between the price they received for the exports and the guaranteed price. Such export subsidies technically constitute what is known as the 'dumping' of products on world markets. It had the adverse effect of lowering world prices by adding to supply; but it also encouraged other agricultural producers to subsidize their own farmers so that they could compete with the EC farmers. This move from storage to export of surpluses was eventually to produce irresistible external pressure for reform of the CAP, although these pressures did not hit home until the 1980s.

Agricultural Reform

From the 1980s onwards, a series of internal and external pressures built up for reform of the CAP (see Insight 21.1), resulting in a series of changes described by Daugbjerg and Swinbank (2016) as policy layering. In short, a series of incremental changes and additions have been layered over the original CAP structures and processes gradually transforming the policy so that the CAP today is a very different beast from that created in the aftermath of the Second World War. First, the share of the EU budget dedicated to the CAP has shrunk from 70 per cent of the overall budget to a projected 28.5 per cent for the 2021–27 period. The link between the size of payment received and the level of production has been reformed—so called 'decoupling'—to reduce the incentives to overproduce; there is an emphasis upon the use of greening measures; and member-state governments are more directly involved in deciding how funds are spent within their countries. Spending is divided between Pillar 1, which channels direct payments to farmers and landowners and Pillar 2, which is dedicated to rural development. There have been numerous reforms to get the CAP to its current structure (see Daugbjerg and Swinbank 2016; Roederer-Rynning 2019; Buonanno and Nugent forthcoming for detail). The key recent changes were made in the 1990s via the MacSharry reforms, in 2000 and 2003 as part of the *Agenda 2000* process, largely in anticipation of the 2004 and 2007 enlargements and in 2013 against a backdrop of austerity and crisis. These revisions are detailed in Insight 21.1.

Insight 21.1 Main Reforms to the Common Agricultural Policy

Reform	Year	Driver for change	Main changes
MacSharry reforms	1992	External trade (Uruguay GATT round) Costs	Decrease in price support to bring European products in line with world prices Initial move towards decoupling of production from funding: direct support was introduced for incomes rather than production Land taken out of production Retirement scheme to encourage older farmers to cease production
Agenda 2000 reforms	1999	External trade Enlargement Costs	Further decrease in price support Introduced rural development policy under pillar structure with direct payments made under Pillar I and rural development delivered via Pillar II Extended decoupling Introduced voluntary cross compliance, which made direct income payments conditional on environmental and animal husbandry measures Introduced modulation, which allowed member states to reduce the direct payments in Pillar I by a small percentage and shift these funds to Pillar II Tight budgetary limits imposed
2003 Reform	2003	External trade (Doha GATT Round) Enlargement Costs	Effectively an extension of *Agenda 2000* Further cuts in price support Made cross-compliance and modulation compulsory
2013 Reform	2013	Costs	Introduced *greening* criteria, which made the payment of 30 per cent of the direct income payments dependent on compliance with environmental requirements Enabled (but did not require) member states to decrease direct income payments (Pillar I) above a certain level and to divert those funds into Pillar II Brought about a more equal distribution of agricultural support within regions and amongst member states (so-called harmonization)

Internal Pressures

There have been four key internal (endogenous) pressures for reform of the CAP: increasing costs, enlargement of the EU, environmental concern, and parliamentarization.

The Cost of the CAP

As noted in 'History' above, the CAP was based on the principle of price support. Under the policy the EU guaranteed prices and bought up surplus to support the price of agricultural produce, an approach that incentivized farmers and landowners to overproduce. Moreover, rational member-state governments would seek to increase their share of the CAP pie. As more and more food was produced and bought up by the Commission, it also had to be stored, further adding to costs.

Between 1974 and 1979 the cost of the CAP rose by 23 per cent, twice the rate of increase of incomes. It then stabilized between 1980 and 1982, but in 1983 the cost soared by 30 per cent, and the EC reached the ceiling of expenditure that could be covered from its own resources. Agreement to lift the limit had to be unanimous, and the British government refused to agree to any increase without firm measures to curb the cost of the CAP. This led to an agreement in 1984 on dairy quotas, and on a system of budgetary discipline whereby a maximum limit would be set to the size of the budget each year before the annual round of negotiations on agricultural prices. Ministers of Agriculture would therefore be negotiating within fixed parameters. Any budgetary overshoot would be clawed back in the following years.

In the event, this system did not work because there was no automatic mechanism for making the necessary adjustments to costs in the years following an overrun. Whilst these reforms marked significant departures from earlier policies, they 'failed to halt the relentless rise in the budget required for the CAP' (Colman 2007: 81). Pressures for reform continued to build, driven by the EU southern enlargement and external pressures, resulting in the MacSharry reforms of the 1990s. However, as the EU enlarged to encompass countries with large agricultural sectors, concerns about the budgetary implications of extending the CAP to new entrants prompted the *Agenda 2000* and 2003 reforms. Similarly, the advent of the eurozone crisis and the parallel negotiations over the multi-annual financial framework and the new CAP saw pressure to cut costs exerted once again in the run-up to the 2013 reforms (see Insight 21.1 on all these reforms). The 2021–27 CAP and multi-annual financial framework are being negotiated at the time of writing and, like the 2013 reforms, take place in a context of budgetary constraint, this time imposed by Brexit, which will see a net contributor to the EU budget leaving the Union.

Enlargement

The southern enlargements of the 1980s (see Chapter 26, 'History') brought new demands on the budget that could only be met by either diverting money away from existing beneficiaries or expanding the size of the budget. This situation was compounded by the insistence of the Spanish, Portuguese, and Greek governments that they would not be able to participate in the freeing of the internal market of the EC by the end of 1992 unless the structural funds were substantially increased. At the London meeting of the European Council in December 1986, agreement was reached in principle on the doubling of the structural funds by 1993, thus requiring an increase in resources. The first enlargement therefore added to the pressure for reform of the CAP to make room within the existing budget for these new items of expenditure.

With the collapse of communism at the end of the 1980s, Germany moved rapidly to reunification. In effect, this constituted an enlargement of the EC. The former East German territories included areas that were considerable agricultural producers, so threatening a big increase in the cost of the CAP.

Pressure on the EU to continue the process of reform of the CAP became greater as the former communist states of east-central Europe began to press ever more strongly for full membership of the EU in the 1990s. After some initial reluctance, most member states came around to the realization that it would be necessary to grant membership to most of these states (see Chapter 26, 'The "Eastern" Enlargement'). Germany in particular became a strong advocate of eastern enlargement. However, reports prepared by the Commission indicated that the existing CAP could not simply be applied to the applicant states without dramatic budgetary consequences.

Extension of the CAP to the acceding countries posed a number of difficulties. Given existing price gaps between candidate countries and generally substantially higher CAP prices, and despite prospects for some narrowing of these gaps by the dates of accession, even gradual introduction of CAP prices would tend to stimulate surplus production, in particular in the livestock sector, thus adding to projected surpluses. World Trade Organization (WTO) constraints on subsidized exports would prevent the enlarged Union from selling its surpluses on third markets (Avery and Cameron 1998: 153).

It was against this context that the *Agenda 2000* and the 2003 Reform of the CAP were brought forward. *Agenda 2000* was an ambitious package developed in response to the EU's imminent enlargement, in which the Commission spelt out its recommendations for the Union's financial framework for the period 2000–06 and for the future development of the Union's policies, and in particular its two most important spending policies—the cohesion and structural funds, and the CAP (Avery and Cameron 1998: 101). On CAP, it proposed large reductions in support prices that would be offset by compensation to farmers in the form of direct payments, with a ceiling on the level of aid that any one individual could receive. Although explicitly linked to the eastern enlargement in *Agenda 2000*, these reforms were in line with the direction of travel in international markets via the General Agreement on Trade and Tariffs (GATT).

When negotiations began on the CAP proposals of *Agenda 2000* in February 1999, the French government predictably pressed for more limited reform. This position was supported by 30,000 farmers—mainly from France, Germany, and Belgium—protesting on the streets of Brussels. After a temporary suspension of the negotiations, the agriculture ministers agreed, on 11 March, to cut cereal prices by 20 per cent, as proposed by the Commission, but to do so in two stages—one-half in 2000–01 and the other half in 2001–02. They agreed to lower milk prices by 15 per cent in line with the Commission's proposals, but only over three years starting in 2003, and dairy production quotas were actually raised slightly. They also agreed that beef prices should be cut by 20 per cent, but this was only two-thirds of the cut proposed by the Commission.

Commissioner for Agriculture Franz Fischler hailed the agreement as the most far-reaching reform of the CAP for forty years; but the states that had most strongly

403

supported reform—Britain, Italy, Sweden, and Denmark—expressed their disappointment. They did not like the delays in implementing the cuts that had been forced through by France and Germany (which held the presidency of the Council). They were to be even more disappointed following the Berlin European Council in March 1999, which was intended to approve the reform.

In Berlin, President Chirac of France simply refused to accept what the French Minister of Agriculture had negotiated. However, the German government was keen to secure agreement during its presidency, and not to break publicly with France, so Chancellor Schröder eventually agreed to support a significant further dilution of the reform package. The dairy reforms were further delayed, and the cuts in cereal prices were scaled back from the compromise level reached by the ministers of agriculture. The other member states went along in return for side-payments: Spain and Greece got agreement to a continuation of the Cohesion Fund (see Bache et al. 2015; 412–18); Britain got agreement to the continuation of the British budgetary rebate with only minor concessions.

> The Agenda 2000 outcome was thus deeply compromised and must be judged a missed opportunity to reform the CAP.
>
> (Lowe et al. 2002: 4)

But Commissioner Fischler did not give up. The 1999 reforms, although not as far-reaching as the Commission had wanted, did continue with the principle, first conceded in the MacSharry reforms (see Insight 21.1), that reduced production subsidies would be compensated by direct payments that were decoupled from production. In July 2002, Fischler put forward a revised proposal for the full decoupling of agricultural subsidies from production in the existing EU by the end of 2004. Under these proposals, the amounts of money that each member state would receive would be the same as under the system that had been agreed in Berlin, but the money would be paid in a lump sum to the governments, which could then distribute between their farmers as they saw fit, so long as it was not paid in the form of a production subsidy. So, governments that did not wish to enter into a confrontation with their larger farmers, who received the bulk of the subsidies under the existing system, could simply pay the money out according to historic distributions. Those that were keen to bring about a domestic restructuring of agricultural holdings could divide the money up differently. In either case, the payment would be linked to requirements for farmers to comply with EU-wide standards on environmental protection, food safety, and animal welfare. After almost a year of debate, the Council of Agriculture Ministers reached a compromise at the end of June 2003. The essence of the Commission's proposals was adopted, although the shift to direct payments was deferred until 2005, and individual member states could apply for exceptions until 2007 to continue to subsidize production where there was a risk of farmers withdrawing from production altogether.

Environmental Pressures

Since the 1980s, there has been increased concern about the environment in general, and about the effect of the CAP in particular (Lynggaard 2007: 300). As detailed in 'History' above, the main beneficiaries of the CAP were large farmers, who responded to the high prices by maximizing output through intensive agricultural practices, such as using fertilizers and pesticides. Increasing evidence of the link between intensive agriculture and declines in bird and insect populations, pollution of water sources, and contribution to greenhouse gas emissions led to increased green pressure to reform the CAP (Feindt 2010). The rise of environmentalism in Europe and the increased electoral success of green parties from the 1980s onwards (see Chapter 22, 'History') provided a counterweight to the general sympathy of European public opinion for farmers, and made it politically easier for governments to respond to the financial pressures with reform measures. The creation of a Directorate General (DG) of the Environment and the inclusion of the 'polluter pays' and precautionary principles into the Treaties also added to the impetus for reform (Feindt 2010).

Sympathy for modern farming methods was also adversely affected in the late 1980s and early 1990s by the outbreak of a number of scares about the safety of food. These included the growing concern over the use of genetically modified organisms (GMOs), salmonella and dioxins in poultry products, and the epidemic of 'mad cow disease', or bovine spongiform encephalopathy (BSE) in the United Kingdom, which reached its height in 1992. Blame for these food scares was attributed to intensive farming methods that ignored the welfare of animals. The issue of food safety is not strictly an environmental concern, but it is closely related and was associated with concerns about damage to the environment in the minds of the European public.

These problems led to a change in the perception of the CAP, even among those institutions and groups most closely associated with it, so that 'by 1992, the conception that intensive farming is the source of both problems of agricultural surplus production and environmental depletion was institutionalized among all the central agents within the CAP' (Lynggaard 2007: 302). Since the 1990s, this shift in perception, coupled with external pressure for reform, has led to the inclusion of funding for environmental measures. A key innovation of the 2013 reforms was to introduce green payments under Pillar 1 of the CAP, for which all farmers in receipt of Pillar 1 funds must apply. However, this green payment scheme has been widely derided as ineffective (Pe'er et al. 2014; Hart 2015). In 2017, the European Court of Auditors (ECA) found that the greening measures adopted since the 2013 reforms had only secured a positive change in 5 per cent of EU farmland, mostly because a majority of the audited farmers (65 per cent) did not have to change their farming practices to qualify for green payments (European Court of Auditors 2017). The ECA also found that member states have implemented greening in ways that minimize the burden on themselves and their farmers. In addition, the Commission failed to set specific objectives for assessing the performance of greening measures (Tamma 2017). Unsurprisingly, given these problems, initial proposals for the 2021–27 CAP reform were subject to criticisms from environmental campaigners, and there were calls for the system of greening payments to be strengthened (Matthews 2018).

Parliamentarization

The increase in budgetary and legislative powers of the European Parliament (EP) has had direct and indirect effects upon the CAP. First, indirectly, the EP has persistently used its budgetary powers to call for the percentage of budget spent on the CAP to be reduced. The main budgetary battles between the EP and the Council were focused around trying to move funding from compulsory spending to non-compulsory spending, over which the EP had more say. The EP also campaigned for the right to exercise powers of co-decision over all policy areas. The extension of the ordinary legislative procedure to agriculture in the Lisbon Treaty and the simultaneous abolition of the distinction between compulsory (i.e. agriculture) and non-compulsory expenditure represented the culmination of a long battle to achieve parity with the Council in relation to agriculture (Roederer-Rynning and Schimmelfennig 2012), and gave the EP a direct role in amending the CAP and its budget.

The EP has long been identified as an 'environmental champion' within the EU's institutional structures (Burns 2013), and it was anticipated that the greater involvement of the EP could lead to further pressure for greening the CAP and the scope for a wider array of actors to become involved in decision making. The EP was certainly closely involved in the 2013 reform to the CAP. There were over forty meetings involving Members of the European Parliament (MEPs) from the Committee on Agriculture and Rural Development (COMAGRI) and representatives of the Council to negotiate an agreement (Greer 2017). However, the anticipated opening up of policy making to bring in a wider array of actors failed to materialize. Parliamentary negotiators are drawn from the lead committee within Parliament, and COMAGRI is dominated by producerist interests and is traditionally quite conservative (Roederer-Rynning and Schimmelfennig 2012). Matthews (2013) argued that the idea that the EP 'would bring new ideas to the debate and help to widen the range of interests that could influence agricultural policy … proved to be hopelessly naïve'. Indeed, the principal impact of the EP's closer involvement in CAP policy making was to extend the length of time it took to negotiate a final package. The EP elected in 2019 had a greater percentage of Green MEPs and, had within a few months declared a climate emergency and called for a green new deal in Europe, which may mean that MEPs will be more inclined to push for a greener CAP in the next round of negotiations.

External Pressures

External (or exogenous) pressures proved a strong incentive for change. As noted in 'History' above, the CAP was underpinned by subsidies, coupled with a high external tariff to protect European producers. When oversupply became an issue the Commission effectively dumped produce on the world markets, driving down prices. This action had particularly negative effects for poorer countries in the Global South, where domestic products were unable to compete with cheaper European ones. This system consequently attracted opprobrium from development non-governmental organizations (NGOs), but also crucially from other large agricultural producers, such as the United States, which also found it hard to compete (see Chapter 24, 'External Trade Policy'). The US made the phasing out of agricultural subsidies a central part of its negotiating position for the trade talks under the General Agreement on Tariffs and Trade (GATT), which began in 1986 and were known as the Uruguay Round. It was joined by the Cairns Group of fourteen agricultural-producing states, including Australia, Canada, New Zealand, and several Latin American states. All felt that they suffered from the dumping of the EC's agricultural exports onto world markets.

The 'MacSharry reforms' of 1992 allowed Ray MacSharry (See Insight 21.1), the Commissioner for Agriculture, to negotiate a deal on agricultural trade that temporarily satisfied the United States and the Cairns Group, and meant that it was possible to conclude the Uruguay Round. That was not the end of the story, though. At the conclusion of the Uruguay Round, it was agreed to open a further round of trade talks at the end of 1999. It was clear that the compromises on agricultural trade reached in the Uruguay Round were provisional, and that agriculture would be a central element of the new round.

At the end of the Uruguay Round, agreement had been reached to allow both the EU and the United States to continue to subsidize cereal and livestock farmers. These measures had, in the terminology of the agreement, been placed in a 'blue box'. This meant that the subsidies distorted production, but could be continued without legal challenge until 2003, provided that they were not increased. Another 'green box' was created, consisting of support for farmers that did not distort production. These included measures such as those that had already been introduced into the CAP by the MacSharry reforms: measures to take land out of production, or to encourage environmental protection. Since the agreement, the United States had unilaterally moved almost all of its support measures out of the blue box into the green box, leaving the EU alone in the blue box. Although the blue box measures were sustained until 2003, the EU was under tremendous pressure to reciprocate the unilateral US gesture (National Farmers' Union (NFU) 1996).

It was in this context that Franz Fischler, Agriculture Commissioner in the Santer Commission, produced a package of proposals for further reform in November 1995. These continued the pattern of the 1992 reforms, decoupling support for farmers from production and linking it to social and environmental objectives (European Commission 1995). They were subsequently incorporated into the Commission's *Agenda 2000* proposals (European Commission 1999a). Following the 2003 reforms, external pressure for further changes to the CAP eased, as negotiations under the Doha Round of the GATT stalled and were then effectively suspended in 2008.

The Effect of Reform

Although it had been a long and sometimes frustrating series of negotiations, the cumulative effect on the CAP of the reform process has been to bring about a considerable shift in the pattern of support for farmers away from price support to direct support. By 2002–03, direct payments, or 'compensatory payments', accounted for 65 per cent of CAP support, and the June 2003 agreement meant that by 2007 all support would be in this form. This, when combined with 'set-aside' requirements, reduced the production surpluses that had plagued the system since it was set up, but did nothing to redress the problem that the bulk of receipts from the CAP went to a small number of large farmers. In 2003, the Organization for Economic Co-operation and Development (OECD) estimated that 70 per cent of CAP support still went to the richest 25 per cent of farms.

Large farmers had always benefited more than small farmers from the CAP because they were able to achieve higher yields. Thus, when payments were related to output, the larger and more efficient farmers pocketed the largest share. Direct payments were introduced under MacSharry to compensate farmers for the reduction in guaranteed prices towards world market prices. In order to minimize opposition to the changes, the direct payments were based on the size of farms. Farmers received payments linked to the number of hectares that they farmed. This reduced the incentive to maximize yields, which was the primary aim of the exercise. Production was further curtailed by making it a requirement of receiving the direct payments that 15 per cent of arable land be set aside and not used to produce crops. Similarly, meat producers were required to reduce the density of livestock per hectare in order to qualify for the direct payments. *Agenda 2000* extended the same principle further. It did nothing, though, to redirect subsidies from rich farmers to poor farmers. This political hot potato was effectively dropped into the laps of national governments by the June 2003 agreement to move to a 'single farm payment' that governments could distribute between different categories of farms as they chose.

The 2013 reform was driven primarily by overall budgetary concerns, and the desire of the governments of the member states to save money over the period of the next multi-annual financial framework (MFF). As the CAP, despite previous reforms, still accounted for 40 per cent of the EU's overall budget, it was obvious from the outset that it would have to take its share of the austerity in public spending that set in with recession and the crisis in the eurozone. Although the hand of the big farmers had been strengthened by developments since the 2003 negotiations, they were only able to play this hand within agricultural negotiations: the financial decisions were taken in a different forum. The result was an agreement that reversed some of the previous gains in environmental protection and rural development, and did nothing to resolve the imbalance in payments to large and small farmers. It did, though, mean that CAP expenditure declined to below 40 per cent of the overall budget for the first time ever, and this is a remarkable difference from the 70 per cent that it took immediately before the reform processes that were initiated from the 1980s onwards.

Future Prospects: 2021–27

In 2016, negotiations began over the future of the CAP and its funding from 2021 to 2027. The initial proposals for the MFF sought to reduce the percentage of the budget dedicated to the CAP to below 30 per cent (to 28.5 per cent). The Commission's stated aims for the new CAP were to streamline and simplify it, to secure a fairer distribution of support, to encourage generational renewal, and to improve environmental outcomes. Nine key priorities have been identified (see Figure 21.1).

The plans will maintain the current two-pillar structure, with direct payments continuing. In order to address the ongoing issue of a high percentage share of support going to large holdings, the Commission has proposed capping the maximum amount that a single beneficiary can receive to €100,000. In a break with the 2013 reforms, the greening payment will be replaced by climate and environment programmes and the responsibility for those programmes will be handled by national authorities (European Commission 2019c). However, every time there have been moves to reform the CAP farming organizations and national governments have mobilized to water down plans, and similar dynamics have already emerged for these proposals, which have,

Figure 21.1 Nine objectives of the CAP 2021–2027

Source: https://ec.europa.eu/info/food-farming-fisheries/key-policies/common-agricultural-policy/future-cap_en. © European Union, 1995–2020.

unsurprisingly, generated opposition from farming organizations. However, a key change for the 2021–27 reforms, especially compared to 2013, is the heightened level of public concern over climate change and the environment. There is also a new Commission President, Ursula von der Leyen, who has identified the environment as a key concern for her term of office. In combination, these factors could provide a counterweight to the watering down of greening measures.

Explaining and Critiquing the CAP

Hardly surprisingly, intergovernmentalism (see Chapter 1, 'Theories of European Integration') can be used to explain the establishment of the CAP. Until the signing of the Treaties, there were no European institutional actors to take into account. The importance of agriculture has to be understood in terms of the perceived national interests of the six states that came together to form the European Economic Community (EEC). It is often told as the story of how French agricultural interests made a deal with German industrial interests to produce an EEC founded on the twin pillars of the industrial common market and the guided price support system of the CAP. This, though, is an oversimplification, and liberal intergovernmentalism, which looks at the domestic politics that produce the positions taken up by national governments in international negotiations, directs our attention to the importance of agriculture and of farmers in all the member states.

Neofunctionalism (see Chapter 1, 'Theories of European Integration') could only come into play once the EEC and the CAP existed, with institutional actors being formed at the European level, but several elements of neofunctionalism can be seen in the history of the CAP. Setting up a system of support for agriculture that was based on fixing the prices of commodities, in a context of mixed farming sizes, inevitably caused problems. The price level that was needed to keep inefficient small farmers in business was so high that it encouraged more efficient farmers to increase output to the maximum level. When combined with technological advances, this led to the food surpluses that became one of the biggest headaches of the EC. This outcome was not an unanticipated consequence of the CAP, though. It was foreseen by the Commission, which used it as a lever to get member states to take the next step of rationalizing farm sizes. So, this was a potential example of cultivated spillover. However, it did not work because the governments of the member states retreated from radical reform in the face of domestic political pressures, thus providing some support for the liberal intergovernmental critique of neofunctionalism (see Chapter 1, 'Theories of European Integration').

Turning to the theories of governance (see Chapter 2, 'Governance'), the CAP appears at first sight to be a prime example of a sector where supranational governance applies. Support for agriculture had been transferred from the national to the EC/EU level. Policy communities of national farmers' organizations and bureaucrats in national ministries of agriculture were apparently replaced by a European policy community of EU farmers' organizations and Commission officials in the Directorate General for Agriculture. However, decisions both on fixing annual price levels and on the regulation and reform of the system remained firmly with national ministers of agriculture meeting in the Council of Ministers. The extent to which these ministers became identified with the interests of their sector, rather than with the interests of their governments, is a question for empirical research, but examples of ministers having to be overruled by the heads of government suggest that this particular Council may have developed a supranational tinge. More significantly, perhaps, the national bureaucrats in agriculture ministries remained involved, if for no other reason than that the actual implementation and administration of the policy remained at national level. The CAP may always, then, have been more accurately analysed as a system of multi-level governance (MLG) rather than an example of supranational governance, and the reform process that was concluded in June 2003 enhanced the multi-level nature of the sector by restoring considerable discretion over the expenditure of CAP receipts to the national level.

That reform of the CAP became possible at all in the 1980s and 1990s has been explained through a variety of different theoretical perspectives.

Fouilleux (2007: 345), without using the term 'epistemic community' (see Chapter 2, 'EU Governance Approaches'), adopted an explanation that invoked the importance of academic experts. She emphasized a learning process within the international agricultural policy community, a process that was sparked off by an exercise that the OECD initiated to review the agricultural policies of its member states. The responsible officials asked academics, mainly agricultural economists, to undertake a critique of existing policies, and, '[t]his process engendered a learning process within the international agricultural policy community and induced a profound change in the way agricultural policy issues were defined'.

The MacSharry reforms were the result of a combination of internal and external pressures, but there is a vigorous academic debate about how important the different pressures were in producing the reforms. Rieger (2000: 193–6) argued that it was the mounting cost of the CAP that forced reform. Swinbank and Daugbjerg (2006; and Daugbjerg and Swinbank 2008) dismissed this argument and sided with Grant (1997: 196) in emphasizing the central importance of the international trade negotiations; indeed, according to Daugbjerg and Swinbank (2008: 637), this pressure 'had a decisive impact on the EU's decision to embark on CAP reform'.

More recent work using a political economy approach (See Chapter 4, 'Critical Political Economy') has used the theoretical lens of post-exceptionalism to analyse the ways in which the neoliberal paradigm has impacted the CAP. The argument advanced within this work is that the CAP was treated as a special or exceptional case by policy makers, characterized by a closed policy community and insulated against market pressures. However, as international trade negotiations intensified the spread of neoliberal practices and approaches, the pressures for CAP reform grew. Scholars have therefore sought to uncover whether the CAP has changed fundamentally to become a post-exceptional policy—i.e. one that is no longer afforded special treatment due to the entry of new actors and processes (see Daugbjerg and Feindt 2017). Greer (2017) suggests that there has only been 'shallow' post-exceptionalism: the agricultural policy subsystem has opened up to new actors and there has been a limited degree of programme change, but the ideational framework underpinning the CAP has been left largely intact, thereby limiting the extent of genuine change. It is worth noting though that Greer's (2017) analysis focuses upon the 2013 reforms, which have been acknowledged to be relatively limited.

The 2013 reforms were undertaken against the background of faltering negotiations on world trade, which considerably reduced the pressure for change in the CAP. Global economic conditions deteriorated rapidly after 2008, and governments faced a tide of public opinion against further liberalization of trade in a context of rising domestic unemployment. At the same time, the need to reduce government debt put a premium on reining-in public expenditure, especially in the eurozone (see Chapter 20, 'The Eurozone Crisis'), which meant that finance ministers and heads of government insisted on a tight overall budgetary settlement for the EU. It was this budgetary squeeze, rather than the pressure from international trade negotiations, that drove the 2013 reforms. The difference from 2003 was that then the requirements of the WTO talks implied a particular direction of reform for the CAP, whereas the budgetary constraint in 2013 required only that CAP expenditure be reduced. In this context, and with a relaxation of the level of public concern about the environment, the strength of the traditional agricultural lobbies came to the fore once more to produce an agreement that did little to green agriculture policy (Alons 2017), to restructure agriculture, or to promote rural development, and left crucial questions about issues such as the balance of payments between large and small farms to national governments, further contributing to the fragmentation and renationalization of the CAP. Intergovernmental theories of the EU seem most relevant here. Budgetary constraints imposed by Brexit, coupled with heightened public concern over the environment, will be subject to further change during the next round of negotiations.

CONCLUSION

For three decades, from the late 1950s to the late 1980s, agricultural policy was absolutely central to both European integration and to academic attempts to understand the process. Then, at the end of the 1980s, a programme of reform began that rapidly moved the policy sector to the periphery of the EU. After many unsuccessful attempts to bring about reform, the CAP was beginning to look entrenched and immutable. Yet, when reform began, it moved remarkably quickly. Within a few years, one of the pillars of European integration had been effectively dismantled, and the policy had been effectively renationalized.

Although new policy areas have pushed agriculture out of its central role within the EU, the explanation for the evolution of the CAP remains an interesting historical and theoretical case study. The variety of explanations offered for the CAP's movement from core to peripheral policy covers a wide range of the theoretical perspectives identified in Part One of this book, and whilst the CAP is a less central policy, it still accounted for just less than 40 per cent of the EU budget from 2014–20.

KEY POINTS

History

- France made it a condition of its participation in the EEC that agricultural policy be a joint pillar alongside the common market in industrial goods.
- The policy that was set up was based on supporting the price of agricultural products so as to maintain the incomes of farmers.
- Prices were set through political bargaining and tended to be high, so as to give an adequate income to small, inefficient farmers, who were politically influential.
- The high prices encouraged large, efficient farmers to produce large surpluses.
- Storing the surpluses put a huge strain on the budget of the EC, and disposing of them through export subsidies attracted hostility from other agricultural-producing states.
- There have been a series of reforms driven by the internal and external pressures.
- Internal pressures have included the increasing budgetary cost of the CAP, enlargement, environmental pressures, and parliamentarization.
- External pressures have stemmed from other states in the context of world trade negotiations and the growing neoliberalization of world trade.

The Effect of Reform

- Decoupling subsidies from production allowed for better budgetary control and put the EU in a stronger position in world trade negotiations.
- The subsidies were only gradually extended to new member states in central and eastern Europe, thus preventing the feared sudden hike in budgetary costs.
- As a result of the 2013 reform, agricultural expenditure declined below 40 per cent of the overall EU budget for the first time, but several decisions were left to heads of government, and some, such as the balance in payments to large and small farmers, were decentralized to national level.

Explaining and Critiquing the CAP

- Intergovernmentalism and liberal intergovernmentalism explain the establishment of the CAP.

- Neofunctionalists expected spillover from the initial CAP both to lead to the reform of agriculture and to produce other common policies, but governments managed to resist these pressures for a long time.

- Both supranational governance and MLG capture key elements of the CAP prior to the 2003 reforms, but following these reforms the analytical lens of MLG is more appropriate.

- Various explanations have been given of the reform of the CAP, emphasizing the role of ideas, of policy communities, of internal pressures, and external pressures.

 For additional material and resources, please visit the online resources www.oup.com/uk/bache5e.

QUESTIONS

1. What was the primary purpose of the CAP?

2. How and why have the CAP's aims changed over time?

3. What are the main challenges associated with the CAP in the current era?

4. Which integration theories best capture and explain the EU's CAP?

5. Do you think agricultural policy should still be treated as an exceptional policy that requires special protection?

FURTHER READING

C. Roederer-Rynning provides an excellent review of the literature and overview of the evolution of the CAP in 'The Common Agricultural Policy: A Case of Embedded Liberalism', *Oxford Research Encyclopaedia Politics* (2019). DOI: 10.1093/acrefore/9780190228637.013.1032. **C. Daugbjerg and P. Feindt's** special issue 'Post-Exceptionalism in Public Policy: Transforming Food and Agricultural Policy', *Journal of European Public Policy* 24 (2017), provides a useful collection of articles reviewing whether and how agricultural policy has changed in recent years. On greening the CAP, **G. Alons** provides a detailed account of the limits of greening reform in 2013 in 'Environmental Policy Integration in the EU's Common Agricultural Policy: Greening or Greenwashing?', *Journal of European Public Policy*, 24 (2017): 1604–22. A comprehensive analysis of the key reforms pre-2013, drawing on the evidence of some of those involved in making the decisions (including Ray MacSharry and Franz Fischler) is presented in **A. Cunha with A. Swinbank**, *An Inside View of the CAP Reform Process: Explaining the MacSharry, Agenda 2000, and Fischler Reforms* (Oxford: Oxford University Press, 2011). **Alan Matthews** runs a useful blog on the CAP with regular updates of reforms: http://capreform.eu/.

Chapter 22

Environment and Climate

Chapter Overview

When the European Union was established, environmental issues were low on the political agenda. However, from the 1960s onwards they became more prominent at both national and European levels. As the Single European Market was created, policy makers moved to address the negative environmental externalities associated with economic growth through creating market-cushioning policies to mitigate harm to the environment. Today, the EU has a comprehensive suite of environment and climate policies, with two Directorates General in the Commission responsible for policy development. The EU has experimented with new environmental policy instruments and has attempted to become a major player, especially in relation to climate change, at the global level. However, implementation deficits have raised concerns over its ability to resolve environmental problems and at the international level its leading role has been compromised by its inability to speak with one voice. Moreover, after years of expansion there has been a slowdown in policy activity since the late 2000s, which has been attributed to the global financial and economic crisis, the enlargement of the Union, and policy saturation. Nevertheless, EU environmental policy has remained resilient in the face of these challenges, and since 2019 there has been a renewed emphasis on this policy area.

This chapter gives a brief historical account of environmental policy, examines recent developments, and discusses some of the major issues of current concern. Finally, the policy's evolution is discussed, drawing on the theories presented in Part One of this book.

History

There was no reference to the environment in the founding Treaties. At the national level, there were also no coherent environmental policies in most member states, so there was no pressure to co-ordinate policy measures at the EU level, other than to avoid trade distortions. Hence until 1973, environmental measures taken by the EU were few and far between (see Table 22.1).

This situation altered substantially over the ensuing years (see Table 22.2 for a timeline), which saw EU environmental policy move steadily up the policy agenda, eventually becoming a major focus for Commission President Ursula von der Leyen, who committed the EU to a European Green Deal in 2019 (see Insight 22.1). Yet, initial legislative activity in this area was characterized by reactive incrementalism, which gradually became more programmatic through the adoption of a series of Environmental

Table 22.1 Environmental Measures Taken Prior to 1973

Directive 59/221 on ionizing radiation (amended with directives 62/1633 and 66/45)

Directive 67/548 on the classification, packaging and labelling of dangerous substances (amended with directive 71/144)

Directive 70/157 on noise from vehicle exhaust systems

Directive 70/220 on carbon monoxide and hydrocarbon emissions from road vehicles

Directive 72/306 on emissions from diesel-engine vehicles

Source: Based on McCormick (2001: 45). Reproduced with permission of Springer Nature through PLSclear.

Table 22.2 EU Environment and Climate Policy: Key Milestones

1972	Heads of state and government ask the Commission to develop environmental policy
1973	First Environmental Action Plan
1977	Second Environmental Action Plan
1981	DG Environment created
1982	Third Environmental Action Plan
1986	Single European Act (SEA) adopted, which introduced formal legal base for environmental policy *Danish Bottle* case
1992	The Treaty of Maastricht established environmental protection as a key goal of the EU and extended qualified majority voting and the co-decision procedure to cover many areas of environmental policy
1993	Fifth Environmental Action Plan adopted, committing the EU to the pursuit of sustainable development
1997	Treaty of Amsterdam made promotion of sustainable development and environmental policy integration key goals of the EU Also introduced Environmental Guarantee Article (Article 193 TFEU) and further extended QMV and co-decision to cover most areas of environmental policy
2002	Sixth Environmental Action Programme adopted
2005	EU Emissions Trading Scheme launched
2009	Treaty of Lisbon committed EU to combatting climate change Failed EU diplomacy at Conference of the Parties climate meeting in Copenhagen.
2010	DG Climate Action created
2013	Seventh Environmental Action Programme adopted
2019	Green New Deal launched and EU commits to carbon neutrality by 2050

> **Insight 22.1 The European Green Deal**
>
> The European Green Deal was proposed by the incoming Commission President, Ursula von der Leyen, in 2019. In a decisive break with the Juncker Commission, which had showed limited interest in environmental and climate policy, von der Leyen moved swiftly to establish her environmental credentials. One reason for this initiative was to secure the support of the European Parliament for her candidacy as Commission President. The proposed Green Deal committed the EU to carbon neutrality by 2050 and a suite of policies were promised to help deliver that goal. These included:
>
> - a 'just transition' fund that could be used to ease the financial burdens of transition in states that were still dependent upon fossil fuels. This fund was central to securing buy-in from central and east European states, although as of December 2019 Poland had refused to sign up to the 2050 target;
> - a new 'climate law' designed to set the EU onto an irreversible path to climate neutrality;
> - a suite of sectoral policies to support and facilitate achieving carbon neutrality.
>
> *Source*: https://ec.europa.eu/info/strategy/priorities-2019-2024/european-green-deal_en.

Action Plans that articulated the principles and goals of environmental policy. A Directorate General (DG) of the Environment was created in 1981, signalling the importance of the issue area, and the environment was given increasing prominence in the Treaties from 1986 onwards. Today, the EU's environmental *acquis communautaire* covers the main media (air, water, soil), nature protection, and a range of pollutants. This evolution of environmental policy from being an afterthought to a major component of EU action has been driven by a range of factors: the state of the European environment; the growth of public concern and emergence of the environmental movement; the growth of international environmental agreements; economic drivers; and the behaviour of key policy entrepreneurs.

The European Environment

The principal explanation for the development of EU environmental policy was the increasing awareness of the negative environmental consequences of economic activity. A main turning point was the recognition of acid rain as a source of forest death (*Waldsterben*) in West Germany and Scandinavia. The UN Stockholm Conference on the Human Environment in 1972 saw governments recognize that economic and industrial activity was generating environmental damage, with negative implications for human health. The EU's member states were called upon to act together to address these challenges in an early acknowledgement of the suitability of the EU and its supranational institutions to tackle what is essentially a transboundary collective-action problem. The understanding of human impacts on the environment has expanded exponentially, with a range of high-profile issues (e.g. acid rain, the hole in the ozone layer, Chernobyl, deforestation, and climate change) driving up awareness and concern and justifying the development of a range of policies. These tend to emerge in waves, depending upon the agenda of the Commission and the perceived need for activity. The main policy preoccupations of the EU since the late 2000s have been upon climate change, plastics, and the development of a circular economy.

Public Awareness

Related to the scientific and governmental recognition of environmental problems was the growth of public awareness of environmental pollution. The 1960s saw the emergence of a range of radical social movements on peace, the rights of women, and the environment. The environmental movements evolved over time into a sophisticated network of environmental non-governmental organizations (ENGOs) and looser movements such as the school climate strikes of 2019 and Extinction Rebellion (see Insight 22.2). The 1980s also saw burgeoning electoral successes for green parties, many of which emerged from those social movements. Whilst levels of concern have changed over time, typically dipping in times of economic contraction, European citizens continue to express concern for the environment. Hence, Eurobarometer polls from 2019 show that 93 per cent of the European public thought that climate change was a serious concern (Eurobarometer 2019*a*) and 14 per cent of the European public identified environment and climate as one of the top two issues they were most concerned about (Eurobarometer 2019*b*).

International Environmental Policy

As noted in 'History' above, from the 1970s onwards states across the world increasingly recognized the environmental consequences of economic and industrial activity and started developing international environmental agreements. However, EU states

---

Insight 22.2 2019: The Year of Climate Crisis

> You have stolen my dreams and my childhood with your empty words.
> (G. H. G. Thunberg, 2019)

Climate Change unexpectedly ascended European and international policy agendas in 2019. The planet was blighted by deadly heatwaves across Europe, wildfires in Australia, and record high global temperatures. But it was children who made the difference: school climate strikes saw young people forsake their studies to take to the streets in protest at the failure of their elders to act to mitigate the problem. Their spokesperson was the passionate Swedish teenager Greta Thunberg, whose rise to global prominence saw her address the United Nations and national parliaments, and attract the ire of climate-sceptic world leaders such as Brazilian President Bolsonaro, Australian Prime Minister Morrison, and President Trump. A new protest movement, Extinction Rebellion, embraced bolder, disruptive climate activism, frequently bringing European cities temporarily to a halt. Climate change was a major issue in the European Parliament (EP) elections in June, contributing to the success of green parties (see Chapter 15, 'Composition and Functions'). The EU and a range of member-state parliaments and governments adopted the language of 'climate crisis' or 'climate emergency' rather than 'climate change' to capture the scale of the challenge facing policy makers and society. However, the year 2019 ended on a low note, as international negotiations held in Madrid failed to reach agreement on tougher emission reductions.

signing up individually to international environmental agreements threatened to derail the common market. Hence, the Commission felt the need to expand its competence in the field, in order to protect the goal of economic integration in Europe. Its case for doing so was strengthened by a Court of Justice of the EU (CJEU) ruling in 1971 on a case concerning the European Road Transport Agreement (ERTA), which held that when the EU was given the right to legislate in a policy area, it would automatically be given external competence in that area, thereby paving the way for the EU to develop as an international environmental actor. The inclusion of a legal base for environmental policy in the Single European Act (SEA) (see Table 22.2) further enhanced the case for the Commission to take a leading role in international negotiations, and for the EU to become a party in its own right. When the 1987 Montreal Protocol on the ozone layer was signed, the EU became a signatory, alongside the member states. From then onwards, the joint participation of both the EU and the member states in world environmental conferences became the norm. The Commission and member states now routinely participate jointly in international environmental negotiations and have played a positive role in advancing some areas of policy, most notably in relation to climate change (see 'EU and Climate: From Leader to Leadiator' below).

Economic Rationale

The primary driver of EU environmental action has been economic. The completion of the internal market required harmonization of regulatory standards to prevent trade distortions and a race to the bottom. Those states with higher environmental standards

---

Insight 22.3 The CJEU as an Environmental Actor: The *Danish Bottle* Case (Case 302/86)

Rulings by the CJEU have played a key role in the evolution of the EU's environmental *acquis*. One of the most important was the *Danish Bottle* case. This case concerned a Danish legislation that required all soft-drink and beer bottles to be recyclable, but had strict rules around what kinds of containers could be recycled, which raised the prospect of excluding lots of products imported from other states. The Commission reacted by taking the Danish government to the CJEU, arguing that the new rules constituted a trade barrier. In the end, the CJEU ruled in favour of Denmark, insisting that environmental protection was of such importance for the Community that under certain circumstances it could even justify measures that distorted trade. The significance of the decision was that, for the first time, the environment was put on an equal footing with the common market and the ruling also laid the groundwork for the inclusion of the environmental guarantee article in the Treaty of Amsterdam. The environmental guarantee (Article 193 TFEU) allows states to pursue higher standards than those stipulated by the EU, as long as the domestic laws are proportionate. The article was included at the insistence of the states that joined the EU in 1995: Austria, Finland, and Sweden. All three of these states had higher environmental standards than the EU and were concerned that they would come under pressure to weaken their domestic environmental laws once the joined the common market. The *Danish Bottle* ruling had, however, established a legal precedent that high environmental standards were permissible within the EU, thereby smoothing the way for the inclusion of the environmental guarantee in the Treaties.

were keen to prevent states with weaker standards from benefiting competitively See Insight 22.3. Establishing common approaches could prevent a race to the bottom. Policy was underpinned by an ideational commitment to ecological modernization, a policy paradigm that accepts capitalism as the most appropriate economic model but seeks to green its practices to make them less damaging. Ecological modernization is based upon the idea that economic growth and environmental protection can go hand in hand through investment in green technologies and efficient resource use. Key EU states, including Germany, Denmark, Sweden, and the Netherlands, have been identified as exemplifying the practices of ecological modernization through developing green industries, such as renewable energy technologies (Mol et al. 2014). Consistent with this paradigm and the EU's status as a market organization, the EU's approach to policy has been underpinned by the use of new environmental policy instruments, such as the Emissions' Trading Scheme (ETS) (see Insight 22.4). The EU has also experimented with other market-based new environmental policy instruments such as

---

Insight 22.4 The Emissions Trading Scheme (ETS)

The ETS is the main tool used by the EU to combat climate change. EU member states, and Norway, Iceland, and Liechtenstein participate in the scheme which covers the power sector, energy-intensive industries, and EU internal aviation. The ETS now includes approximately half of the EU's greenhouse gas emissions. It is a 'cap-and-trade' scheme, which means that it sets an overall emissions cap, but it also allows trade to take place among the companies within the system.

Each company that participates in the scheme receives or buys a certain number of allowances. An allowance is equal to a tonne of CO_2 emissions. The companies that pollute less than anticipated can keep their spare allowances for future use or sell them to other companies that exceed their emission permits. Thus, a carbon market is created that in theory rewards those companies that make efforts to reduce emissions and penalizes companies that do not. The overall cap is progressively lowered, in order to reduce greenhouse gas emissions according to the EU international obligations.

During the first (2005–07) and second (2008–12) phases of the EU's ETS, each member state was obliged to draft a National Allocation Plan (NAP). This determined not only the total number of allowances each country was permitted to allocate, but also contained a detailed plan on how many allowances each company that participated in the scheme received.

The third phase of the ETS covering the years from 2013 until 2020, brought about considerable change. NAPs were abolished and the system amended to be managed centrally at the EU level. In 2013 more than 40 per cent of allowances were auctioned rather than allocated freely, as was the case in the past, to address the ongoing problems of oversupply of permits which had kept the carbon price low. It has been estimated that a price of €30–40 per tonne of carbon was required to bring about a low carbon transition but by 2013 the price was only €5 (Wettestad and Jevnaker 2019). To address this ongoing challenge the Commission introduced a market stability reserve, a mechanism that allows for withdrawing and releasing allowances to stabilize the carbon price. A revised ETS directive was agreed in 2017 for the 2021–30 period, which further tightened the system to reduce the number of permits released on the market (Wettestad and Jevnaker 2019).

eco-labels, and environmental audit schemes that offer information to consumers and citizens to shape their purchasing behaviour (Jordan et al. 2003). Whilst individual states have increasingly adopted eco-taxes, the EU's attempts to develop a carbon tax was thwarted in the 1990s and is unlikely to be developed at European level, as tax policy is subject to unanimity voting in the Council of the EU.

Policy Entrepreneurs

A key explanation for the evolution of EU environmental policy has been the behaviour of key policy entrepreneurs. So-called environmental leaders or pioneers, generally those states that already boasted high environmental standards and burgeoning green industries, have sought to establish higher EU regulations to prevent a 'race to the bottom'. The emergence and increasing electoral success of green parties within EU states, especially the environmental leaders, changed the domestic political landscape. Mainstream parties have sought to squeeze out the greens as an electoral threat by adopting ambitious environmental policies themselves, which has then fed through into government programmes and member-state positions in Council (Carter 2018). In the late 1990s, the Greens did so well in elections in Europe that they sat in government in five states and were a notable presence in Council meetings. Since that heyday the Greens' electoral fortunes have waxed and waned in national and European elections but their presence, even if they do not perform particularly well, has shaped the ambition of other parties and therefore of government programmes (Carter 2013). In 2019, the so-called green surge in the European elections appeared to lead Commission President, Ursula von der Leyen, to commit to a Green New Deal in order to secure the support of the European Parliament for her mandate.

Indeed, generally speaking, the European Commission and key actors within it have also been key environmental policy entrepreneurs. In the 1980s, Commissioner for the Environment, Carlo Ripa Di Meana, worked closely with the EP's environment committee to secure the adoption of ambitious policy (Judge 1992). Jos Delbeke, the first head of DG Climate Action, was widely recognized as playing a central role in persuading EU states to be more ambitious on environmental policy and in the design of the ETS (Skjærseth and Wettestad 2009). The EP has also been identified as a key actor pushing for stronger environmental policy, not least by being an alternative entry point to the legislative system for groups that find it harder to access policy making, such as ENGOs. Green MEPs have used the funding and platform provided by the EP to build and support their activities. However, the evidence suggests that the EP has become less environmentally ambitious over time (Burns et al. 2013; Burns 2019). Moreover, whilst the Environment Committee has been an advocate for more ambitious policy, the Agriculture Committee is traditionally quite conservative and played a key role in watering down the ambition of the 2014–20 CAP (see Chapter 21, 'Future Prospects 2021–27').

Finally, the CJEU has played a key role through important rulings in shaping the environmental *acquis*. As noted in 'International Environmental Policy' above, the ERTA case gave the EU scope to develop as an external actor, which has been critical to its development as an external environmental actor. Another important case for the development of environmental policy was the *Danish Bottle* case of 1986 (Case 302/86) (see Insight 22.3), which ruled that environmental protection was permissible, even if it interfered with the operation of the common market, as long the policy was proportionate to the aim to be achieved. ENGOs have also been able to take cases the CJEU to secure implementation of policy.

Current Policy Context

Whilst these factors have contributed to the expansion of the EU's environmental *acquis* over time, there have been several policy developments in recent years that have led to a reappraisal of this sector's trajectory (see Zito et al. 2019). A substantial body of legislation is now in place, which has reduced the demand for new laws. Key voices have even called for policy to be rolled back (so-called dismantling). Such calls have long been a feature of EU environmental policy (Gravey and Jordan 2016); however, the Commission decided to review the habitats and birds directives in 2016 as part of its Regulatory Fitness programme, designed to determine whether policies are fit for purpose, which prompted concerns that there would be attempts to actively dismantle the environmental *acquis*. However, the evidence as to whether such dismantling is happening is mixed. Some studies suggest that dismantling can and does happen (Gravey and Jordan 2016; Steinebach and Knill 2017; Pollex and Lenschow 2020), but a large-scale review of policy over a ten-year period suggests that in general policy has slowed down, rather than being actively removed (Burns et al. 2020). There are several explanations for this slow down.

Some scholars suggest that the economic and financial crisis limited the appetite for ambitious environmental policy amongst member states and the European Commission (Burns et al. 2020) and saw the environment downgraded on the policy agenda. The enlargement of the EU has also clearly played a central role in shaping the ambition and character of environmental policy. The priorities of the northern green pioneers are different from those of southern, central, and eastern European states that have joined the Union. Accommodating this diversity has become more challenging. When Greece, Spain, and Portugal joined the EU in the 1980s, a series of side-payments were made to facilitate the implementation of the *acquis* through the creation of cohesion funds (see Chapter 18, 'Major Policy Areas'), although implementation of policy within those states continues to be an issue. The enlargement of the EU in the 2000s to bring less affluent states from central and eastern Europe with no history of environmental policy and a host of environmental problems has had more profound implications. On the one hand, the EU has had a positive impact upon those states in driving policy development and funding infrastructure projects. However, since the 2000s the key focus of EU environmental policy has been upon climate policy, which poses particular challenges for those states still heavily dependent upon fossil fuels. Increasingly, the so-called 'Visegrad' group of Czech Republic, Hungary, Poland, and Slovakia have met separately to determine their policy agenda ahead of the Council of the EU meetings (Wurzel et al. 2019). The EU also struggled to agree a zero-carbon target for 2050 due to the reluctance of central and eastern European states to sign up. A partial agreement on the target was eventually reached on 13 December 2019, with all states except Poland agreeing to commit the EU to being climate neutral by 2050 (Morgan 2019).

Whilst the EU has long regarded itself as an environmental leader, that role has been underpinned by the ambition exhibited by the European Commission and key green pioneer states and their ability to work with others to secure the adoption of progressive environmental policy. However, Wurzel et al. (2017) suggest that the environmental leader states are no longer interested in pushing for ambitious policy at the European level. The Juncker Commission (2014–19) showed limited interest in environmental or climate policy. Moreover, the appointment in 2014 to the Commission of Manuel Arias Cañete to take the climate and energy portfolio whilst holding shares in a family oil company, was seen as indicating a lack of understanding or concern for the environment (Čavoški 2015). A further significant challenge to environmental policy came via the dieselgate scandal (see Insight 17.3), which erupted in 2015 and revealed that car companies had cheated laboratory emissions tests to make it appear that vehicles emitted lower levels of nitrous oxides than they did in real-world situations. The scandal revealed a close relationship between European (especially German) car manufacturers and the European Commission, undermining the EU's claims to environmental leadership.

Implementation Deficit

In addition to recent challenges, a long-standing issue for the field has been an ongoing implementation deficit. Implementation can be understood either in legal or in practical terms. The former refers to the extent that there has been transposition of EU legislation into national laws, whereas the latter refers to whether a law has been implemented in practice (Weale et al. 2000: 297–8).

Problems with the legal aspect of implementation are exacerbated because most EU environmental legislation comes in the form of directives (for the main types of EU legislation see Chapter 12, 'Decision Making Procedures'). Since directives are not directly applicable in the member states, national governments are responsible for translating them into national laws. Hence, problems arise when a member state does not take the appropriate action. Additionally, the member states and subnational authorities are responsible for the practical implementation of those laws inside their territory. Consequently, the EU institutions, as in many other policy areas, are in the peculiar position of adopting environmental measures that are to be applied and enforced by national and subnational authorities.

The Commission is formally responsible for overseeing the implementation of EU legislation, commensurate with its role as 'the guardian of the Treaties'. Since DGs Environment and Climate lack the necessary resources to perform this role effectively, they depend on the complaints procedure to be notified of infringements of the law. Non-governmental organizations (NGOs), the general public, governments, parliaments, and corporations can all file a complaint with the Commission when there is incomplete implementation of an environmental law by a member state. The role of the Commission is to investigate the complaint and, if the complaint holds, to begin infringement proceedings against the member state. This can ultimately lead to a referral to the CJEU.

Initially, the CJEU lacked the 'teeth' to enforce its verdicts on the member states. However, since the Treaty of Maastricht, the Commission can request the CJEU to fine member states that have failed to comply with previous Court decisions (Article

171; now Article 260 TFEU). The Commission was quick to threaten the use of the amended article in a number of cases. Greece was the first member state to be required to pay a fine because of non-compliance with a previous CJEU decision (see Chapter 16, 'CJEU Rulings and Policy Impact').

Greece had already been found guilty of the maintenance of an illegal landfill site at Kouroupitos in the prefecture of Chania, Crete. However, the government failed to close the site as requested and so was referred back to the CJEU by the Commission. The CJEU, in a seminal decision, obliged Greece to pay €20,000 daily until it stopped the operation of the landfill (Case C-387/97). Introducing fines has consequently played a role in helping to secure the enforcement of EU environmental legislation.

The Commission has adopted a number of other strategies to increase the efficiency of environmental law and subsequently reduce the implementation deficit. For example, it has simplified and codified existing regulations (European Commission 2007: 14). Additionally, it has adopted a bottom-up approach when dealing with implementation issues. It has thus opted for wider consultation with a number of environmental policy actors during the early stages of policy making, in order to enhance legitimacy and acquire the highest level of agreement with its proposals. Hofmann (2019) suggests that another approach used by the Commission has been to decentralize enforcement, so that rather than the Commission taking cases against member states, ENGOs have been encouraged to do so instead. This trend raises some concerns, however, as access to the legal process varies across EU member states, leading to potentially patchy implementation. Indeed, despite the adoption of these strategies, implementation and enforcement continue to be a challenge for the EU: there were still 333 environmental infringement cases open at the end of 2018 (European Commission 2019*d*).

The EU as a Climate Actor: From Leader to 'Leadiator'

A key element of EU environmental policy, especially since the 2000s, has been climate policy. The significance of this area was underscored by the creation of a new DG for Climate in 2010 to help implement the emissions trading scheme and to develop future-facing policies for climate and energy policy.

Climate change had emerged as a key feature of international environmental diplomacy in the early 1990s, when it became accepted that action should be taken to reduce emissions of greenhouse gases in order to combat climate change. As the debate on climate change was gradually pushed higher up the environmental agenda, the EU managed to develop a reputation as a world leader due to its ability to strike a burden-sharing agreement among its member states, and to the unwillingness of the United States to commit to binding reductions in emissions.

The Council initially agreed in 1997 that, although the EU as a whole was committed to reducing the emission of greenhouse gases, the poorest member states should be allowed to increase their emissions, with those increases being offset by higher reductions in the most developed countries. In the 1997 Kyoto Protocol, the EU agreed to reduce its emissions of greenhouse gases by 8 per cent from their 1990 levels by

2008–12. The final, post-negotiation burden-sharing agreement saw Greece, Portugal, Spain, and Ireland being allocated an increase of more than 10 per cent and countries such as Germany, Denmark, and Luxembourg accept reductions higher than 20 per cent. Because of the success of this initial burden-sharing agreement, the member states decided to adopt a similar strategy for the second Kyoto commitment period up to 2020. The ability of the member states to distribute the burden of the Kyoto Protocol between themselves showed the degree of solidarity within the EU. Alongside the reluctance of the United States to ratify the agreement, this gave the EU the necessary credibility to lead the talks on climate change.

However, this leadership position was challenged at the 2009 Copenhagen Conference of the Parties' (COP) meeting to reach a new international climate change agreement for the post-Kyoto period. The EU pushed hard for agreement, but was quickly side-lined by the United States and China, who engaged in bilateral meetings from which EU representatives were excluded. The EU delegation also struggled to respond swiftly to changes in the negotiations due to the need to reach internal consensus. The 2009 COP failed to reach an agreement and was largely judged a failure for climate diplomacy and for the EU's reputation as a climate leader (Parker et al. 2012).

A key theme emerging from Copenhagen was the ongoing challenge facing the EU when it acts in the international arena: namely who speaks on its behalf. As a rule of thumb, the Commission speaks for the EU in all areas where it has exclusive competence, and the Council when there is mixed competence. In practice, the situation is much more complicated. First, there is rivalry within the Commission about who is to take the lead in global negotiations, especially when complicated issues are discussed that relate to a number of different DGs. Second, there are grey areas as to whether the Commission or the Council takes the lead, although co-ordination processes have been improved. Finally, questions arise about the stance of the member states in the negotiations and the extent to which they follow the official EU line.

Nevertheless, an 'informal division of labour' has emerged (Delreux and van den Brande 2013). The rotating Council presidency is officially responsible for leading negotiations, but in many instances assigns responsibilities to the Commission and/or member states. This allows burden sharing and the exploitation of different sources of expertise, thus increasing EU efficiency in international negotiations (Delreux and van den Brande 2013: 125–6). The EU has also adjusted its strategy to reflect the changing nature of climate dynamics on the international stage, such as the increasing importance of emerging economies like China, India, and Brazil in international negotiations (Parker et al. 2017). Bäckstrand and Elgström (2013) capture this strategy with the term 'leadiator', which combines leader with mediator to reflect the more nuanced role that the EU has developed. Bäckstrand and Elgström (2013) argue that since the Copenhagen COP the EU has worked more effectively to find compromise and to build coalitions with and between developing countries. This strategy has generally been effective in the post-Copenhagen period for climate policy and has also been deployed effectively in relation to international biodiversity policy (Groen 2019).

However, despite these positive advances the EU continued to struggle to reach internal consensus on climate policy. Some states were keen to adopt ambitious targets and others (notably Poland) resisted. States made commitments up to 2030 to deliver a 40 per cent reduction in greenhouse gas emissions. Each state was obliged to produce a national climate and energy plan (NCEP) by the end of 2019, spelling out its contribution to the overall target. At the time of writing, the final NCEPs were not available, but initial drafts were criticized by the Commission for failing to be sufficiently ambitious or detailed (European Commission 2019e). As noted in 'Current Policy Context' above, a further commitment to achieve carbon neutrality by 2050 was agreed in late 2019, although Poland refused to participate. The burden-sharing principles developed to implement the Kyoto Protocol informed the design of how the 2050 goal will be implemented to allow some states to push ahead with more ambitious policies, while others reduce emissions at a slower rate.

A further element of uncertainty for EU climate policy is Brexit. The UK has a mixed reputation on environmental policy, but was typically regarded as a climate leader within the EU, prompting fears that its exit could change policy dynamics in Council by tipping the balance of opinion in favour of more climate-sceptic states (Farstad et al. 2018). However, Wettestad and Jevnaker (2019) note that the UK was a less important actor in the negotiation of ETS reforms for the 2021–30 period and that France emerged as a key player to fill the leadership gap. Brexit may therefore be less disruptive to EU climate politics than some commentators originally feared.

Explaining EU Environmental Policy

The rapid expansion and increasing importance of EU environmental policy make it an interesting test case for theorizing. Why was the policy created in the first place and what has been the motor behind its apparently impressive expansion? This section discusses the contrasting explanations of the policy's creation and evolution offered by different theoretical perspectives.

There are not many pure intergovernmentalist analyses (see Chapter 1, 'Theories of European Integration') of EU environmental policy (Lenschow 2007). This is not surprising, given the key role that the EU institutions have played. Intergovernmentalist accounts put emphasis on the role of the member states in advancing or containing environmental policy. They explain its emergence as a rational decision made by the member states aimed at decreasing the possible negative consequences of environmental competition. Thus, the member states initially delegated power to the EC institutions in the environmental field in order to protect the goal of the common market, which was beneficial to all of them.

Intergovernmentalist interpretations suggest that lowest-common-denominator (LCD) outcomes should have prevailed, at least during the initial development of environmental policy when unanimity applied in the Council of the EU. However, as Lenschow (2007: 415) points out, 'the rather remarkable expansion of the field did not usually come at the price of LCD decisions'. If LCD had been the case, the poor countries of the South would have dictated the pace of environmental policy evolution. Rather, these countries had to increase their environmental standards considerably, converging upwards with the other member states, although both southern states and central and east European states have often secured side-payments as a price for converging upwards.

Intergovernmentalists would also stress that, even after the SEA, unanimity has been retained for the most important issues, such as energy use and taxation. Although QMV was progressively expanded, a cluster of these core issues has remained untouched. Long negotiations prior to the Amsterdam and Nice Treaties did not succeed in expanding QMV to those areas. The member states have retained the initiative where it matters. The case of the failed carbon tax proposal is a good example. As noted in 'Economic Rationale' above, the Commission did try in the 1990s to advance the idea of an EU-wide energy tax but was defeated in the Council of the EU. So, while the member states have chosen to concede some powers on environmental issues, they have kept control in core areas.

Europeanization (see Chapter 3, 'Europeanization') has been used extensively to analyse the dynamics of environmental policy and relationship between environmental leaders and laggards. Denmark, the Netherlands, Germany, Austria, Sweden, and Finland are generally considered as leading countries in promoting legislation, whereas Greece, Portugal, Ireland, and Spain—together with the central and east European states—are considered to put obstacles in the way of the adoption of tougher environmental measures. The push-and-pull between these two camps has played a key role in shaping the character of EU environmental policy.

However, a model that crudely divides the member states into opposing camps is far too simplistic. Börzel (2000) demonstrated that there is no clear-cut divide between the rich North and the poor South in promoting and implementing environmental legislation. Hence, although the state-centric, push– pull model is parsimonious and gives a robust explanation of the policy, it could lead to oversimplifications.

A member state might resist a policy measure not because it is an environmental laggard, but rather because this measure does not relate either to its regulatory policy tradition or to the relevant policy measures it has adopted at home. It has thus been proposed that what primarily matters is the extent of 'fit' or 'misfit' between the domestic environmental policies of a member state and environmental policies at the EU level (Risse et al. 2001). In order to minimize the costs of EU environmental policy, the member states attempt to upload their own environmental policies to the EU level, which can lead to regulatory competition among them (Jordan and Liefferink 2004).

Neofunctionalist analyses (see Chapter 1, 'Theories of European Integration') stress the importance of spillover effects following the creation of the common market to explain the emergence and evolution of environmental policy. The argument here is that the environmental measures that several member states took from the late 1960s onwards threatened to derail the goal of economic integration (Zito 1999). The environmental issues that affected the smooth functioning of the common market had to be tackled at the EU level. Once a distinct environmental policy was created, it could not be contained by national governments. Unanimity was progressively replaced by QMV, and the role of the EP increased, whereas environmental issues not relevant to the common market were finally brought within the EU policy-making remit. Weale (1999b: 40) described the expansion of environmental policy as integration by stealth and argued that it could 'be regarded as a textbook illustration of the [Monnet] method at work' (on the Monnet method, see Chapter 1, 'The Intellectual Background').

The strength of this theoretical perspective lies in its ability to accommodate more fully the role of the EU institutions. According to neofunctionalism, the European Commission was quick to respond to the European Council's calls for environmental measures. It thus exploited the window of opportunity that opened at the beginning of the 1970s to promote the idea of an EU environmental policy. Throughout the following years, the Commission showed policy entrepreneurship in advancing important legislation.

However, while the Commission has been of paramount importance in promoting EU environmental policy, closer scrutiny reveals that, as a result of its inherent internal divisions, it has not always been in favour of unconditional policy expansion. There is great competition between the economic DGs (Trade, Competition) and the DGs for Environment and Climate, which can struggle to gain sufficient support for green legislation within the college of Commissioners.

The environment is a policy area where science and expertise are central to policy making. Hence, the epistemic communities approach (see Chapter 2, 'Governance' and 'Policy Networks') can be used to explain some of the policy shifts that have been observed during recent years. Acid rain, ozone depletion, and climate change are complicated phenomena that politicians have had difficulty in grasping. Practitioners have turned to environmental experts to increase their information on the causes of these phenomena and how to combat them. Thus, through the channel of epistemic communities, ideas have been diffused and environmental policies reshaped.

A very good example of the influence of epistemic communities is the issue of climate change. The broad agreement among environment experts that there is a strong causal relationship between climate change and the level of greenhouse gases was decisive in pushing measures to reduce CO_2 onto the policy agenda. Moreover, not only did policy experts dictate what gases had to be reduced, but they also helped shape the policy schemes for this to happen, namely the creation of the ETS. Their influence was fundamental in providing technical expertise and changing the broader framework within which EU environmental policy functioned.

Critiquing EU Environmental Policy

There is an increasing number of critical perspectives and evaluations of EU environmental policy. From a radical green position, the EU's pursuit of economic growth has limited its environmental ambition and framing the EU as a green leader seems wide of the mark. Machin (2019), deploying critical discourse theory, suggests that the use of market rationality to justify environmental policy has served to marginalize alternative and contesting discourses that suggest limiting growth to protect the environment. Post-structural critiques of climate policy suggest that the EU approach is effectively reinforcing the status quo, rather than facilitating the changes required to enable effective climate policy adaptation (Remling 2018).

Recent literature has pointed to the declining ambition of environmental policy and suggested that the period of policy expansion may be over (Gravey and Jordan 2016; Burns et al. 2020). For much of the 2014–19 period, the EU seemed to be in stasis, with limited environmental leadership on display and a core group of states and industrial interests prepared to block or water down environmentally ambitious legislation. This trend fits with a new intergovernmentalist interpretation, which has suggested that states have been more assertive on policies touching on core state powers (see Chapter 2, 'New Intergovernmentalism'). Climate change, with its implications for growth and—crucially—a state's energy mix and industrial strategy has seen central and east European countries in particular assert state power and be prepared to block agreement. This behaviour has undermined the EU's attempts to develop a coherent, external-facing climate position.

Another trend since the late 2000s has been the retreat of policy entrepreneurs and leaders. The Commission continues to be discursively committed to environmental leadership but it is not delivering on that rhetoric, leading Knill et al. (2018) to label it a hypocritical policy entrepreneur. Wurzel et al. (2019) suggest that the traditional green leaders within Council no longer wish to be in the vanguard of EU policy ambition. Hofmann (2019) has pointed to the ways in which the Commission has sought to devolve policy implementation to other actors. This more critical reading of the history of the EU's environmental policy suggests that the period of expansion and ambition may now have plateaued (Zito et al. 2019).

CONCLUSION

The environment is a good example of how a once peripheral policy area can transform in importance. However, since the eurozone crisis, environmental policy has occupied less importance on the EU's agenda. On the positive side, after a struggle at the 2009 Copenhagen climate conference to assert its position, the EU has adjusted its climate diplomacy to play a role that combines leading with mediating to secure agreement. By doing so, it has retained its international reputation as a climate leader. However, the different policy priorities and traditions amongst EU states mean that securing agreement continues to be a struggle, especially in relation to climate change. In 2019, the high profile of the climate issue and the success of green parties in the European Parliament elections appeared to have prompted Commission President von der Leyen's decision to commit to a European Green New Deal and to make the environment a key part of her mandate for the 2019–24 period. The EU has also agreed to be carbon neutral by 2050, which will require a step change in ambition and activity. The environment and, crucially, climate change look set to continue to be a key part of EU policy activity for the foreseeable future.

KEY POINTS

History

- The initial Treaties did not contain any environmental provisions.
- 1973 marked the beginnings of environmental policy at Community level.
- The SEA formalized EC environmental policy.
- The Treaty of Maastricht increased the visibility of the environment in the Treaties.
- The Amsterdam Treaty provided for the integration of environmental objectives into all other EU policies and eliminated the previous duality of decision making procedures.
- The Lisbon Treaty mentioned climate change for the first time, and explicitly identified environmental policy as a shared competence.

Current Policy Context

- The combination of enlargement, the era of crises, and policy saturation appear to have slowed the production of EU environmental policy.

- The EU struggled to achieve its ambitions at the 2009 Climate COP, so adjusted its strategy at international meetings to combine leadership with a mediation role (leadiator).

- There was a green 'surge' in the European elections in 2019 and climate change achieved prominence internationally following the climate school strikes and Extinction Rebellion activities.

- The Commission President committed the EU to a Green New Deal, as part of which a plan to achieve carbon neutrality EU by 2050 was agreed in 2019.

Explaining and Critiquing EU Environmental Policy

- No individual theory or approach can adequately explain the origins and evolution of EU environmental policy.

- Intergovernmentalism captures best the influence of certain member states in advancing the case for EU policy.

- Neofunctionalism explains the active role that the Commission, the CJEU, and the EP have played in shaping the content of environmental policy.

- Critics of EU environmental policy suggest that the focus upon marrying growth to environmental protection undermines the EU's claims to green leadership and has crowded out discussion of more radical policy alternatives.

 For additional material and resources, please visit the online resources www.oup.com/uk/bache5e.

QUESTIONS

1. Why does the EU have policies on the Environment and Climate Change?
2. How has this policy area changed over time and why?
3. What are the main challenges facing the EU in the field of environmental and climate change?
4. What impacts have the successive enlargements of the EU had upon its environmental ambition?
5. Do you think the EU can credibly claim to be a green leader?

FURTHER READING

For excellent overviews of EU environmental policy, see a special issue of *Environmental Politics*, edited by **A. Zito**, **C. Burns**, and **A. Lenschow**, 'The Future of European Union Environmental Politics and Policy', *Environmental Politics*, 29 (2019), which brings together nine articles updating and analysing different aspects of EU environmental politics and policy. analysing different aspects of EU environmental politics and policy. **T. Delreux and S. Happaerts** provide a useful textbook introduction to the field in *Environmental Policy and Politics in the European Union* (London: Palgrave Macmillan, 2016). **J. Wettestad** and **T. Jevnaker** provide an excellent account of the evolution of Emissions Trading Scheme in *Rescuing EU Emissions Trading, The Climate Policy Flagship* (London: Palgrave Macmillan, 2016), which is brought up to date by the same authors in, 'Smokescreen Politics? Ratcheting Up EU Emissions Trading in 2017', *Review of Policy Research*, 36 (2019): 635–59. Analysis of the impact of the economic crisis upon EU policy is provided by **C. Burns**, **P. Eckersley, and P. Tobin** in 'EU Environmental Policy in Times of Crisis', *Journal of European Public Policy* 27 (2020):1–19. The EU's role as a climate leader is covered by **C. Parker**, **C. Karlsson**, **M. Hjerpe**, **and B-O Linnér** in 'Fragmented Climate Change Leadership: Making Sense of the Ambiguous Outcome of COP-15', *Environmental Politics*, 21 (2012): 268–86, and **K. Bäckstrand and O. Elgström** in 'The EU's Role in Climate Change Negotiations: From Leader to "Leadiator"', *Journal of European Public Policy*, 20 (2013): 1369–86.

Chapter 23

Freedom, Security, and Justice

Chapter Overview

The policy activity of the European Union (EU) in Justice and Home Affairs (JHA) was given formal recognition in the 1992 Treaty on European Union (TEU). Through subsequent reforms, culminating in the Lisbon Treaty, the policy was recast around creating an area of freedom, security, and justice (AFSJ). This chapter initially explores the emergence and growth of JHA policy in the EU, and the Treaty reforms that led to the emphasis on creating an AFSJ. It looks at the policies related to the AFSJ, as well as the associated political struggles. Foremost amongst these has been the refugee crisis during the 2010s. Finally, the chapter explores the debates and interpretations that have been offered for the policy area's dynamics.

Context

Freedom, security, and justice are areas that have traditionally been understood as the core responsibilities of the nation state. It is an indication of the wide-ranging nature of the integration process that these policy areas have come under the EU's umbrella. In terms of policy purpose (see Table 18.2) AFSJ is a 'political' policy, rather than one concerned with economic markets. Introduced principally by the Maastricht Treaty of 1992, the policy area initially was termed JHA and was located in its own 'third' pillar of the EU (on pillars, see Figure 12.1). However, the Amsterdam Treaty moved immigration and asylum policy to Pillar 1 as part of an aim to create an AFSJ. The AFSJ was greatly enhanced by the Lisbon Treaty, which ended the separate existence of the third pillar, consolidating police and judicial co-operation into mainstream EU business. Accordingly, this chapter is entitled 'Freedom, Security, and Justice', although the historical part is framed in terms of JHA. The policy area has matured over time, even though it remains contested because of the way in which its content strikes at national sovereignty. This aspect was demonstrated most vividly with the refugee crisis that developed in 2015/16, as the EU's policy arrangements were almost overwhelmed by the flow of people from the political turbulence of Syria and other states (see Chapter 11, 'The Refugee Crisis'). The EU proved unable to reform its policies swiftly enough to respond to the new circumstances, owing to differences between member states.

The AFSJ has developed its own governance arrangements, with three notable characteristics. First, despite the development of EU policies, responsibility largely remains shared with the member governments. Second, another key characteristic of JHA and

AFSJ has been the use of differentiated integration, whereby not all member states participate in all of the arrangements. Both these features reveal the political sensitivity of the policy issues. Third, the governance of AFSJ entails a strong reliance on EU agencies (working with member state counterparts) and the exchange of data. Together, border control, police, customs, judicial agencies, and others are networked across the EU.

History

Early Co-operation: Before the Treaty on European Union

The founding Treaties of the 1950s made few provisions relating to what has emerged since the 1990s. The commitment to the free movement of persons, and specifically of workers, amongst member states was notable (Article 48 EEC Treaty). However, this provision only became significant with the developing momentum in the mid-1980s to create the single market (see Chapter 19, 'Project 1992: Freeing the Internal Market'). Other very limited rights bestowed on individuals in the early decades of integration were economic and market related. Even with the fragmented policy initiatives of the 1980s, there was no indication of the scope that the AFSJ would take in the EU of today, where two Commission Directorates General (DGs) oversee a range of policy issues (see Insight 23.1).

Insight 23.1 The Scope of the Area of Freedom, Security, and Justice

Migration and Home Affairs	Justice and Fundamental Rights
Legal migration and integration	EU citizenship
Irregular migration and return	Civil justice and criminal justice
Common European Asylum System	Data protection
Schengen, borders and visas	Upholding the rule of law
Innovation and industry for security	Combating discrimination
Organized crime and human trafficking	Gender equality
Cybercrime	Rights of the child
Crisis and terrorism	External aspects of the above: international
Police co-operation	gender equality, human rights, and
International affairs (e.g. in managing	anti-discrimination
migration or security challenges)	
Europe for Citizens programme	
European Agenda on Migration	
European Agenda on Security	
Securing EU borders	

Source: this listing is based on responsibilities listed by the Commission on its website in December 2019. Full details of the policy measures in force are obtainable at the webpages of the Commission's directorate-generals for justice and home affairs, respectively:

https://ec.europa.eu/info/policies/justice-and-fundamental-rights_en#policies;

https://ec.europa.eu/home-affairs/what-we-do/policies_en;

http://ec.europa.eu, © European Union, 1995–2019.

Until the 1990s, the driving forces behind co-operation lacked real ongoing salience. In consequence, the policy responses resembled a patchwork. Accordingly, one of the key characteristics in this early period, and still relevant today, was the use of a 'laboratory' approach to the policy area (Monar 2001: 748–52). Co-operation took place in different forums and was not confined to the European Community (EC)/EU. Three particular 'laboratories' undertook experiments that prepared the ground for the rapid policy advances of the 1990s. These were the Council of Europe, 'Trevi', and the Schengen group.

The Council of Europe's (see Insight 5.2) texts on extradition, mutual legal assistance in criminal matters, the international validity of criminal judgments, and the transfer of sentenced persons—some dating back to the late 1950s—were to become central to JHA co-operation between EU member states. Indeed, they have become part of the *acquis* that applicant states are required to adopt before they can become new members (Monar 2001: 749). More importantly, though, through co-operation in the Council of Europe, the traditionally parochial outlook of interior ministries began to be broken down, and experience was gained of working co-operatively with European counterparts. Awareness was raised of national sensitivities and peculiarities, and of the problems involved in co-operation.

'Trevi' was a loose form of co-operation within the European political co-operation (EPC) machinery (see Chapter 25, 'European Political Co-operation (EPC)'). It was an intergovernmental process comprising EC member governments, set up in 1975 as a response to increasing terrorist activity in Europe. It was later extended to the fight against drugs trafficking and organized crime. It paved the way for more structured co-operation once the TEU was put into effect in 1993. The work of Trevi was particularly influential for the development within JHA of Europol (the European Police Office) (see 'The Area of Freedom, Security, and Justice').

The third 'laboratory' was the 'Schengen group' of member states that agreed to eliminate internal border controls. This initiative can be traced back to Franco–German efforts in 1984 to include some components of JHA activity in what became the Single European Act (SEA). It became clear that one of the core components—the lifting of passport controls to accompany the opening of the single market—was not acceptable to Britain, Ireland, and Denmark. In consequence, the Schengen group emerged outside the EC as a laboratory for developing a passport-free zone (see Insight 23.2). The implications of removing passport controls proved to be more far-reaching than envisaged, and the scope of JHA co-operation widened to include compensatory control measures.

Insight 23.2 The Schengen Area

The name 'Schengen' comes from a small town in Luxembourg located at the border with both Germany and France. The signing of the Schengen Agreement on 14 June 1985 took place on board the pleasure boat, *Princesse Marie-Astrid*, moored on the river Moselle, which, at Schengen, forms the boundary between Luxembourg and Germany. Initial members were France, Germany, Belgium, Luxembourg, and the Netherlands. The Agreement's implementing arrangements were agreed in 1990 through the Schengen Convention. The term 'Schengen' is still utilized to denote the area comprising those states that have given up border controls with each other (see Figure 23.1).

The Schengen 'laboratory' undertook valuable work that paved the way for JHA agreements on asylum and immigration policies, extradition, and police co-operation. It also created a 'culture of co-operation' (Monar 2001: 752) and laid the basis for the transnational networks of police and judicial authorities that are essential to the successful implementation of JHA measures. The EU's Amsterdam Treaty (1997) incorporated policy agreed under the Schengen provisions into the EU Treaties, giving it a new legal personality.

One consequence of the Schengen arrangements was the need to start work on complementary external measures. The Dublin Convention, signed in 1990 and coming into force in 1997, was designed to stop 'asylum shopping': a tactic whereby asylum seekers might try to find the member state offering the easiest access to the EU by making multiple applications. Instead, only one application was permissible, and the outcome applied across all states. Unlike with the Schengen arrangements, Britain, Ireland, and Denmark chose to participate. In 2003, the Convention was revised and subsequently became known as the Dublin Regulation.

Policy Dynamics and JHA Structures under the Treaty on European Union

How did the policy co-operation in these laboratories culminate in the creation of the JHA 'pillar' within the EU, as agreed at Maastricht in 1991? A number of overlapping dynamics were at play and became irresistible during the negotiation of the TEU. First, the Treaty was negotiated when European integration had attained a new level of dynamism from the SEA and the creation of the single market. Giving JHA prominence in the new Treaty was championed by the German Chancellor, Helmut Kohl. Second, specific consequences of the single market, with its removal of border controls, gave new urgency to intensified co-operation in order to provide control over illegal immigration and cross-border criminality. Free movement of goods could facilitate smuggling, especially of goods such as cigarettes, which attracted very different levels of tax in different parts of the EU. Free movement of people could allow criminals to commit a crime in one of the member states and retreat to another to evade detection and capture. Free movement of capital could facilitate financial crime, such as 'money laundering' from criminal activities. Also, individuals and businesses that took advantage of the single market to buy or sell in other member states found it difficult and prohibitively expensive to gain access to another state's system of justice if things went wrong.

A third dynamic arose from the interaction between globalization and new security challenges. While the single market raised the scope for cross-border criminality, this was part of a larger-scale phenomenon. The end of the Cold War dramatically increased the opportunity for international crime and cross-border migration from the former communist states, although the scale of the threat was not as great as some of the predictions (Geddes 2006: 453). Economic migrants and asylum seekers were drawn to EU states. The civil wars in former Yugoslavia led to increases in asylum applications. Subsequently, the threat from terrorism took on particular salience with the Al-Qaeda '9/11' terrorist attacks in the United States in September 2001 and subsequent bombings in Madrid (March 2004) and London (July 2005). These actions produced further rapid escalation in JHA policy making within the EU. Alongside these developments, the growth of the internet introduced new challenges associated with 'cyber crime'.

The new global challenges were intrinsically linked to a redefined security agenda. Traditionally, security was seen as how states guaranteed their defence in military terms: as part of foreign policy in a state-centred system of international relations. However, this understanding was challenged on two fronts. First, security came to be understood differently: for instance, as societal security. Issues such as cross-border criminality or illegal immigration took on greater importance on the political agenda. Second, the international concern with terrorism after 9/11 emphasized the role of non-state actors, such as Al-Qaeda and ISIS (Islamic State), in internal security. Thus, security established itself as a key part of *home* affairs policy—or to use the academic terminology, home affairs policies became 'securitized'.

A final dynamic for JHA policy came from a small number of states that, recognizing such dynamics, advocated the development of the EU's capacity to address the new internal security agenda. Foremost among these was Germany, the member state with the largest number of borders with different states: a situation exacerbated by the opening up of frontiers to its east with the end of the Cold War. At the same time, its relatively liberal asylum policy was attracting increasing numbers of applicants. The Kohl government sought to utilize the EU's new role as an argument for making its asylum rules more restrictive, thus justifying the necessary domestic reforms.

As a result of these developments, the interior and justice ministry officials, the police, and the customs authorities gradually came to realize that they were 'increasingly sitting in "the same boat" as regards a broad range of issues' (Monar 2001: 754). There was therefore a strong logic to providing a common EU framework for the policy responses.

The agreement reached in the Maastricht Treaty was to create a separate intergovernmental 'third pillar' within which JHA co-operation could be developed. The Treaty identified some of the policy issues detailed in Insight 23.1. However, the institutional arrangements proved far from satisfactory. During the Maastricht negotiations, a majority of states had unsuccessfully favoured integrating JHA policy into EC business. At the same time, a few states, but primarily Britain, were insistent on not giving authority to the European Commission and other supranational bodies, notably the Court of Justice of the EU (CJEU). Consequently, the institutional arrangements in the third pillar were an intergovernmental compromise.

The JHA Council and the Commission shared the right to initiate policy. Much of the detailed work was undertaken under the auspices of three steering groups, which reflected sub-areas of JHA work: asylum and immigration; police and customs co-operation (the busiest); and judicial co-operation in civil and judicial matters (den Boer and Wallace 2000: 502–3). Officials from different national agencies, including customs and the police, as well as the judicial authorities, worked more intensively than in the past, leading to changes in their working practices as well as those of interior and justice ministries. Some non-governmental organizations concerned with human rights and asylum issues began to emerge at EU level in response to the EU's new powers.

The main policy-making difficulty, however, was that JHA showed the pitfalls of an intergovernmental system. Decision making was slow and unwieldy; decisions, if taken, tended towards the lowest common denominator. In addition, the visibility of

JHA decision making was low and parliamentary control virtually non-existent. Dissatisfaction led to pressure for institutional reform, which came about with the 1997 Amsterdam Treaty.

The Reforms of the Amsterdam Treaty

The Amsterdam Treaty brought about a number of significant changes to JHA policy, most significantly the new overarching mission to create an AFSJ (see Insight 23.3). This terminology was used in order to present the reforms as a major new programme in integration that, according to the Amsterdam Treaty, 'would provide citizens with a high degree of safety'. The AFSJ therefore sought to engage with the European public on societal security. Once again, the new arrangements represented a compromise between the different member governments in the Treaty negotiations (for details, see den Boer and Wallace 2000: 513). The Benelux states were among the most supportive of communitarization of JHA policy into the first pillar. Britain, by contrast, was opposed.

The most important institutional change was the transfer of visa, asylum, and immigration policies to the first pillar. The policy provisions went hand in hand with new decision making rules: namely, qualified majority voting (QMV) in the Council. These rules in fact only came into operation from January 2005, by which time much legislation was agreed, but on the basis of unanimity. Pillar 3 remained, but with a narrower set of JHA responsibilities: namely, police and judicial co-operation in criminal matters (PJCCM).

At a relatively late stage in the negotiations leading to the Amsterdam Treaty, several states proposed the incorporation of the Schengen system into the EU. The Dutch government was extremely influential in securing this outcome. A major immediate task, once the Amsterdam Treaty came into force in May 1999, was actually to catalogue the accumulated decisions taken within the Schengen 'laboratory'. This task was made complex by the fact that some of the decisions and associated policy instruments were matters for the first pillar and others for the third pillar. Greater complexity arose because the British and Irish governments had negotiated opt-outs in view of their non-participation in the Schengen system. These opt-outs stemmed primarily from the UK governments' preference to maintain passport controls. In order to maintain its common travel area with the UK, Ireland maintained a similar opt-out. Denmark's participation in the Schengen zone had by this time increased, since the 1995 EU enlargement had brought in other states within the Nordic passport area.

Insight 23.3 The Key Changes to JHA in the Amsterdam Treaty

- Visa, asylum, and immigration policies were 'communitarized'—that is, transferred from the third pillar to the first pillar.
- The residual responsibilities in the third pillar were confined to police and judicial co-operation in criminal matters (PJCCM), although provisions were enhanced.
- The Schengen Conventions and associated decisions within that framework were to be transferred to the responsibility of the EU.

The Area of Freedom, Security, and Justice (AFSJ): From Amsterdam to Nice

The ambition to develop the AFSJ as a new 'project' for the EU bore fruit. In 1999, the European Commission created a fully fledged Directorate General (DG) (DG for Justice, Freedom, and Security). The European Parliament (EP) was given consultation rights on first-pillar JHA decision making during the transition period. It increased its policy engagement and strengthened its committee, eventually called the Civil Liberties, Justice, and Home Affairs Committee. The CJEU for the first time obtained some very restricted powers over first-pillar JHA policy. A final key institutional development arose from the engagement of the heads of government. In October 1999, the European Council, meeting in Tampere (Finland), agreed on a substantial programme of AFSJ work for the period ahead: the first of three five-yearly programmes underpinned by scorecards and other mechanisms to ensure that momentum would be maintained. The Hague Programme (2004) and the Stockholm Programme (2009), which was the last of its kind, were agreed subsequently to maintain the policy momentum.

The Treaty of Nice made fewer fundamental changes to JHA. QMV was extended to limited parts of judicial co-operation as well as to anti-discrimination measures and matters relating to refugees. The first two of these were also to be covered by the co-decision process, thus making small inroads into a policy area in which the EP had historically lacked real powers. Another change was the approval of the Charter of Fundamental Rights of the EU, comprised of six chapters spelling out a set of principles. They covered dignity (e.g. the right to life and the prohibition of the death penalty), freedoms, equality, solidarity, citizens' rights, and justice. The British government was opposed to the Charter of Fundamental Rights being given legal status as part of the Treaty of Nice. Consequently, the Charter was 'solemnly proclaimed' at Nice in December 2000. For the time being, its status was to be political, but it was then subject to discussion as part of the subsequent constitutional debate.

The Lisbon Treaty

The Lisbon Treaty brought about major reforms to JHA policy (Kietz and Parkes 2008; Duff 2009: 95–102) (see Insight 23.4). The first point to note is the new, upgraded commitment that:

> The Union shall offer its citizens an area of freedom, security and justice without internal frontiers, in which the free movement of persons is ensured in conjunction with appropriate measures with respect to external border controls, asylum, immigration and the prevention and combating of crime.

(Article 3 TEU)

Symbolically, this objective was located ahead of such priorities as the single market and the single currency. In addition, the abolition of the three-pillar system meant

> ### Insight 23.4   The Key Changes to the AFSJ in the Lisbon Treaty
>
> - The third pillar was abolished and police and judicial co-operation (PJCCM) transferred into a new chapter within the TFEU's provisions on the AFSJ.
> - All AFSJ proposals were to be adopted by the 'Union method', but with five-year transitional rules for PJCCM, as well as various other exceptional policy-making rules.
> - The EU Charter on Fundamental Rights became legally binding, but with special provisions weakening its application in the UK, Poland, and the Czech Republic.
> - There were new opt-out provisions for the UK, Ireland, and Denmark.

that those parts of JHA that remained in the third pillar—namely PJCCM—were brought into mainstream EU business. AFSJ was incorporated in a single part (or 'Title') of the Treaty on the Functioning of the European Union (TFEU). Thus, the whole of AFSJ policy in principle moved to a single pattern of policy making: one in which the Treaty provides for QMV in the Council, co-decision rights for the EP, and, with some restrictions, the jurisdiction of the CJEU. The work of AFSJ agencies was brought under closer parliamentary scrutiny.

However, it was not quite as straightforward as that, as a number of exceptional arrangements were written into the Treaties, reflecting the fact that the member governments were unwilling to give up their powers quite so easily:

- the Commission continued to lack the exclusive right of initiative on some AFSJ matters, notably PJCCM, since one-quarter of the member states could also launch initiatives;
- the European Council was given the powers to set the strategic guidelines of policy;
- an 'emergency brake' procedure was introduced into PJCCM whereby a member state could declare a matter to be of national interest through appeal to the European Council;
- PJCCM only became subject to the Union method in late 2014, after a five-year transition period, and there were some special exceptions because member states wished to limit the possible impacts on their systems of criminal justice;
- Britain, Ireland, and Denmark secured new opt-outs from PJCCM.

The Area of Freedom, Security, and Justice

In exploring the post-Lisbon AFSJ, we review first the range of policies covered and then the institutions delivering them and the political struggles that they reflect.

AFSJ Policy Measures

Many of the policy activities entailed by the AFSJ can be identified from the evolution of JHA co-operation and are reflected in the work of the EU's executive agencies. Table 23.1 summarizes the policy work, as well as indicating the relevant agencies and where pioneer groups have played an important role.

Free movement of persons enshrines the right of all EU citizens to travel freely around the member states of the EU and to settle anywhere within the EU. This provision means that no special requirements are needed other than a valid travel document to enter the member state concerned. Free movement is one of the cornerstones of the single market (Chapter 19, 'History'). It was because of this status that British Prime Minister Cameron was unable to achieve significant restriction to free movement in negotiations with the EU as part of the 're-negotiations' exercise ahead of the June 2016 referendum on EU membership (see online Brexit Supplement).

 Visit the online resources for access to a Supplement including coverage of Brexit www.oup.com/uk/bache5e.

Table 23.1 An Overview of the AFSJ

Policy area	EU-level agencies or other bodies involved	'Pioneer groupings'
Free movement	None directly	Schengen zone, including Schengen Information System
Immigration and asylum	Frontex, European Asylum Support Office	Prüm Convention
Combating human trafficking	Europol, Eurojust, Frontex	
Police and customs co-operation	Europol, EU Agency for Law Enforcement Training (CEPOL)	Schengen provisions, Prüm Convention
Combating organized crime, including drugs strategy and cybercrime	Europol, Eurojust, European Monitoring Centre for Drugs and Drug Addiction	
Counterterrorism	Europol, Eurojust	
Judicial co-operation in civil and criminal matters	EU Judicial Cooperation Unit (Eurojust), European Judicial Network	
Fundamental rights and anti-discrimination	Fundamental Rights Agency, European Institute for Gender Equality	

The same principle of free movement of people is extended to Norway, Iceland, and Liechtenstein (as member states of the European Economic Area; see Insight 26.2) and to Switzerland on the basis of a bilateral accord. For the Schengen-zone states (see Figure 23.1), internal border checks have been abolished. Their abolition has been accompanied by harmonized controls at the external frontiers of the Schengen zone, supported by the Schengen Information System (see later in this section). No travel document is therefore needed by citizens of Schengen states to travel within the zone.

Figure 23.1 Member State Participation in the Schengen Zone 2014

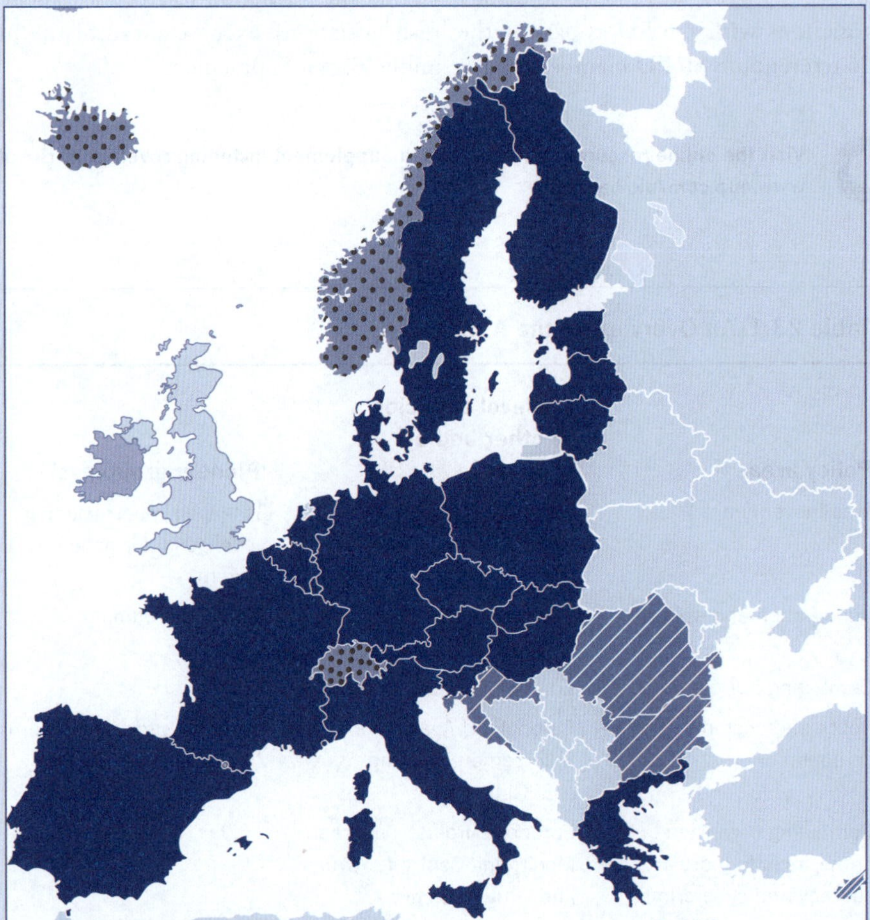

Key

■ Fully Schengen members (EU member states that have implemented the Schengen Agreement)

• Associated Schengen members (non-EU member states that have implemented the Schengen Agreement)

▨ Other EU member states (EU member states that have not implemented the Schengen Agreement yet)

▨ EU member state that applies only some Schengen laws and is not in the passport-free zone

□ Non-member states

The EU member states have committed themselves to a common *immigration and asylum* policy. Large numbers of legal and illegal migrants, as well as asylum seekers, have sought to come to the EU. Asylum is granted to a person who fears persecution for reasons of race, religion, nationality, membership of a particular social group, or political opinion and should be in conformity with the international standards set by the **Geneva Convention**. The EU aims to have a fully harmonized system in which applicants for asylum would receive equivalent treatment across member states. Work continues on creating this common system, but progress has been greater on procedures rather than on some of the key policy content. Moreover, the refugee crisis of 2015/16 opened up divisions between states (see 'The Refugee Crisis' below and Chapter 11, 'The Refugee Crisis').

The European Asylum Support Office, based in Malta, supports member states in implementing the EU's common asylum system. For example, it monitors numbers of asylum applications and changing patterns in the countries of origin. The European Border and Coastguard Agency (Frontex) has the task of co-ordinating integrated external border management. However, front-line border controls continue to be carried out by member state officers except in the case of a crisis, where Frontex resources may be brought in as well.

The work on immigration entails: spelling out who may legally enter the EU, for example as an economic migrant; monitoring irregular immigration and developing an action plan against it; and encouraging policies to enable integration of legitimate immigrants within member states. In May 2009, the EU adopted a so-called 'blue card' visa system to attract young, highly skilled workers to Europe in areas in which their skills are needed. The scheme drew on the US green card system, but the colour was changed to reflect the EU flag. The card gives recipients a specified set of rights. Danish, British, and Irish opt-outs apply. The scheme failed to attract large numbers of applicants and had to compete with similar national schemes. This led to Commission calls for the scheme's reform in 2016. However, these moves were stalled by key member states, many of which feared proposals that could potentially limit their control over the numbers and profiles of economic migrants from third countries who would be allowed to enter their country.

Following the 2015/16 refugee crisis, the EU has paid particular attention to irregular migration and return. As part of this, the European Commission is given responsibility to negotiate 'return and readmission' agreements with a number of third countries. It is assumed that citizens seeking to enter the EU from these states are ineligible for asylum and so can be returned in accordance with the minimum rules laid out in the Return Directive. Sri Lanka, Russia, Ukraine, the western Balkan countries, Moldova, Turkey, and Pakistan are amongst those with readmission agreements in force, while others are under negotiation.

Police and customs co-operation has become increasingly necessary as a result of European integration itself, but also because of globalization and the securitization of home affairs. Police co-operation concentrates on crime prevention, as well as specific tasks such as combating cross-border hooliganism at international sport events. Operational co-operation of police forces is the task of Europol, while the European Police Chiefs' Convention provides a top-level arena for exchange on policy. CEPOL (EU Agency for Law Enforcement Training) was set up as an EU agency in 2005. Its task is to bring together senior police officers from across the EU in a network enabling cross-border co-operation in the fight against crime, and promoting public security and law and order. It does so specifically by organizing training activities and presenting research findings.

More intensive police co-operation can take place under the auspices of Schengen, including the 'hot pursuit' by police authorities of suspected criminals into the territory of a neighbouring Schengen state. Such measures are a logical consequence of removing border controls, otherwise escape across borders would obstruct criminal justice. 'Hot pursuit' is a clear departure from traditional notions of national sovereignty and borders. It necessitates a strong degree of trust between police forces, possibly including joint patrols or investigation teams in border regions, as well as a likely need for language training. Customs administrations of the member states also contribute to the fight against cross-border crime through the prevention, detection, investigation, and prosecution of illegal movement of goods, the trafficking of prohibited goods, money laundering, and so on.

Combating organized crime, drugs, cybercrime, and human trafficking represent four areas of intensive co-operation in which member state police and customs authorities play a key role. In each area, a strategy and programme/action plan has been agreed. The EU's engagement is designed to enhance member states' capabilities, with agencies—notably Europol—playing an active role in adding resources.

The EU's *counterterrorism* strategy has developed significantly over recent decades. It has numerous component parts, focused around prevention, protection, prosecution, and response. Detailed measures include: analysis of radicalization and disrupting terrorist-related flows of money (prevention); countering chemical and biological threats (protection); information exchange between law-enforcement agencies and retention of telecommunications data (prosecution); and improving 'consequence management' (response). The launch of a European Security Strategy in 2015 intensified measures, for example, with the creation in 2016 of a European Counter Terrorism Centre within Europol to act as a strategic and operational hub to tackle the changing patterns of terror attacks.

Judicial co-operation in civil and criminal matters did not proceed as rapidly as work in other issue areas, for member governments took longer to recognize the EU's role. Member states have agreed to 'approximate' the definition of, and the level of sanctions for, specific types of offence, in particular those with transnational aspects. Mutual recognition of decisions taken by judges in other member states has also developed as part of judicial co-operation in criminal matters. Additionally, the EU started to be perceived as an international actor in judicial co-operation.

It was particularly in this part of policy that new momentum was gained following the 11 September 2001 bombings in the United States. This culminated in the best-known development, the European Arrest Warrant (EAW), which replaced conventional extradition between member states with a judicial procedure. The challenge faced by the EU was that it was possible for criminals to exploit differences in criminal justice systems to their advantage.

Similar principles underpin action in civil law, except that it is usually in recognition of the rights of citizens and companies. For instance, greater mobility has increased the number of international marriages/partnerships and these may result in the need for access to another member state's system of justice, such as over child custody when a relationship breaks down. Similarly, the increase in cross-border commerce results in the need for access to justice beyond the 'home' member state. As with co-operation on criminal matters, policy making has taken on a new legislative character following implementation of the Lisbon Treaty. The European Judicial Network, which has national contact points in each of the member states, is a means of facilitating judicial co-operation and access to justice in other member states. Eurojust is the agency enabling co-operation between prosecuting authorities in the member states.

As can be seen from the above, internal security looms large in many of the EU's policy measures. However, there is more to the 'freedom' component of the AFSJ than free movement. A key contribution comes in the form of the protection of *fundamental rights*, which is closely linked with action taken to *combat discrimination*, such as on racism and xenophobia, as well as on gender. These components of AFSJ complement the more security-focused policy activities.

The EU's effort to secure a role in assuring fundamental rights has been far from straightforward. On the one hand, a core of fundamental rights is associated with the 1950 European Convention on Human Rights. The Convention, which all member states have signed, is attached to the Council of Europe (the quite separate European organization, based in Strasbourg—see Insight 5.2). Principles of non-discrimination were agreed in the Amsterdam Treaty enabling the EU to 'combat discrimination based on sex, racial or ethnic origin, religion or belief, disability, age, or sexual orientation' (now in Article 19 TFEU). On the other hand, as Joseph Weiler (1999: 102) noted, 'the definition of fundamental human rights often differs from polity to polity'. Consequently, a few member states have been concerned about the development of the EU's profile on fundamental rights, while there have also been substantive issues arising from the jurisprudence of the CJEU. Under Article 6 TEU, the EU is committed to adhere to the Convention's principles; indeed, the EU committed to accede to the Convention in its own right. A draft accession agreement was reached in April 2013, but in 2015 the CJEU ruled the agreement incompatible with EU law, thereby blocking the commitment to accede.

The most obvious example of the different member-state attitudes was the fact that three states obtained assurances in Protocols to the Lisbon Treaty that make exceptions to the 'justiciability' of the Charter (in other words, the ability to invoke the Charter in domestic courts): the UK, Poland, and the Czech Republic. By contrast, the German Constitutional Court had challenged the primacy of European law until the treaties embodied a set of fundamental rights. Thus, the granting of legal status to the EU Charter of Fundamental Rights was not welcomed unanimously, and the EU's accession to the European Convention of Human Rights (ECHR) remains a mere aspiration.

In March 2007, the EU's Fundamental Rights Agency was established to: collect information and data; provide advice to the EU and its member states; and promote dialogue with civil society to raise public awareness of fundamental rights. It built on the work of the European Monitoring Centre on Racism and Xenophobia, but the remit was widened to reflect the EU's explicit concern with fundamental rights after 2000.

Citizenship is the final area of rights-related policy on the part of the EU. The Maastricht Treaty initiated the notion of EU citizenship, which supplements rather than replaces national citizenship of a member state. By developing fundamental rights in EU law and in political declarations, as outlined above, the objective is to flesh out

---

Insight 23.5 Citizenship of the EU

Citizens of the Union shall enjoy the rights and be subject to the duties provided for in the Treaties. They shall have, inter alia:

(a) the right to move and reside freely within the territory of the Member States;

(b) the right to vote and to stand as candidates in elections to the European Parliament and in municipal elections in their Member State of residence, under the same conditions as nationals of that State;

(c) the right to enjoy, in the territory of a third country in which the Member State of which they are nationals is not represented, the protection of the diplomatic and consular authorities of any Member State on the same conditions as the nationals of that State;

(d) the right to petition the European Parliament, to apply to the European Ombudsman, and to address the institutions and advisory bodies of the Union in any of the Treaty languages and to obtain a reply in the same language.

Source: Article 20 TFEU.

---

what it means to be an EU citizen. The four, specific citizenship rights provided for in the Maastricht Treaty are set out in Insight 23.5. These rights having been established, citizenship policy is now located in the European Commission's DG for Justice and Fundamental Rights, which hosts the Europe for Citizens Programme. This programme deals with promoting projects that help the public understand the history, values, and diversity of the EU, and with encouraging citizens to participate and engage in democracy at the EU level.

All of the above components of AFSJ policy have an *external dimension* beyond enlargement (Lavenex 2010: 474–5). Some of these external activities have already been outlined: the liaison of Europol and Eurojust with US authorities in combating terrorism, for example, and of Frontex with states from which there are significant flows of illegal immigrants. Initially developed in a somewhat ad hoc manner, the Hague Programme called for the development of a strategic approach covering all external aspects of the AFSJ. The document—*A Strategy for the External Dimension of JHA: Global Freedom, Security and Justice*—was adopted by the Council in December 2005 (Council of the EU 2005). Themes addressed included combating corruption, organized crime, terrorism, illegal immigration, drug production, and trafficking. In geographical terms, the immediate focus was on stability in the western Balkans and preparing candidate states to meet EU standards; freedom, security, and justice work in relation to the European Neighbourhood Policy (see Chapter 24, 'The European Neighbourhood Policy'); co-operation with strategic partners such as the United States or Russia; and working with international organizations, such as the United Nations. The international dimension of AFSJ policy has grown over the years, reflecting the policy's widening scope within the EU.

A prominent component of the international dimension of AFSJ policy relates to immigration and asylum policy. Geddes (2008: 170–85) outlined the evolution of this work and highlighted two phases of development. Its initial concern was with enlargement (ahead of the 2004 and 2007 expansions). In a second phase, policy attention shifted to the European 'neighbourhood': an arc of states bounding the EU from Belarus on the north-eastern flank to Morocco on the southern one. In order to try to discourage illegal immigration, various measures have been taken: information campaigns in the sending states; financial aid to try to improve economic conditions in the sending states; the creation of a 'return fund' to repatriate illegal immigrants; and financial support for the integration of third-country nationals in the EU. As Geddes (2008: 184) noted, while it was straightforward to obtain the co-operation of accession states, since the incentive of membership was clear enough, the EU's leverage over other countries addressed by the external dimension of asylum and immigration policy is both reduced and very variable between states. The refugee crisis of the mid-2010s revealed the limitations of the attempts to prevent immigration from the EU's south-eastern flank when that area was suffering political turmoil, notably the Syrian civil war.

AFSJ Institutions and Politics

The AFSJ is a policy area comparable to others of the EU in that it shares a common problem of balancing member-state sovereignty with a competing functional logic that suggests many problems can be better tackled by collective action. Even following the Lisbon Treaty, the member governments maintain strong powers because, distinctively, the Commission does not have the exclusive right of initiative. In addition, the European Council maintains a close interest in the overall strategy, given the political salience of issues such as migration from outside the EU or terror attacks.

The AFSJ is also characterized by strong traits of differentiated integration: Ireland and—to a lesser degree—Denmark do not apply the full set of rules. Romania, Bulgaria, and Croatia are also affected by differentiated integration. They have not been deemed to have attained high enough standards to be admitted to the Schengen border-control system. However, there were signs that Croatian accession to Schengen might take place in the near future, as it had been evaluated positively with regard to the technical requirements of membership in autumn 2019. The special situation in Cyprus means that it also is not a Schengen member state. Ireland has opt-outs. Five of the EU27 remain outside the Schengen border system, but with Norway, Iceland, Liechtenstein, and Switzerland being EU non-members within the Schengen border regime.

In 2010, enhanced co-operation was used in this policy area for the first time when fourteen states agreed to legislation in judicial co-operation on matters relating to divorce and separation. This use of enhanced co-operation or pioneer groupings—see Table 23.1—is a variation within the EU of the laboratory approach that the Schengen Convention initially offered outside the EU. Another example, comparable with Schengen, was the Prüm Convention. Initiated by the German government, the Convention was to facilitate the exchange of data (including access to other signatory states' DNA databases) for crime prevention and prosecution purposes. Signed by seven EU states on 27 May 2005, it seemed designed to circumvent possible obstruction by some states and to avoid the scrutiny anticipated by the EP after treaty reform. However, it included explicit provision for later adoption by the EU, which duly occurred, albeit with some controversial provisions excluded, during the 2007 German presidency. In short, differentiated integration is arguably more embedded in AFSJ policy than any other.

As for the supranational institutions, the Commission divided its AFSJ responsibilities across two DGs following the implementation of the Lisbon Treaty: DG Justice and DG Home Affairs. The constraints on its powers were highlighted in 2010, when its efforts to shape the European Council's five-year Stockholm Programme for AFSJ into an action plan of its own were met with criticism from member state ministers, who refused to endorse the plan on the grounds that it had departed too far from their own programme. Its responsibilities have grown over the subsequent decade, as reflected in the December 2019 listing (see Insight 23.1). For instance, responsibilities in relation to immigration have been expanded, with the Commission having its own 'European Agenda on Migration', which was launched in May 2015, just ahead of the peak of the refugee crisis. The Commission's capacity has had to be increased to encompass issues such as people smuggling. It has also been negotiating return and readmission agreements with third countries to deter migration flows from countries that are deemed 'safe', meaning refugee status is very unlikely to be granted in the EU.

The EP has become a more important player, flexing its muscles in February 2010, just months after the Lisbon Treaty entered into force, when it made first use of its new powers to reject, on civil liberties grounds, a counterterrorist agreement between the EU and the United States to exchange data on bank transfer payments. The EP has emerged as an important defender of privacy, including in relation to the 2013 revelations by Edward Snowden about the work of the American National Security Agency and others in data gathering, including allegations of spying on the Commission (*European Voice*, 25 July 2013: 4).

A final distinctive feature of AFSJ governance is the plethora of data systems, agencies, and networks that have been developed in order to operationalize policy on the basis of co-operation between member-state administrations. As illustrations, we explore the role of the Schengen Information System, Europol, Eurojust, and Frontex.

Schengen Information System

The Schengen Convention provided for a multinational database for use by immigration, border control, police, and judicial authorities in any of the Schengen member states. This database is called the Schengen Information System (SIS). It is a key policy instrument put in place to accompany removal of border and passport controls. Another policy instrument is the 'Schengen visa', which allows the holder to visit—in the absence of border controls—any of twenty-six states (see Figure 23.1). The SIS is therefore an important instrument linking together participants' databases in order to facilitate JHA co-operation. According to the European Commission (2019f) 'at the end of 2017, SIS contained approximately 76.5 million records, it was accessed 5.2 billion times and secured 243 818 hits (when a search leads to an alert and the authorities confirm it)'. A new generation of the system with wider scope and including biometric data is expected to come into operation by 2021.

The SIS can be used to pursue AFSJ policies in a range of situations. Someone taken into custody in one of the member states might be found to be the subject of an extradition request or EAW, listed in the SIS. A Schengen visa might be refused because of a ban from another member state emerging from SIS. A suspicious vehicle might turn out via SIS to have been reported stolen in another member state.

A separate database exists in relation to the asylum regime under the Dublin Regulation. Known as EURODAC, this Commission-run database is designed to identify whether an asylum applicant or a foreign national found illegally present within a member state has previously claimed asylum in another member state, or whether an asylum applicant entered the EU territory unlawfully. All member states plus Norway, Iceland, and Switzerland—the signatories to the Dublin Regulation—participate in EURODAC.

Europol, Eurojust, and Frontex

Europol, Eurojust, and Frontex (see Table 23.2) are three key agencies in charge of particular aspects of the AFSJ (on agencies more generally, see Lavenex 2010: 467–70; see also Table 23.1). They aim to facilitate co-operation between member-state agencies in different areas of policy that are all of centrality to achieving the AFSJ. Each has grown in size and been allocated new tasks as policy has developed in the face of new threats and as the confidence of domestic agencies, such as the police, has developed.

Frontex's role has evolved particularly in recent times, not least as a result of conclusions drawn from the refugee crisis. Frontex was originally established in the 1990s as the European Agency for the Management of Operational Co-operation at the External Borders of the Member States of the EU. Its work focused on states serving as major transit points for illegal immigrants or that were the ultimate sources of the migration flows. Its work was to tackle the perceived weak spots in the EU's frontiers: the EU's external land borders in south-eastern Europe and the western Balkans and with Ukraine; the sea borders in the Atlantic and the western Mediterranean; and air borders at major international gateways. All of these are recognized routes for irregular immigration and, in the case of land and sea routes, for people smuggling.

Frontex was fundamentally upgraded in 2019 (Bossong 2019). In fact, its official title has changed to the European Border and Coastguard Agency. As a response to the problems experienced at the time of the refugee crisis, its capacity is being significantly enhanced. It is developing its own uniformed border force, with eventually 10,000 border and coast guard officers to support the work of member state officers (and in addition to the staff in its Warsaw headquarters). Its expanded scale reflects two lessons from the refugee crisis: that migrant flows will seek out, or benefit from, the weakest link in the EU's external borders (in 2015/16 this was Greece); and that a Europeanized border guard might have provided a much more effective response to the flow of migrants to the EU than the patchwork of member-state responses. Frontex therefore is in the process of becoming a key instrument for tackling any similar refugee crisis in the future. Frontex's tasks following the 2019 reform are set out in Insight 23.6.

The Refugee Crisis

The highest-profile crisis for the AFSJ policy came with the 2015/16 refugee crisis (see Chapter 11, 'The Refugee Crisis'). It exposed weaknesses in the EU's AFSJ policies, and for a period the Schengen zone of free movement amongst member states seemed

Table 23.2 Europol, Eurojust, and Frontex

Agency	Europol	Eurojust	Frontex
Responsibility	European law enforcement agency	EU's judicial co-operation unit	Securing the external borders of the EU
Date of establishment (decision; operational)	1992; 1999	1999; 2002	2004; 2005; 2019 (re-named)
Location	The Hague, Netherlands	The Hague, Netherlands	Warsaw, Poland
Mode of operation	Facilitates bilateral exchange of information between all member state police forces	Facilitates co-operation between investigating and prosecuting authorities in the member states Exchange of personal data and judicial information	Exchange of information and co-operation between member states' border guards, customs, and police
Policy remit	Combating international crime: motor vehicle crime; organized crime; drug trafficking; illicit immigration networks; terrorism; forgery of money (counterfeiting of the euro); trafficking in human beings; and money laundering	Largely as for Europol	Integration of member states' national border security systems to deal with threats at the EU's external frontier Tasks include immigration, repatriation, surveillance, border checks, and risk analysis
Staffing/ structure	Almost 800 staff, including 145 police liaison officers from the member states	Twenty-seven 'national members', typically senior judges or public prosecutors (one per member state)	Approximately 1000, plus a standing corps of up to 750 that can support border control forces of the member states Standing corps is to grow to 10,000 by 2027.

to be under threat as a result of the impact of the flow of migrants from third countries. However, the EU eventually responded with some reforms, including the major reform of Frontex just outlined, resulting in the fears of disintegration subsiding and, indeed, an outcome of more integration than at the outset.

Insight 23.6 Frontex Tasks from 2019

- to develop and strengthen EU's border management capacities through the development of the integrated planning;

- to become more active outside the European Union, able to conduct operations in states that do not border the EU;

- to upgrade its management system to ensure that Frontex remains fully accountable and transparent as it continues to grow;

- to ensure well-functioning border controls for EU citizens and travellers from other countries;

- to build resilience at Europe's borders thanks to its annual assessments;

- to maintain safe and secure external borders by providing national authorities with operational support (land, sea and air);

- to contribute to the fight against cross-border crime by providing experts and training;

- to assist national authorities in effective returns of those who are not eligible to remain in the EU;

- to be the eyes and ears of law enforcement at the external borders with constant situation-monitoring, risk analyses, and information exchange on what is happening at EU's borders and beyond; and

- to remain committed to the respect of fundamental rights (with 40 fundamental rights monitors in its operations).

Source: Frontex (2019).

A problem with external migration into the EU had existed for some time, but the number of refugees dramatically increased in 2015/16 (see Chapter 11, Table 11.1). As a result, concern grew that the scale of arrivals was beginning to overwhelm the capacity of border guards at the local level. The consequence was to make it very difficult to check the status of those arriving at their first point of entry into the EU, as per the Dublin Regulation. Not only was this situation undermining the EU's immigration policy, but those arriving could then take advantage of the Schengen zone's lack of frontier controls.

As early as 2011, for example, the French government had expressed concern that Tunisians arriving in Italy might make their way to France, which has a significant Tunisian community. This linkage highlights the point that a weakness in the immigration policy for third-country nationals can quickly transform into a challenge to the Schengen passport-free travel regime.

As the crisis began to build, it was increasingly Greece that was at the front line of flows of migrants from Syria, Afghanistan, and other states, who crossed the Aegean Sea from Turkey (see Table 11.1). Greece quickly became a weak point in the EU's external borders. Other member states began to respond to the influx with unilateral measures to protect their own borders, most visibly Hungary, which in July 2015 began erecting a literal, physical fence along its border.

It was clear that a significant number of the migrants were seeking to reach Germany. In late August 2015, the German Federal Office for Migration and Refugees invoked the 'sovereignty clause' (Article 3.2) of the Dublin Regulation. This had the effect of allowing migrants to be 'waved through' the controls at front-line and intermediate states if they were seeking refuge in Germany. While the German action was taken in the knowledge that the registration system of the Dublin Regulation was failing, it placed pressure on the Schengen regime. Other member states started to make border checks to deal with potentially large flows of migrants; for instance, Austria began checks at its border with Germany.

The difficulty was that the sheer scale of migrants was not abating, and it was creating divisive effects between member states, putting a tremendous strain on what was an incomplete EU policy regime. Those at the front line of migration flows, such as Greece or Italy, had different interests from those ultimately receiving the most asylum applications, such as Germany, Sweden, and Austria. The former group of states had large numbers of migrants stuck in reception centres and were bearing many of the immediate costs, including dealing with the humanitarian tragedies of people trafficking, notably capsizing dinghies and other vessels (see Table 11.2). They felt other EU states were showing a lack of solidarity in the face of the costs they were bearing and the fact that there was supposedly a commitment to a common policy. The states in the latter group were involved with setting up reception and integration arrangements as well as managing the asylum application process. 'Non-affected states' with few applications, such as Slovakia or Romania, had different interests again, and formed a third category (Biermann et al. 2019: 255–7). They were in many cases not sympathetic to efforts to distribute refugees across the EU because of concerns about multiculturalism.

In May 2015, the EU started work on an integrated policy approach: the European Agenda on Migration (European Commission 2015). However, the initiative that received the greatest attention in the short term was its legislative proposal to distribute migrants held in key front-line states across the EU: a proposal that Germany supported, but which was opposed in the Council by the central and east European (CEE) member states: the Czech Republic, Hungary, Romania, and Slovakia. After a change of government, Poland joined these opponents.

Although the legislation was passed in the Council using QMV, the CEE states effectively ignored it and the whole matter went to a ruling of the CJEU, which found these states to be in breach of the law.

The way out of the problem in the short term was a 'cash for co-operation' agreement between the EU and Turkey, whereby Turkey received substantial funding from the EU (€6 billion was to be allocated by 2018) in return for holding migrants in camps inside its territory (see also Chapter 11, 'The Refugee Crisis'). This step corresponded to more long-standing attempts to 'externalize' EU migration policy: instead of sorting out internal divisions on how to proceed, money was offered to third countries to stem the flow of migrants leaving for the EU.

Less controversial was legislation for a European Border and Coast Guard, which was adopted in 2019 (see 'Europol, Eurojust, and Frontex' above). Member states found it easier to agree on strengthening external control measures. However, while this step resulted in more integration, it was clearly only one part of what would be needed for a solution to any future migration crisis.

The EU made efforts to improve its immigration regime in line with the Commission's European Agenda on Migration (Buonanno 2017: 118–19; European Commission 2018). A range of steps was taken, including revised procedures, a revised

Dublin Regulation, and attempts to improve the conditions for asylum seekers in reception centres. However, the European Asylum Support Office (2019) reported in November 2019 that asylum applications had reached over 500,000 in the first nine months of 2019, an increase of 10 per cent, indicating that the policy challenge has not ended and raising the question of how resilient the EU policy would be to further spikes in numbers.

Explaining the AFSJ

Neofunctionalist accounts of AFSJ-related policy emphasize a functional spillover from the lifting of border controls as part of the single market project (see Geddes 2006: 455–6; Boswell 2010: 281–2). However, there do seem to be some limits to this explanation. Important early developments took place in the Schengen Agreement, and not the EU. The murky procedures gave little scope for interest groups to pursue 'political spillover', never mind 'cultivated spillover' from central institutions, since they were absent from Schengen arrangements until communitarization in the late 1990s. A more plausible interpretation in terms of 'institutionalizing European space' is offered by Turnbull and Sandholtz (2001), emphasizing the early (functional) spillover but linking it to external factors (the end of the Cold War) and the advocacy role of Helmut Kohl. However, this analysis only covers the period to mid-1995.

An alternative account of policy dynamics is offered by Virginie Guiraudon (2000). It draws on the public policy literature on 'venue-shopping' and applies it to immigration policy. It is argued that interior and justice ministries sought to escape control from their respective domestic justice and rights regimes. Anticipating further migratory flows arising from greater openness of borders, they sought increased control through developing new policy arenas within an international institutional setting in which their interests would be strengthened. This explanation looked plausible both for the EU and for the 'laboratories' such as Schengen. However, it did not sit well with the way in which it was German Chancellor Kohl and French President Mitterrand who advocated lifting passport controls. They had to put pressure on their interior ministries, who dragged their feet in the early period (Bulmer 2011).

A more orthodox intergovernmentalist account of policy appears to have some importance, given that member governments retained the key decision making powers for a significant period (Lavenex 2010: 466–7). However, this position has become less persuasive than was originally the case, due to the communitarization of immigration and asylum policy after Amsterdam and of PJCCM after Lisbon.

With regard to the refugee crisis, integration theories have offered competing interpretations (see Insight 1.2, where these insights are spelt out). Whilst the division between groupings of states would lead to an expectation of intergovernmentalism assuming a dominant position in explanatory accounts, that is not so clearly the case. Neofunctionalism offers insights, namely into how 'more Europe'—notably, the strengthening of Frontex—has been one consequence of the crisis. And postfunctionalism (see Chapter 1, 'Postfunctionalism') offers key insights into how EU migration policy became highly politicized and became linked to the rise of populism (Chapter 11, 'The Populist Challenge').

A different kind of account of the refugee crisis is offered by Scipioni (2018). He draws on an historical-institutionalist approach that was deployed by Jones et al. (2016) to analyse the evolution of European monetary policy in the aftermath of the euro-zone crisis. As with that case, Scipioni (2018) outlines how the gaps in EU policy combine with a crisis to advance policy through incremental policy responses: understood as 'failing forward'. In other words, policy failure enables policy advance. Thus, crises may form part of a cycle of integration and fit in with the temporal focus of historical institutionalism (Chapter 2, 'Historical Institutionalism'). Scipioni's account therefore offers an interesting explanation of the refugee crisis from the governance literature.

Critiquing the AFSJ

A number of critical voices have engaged with the evolving area of AFSJ. Such critique has often involved the assertion that the EU promotes a 'fortress Europe' that permits free movement for 'insiders'—EU citizens—while making it increasingly difficult for 'outsiders'—migrants of various categories—to enter, reside in, and work in the EU. Such concerns were exacerbated by the number of tragic cases where those seeking to reach EU territory have lost their lives.

Such critiques are often made via the concept of 'securitization'—a much-debated term emanating from critical security studies within international relations (Waever 1996; Bigo 2000). In its simplest form, the term refers to the way in which certain issues, such as migration, become conceived primarily through the lens of security and often at the expense of human rights and justice considerations. In the aftermath of 11 September 2001, and in the context of growing concerns about terrorism, scholars debated whether AFSJ policies had become securitized in this way (Boswell 2010). Exponents of this claim emphasized the ways in which experts in home affairs, or more recently right-wing populists, played upon popular insecurity to promote new controls, such as over immigration (see, for instance, Huysmans 2006; Guild et al. 2008; Van Munster 2009). Other critics have claimed that when it comes to anti-terrorism measures which have encroached on the rights and freedoms of EU citizens (as well as non-citizens) the EU is 'world leader rather than reluctant follower' of the United States (De Goede 2008: 162). Adopting a post-structuralist framework (see Chapter 4, 'Post-Structuralism'), Vaughan-Williams (2015) has made the similar point that a security logic potentially undermines the very values that the EU seeks to protect.

It has been argued that the term 'fortress Europe'—and the associated concept of 'securitization'—may be somewhat misleading when applied to the EU, since large numbers of visitors are permitted to enter legally, as do many migrants, especially for reasons of family reunification or work (Boswell 2007; Boswell and Geddes 2011: 42–3). Moreover, wealthy outsiders have been increasingly able in recent years to acquire residence and, controversially, even EU citizenship as a consequence of their financial investments in particular member states (Parker 2017). Indeed, if the EU is a fortress, it is one that selectively opens its gates to certain 'outsiders' and works according to a variety of rationales which go beyond classic security concerns.

A critical perspective has also highlighted that not all EU citizens are regarded as 'insiders', able to take advantage of the freedoms of movement and residence associated with that status. With reference to the high-profile expulsions of Roma EU citizens from France in 2010, Parker (2012*b*) noted that such freedoms are granted conditionally by member states—often in accordance with an economic logic—and this may be in conformity with an EU law which permits such conditions.

CONCLUSION

The development of the AFSJ has been a very significant development for European integration. Starting from modest beginnings and in large part outside the EC itself, the policy area was established as an intergovernmental pillar and then communitarized over a staged process. The development is striking, given that JHA policy areas—not least the issue of border control—have traditionally been seen as key powers of the nation state. It is not surprising then that these areas of policy only reached the EU agenda after many others. However, it is also clear that there was some linkage arising from the dismantling of barriers to trade as part of the single market.

The refugee crisis not only heightened the salience of AFSJ policy in European politics, but it also led to much-strengthened engagement of integration theory with the subject matter. While different integration theories shed different insights, in line with intergovernmentalism member governments have been extremely reluctant to delegate their sovereign powers to the EU unless there is a clear demonstration that an issue cannot be addressed without co-operation among the EU states. Despite these concerns, the delegation of tasks to the EU at times has been rapid, often for functional reasons.

A number of scholars researching AFSJ focus less on its evolution as an EU competence and more on emphasizing the ways in which the EU has increasingly contributed to the establishment of a 'fortress Europe', preoccupied with security concerns often to the detriment of professed EU ideals of freedom and justice. Whatever one's view on such assertions, the political and normative debates over the issues falling within the AFSJ look set to play a key role in the EU's development.

KEY POINTS

History

- JHA was not envisaged in the founding Treaties.
- The initial steps in co-operation were taken in diverse forums ('laboratories'), such as the Council of Europe, Trevi, and Schengen.
- The free movement of goods and people in the single market increased the number of problems that demanded a collective policy response.
- Globalization and changes in the international system posed new security threats. Security became more widely defined and more politically salient.
- In the Maastricht Treaty, JHA was made a 'third pillar' of the EU. The institutional arrangements were a compromise between those who wanted closer co-operation and those who wanted to retain more national control.
- The Amsterdam Treaty committed the EU to creating an area of freedom, security, and justice. Visa, asylum, and immigration policies were transferred to the first pillar and came under QMV. Pillar 3 became PJCCM. Schengen was incorporated into the EU.

453

- At Nice in 2000, the heads of government solemnly declared their commitment to a Charter of Fundamental Rights.

- The evolution of the policy area has been marked by the use of differentiated integration.

The Lisbon Treaty

- Lisbon abolished the third pillar and incorporated PJCCM into a Title on the AFSJ.

- In line with broader trends in public administration, new policy tasks were delegated to expert bodies and new technology was deployed.

The Area of Freedom, Security, and Justice

- Creating an AFSJ has become a central objective of the EU.

- The AFSJ involves: free movement of persons; common immigration and asylum policies; judicial co-operation in civil and criminal matters; police and customs co-operation; combating organized crime, terrorism, drugs, and human trafficking; the protection of fundamental rights; action to avoid unjust discrimination; and citizenship.

- Many of these activities have a wider international dimension.

- Differentiated integration is a striking characteristic of the politics of the AFSJ.

- The EP and the Commission have sought to assert their new, post-Lisbon authority, but with variable results.

- Agencies, networks, and data systems are a key component of the practical operationalization of AFSJ policies.

The Refugee Crisis

- The 2015/16 refugee crisis was caused by a large rise in people seeking to enter the EU after turmoil in Syria and other states.

- The crisis revealed fundamental weaknesses in existing policy and divisions between member states.

- The crisis resulted in some (but not all) of these weaknesses being addressed.

Explaining the AFSJ

- Intergovernmental explanations were plausible for early developments of JHA/AFSJ policies and shed important insights into the difficulties of addressing the refugee crisis.

- Neofunctionalist explanations of the origins of JHA stressed spillover dynamics, and they have found application in explaining policy integration following the refugee crisis.

- Related analyses invoked the concepts of 'institutionalizing European space' and 'venue-shopping'.

- Postfunctionalism helps explain how controversies over immigration and other policies have formed a new, populist challenge to the EU.

- More critical debates have emerged around the themes of 'fortress Europe' and 'securitization'.

Critiquing the AFSJ

- The AFSJ has been critiqued on different grounds. First it has been seen as a fortress privileging insiders over migrants from outside. Against this, it is pointed out that a significant number of outsiders are still allowed in.

- A second criticism is that the AFSJ has become 'securitized'; that is, that it has come to be dominated by security concerns, emphasizing controls of various kinds at the cost of human rights and liberties of EU and other migrants.

 For additional material and resources, please visit the online resources www.oup.com/uk/bache5e.

QUESTIONS

1. Why did the EU take on responsibilities in JHA?
2. Assess the importance of differentiated integration to the AFSJ.
3. What are the distinctive characteristics of the governance of the AFSJ?
4. To what extent does the 2015/16 refugee crisis highlight the political contestation over AFSJ policy?
5. Does the AFSJ have a bias towards security and borders that collides with its commitment to upholding freedoms?

FURTHER READING

Useful analysis of the early evolution of this policy area is offered by: **J. Monar**, 'The Dynamics of Justice and Home Affairs: Laboratories, Driving Factors and Costs', *Journal of Common Market Studies*, 39 (2001): 747–64. Alternative overviews of AFSJ policy and governance can be found in: **S. Lavenex**, 'Justice and Home Affairs: Institutional Change and Policy Continuity', in **H. Wallace, M. Pollack, and A. Young (eds)**, *Policy-Making in the European Union*, 7th edn (Oxford: Oxford University Press, 2015), 367–87; and **E. Uçarer**, 'The Area of Freedom, Security and Justice', in **M. Cini and N. Pérez-Solórzano Borragán (eds)**, *European Union Politics*, 6th edn (Oxford: Oxford University Press, 2019), 323–42. On migration, see **A. Geddes, L. Hadj-Abdou, and L. Brumat**, *Migration and Mobility in the European Union* (London: Macmillan/Red Globe, 2020).

For reviews of the dynamics of the policy area, see: **C. Boswell**, 'Justice and Home Affairs', in **M. Egan, N. Nugent, and W. Paterson (eds)**, *Research Agendas in EU Studies: Stalking the Elephant* (Basingstoke: Palgrave Macmillan, 2010), 278–304. On the refugee crisis, see **L. Buonanno**, 'The European Migration Crisis', in **D. Dinan, N. Nugent, and W. Paterson (eds)**, *The European Union in Crisis* (London: Palgrave), 100–30. A useful summary of annual-policy developments is provided until 2017 by **J. Monar** in the special Annual Review edition of the *Journal of Common Market Studies*. A review of migration policy is provided in the 2018 edition by **A. Geddes**, 'The Politics of European Migration Governance', *Journal of Common Market Studies: Annual Review*, 58: 120–30. Also useful is the special issue of *Journal of Ethnic and Migration Studies*, 42: 537–664, introduced by **J. Hampshire** (2016).

Chapter 24

Trade and Development Aid

Chapter Overview

Up to now, this part of the book has dealt primarily with the internal policies of the European Union (EU). In this chapter and Chapter 25, the focus shifts to policies that concern the relations of the EU with the rest of the world. This chapter looks at the external trade relations of the EU in the context of the wider framework of global trade agreements, and at its related policies on development aid, particularly with the African, Caribbean, and Pacific (ACP) states. It also looks at the combination of trade and aid policies towards the near neighbours of the EU in the rest of Europe and in North Africa. From this examination of policy, it becomes clear that too sharp a distinction cannot be drawn between economic (or 'market building'—see Chapter 18, 'The European Union's Policy Agenda') and political aspects of the external relations of the EU.

History

From the outset, the European Economic Community (EEC) aimed to become a major international economic actor. The creation of a customs union and common market (see Chapter 19, 'History') had as its natural corollary a common commercial or trade policy. The EEC's main pattern of bilateral and multilateral trade relations was structured through the international institutions that were set up after the Second World War to promote the emergence of the post-war trading system. It also pursued an active policy of cultivating special relations with former European colonies, which sometimes created a tension with its commitments under the wider trading arrangements. The EU later used economic and trade instruments to help to stabilize the economies of its near neighbours in other parts of Europe and in North Africa. These instruments are concerned with trade, but also tend to have a political or foreign policy dimension. The EU has in recent years pursued 'deep trade' deals, often on a bilateral basis, which focus not only on trade in goods, but also services, investment, and non-tariff issues such as regulation. These have often been politically controversial.

The International Context for EU Policy

When the EEC came into existence, international economic relations were governed by the agreements reached at negotiations in Bretton Woods, New Hampshire, in 1944. These agreements set up several institutions designed to help an international economic system to emerge. At the heart of the structure was a monetary system nominally based on gold, but in practice with the US dollar as the anchor. To assist the development of states' economies, the International Bank for Reconstruction and Development (IBRD), or World Bank, was created. To help states that got into temporary difficulties with their balance of payments, the International Monetary Fund (IMF) was set up. There was also intended to be an International Trade Organization (ITO), to facilitate the gradual introduction of global free trade agreements, and to regulate trade disputes between states. However, the US Congress would not agree to the ITO, so instead a series of intergovernmental negotiations were initiated, known as the General Agreement on Tariffs and Trade (GATT).

One important feature of the GATT framework was that the EEC, after its formation, had a single representative. This followed from the commitment in the Treaty of Rome to have a common commercial policy that was solely a Community competence (Article 113, now Article 207 of the Treaty on the Functioning of the European Union (TFEU)).

Within the GATT framework, a key concept was that of 'most favoured nation' (MFN) treatment. This meant that states would not negotiate more favourable deals with some partners than they were prepared to offer to all of the participants in GATT. Exceptions were allowed, though, and the EEC was able to dismantle tariffs on internal trade between the member states, because there was provision in the rules to allow the creation of **customs unions** and **free trade areas** that might speed up the process of dismantling barriers to free trade globally. Another area in which the EEC concluded preferential trading deals was in relation to the former colonies of the member states. There were also special agreements with prospective future members of the EEC. These arrangements were not uncontroversial, though, and they became more liable to challenge when the GATT was superseded by the World Trade Organization (WTO) in 1995.

The GATT was a weak organization. It was never intended to stand alone, and only became the arbiter of international trade relations because the ITO failed to appear. Although the GATT had a procedure for resolving disputes, it was easy for a state that was losing a case to block a ruling against it. The arrangements began to collapse in the late 1970s and 1980s with the growth of protectionism in the face of a global economic downturn. In response, GATT launched a marathon round of trade negotiations in 1986, known as the Uruguay Round. The negotiations were scheduled to be completed by 1990, but stretched out until 1994. The difficulty of reaching agreement, and the prospect of having to enforce a much more complex package of arrangements, led to the creation of the WTO, a far stronger body than GATT.

Development Policy

One area of considerable concern to the original EEC was its relations with member states' ex-colonies. When the Treaty of Rome was signed in 1957, the vast majority of independent countries that eventually became the ACP group remained the responsibility of colonial powers. In 1956, France, which of the original EEC member states had the largest number of colonies, requested that its overseas territories be granted associated status with the proposed EEC.

Relations were initially dealt with in an Implementing Convention, which was replaced in July 1963 by the Yaoundé Convention, named after the capital of

Cameroon, where it was signed. Both these instruments had the objective of gradually moving towards a free trade area between the EEC and the former French colonies, and there was a European Development Fund (EDF) for the purpose of granting European Community (EC) financial aid to the associated countries and territories to promote their social and economic development (Frey-Wouters 1980: 14).

Neither the Implementing Convention nor the Yaoundé agreements marked a serious attempt to break with the traditional pattern of relations between Europe and the developing world. A. H. Jamal, a former Tanzanian Minister of Communications, described the Yaoundé Convention as providing 'an institutional dependence on the part of some African countries on one particular metropolitan power—France' (Jamal 1979: 134), and the EDFs under the Implementing Convention and Yaoundé were described by another commentator as 'basically a device to offload the costs of French colonial mercantilism on the EEC in return for other EEC states receiving access to their markets and sources of supply' (Green 1976: 50).

Many hoped that the first Lomé agreement would mark a turning point in these relations. Lomé was negotiated in the early 1970s as a result of the accession of Britain to the EC. Like France, Britain was a former imperial power, and the addition of its former colonies brought to forty-six the number of associated states. The Lomé agreement was received by the ACP states more enthusiastically than its predecessors had been. As one observer put it:

> When Lomé 1 was signed, both sides claimed that it was qualitatively different from anything that had gone before; a contract between equal partners and a step towards a New International Economic Order.
>
> (Stevens 1984: 1)

The Lomé agreement did enable non-reciprocal trade preferences, whereby the EC granted access to its market without itself insisting on equivalent access. Under such arrangements the ACP countries enjoyed duty-free access for many of their exports, including preferential access for important commodities (see Chapter 21, 'External Pressures'). Revised Lomé agreements were reached in the late 1970s and the 1980s. However, in most respects, the terms of the subsequent Lomé Conventions were disappointing. The terms of trade with the EC perpetuated the dependence of ACP states and at least contributed to a lack of economic diversification in those countries. Moreover, the EU consistently used its power to close its market when EU (particularly agricultural) producers were facing competition (De Bièvre and Poletti 2013: 144–5).

Although aid was increased in each agreement, it was not by enough to take account of the combined effects of increases in inflation and in population. When inflation and population growth were taken into account, the period leading up to Lomé 3 (1976–85) saw a fall in EC real *per capita* transfers to ACP states of 40 per cent (Hewitt 1989: 291). In the period 1980–87, Africa's *per capita* gross domestic product (GDP) fell by an average of 2.6 per cent and its returns on investment were substantially down (Glaser 1990: 26). This meant that, on top of the unfulfilled hopes of various aid schemes, many ACP countries were under intense pressure to repay loans. By 1983, the IMF and the World Bank were implementing stabilization and structural adjustment programmes in those countries, and the EC response to ACP problems had to be implemented in close co-ordination with these institutions. This situation placed the IMF in the driving seat 'with its own short-run conditions overwhelming those of all the other partners' (Hewitt 1989: 296).

Thus, by the late 1980s, ACP states believed that Lomé seriously neglected their main concerns: the impossibility of servicing debt, and the increasing demands of the World Bank and the IMF for changes in economic and social policies. By the early 1990s, concerns also arose over the effect of the completion of the single European market and over the aid demands on the EC from the former communist countries of eastern Europe.

Relations with Near Neighbours

With the collapse of communism and the end of the Cold War, the EU faced the problem of instability among its near neighbours. It was against this backdrop that the Maastricht Treaty (1992) provided the legal basis for development policy to focus on the promotion of democracy and human rights (as well as the challenge of economic development and poverty). Lomé IV (1990–2000) introduced a human rights clause, which in 1995 became a 'fundamental part' of cooperation (Gstöhl and De Bièvre 2018: 144–5).

The EC also signed technical co-operation agreements with the central and eastern European countries (CEECs). These were subsequently replaced with 'Europe Agreements': Association Agreements that fell short of envisaging full membership. Then, in June 1993, the Copenhagen European Council accepted the legitimacy of the aspirations of the newly independent states to become members (see Chapter 26, 'History').

In the Balkans, as part of its stability pact for south-eastern Europe, the EU agreed a Memorandum of Understanding (MoU) on Trade Liberalization and Facilitation with Albania, Bosnia and Herzegovina, Croatia, the Federal Republic of Yugoslavia (Serbia and Montenegro), and the former Yugoslav Republic of Macedonia. This was the first stage in what became known as the Stabilization and Association Process (SAP), which led to formal accession processes in a number of cases (see Chapter 26, 'History').

While the governments of France and the southern member states could see the arguments for enlargement to the east, and even accepted them, they were concerned that the problems of the Mediterranean, which affected them more than did instability in the east, would be relegated to a secondary issue. Instability in North Africa, particularly a civil war in Algeria, was already having an impact on them in the form of refugees, and in terms of threats to their companies' investments in the region.

Their concern that attention would be diverted from the problems of the Mediterranean was recognized by the German government when it held the presidency of the EU in the second half of 1994. Agreement was reached at the Essen meeting of the European Council in December 1994 to launch an initiative on North Africa and the Middle East. This assumed more tangible form during 1995 under the successive French and Spanish presidencies, culminating in a major conference in Barcelona on 23–29 November 1995 involving the EU member states, the Maghreb states (Algeria, Morocco, and Tunisia), Israel, Jordan, Lebanon, Syria, Turkey, Cyprus, and Malta. From this emerged the Euro-Med Partnership Agreement.

External Trade Policy

The EU is the world's largest trading entity. In 2017, its twenty-eight member states accounted for 17 per cent of total world trade. The EU exported more than any state (worth 2.6 trillion euros versus around 2 trillion euros for the United States) while the EU and United States imported a similar amount (around 2.5 trillion euros) (European Commission 2018). These enormous figures mean that trade policy is central to the EU's external activities.

The Common Commercial Policy

In the negotiation of multilateral and bilateral trade agreements, the EU operates under the rules of its own common commercial policy. Article 207 TFEU gives the EU exclusive competence in commercial policy, including external trade negotiations. This exclusive competence is the logical corollary of the EU's common or single market (see Chapter 19) and, in particular, its customs union, which means the removal of internal tariffs and the establishment of a common external tariff.

However, this is an *EU* competence, which is not the same as a Commission competence. Before it can even enter into trade negotiations, the Commission (its Trade Directorate General) has to get the agreement of the Council of Ministers on a negotiating mandate. The negotiations are then to be conducted 'in consultation with a special committee appointed by the Council' (Article 207(3) TFEU). This committee, known as 'the Trade Policy Committee' since the Lisbon Treaty, consists of senior civil servants of the member states who monitor the position taken by the Commission at every stage of trade negotiations to ensure that it is in line with the negotiating mandate laid down by the Council of Ministers. The senior committee meets monthly throughout the year, and there are weekly meetings of deputies. Once an agreement has been reached in the negotiations, it has to be ratified by the member states meeting in full Council, using qualified majority voting (QMV) (see Chapter 12, 'The Council of the EU (the Council)'), although in practice consensus is the norm. Since the Lisbon Treaty, the Commission must also report regularly to the European Parliament (EP), which has to ratify any agreement. As such, the Commission will tend to ensure Parliament support early in any negotiation. A range of non-governmental actors also play a role in trade negotiations, including private business interests and public interest civil society organizations (for more detail, see Gstöhl and De Bièvre 2018: 47–54). Those interests will often have starkly different views (see Insight 24.1).

For a long time, not only was the Commission bound by the mandate and closely monitored in trade negotiations, but also the EC/EU did not even have formal full competence except for trade in goods. Until the Lisbon Treaty, trade in services and in intellectual products were not included. Originally, this was because they were not the subjects of trade negotiations when the Treaty of Rome was drawn up. In 1994, the Court of Justice of the European Union (CJEU) ruled that the EU did not have sole competence in negotiations on such matters, but shared competence with the member states. In September 1996, the Commission asked the Council of Ministers to extend its remit to these sectors, but met with a cool response. Member states, and especially the larger of them, were reluctant to extend competence in these new trade issues to

> **Insight 24.1 The 1997 Internal Dispute over Measures against Imports of Unbleached Cotton Cloth**
>
> The measures against China, Egypt, India, Indonesia, and Pakistan were demanded by Eurocoton, the association of European producers of cotton fabrics—but they were opposed by European producers of finished cotton goods, who benefited from the cheaper semi-finished products imported from the non-EU countries. The member states were evenly divided, with Germany abstaining when the first vote was taken in March 1997. This reflected the balance of industrial interests between producers of raw cotton cloth and producers of finished cotton goods in the different member states. Eventually, in May 1997, the German government decided to oppose the anti-dumping measures, to the fury of the French.

the EU because the new issues are more sensitive domestically than trade in goods; some member states did not trust the Commission to represent their interests in these areas; and if competence were ceded to the EU, where common agreement was blocked by a coalition of unwilling member states, there would be no possibility of those states that wanted to go further in liberalizing such areas concluding agreements independently of the EU (Young 2000: 101).

Today, however, the common commercial policy (and the EU competence it implies) applies to all areas where the EU has established competence internally. Such areas have, of course, expanded significantly via, in particular, the single market project (see Chapter 19). This principle (of 'implied powers') was codified with the Lisbon Treaty, which, more generally, 'consecrated the extension of EU exclusive competences in trade policy matters in line with the broadening of the trade agenda in general' (Gstöhl and De Bièvre 2018: 42). On this basis, the EU was empowered to pursue what some have called a new trade agenda (Young 2007) and negotiate 'deep trade' agreements covering aspects of policy that extend far beyond traditional trade in goods, including services and intellectual products.

However, member state unanimity still formally applies in relation to agreements that include provisions for which unanimity applies internally and for trade in some politically sensitive services (such as culture and audiovisual, social, education, and health services). Moreover, the CJEU clarified in Opinion 2/15, published in 2017, that the EU did not have exclusive competence in relation to 'portfolio investment' (non-direct forms of foreign investment) and investor-to-state dispute settlement. Most recent agreements (see below) have included references to one or both of these issues, meaning that they have been negotiated as mixed agreements, requiring ratification by all member states and therefore a de facto consensus between them (Gstöhl and De Bièvre 2018: 55).

Other important aspects of the common commercial policy are defensive and offensive instruments. The former constitute exceptions to the general WTO rule not to raise customs tariffs above agreed levels. They are designed to protect the EU from unfair trade practices by non-members. These instruments include restrictions that can be imposed where non-members are suspected of dumping produce on the EU market at less than the cost of production, and similar measures to counter unfair subsidies.

461

The Commission's power to impose such measures has increased over time. One example of their recent use was against Chinese steel imports in 2017. Offensive measures involve the EU ensuring market access when countries outside of the EU impose barriers to their markets in breach of agreed rules. In recent years the EU has, for instance, explored ways in which it might open foreign public procurement markets to European companies (Gstöhl and De Bièvre 2018: 69–82).

It is not always easy for the member states to reach common positions on external trade policy. For example, in 1997, there was internal dispute over the imposition of anti-dumping measures against imports of unbleached cotton cloth (see Insight 24.1). The divisions between member states in this case illustrated two aspects of the difficulty in reaching common positions: there was a straight division on the basis of national economic interest, and a more general issue about free trade versus managed trade. Among the EU fifteen (that is, prior to the eastern enlargement), generally the northern member states were more in favour of liberalization, while suspicions of market opening were felt most strongly in the southern member states. France has had particular difficulties with the idea of unmanaged global free trade. The eastern enlargement, on balance, probably made the EU slightly more protectionist, while the UK's intended departure could push the EU slightly further in that direction.

Despite such difficulties, the thrust of EC commercial policy has been consistently in the direction of free trade. In the most recent WTO Doha Round of trade negotiations, which began in 2001, the EU's negotiating position with respect to traditional trade policy was described by Young (2007: 798) as 'aggressive, with a heavy emphasis on increasing market access in non-agricultural products, . . . rather than a preoccupation with protecting European industrial sectors'. That said, the Doha round broke down in 2008 due to the conflicting interests of the developed and developing world.

Since this failure, the EU has shifted away from its pursuit of multilateralism to once again explicitly pursue bilateral free trade agreements (FTAs). This has allowed the EU to pursue a so-called 'deep trade' agenda (for reasons that are considered in 'Critiquing Trade and Development Aid Policies' later in the chapter). The EU has agreements in place with a number of countries and, in 2019, agreements recently completed, or close to completion, with Canada, South Korea, Singapore, Japan, Vietnam, and India, among others.

In 2013, the EU began negotiating the Transatlantic Trade and Investment Partnership (TTIP) with the United States, but negotiations stalled in 2016 and were halted by President Trump when he took office in 2017. TTIP was qualitatively different from previous trade deals in terms of its depth, particularly the extent to which it emphasized regulatory co-operation and investment protection, with the ultimate aspiration of creating a transatlantic market (De Ville and Siles-Brügge 2017). While the aspirations on both sides to establish TTIP were very real, even prior to the Trump presidency, achieving a deal was never going to be easy. As noted in 'Critiquing Trade and Development Aid Policies' below, TTIP was politically controversial. Moreover, a history of disputes between the two trading partners rendered the talks difficult in certain areas (on historical disputes, see Insights 24.2, 24.3, and 24.4). In a further demonstration of the shift towards deep trade agreements, in 2013 the EU started negotiations on a 'plurilateral' Trade in Services Agreement (TiSA) with twenty-three other WTO members.

Insight 24.2 The WTO Dispute over the EU Banana Regime

This was part of the Lomé Agreements with former French and British colonies. It gave preferential access to the EU market for bananas grown in those Caribbean and Pacific states that were parties to the agreement. The United States objected to the discrimination against bananas produced in Latin America, mainly by US-owned companies. Eventually, in April 1999, the WTO did authorize the imposition of sanctions by the United States, although at a much-reduced level from those originally proposed. This generated significant tension between the EU and the United States. The dispute was eventually settled in December 2009 by an agreement under which the EU would reduce its tariffs on imported bananas progressively over seven years, and the United States and banana-producing countries from Latin America agreed to drop litigation against the EU.

Insight 24.3 WTO Disputes over Hormone-Treated Beef and Genetically Modified Crops

In 1999, the United States won a complaint to the WTO against a ban by the EU on the import of hormone-treated beef. The ban reflected the strong prejudice of EU consumers against meat that contained hormones, and was first imposed in 1987. The United States maintained that this action was against WTO rules because there was no scientific evidence that there was any risk to human health from eating such meat. The EU insisted that it wanted to complete its own scientific tests before agreeing to lift the ban. Early in 1999, the WTO ruled against the EU, and the United States said that it would impose retaliatory sanctions unless the ban was lifted, but the EU refused to lift the ban in the face of intense consumer opposition. It did offer to allow the import of hormone-treated beef if it was clearly labelled as such, but the United States rejected this compromise because it said that the labelling itself implied that there was something wrong with the beef.

Also in 1999, the EU placed an effective moratorium on the granting of licences for genetically modified (GM) crops. This move was attacked by the United States as imposing a non-tariff barrier on agricultural trade. In 2001, the Commission introduced an EU-wide system of authorization for GM crops, which led to a number of crops being approved for the EU market. However, due to different views among member states, in 2015 it was decided that each EU state would have discretion to decide whether or not to introduce any EU-authorized GM crop.

Insight 24.4 WTO Dispute over 'Chlorinated Chicken'

In 1997, the EU started to block imports of US products that had been treated with 'pathogen reduction treatments' (PRTs) designed to kill pathogens commonly found on meat. Such methods are commonly used in the United States, particularly on poultry (in public debate in Europe in relation to the TTIP and Brexit, this was often referred to as 'chlorinated chicken'). While there is no particular scientific evidence to suggest that such treatments are unsafe, concerns on the EU side relate to the fact that such measures are used to offset unhygenic and potentially harmful practices in the process of meat production prior to the use of PRTs. In 2009, the United States requested the establishment of a WTO dispute settlement panel to adjudicate on the restrictions, citing the impact on US poultry exports. Since then the EU has permitted the use of some PRTs, while continuing to restrict the use of others. The issue arose also in relation to the now-stalled TTIP negotiations and, as of 2019, was the source of ongoing dispute.

Disputes within the World Trade Organization

Partly because of the increased complexity of the rules, and partly because of the advent of more effective machinery, recourse to dispute panels has increased considerably under the WTO, averaging forty disputes a year as compared to six per year under the GATT procedures (McQueen 1998: 436). This has affected the EU because of increased challenges to its practices, particularly from the United States.

Since the WTO began operation in January 1995, both the United States and the EU have attempted to dominate the procedures and the agenda, or at least to ensure that the other does not dominate. Each side has brought complaints against the other. In 1998, the US disputed the EU's banana regime (see Insight 24.2), in 1999 it twice disputed the EU's restrictions on the use of biotechnology in agricultural produce (see Insight 24.3), and the United States has consistently challenged EU restrictions on the use of products for cleaning meat, particularly poultry (see Insight 24.4). In 1998, the EU launched its own WTO appeal against the foreign sales corporation (FSC) provisions of US tax law (see Insight 24.5).

Insight 24.5 The WTO Dispute over the US Foreign Sales Corporation (FSC) Tax Provisions

The FSC came into effect in 1984, and allowed US corporations to claim exemption on between 15 and 30 per cent of their earnings from exports. The EU maintained that this amounted to an export subsidy in breach of WTO rules. The United States considered that the appeal was simply EU retaliation against its appeals on bananas and beef, pointing out that it had taken the EU fourteen years to get round to protesting about the FSC, and that there was no evidence of pressure on the Commission from European businesses for the complaint to be made at this time (Ahearn 2002: 4). However, in October 1999, a WTO disputes panel found in favour of the EU, and the United States was told to come into compliance with its WTO obligations by October 2000. In November 2000, the FSC was repealed and replaced by the Extraterritorial Income (ERI) provisions. This allowed tax breaks up to the same amount to US corporations on all foreign earnings, including their earnings from foreign investments. By extending the provision beyond export earnings in this way, Congress hoped to redefine the tax provision. Predictably, the EU appealed and the WTO ruled against the ERI, and against the counter-appeal from the Bush Administration (Ahearn 2002: 5). In August 2002, the WTO disputes panel ruled that the EU could impose up to US$4 billion of sanctions in retaliation.

464

The result of these moves and countermoves was that the United States and the EU entered the twenty-first century each armed with the right to impose WTO-approved sanctions on the other. Further tensions emerged over accusations and counteraccusations of illegal subsidies by both sides to their major producers of civil aircraft (in Europe, Airbus and in the United States, Boeing). Perhaps because of the awareness of both sides of the potential for damage to themselves as well as to the global trading system, restraint has generally been shown in the application of sanctions. However, President Trump, who campaigned on a protectionist platform, has been less restrained than his predecessors. In mid-2018, he imposed tariffs on aluminium and steel imports from a number of trading partners, including the EU, triggering a tit-for-tat trade war. That said, as of late 2019 both sides still agreed on the value of tackling regulatory 'barriers' and it was not impossible that agreements on such issues would be possible at some point in the early 2020s.

Development and Trade

Trade and development issues are closely connected in EU policy. The EU has historically used its trade policy to push a development agenda as well as other political goals, such as human rights and environmental protection. It has offered preferential trading terms to developing states and sometimes development aid, with various conditions attached. Such policies focused historically on the former colonies of member states, but later expanded to include a broader range of developing countries and also states in its near neighbourhood. Development and trade logics often conflict, however, as was apparent with the failure of the multilateral Doha WTO trade round, but also in the EU's frequent failure to conclude bilateral deals with the developing world.

Relations with African, Caribbean, and Pacific States

The original ACP states were all former colonies of the member states of the EU, although, as the Lomé Convention was regularly updated, other states joined that had never been colonies of EU members. When the Cotonou Agreement was signed in June 2000, more ACP states joined. In 2018, there were eighty in total (see Table 24.1).

Negotiations on what became Cotonou followed a Commission 'Green Paper' highlighting the ongoing problems of ACP countries (European Commission 1996). The Green Paper identified two main reasons why the Lomé pattern could not continue, as follows:

- The preferences under Lomé were becoming less valuable as the liberalization of global trade proceeded; this was evidenced by a decline in the ACP share of the EU market.
- Lomé was incompatible with WTO rules. Although various waivers had been granted, the rules were quite clear. Article 1 of the WTO Charter requires participants not to discriminate between other WTO members in trade concessions. Exceptions are allowed to this rule for less developed countries (LDCs), but the concessions must apply to all LDCs. There were two problems about the compat-

ibility of Lomé with these WTO rules: first, many of the ACP states covered by Lomé were not classified as LDCs by the WTO; second, there were nine LDCs that were not included in Lomé.

In response to these problems with the existing arrangements, the Commission proposed dividing the ACP states into the LDCs, which could choose to continue to receive non-reciprocal trade concessions that would also be offered to the nine LDC states that had previously been excluded, and the non-LDCs, which would be offered Economic Partnership Agreements (EPAs). The EPAs would involve some measure of reciprocity, so the ACP states would have to offer free market access to EU goods. To be WTO-compatible, they would also have to cover 'substantially all' trade, which was interpreted by the EU as 90 per cent of products, so agricultural produce that had been excluded from Lomé to protect areas that were adjudged 'sensitive' by EU member states would have to be included. The EU agreed that it would conclude such agreements either with individual states or regional groupings, but indicated a strong preference for Regional Economic Partnership Agreements (REPAs). The

---

Table 24.1 ACP Regional Groups for EPA Negotiations (and LDCs)

EPA Region	Members (LDCs in bold)
Caribbean (Cariforum)	Antigua and Barbuda, Bahamas, Barbados, Belize, Dominica, Dominican Republic, Grenada, Guana, **Haiti**, Jamaica, St Kitts and Nevis, St Lucia, St Vincent and the Grenadines, Surinam, Trinidad and Tobago
Central Africa	Cameroon, **Central African Republic, Chad**, Congo, **Democratic Republic of Congo, Equatorial Guinea**, Gabon, **Sao Tome and Principe**
East African Community	**Burundi**, Kenya, **Rwanda, Tanzania, Uganda**
Eastern and Southern Africa	**Comoros, Djibouti, Eritrea, Ethiopia, Madagascar, Malawi**, Mauritius, Seychelles, **Somalia, Sudan, Zambia**, Zimbabwe
Pacific (Pacific Islands Forum except Australia and New Zealand)	Cook Islands, Federated States of Micronesia, Fiji, **Kiribati**, Marshall Islands, Nauru, Niue, Palau, Papua New Guinea, **Samoa, Solomon Islands, Timor Leste**, Tonga, **Tuvalu, Vanuatu**
Southern African Development Community	**Angola**, Botswana, **Lesotho, Mozambique**, Namibia, South Africa, Swaziland
West Africa	**Benin, Burkina Faso**, Cape Verde, **Gambia**, Ghana, **Guinea, Guinea Bissau**, Ivory Coast, **Liberia, Mali, Mauritania, Niger**, Nigeria, **Senegal, Sierra Leone, Togo**

Source: Gstöhl and De Bièvre (2018: 150). © Sieglinde Gstöhl and Dirk De Bièvre 2018. Reproduced with permission of the Licensor through PLSclear.

most significant change from Lomé was the gradual replacement of the system of trade preferences by a series of new economic partnerships based on the progressive and reciprocal removal of trade barriers (European Commission 2000: Chapter 2, Articles 36–38).

The negotiation of EPAs saw ACP states deal for the first time with DG Trade rather than DG Development, which some regarded as symbolically important. Negotiations repeatedly stalled and were seen as controversial in many ACP states due to the perception that market opening could harm development prospects, particularly in areas related to the new trade agenda. A number of ACP states agreed only to interim EPAs focused on trade in goods and development aid. At the end of 2018, only the Caribbean region and the Southern African Development Community had signed a full EPA (covering services as well as goods) (see Table 24.1). The EU is keen that EPAs will remain an important instrument beyond the Cotonou agreement (which is due to expire in 2020), but there is some uncertainty with respect to future relations between the EU and ACP states (for an excellent analysis attempting to understand the EU's general failure on EPAs, see Murray-Evans 2018).

Many LDC states among the ACP states preferred to rely on the EU's 'Generalised System of Preferences' (GSP). In a derogation to normal WTO rules, which do not permit preferential treatment, there are, broadly, three GSP tiers. First, a standard GSP can be applied to any country that declares itself to be a developing country and is formally classified as lower than 'upper middle income'. Second, GSP+ can be applied to countries meeting particular vulnerability criteria and willing to sign up to EU social, environmental and good governance conditions. Finally, there is the 'Everything-but-Arms' initiative, launched in the context of the WTO Doha Round in an attempt to build confidence in the talks among developing countries. This grants duty- and quota-free access to EU markets for all imports from participating LDCs (for more detail, see Gstöhl and De Bièvre 2018: 153–62).

Relations with Asia and Latin America

The EU has historically had a weaker trading relationship with Asia and Latin America than with the ACP states. That said, the EU has negotiated with regional bodies such as Mercosur in Latin America and ASEAN (the Association of Southeast Asian Nations) in Asia (although as of 2018, talks were ongoing with the former and suspended with the latter). The EU has also managed to establish FTAs with countries in both regions over the past couple of decades. The first comprehensive FTAs with Asian countries were agreed in 2010 (South Korea) and 2018 (Singapore). Like LDCs among the ACP states, LDCs in both regions have been able to benefit from the EU GSP.

The European Neighbourhood Policy

In 2004, the relations of the EU with neighbouring states were brought together under the European Neighbourhood Policy (ENP). Its objectives were: to share the benefits of the 2004 enlargement with neighbouring countries without offering the perspective of membership, and so to prevent the emergence of stark dividing lines between EU and non-EU states; and to build security in the area surrounding the EU. Although the ENP is not a purely economic arrangement (it is also an important aspect of the EU's broader foreign policy—see Chapter 25, 'CFSP and CFDP in Action'), the provision of financial assistance and economic co-operation, including access for the neighbouring states to the EU's internal market, are central to its operation. In 2013, there were sixteen ENP countries to the south and east of the EU: Algeria, Armenia, Azerbaijan, Belarus, Egypt, Georgia, Israel, Jordan, Lebanon, Libya, Moldova, Morocco, Palestine, Syria, Tunisia, and Ukraine. It does not cover states to the east that already have a prospect of membership—Turkey, and the western Balkan states of Serbia, Montenegro, Bosnia-Herzegovina, Albania, and North Macedonia (see Chapter 26, Table 26.2), nor does it cover Russia.

In line with the objective of avoiding stark dividing lines between the EU and its neighbours, it was intended from the outset that the European Neighbourhood and Partnership Instrument (ENPI) would have a specific focus on cross-border co-operation and intra-regional co-operation. The principles used in the management of the ENPI are those that were pioneered first in the management of the structural funds for regional development in the EU—multi-annual programming, partnership, and co-financing (see Chapter 18, 'Cohesion Policy')—and later deployed in the context of enlargement policy (see Chapter 26).

Throughout the political and economic dialogue with neighbouring states, the emphasis has been on the development of the rule of law, good governance, respect for human rights (including minority rights), the promotion of good-neighbourly relations, and the principles of the market economy and sustainable development. While the ENP consists in the main of bilateral relations between the EU and partner countries, it co-exists and overlaps with ongoing multilateral regional-based initiatives in the 'neighbourhood', such as the Euro-Med Partnership, the Eastern Partnership, and the Black Sea Synergy.

In the context of the ENP, the EU has been able to negotiate association agreements with many countries in the EU 'neighbourhood'. These agreements typically provide for the liberalization of trade to various degrees and often (though not necessarily) pave the way to formal accession processes. One of the earliest such agreements was with Turkey in 1973. In recognition of the disappointment of Turkey at not being treated as a candidate for membership of the EU in the enlargement round that ended in 2004, in 1996, the association agreement with it was extended into a special customs union (on Turkey, see also Chapter 26, 'Turkey').

In the late 1990s and throughout the 2000s, the EU negotiated association agreements with a number of countries in the Mediterranean region geared towards the liberalization of trade in goods. Since the late 2000s and in the context of its Eastern Partnership, the EU has sought to negotiate further such agreements. As of early 2014, it had made significant progress towards the signature of agreements with Georgia and Moldova. Despite having negotiated and initialled an agreement with the EU, Ukraine opted in late 2013 not to sign this in response to Russian pressure. This led to widespread political opposition and upheaval in Ukraine in early 2014 and significant tensions between Russia and the West (for more on these events, see Chapter 25, 'The CFSP and CSDP in Action'). Russia is generally concerned about the extension of EU economic and political influence in the East, and particularly into soviet successor states.

Explaining and Critiquing Trade and Development Aid Policies

Theoretical explanations of the external trade and development aid policies of the EU have focused on the politics of formulating a common commercial policy and on the relations of the EU with the ACP states. In both cases, use has been made of the idea of a 'multi-level game', derived from Robert Putnam's (1988) concept of a 'two-level game', combined with insights from institutionalist approaches. However, it is questionable whether such models entirely capture the ever-increasing complexity of contemporary trade policy. Critical scholarship has engaged with this policy area from a different angle, focusing on and questioning its normative underpinnings.

Explaining External Trade Policy

Explanations of the external trade policy of the EU have not generally supported supranational theories, although, given the qualms of France and some of the other member states about policies of liberalization, the idea of the Commission playing an autonomous role can be put forward. Most analyses, though, adopt an approach based on the idea of a multi-level game, to which has been added an institutionalist perspective.

One possible explanation of the trade policy of the EU is that the Commission is able to play a role as an autonomous actor (Damro 2007). On this view, divisions within the EU between member states, combined with the need for the Council to approve trade agreements by a qualified majority rather than unanimity, opened up an opportunity for active and committed Commission leadership to influence the direction of policy. Such leadership was provided by a succession of Trade Commissioners, all of whom favoured trade liberalization. In the Santer Commission, Sir Leon Brittan held the portfolio from 1994 to 1999, and set a strong free trade agenda; he was followed by Pascal Lamy (1999–2004), who, despite his French nationality, continued to push the EU in the same direction during the Prodi Commission, as did his successor in the Barroso Commission, Peter Mandelson (2004–08).

This does not mean that there were no differences in emphasis between the Commissioners. Meunier (2007a) looked at the differences between the 'managed globalization' favoured by Lamy and the position of his successor, Mandelson, as expressed in the 2006 communication *Global Europe: Competing in the World* (European Commission 2006). 'Managed globalization' made multilateralism the central doctrine of EU trade policy, and linked trade to political objectives such as social justice and sustainable development. This was very much the EU approach to the Doha round of negotiations led by Lamy. In contrast, 'Global Europe' argued that the central objective of EU trade policy should be to open markets abroad for European companies. To this end, and also in part as a consequence of the failure of Doha, a 'new generation' of bilateral FTAs have been agreed over the past decade, focused, as noted in 'The Common Commercial Policy' above, not only on goods and services, but also on 'behind-the-border' issues, such as the adverse trade effects of national rules, state subsidies, intellectual property, and public procurement. The shift of emphasis within the Commission was continued with the 2010 EU trade strategy, *Trade, Growth and World*

Affairs (European Commission 2010*b*), which emphasized the importance of pushing for increased market access and bilateral deals.

Meunier (2007*a*) noted that neither the adoption of the approach of multilateral managed globalization nor the shift towards bilateralism involved a new mandate from the member states. This seemed to indicate a degree of autonomy for the Commission in making EU policy on external trade. However, little evidence was found to sustain the argument that the Commission had a significant autonomous effect on the policy. The autonomy of the Commission was judged to be limited to reframing and repackaging the interests of the member states, and perhaps tweaking them at the margins (Meunier 2007*a*: 922). Indeed, the member states as principals are keen to maintain some measure of control of the Commission as agent, while maintaining the benefits of delegation (see Chapter 2, 'Rational Choice Institutionalism' on principal–agent theory). In relation to our example, they broadly endorsed the shift from multilateralism to bilateralism.

Intergovernmental explanations have centred on the idea of trade negotiations as a multi-level game. Putnam (1988) described the making of foreign policy for a state as a 'two-level game' (see also Gstöhl and De Bièvre 2018: 100–3). Moravcsik (1991*a*, 1993, 1998) incorporated this insight into his 'liberal intergovernmental' theorizations of the nature of the relationship between the EC/EU and its member states (see Chapter 1, 'Theories of European Integration'). At one level, the government of each member state has to find a position that will satisfy the balance of pressures in its domestic political arena. It then has to play a game at the level of negotiations with the other member states to try to achieve an agreement that falls within the parameters of what is acceptable domestically.

However, the position in EC trade negotiations is even more complex. The nature of the relationship between the member states, the Commission, and the trade partners means that it is a three-level, rather than a two-level, game (Collinson 1999). The three levels are as follows:

1. The government of each of the member states has to find a negotiating position that reflects its own domestic constraints.

2. All of the governments then have to negotiate around these positions in determining together the negotiating mandate for the Commission in the wider trade talks.

3. The Commission then has to negotiate in the wider talks within the tight parameters of this mandate.

If it is necessary to go beyond these parameters to reach a deal, the Commission has to refer back to its constituency in the Council, and the members of that constituency (the governments of the member states) have to refer back to their domestic constituencies.

Matters are complicated by the increased role of the EP (see 'The Common Commercial Policy' above) and, more generally, the expansion of interested actors in trade policy. This is a consequence of the multi-issue nature of contemporary trade. Agriculture, which was effectively excluded from the earliest rounds of GATT negotiations by a tacit agreement between the participants, has become a central issue. More significantly, with the new trade agenda, trade is no longer only about goods. There is also trade in services and intellectual property and the liberalization of foreign direct investment (FDI) became an explicit part of the EU agenda with the Lisbon Treaty. In general, a new trade agenda is no longer concerned only with restrictions that occur at the border of national economies, but also with 'behind-the-border' issues and domestic policy and regulation. The EU increasingly attempts to harmonize such regulation and, indeed, can be considered a significant 'regulatory power' in world politics (see Chapter 25, 'EU Power in World Politics'; and Webber 2016).

Such complexity means that as well as trade officials, non-trade departments, both of the Commission and national governments, have increasingly important roles in trade policy. New actors are less likely to share the acceptance of the benefits of free trade that forms the ideational context for policy making among trade officials. Also, the sorts of issues covered by the new agenda have much wider direct political implications within states. This is particularly true of the 'social trade' agenda, which affects such issues as measures to protect the environment or consumers. Here, both politicians and campaigning interest groups, such as environmental groups and consumer groups, have an incentive to become active within the policy-making process.

In short, we can see that a multitude of actors are involved in contemporary trade policy and politics, including supranational institutions and member states, but also a range of other actors. As discussed in the following section, critical approaches to EU trade policy have, among other things, started to engage with the role that such actors are playing.

Critiquing Trade and Development Aid Policies

The general orientation of EU trade policy has been, in accordance with its internal single market policy, towards a free-trade agenda (agriculture being a notable exception—see Chapter 21). However, just as the single market project has provoked critiques from a critical political economy perspective (see Chapter 4, 'Critical Political Economy' and Chapter 19, 'Evaluating the Single Market'), so have trends in EU trade policy. These interventions have tended to focus on the EU's relationship with the developing world, but increasingly they also consider trade and development policy as a whole and the 'deep trade' or 'behind-the-border' issues discussed in 'Explaining External Trade Policy' above.

Deploying a neo-Gramscian perspective, Gibb (2000: 477–8) analysed the shift from Lomé to Cotonou. He argued that the Commission, in its Green Paper, had presented the requirements of the WTO as an insuperable barrier to the continuation of Lomé, but, in reality, the WTO system was one that the EU had been involved in installing. An alternative to changing the Lomé principles to make them compatible with the WTO would have been to change the WTO rules to make them compatible with the Lomé principles. Some ACP delegations had suggested that the EU and ACP jointly argue for the acceptance by the WTO of a new category of free trade agreement, a 'soft' or 'low' agreement, that would not be subject to the same stringent requirements as were implied by existing WTO rules. The EU chose not even to raise this issue during the Millennium Round of trade negotiations. The conclusion was that, '[t]he WTO is . . . at the centre of the post-Lomé negotiations because the EU placed it there. And it placed it there because it is in its own best interests to do so' (Gibb 2000: 478).

Hurt (2003) went further by analysing the aid provisions as well as the trade provisions of the agreement. He drew attention to the similarity of principles underpinning Cotonou to the principles of other institutions of international economic management, including not only the WTO, but also the IMF and the World Bank. This similarity was again attributed to the dominance of neoliberal ideas, which served the interests of powerful actors within the developed world.

> The current neoliberal hegemony of ideas sits broadly compatibly with the self-interests of political élites and the outward-orientated fraction of the capitalist class within the EU member states.

(Hurt 2003: 174)

More generally, the shift in agenda from multilateralism to bilateralism associated with the 'Global Europe' agenda can also be considered in terms of such a 'neoliberal hegemony of ideas', or what Siles-Brügge (2014) has termed a shift towards 'competitive liberalization'.

Moves to pursue bilateral agreements which focus on liberalization in areas with significant 'behind-the-border' implications, such as services and investment, have been understood as exemplary of this shift. Heron and Siles-Brügge (2012) emphasized the importance of broader systemic factors in explaining such a shift: in particular, the efforts of competitor nations such as the United States and Japan to pursue such policies themselves. It can also, according to their analysis, be understood in terms of the increasing power and influence of services and investment-industry interest groups, seen as vital to the fortunes of the EU and developed economies more generally. These broader structural political-economy factors perhaps go some way to explaining why the Commission has increasingly been given the mandate to negotiate 'deep trade' agreements that focus on regulatory alignment.

This has, however, met with political controversy. This was particularly true of TTIP, which was described as a 'game-changer' by some analysts (De Ville and Siles-Brügge 2017) in terms of its attempt to establish a transatlantic market. The draft agreement had the potential, according to its numerous critics, to erode European domestic and EU regulation. This would effectively diminish the ability of states or the EU to make democratic decisions on politically salient issues relating to, for instance, food safety (see Insights 24.3 and 24.4), environmental protection, or even certain public services. Such issues also animated debates in relation to the Comprehensive Economic and Trade Agreement (CETA) with Canada, signed in 2017. In the context of growing politicization around trade issues, the final agreement was initially rejected in 2016 by the Belgian regional government in Wallonia (its agreement was required for the Belgian signature) and only agreed once significant reassurances, pertaining in particular to the preservation of autonomous economic governance, were written in to the agreement (Gstöhl and De Bièvre 2018: 200–1).

There are important parallels here with the controversial shifts towards liberalizing services associated with the single market project (see Chapter 19, 'Beyond 1992'). Both trends can be understood within the context of emerging understandings of competitiveness and the 'knowledge economy' (see Chapter 10, 'The Lisbon Strategy') and perceptions of regulation as 'red-tape' or a 'barrier to trade' (associated, for instance, with the EU's 'Better Regulation' agenda (see Chapter 19, 'The Single

Market beyond the Eurozone Crisis')). Indeed, adopting a 'radical' constructivist perspective (see Chapter 4, 'Social Constructivism'), Orbie and De Ville (2014) argued that EU discourse had increasingly used internal neoliberal policy to legitimize external trade policy and vice versa.

While these critical political economy approaches (see Chapter 4, 'Critical Political Economy') may at times understate the plurality and complexity of competing interests at play in the trade arena, they offer an important alternative perspective to mainstream approaches that do not explicitly question the normative assumptions underpinning EU trade policy. Critical political economy approaches point to the important potential impacts of a liberalizing trend, which remains strong despite growing challenges from within and beyond the EU.

CONCLUSION

Examination of the external economic relations of the EU brings to the fore several of the theoretical themes that have appeared throughout this book: the tension between nationalism and supranationalism; the complexities of bargaining within multiple international forums; and the dominance of particular ideas across different forums. It also shows the difficulty entailed in clearly separating internal and external policies, and economic and political issues.

The complex decision making rules for the common commercial policy demonstrate the dangers of any oversimplification of the relationship between intergovernmentalism and supranationalism. The Commission clearly plays an important role, and has a certain autonomy over the conduct of trade negotiations under the Articles of the original Treaty dealing with the common commercial policy. The member states have always been influential, though. They have to agree the negotiating mandate within which the Commission works, and they have to secure sufficient domestic support before their representatives dare vote for the ratification of the agreements, which acts as a further constraint on the Commission's scope for making deals. The EP has become an increasingly important actor in recent years and the CJEU has played an important role in adjudicating on matters of competence as trade has become increasingly complex. The theoretical concept of the multi-level game is helpful for understanding the functioning of trade policy, especially when supplemented by an institutionalist analysis that takes into account variations in the constellations of actors, established practices, and ideational contexts of the different issue areas.

From a more explicitly critical perspective, the dominant ideas that underpin EU trade policies have been called into question. Such analyses have, in particular, highlighted the free market and increasingly neoliberal bias inherent in recent EU policy. They emphasize the broader power relations that have supported this bias and draw attention to the often adverse consequences that it has for developing countries and other constituencies, both within and beyond the EU. In many cases, they have also highlighted the close connections between these external policies and the internal EU economic policies discussed in earlier chapters. Such critical voices have had some purchase in the 'real world' in recent years, with the politicization of recent EU trade agreements within many member states and the protectionist turn of a major EU trading partner, the United States.

Whatever the approach adopted in considering trade policies, it is an area which makes clear that economic and political issues are interrelated in important and complex ways. This makes it difficult to distinguish clearly the economic external relations examined in this chapter from the political external relations discussed in Chapters 25 and 26, even if they have traditionally operated under different institutional arrangements.

KEY POINTS

History

- When the EEC was set up in the 1950s, world economic relations were governed by the 1944 Bretton Woods agreements. Trade relations were governed by the GATT.

- A key principle of the GATT was MFN: members had to offer to all other member states terms of trade as favourable as the best terms they offered to any other state. The EEC gained exemption from MFN for the internal common market and for its relations with former colonies of EEC members.

- Relations with the former colonies initially continued their dependence on France in particular. When Britain joined the EEC, the Lomé Convention provided the ACP states with a fairer deal.

- Following the collapse of communism in eastern Europe, the EU concluded special trade and aid agreements with the CEECs in an attempt to ensure the stability of its near neighbours. For the same reason, special agreements were reached with the states of the southern Mediterranean.

External Trade Policy

- Trade negotiations are conducted by the Commission on behalf of the EU as a whole, working to a mandate agreed by the Council of Ministers and supervised by a committee of national representatives.

- Until the Lisbon Treaty came into force, trade in services and intellectual products were not automatically covered by this arrangement: the governments of the member states had to agree ahead of each round of negotiations to allow the Commission authority in these areas.

- Trade policy traditionally covered trade in goods, but has expanded to cover trade in services and 'behind-the-border' areas pertaining to regulations and intellectual property. The competence of the EU has expanded accordingly.

- Under the terms of the Lisbon Treaty, trade in services and intellectual products are an EU competence, but unanimity remains the voting rule where sensitive domestic issues are concerned.

- The Commission has the power to impose duties and other restrictions on imports of goods to the EU where dumping or unfair subsidies are suspected.

- Member states are often divided over trade issues both by conflicting economic interests and by their general attitude to free trade.

- Since the introduction of the WTO, the EU has been involved in a series of trade disputes, mainly with the United States, which took a protectionist turn with the Trump presidency.

Development and Trade

- Between 1975 and 2000, the relations of the EC/EU with the ACP states were governed by the Lomé Conventions. The terms of Lomé were more favourable to the ACP states, reflecting the international economic circumstances in which they were negotiated in the 1970s.

- By the end of the 1990s, when Lomé was renegotiated, it was clear that its terms were incompatible with the rules of the WTO in several respects. A new agreement was signed in 2000 in Cotonou, Benin. The Lomé system of trade preferences was replaced by a series of new economic partnerships based on the progressive and reciprocal removal of trade barriers.

- Beyond the ACP states, the EU has in recent decades intensified its trading relations with Asia and Latin America.

- The European Neighbourhood Policy (ENP) aims to prevent the emergence of stark dividing lines between EU and non-EU states in its neighbourhood by offering many of the

474

advantages of association to those states that do not have a prospect of membership. The EU has negotiated association agreements with many such states. These agreements lead to the liberalization of trade between the EU and association countries.

Explaining and Critiquing Trade and Development Aid Policies

- Shared responsibility for trade negotiations produces a complex pattern of bargaining that has been characterized as a 'three-level game'.
- Such rational-choice analyses of trade negotiations have been supplemented by institutional analysis.
- Both types of analysis have also been applied to relations with the ACP states.
- Critical political economists have emphasized the increasingly neoliberal bias in EU trade policy—reflected in a growing emphasis on 'deep trade' and 'behind-the-border' issues—and drawn attention to its negative consequences.

 For additional material and resources, please visit the online resources www.oup.com/uk/bache5e.

QUESTIONS

1. What does it mean to say that the EU has exclusive competence in relation to its common commercial (trade) policy?

2. Is the Commission an autonomous actor in the development of EU trade policy?

3. Assess the usefulness of the concept of a 'multi-level game' for understanding the formulation of EU trade policy.

4. Has EU development and trade policy been a positive force for countries in the global south?

5. Why have recent proposed trade deals, such as the TTIP, been politically controversial?

FURTHER READING

Two excellent recent sources on the EU and its trade policy are **S. Gstöhl and D. De Bièvre**, *The Trade Policy of the European Union* (Palgrave Macmillan, 2018) and **S. Khorana and M. García**, *Handbook on the EU and International Trade* (Cheltenham: Edward Elgar, 2018). A little older, but also excellent is **S. Meunier**, *Trading Voices: The European Union in International Commercial Negotiations* (Princeton, NJ: Princeton University Press, 2007). A useful literature review is offered by **A. Poletti and D. De Bièvre**, 'The Political Science of European Trade Policy: A Literature Review with a Research Outlook', *Comparative European Politics*, 12 (2014): 101–19. The chapters in **G. Faber** and **J. Orbie (eds)**, *Beyond Market Access for Economic Development: EU Africa Relations in Transition* (Abingdon: Routledge, 2009), address the emergence of EPAs in the context of the ACP. **G. Siles-Brügge**, *Constructing European Union Trade Policy: A Global Idea of Europe* (Palgrave Macmillan, 2014) offers an example of the critical approach enunciated in this chapter with reference to recent FTAs. For an introduction to the debates pertaining to TTIP, see the debate in the *Journal of European Public Policy*, 10 (2017): 1491–1533. For greater detail, see **F. De Ville and G. Siles-Brügge**, *TTIP: The Truth about the Transatlantic Trade and Investment Partnership* (London: Polity Press, 2015) and **A. R. Young**, *TTIP and the New Politics of Trade* (Newcastle: Agenda, 2017).

Chapter 25

Common Foreign and Security Policy

Chapter Overview

External political relations were always handled outside of the European Community (EC) frame-work, and initially were outside of the Treaty framework altogether. From 1993 to 2009, they formed the second pillar of the European Union (EU), on Common Foreign and Security Policy (CFSP) (the Lisbon Treaty abolished the three pillars). Although CFSP was officially an intergov-ernmental pillar, the Commission came to play an important role, and informally there were some similarities between the way in which the CFSP pillar operated and the way in which the EC pillar operated, even though the formal rules were different. Serious attempts were made to strengthen the security and defence aspects of the CFSP in the face of the threats that faced the EU from instability in its neighbouring territories. However, the EU remains far from having a truly supranational foreign policy and its status as a 'power' in international relations is debatable.

History

Prior to the Lisbon Treaty taking effect in December 2009, the external economic relations of the EC with the rest of the world were covered by the Treaty establishing the European Community (TEC), and generally came within the competence of the Commission (see Chapter 24, 'The Common Commercial Policy')—but the member states also separately developed machinery for formulating common positions on political issues of foreign policy. This initially developed outside of the framework of the Treaties under the name of European Political Co-operation (EPC). It entered the Treaties as Title III of the Single European Act (SEA) in July 1987, although still on an intergovernmental basis. Title V of the Treaty on European Union (TEU) (the Maastricht Treaty) set up a Common Foreign and Security Policy (CFSP) as the sec-ond pillar of the EU, and some additions were made to the machinery of the CFSP in the 1997 Amsterdam Treaty, including the creation of the 'High Representative for Common Foreign and Security Policy' (HRCFSP). In the late 1990s, efforts were made to establish a European Security and Defence Policy (ESDP), and this was brought into the EU by the Nice Treaty, which came into effect at the start of 2003. The Lisbon Treaty introduced further institutional reforms in the late 2000s through the creation of the post of 'High Representative of the Union for Foreign Affairs and

Security Policy' (HRUFASP)—with greater powers than the HRCFSP—and the 'European External Action Service' (EEAS). This Treaty also renamed the ESDP, which became the Common Security and Defence Policy (CSDP): (it will be referred to as CSDP hereafter). Since 2016, there has been a renewed push to reinforce co-operation in defence, with the establishment of permanent structured co-operation (PESCO) in the area of security and defence (see Insight 25.2).

European Political Co-operation (EPC)

EPC was suggested by French President Pompidou at the Hague Summit in 1969, but was seen at the time as little more than a sop to his Gaullist supporters. Few participants or observers thought that it would amount to anything, because it closely resembled the Fouchet Plan, which had already been rejected (see Insight 7.2), and because it proposed co-operation in the field of 'high politics' as defined by Hoffmann (1964, 1966), an area in which concerns about national sovereignty would be expected to get in the way of common action (see Chapter 1, 'Theories of European Integration'). Nevertheless, the initiative led to the setting up of a committee under the chairmanship of the Belgian Étienne Davignon, and its report—the Davignon or Luxembourg Report—recommending increased co-operation on international political issues, was adopted by foreign ministers meeting in Luxembourg in October 1970.

The machinery of EPC consisted mainly of regular meetings to co-ordinate national stances to particular areas of the world, or to particular issues. Foreign ministers were required to meet at least twice a year, but in practice met much more often. Immediately below the ministerial level, Foreign Office political directors met, on the original plan every three months, but in practice monthly. In addition to the meetings of foreign ministers and political directors, other institutional innovations were the COREU (*Correspondance Européenne*) telex link, and working groups on a range of policy and geographical issues. In the days before email and encryption, COREU allowed officials in the foreign ministries of member states to communicate with each other as frequently as they wished on a confidential line. By the mid-1970s, the Foreign Offices of member states were exchanging an average of 4,800 confidential telexes a year in an intensive process of consultation (Smith 2004: 107). By the time that the EPC was superseded by CFSP in the Maastricht Treaty, there were more than twenty quasi-permanent Working Groups (Smith 2004: 105).

Until 1987, EPC had no secretariat to provide administrative back-up. This was provided by whichever member state held the presidency of the Council at the time, imposing additional strain on the state holding the presidency, and also working against proper continuity across changes of presidency. Disappointment at the failure of the EC to respond effectively to the Iranian crisis in 1979 led to a review of EPC—the London Report—that recommended improved procedures for use in a crisis, and the creation of a small permanent secretariat. These recommendations were adopted in October 1981, and led directly to the creation in the SEA of a small secretariat, situated in Brussels.

EPC was originally set up as a parallel process to that of economic integration within the EC, but the two became closely linked. The distinction between matters proper to EPC and EC matters was rigidly maintained in the early years of the operation of EPC, at the insistence of the French, but it broke down with the opening of the 'Euro–Arab dialogue' in 1974. This was a structured series of regular meetings between representatives of the EC and representatives of the Arab states, prompted by the oil crisis of 1973–74. The Arab participants in the talks insisted on maintaining a clear linkage between trade and political questions, which forced the EC to fudge the lines of demarcation on its side. Once the artificial distinction had broken down here, it soon became less evident elsewhere in the external relations of the EC.

Once the EPC/EC distinction had been eroded, the Commission, originally excluded from meetings under the machinery of EPC, had to be admitted. One of the most compelling reasons for involving the Commission was that it proved difficult to do anything other than make declarations under EPC without having the use of the normal instruments of foreign policy. As military capabilities were unlikely to be made available to EPC, the obvious 'soft' weapon to use was economic sanctions, together with economic rewards, such as loans. These economic instruments fell within the competence of the EC, and were administered by the Commission. In theory, national economic mechanisms could have been used to back up EPC declarations, but this would have been less efficient than using centralized EC mechanisms, and might have worked against EC external economic policies. Consequently, the Commission's role in EPC became gradually more significant. The European Parliament (EP), while less significant, was not entirely excluded from the EPC. Reports were made in a full plenary session, usually as part of the same statement on progress in Community affairs that was made by the foreign minister of the state holding the Council presidency. Members of the EP were allowed to question the minister about EPC matters, as well as about more strictly Community matters.

Procedurally, then, EPC made big strides in the course of the 1970s, and became intertwined with the institutions and procedures of the EC. These advances were then formalized in the SEA in 1985–86. The SEA gave EPC a written basis for the first time, but the Articles relating to it were not subject to judicial interpretation by the Court of Justice of the European Union (CJEU).

Although EPC was at one time described as an example of 'procedure substituting for policy' (Wallace and Allen 1977), it had several substantive successes. For example, the member states achieved a high degree of unity in the United Nations (UN), voting together on a majority of resolutions in the General Assembly, and developing a reputation for being the most cohesive group there at a time when group diplomacy was becoming much more common.

Perhaps even more impressively, EPC formulated a common position on the Arab–Israeli conflict. This in itself was quite an achievement, given that prior to EPC there had been wide divergences in the extent of sympathy for Israel and for the Arab states in different member states. Reaching an agreed position allowed the EC, through the Euro–Arab dialogue, to pursue its clear interest in improving trade with the Arab Organization of the Petroleum Exporting Countries (OPEC) states in the 1970s. In June 1980, this common policy culminated in the Venice Declaration, which went further than the United States was prepared to go in recognizing the right of the Palestinians to a homeland.

The then nine member states were also extremely successful in formulating a common position at the Conference on Security and Co-operation in Europe (CSCE) in Helsinki in 1975, and at the follow-up conferences in Belgrade in 1977, and Madrid in 1982–83. Indeed, the whole CSCE process was an initiative of the EC states. Again, the common position adopted by the EC ran somewhat contrary to the position of the United States. The Americans regarded the Helsinki process with some suspicion because they thought it risked legitimating communist rule in eastern Europe. In January 1995, the CSCE took on more permanent form as the Organization for Security and Co-operation in Europe (OSCE).

Admittedly, there were also failures. It proved difficult to find a joint position on the invasion of Afghanistan by the Soviet Union in December 1979. The British government argued strongly for following the lead of the United States in boycotting the Olympic Games in Moscow, while the French in particular were not prepared to do so, and the West German government was unhappy at the way in which the United States used the issue to heighten East–West tension. On balance, though, there were more successes than there were failures.

The Common Foreign and Security Policy (CFSP) and Common Security and Defence Policy (CSDP)

At the beginning of the 1990s, the EC failed to respond adequately to two separate international crises. The first was in the Persian Gulf, where Iraq invaded its neighbour, Kuwait, in August 1990. The second was in Yugoslavia, where fighting broke out in June 1991 between the former Yugoslav army and Croat and Slovenian separatist forces. In both cases, the immediate response of the EC was positive, but as the crises developed, differing national interests paralysed the process of political co-operation, and the United States ended up having to take the lead in resolving both.

While it was struggling to deal with these crises, the EC was also transforming itself into the EU. The intergovernmental conference (IGC) on political union, which began in January 1991, had the future evolution of EPC as a central item on its agenda. The more radical agenda, supported by Commission President Jacques Delors and by the German government, was to bring EPC into the framework of the EC, with the Commission perhaps not having the sole right of initiative but being centrally involved, and qualified majority voting (QMV) applying to decisions in the Council of Ministers. Security and defence would be added to the remit of this new mechanism for a common foreign policy. The opposite pole was marked out by the British, who argued against QMV on issues that were central to the sovereignty of the member states, and were particularly concerned that any moves to establish a common policy for security and defence should not undermine the North Atlantic Treaty Organization (NATO) alliance.

The two voices in this debate drew opposite conclusions from events in the Gulf. Both sides agreed that the failure of the EC to respond effectively to the crises indicated how far there still was to travel to a common policy. However, whereas Delors told the EP that the ineffective response indicated the urgency of pushing forward to political union (*Debates of the European Parliament*, 23 January 1991, 3–398/139), British Prime Minister John Major told the House of Commons that this failure clearly indicated that Europe was not ready for a common policy (Hansard, 22 January 1991, col. 162).

In a compromise between these two positions, a three-pillar structure was adopted at Maastricht, with the CFSP and Justice and Home Affairs (JHA) forming intergovernmental pillars of the new EU alongside the EC pillar (see Chapter 12, Figure 12.1). Majority voting in the second pillar was restricted to the implementation measures needed to carry through decisions of principle that would have to be taken by consensus, and even then, the QMV would only apply if all states were to agree to accept it in a particular case. There were some other enhancements of EPC, including moving the old EPC Secretariat into the Council Secretariat and giving it a larger staff and budget. Overall, though, the TEU really represented a victory for the minimalist position on the CFSP.

The crisis in former Yugoslavia did have the effect of bringing France and Britain closer together on security and defence. The common experience of operating under UN auspices in Bosnia led to increased co-operation on the ground, which spread into the creation of a joint air-force command unit. Nevertheless, when, in 1998, a further crisis occurred in the Kosovo province of Serbia, the EU again proved unequal to the task of making a rapid response. It was NATO that undertook a bombing campaign against Serbia to force it to retreat from the persecution of the ethnic Albanians in Kosovo. The United States spearheaded the NATO effort.

The failure of the EU to act in Kosovo provided the impetus for a move to extend CFSP to security and defence. In December 1998, at a bilateral Franco–British summit in Saint-Malo, France, French President Jacques Chirac and British Prime Minister Tony Blair jointly announced their support for a CSDP (at the time, and until the Lisbon Treaty, called *European* Security and Defence Policy—ESDP). A year later, the Helsinki European Council announced what was called the 'headline goal' of creating, by the end of 2003, a European Rapid Reaction Force of 50,000–60,000 troops, plus naval and air back-up that could be sustained in the field for up to one year. In March 2000, the institutions of the CSDP began provisional operation: a political and security committee, known by its French acronym COPS (standing for *Comité Politique et de Sécurité*); a military committee; and the basis for a joint military command structure.

The Amsterdam Treaty had already made some modifications to the CFSP, particularly in creating the post of HRCFSP, the holder of which would be the first point of contact for CFSP matters. In November 1999, it was agreed to appoint the then NATO Secretary-General, Javier Solana, to this post. The Commission had argued that the post should go to one of the Commissioners, but the heads of government decided to make it a position within the Council framework, thus storing up potential for problems in the co-ordination of the work of the two institutions.

Amendments to the TEU at Amsterdam drew a distinction between, on the one hand, deciding the principles and general guidelines of the CFSP, and common strategies in pursuit of these, and on the other, the adoption of joint actions, common positions, and implementing decisions. The first category of decision had to be unanimous; QMV could decide the second. Also, a member state could abstain in a vote and make a formal declaration that it would not be bound by the vote. This would allow the EU as a whole to be committed to the decision, but not the individual abstaining state, which would only be obliged not to act in any way that would conflict with the pursuit of the action by the EU.

Amsterdam also incorporated the so-called 'Petersberg Tasks' into the EU. In June 1992, the Western European Union (WEU) Petersberg Declaration had said that member states would allocate armed forces to peace-keeping and humanitarian tasks in Europe (see Insight 25.1). This had committed only the members of WEU, but the 1997 Amsterdam Treaty committed all EU member states to the tasks. CSDP was officially brought into the TEU by amendments made in the 2000 Nice Treaty, which took effect at the start of 2003. The 'European Security Strategy' (ESS) established the context and strategic principles for the CSDP. The context was growing concerns with respect to terrorism, state failure, and organized crime in a post-Cold War environment. The strategic aspiration was to create an effective military dimension and included a concern with preventative action and 'human security'.

Further amendment was made to the institutions of the CFSP in the Lisbon Treaty. First, the three-pillar structure was abolished, and CFSP became an integral part of an EU that now had a consolidated legal personality. However, this does not mean that CFSP has become regular EU business: it is still 'subject to specific rules and procedures' (Article 24(1) TEU).

Insight 25.1 The Western European Union (WEU)

The WEU was set up in 1954 following the collapse of the Pleven Plan for a European Defence Community (see Chapter 6, 'The Pleven Plan'). The original members were Belgium, France, Luxembourg, the Netherlands, Britain, West Germany, and Italy, while Portugal and Spain became members in 1990 and Greece in 1995, bringing the membership to ten. By the 1980s, the WEU had become effectively moribund, but proposals to revive it as a vehicle for co-ordinating European positions were made by the Belgian and French governments in 1984. Prior to the Gulf War of 1990, the WEU co-ordinated mine-sweeping operations in the Persian Gulf, which had been mined during the Iran–Iraq war. It was therefore in a strong position to provide a co-ordination mechanism for the member states involved in the Gulf War, which it did, and continued with mine-sweeping operations afterwards.

The WEU co-operated with NATO to monitor the embargo against former Yugoslavia in 1993, providing a joint naval task force. It also helped to enforce the sanctions on the Danube, providing patrol boats, vehicles, and personnel to work alongside the national agencies of Bulgaria, Hungary, and Romania. From 1994 to 1996, the WEU provided a police contingent to the EU administration in Mostar in Bosnia-Herzegovina, to assist in the setting up of a Bosnian–Croat joint police force. These activities, which prefigured the missions later undertaken by the EU under its CSDP, continued with a police mission in Albania from 1997 to 2001, a De-mining Assistance Commission to Croatia in 1999, and a General Security Surveillance Mission in Kosovo in 1998–99.

To facilitate closer co-ordination, in 1992 the WEU Secretariat was moved from London to Brussels, where both the European Commission and NATO headquarters were located. In 1999, Javier Solana, the EU High Representative for the CFSP, was appointed Secretary General of the WEU as well. Following the effective transfer of its crisis-management functions to the EU, the WEU was fully closed in 2011.

Until the Lisbon Treaty came into effect, it could be argued that the Brussels Treaty still formed the basis of a mutual defence pact between the ten member states, but Lisbon amended the TEU so as to envisage a possible future common defence under Article 42, which says that should a member state experience armed aggression on its own territory, the other states shall assist it by all means in their power.

Second, the HRCFSP became the 'High Representative of the Union for Foreign Affairs and Security Policy' (HRUFASP). This was more than a change of name. Whereas the original post was combined with that of Secretary General of the Council, and there was a separate Commissioner for External Relations, the new post carried with it the position of Vice-President of the European Commission, and the incumbent was to chair all meetings of the Council of Foreign Ministers, thus making it a position that straddled both institutions, and acted as a bridge between external economic relations and the CFSP/CSDP. At the Brussels European Council in September 2009, the heads of government agreed to appoint Baroness Catherine Ashton, until then the Commissioner for Trade, to the HRUFASP post with effect from the Treaty coming into force on 1 December 2009. The Lisbon Treaty also established the EEAS (which came into operation in 2011), the EU's diplomatic service, to assist the HRUFASP. It is formed by staff drawn from the external relations departments of the Council and Commission, with provision for additional staff to be seconded from the national diplomatic services of the member states.

In 2016, the second HRUFASP, Federica Mogherini (2014–19), launched the 'EU Global Strategy: Shared Vision, Common Action' (EUGS) in an attempt to renew the ESS in the light of new geopolitical challenges (Tocci 2017). The EUGS called, in particular, for further co-operation on defence and military matters. PESCO represents the first concrete attempt to deepen cooperation in this way (see Insight 25.2). While some commentary declared this as a decisive step towards a European army, others wondered whether it would go much further than the CSDP in practice. At the time of writing in 2019, it was too early to reach a proper assessment. It will fall to Josep Borrell—the third HRUFASP, appointed in 2019—to lead the development of further initiatives in this area.

Insight 25.2 Permanent Structured Co-operation (PESCO)

Emerging following the publication of EUGS, PESCO was established in December 2017. Twenty-five member states (all except the UK, Denmark, and Malta) signed up to participate in the treaty-based framework. The foundations for this were laid out in the Lisbon Treaty:

> Those Member States whose military capabilities fulfil higher criteria and which have made more binding commitments to one another in this area with a view to the most demanding missions shall establish permanent structured cooperation within the Union framework.
> (Article 42.6 the TEU)

PESCO allows participating states to jointly plan, develop, and invest in shared capability projects. The aim is to harmonize the interoperability of militaries in various ways, co-develop and pool military capabilities through the 'European Defence Agency', and thereby have the capacity to coordinate joint missions more closely and effectively. Participating states are required to adopt annual national implementation plans to ensure they are making the required reforms. In 2018, the Council committed to seventeen projects geared towards standardizing and harmonizing a range of military capabilities ranging from medical support to communications.

The impact of Brexit (see the online Brexit Supplement) on CFSP/CSDP may be significant, but was unclear at the time of writing in 2019. On the one hand, both Britain and the EU are keen to maintain a close relationship in this area post-Brexit. The largely intergovernmental nature of EU cooperation would perhaps allow for that in a way that would not be possible in many other policy areas. On the other hand, Britain's departure—given its traditional hostility to significant integration in CFSP/CSDP—may have paved the way for PESCO and further integration that would make it increasingly difficult for Britain to participate. That said, if such integration were not to include Britain, that could come with a cost to the EU's security and defence capabilities, given Britain's relative military strength and high defence expenditure (see Whitman 2016; Cardwell 2017).

 Visit the online resources for access to a Supplement including coverage of Brexit www.oup.com/uk/bache5e.

The CFSP and CSDP in Action

The start of CFSP did not suggest a great leap forward in either the capabilities or the ambitions of the EU. The first actions undertaken were modest, and were all in areas that built on EPC. Monitors were sent to observe the elections in Russia in December 1993; humanitarian aid for Bosnia was co-ordinated; and a new political framework was developed for aid to the West Bank and Gaza. Subsequently, observers were sent to monitor the first non-racial elections in South Africa, and the EU played an active role in the preparations for elections in the Palestinian homeland.

A more ambitious proposal, which originated with French Prime Minister Edouard Balladur, came to fruition in March 1995, when fifty-two states from western and eastern Europe signed a stability pact binding themselves to be good neighbours, and to respect the rights of minorities. Although there were several flaws in the pact, especially the exclusion for one reason or another of all of the Yugoslav successor states, the pattern was adopted later in the year by the Spanish presidency to develop a regional pact for the Mediterranean, in the face of growing concern in southern Europe about Islamic fundamentalism in the Arab world and about illegal immigration from there.

Following the so-called '9/11' (11 September 2001) terrorist attack on the United States (a series of four co-ordinated attacks on the United States by the Islamic terrorist group al-Qaeda), the EU, as in previous crises, initially reacted positively and decisively. Within thirty-six hours, declarations in support of the United States had been made by the Commission President, the Commissioner for External Relations, the Special Representative for Foreign Affairs, and the General Affairs Council. The Commission rapidly tabled proposals for a European arrest warrant (EAW), and agreement on this was reached in December, despite reservations by Italy (Hill 2004: 145–7). Indeed, the EU responded with 'an unforeseeable speed, range and flexibility' (Hill 2004: 150). EU solidarity was maintained during the subsequent US campaign in Afghanistan to unseat the Taliban government.

Both this solidarity with the United States and EU internal unity began to break down with the identification of an 'axis of evil' by US President George W. Bush in his 2002 'State of the Union' speech. Three states were identified as part of this axis: Iraq, Iran, and North Korea. The EU was working diplomatically with the latter two states, and the bellicose tone of President Bush worked against these efforts. In the case of Iraq, the EU was not following a strategy of its own, but the general view of member states was that the existing UN policy of sanctions was working. Of its 'axis of evil' states, it was Iraq that the United States chose to tackle first, and this precipitated a serious split within the EU. In the build-up to the eventual invasion, France and Germany led a group of states that opposed any military action, while Britain, Spain, and Italy were the leading supporters of a group (including the then accession states) that backed the US action. In March 2003, France publicly declared that it would veto any UN Security Council resolution in support of military action against Iraq that might be presented by the United States and Britain. This led to a bitter verbal attack on France by Tony Blair in the House of Commons on 18 March 2003.

As Howorth (2003: 179–80) made clear, the tensions had started to rise before this. Blair's response to the '9/11' attacks had been to reaffirm Britain's attachment to NATO. When the Spanish presidency attempted to reorient the European Rapid Reaction Force to turn it into a weapon that could be used against terrorism, Blair opposed the change, arguing that the war against terror should be handled through NATO. He subsequently supported a US proposal to the November 2002 NATO Summit in Prague for a NATO Response Force to react to terrorist incidents, and in April 2003, he was critical of the French position of rivalry with the United States, which he contrasted with the British position of partnership.

Following the invasion of Iraq by a US-led coalition backed by Britain in March 2003, Franco–British relations were at a very low ebb, and the prospects for CSDP looked poor. Yet Howorth (2003: 187) reported that there were already signs at the end of 2003 of both sides trying to improve matters. In August, at a meeting of European states in Rome, a clash was expected over whether CSDP needed its own planning headquarters, which France insisted it must have, or whether the EU should develop a permanent planning cell within the Supreme Headquarters Allied Powers Europe (SHAPE) of NATO. But the clash did not happen: the meeting agreed that both developments would be useful, and that they would complement one another. Then, in September, Blair agreed in principle that the EU should have the joint planning capacity to conduct operations without the involvement of NATO, a concession that appeared to alarm the United States. Britain also signed up to the ESS in December 2003, the development of which had been heavily influenced by a former Blair foreign policy advisor, Robert Cooper, who worked closely with Solana on the strategy. In short, the signs were that the British wanted to facilitate the relaunch of the CSDP.

There were also three successful international operations under the CSDP in the course of 2003 (Allen and Smith 2004: 97). In March, an EU force replaced the NATO force in the Former Yugoslav Republic of Macedonia (from 2018, the Republic of North Macedonia—see 'History' above), a move that had been scheduled for 2002 but had been delayed by Greek objections. In the middle of the year, there was a successful EU intervention to restore order in the Republic of Congo. Then, in December, the European Council agreed to provide a replacement for the NATO stabilization force in Bosnia. Subsequently, the EU conducted a number of missions. The majority of these were civilian, though some involved the deployment of military personnel, albeit only rarely in a combat capacity (see the EEAS website, https://eeas.europa.eu/headquarters/headquarters-homepage_en for a full and up-to-date list of missions).

There has been some evidence of success since the post-Lisbon architecture was put in place. EU missions in the troubled Sahel region of northern Africa and on the Horn of Africa suggested that greater cohesion between various actors in EU foreign policy was starting to emerge. Catherine Ashton also became an important and visible actor in certain international contexts. She played an important role in the western Balkans, successfully diffusing ethnic tension in Bosnia in 2011 and facilitating the negotiation of an unlikely agreement between the Kosovo and Serbian authorities in 2013, with the latter recognizing the autonomy of the former (which, in turn, paved the way for EU accession negotiations to commence with Serbia in 2014—see Chapter 26, 'Further Applications'). Despite ongoing tensions between the two sides, the implementation of this agreement was ongoing at the time of writing in 2019. Baroness Ashton was also centrally involved with the brokering of a deal with Iran in 2013, which led to an agreement in 2015 on the halting of Iran's nuclear programme in exchange for the removal of long-term sanctions on Iran. That said, at the time of writing in late 2019, the deal looked to be at breaking point; primarily as a result of President Trump's 2018 decision to remove the United States from the agreement and re-impose sanctions on Iran and increased tensions between the United States and Iran.

The post-Lisbon foreign policy architecture has also faced a number of challenges. An early test emerged in 2008 when, following a period of deteriorating relations between Russia and Georgia, the Russian military launched an offensive on Georgian territory. The proximate cause was the push for secession by two Georgian regions bordering Russia, although Putin was also exercised about Georgia's aspiration for NATO membership, which was supported by the United States. The EU collectively condemned Russian aggression and French President Sarkozy, as holder of the European Council's rotating presidency, was central to brokering a ceasefire. However, in some quarters the EU's reaction was characterized as weak; a function of divisions between member states and the lack of any credible military threat (in September 2008, *The Economist* described the EU as a 'chocolate fireguard').

A further test arose as a series of popular uprisings unfolded in the Middle East and North Africa in 2011. In some instances, these rebellions ousted incumbent authoritarian regimes from power (in Tunisia, Egypt, Libya, and Yemen), while in others they led to sustained campaigns of civil resistance (Bahrain), or drawn-out civil war (Syria). This upheaval has, notably, contributed to the EU's 'refugee crisis' that became particularly acute after 2015 (see Chapter 11, 'The Refugee Crisis' and Chapter 23, 'The Refugee Crisis'). The EU response to the so-called 'Arab Spring' was in many respects similar to its response to other crises. Individual member states led the way in terms of diplomacy and military initiatives, and the visibility of EU-level actors, such Catherine Ashton, was limited. For instance, French and British actors—notably President Sarkozy and Prime Minister Cameron—were key players in promoting and enacting the military intervention in Libya in 2011, which supported the opposition movement in ousting Colonel Gaddafi's regime. The EU's role was, in this case, limited to imposing sanctions. In other cases, it sought to engage with the new regimes economically, although in practice this did not amount to much more than a reinforcement of existing policy conducted under the auspices of the European Neighbourhood Policy (ENP) (see Chapter 24, 'Development and Trade'). Notwithstanding the new foreign policy architecture, the Arab Spring and its aftermath exposed certain long-standing weaknesses in CFSP/CSDP, both in terms of its horizontal cohesiveness (between EU institutions) and vertical cohesiveness (between member states and the EU).

Russia again presented a major challenge for EU foreign policy from around 2013. The Ukraine decided in late 2013, and at the last minute, not to sign an already-negotiated Association Agreement with the EU (see Chapter 24, 'Development and Trade'). This 'u-turn' prompted widespread, and at times violent, demonstrations in the Ukraine in support of its association with the EU and in opposition to its government. These led in early 2014 to the ousting of its President, Viktor Yanukovych. Russia's support for the ousted President and its subsequent dramatic annexation of the Crimea, a strongly pro-Russian region of Ukraine, created significant tensions with the West, including with the EU. In March 2014, the EU (as well as the United States) agreed to impose sanctions on Russia, although member states only agreed on a limited range of sanctions given divergent interests and relations with Russia. The case revealed the difficulty for the EU of pursuing closer relations with countries that the current Russian administration perceived, for various reasons, as an important part of its sphere of influence. Certainly, anxieties vis-à-vis an increasingly emboldened Russia were acute in the east of the EU following these events (and those in Georgia), particularly in the small Baltic nations.

This growing tension with Russia was an important context for the formulation of the 2016 EUGS (mentioned in 'The Common Foreign and Security Policy (CFSP) and Common Security and Defence Policy (CSDP)' above). However, other factors were also relevant, including: continued instability in the Middle East following the Arab Spring and ongoing Israeli–Palestinian conflict; a number of terrorist attacks within the EU itself since 2015 (including in Paris (2015), Brussels (2016), Nice (2016), Munich (2016), Berlin (2016), Manchester (2017), London (2017), and Barcelona (2017)); the election of Donald Trump as US President (particularly with respect to his uncertain commitment to NATO); and the continued rise of new global powers such as China. Given these and various other issues, the EUGS was far less bold than the ESS with respect to the EU's potential status and role in the world, calling for an approach characterized by 'principled pragmatism' (for an overview by an inside actor, see Tocci 2017). Concretely, the EUGS paved the way for, in particular, increased defence co-operation via PESCO (see Insight 25.2).

Explaining CFSP and CSDP

For a long time, explanations of political co-operation were rather weakly linked to theory. There were many detailed empirical accounts, some of the best written by practitioners, but although all such accounts were inevitably underpinned by theoretical assumptions, these were rarely made explicit. Most discussion was around the idea of the 'capability–expectations' gap, which was a valid concept, but was explicitly not intended as an explanatory theory (Hill 1993: 306), and which therefore did not address the central question of why political co-operation took place.

Perhaps the difficulty was that the academic community that initially emerged around political co-operation was dominated by 'realists' who started their analysis from the assumption that national interest was the sole motivating force of national foreign policy. As Glarbo (1999: 634) observed, although realist analyses differed from one another in detail, they all held to the common core proposition 'that the interests of single European nation states will eternally block integration within the high politics realms of foreign, security and defence policy'. Where common policies were devised, this would be explained by the coincidence of converging national interests; more often, such common positions were dismissed as trivial. Only with the later deployment of social constructivism (see Chapter 4, 'Social Constructivism') and other similar perspectives to the understanding of political co-operation did the debate become more theoretically sophisticated.

The Capability–Expectations Gap

Between the agreement of the TEU and its final ratification, Christopher Hill (1993) produced an assessment of political co-operation in which he developed a concept that was to become widely used in the subsequent literature: the 'capability–expectations gap'. Hill (1993: 309) cast doubt on whether the EC should be conceived as an actor in international affairs. It lacked autonomy, and was not distinct from other actors: notably, the member states. Many foreign policy practitioners external to the EC, and some internal practitioners too, had mistaken the EC for an actor. For instance, former US Secretary of State Henry Kissinger is said to have asked: 'Who do I call if I want to call Europe?' The mistake arose because the EC did have a distinct international 'presence'.

To mistake it for an actor, though, was to raise expectations of what it could achieve. It was expected to perform certain functions in the international system, such as acting as a counterweight to the dominance of the United States. Yet, the EC lacked the capability to meet these expectations. It lacked the resources, and the instruments—but also, because it was not an actor, it lacked the ability to reach agreement internally (Hill 1993: 310–15). This was why the capability–expectations gap existed, and Hill (1993: 315) believed that the gap had only been increased by the SEA and the TEU, which suggested advances in the international activity of the EC/EU that it was incapable of making.

In a review of the factors that have strengthened the 'actorness' of the EU since Hill's 1993 assessment, and those that continued to weaken it, Krotz (2009) argued that the EU was still a long way from being an international actor, although the forces making for 'actorness' were strengthening and those working against it might be weakening, opening up the future possibility of 'a fully grown high-politics actor Europe on the world stage'. It has been claimed in this respect that the Lisbon Treaty's reforms, highlighted in 'The Common Foreign and Security Policy (CFSP) and Common Security and Defence Policy (CSDP) above, contributed to increasing EU 'actorness'. For instance, Commission President Barroso claimed in 2009 that, with the appointment of Catherine Ashton as HRUFASP, 'the so-called Kissinger question is now solved' (Barroso 2009).

Finally, it is worth noting that the EU's 'actorness' in the world extends beyond CFSP. Indeed, particularly since the Lisbon Treaty, it has been practically difficult to sustain a clear distinction between a supposedly political and legally intergovernmental CFSP and a range of supranational policy areas that also involve 'external' action: most notably, trade and development policy (Chapter 24), but also freedom, security, and justice (Chapter 23), environment (Chapter 22), and energy policy (for a legal analysis, see Cardwell 2013). As such, while the EU's ability to act in the world may, in general, be declining as a consequence of recent geopolitical dynamics and the EU's own crises (Chapter 11), any adjudication on the EU's influence in world politics requires us to differentiate between the various ways in which it acts in the world (see ' EU Power in World Politics' below and Webber 2016).

Theoretical Explanations of Political Co-operation

Glarbo (1999) put forward two alternatives to realist approaches. The first was that important developments in political co-operation could only be understood as the outcome not only of national interest, but also of a growing level of communication between national officials. The second was that, contrary to realist analyses, integration *had* occurred within the field of political co-operation; it was a form of social integration stemming from the communication processes that the institutions of EPC and CFSP had set up.

This perspective had affinities with sociological institutionalism and social constructivism (see Chapters 2, 'Sociological institutionalism' and 4, 'Social Constructivism') inasmuch as it emphasized how institutional cultures can change over time. According to this thesis, the 'continuous communicative process' (Glarbo 1999: 644) that the EPC set going shifted the perceptions of the actors. They became sensitive to the constraints on the other actors, and tried to accommodate them. A code of conduct emerged whereby actors tried not to surprise their partners with *faits accomplis*. They also came to define the national interest differently, taking account of the emerging *acquis politique*: the accumulation of decisions and policy positions adopted through the EPC process. These developments were recognized by the actors, who were quite prepared to acknowledge in interviews with academics that their national practices had been modified as a result of participation in EPC, and who themselves contributed in surprisingly large numbers to the literature on the process, thereby coming to 'participate in the epistemic community surrounding this field' (Glarbo 1999: 659). In public statements, the advantages of EPC were presented in terms of how the process served national interests, but only because this was the language that was expected and understood by the wider public.

In a series of articles, Michael E. Smith (1999, 2000, 2001, 2003, 2004) developed a perspective on political co-operation that drew on the insights of both social constructivism and historical institutionalism. In this perspective, while the process of political co-operation began as an intergovernmental bargain, once the process was under way, it took on a different aspect. There were three linked elements in this transition. In decreasing order of importance, these were: the development of transgovernmental relations; the development and codification of EPC rules; and the forging of links with EC actors, especially the Commission (Smith 1999: 309–10).

Initial negotiations within EPC were conducted on the basis of existing national positions, so that, in its early years, EPC looked like classic intergovernmentalism— but this did not last. The intensive interaction between national representatives that was implicit in the idea of political co-operation constituted a system of transgovernmental relations in which these discrete national positions began to be modified as mutual trust developed (Smith 2004: 114–22). Out of this trust, and the constant process of discussion, emerged a socialization of participants, which led naturally to the gradual displacement of instrumental rationality by social rationality: the replacement of a bargaining approach by a problem-solving approach (Smith 2004) (note the similarities here with Glarbo (1999)).

The second aspect of the movement of EPC away from intergovernmentalism was the development and codification of EPC rules. This process, which can be described as the 'institutionalization' of EPC, has been discussed in 'European Political Co-operation' above. The increasingly rich institutional structure provided the forum for intensive interaction between officials from different levels in national foreign ministries. The transgovernmental network of diplomats and technical experts was thus extended and deepened. Such intensive interaction could not but influence the attitudes of professional diplomatic actors, and through them the process of defining the national interest. It fed back into national institutional structures, too. Political co-operation required the creation of new posts to serve it. This led to the expansion of national diplomatic services, and a reorientation of internal structures, sometimes amounting to complete reorganizations (M. E. Smith 2000: 619–23).

The third element in the transformation of EPC was the forging of links with EC institutions, especially the Commission. The reasons for involving the Commission and the EP in political co-operation have been outlined in 'European Political Co-operation (EPC)' above. Eventually, the role of the Commission in ensuring the consistency of EPC and EC actions was codified in the SEA (Smith 2001: 90). From this point on, the involvement of the Commission in political co-operation was not only customary, but it was also mandatory.

Explaining CSDP

The initiation of the security and defence dimension to CFSP is usually explained in terms of intergovernmental politics and coinciding national interests. The experience of the crises in the Gulf, in Bosnia, and in Kosovo all pointed to the weakness of the EU; something that the key member states came to accept required action. From the French point of view, awareness of the gap that had opened up between US and European military capabilities, and especially the dependence of the French armed forces on the United States for reconnaissance and for transport of equipment, pushed towards closer collaboration with NATO in the short term. In the longer term, however, the gaps might be filled by collaboration between European states. Co-operation of the British would be essential to achieve this, given that Britain was the other main military power in the EU. From the British point of view, the rapprochement between France and NATO was encouraging, but in the wake of the two Balkan crises, the United States began to pressurize the Europeans to get their act together so that they could make a bigger contribution to policing their own hinterland.

It is possible, though, that socialization became an increasingly important explanatory factor following the initial push towards defence integration. Howorth (2004) identified an 'epistemic community' (see Chapter 2, 'Related Literatures') that had formed around the issue of defence. He argued that one of the facilitating factors in the determination of Britain and France to take forward the project of CSDP in 2001 was 'the close-knit epistemic community of senior officials in London and Paris who, from the early 1990s onwards, had gradually developed a common mindset around the necessity and legitimacy of CSDP' (Howorth 2003: 175). More recently, and continuing his prior analysis (see 'Theoretical Explanations of Political Co-operation' above), M. E. Smith (2017) deployed a historical institutionalist approach to emphasize the importance of what he called 'experiential institutional learning' in this area. CSDP initiatives meant establishing new and intensified transgovernmental links between officials of national ministries of defence, and between military personnel. Some links already existed, of course, because of co-operation in NATO and the WEU, although the links were less intense for France, which was outside of the NATO command structure, and for those EU member states that were not members of NATO or WEU. Smith (2017) argued that as a consequence, certain CSDP missions could be judged to have been successful. That said, he also noted that continued intergovernmentalism in this sensitive policy area and bureaucratic complexity reduced what was possible (in Hill's terms, it reduced the EU's 'capabilitities') in the context of CSDP.

EU Power in World Politics

A number of academic discussions of developments in CFSP/CSDP are situated within a broader debate about what kind of power the EC/EU is in international affairs. While at one level this debate is about understanding the nature of the EU as a global power, at another level it is a normative debate about what kind of power the EU should be. The positions taken in this debate are important in terms of how EU external actions and policies are judged.

Duchêne (1973: 19) famously described the EC as a 'civilian power', 'long on economic power and relatively short on armed forces', and argued that it should not seek to increase its military power. As discussed in Chapter 24, the EC/EU has long been influential in global economic governance, and its member states have delegated significant responsibilities to supranational authority in this area. The linking of foreign policy with economic relations has given the EC/EU significant leverage in international affairs and allowed it to pursue European interests and promote ostensibly European values (such as free trade, democracy, and human rights) in the absence of military power. For Duchêne, this commitment to multilateral economic diplomacy was characterized as a 'domestication' of international relations and distinct from a then-prevalent Cold War power politics. This was a welcome feature of EC external relations that the development of a military capability would threaten. His argument had affinities with various liberal approaches to international relations, which emphasized the importance of economic interdependence.

Bull (1982) countered Duchêne's argument, making the case that the effectiveness of 'civilian power' would always require some form of 'military power' and advocating an increase in the EC's military capabilities. In this respect, Bull's argument had affinities with a realist perspective in international relations, although he was an advocate of international co-operation, so by no means a hard-line realist. As discussed in

Insight 25.1 above, the development of a common defence capacity was a long-standing goal of many actors in European affairs, but substantive steps in this direction were only achieved in the late 1990s with CSDP. For some advocates of 'civilian power Europe' such steps were a source of concern because they indicated the continued necessity of military force (K. Smith 2000: 28). However, for others the missions conducted in the context of CSDP were not necessarily incompatible with 'civilian' goals inasmuch as their primary aim was the promotion of sustainable peace (Whitman 2002). Moreover, EU capabilities in this area remained limited.

Manners (2002, 2008) drew attention to a third aspect of EU external power—its 'normative power'—which is rooted in neither its economic nor its military power, but in its ability to promote certain 'norms' or ideas in international affairs. This can refer to the promotion of values such as democracy and human rights, or to the way in which the very evolution and existence of the EU serves as a model for peaceful relations between states based on a set of common values. From this perspective, the novelty of the EU as an actor in international affairs means that it is particularly well positioned to promote these ostensibly 'normative' values. The concept of normative power spawned a significant debate. It was criticized for understating the ways in which the EU's 'normative' agendas are in practice tied to strategic economic and geopolitical interests (Youngs 2004; Damro 2012) and for dangerously (even complacently) overstating the value of the EU as a force for 'good' (Diez 2005; Parker and Rosamond 2013). However, Manners's argument was as much normative as descriptive: it was about promoting a cosmopolitan agenda for the EU and in international affairs more generally (see Chapter 4, 'Critical Social Theory').

Webber (2016) more recently assessed the EU's capabilities in relation to the three notions of power articulated (while he termed them economic, military, and ideological power, they align closely with, respectively, civilian, military, and normative). He also considered whether in each area the EU's power had increased or declined since 2003. Webber concluded that as a trade and environmental actor the EU remained a significant power. However, this power was on the wane, with the exception of its status as a regulatory power, which was increasing over the period (see also Chapter 24, 'Explaining External Trade Policy'). As an ideological or normative power, the EU remained, according to Webber, a somewhat important actor, but its power of influence had decreased. And as a military or defence power, its capabilities had always been limited (in accordance with Hill's capabilities–expectations gap), and remained so throughout the period.

The notion of 'principled pragmatism' that appears in the EUGS (see 'The Common Foreign and Security Policy (CFSP) and Common Security and Defence Policy (CSDP)' above) can be considered as an attempt to reconcile in practice very different understandings of the EU as a power in world affairs, while recognizing the kinds of limitations identified by Webber. As HRUFASP Federica Mogherini put it in 2016:

> We will be guided by clear principles. These stem as much from a realistic assessment of the strategic environment as from an idealistic aspiration to advance a better world. In charting the way between the Scylla of isolationism and the Charybdis of rash interventionism, the EU will engage the world manifesting responsibility towards others and sensitivity to contingency.

(cited in Tocci 2017: 499)

CONCLUSION

European co-operation on the political aspects of external relations arose partly out of necessity and partly out of the ambitions of some EC member states, particularly France, to use the EC as a platform to exert greater global influence than any one European state could exercise acting alone. It expanded partly as a result of its own momentum, and partly through the member states trying to learn the lessons of their failures to deal adequately with a series of international crises.

The necessity for EPC came from the inextricable tangling of external economic and external political relations. For the EC to maximize its economic influence, it had to have a coherent relationship between the economic and the political. From an early stage, other states expected the EC to behave as a single unified actor on the world stage, placing a burden of expectation on the member states for which they were partly responsible, because they spoke of European integration in terms that represented aspirations rather than realities. The practice of collaboration between national foreign ministries led to a habit of consultation that eroded stark national positions on issues that did not become overtly politicized. However, major crises proved difficult for the Europeans to handle jointly because they had a high domestic profile and senior politicians took control of the decisions. Between crises, though, a web of procedures and a growing *acquis* of joint positions were imperceptibly eroding the separate national foreign policies and slowly putting a European policy in their place.

Paradoxically, the crises themselves contributed to furthering EPC. Each time the EC/EU failed to act decisively in a crisis, or each time the United States was able to take the lead or had to do so because of European failings, there was a round of soul-searching and attempts to make future co-operation more effective. This produced the transition from EPC to CFSP and the efforts to create a CSDP. While the 'capability–expectations' gap remained, the weight of international expectation acted as a spur to continued efforts to increase capabilities. The creation of the role of HRCFSP in the Amsterdam Treaty, and the extension of the role and responsibilities of this post in the Lisbon Treaty (with the creation of the role of HRUFASP), were indicative of a desire to reduce the gap by increasing the 'actorness' of the EU. That said, in the context of an increasingly complex and rapidly changing geopolitics and various internal crises, the EU has become less powerful in global politics and less bold in terms of its aspirations. This is apparent if we compare the EU's 2003 (ESS) and 2016 (EUGS) foreign and security policy strategies.

Academic discussions of EC/EU foreign policy often have an underlying normative dimension which relates to different visions of the EU's purpose in global politics. In particular, a debate about what kind of international power the EU should be has been ongoing since the 1970s, with some arguing that it should develop its military power and others arguing that it should maintain its focus on its already significant 'civilian' economic power. Recent contributors to this debate have made the case that the EU is well positioned to promote important values such as democracy and human rights and this should be its primary foreign policy focus. Different perspectives in this debate will have different views on the EU's CFSP, both in terms of what it has done and where it should be headed.

KEY POINTS

History

- EPC was set up in 1970. It consisted of regular meetings of Foreign Ministers and of senior Foreign Office officials to try to co-ordinate national foreign policies. It was incorporated into the Treaties for the first time with the SEA, which also created a small EPC secretariat.

- Initially, the Commission was excluded from meetings of foreign ministers under EPC, but gradually the role of the Commission increased.
- EPC had several substantive successes to its name: achieving a high degree of unified voting at the UN; conducting an effective 'Euro–Arab dialogue'; and launching and sustaining the CSCE process.
- Failures of EPC occurred in responding to the invasion of Afghanistan by the USSR in December 1979, over the Gulf Crisis in 1990–91, and over successive crises in former Yugoslavia.

The Common Foreign and Security Policy (CFSP) and Common Security and Defence Policy (CSDP)

- The TEU made CFSP a separate pillar of the EU from the EC; QMV was restricted to implementation of agreed measures, and could only be used if all participants agreed.
- In 1998–99, as a reaction to the failure of the EU to respond effectively to the crisis in Kosovo, the first steps were taken towards the CSDP. The institutions of CSDP began work in 2000. It was incorporated into the EU by the Nice Treaty.
- The Treaty of Amsterdam created the post of High Representative for CFSP; the Lisbon Treaty renamed this the High Representative for Foreign Affairs and Security Policy (HRUFASP) and increased its functions. Lisbon also created the EEAS.
- The 2003 ESS represented an attempt by the EU to consider in broad terms its role in the world. The 2016 EUGS offered an update of this vision in a very different geopolitical context.
- With the establishment of PESCO in 2017, twenty-five member states undertook to deepen military and defence cooperation.

CFSP and CSDP in Action

- The terrorist attacks in the United States in September 2001 caused a series of setbacks to the progress that had been made on the CSDP. Initial support for the United States began to waver in the light of the Bush Administration's identification of an 'axis of evil'.
- The US-led invasion of Iraq led to an open rift, especially between Britain—which supported the US action—and France and Germany, which condemned it.
- Despite these setbacks, by the end of 2009 CSDP had undertaken some twenty-two crisis-management missions.
- The EUGS was formulated in 2016 against a backdrop of growing geopolitical instability.

Explaining CFSP and CSDP

- Hill (1993) identified a 'capability–expectations gap' in the international activities of the EC, which he expected would only increase when it became the EU.
- Realists assumed that political co-operation would never amount to more than trivial actions, or would only achieve success where national interests coincided.
- Social constructivist perspectives emphasized the extent to which social interaction between foreign policy practitioners has led to a changing of their perspectives and the emergence of a common outlook.

EU Power in World Politics

- How the EU's impact in the world is judged from a normative perspective depends to a large extent on what kind of actor or power one thinks the EU should be in international affairs.

- Academics have variously promoted visions of the EU as a civilian (economic), military, and normative (cosmopolitan) power. Aspects of these visions have been taken up by the EU institutions in the formulation of foreign and security policy strategies.

- Recent assessments suggest that the EU is, in general, a declining power in world politics, although its economic and normative (or ideational) power remains significant and its military power limited.

 For additional material and resources, please visit the online resources www.oup.com/uk/bache5e.

QUESTIONS

1. Why did the member states decide to develop a common foreign policy?

2. What does it mean to say that the EU's CFSP is 'intergovernmental'?

3. Is the EU a significant 'actor' in world politics?

4. What are the possible implications of Brexit for the EU's CFSP?

5. Is the EU a declining power in world politics?

FURTHER READING

A clear and up-to-date introduction to the complexity of the EU's external relations is provided by the third edition of **C. Hill**, **M. Smith, and S. Vanhoonacker (eds)**, *International Relations and the European Union* (Oxford: Oxford University Press, 2017). The second edition of **K. Smith**, *European Union Foreign Policy in a Changing World* (Cambridge: Polity Press, 2013) is also very useful. For an up-to-date analysis of CSDP, see **M. E. Smith**, *Europe's Common Security and Defence Policy: Capacity-Building, Experiential Learning and Institutional Change* (Cambridge: Cambridge University Press, 2017).

An intresting reflection on the EUGS by someone with an insider view is offered in **N. Tocci**, 'From the European Security Strategy to the EU Global Strategy: Explaining the Journey', *International Politics,* 54 (2017): 487–502. For a discussion of the 'power' debate with a particular focus on Ian Manners's concept of 'normative power Europe', see the special issue of *Co-operation and Conflict*, 48, 2 (2013), edited by **K. Nicolaïdis and R. Whitman**. For an accessible assessment of the contemporary status of EU power in relation to different aspects of its external relations (including political and economic relations), see **D. Webber**, 'Declining Power Europe: The Evolution of the European Union's World Power in the Early Twenty-First Century', *European Review of International Studies*, 1 (2016): 31–52.

Given its importance to so many later contributions, an article that should certainly be read is **C. Hill**, 'The Capability–Expectations Gap, or Conceptualising Europe's International Role', *Journal of Common Market Studies*, 31 (1993): 305–28.

Chapter 26

Enlargement

Chapter Overview

Starting with six member states originally, the European Community (EC)/European Union (EU) has grown through successive enlargements—from six to nine, then ten, twelve, fifteen, twenty-five, twenty-seven, and now twenty-eight (although 'Brexit' makes that twenty-seven). This chapter looks at each of the main enlargement rounds in turn, outlining what happened and what the effect was on the EC/EU, and at the outstanding applications that are still under consideration at the time of writing. A procedure emerged over the six rounds of enlargement that is being applied to the present applications, and this is explained. Academic explanations of why the various applications for membership were made, and why they were accepted by the EC/EU, are reviewed. Finally, a closer analysis of the controversial case of Turkey is offered, and consideration is given to the concept of 'enlargement fatigue'.

History

The EC/EU has preferred to negotiate enlargements with groups of states together. This has produced six distinct rounds of enlargement (see Table 26.1), starting in 1973 when Britain, Denmark, and Ireland became members.

The second enlargement was in 1981, when Greece became a member, and the third was in 1986, when Portugal and Spain joined. For analytical purposes, the second and third enlargements are often treated as a single 'southern enlargement', as they were undertaken for similar reasons and involved similar issues.

The fourth enlargement was that of 1995, which admitted Austria, Finland, and Sweden. Because the applicants (including Norway, which rejected membership in a referendum) were the leading members of the European Free Trade Association (EFTA) (see Insight 26.1), this is usually referred to as 'the EFTA enlargement'.

The fifth and sixth enlargements, in 2004 and 2007, are often referred to collectively as 'the eastern enlargement' because most of the new entrants were former communist states in central and eastern Europe. Strictly speaking, this name is inaccurate, because two of the entrants in 2004—Cyprus and Malta—were Mediterranean island states.

The seventh enlargement saw the admittance of Croatia in 2013. It was the first of the western Balkan states to complete its accession process.

Table 26.1 Enlargements of the EEC/EC/EU

Year	1973	1981	1986	1995	2004	2007	2013
New members	Denmark, Ireland, UK	Greece	Portugal, Spain	Austria, Finland, Sweden	Cyprus, Czech Republic, Estonia, Hungary, Latvia, Lithuania, Malta, Poland, Slovakia, Slovenia	Bulgaria, Romania	Croatia

Source: http://ec.europa.eu © European Union, 1995–2020.

Insight 26.1 EFTA at the End of the 1980s

The European Free Trade Association (EFTA) was set up in 1959 and entered into force in January 1960. It was a response to the setting up of the European Economic Community (EEC) in 1958. The original members of EFTA were Austria, Britain, Denmark, Norway, Portugal, Sweden, and Switzerland.

By the late 1980s, EFTA consisted of seven states of varying size:

Country	Population (000s)
Sweden	8,640
Austria	7,820
Switzerland	6,790
Finland	5,030
Norway	4,260
Iceland	256
Liechtenstein	30

The economies of the EFTA states had been linked with those of the EC since the 1970s by a series of bilateral free-trade agreements. By the end of the 1980s, EFTA was, economically, closely integrated with the EC. The EC did 25 per cent of its trade with EFTA, a higher proportion than with the United States, while the EFTA states sent 56 per cent of their exports to the EC, and bought 60 per cent of their imports from the EC.

The First Enlargement

In August 1961, Britain, Denmark, and Ireland applied for membership of the EC. In April 1962, Norway also applied. The key applicant here was Britain. The other applicants were highly dependent on their economic links with Britain, which were fostered through their membership of EFTA. None of these states could afford to risk the loss of trade with their biggest customer that might result from Britain going into the European Economic Community (EEC) while they remained outside.

Negotiations went on throughout 1962, until, in January 1963, President de Gaulle of France unilaterally announced that France was not prepared to accept British membership. As any member state could veto entry, and as the other applications were dependent on British entry, the enlargement round collapsed.

In May 1967, Britain, Denmark, and Ireland applied again, and Norway joined the second application in July. This time, negotiations did not even get under way: France blocked agreement on opening negotiations in December 1967. Following the replacement of de Gaulle by Georges Pompidou as French President in 1969, a summit meeting at The Hague agreed on a package of measures to 'relaunch Europe' that included opening negotiations with the applicants, the 1967 applications of which remained on the table (see Chapter 7, 'The Hague Summit'). On 1 January 1973, Britain, Denmark, and Ireland became members of the EC. Norway negotiated terms of entry, but the Norwegian people rejected membership in a subsequent referendum in 1972.

The impact of the first enlargement on the EC was profound. In terms of bargaining games, not only did the total number of member states increase by 50 per cent, but there was also another 'big state' among the new members (Britain), which changed the coalition dynamics that had previously been dominated by France and West Germany. In terms of the sense of self-identity of the EC, the admission of two states—Britain and Denmark—that were sceptical of the 'European ideal' made it much more difficult to find a common discourse to conceptualize the mission of the organization.

The Southern Enlargements

As explained earlier, the second and third enlargements of the EC are often treated as a single 'Southern' enlargement. Greece became a member state in January 1981, and Spain and Portugal in January 1986. In all cases, political considerations overrode economic in the decision to enlarge.

All three of the states concerned had just emerged from periods of dictatorship, and the desire to consolidate democracy and guard against a resurgence of authoritarianism featured strongly in the reasons for the applications and the reasons for their acceptance. It was assumed that EC membership, conditional on democratic government, would help to achieve that. The impact of this enlargement on the EC/EU was in its way as great as that of the first enlargement. Again, it changed the bargaining dynamics of the organization. The three new members shifted the orientation of the EC to the south, and the membership of Greece and Spain ensured that there would be a stronger Mediterranean dimension to policy. In political co-operation, the influence of Spain and Portugal led to a greater emphasis on relations with Latin America. Perhaps most significantly in the short run, Spain, with the support of the other new entrants, took the lead in demanding larger structural funds (see Chapter 18, 'Cohesion Policy') and soon showed itself adept at playing the EC negotiating game to get them.

On the other hand, Greece's membership had some less positive consequences. Its long-standing disputes with Turkey proved an embarrassment to the EC/EU on more than one occasion, and spilled over into a hard EC/EU line on Cyprus. Also, its position on the edge of the Balkans meant that Greece had sensitivities in the region that were difficult for other EU members to understand. These became particularly pertinent in the early 1990s, following the break-up of Yugoslavia (see also Chapter 25, 'The Common Foreign and Security Policy (CFSP) and Common Security and Defence Policy (CSDP)').

The EFTA Enlargement

In the early 1990s, several member states of EFTA enquired about membership. At first, they were offered a form of close association that fell short of full membership. Subsequently, though, they lodged formal applications, and eventually Austria, Finland, and Sweden became members of the EU on 1 January 1995. Norway again rejected membership in a referendum in 1994, after terms of entry had been agreed.

Because the new members were wealthy, were already culturally aligned with the prevailing values of the existing member states, and had been closely associated with the EC prior to their membership, the effects of this enlargement were smaller than those of any other enlargement.

One effect was the emergence of a Nordic bloc within the Council of Ministers. From 1995, Denmark received support from Sweden and Finland for positions that it had long defended on issues such as environmental protection and human rights, and the Nordic states combined to press the membership claims of the Baltic states (Estonia, Latvia, and Lithuania) in the eastern enlargement round. Austria joined the Nordic states in reinforcing the coalition of member states for which environmental protection was a significant issue. Because the new members were all net contributors to the budget, their presence reinforced the coalition in favour of reform of the budgetary rules.

The 'Eastern' Enlargement

With the collapse of communism in 1989, the EC was faced with a large number of potential new members, all of which expressed an aspiration to join. The first response was to conclude 'Europe Agreements', Association Agreements that fell short of envisaging full membership. Then, in June 1993, the Copenhagen European Council accepted the legitimacy of the aspirations of the newly independent states to become members, and laid down criteria that they would have to fulfil in order for their applications to be considered. Applications came in rapidly from ten central and eastern European countries (CEECs)—Bulgaria, the Czech Republic, Estonia, Hungary, Latvia, Lithuania, Poland, Slovakia, Slovenia, and Romania—plus Cyprus, Malta, and Turkey.

In December 1997, the Luxembourg European Council agreed that negotiations should open with five of these states—the Czech Republic, Estonia, Hungary, Poland, and Slovenia—plus Cyprus (Malta had withdrawn its application), but hold back on the five others. In December 1999, the Helsinki European Council agreed to open negotiations with the remaining five CEECs, plus Malta, which had resubmitted its application. On 1 May 2004, eight CEECs—the ten listed above not including Bulgaria and Romania—plus Cyprus and Malta, became members of the EU.

The two outstanding applications from former eastern European communist states were from Bulgaria and Romania. Starting from a lower base of both economic development and legal stability than the other applicants, they took longer to satisfy the basic criteria, but both became members in 2007.

The effects of this enlargement were profound. In order to be ready to take as many as twelve new members, the EU had to deal with some difficult issues requiring reforms of both policies and institutions. Two policy issues were particularly crucial to the prospects for enlargement: agriculture (see Chapter 21) and the structural funds (see Chapter 18, 'Cohesion Policy'). In both cases, the existing member states that were beneficiaries from the funds proved very reluctant to surrender their benefits to facilitate enlargement. The institutional questions were those that were already apparent at the time of the EFTA enlargement: the weighting of votes under qualified majority voting (QMV), and the size of the blocking minority; the abandonment of the national veto in more policy sectors; and the size of the Commission.

Croatia

With the completion of the eastern enlargement, the EU faced the question of how far it would continue to expand geographically. There was no shortage of prospective applicants. In particular, there was the prospect of applications from the Yugoslav successor states.

Most of these states were not expected to be ready to make applications for some time, but in March 2003, Croatia applied for membership, and was granted candidate status in June. In April 2004, the Commission recommended the opening of negotiations with Croatia, which had made remarkable progress in a short time on both the political and economic fronts. Accession negotiations began in December 2005 and Croatia became a member in 2013.

Further Applications

Beyond Croatia, five western Balkans states have applied for membership and Kosovo is likely to apply at some point in the near future. Two of these states are already engaged in accession negotiations. Montenegro applied for membership in December 2008, was granted candidate status in December 2010, and accession negotiations began in June 2012. Serbia applied for membership in December 2009, and became a candidate in March 2012. Following the EU-brokered agreement that was reached on the status of Kosovo in 2013, accession negotiations began in January 2014.

Two other states have been granted official candidate status. The Former Yugoslav Republic of Macedonia (FYROM) applied for membership only shortly after Croatia in March 2004, and was granted candidate status in December 2005. Accession negotiations were, however, blocked by Greece because of a long-standing dispute over the applicant country's name. In 2018, agreement was reached to change the country's name to the Republic of North Macedonia (or North Macedonia for short), and Greece removed its veto to accession talks. Albania submitted a membership application in April 2009 and was granted candidate status in June 2014. However, in October 2019, France controversially vetoed the commencement of accession negotiations with both North Macedonia and Albania (and in the latter case was supported by Denmark and the Netherlands).

> **Table 26.2 Prospective Members (as of the end of 2019)**
>
> | | |
> |---|---|
> | Accession negotiations open | Turkey (suspended), Iceland (suspended), Serbia, Montenegro |
> | Candidate status | North Macedonia, Albania |
> | Applied | Bosnia and Herzegovina |

Finally, Bosnia and Herzegovina applied for EU membership in February 2016 and remains a potential candidate for EU membership. Kosovo had not applied for membership as of the end of 2019, but the EU had consistently affirmed its status as a prospective future candidate. Kosovo's application was complicated, however, by its non-recognition as an independent state by five EU member states (Spain, Slovakia, Cyprus, Romania, and Greece).

Beyond the western Balkans, two other countries—Iceland and Turkey—have applied for membership, but their accession negotiations remained suspended as of the end of 2019. Following the financial crisis of 2008–09, in which Icelandic banks suffered badly, the Icelandic parliament, the Althingi, narrowly voted (by thirty-three votes to twenty-eight, with two abstentions) to apply for EU membership. Iceland was granted candidate status in June 2010 and accession negotiations began immediately. However, following elections in April 2013 that brought to power Eurosceptic parties, negotiations with the EU were suspended.

Turkey has been an applicant for membership for longer than any of the states that gained entry in 2004. An Association Agreement envisaging eventual membership was signed over fifty years ago, in 1963. The agreement was suspended in 1970 and again in 1980, following military takeovers of power, but reinstated following elections and a return to civilian government in 1973, and again in 1983. In 1987, Turkey lodged its first formal application for membership of the EU. Two years later, the EU responded by saying that no further enlargement was envisaged in the foreseeable future. In 1995, a customs union agreement was signed with Turkey, the first time that such an agreement had been part of a process of accession. Then, in 1997, came the Luxembourg European Council and the decision to move forward with various applications, but excluding Turkey. In 1999, the Helsinki European Council reversed this decision and recognized Turkey as a candidate. Accession negotiations began in October 2005, at the same time as those for Croatia, but these quickly stalled in many areas and have been effectively frozen since 2016 (for an overview of the status of prospective members, see Table 26.2 and for further discussion of Turkey, see 'Turkey' below).

The Enlargement Procedure

Over the course of the five rounds of enlargement, a procedure gradually evolved. Each of the enlargements added something to this emerging approach.

When a potential applicant approaches the EU, the first step is for the European Council to consider whether the application is acceptable in principle. If it is, then the

Commission produces an official Opinion on the application. This consists of a report on the economic and political position of the applicant state, and a recommendation on whether to proceed to negotiations immediately, or whether to delay. Usually, the recommendation to delay is to give the applicant time to strengthen its claim to be ready for membership. If so, then a plan of action is produced to facilitate this, which will normally involve an Association Agreement or the strengthening of existing agreements.

If the decision of the European Council is to proceed with the application immediately, it will set a date for the opening of negotiations. The Commission will then convene meetings of various sectoral groups of experts to work out the detail of the EU's negotiating position. Negotiations then commence with the applicant(s). These are handled on a day-to-day basis by the groups of experts, often by correspondence rather than in formal meetings. They are co-ordinated by the Commission, and overseen by the Council of Foreign Ministers.

When agreement has been reached by the expert working groups in all sectors, and has been pronounced acceptable by the foreign ministers, the terms are passed to the European Council for formal approval. Assuming that approval is given, an Accession Treaty is drawn up with each applicant state. The Accession Treaty then has to be ratified by the European Parliament (EP) on the side of the EU, and by either the national parliament of the applicant state, or by referendum, depending on the constitutional procedures of each state.

In the context of the first enlargement, it was established that prospective member states would be required to accept and transpose into domestic law the complete body of EC law, or the **acquis communautaire** (Preston 1995: 452). In other words, they would have to adopt the full range of market building, correcting, cushioning, and political policies (see Chapter 18, 'The European Union's Policy Agenda'), with only very limited and usually temporary opportunities to opt out of policies.

The southern enlargement established the precedent that membership applications could be accepted for geostrategic and political reasons, even where the economic conditions were not ideal. This was relevant to the applications from a range of economically weak CEECs following the collapse of communism in 1989. The relatively straightforward EFTA enlargement did not produce any new principles.

In the negotiation of the eastern enlargement, formal criteria were laid down for the first time. These criteria arose from concern about the preparedness of the former communist states for membership. Agreed at the June 1993 Copenhagen European Council, they became known as the Copenhagen criteria (1993). They are:

- a political criterion—that an applicant must have stable institutions guaranteeing democracy, the rule of law, human rights, and the protection of minorities;

- an economic criterion—that an applicant must have a functioning market economy and the capacity to cope with competitive pressures within the single market of the EU;

- a criterion relating to the *acquis communautaire*—that an applicant must be able to take on the obligations of membership, including adherence to the aims of political, economic, and monetary union.

Although these were originally criteria for the acceptance of applications, they came to structure the negotiations on membership, and were applied in the negotiations

501

with subsequent applicants. Adherence to these criteria on the part of prospective member states amounts to a significant 'Europeanization' of their politics, economy, and institutions (see Chapter 3, 'Europeanization').

Explaining Enlargement

Schimmelfennig and Sedelmeier (2002) produced a typology of the academic literature on enlargement, classifying it according to the research focus along four dimensions:

- the enlargement policies of the applicants;
- the enlargement policies of the existing member states;
- the enlargement policies of the EU;
- the impact of enlargement.

Structuring existing studies along these dimensions, Schimmelfennig and Sedelmeier (2002: 523–4) were able to conclude that:

- the bulk of analytical studies were on the EFTA and eastern enlargements;
- the analyses of the EFTA enlargement focused primarily on their first dimension— questioning why the EFTA states applied for membership;
- the analyses of the eastern enlargement focused primarily on their second and third dimensions—questioning why the applications were accepted, and on what conditions the applicants were offered membership.

Schimmelfennig and Sedelmeier (2002: 508–15) also divided existing studies of enlargement according to whether they emphasized interests or ideas in their analysis. They referred to these as 'rationalist' and 'constructivist' institutionalism (see Chapter 4, 'Social Constructivism' and 2, 'New Institutionalism').

Explanations that emphasize interests—both economic and geopolitical—are in most cases able at least partially to account for the desire of prospective members to join the EU and the desire of the EU and its constituent states and institutions to permit membership. However, they are liable to understate the costs incurred on both sides: for prospective members in terms of the often domestically unpopular adjustment processes required in order to meet membership criteria and for current members in terms of diminished influence within the EU, as well as the potential financial costs of accepting new members (relevant in many enlargement rounds). Constructivist explanations that emphasize the importance of ideas can usefully account for a willingness on all sides to overlook such costs. Such ideas can consist of general normative conceptions about 'Europe', its identity, and its limits (see Chapter 4, 'Critical Social Theory'), and also more specific technical norms associated with policy and law that are 'diffused' during the enlargement process.

Explanations of the First Enlargement

It is generally agreed that to understand why the applicant states of the first enlargement decided to seek entry, it is primarily necessary to consider the reasons for the British application. The other applicants were so tightly bound economically to

Britain that they could not afford to stay outside the EC if Britain went in. There were two main factors behind the British application: economic and geostrategic.

Sluggish economic growth in Britain in the late 1950s was increasingly blamed by economists both inside and outside government on the pattern of trade. Britain, at the end of the 1950s, still did a high proportion of its trade with the countries of its former empire, now voluntarily grouped together as the Commonwealth—but the fastest growth in trade was between industrialized countries, including within the newly formed EEC. The success of the EEC surprised British policy makers, and led to efforts in the late 1950s to conclude a free-trade agreement with the six. When this failed, an application for British entry for economic reasons began to be taken seriously.

Political considerations started to point in the same direction when de Gaulle began to dominate the EEC, and became especially influential when he made proposals for political co-operation in the Fouchet Plan (see Insight 7.2). British concern centred on the known hostility of de Gaulle to US hegemony in the capitalist world. Camps (1964: 336) recorded that the British government came under pressure from the United States to join the EEC so as to act as a counterweight to French influence, and she believed that this was 'a very important—perhaps the controlling—element in Macmillan's decision to apply'. The same perception seems to have been one of the significant factors in de Gaulle's decision to block enlargement throughout the 1960s.

Initially, the EC member states other than France were interested in British membership for predominantly political reasons. They saw Britain as a future counterweight to French domination of the EC. The reason why France finally accepted the British application in 1972 was primarily economic. The post-war economic boom faltered in the late 1960s, and British entry offered the prospect of giving a boost to the EC economies.

Explanations of the Southern Enlargements

As suggested in 'The Southern Enlargements' above, the reasons for the applications of Greece, Portugal, and Spain have not generally been considered problematic. Each emerged from a period of right-wing dictatorship in the course of the 1970s, and the democratic government of each was anxious to embed the democratic constitution by tying in the state to the EC. It seemed equally clear that the existing member states were prepared to accept the applications for essentially the same reason: to stabilize their own southern flank.

Explanations of the EFTA Enlargement

The EFTA enlargement was the first to be systematically analysed in the literature. As Schimmelfennig and Sedelmeier (2002: 517) put it: 'The key question pursued is: why did the EFTA countries, after a long period of deliberate non-membership in the EC, develop an interest in closer ties with, and membership of, the EC at the beginning of the 1990s?'

In the course of the 1980s, the member states of EFTA became concerned about the impact on investment in their economies of the EC's decision to create the single internal market (see Chapter 19, 'History'). Export-oriented businesses in the EFTA states experienced difficulties in selling to the EU, with the result that, increasingly, businesses wanted to be inside the single market, and investment began to flow in that direction. Even large national companies of the EFTA states, such as Volvo of Sweden, were locating their investments inside the EC and not in the EFTA countries. This led the EFTA states to enquire about closer links with the EC, despite the unpopularity of the idea of membership inside some of the states concerned.

The other factor that affected the decision was the end of the Cold War. Events in 1989 removed one of the main objections of opponents of membership within the EFTA states. Austria, Finland, and Sweden were all neutral during the Cold War, and there had been doubts about whether membership of an organization that was developing a Common Foreign and Security Policy (CFSP) (see Chapter 25) was compatible with neutrality. The end of the Cold War called into question the meaning of neutrality, and effectively dissipated the doubts on that score.

Sweden is the most studied of the cases from this enlargement. It illustrates well why analysts have considered their main problem to be explaining the reasons for the EFTA states' applications. Sweden was an exemplar of a social-democratic neo-corporatist type of state, and its social-democratic governments had previously rejected membership of the EC on the grounds that the free-market orientation of the organization would jeopardize the Swedish model of capitalism. Yet, in 1991 a social-democratic government applied for membership at just the time that the EC was taking a major step in a neoliberal direction with the single market programme (Bieler 2002: 576). Why?

In separate analyses, both Fioretos (1997) and Ingebritsen (1998) offered rational-choice explanations for the decision in the mould of liberal intergovernmentalism (see Chapter 1, 'Theories of European Integration'). Both emphasized the importance of export-oriented and transnational corporations in setting the agenda. In the course of the 1980s, these actors began to increasingly transfer production abroad. Swedish governments were already concerned about the country's lack of competitiveness, and the internal market programme offered a means of injecting more competitiveness into the economy. At first, the EFTA states were offered membership of a new organization called the European Economic Area (EEA), which gave access to that market (see Insight 26.2). The Swedish government tried this approach, but it was abandoned in favour of an application for full membership because it did not satisfy the large Swedish manufacturers and did not stop the outward flow of **investment capital**.

Bieler (2000, 2002) offered a neo-Gramscian analysis of the EFTA enlargement (see Chapter 4, 'Critical Political Economy') that placed more emphasis on the role of ideas. Comparing Sweden with Austria, he notes that while transnational sectors were the key economic actors in Sweden, in Austria the dominant sectors were not transnational. They consisted rather of internationally oriented national firms, which were dependent on exports to the EC but did not have production facilities outside their own country that the larger Swedish firms had acquired during the 1980s. This meant that these economic actors had not been as powerful in dictating terms to their national government as their Swedish counterparts. Consequently, Austrian business groups pursued what Bieler (2002: 583) called a 'hegemonic project'. This involved issuing a series of studies that not only advanced a strong version of the neoliberal economic argument, but also dealt with the constitutional implications of membership and the issue of what it implied for Austria's post-war neutrality. These arguments eventually won over the leadership of both major political parties, thus setting the course for the application. By the time of the Austrian referendum in June 1994, a new orthodoxy had emerged around membership, thus ensuring a comfortable 'Yes' vote by 66.6 per cent to 33.4 per cent.

Explanations of the 'Eastern' Enlargement

As with the membership applications of Greece, Portugal, and Spain in the 1970s, the wish of the former communist states to become members of the EU was widely understood. The states that had emerged from Soviet domination wanted to cement their status as Europeans, and to foreclose any possibility of being drawn back into the Russian sphere of influence. From this point of view, membership of the North Atlantic Treaty Organization (NATO) was the more important objective, but membership of the EU was also important. The former communist states also saw EU membership as essential to their future economic success, and it fitted with a widespread desire to reaffirm a European identity.

Bieler (2002: 588–9) applied neo-Gramscian concepts to the analysis of why the applications by the former communist states were made. He suggested that the decision to apply was taken by what he called 'cadre élites within state institutions'. These elites had taken advantage of the collapse of the previous regimes to take power and to introduce programmes of neoliberal reconstruction, supported by external forces. When the restructuring programmes precipitated big falls in gross domestic product (GDP), the legitimacy of the elites and of their reform programmes were jeopardized. EU membership was pursued as a buttress against resistance and reversion to anti-capitalist politicians and policies. It was sold to the populations of the CEECs as a historical 'return to Europe'. However, the volatility of society and politics in the CEECs ruled out the construction of a pro-EU historical bloc organized around a hegemonic project such as Bieler had identified in Austria (2002 : 582–5). Instead, the process in the CEECs was conceptualized as a Gramscian 'passive revolution', led from above by the state elites. This had implications for the commitment of a broader array of socio-economic actors to the project and may account for what some regard as recent reversals in processes of Europeanization in some of these now member states (see Chapter 11, 'The Populist Challenge').

The immediate reaction of the EC to the collapse of communism was to offer the Europe Agreements, which did not make a commitment to eventual membership. In explanation of this, Friis (1998) pointed out that the collapse of communism came quickly and was not anticipated. First, the European Commission was preoccupied with the prospect of a sudden increase in the territory of the EC, and the adaptation of common policies to the addition of another 17 million people with a GDP per head well below the EC average. Second, the negotiation of the EFTA enlargement was still at an early stage in 1989. Indeed, the EC was still following a policy of trying to persuade the EFTA applicants to become part of the single market without becoming members of the EC—that is, the EEA negotiations. Indeed, the deal offered in the original Europe Agreements was similar to that on offer to the EFTA states at that stage: membership of the single market without membership of the EC. Third, the EC in 1989 was about to embark on the process of agreeing to a monetary union, a further issue that occupied the attention of the member states and the Commission.

However, between 1990 and 1995, the three pressing issues identified here were all cleared out of the way. Formal reunification of Germany took place on 3 October 1990. The timetable and conditions for monetary union were agreed with Maastricht in 1992 (see Chapter 20, 'History'). Terms of entry for Austria, Finland, and Sweden were agreed in March 1994.

The EU was thus more amenable to the prospect of a significant enlargement by the mid-1990s. The persistence of the CEECs in pressing for entry to the EC/EU was strengthened by the acceptance of the EC that the EEA scheme was not going to work for the EFTA applicants. It would have been difficult to convince the CEECs that membership of the single market without membership of the EU would be any more successful or acceptable for them once the argument had been conceded for the EFTA applicants. It would have appeared that the EC/EU was prepared to accept prosperous member states and not those most in need of support.

Security considerations also became more urgent in the context of growing instability in Russia (Friis and Murphy 1999: 220). The USSR broke apart rapidly between August and December 1991 and it formally ceased to exist on 31 December 1991. The Russian state that emerged after many of the former Soviet republics had proclaimed independence was an insecure place in which nationalist voices received a hearing from the population, and in turn the government under President Boris Yeltsin came under pressure to talk tough with 'the near abroad'. In these circumstances, the concern of the CEECs for security from an aggressive Russia led to increased demands for membership of both the EC and NATO. These two issues became intertwined. The United States was concerned not to expand NATO membership too precipitately for fear of alarming Russia, so it put pressure on the EC to offer membership as a second-order guarantee of independence to the states most affected. There was particular pressure on the EC to offer membership to the three Baltic states—Estonia, Latvia, and Lithuania—because they were too close to Russia to make NATO membership feasible, but they were also too close to Russia for comfort, given the rising nationalist sentiment there. Although it was never likely that the EC would accede directly to any such demand from the United States, it had to show that it was prepared to move some way to contributing to the stabilization of eastern Europe. Also, as Yugoslavia began to disintegrate on the very doorstep of the EC, concerns about security grew in the member states themselves.

The prevarication on whether to proceed with all twelve applications together or whether to prioritize some of the applicants reflected the different stakes that different member states had in the enlargement. Germany was particularly keen to see early enlargement to take in at least its closest neighbours: Poland, Hungary, and the Czech Republic. This was both for security and economic reasons. The security reasons are obvious: reunification rendered Germany once more a central European state itself; and instability in neighbouring states was highly undesirable. The economic motivations reflected the traditional economic links between Germany and its central European neighbours. France, on the other hand, had less of a stake in either consideration, as it had no contiguous land frontier with the central European states, and had fewer economic links. For France and the other Mediterranean member states, there was a real risk that eastern enlargement would reduce their influence in the EU, shifting the centre of gravity away from them towards Germany. The French government was therefore more prepared to take a leisurely approach, whereas the German government wanted as few obstacles as possible placed in the way of early accession for its favoured candidates.

The European Commission's motivation in proposing to proceed with only some of the applications reflected particularly its concerns about its limited resources. The process of accession is long and complex, and can tie up a lot of the available resources of the Commission. Member states have never been prepared to provide all of the extra resources necessary to allow it to perform efficiently the task set for it, and there was no indication that they would do so on this occasion.

Acceptance of the Commission's proposal to limit the number of applicants with which accession negotiations would begin reflected a temporary meeting of minds between Germany and France.

The change of tactic at Helsinki, to open negotiations with the remaining applicants, reflected a number of changed circumstances. First, the CEECs that had not been placed in the first group had become increasingly restive about their treatment. Second, the pressure from the United States had receded as the security threat posed by Russia appeared also to recede. Third, the change of heart in Malta opened the prospect to France, Spain, Portugal, Italy, and Greece of having another Mediterranean small state in the first group of members to offset the influx of small and medium-sized CEECs. Of the second six, Malta was the most equipped to catch up with some of the first six applicants and get membership early.

507

Bieler (2002: 590) also offered an analysis of why the applications were accepted. He identified the key to the acceptance of the applications as the support given after 1997 by the European Round Table of Industrialists (ERT). Bieler maintained that the ERT was recruited as an ally by the Commission, but was willingly recruited because many of the transnational corporations that made up the membership of the ERT had invested heavily in the CEECs and therefore had an interest in consolidating the conditions for profitable production there.

From a constructivist perspective (see Chapter 4, 'Social Constructivism'), others (for instance, O'Brennan 2006) have emphasized the way in which certain actors invoked a moral or ideational argument in favour of CEEC membership during the course of the negotiations. Such rhetoric usually referred in some way to the 'European vocation' of the CEECs and their enforced exclusion from the integration project during the Cold War. This rhetoric was particularly prevalent within the Commission, whose 'policy entrepreneurship' under President Prodi and Enlargement Commissioner Verheugen was for many a critical driver of this enlargement.

Explanations of the Western Balkans Enlargement

Croatia became the first Balkan state to join in 2013, by which time negotiations with other states in the region were under way. These states had similar motivations to the CEECs in their desire to become members: in short, twin economic and security concerns. The EU is also interested in guaranteeing long-term stability in the western Balkans. Following the destructive wars in the 1990s, which led to the break-up of Yugoslavia, the EU became an active presence in the region, involved in peace-keeping and policing missions and various forms of reconstruction project (see Chapter 25, 'The Common Foreign and Security Policy (CFSP) and Common Security and Defence Policy (CSDP)').

The EU sought to use the prospect of enlargement as leverage to promote peace and reconciliation in the region. Through the so-called stabilization and association process (SAP), it established a set of conditions which largely mirrored those contained in the Copenhagen criteria. In addition, via this process it successfully pressed for co-operation with the International Criminal Tribunal for the Former Yugoslavia (ICTY), the body responsible for prosecuting those accused of serious crimes committed during the conflicts within the former Yugoslavia.

However, despite stating at the Thessaloniki European Council of June 2003 that, 'the future of the Western Balkans is in the European Union', the accession process for these states has proceeded slowly due to a combination of 'enlargement fatigue' on the part of the EU (see 'Enlargement Fatigue?' below) and domestic turbulence in a number of these states. O'Brennan (2013) has argued that while normative and ideational factors were key drivers of recent enlargements, in the context of negotiations with western Balkans states, member state self-interest had become more important and intergovernmental decision making more prominent. That said, in February 2018 the European Commission published a strategy paper that sought to generate new momentum for the accession prospects of the six states in the region yet to join the EU, calling for a 'credible enlargement perspective' (O'Brennan 2018; also see above, 'Further Applications'). While many member states appeared to support this agenda, France's veto in 2019 of the start of accession negotiations with Northern Macedonia and Albania was indicative of continued resistance to it.

Turkey

Turkey's 1959 application for associate membership of the EC can be understood as an attempt by certain elites and sections of the population to strengthen the contested identity of Turkey as a western European nation rather than as an eastern, Muslim nation (for a useful summary of Turkish modern history see, for instance, Ahmad 2001). For the EC, the decision in the 1960s to conclude an Association Agreement with Turkey envisaging eventual membership can be explained largely in geostrategic terms. Turkey had just emerged from a period of military rule, and the political scene was volatile. The predominant strategic concern of the period was the Cold War, and Turkey stood on the cusp of the communist world. It was important for the capitalist states to shore up this flank of NATO, and to do that it was important to strengthen the democratic forces that favoured a western and capitalist orientation for the state.

Further military intervention in 1970 indicated that this tactic had not worked, and led to the suspension of the Association Agreement. The restoration of democracy in 1973 reactivated the Agreement, but tensions between the neo-fascist right and the extreme left precipitated a further military intervention in 1980. Democracy was restored in 1983, but it was not until 1987 that Turkey was sufficiently stable for a formal application to the EU to be a credible move.

Müftüler-Bac and McLaren (2003) analysed the reasons for the decision of the EU to exclude Turkey from the list of prospective members in 1997, and for the change of position in 1999. They considered this to be a puzzle because nothing significant had changed in Turkey in the intervening period. Adopting an intergovernmental perspective, they argued that the explanation lay in the changing preferences of the governments of existing member states, which in turn reflected their national interests. Turkey not only had no champion among the existing member states, but in Greece it had an adversary. Germany also had grave doubts about the acceptability of Turkish entry. The ability of Greece to exercise a veto over moves towards Turkish membership, and the opposition of Germany to any such moves, explained the omission of Turkey from the list of candidates in 1997. By the end of 1999, though, both of these opponents had changed position.

In late 1999, there was a dramatic improvement in relations between Greece and Turkey. There were a number of reasons for this, including a wave of sympathy among the Greek population following a terrible earthquake in Turkey. The fact that Greece had used up a lot of political capital within the EU in blocking Turkey's ambitions was also probably significant.

There was also a change in the German position between 1997 and 1999. For the German government of Helmut Kohl, the main objection to Turkish membership, which was often unspoken, was a concern that it was not culturally compatible with the image that the German Christian Democratic Union (CDU)/Christian Social Union (CSU) parties held of Europe: in other words, Turkey was not Christian. The change of position in Germany came about as a result of the replacement of the CDU–CSU government in 1998 with a Social Democratic Party (SPD)–Green government under Gerhard Schröder. Müftüler-Bac and McLaren (2003: 23–4) represented the issue for the new government as one of domestic politics: the need to integrate the

509

large Turkish minority more securely into German society. The shifts in Greece and Germany were significant in the decision to grant candidate status in 1999.

Moreover, Britain, always sympathetic to Turkey's claims, became a strong advocate of its case during the early 2000s. In the aftermath of a spate of terrorist bombings in Ankara in November 2003, the British Foreign Secretary, Jack Straw, called for Turkish membership 'as soon as possible', and the Europe Minister, Denis MacShane, said, 'Europe is incomplete without Turkey' (Foreign and Commonwealth Office 2004). The dominant reason for British support was geostrategic. Turkey occupied a geographical position between the EU and the Middle East. It bordered Iran, Iraq, and Syria. It had a majority of Muslims among its population, at a time when the EU was increasingly being accused of bias against Muslims. A stable and western-oriented Turkey was therefore an important strategic goal for the West, and the best way of ensuring the stability and western orientation of Turkey was to admit it to the EU.

As Parker (2009b) noted, changes within Turkey facilitated these pro-Turkish perspectives in the early 2000s. In November 2002, the Justice and Development Party (AKP) came into office. A self-proclaimed moderate Islamic party, it was committed to pursuing Turkey's bid for EU membership. Under the premiership of Recep Tayyip Erdogan, the AKP vigorously set about trying to satisfy the political prerequisites ('Copenhagen political criteria') for the opening of accession negotiations. These reforms paved the way for the opening of accession negotiations in 2005.

Although member states endorsed the Commission's recommendation to begin negotiations, there remained significant reluctance in certain national contexts. Some have argued that in this instance, as with the CEECs, the EU's collective 'rhetorical entrapment' made it difficult to shun Turkey at this stage (Bürgin 2010). Such rhetoric consisted of commitments to Turkey's 'European vocation', the political criteria as a basis for assessment, and a clear decision making time frame that required a decision in 2004.

However, after 2006, negotiations progressed slowly. Formally, this was due to the failure of Turkey to open its land and seaports to the Republic of Cyprus (an EU member state). However, changes in key member states are also relevant. When the Christian Democrats returned to office in Germany in 2004, the German position became far less positive towards Turkish membership, with Chancellor Merkel arguing in favour of a 'privileged partnership' instead of full membership for Turkey; and, before he took office in 2007, French President Sarkozy stated unequivocally that 'Turkey has no place inside the EU' (Parker 2009b: 1095).

The situation in Turkey also changed. Erdogan's hard-line response to a wave of protests during the summer of 2013 served to reinforce the already growing doubts among some within both Turkey and the EU regarding the sincerity of his government's pledges on democracy and human rights (*The Economist* 2013). This situation worsened significantly when, following a failed *coup d'état* in 2016, the Turkish government declared a state of emergency, clamped down on its opponents, and—via a narrowly won referendum—secured reforms to the constitution that granted increased powers to an increasingly autocratic President Erdogan. Citing these and other issues, the EU effectively froze accession negotiations after 2016. On the Turkish side, it appeared that, for Erdogan at least, EU membership was no longer a clear foreign policy priority. However, the EU continued to preserve a working relationship with Turkey, particularly in light of its co-operation on migration and the refugee crisis (Chapter 23, 'The Refugee Crisis').

Perhaps more than in any other case, Turkey's bid for membership has brought into sharp focus a number of fundamental normative and sociological questions (Chapter 4, 'Critical Social Theory') about the limits and nature of the EU. Such questions as: 'Where do the EU's geographical borders lie?', 'Are identity, culture, and religion relevant factors in the enlargement process and should they be?', 'If they are relevant, what is the "European" identity against which prospective members are to be judged?', and 'Is this identity a fixed one to which others must adjust or does the EU (and *should* it) adapt itself to its new members?' (Parker 2009*b*).

Enlargement Fatigue?

Following the 2004 enlargement, many scholars invoked the concept of 'enlargement fatigue' to encapsulate the notion that after June 2004, the EU's appetite for further enlargement was diminished. Certainly, that seemed to be the case in the immediate aftermath of the CEEC enlargement. The economic crisis (see Chapter 11, 'The Unfolding Eurozone Crisis') may have further reduced the attractiveness of enlargement, both for the EU and for prospective members.

Following the CEEC enlargement, the borders of the enlarged EU abutted states that had formerly been part of the Soviet Union itself: Armenia, Azerbaijan, Georgia, Moldova, and Ukraine. However, there was little prospect that they would be accepted as applicants. In May 2004, the then Enlargement Commissioner Günter Verheugen appeared to rule it out when he said: 'Membership is not on the agenda for these countries. Full stop' (*Financial Times*, 13 May 2004). His statement applied also to North African states such as Morocco and Tunisia, which had expressed an interest in eventual membership. Unlike Turkey, these latter states were defined as beyond Europe, which allowed membership to be ruled out. Reluctance on the EU side at this time to engage in further large-scale enlargements can be related in particular to difficulties encountered in reforming EU institutions (and associated treaties) in preparation for the CEEC enlargement (see Chapter 10, 'Enlargement').

The economic crisis in the EU which dominated the agenda after 2009 further diminished the EU's appetite for significant enlargement (see Chapter 11, 'The Unfolding Eurozone Crisis'). The cost implications of future enlargement became a particular concern, given the economic situation within certain member states. Concerns that further enlargement would undermine the prospects of pushing forward further and deeper integration (in response to the crisis) also re-emerged in some quarters. When he came to office in 2014, Commission President Juncker made clear that there would be no further enlargement during his mandate (which ended in 2019). President Macron's decision in October 2019 to veto the start of accession negotiations with North Macedonia and Albania cited such concerns.

The attractiveness of the EU for prospective members may have also been adversely affected. Public opinion in favour of enlargement diminished not only within the EU, but also within a number of prospective members (Di Mauro and Fraile 2012). That said, EU membership remains an attractive long-term proposition for certain prospective states and some populations beyond the EU. For instance, as noted in 'Explanations of the Western Balkans Enlargements' above, many western Balkan states have been frustrated at the slow progress in their EU membership trajectories.

A further reason for this enlargement fatigue relates to 'retrospective doubts about the EU's alleged "transformative effect"' (O'Brennan 2018: 2). In other words, the Europeanization (see Chapter 3, 'Europeanization') that it was thought the enlargement process would set in motion may not be as deeply embedded or as irreversible as many thought it would be. These doubts are the product of a perceived backsliding on core values, such as the rule of law and fundamental rights in some prospective and recently joined member states (perhaps most notably, Turkey, Poland, and Hungary—see also Chapter 11, 'The Populist Challenge'). President Macron also cited concerns on this issue when vetoing the commencement of accession negotiations with North Macedonia and Albania, suggesting that the EU needed to ensure it could properly address backsliding before embarking on further enlargements. However, as an October 2019 *Financial Times* editorial argued, the decision itself had the potential to precipitate just such backsliding in the western Balkans.

CONCLUSION

It was surely never envisaged by the founders of the European Coal and Steel Community (ECSC) and the EEC that these organizations of six states would expand over the next half century to a membership of twenty-eight, with more applicants waiting to join. Perhaps more than any other policy, enlargement demonstrates the stark difference between the EU and a nation state. This is a policy—often described as the EU's most successful policy—which has allowed the EC/EU to expand geographically but without the violence of national empire building.

The effects of the enlargements have been significant. They have certainly had a major impact both on the EU and on the new members. Within the EU, enlargement has necessitated European institutional reforms and associated Treaty change. It has also changed the EU socially and culturally, as has become evident for EU citizens as a consequence of freedom of movement. For new members, processes of Europeanization (see Chapter 3, 'Europeanization') have significantly altered their economies, politics, and institutions. That said, it has been argued that we have seen the reversal of those processes in some prospective and member states in recent years. Moreover, the UK's departure from the EU in 2020 of course marks the first instance of a 'shrinking' of the EU.

The reasons for enlargement have been much debated, both as to why the applications were made and why they were accepted, but they come down to some mix of economic and political considerations. Scholars have considered the motives on both sides in terms of some combination of rational interests and the role of ideas and norms. Rational interests consist of the various perceived economic and geopolitical advantages and disadvantages of enlargement. Ideas and norms refer to the importance of fundamental normative conceptions about the geographical, cultural, and political limits of the EU.

Considered as a whole, and in relation to all enlargement processes, scholarship has attributed importance to a variety of agents, including governments on different sides of the process, supranational actors (particularly the European Commission), and non-governmental entities. The relative importance given to these actors has varied across different enlargement processes, and the emphasis that different scholars have placed on them has also depended on the broader theoretical perspective that each has adopted.

A number of commentators noted that after 2004, and particularly following the 2008 economic crisis (see Chapter 11, 'The Unfolding Eurozone Crisis'), the incentives on all sides for further significant enlargements were substantially diminished. However, the EU will need to balance its understandable 'enlargement fatigue' against the imperative to ensure stability in its near neighbourhood.

KEY POINTS

History

- There have been seven rounds of enlargement.
- The first enlargement brought into the EC two states, Britain and Denmark, that were sceptical about European integration.
- The second and third enlargements are often treated together as the 'southern enlargement'. It gave the EC a stronger Mediterranean orientation, and raised the profile of Latin America in external relations. Greece's membership caused some problems for relations with other states in the Balkans.
- As a result of the fourth enlargement, environmental protection became more important, the coalition in favour of budgetary reform was strengthened, and a Nordic bloc was formed.
- The fifth and sixth enlargements are often treated together as an 'eastern enlargement'. It forced reform of the institutions and of key policies.
- The seventh enlargement saw Croatia become the first western Balkan country to join.
- At the end of 2019, accession negotiations were under way with Montenegro and Serbia (and effectively stalled with Turkey). North Macedonia and Albania had candidate status and Bosnia Herzegovina had applied.

The Enlargement Procedure

- A procedure was developed over the seven rounds of application.
- Once an application has been approved by the European Council, the Commission prepares an Opinion. Negotiations proceed in sectoral groups. Agreed terms have to be ratified by the Council of Foreign Ministers and the European Council.
- Existing member states try to sort out problems that might be caused by the new members before the enlargement is completed.
- The southern enlargement set a precedent for member states to overrule an unfavourable Commission Opinion on political grounds.
- The eastern enlargement led to the development of a set of criteria for membership that have come to structure negotiations with applicants.

Explaining Enlargement

- The first enlargement was driven by both economic and geostrategic considerations.
- The EFTA enlargement was a response to the success of the single market programme.
- The eastern enlargement was a result of a wish to consolidate democracy and capitalism in the former communist states.
- The enlargement processes with the western Balkans were rooted in a desire to guarantee stability in this previously troubled region.
- Turkey's fluctuating EU membership prospects have been driven by both domestic politics and factors within the EU.

Turkey

- Turkey signed an Association Agreement with the EU in 1963, but only began formal accession negotiations with the EU in 2005. These negotiations have stalled in recent years, not least as a result of domestic instability in Turkey.

- Perhaps more than in any other case, Turkey's accession process has prompted fundamental normative and sociological questions about the limits and nature of the EU and enlargement.

Enlargement Fatigue?

- After 2004, and certainly in the context of the eurozone crisis, the prospects of further significant enlargements were diminished due to 'enlargement fatigue'.

 For additional material and resources, please visit the online resources www.oup.com/uk/bache5e.

QUESTIONS

1. Are rationalist or constructivist accounts most convincing in explaining the drivers of EU enlargement (consider with reference to one or more enlargement round)?

2. Does EU enlargement reflect the success of processes of 'Europeanization'?

3. To what extent have neoliberal preferences in prospective member states and the EU driven the most recent enlargement rounds?

4. Why has Turkey's long-standing pursuit of EU membership proved so difficult and politically controversial?

5. Why has the EU been regarded as suffering from 'enlargement fatigue'?

FURTHER READING

Comprehensive coverage of the first four enlargements is contained in **C. Preston**, *Enlargement and European Integration in the European Union* (London: Routledge, 1997). It contains sections on the accession process for each new member state and information on other applications. It considers the effects of enlargement on each member state, on the EU's policies and on the structure and processes of the EU. A complete narrative of how those enlargement negotiations developed, with copious quotations from official documentation, is provided in **G. Avery and F. Cameron**, *The Enlargement of the European Union* (Sheffield: Sheffield Academic Press, 1998).

For analyses using conditionality and Europeanization interpretations, see **F. Schimmelfennig and U. Sedelmeier (eds)**, *The Europeanization of Central and Eastern Europe* (Ithaca, NY: Cornell University Press, 2005), and **H. Grabbe**, *The EU's Transformative Power: Europeanization through Conditionality in Central and Eastern Europe* (Basingstoke: Palgrave Macmillan, 2005).

For a full neo-Gramscian analysis, the conscientious student will look at **A. Bieler**, *Globalization and Enlargement of the European Union: Austrian and Swedish Social Forces in the Struggle over Membership* (London: Routledge, 2000), although others may find enough information in **A. Bieler's** later article, 'The Struggle over EU Enlargement: A Historical Materialist Analysis of

European Integration', *Journal of European Public Policy*, 9 (2002): 575–97. This analysis can be usefully compared with that of **C. Ingebritsen**, *The Nordic States and European Unity* (Ithaca, NY: Cornell University Press, 1998).

For a discussion of the drivers behind Turkey's EU membership process, see **A. Bürgin**, 'Cosmopolitan Entrapment: The Failed Strategies to Reverse Turkey's EU Membership Eligibility', *Perspectives: Review of International Affairs*, 18 (2010): 33–56. For a discussion of the political and normative dilemmas associated with this case, see **O. Parker**, '"Cosmopolitan Europe" and the EU–Turkey Question: The Politics of a "Common Destiny"', *Journal of European Public Policy*, 16 (2009), 1085–101. And **T. Diez**, 'Expanding Europe: The Ethics of EU–Turkey Relations', *Ethics and International Affairs*, 21 (2007): 415–22.

For a discussion of the contemporary situation pertaining to the western Balkans (the site of the next likely enlargement), see **J. O'Brennan,** 'EU Enlargement to the Western Balkans: Towards 2025 and Beyond', *The Institute of International & European Affairs,* 17 May 2018. https://www.iiea.com/publication/iiea-publication-eu-enlargement-to-the-western-balkans-towards-2025-beyond.

References

Adnett, N. (2001). 'Modernizing the European Social Model: Developing the Guidelines'. *Journal of Common Market Studies*, 39: 353–64.

Ahearn, R. (2002). 'US–European Union Trade Relations: Issues and Policy Challenges'. *CRS Issue Brief for Congress*. http://fpc.state.gov/documents/organization/9546.pdf.

Ahmad, F. (2001). 'Turkey', in J. Krieger (ed.), *The Oxford Companion to the Politics of the World* (2nd edn). New York: Oxford University Press, 850–1.

Allen, D. and Smith, M. (2004). 'External Policy Developments'. *Journal of Common Market Studies: The European Union*, 2003, *Annual Review of Activities*: 95–112.

Allen, D. and Smith, M. (2012). 'Relations with the Rest of the World'. *Journal of Common Market Studies: Annual Review of Activities*: 162–77.

Alons, G. (2017). 'Environmental Policy Integration in the EU's Common Agricultural Policy: Greening or Greenwashing?' *Journal of European Public Policy*, 24: 1604–22.

Alter, K. (1996). 'The European Court's Political Power'. *West European Politics*, 19: 458–87.

Alter, K. (1998). 'Who Are the "Masters of the Treaty"? European Governments and the European Court of Justice'. *International Organization*, 52: 121–47.

Alter, K. (2001). *Establishing the Supremacy of European Law: The Making of an International Rule of Law in Europe*. Oxford: Oxford University Press.

Amato, G. and Ziller, J. (eds) (2007). *The European Constitution: Cases and Materials in EU Member States' Law*. Cheltenham: Edward Elgar.

Amoore, L. (2008). 'Foucault against the Grain'. *International Political Sociology*, 2: 274–6.

Anderson, J. (2003). 'Europeanization in Context: Concept and Theory', in K. Dyson and K. Goetz (eds), *Germany, Europe and the Politics of Constraint*. Oxford: Oxford University Press, 37–54.

Armstrong, K. and Bulmer, S. (1998). *The Governance of the Single European Market*. Manchester: Manchester University Press.

Arnull, A. (2010). 'European Union Law: A Tale of Microscopes and Telescopes', in M. Egan, N. Nugent, and W. Paterson (eds), *Research Agendas in European Union Studies: Stalking the Elephant*. Basingstoke: Palgrave Macmillan, 168–88.

Aspinwall, M. and Schneider, G. (2000). 'Same Menu, Separate Tables: The Institutionalist Turn in Political Science and the Study of European Integration'. *European Journal of Political Research*, 38: 1–36.

Avery, G. and Cameron, F. (1998). *The Enlargement of the European Union*. Sheffield: Sheffield Academic Press/University Association for Contemporary European Studies.

Bache, I. (1998). *The Politics of European Union Regional Policy: Multi-Level Governance or Flexible Gatekeeping?* Sheffield: Sheffield Academic Press/University Association for Contemporary European Studies.

Bache, I. (2008). *Europeanization and Multi-Level Governance: Cohesion Policy in the European Union and Britain*. Lanham. MD: Rowman and Littlefield.

Bache, I. (2015). 'Cohesion Policy: A New Direction for New Times?', in H. Wallace, M. Pollack, and A. Young (eds), *Policy-Making in the European Union* (7th edn). Oxford: Oxford University Press, 243–62.

Bache, I. and Chapman, R. (2008). 'Democracy through Multi-Level Governance? The Implementation of the Structural Funds in South Yorkshire'. *Governance*, 21: 397–418.

Bache, I. and Flinders, M. (2004). 'Conclusions and Implications', in I. Bache and M. Flinders (eds), *Multi-Level Governance*. Oxford: Oxford University Press, 195–206.

Bache, I. and George, S. (2006). *Politics in the European Union* (2nd edn). Oxford: Oxford University Press.

Bache, I. and Jordan, A. (2006*a*). 'Europeanization and Domestic Change', in I. Bache and A. Jordan (eds), *The Europeanization of British Politics*. Basingstoke: Palgrave Macmillan, 17–36.

Bache, I. and Jordan, A. (eds) (2006*b*). *The Europeanization of British Politics*. Basingstoke: Palgrave Macmillan.

Bache, I. and Marshall, A. (2004). 'Europeanisation and Domestic Change: A Governance Approach to Institutional Adaptation in Britain'. *Europeanisation* Online *Papers* No. 5/2004, Queen's University Belfast. http://qub.ac.uk/schools/SchoolofPolitics InternationalStudiesandPhilosophy/Research/PaperSeries/EuropeanisationPapers/.

Bache, I., Bulmer, S., and Gunay, D. (2012). 'Europeanization: A Critical Realist Perspective', in C. Radaelli and T. Exadaktylos (eds), *Research Design in European Studies*. Basingstoke: Palgrave Macmillan, 64–84.

Bache, I., Bulmer, S., George, S., and Parker, O. (2015). *Politics in the European Union* (4th edn). Oxford: Oxford University Press.

Bäckstrand, K. and Elgström, O. (2013). 'The EU's Role in Climate Change Negotiations: From Leader to "Leadiator"'. *Journal of European Public Policy*, 20: 1369–86.

Baker, D., Gamble, A., and Ludlam, S. (1993). '1846–1906–1996? Conservative Splits and European Integration'. *Political Quarterly*, 64: 420–34.

Baker, D., Gamble, A., and Ludlam, S. (1994). 'The Parliamentary Siege of Maastricht 1993: Conservative Divisions and British Ratification of the Treaty of European Union'. *Parliamentary Affairs*, 47: 37–60.

Barbière, C. (2018). 'European Parliament Votes in Favour of the Revision on Posted Workers', *EurActiv*, 30 May. https://www.euractiv.com/section/economy-jobs/news/european-parliament-votes-in-favour-of-the-revision-on-posted-workers/. re (2018).

Barnard, C. and Peers, S. (eds) (2017). *European Union Law* (2nd edn). Cambridge: Cambridge University Press.

Barroso, J. (2009). 'State of the Union: Delivering a "Europe of Results" in a Harsh Economic Climate'. *Journal of Common Market Studies*, *Annual Review*, 57: 7–16.

Bartolini, S. (2005). *Restructuring Europe: Centre Formation, System Building, and Political Structuring between the Nation State and the European Union*. Oxford: Oxford University Press.

Baun, M. (1996a). *An Imperfect Union: The Maastricht Treaty and the New Politics of European Integration*. Boulder, CO: Westview.

Baun, M. (1996b). 'The Maastricht Treaty as High Politics: Germany, France and European Integration'. *Political Science Quarterly*, 110: 605–24.

Beck, U. and Grande, E. (2007). *Cosmopolitan Europe*. Cambridge: Polity Press.

Beetham, D. and Lord, C. (1998). *Legitimacy and the European Union*. London and New York: Longman.

Bellamy, R. and Kröger, S. (2016). 'The Politicization of European Integration: National Parliaments and the Democratic Disconnect'. *Comparative European Politics*, 14: 125–30.

Berghahn, V. and Young, B. (2013). 'Reflections on Werner Bonefeld's "Freedom and the Strong State: On German Ordo-Liberalism"'. *New Political Economy*, 18: 768–78.

Berkhout, J., Beyers, J., Braun, C., Hanegraaff, M., and Lowery, D. (2018). 'Making Inference across Mobilisation and Influence Research: Comparing Top-Down and Bottom-Up Mapping of Interest Systems'. *Political Studies*, 66: 43–62.

Beyers, J. (2004). 'Voice and Access: Political Practices of European Interest Associations'. *European Union Politics*, 5: 211–40.

Beyers, J. (2010). 'Conceptual and Methodological Challenges in the Study of European Socialization'. *Journal of European Public Policy*, 17: 909–20.

Beyers, J. and Dierickx, G. (1998). 'The Working Groups of the Council of the European Union: Supranational or Intergovernmental Negotiations?' *Journal of Common Market Studies*, 36: 289–317.

Beyers, J., Eising, R., and Maloney, W. (eds) (2009). *Interest Group Politics in Europe: Lessons from EU Studies and Comparative Politics*. Abingdon: Routledge.

Bickerton, C., Hodson, D., and Puetter, U. (eds) (2015a). *The New Intergovernmentalism: States and Supranational Actors in the Post Maastricht Period*. Oxford: Oxford University Press.

Bickerton, C., Hodson, D., and Puetter, U. (2015b). 'The New Intergovernmentalism: European Integration in the Post-Maastricht Era'. *Journal of Common Market Studies*, 53: 703–22.

Bickerton, C., Hodson, D., and Puetter, U. (eds) (2015c). 'The New Intergovernmentalism and the Study of European Integration', in C. Bickerton, D. Hodson, and U. Puetter (eds), *The New Intergovernmentalism: States and Supranational Actors in the Post Maastricht Period*. Oxford: Oxford University Press, 1–48.

Bieler, A. (2000). *Globalization and Enlargement of the European Union: Austrian and Swedish Social Forces in the Struggle over Membership*. London: Routledge.

Bieler, A. (2002). 'The Struggle over EU Enlargement: A Historical Materialist Analysis of European Integration'. *Journal of European Public Policy*, 9: 575–97.

Bieler, A. (2011). 'Labour, New Social Movements and the Resistance to Neo-Liberal Restructuring in Europe'. *New Political Economy*, 16: 163–83.

Bieler, A., Bonefeld, W., Burnham, P., and Morton, D. A. (2006). *Global Restructuring, State,*

517

Capital, and Labour: Contesting Neo-Gramscian Perspectives. Basingstoke and New York: Palgrave Macmillan.

Biermann, F., Guérin, N., Jagdhuber, S., Rittberger, B., and Weiss, M. (2019). 'Political (Non)reform in the Euro Crisis and the Refugee Crisis: A Liberal Intergovernmentalist Explanation'. *Journal of European Public Policy*, 26: 246–66.

Bigo, D. (2000). 'When Two Become One: Internal and External Securitisations in Europe', in M. Kelstrup and M. C. Williams (eds), *International Relations Theory and the Politics of European Integration: Power, Security, and Community*. London: Routledge, 171–204.

Blyth, M. (2013). *Austerity: The History of a Dangerous Idea*. Oxford: Oxford University Press.

Bomberg, E. and Peterson, J. (2000). 'Policy Transfer and Europeanization'. *Europeanisation Online Papers*, No. 2/2000, Queen's University, Belfast.

Bonefeld, W. (2012). 'Freedom and the Strong State: On German Ordo-Liberalism'. *New Political Economy*, 17: 633–56.

Borras, S. and Jacobsson, K. (2004). 'The Open Method of Co-ordination and New Governance Patterns in the EU'. *Journal of European Public Policy*, 11: 185–208.

Börzel, T. (1998). 'Organizing Babylon: On the Different Conceptions of Policy Networks'. *Public Administration*, 76: 253–73.

Börzel, T. (2000). 'Why There is No "Southern Problem". On Environmental Leaders and Laggards in the European Union'. *Journal of European Public Policy*, 7: 141–62.

Börzel, T. (2002). 'Pace-Setting, Foot-Dragging, and Fence-Sitting: Member State Responses to Europeanization'. *Journal of Common Market Studies*, 40: 193–214.

Börzel, T. (2010). The Transformative Power of Europe Reloaded: The Limits of External Europeanization'. KFG 'The Transformative Power of Europe'. Working Paper No. 11, February. http://userpage.fu-berlin.de/kfgeu/kfgwp/wpseries/WorkingPaperKFG_11.pdf.

Börzel, T. (2019). 'Governance Approaches to European Integration', in A. Wiener, T. Börzel, and T. Risse (eds), *European Integration Theory*. Oxford: Oxford University Press, 87–107.

Börzel, T. and Risse, T. (2000). 'When Europe Hits Home: Europeanization and Domestic Change'. *European Integration Online Papers*, 4(15). http://www.eiop.or.at/eiop/pdf/2000-015.pdf.

Börzel, T. and Risse, T. (2003). 'Conceptualising the Domestic Impact of Europe', in K. Featherstone and C. Radaelli (eds), *The Politics of Europeanization*. Oxford: Oxford University Press, 57–82.

Börzel, T. and Schimmelfennig, F. (2017). 'Coming Together or Drifting Apart? The EU's Political Integration Capacity in Eastern Europe'. *Journal of European Public Policy*, 24: 278–96.

Bossong, R. (2019). 'The Expansion of Frontex: Symbolic Measures and Long-Term Changes in EU Border Management'. SWP Comment 2019/C 47, December. https://www.swp-berlin.org/en/publication/the-expansion-of-frontex/.

Boswell, C. (2007). 'Migration Control in Europe after 9/11: Explaining the Absence of Securitization'. *Journal of Common Market Studies*, 45: 589–610.

Boswell, C. (2010). 'Justice and Home Affairs', in M. Egan, N. Nugent, and W. Paterson (eds), *Research Agendas in EU Studies: Stalking the Elephant*. Basingstoke: Palgrave Macmillan, 278–304.

Boswell, C. and Geddes, A. (2011). *Migration and Mobility in the European Union*. Basingstoke: Palgrave Macmillan.

Bouwen, P. (2002). 'Corporate Lobbying in the European Union: The Logic of Access'. *Journal of European Public Policy*, 9: 365–90.

Bouwen, P. (2009). 'The European Commission', in D. Coen and J. Richardson (eds), *Lobbying the European Union, Institutions Actors and Issues*. Oxford: Oxford University Press, 19–38.

Branch, A. P. and Øhrgaard, J. C. (1999). 'Trapped in the Supranational-Intergovernmental Dichotomy: A Response to Stone Sweet and Sandholtz'. *Journal of European Public Policy*, 6: 123–43.

Braun, B. and Hübner, M. (2018). 'Fiscal Fault, Financial Fix? Capital Markets Union and the Quest for Macroeconomic Stabilization in the Euro Area'. *Competition and Change,* 2: 117–38.

Bressanelli, E. and Chelotti, N. (2018). 'The European Parliament and Economic Governance: Explaining a Case of Limited Influence'. *The Journal of Legislative Studies*, 24: 72–89.

Bressanelli, E. and Chelotti, N (eds) (2019). 'Power without Influence? Explaining the Impact of the European Parliament Post-Lisbon'. *Journal of European Integration*, 41(3): 265–76.

Brunnermeier, M., James, H., and Landau, J.-P. (2016). *The Euro and the Battle of Ideas*, Princeton, NJ: Princeton University Press.

Buch-Hansen H. and Wigger, A. (2010). 'Revisiting 50 Years of Market-Making: The Neoliberal Transformation of European Competition Policy'. *Review of International Political Economy*, 1: 20–44.

Buckel S. (2011). 'Staatsprojekt Europa'. *Politische Vierteljahresschrift*, 52: 636–62.

Budden, P. (2002). 'Observations on the Single European Act and the "Relaunch of Europe": A Less "Intergovernmental" Reading of the 1985 Intergovernmental Conference'. *Journal of European Public Policy*, 9: 76–97.

Bull, H. (1982). 'Civilian Power Europe: A Contradiction in Terms?' *Journal of Common Market Studies*, 21: 149–64.

Buller, J. (1995). 'Britain as an Awkward Partner: Reassessing Britain's Relations with the EU'. *Politics*, 15: 33–42.

Buller, J. and Gamble, A. (2002). *'Conceptualising Europeanization'. Public Policy and Administration*, 17: 4–24.

Bulmer, S. (1983). 'Domestic Politics and European Policy-Making'. *Journal of Common Market Studies*, 21: 349–63.

Bulmer, S. (1993). 'The Governance of the European Union: A New Institutionalist Approach'. *Journal of Public Policy*, 13: 351–80.

Bulmer, S. (1998). 'New Institutionalism and the Governance of the Single European Market'. *Journal of European Public Policy*, 5: 365–86.

Bulmer, S. (2007). 'Theorizing Europeanization', in P. Graziano and M. Vink (eds), *Europeanization: New Research Agendas*. Basingstoke: Palgrave Macmillan, 46–58.

Bulmer, S. (2009). 'Politics in Time Meets the Politics of Time: Historical Institutionalism and the EU Timescape'. *Journal of European Public Policy*, 16: 307–24.

Bulmer, S. (2010). 'Germany: From Launching the EU Constitutional Debate to Salvaging a Treaty', in M. Carbone (ed.), *National Politics and European Integration: From the Constitution to the Lisbon Treaty*. Cheltenham, UK and Northampton, MA: Edward Elgar, 51–70.

Bulmer, S. (2011). 'Shop Till You Drop? The German Executive as Venue-Shopper in Justice and Home Affairs?', in P. Bendel, A. Ette, and R. Parkes (eds), *The Europeanization of Control: Venues and Outcomes of EU Justice and Home Affairs Cooperation*. Berlin: Lit Verlag, 41–76.

Bulmer, S. and Burch, M. (1998). 'Organising for Europe: Whitehall, the British State, and the European Union'. *Public Administration*, 76: 601–28.

Bulmer, S. and Burch, M. (2009). *The Europeanisation of Whitehall: UK Central Government and the European Union*. Manchester: Manchester University Press.

Bulmer, S. and Joseph, J. (2016). 'European Integration in Crisis? Of Supranational Integration, Hegemonic Projects and Domestic Politics'. *European Journal of International Relations*, 22: 725–48.

Bulmer, S and Lequesne, C. (eds) (2020). *The Member States of the European Union* (3rd edn). Oxford: Oxford University Press.

Bulmer, S. and Padgett, S. (2005). 'Policy Transfer in the European Union: An Institutionalist Perspective'. *British Journal of Political Science*, 35: 103–26.

Bulmer, S. and Paterson, W. (2010). 'Germany and the European Union: From "Tamed Power" to Normalized Power?' *International Affairs*, 86: 1051–73.

Bulmer, S. and Paterson, W. (2015 [1987]). *The Federal Republic of Germany and the European Community* (Abingdon and New York: Routledge). (Original work published London: Allen and Unwin, 1987).

Bulmer, S. and Paterson, W. (2019). *Germany and the European Union: Europe's Reluctant Hegemon?* London: Macmillan/Red Globe.

Bulmer, S. and Radaelli, C. (2013). 'The Europeanization of Member State Policy', in S. Bulmer and C. Lequesne (eds), *The Member States of the European Union* (2nd edn). Oxford: Oxford University Press, 357–83.

Bulmer, S. and Wessels, W. (1987). *The European Council: Decision Making in European Politics*. Basingstoke: Macmillan.

Bulmer, S., Dolowitz, D., Humphreys, P., and Padgett, S. (2007). *Policy Transfer in European Union Governance: Regulating the Utilities*. Abingdon: Routledge.

Buonanno, L. (2017). 'The European Migration Crisis', in D. Dinan, N. Nugent, and W. Paterson (eds), *The European Union in Crisis*. London: Palgrave, 100–30.

Buonanno, L. and Nugent, N. (2013). *Policies and Policy Processes of the European Union*. Basingstoke: Palgrave Macmillan.

Buonanno, L. and Nugent, N. (forthcoming). *Policies and Policy Processes of the European Union* (2nd edn). London: Macmillan/Red Globe.

Burgess, M. (ed.) (1986). *Federalism and Federation in Western Europe*. London: Croom Helm.

Burgess, M. (1989). *Federalism and Federation in the European Union: Political Ideas, Influences and Strategies*. London and New York: Routledge.

Bürgin, A. (2010). 'Cosmopolitan Entrapment: The Failed Strategies to Reverse Turkey's EU Membership Eligibility'. *Perspectives: Review of International Affairs*, 18: 33–56.

Burley, A-M. and Mattli, W. (1993). 'Europe before the Court: A Political Theory of Legal Integration'. *International Organization*, 47: 41–76.

Burns, C. (2004). 'Co-Decision and the European Commission: A Study of Declining Influence?' *Journal of European Public Policy*, 11: 1–18.

519

Burns, C. (2013). 'Consensus and Compromise Become Ordinary—But at What Cost? A Critical Analysis of the Impact of the Changing Norms of Codecision upon European Parliament Committees'. *Journal of European Public Policy*, 20: 988–1005.

Burns, C. (2019). 'In the Eye of the Storm? The European Parliament, the Environment and the EU's Crises'. *Journal of European Integration*, 41: 3, 311–27.

Burns, C., Carter, N., Davies, G. A. M., and Worsfold, N. (2013). 'Still Saving the Earth? The European Parliament's Environmental Record'. *Environmental Politics*, 22(6): 935–54.

Burns, C., Eckersley, P., and Tobin, P. (2020). 'EU Environmental Policy in Times of Crisis'. *Journal of European Public Policy*, 27: 1–19.

Cafruny, A. W. and Ryner, J. M. (2007). *Europe at Bay: In the Shadow of US Hegemony*. London: Lynne Rienner.

Cafruny, A. W. and Ryner, J. M. (2009). 'Critical Political Economy', in A. Wiener and T. Diez, *European Integration Theory* (2nd edn). Oxford: Oxford University Press, 221–40.

Calingaert, M. (1999). 'Creating a European Market', in L. Cram, D. Dinan, and N. Nugent (eds), *Developments in the European Union*. Basingstoke and London: Macmillan, 153–73.

Cameron, D. R. (1992). 'The 1992 Initiative: Causes and Consequences', in A. Sbragia (ed.), *Euro-Politics: Institutions and Policymaking in the 'New' European Community*. Washington, DC: Brookings Institution, 23–74.

Cameron, D. R. (1997). 'Economic and Monetary Union: Underlying Imperatives and Third-Stage Dilemmas'. *Journal of European Public Policy*, 4: 455–85.

Camps, M. (1964). *Britain and the European Community 1955–1963*. London: Oxford University Press.

Camps, M. (1967). *European Unification in the Sixties: From the Veto to the Crisis*. London: Oxford University Press.

Caporaso, J. (1999). 'Toward a Normal Science of Regional Integration'. *Journal of European Public Policy*, 6: 160–4.

Caporaso, J. and Keeler, J. T. S. (1995). 'The European Union and Regional Integration Theory', in C. Rhodes and S. Mazey (eds), *The State of the European Union Vol. 3, Building a European Polity?* Boulder, CO, and Harlow, Essex: Lynne Rienner and Longman, 29–62.

Carbone, M. (2010). 'Conclusion: Preference Formation, Inter-Itate Bargaining and the Treaty of Lisbon', in M. Carbone (ed.), *National Politics and European Integration: From the Constitution to the Lisbon Treaty*. Cheltenham, UK; Northampton, MA: Edward Elgar, 215–32.

Cardwell, P. (2013). 'On "Ring-Fencing" the Common Foreign and Security Policy in the Legal Order of the European Union' *Northern Ireland Legal Quarterly*, 64(4): 443–63.

Cardwell, P. (2017). 'The United Kingdom and the Common Foreign and Security Policy of the EU: From Pre-Brexit "Awkward Partner" to Post-Brexit "Future Partnership"?' *Croatian Yearbook of European Law and Policy*, 13: 1–26.

Cardwell, P. J. and Hervey, T. (2015). 'The Roles of Law in a New Intergovernmentalist EU', in C. Bickerton, D. Hodson, and U. Puetter (eds), *European Politics in the Post Maastricht Period: States, Supranational Actors and the New Intergovernmentalism*. Oxford: Oxford University Press, 73–89.

Carrubba, C. J. (2003). 'The European Court of Justice, Democracy, and Enlargement'. *European Union Politics*, 4: 75–100.

Carter, N. (2013). 'Greening the Mainstream: Party Politics and the Environment'. *Environmental Politics*, 22: 73–94.

Carter, N. (2018). *The Politics of the Environment, Ideas, Activism and Policy*. Cambridge: Cambridge University Press.

Čavoški, A. (2015). 'A Post-Austerity European Commission: No Role for Environmental Policy?' *Environmental Politics*, 24(3): 501–5.

Cecchini, P. (1988). *The European Challenge 1992: The Benefits of a Single Market*. Aldershot: Gower.

Chakrabortty, A. (2011). 'Q&A: Greece's Debt Crisis'. The *Guardian*, 31 July. http://theguardian.com/world/2011/jul/31/greece-debt-crisis-how-bad.

Chalmers, D., Davies, G., and Monti, G. (2010). *European Union Law* (2nd edn; 3rd edn, 2014). Cambridge: Cambridge University Press.

Chang, M. (2009). *Monetary Integration in the European Union*. Basingstoke: Palgrave Macmillan.

Checkel, J. and Moravcsik, A. (2001). 'A Constructivist Research Programme in EU Studies?' *Journal of European Union Politics*, 2, 219–49.

Christiansen, T. (2010). 'The EU Reform Process: From the European Constitution to the Lisbon Treaty', in M. Carbone (ed.), *National Politics and European Integration: From the Constitution to the Lisbon Treaty*. Cheltenham, UK; Northampton, MA: Edward Elgar, 16–33.

Christiansen, T., Jørgensen, K., and Wiener, A. (eds) (1999). 'Social Constructivism and European Integration'. *Journal of European Public Policy*, special issue, 6: 527–720.

Church, C. and Phinnemore, D. (2006). *Understanding the European Constitution: An Introduction to the EU Constitutional Treaty*. London: Routledge.

Cini, M. and Pérez-Solórzano Borragán, N. (eds) (2010). 'From the Constitutional Treaty to the Treaty of Lisbon', in M. Cini and N. Perez-Solórzano Borragán (eds), *European Union Politics* (3rd edn). Oxford: Oxford University Press, 48–68.

Cocks, P. (1980). 'Towards a Marxist Theory of European Integration'. *International Organization*, 31: 1–40.

Coen, D. and Katsaitis, A. (2013). 'Chameleon Pluralism in the EU: An Empirical Study of the European Commission Interest Group Density and Diversity across Policy Domains'. *Journal of European Public Policy*, 20, 1104–19.

Coen, D. and Richardson, J. (2009). 'Learning to Lobby the European Union: 20 Years of Change', in D. Coen, and J. Richardson, J. (eds), *Lobbying the European Union, Institutions Actors and Issues*. Oxford: Oxford University Press, 1–13.

Cohen, B. J. (2012). 'The Future of the Euro: Let's Get Real'. *Review of International Political Economy*, 19: 689–700.

Collinson, S. (1999). '"Issue Systems", "Multi-Level Games" and the Analysis of the EU's External Commercial and Associated Policies: A Research Agenda'. *Journal of European Public Policy*, 6: 206–24.

Colman, D. (2007). 'The Common Agricultural Policy', in M. Artis and F. Nixson (eds), *The Economics of the European Union: Policy and Analysis* (4th edn). Oxford: Oxford University Press, 77–104.

Committee of the Regions (2009). *The Committee of the Regions White Paper on Multi-Level Governance*. CdR 89/2009 in FR/EXT/RS/GW/ym/ms. Brussels: Committee of the Regions.

Coombes, D. (1970). *Politics and Bureaucracy in the European Community*. London: Allen & Unwin.

Cooper, I. (2013). 'A Yellow Card for the Striker: How National Parliaments Defeated EU Strikes Regulation', paper prepared for the European Union Studies Association conference, Baltimore, MD, 9–11 May.

Copeland, P. (2012). 'Conclusion: The Lisbon Strategy—Evaluating Success and Understanding Failure', in P. Copeland and D. Papadimitriou (eds), *The EU's Lisbon Strategy*. Basingstoke: Palgrave Macmillan, 229–37.

Copsey, N. and Haughton, T. (2009). 'The Gathering Storm: A Drama in Two Acts'. *Journal of Common Market Studies, Annual Review*, 57: 1–5.

Corbett, R., Jacobs, F., and Shackleton, M. (2003). 'The European Parliament at Fifty: A View from the Inside'. *Journal of Common Market Studies*, 41: 353–73.

Corbett, R. Jacobs, F., and Neville, D. (2016). *The European Parliament* (9th edn). London: John Harper Publishing.

Corporate Europe Observatory (2017). 'Lobby Planet Brussels', 29 June 2017. https://corporateeurope. org/en/2017/06/lobby-planet-brussels.

Corporate Europe Observatory (2018). 'Copyright Directive: How Competing Big Business Lobbies Drowned Out Critical Voices', 10 December 2018. https://corporateeurope.org/en/2018/12/copyright-directive-how-competing-big-business-lobbies-drowned-out-critical-voices.

Council of the EU (2005). *A Strategy for the External Dimension of JHA: Global Freedom, Security, and Justice*, 14366/3/05 REV 3 Brussels: General Secretariat of the Council, 30 November.

Council of EU (2018a). 'List of Council Preparatory Bodies', 13 December 2018. https://www.consilium.europa.eu/media/37507/st15131-en18.pdf.

Council of the EU (2018b). '18-Month Programme of Council (1 January–30 June 2020)'. Council of the European Union, Brussels, 30 November 2018. http://data.consilium.europa.eu/doc/document/ST-14518-2018-INIT/en/pdf.

Cowles, M. G. (1995). 'Setting the Agenda for a New Europe: The ERT and EC 1992'. *Journal of Common Market Studies*, 33: 501–26.

Cowles, M. G. (2003). 'Non-State Actors and False Dichotomies: Reviewing IR/IPE Approaches to European Integration'. *Journal of European Public Policy*, 10: 102–20.

Cowles, M. G., Caporaso, J., and Risse, T. (eds) (2001). Transforming *Europe: Europeanization and Domestic Change*. Ithaca, NY, and London: Cornell University Press.

Cox, R. (1981). 'Social Forces, States, and World Orders: Beyond International Relations Theory'. *Millennium: Journal of International Studies*, 10: 126–55.

Craig, P. and De Búrca, G. (2015). *EU Law: Text, Cases and Materials* (6th edn). Oxford: Oxford University Press.

Cram, L. (1997). *Policy Making in the EU: Conceptual Lenses and the Integration Process*. London and New York: Routledge.

Cram, L. (2001). 'Whither the Commission? Reform, Renewal and the Issue-Attention Cycle'. *Journal of European Public Policy*, 8: 770–86.

Criddle, B. (1993). 'The French Referendum on the Maastricht Treaty, September 1992'. *Parliamentary Affairs*, 46: 228–38.

Crombez, C. (1996). 'Legislative Procedures in the European Community'. *British Journal of Political Science*, 26: 199–228.

Crombez, C. (1997). 'The Co-Decision Procedure in the European Union'. *Legislative Studies Quarterly*, 22: 97–119.

Crombez, C. (2000). 'Understanding the EU Legislative Process-Co-Decision: Towards a Bicameral European Union'. *European Union Politics*, 1: 363–8.

Cunha, A. with Swinbank, A. (2011). *An Inside View of the CAP Reform Process: Explaining the MacSharry, Agenda 2000, and Fischler Reforms*. Oxford: Oxford University Press.

Damro, C. (2007). 'EU Delegation and Agency in International Trade Negotiations: A Cautionary Comparison'. *Journal of Common Market Studies*, 45: 883–903.

Damro, C. (2012). 'Market Power Europe'. *Journal of European Public Policy,* 19: 682–99.

Dang-Nguyen, G., Schneider, V., and Werle, R. (1993). 'Networks in European Policy-Making: Europeification of Telecommunications Policy', in S. S. Andersen and K. A. Eliassen (eds), *Making Policy in Europe: Europeification of National Policy-Making*. London: SAGE Publications, 93–114.

Daugbjerg, C. and Feindt, P. (2017). 'Post-Exceptionalism in Public Policy: Transforming Food and Agricultural Policy', Special Issue, *Journal of European Public Policy*, 24(11) : 1565–84.

Daugbjerg, C. and Swinbank, A. (2008). 'Curbing Agricultural Exceptionalism: The EU's Response to External Challenge'. *World Economy*, 31: 631–52.

Daugbjerg, C. and Swinbank, A. (2016). 'Policy Layering and Politically Sustainable Reform'. *Governance*, 29: 265–80.

De Bièvre, D. and Poletti, A. (2013). 'The EU in EU Trade Policy: From Regime Shaper to Status Quo Power', in G. Falkner and P. Müller (eds), *EU Policies in a Global Perspective*. London: Routledge, 20–37.

De Búrca, G. (1998). 'The Principle of Subsidiarity and the Court of Justice as a Political Actor'. *Journal of Common Market Studies*, 36: 217–35.

Dedman, M. (2010). *The Origins and Development of the European Union 1945–2008* (2nd edn). London: Routledge.

De Goede, M. (2008). 'The Politics of Pre-Emption and the War on Terror in Europe'. *European Journal of International Relations*, 14: 161–85.

De Gucht, K. (2003). 'The European Commission: Countdown to Extinction?' *European Integration*, 25: 165–8.

Delanty, G. and Rumford, C. (2005). *Rethinking Europe: Social Theory and the Implications of Europeanization*. Abingdon and New York: Routledge.

Dell, E. (1995). *The Schuman Plan and the British Abdication of Leadership in Europe*. Oxford: Clarendon Press.

Delreux, T. and Happaerts, S. (2016). *Environmental Policy and Politics in the European Union*. London: Palgrave Macmillan, 2016.

Delreux, T. and van den Brande, K. (2013). 'Taking the Lead: Informal Division of Labour in the EU's External Environmental Policy-Making'. *Journal of European Public Policy*, 20: 113–31.

den Boer, M. and Wallace, W. (2000). 'Justice and Home Affairs: Integration through Incrementalism?', in H. Wallace and W. Wallace (eds), *Policy-Making in the European Union* (4th edn). Oxford: Oxford University Press, 493–519.

De Schoutheete, P. (2017). 'The European Council: A Formidable Locus of Power', in D. Hodson and J. Peterson (eds), *The Institutions of the European Union* (4th edn). Oxford: Oxford University Press, 55–79.

Deutsch, K. (1953). *Nationalism and Social Communication: An Inquiry into the Foundations of Nationality*. Cambridge, MA: MIT Press.

Deutsch, K., Burrell, S. A., Kann, R. A., Lee, M. Jr, Lichterman, M., Lindgren, R. E., Loewenheim, F. L., and van Wagenen, R. W. (1957). *Political Community and the North Atlantic Area: International Organization in the Light of Historical Experience*. Princeton, NJ: Princeton University Press.

De Ville, F. and Siles-Brügge, G. (2015). *TTIP: The Truth about the Transatlantic Trade and Investment Partnership*. London: Polity Press.

De Ville, F. and Siles-Brügge, G. (2017). 'Why TTIP is a Game-Changer and its Critics Have a Point'. *Journal of European Public Policy*, 24: 1491–505.

De Vries, C. (2017). 'Benchmarking Brexit: How the British Decision to Leave Shapes EU Public Opinion'. *Journal of Common Market Studies*, 55: 38–53.

De Vries, C. (2018). *Euroscepticism and the Future of European Integration*. Oxford: Oxford University Press.

De Wilde, P. (2011). 'No Polity for Old Politics? A Framework for Analyzing Politicization of European Integration'. *Journal of European Integration*, 33: 559–75.

De Wilde, P. (2019). 'Media Logic and Grand Theories of European Integration'. *Journal of European Public Policy*, 26: 1193–212.

De Wilde, P., Leupold, A., and Schmidtke, H. (2016a). 'The Differentiated Politicisation of European Governance'. *West European Politics*, special issue, 39: 1–182.

De Wilde, P., Leupold, A., and Schmidtke, H. (2016b). 'Introduction: The Differentiated Politicisation of European Governance'. *West European Politics*, 39: 3–22.

Diebold, W., Jr (1959). *The Schuman Plan: A Study in Economic Cooperation, 1950–1959*. New York: Praeger.

Diez, T. (1999). 'Speaking "Europe": The Politics of Integration Discourse'. *Journal of European Public Policy*, 6: 598–613.

Diez, T. (2005). 'Constructing the Self and Changing Others: Reconsidering "Normative Power Europe"'. *Millennium: Journal of International Studies*, 33: 613–36.

Diez, T. (2007). 'Expanding Europe: The Ethics of EU–Turkey Relations'. *Ethics and International Affairs*, 21: 415–22.

Diez, T. and Wiener, A. (2004). 'Introducing the Mosaic of Integration Theory', in A. Wiener and T. Diez (eds), *European Integration Theory*. Oxford: Oxford University Press, 1–21.

Di Mauro, D. and Fraile, M. (2012). 'Who Wants More? Attitudes Towards EU Enlargement in Time of Crisis'. European Union Democracy Observatory (EUDO), Spotlight 04, October.

Dinan, D. (1994). *Ever Closer Union? An Introduction to the European Community*. London: Macmillan.

Dinan, D., Nugent, N., and Paterson, W. (eds) (2017). *The European Union in Crisis*. London, Palgrave Macmillan.

Dionigi, M. (2017). *Lobbying in the European Parliament. The Battle for Influence*. Basingstoke, Palgrave Macmillan.

Dolowitz, D. and Marsh, D. (1996). 'Who Learns What from Whom?'. *Political Studies*, 44: 343–57.

Dougan, M. (2008). 'The Treaty of Lisbon 2007: Winning Minds not Hearts'. *Common Market Law Review*, 45: 617–701.

Duchêne, F. (1973). 'The European Community and the Uncertainties of Interdependence', in M. Kohnstamm and W. Hager (eds), *A Nation Writ Large? Foreign-Policy Problems before the European Community*. London: Macmillan, 1–21.

Duchêne, F. (1994). *Jean Monnet: The First Statesman of Interdependence*. New York and London: W.W. Norton & Company.

Duff, A. (1997 *The Treaty of Amsterdam: Text and Commentary*. London: Federal Trust/Sweet and Maxwell.

Duff, A. (2009). *Saving the European Union. The Logic of the Lisbon Treaty*. London: Shoehorn Media.

Dullien, S. (2012). 'Why the Euro Crisis Threatens the Single Market', European Council of Foreign Affairs, Policy Memo 64, October.

Dumoulin, M. and Bitsch, M.-T. (2007). *The European Commission, 1958–1972: History and Memories*. Luxembourg: Office for Official Publications of the European Communities.

Dür, A. Bernhagen, P., and Marshall D. (2015). 'Interest Group Success in the European Union: When (and Why) does Business Lose?' *Comparative Political Studies*, 48: 951–83.

Dür, A., Bernhagen, P., and Marshall D. (2019). *The Political Influence of Business in the European Union*. Ann Arbor, MI: Michigan University Press.

Dyson, K. (1994). *Elusive Union: The Process of Economic and Monetary Union in Europe*. Harlow: Longman.

Dyson, K. and Featherstone, K. (1999). *The Road to Maastricht: Negotiating Economic and Monetary Union*. Oxford: Oxford University Press.

Dyson, K. and Goetz, K. (2002). 'Germany and Europe: Beyond Congruence', paper given to the British Academy Conference, Germany and Europe: A Europeanised Germany? London, 11 March.

Dyson, K. and Goetz, K. (eds) (2003). *Germany, Europe and the Politics of Constraint*. Oxford: Oxford University Press/British Academy.

The Economist (2013). 'Turkey's Protests: Erdogan Cracks Down', 22 June. http://www.economist.com/news/europe/21579873-vicious-police-tactics-have-reclaimed-taksim-square-and-other-places-protest-high.

Edquist, K. (2006). 'EU Social Policy Governance: Advocating Activism or Servicing States?' *Journal of European Public Policy*, 13: 500–18.

Edwards, G. and Pijpers, A. (1997), *The Politics of European Treaty Reform: The 1996 Intergovernmental Conference and Beyond*. London and Washington, DC: Pinter.

Egeberg, M. (2006), *Multilevel Union Administration: The Transformation of Executive Politics in Europe*. Basingstoke: Palgrave Macmillan.

Eichenberg, R. and Dalton, R. (2007). 'Post-Maastricht Blues: The Transformation of Citizen Support for European Integration, 1973–2004'. *Acta Politica*, 42: 128–52.

Eising, R. and Lehringer, S. (2010). 'Interest Groups and the European Union', in M. Cini and N. Pérez-Solórzano Borragán (eds), *European Union Politics* (3rd edn). Oxford: Oxford University Press, 189–206.

Ellina, C. (2003). *Promoting Women's Rights: The Politics of Gender in the European Union*. New York: Routledge.

523

Ellinas, A. and Suleiman, E. (2012). *The European Commission and Bureaucratic Autonomy*. Cambridge: Cambridge University Press.

Eriksen, E. and Fossum, J. (2002). 'Democracy through Strong Publics in the European Union'. *Journal of Common Market Studies*, 40: 401–24.

Eurobarometer (2019a) *Special Eurobarometer 490, Climate Change*, Luxembourg: Eurostat.

Eurobarometer (2019b) *Public Opinion in the European Union, Standard Eurobarometer 91*. Luxembourg: Eurostat.

European Asylum Support Office (2019). 'More than Half a Million Asylum Applications Lodged in the EU So Far in 2019', 19 November. https://www.easo.europa.eu/news-events/more-half-million-asylum-applications-lodged-eu-so-far-2019.

European Commission (1985). *Completing the Internal Market*. COM(85)310. Brussels: European Community.

European Commission (1989). *Guide to the Reform of the Community's Structural Funds*. Brussels/Luxembourg: European Communities.

European Commission (1995). *The Agricultural Situation in the European Union*. Brussels and Luxembourg: European Communities.

European Commission (1996). *Green Paper on Relations between the European Union and the ACP Countries on the Eve of the 21st Century—Challenges and Options for a New Partnership*. Brussels: European Commission.

European Commission (1999a). *Agenda 2000: For a Stronger and Wider Europe*. Brussels and Luxembourg: European Communities.

European Commission (1999b). *The Amsterdam Treaty: A Comprehensive Guide*. Brussels and Luxembourg: European Communities.

European Commission (2000). 'Partnership Agreement between the African, Caribbean, and Pacific Group of States of the One Part, and the European Community and its Member States, of the Other Part, signed in Cotonou, Benin, on 23 June 2000'. http://ec.europa.eu/world/agreements/downloadFile.do?fullText=yes&treatyTransId=818.

European Commission (2001). *European Governance: A White Paper*. COM(2001)428 final, 25 July. Brussels: Commission of the European Communities.

European Commission (2004). *First Report on the Implementation of the Internal Market Strategy 2003–2006*. COM(2004)22 final. Brussels: Commission of the European Communities.

European Commission (2006a). *A European Strategy for Sustainable, Competitive and Secure Energy*. Brussels: European Commission.

European Commission (2006b). *Global Europe: Competing in the World* (4th edn). Brussels: European Commission.

European Commission (2007). *Communication from the Commission to the European Parliament, the Council, the European Economic and Social Committee, and the Committee of the Regions on Mid-Term Review of the Sixth Community Environment Action Programme*. COM(2007)225final. Brussels: Commission of the European Communities.

European Commission (2010a). *Europe 2020: A Strategy for Smart, Sustainable, and Inclusive Growth*. Communication from the Commission 2020 final. Brussels: European Commission.

European Commission (2010b). *Trade, Growth and World Affairs: Trade Policy as a Core Component of the EU's 2020 Strategy*. Brussels: DG Trade.

European Commission (2011). 'White Paper on Transport: Roadmap to a Single European Transport Area—Towards a Competitive and Resource-Efficient Transport System', Brussels. https://ec.europa.eu/transport/sites/transport/files/themes/strategies/doc/2011_white_paper/white-paper-illustrated-brochure_en.pdf.

European Commission (2015a). 'Communication from the Commission to the European Parliament, the Council, the European Economic and Social Committee and the Committee of the Regions: A European Agenda on Migration', COM(2015) 240 final, Brussels: European Commission, 13 May.

European Commission (2015b). 'Completing Europe's Economic and Monetary Policy'. https://ec.europa.eu/commission/sites/beta-political/files/5-presidents-report.en.pdf.

European Commission (2017) 'Communication from the Commission—EU Law: Better Results through Better Application', OJC 18, 19 January 2017. Brussels: European Union.

European Commission (2018). 'DG Trade Statistical Guide', June. Brussels: European Union.

European Commission (2019a). 'Communication from the Commission—Towards a More Efficient and Democratic Decision Making in EU Tax Policy', COM(2019) 8 final. Brussels: European Union.

European Commission (2019b). *European Commission Human Resources Key Figures 2019*. Brussels: European Commission, 16 April.

European Commission. (2019c). 'The Post-2020 Common Agricultural Policy: Environmental Benefits and Simplification'. https://ec.europa.eu/info/sites/info/files/food-farming-fisheries/key_policies/documents/cap-post-2020-environ-benefits-simplification_en.pdf.

European Commission (2019*d*). 'Statistics on Environmental Infringements', 17 July 2019. https://ec.europa.eu/environment/legal/law/statistics.htm.

European Commission (2019*e*). 'Communication from the Commission to the European Parliament, the Council, the European Economic and Social Committee and the Committee of the Regions, United in Delivering the Energy Union and Climate Action—Setting the Foundations for a Successful Clean Energy Transition', COM(2019) 285 final. Brussels: European Union.

European Commission (2019*f*). 'Schengen Information System'. https://ec.europa.eu/home-affairs/what-we-do/policies/borders-and-visas/schengen-information-system_en.

European Commission (2019*g*). 'The European Pillar of Social Rights: From Words to Deeds, from Principles to Concrete Initiatives', Brussels, 9 April. https://ec.europa.eu/social/main.jsp?catId=1288&langId=en.

European Council (2009). 'Rules of Procedure of the European Council—Rules of Procedure of the Council', Luxembourg: Office for Publications of the European Union. https://europa.eu/european-union/sites/europaeu/files/docs/body/rules_of_procedure_of_the_council_en.pdf.

European Court of Auditors (2017). 'Greening: A More Complex Income Support Scheme, Not Yet Environmentally Effective', Special Report No. 21. https://www.eca.europa.eu/Lists/ECADocuments/SR17_21/SR_GREENING_EN.pdf.

European Parliament (1988). *Official Journal of the European Communities*. Annex. Debates of the European Parliament, 1988–9, no. 2–367.

European Parliament (2015). 'European Parliament Decision on Setting Up a Committee of Inquiry into Emission Measurements in the Automotive Sector, its Powers, Numerical Strength and Term of Office', 16 December 2015. https://www.europarl.europa.eu/doceo/document/B-8-2015-1424_EN.html?redirect.

European Parliament (2016). 'Activity Report on the Ordinary Legislative Procedure, 4 July 2014–31 December 2016 (8th Parliamentary Term)', European Parliament, Brussels. http://www.epgencms.europarl.europa.eu/cmsdata/upload/3ef941c7-9e08-44b8-8bb1-f84e0a2562a4/Activity-report-ordinary-legislative-procedure-2014-2016-en.pdf.

European Parliament (2017). 'Activity Report on the Ordinary Legislative Procedure, 4 July 2014–31 December 2016 (8th parliamentary term)', European Parliament: Brussels. http://www.epgencms.europarl.europa.eu/cmsdata/upload/7c368f56-983b-431e-a9fa-643d609f86b8/Activity-report-ordinary-legislative-procedure-2014-2016-en.pdf.

European Parliament (2019*a*). 'Council of the European Union: Facts and Figures', December 2019. https://www.europarl.europa.eu/RegData/etudes/BRIE/2019/646113/EPRS_BRI(2019)646113_EN.pdf.

European Parliament (2019*b*). 'Elections 2019: Highest Turnout in 20 Years, updated 2 July 2019. http://www.europarl.europa.eu/news/en/headlines/eu-affairs/20190523STO52402/elections-2019-highest-turnout-in-20-years.

European Parliament (2019*c*). 'The Impact of the UK's Withdrawal on the Institutional Set-Up and Political Dynamics within the EU'. Policy Department for Citizens' Rights and Constitutional Affairs Directorate General for Internal Policies of the Union, December 2019. https://www.europarl.europa.eu/RegData/etudes/STUD/2019/621914/IPOL_STU(2019)621914_EN.pdf.

European Parliament (2019*d*). 'Rules of the Procedure of the European Parliament, 9th Parliamentary Term', December 2019. https://www.europarl.europa.eu/doceo/document/RULES-9-2019-07-02-TOC_EN.html.

European Parliament (2020). 'The European Parliament after Brexit'. https://www.europarl.europa.eu/regData/etudes/ATAG/2020/642259/EPRS_ATA(2020)642259.EN.pdf.

European Union (2005). *From the ECSC to the Constitution: Treaty of Maastricht on European Union*. Brussels: Europa.

European Voice (2012). 'John Dalli Resigns'. *European Voice*, 16 October 2013. https://www.politico.eu/article/john-dalli-resigns/.

Exadaktylos, T. and Radaelli, C. (2009). 'Research Design in European Studies: The Case of Europeanization'. *Journal of Common Market Studies*, 47: 507–30.

Exadaktylos, T. and Radaelli, C. (eds) (2012). *Research Design in European Studies: Establishing Causality in Europeanization*. Basingstoke: Palgrave Macmillan.

Exadaktylos, T., Graziano, P., and Vink, M. (2020). 'Europeanization: Concept, Theory, and Methods', in S. Bulmer and C. Lequesne (eds), *The Member States of the European Union* (3rd edn). Oxford: Oxford University Press, 47–69.

Fabbrini, S. (2005). *Democracy and Federalism in the European Union and the United States: Exploring Post-National Governance*. Abingdon: Routledge.

Fabbrini, S. (2010). *Compound Democracies: Why the United States and Europe Are Becoming Similar*. Oxford: Oxford University Press.

Fabbrini, S. and Puetter, U. (eds) (2016). 'Integration without Supranationalisation: The Central Role of the European Council in Post-Lisbon EU Politics'. *Journal of European Integration*, 38: 481–95.

Faber, B. and Orbie, J. (2009). *Beyond Market Access for Economic Development: EU Africa Relations in Transition*. Abingdon: Routledge.

Fairbrass, J. (2003). 'The Europeanization of Business Interest Representation: UK and French Firms Compared'. *Comparative European Politics*, 1: 313–34.

Faist, T. and Ette, A. (2007). *The Europeanization of National Policies and Politics of Immigration: Between Autonomy and the European Union*. Basingstoke: Palgrave Macmillan.

Falkner, G. (2000). 'The Council or the Social Partners? EC Social Policy between Diplomacy and Collective Bargaining'. *Journal of European Public Policy*, 7: 705–24.

Farstad, F., Carter, N., and Burns, C. (2018). 'What does Brexit Mean for the UK's Climate Change Act?' *The Political Quarterly*, 89: 291–7.

Favell, A. (2008). *Eurostars and Eurocities: Free Movement and Mobility in an Integrating Europe*. Oxford: Blackwell.

Featherstone, K. and Papadimitriou, D. (2008). *The Limits of Europeanization. Policy Conflict and Reform Capacity in Greece*. Basingstoke: Palgrave Macmillan.

Featherstone, K. and Radaelli, C. (eds) (2003). *The Politics of Europeanization*. Oxford: Oxford University Press.

Feindt, P. (2010). 'Policy-Learning and Environmental Policy Integration in the Common Agricultural Policy, 1973–2003'. *Public Administration*, 88: 296–314.

Feus, K. (ed.) (2001). *The Treaty of Nice Explained*. London: Federal Trust for Education and Research.

Fioretos, K.-O. (1997). 'The Anatomy of Autonomy: Interdependence, Domestic Balances of Power, and European Integration'. *Review of International Studies*, 23: 293–320.

Flinders, M. (2008). *Delegated Governance and the British State: Walking without Order*. Oxford: Oxford University Press.

Flockhart, T. (2010). 'Europeanization or EU-ization? The Transfer of European Norms across Time and Space'. *Journal of Common Market Studies*, 48: 787–810.

Foreign and Commonwealth Office (2004). 'Turkey and the EU'. *Enlargement Update*, Spring 2004. London: FCO.

Forster, A. (1998). 'Britain and the Negotiation of the Maastricht Treaty: A Critique of Liberal Intergovernmentalism'. *Journal of Common Market Studies*, 36: 347–67.

Forsyth, M. G., Keens-Soper, H. M. A., and Savigear, P. (eds) (1970). *The Theory of International Relations: Selected Texts from Gentili to Treitschke*. London: George Allen & Unwin.

Fouilleux, E. (2007). 'The Common Agricultural Policy', in M. Cini (ed.), *European Union Politics* (2nd edn). Oxford: Oxford University Press, 340–55.

Franchino, F. (2007). *The Powers of the Union: Delegation in the EU*. Cambridge: Cambridge University Press.

Freestone, D. (1983). 'The European Court of Justice', in J. Lodge (ed.), *Institutions and Policies of the European Community*. London: Pinter, 45–53.

Frey-Wouters, E. (1980). *The EC and the Third World: The Lomé Convention and Its Impact*. New York: Praeger.

Friis, L. (1998). 'Approaching the "Third Half" of EU Grand Bargaining—The Post-Negotiation Phase of the "Europe Agreement Game"'. *Journal of European Public Policy*, 5: 322–38.

Friis, L. and Murphy, A. (1999). 'The European Union and Central and Eastern Europe: Governance and Boundaries'. *Journal of Common Market Studies*, 37: 211–32.

Frontex (2019). 'News Release: New Frontex Regulation Comes into Force', 12 April 2019. https://frontex.europa.eu/media-centre/news-release/new-frontex-regulation-comes-into-force-S0luwe.

Fuchs, G. (1994). 'Policy-Making in a System of Multi-Level Governance—The Commission of the European Community and the Restructuring of the Telecommunications Sector'. *Journal of European Public Policy*, 1: 177–94.

Fursdon, E. (1980). *The European Defence Community: A History*. London: Macmillan.

Galligan, Y. (2019). 'European Integration and Gender', in A. Wiener, T. Börzel, and T. Risse (eds), *European Integration Theory* (3rd edn). Oxford: Oxford University Press, 174–94.

Galligan, Y., Haupfleisch, R., Irvine, L., Korolkova, K., Natter, M., Schultz, U., and Wheeler S. (2017). 'Mapping the Representation of Women and Men in Legal Professions across the EU', Policy Department for Citizens' Rights and Constitutional Affairs, Directorate General for Internal Polities of the Union, PE596.804, August 2019. http://www.europarl.europa.eu/studies.

Garrett, G. (1995). 'The Politics of Legal Integration in the European Union'. *International Organization*, 49: 171–81.

Garrett, G. and Tsebelis, G. (1996). 'An Institutional Critique of Intergovernmentalism'. *International Organization*, 50: 269–99

Garrett, G., Kelemen, R. D., and Schultz, H. (1998). 'The European Court of Justice, National Governments, and Legal Integration in the European Union'. *International Organization*, 52: 149–76.

Geddes, A. (2006). 'The Politics of European Union Domestic Order', in K. E. Jørgensen, M. Pollack, and B. Rosamond (eds), *Handbook of European Union Politics*. London: SAGE Publications, 449–62.

Geddes, A. (2008). *Immigration and European Integration: Beyond Fortress Europe* (2nd edn). Manchester: Manchester University Press.

Geddes, A. (2018). 'The Politics of European Migration Governance'. *Journal of Common Market Studies: Annual Review*, 58: 120–30.

Geddes, A., Hadj-Abdou, L., and Brumat, L. (2020). *Migration and Mobility in the European Union*. London: Macmillan/Red Globe.

Genschel, P. and Jachtenfuchs, M. (2015). 'More Integration, less Federation: The European Integration of Core State Powers'. *Journal of European Public Policy*, 22: 42–59.

George, S. (ed.) (1992). *Britain and the European Community*. Oxford: Oxford University Press.

George, S. (1998). *An Awkward Partner: Britain in the European Community* (3rd edn). Oxford: Oxford University Press.

George, S. (2004). 'Multi-Level Governance and the European Union', in I. Bache and M. Flinders (eds), *Multi-Level Governance*. Oxford: Oxford University Press, 107–26.

Gibb, R. (2000). 'Post-Lomé: the European Union and the South'. *Third World Quarterly*, 21: 457–81.

Gilbert, M. (2008). 'Narrating the Process: Questioning the Progressive Story of European Integration'. *Journal of Common Market Studies*, 46: 641–62.

Gill, S. (1998). 'European Governance and New Constitutionalism: European Monetary Union and Alternatives to Disciplinary Neo-Liberalism in Europe'. *New Political Economy*, 3: 5–26.

Gillingham, J. (1991a). *Coal, Steel, and the Rebirth of Europe, 1945–1955*. Cambridge: Cambridge University Press.

Gillingham, J. (1991b). 'Jean Monnet and the European Coal and Steel Community: A Preliminary Appraisal', in D. Brinkley and C. Hackett (eds), *Jean Monnet: The Path to European Unity*. Basingstoke and London: Macmillan, 129–62.

Glarbo, K. (1999). 'Restructuring the CFSP of the EU'. *Journal of European Public Policy*, 6: 634–51.

Glaser, T. (1990). 'EEC/ACP Cooperation: The Historical Perspective'. *The Courier*, 120, March/April.

Gold, M., Cressey, P., and Leonard, E. (2007). 'Whatever Happened to Social Dialogue? From Partnership to Managerialism in the EU Employment Agenda'. *European Journal of Industrial Relations*, 13: 7–25.

Grabbe, H. (2001). 'How Does Europeanization Affect CEE Governance? Conditionality, Diffusion, and Diversity'. *Journal of European Public Policy*, 8: 1013–31.

Grabbe, H. (2003). 'Europeanization Goes East: Power and Uncertainty in the EU Accession Process', in K. Featherstone and C. Radaelli (eds), *The Politics of Europeanization*. Oxford: Oxford University Press, 303–27.

Grabbe, H. (2005). *The EU's Transformative Power: Europeanization through Conditionality in Central and Eastern Europe*. Basingstoke: Palgrave Macmillan.

Grant, C. (1994). *Delors: Inside the House that Jacques Built*. London: Nicholas Brealey Publishing.

Grant, W. (1997). *The Common Agricultural Policy*. Basingstoke and London: Macmillan.

Gravey, V. and Jordan, A. (2016). 'Does the European Union Have a Reverse Gear? Policy Dismantling in a Hyperconsensual Polity'. *Journal of European Public Policy*, 23: 1180–98.

Gray, A., Barigazzi J., and De la Baume, M. (2019). 'Who Killed the Spitzenkandidat?' *Politico*, 17 May 2019. https://www.politico.eu/article/who-killed-the-spitzenkandidat-european-parliament-election-2019-transition/.

Gray, M. Stubb, A. (2001). 'Keynote Article: The Treaty of Nice—Negotiating a Poisoned Chalice?', in G. Edwards and G. Wiessala (eds), *The European Union: Annual Review of the EU 2000/2001*. Oxford: Blackwell, 5–24.

Graziano, P. and Vink, M. (2007). *Europeanization: New Research Agendas*. Basingstoke: Palgrave Macmillan.

Green, R. H. (1976). 'The Lomé Convention: Updated Dependence or Departure towards Collective Self-Reliance?'. *African Review*, 6: 43–54.

Greenwood, J. (2003). *Interest Representation in the European Union*. Basingstoke: Palgrave Macmillan.

Greenwood, J. (2011). *Interest Representation in the European Union* (3rd edn). Basingstoke: Palgrave Macmillan.

Greenwood, J. (2017). *Interest Representation in the European Union* (4th edn). Basingstoke: Palgrave Macmillan.

Greenwood, J. (2019). 'Interest Organizations and European Union Politics', in *Oxford Research Encyclopaedias*, Politics. DOI:10.1093/acrefore/9780190228637.013.1162.

Greenwood, J. and Dreger, J. (2013). 'The Transparency Register: A European Vanguard of Strong Lobby Regulation?' *Interest Groups and Advocacy*, 2: 139–62.

527

Greer, A. (2017). 'Post-Exceptional Politics in Agriculture: An Examination of the 2013 CAP Reform'. *Journal of European Public Policy*, 24: 1585–603.

Groen, L. (2019). 'Explaining European Union Effectiveness (Goal Achievement) in the Convention on Biological Diversity: The Importance of Diplomatic Engagement'. *International Environmental Agreements*, 19: 69–87.

Gstöhl, S. and De Bièvre, D. (2018). *The Trade Policy of the European Union*. London: Palgrave Macmillan.

Guerrina, R., Haastrup, T., Wright, K. A. M., Masselot, A., MacRae, H., and Cavaghan, R. (2018). 'Does European Union Studies have a Gender Problem? Experiences from Researching Brexit'. *International Feminist Journal of Politics*, 20: 252–7.

Guild, E., Carrera, S., and Balzacq, T. (2008). 'The Changing Dynamics of Security in an Enlarged European Union', CEPS CHALLENGE Programme (Changing Landscape of European Liberty and Security), Research Paper 12. https://www.ceps.eu/ceps-publications/changing-dynamics-security-enlarged-european-union/.

Guiraudon, V. (2000). 'European Integration and Migration Policy: Vertical Policy-Making as Venue-Shopping'. *Journal of Common Market Studies*, 38: 251–71.

Guth, J. and Elfving, S. (2018). *Gender and the Court of Justice of the European Union*. Abingdon: Routledge.

Guyomarch, A., Machin, H., and Ritchie, E. (1998). *France in the European Union*. Basingstoke: Macmillan.

Haas, E. B. (1958). *The Uniting of Europe: Political, Social, and Economic Forces 1950–57*. London: Library of World Affairs.

Haas, E. B. (1968). *The Uniting of Europe: Political, Social, and Economic Forces, 1950–1957* (2nd edn). Stanford, CA: Stanford University Press.

Haas, E. B. (1970). 'The Study of Regional Integration: Reflections on the Joy and Anguish of Pre-theorizing', *International Organization*, 24: 607–46.

Haas, E. B. (2001). 'Does Constructivism Subsume Neo-Functionalism?', in T. Christiansen, K. E. Jørgensen, and A. Wiener (eds), *The Social Construction of Europe*. London: SAGE Publications, 22–31.

Haas, P. (1992). 'Introduction: Epistemic Communities and International Policy Coordination'. *International Organization*, 46: 1–35.

Habermas, J. (2001*a*). *The Postnational Constellation*. London: Polity Press.

Habermas, J. (2001*b*). 'Why Europe Needs a Constitution'. *New Left Review*, September/October: 11. http://newleftreview.org/II/11/jurgen-habermas-why-europe-needs-a-constitution.

Häge, F. (2013). 'Coalition Building and Consensus in the Council of the European Union'. *British Journal of Political Science*, 43: 481–504.

Hagemann, S. and Høyland, B. (2008). 'Parties in the Council?' *Journal of European Public Policy*, 15: 1205–21.

Hagemann, S., Bailer, S., and Herzog, A. (2019). 'Signals to their Parliaments? Governments' Use of Votes and Policy Statements in the EU Council'. *Journal of Common Market Studies*, 57: 634–50.

Hager, S. B. (2008). '"New Europeans" for the "New European Economy": Citizenship and the Lisbon Agenda', in B. Van Apeldoorn, J. Drahokoupil, and L. Horn (eds), *Contradictions and Limits of Neoliberal European Governance: From Lisbon to Lisbon*. Basingstoke and New York: Palgrave Macmillan, 106–24.

Hall, P. and Taylor, R. (1996). 'Political Science and the Three New Institutionalisms'. *Political Studies*, 44: 936–57.

Hallstein, W. (1962). *United Europe: Challenge and Opportunity*. Cambridge, MA, and London: Harvard University Press and Oxford University Press.

Hampshire, J. (2016). 'European Migration Governance since the Lisbon Treaty: Introduction to the Special Issue'. *Journal of Ethnic and Migration Studies*, 42: 537–53.

Hanf, K. and Soetendorp, B. (eds) (1998). *Adapting to European Integration: Small States and the European Union*. London: Longman.

Hantrais, L. (2000). *Gendered Policies in Europe: Reconciling Employment and Family Life*. Basingstoke: Macmillan.

Hart, K. (2015). 'The Fate of Green Direct Payments in the CAP Reform Negotiations', in J. Swinnen (ed.), *The Political Economy of the 2014–2020 Reforms of the Common Agricultural Policy: An Imperfect Storm*. London: Rowman Littlefield, 245–76.

Haverland, M. (2005). 'Does the EU Cause Domestic Developments? The Problem of Case Selection in Europeanization Research'. *European Integration online Papers (EIoP)*, 9(2). http://eiop.or.at/eiop/pdf/2005-002.pdf.

Hay, C. (2002). *Political Analysis: A Critical Introduction*. Basingstoke: Palgrave Macmillan.

Hay, C. and Rosamond, B. (2002). 'Globalization, European Integration, and the Discursive Construction of Economic Imperatives'. *Journal of European Public Policy*, 9: 147–67.

Hay, C. and Wincott, D. (2012). *The Political Economy of European Welfare Capitalism*. Basingstoke: Palgrave Macmillan.

Hayes-Renshaw, F. (2017). 'The Council of Ministers: Conflict, Consensus and Continuity', in D. Hodson and J. Peterson (eds), *The Institutions of the European Union* (4th edn). Oxford: Oxford University Press, 80–107.

Hayes-Renshaw, F. and Wallace, H. (2006). *The Council of Ministers* (2nd edn). Basingstoke: Palgrave Macmillan.

Hayes-Renshaw, F., Lequesne, C., and Mayor Lopez, P. (1989). 'The Permanent Representations of the Member States to the European Communities'. *Journal of Common Market Studies*, 28: 121–37.

Henry, G. (2019). 'EU Court Dismisses Ex-Commissioner John Dalli's Bid for Compensation'. *Politico* 6 June 2019. https://www.politico.eu/article/eu-court-dismisses-ex-commissioner-john-dallis-bid-for-compensation/.

Héritier, A., Kerwer, D., Knill, C., Lehmkuhl, D., Teutsch, M., and Douillet, A-C. (2001). *Differential Europe. The European Union Impact on National Policymaking*. Lanham, MD: Rowman and Littlefield.

Heron, T. and Siles-Brügge, G. (2012). 'Competitive Liberalization and the "Global Europe" Services and Investment Agenda: Locating the Commercial Drivers of the EU–ACP Economic Partnership Agreements'. *Journal of Common Market Studies*, 50: 250–66.

Hewitt, A. (1989). 'ACP and the Developing World', in J. Lodge (ed.), *The European Community and the Challenge of the Future*. London: Pinter, 285–300.

Higgins, A. (2012). 'Protest of Peace Prize for EU Turns Local'. *New York Times*, 9 December.

Hill, C. (1993). 'The Capability–Expectations Gap, or Conceptualising Europe's International Role'. *Journal of Common Market Studies*, 31: 305–28.

Hill, C. (2004). 'Renationalizing or Regrouping? EU Foreign Policy since 11 September 2001'. *Journal of Common Market Studies*, 42: 143–63.

Hill, C., Smith, M., and Vanhoonacker, S. (eds) (2017). *International Relations and the European Union* (3rd edn). Oxford: Oxford University Press.

Hix, S. (1994). 'The Study of the European Community: The Challenge to Comparative Politics'. *West European Politics*, 17: 1–30.

Hix, S. (1999). *The Political System of the European Union*. Basingstoke and London: Macmillan.

Hix, S. (2008). *What's Wrong with the European Union and How to Fix it*. Cambridge: Polity Press.

Hix, S. and Høyland, B. (2011). *The Political System of the European Union* (3rd edn). Basingstoke: Palgrave Macmillan.

Hix, S., Kreppel, A., and Noury, A. (2003). 'The Party System in the European Parliament: Collusive or Competitive?'. *Journal of Common Market Studies*, 41: 309–31.

Hix, S., Noury, A., and Roland, G. (2005). 'Power to the Parties: Cohesion and Competition in the European Parliament, 1979–2001'. *British Journal of Political Science*, 35: 209–34.

Hix, S., Noury, A., and Roland, G. (2007). *Democratic Politics in the European Parliament*. Cambridge: Cambridge University Press.

Hobolt, S. and De Vries, C. (2016). 'Turning against the Union? The Impact of the Crisis on the Eurosceptic Vote in the 2014 European Parliament Elections'. *Electoral Studies*, 44: 504–14.

Hobolt, S. and Spoon, J.-J. (2012). 'Motivating the European Voter: Parties, Issues and Campaigns in European Parliament Elections'. *European Journal of Political Research*, 51: 701–27.

Hodges, M. and Wallace, W. (eds) (1981). *Economic Divergence in the European Community*. London: Butterworth.

Hodson, D. and Maher, I. (2001). 'The Open Method as a New Mode of Governance: The Case of Soft Economic Policy Co-ordination'. *Journal of Common Market Studies*, 39: 719–46.

Hodson, D. and Peterson, J. (2017). *The Institutions of the European Union* (4th edn). Oxford: Oxford University Press.

Hoffmann, S. (1964). 'The European Process at Atlantic Cross-Purposes'. *Journal of Common Market Studies*, 3: 85–101.

Hoffmann, S. (1966). 'Obstinate or Obsolete? The Fate of the Nation State and the Case of Western Europe'. *Daedalus*, 95: 862–915.

Hoffmann, S. (1989). 'The European Community and 1992'. *Foreign Affairs*, 68: 27–47.

Hofmann, A. (2019). 'Left to Interest Groups? On the Prospects for Enforcing Environmental Law in the European Union'. *Environmental Politics*, 28: 342–64.

Holland, S. (1980). *Uncommon Market*. Basingstoke and London: Macmillan.

Hooghe, L. and Marks, G. (2003). 'Unravelling the Central State, But How?'. *American Political Science Review*, 97: 233–43.

Hooghe, L. and Marks, G. (2004). 'Contrasting Visions of Multi-Level Governance', in I. Bache and M. Flinders (eds), *Multi-Level Governance*. Oxford: Oxford University Press, 15–30.

Hooghe, L. and Marks, G. (2009). 'A Postfunctionalist Theory of European Integration: From Permissive Consensus to Constraining Dissensus'. *British Journal of Political Science*, 39: 1–23.

529

Hooghe, L. and Marks, G. (2018). 'Cleavage Theory Meets Europe's Crises: Lipset, Rokkan, and the Transnational Cleavage'. *Journal of European Public Policy*, 25: 109–35.

Hooghe, L. and Marks, G. (2019*a*). 'Is Liberal Intergovernmentalism Regressive? A Comment on Moravcsik (2018)'. *Journal of European Public Policy*, online first. DOI: 10.1080/13501763.2019.1582684.

Hooghe, L. and Marks, G. (2019*b*). 'Grand Theories of European Integration in the Twenty-First Century'. *Journal of European Public Policy*, 26: 1113–33.

Hopkin, J. (2020). *Anti-System Politics: The Crisis of Market Liberalism in Rich Democracies*. Oxford: Oxford University Press.

Horn, L. (2012). *Regulating Corporate Governance in the EU: Towards the Marketization of Corporate Control*. Basingstoke and New York: Palgrave Macmillan.

Hoskyns, C. (1996). *Integrating Gender: Women, Law, and Politics in the European Union*. London: Verso.

Hoskyns, C. (2004). 'Gender Perspectives', in A. Wiener and T. Diez (eds), *European Integration Theory*. Oxford: Oxford University Press, 217–36.

House of Commons (2012). 'The Treaty on Stability, Coordination and Governance in the Economic and Monetary Union: Political Issues'. *Research Paper* 12/14, 27 March.

Howorth, J. (2003). 'France, Britain, and the Euro-Atlantic Crisis'. *Survival*, 45: 173–92.

Howorth, J. (2004). 'The Role of Discourse, Ideas, and Epistemic Communities in the Forging of ESDP'. *West European Politics*, 27: 211–34.

Hu, Y. (1981). *Europe under Stress*. London: Butterworth.

Hughes, J., Sasse, G., and Gordon, C. (2004). 'Conditionality and Compliance in the EU's Eastward Enlargement'. *Journal of Common Market Studies*, 42: 523–51.

Humphreys, P. and Padgett, S. (2006). 'Globalization, the European Union, and Domestic Governance in Telecoms and Electricity'. *Governance: An International Journal of Policy, Administration, and Institutions*, 19: 383–406.

Hurt, S. R. (2003). 'Co-operation and Coercion? The Cotonou Agreement between the European Union and ACP States and the End of the Lomé Convention'. *Third World Quarterly*, 24: 161–76.

Huysmans, J. (2006). *The Politics of Insecurity: Fear, Migration, and Asylum in the EU*. Abingdon and New York: Routledge.

Ingebritsen, C. (1998). *The Nordic States and European Unity*. Ithaca, NY: Cornell University Press.

Jachtenfuchs, M. (2001). 'The Governance Approach to European Integration'. *Journal of Common Market Studies*, 39: 245–64.

Jamal, A. H. (1979). 'Preparing for Lomé Two'. *Third World Quarterly*, 1: 134–40.

Jenkins, R. (1977). 'Europe's Present Challenge and Future Opportunity: The First Jean Monnet Lecture Delivered at the European University Institute, Florence, 27 October 1977'. *Bulletin of the European Communities Supplement* 10/77: 6–14.

Jenkins, R. (1989). *European Diary, 1977–1981*. London: Collins (republished London: Bloomsbury, 2012).

Joint Transparency Register (2019). 'Transparency Register Statistics', 25 November 2019. https://ec.europa.eu/transparencyregister/public/consultation/statistics.do?locale=en&action=prepareView.

Jones, E., Kelemen, D., and Meunier, S. (2016). 'Failing Forward? The Euro Crisis and the Incomplete Nature of European Integration'. *Comparative Political Studies*, 49: 1010–34.

Jordan, A. (2001). 'The European Union: An Evolving System of Multi-Level Governance … or Government?' *Policy and Politics*, 29: 193–208.

Jordan, A. and Liefferink, D. (eds) (2004). *Environmental Policy in Europe: The Europeanization of National Environmental Policy*. London: Routledge.

Jordan, A., Wurzel, R. K .W., and Zito, A. R. (2003). '"New" Instruments of Environmental Governance: Patterns and Pathways of Change'. *Environmental Politics*, 12: 1–24.

Judge, D. (1992). 'Predestined to Save the Earth': The Environment Committee of the European Parliament. *Environmental Politics*, 1: 186–212.

Judge, D. and Earnshaw, D. (2002). 'The European Parliament and the Commission Crisis: A New Assertiveness?' *Governance*, 15: 345–74.

Judge, D., Earnshaw, D., and Cowan, N. (1994). 'Ripples or Waves: The European Parliament in the European Community Policy Process'. *Journal of European Public Policy*, 1: 27–52.

Juncker, J.-C. (2018). 'State of the Union 2018, The Hour of European Sovereignty, Authorised version of the State of the Union Address 2018'. https://ec.europa.eu/commission/priorities/state-union-speeches/state-union-2018_en.

Kaiser, W. and Elvert, J. (eds) (2004). *European Union Enlargement: A Comparative History*. London: Routledge.

Kaltenthaler, K. (2002). 'German Interests in European Monetary Integration'. *Journal of Common Market Studies*, 40: 69–87.

Kaltenthaler, K. (2006). *Policymaking in the European Central Bank: The Masters of Europe's Money*. Lanham, MD: Rowman and Littlefield.

Kantola, J. (2010). *Gender and the European Union*. Basingstoke: Palgrave Macmillan.

Kantola, J. (2019). 'European Integration and Disintegration: Feminist Perspectives on Inequalities and Social Justice'. *Journal of Common Market Studies*, 57 (Annual Review): 62–76.

Kantola, J. and Rolandsen Agustín, L. (2019). 'Gendering the Representative Work of the European Parliament: A Political Analysis of Women MEP's Perceptions of Gender Equality in Party Groups'. *Journal of Common Market Studies*, 57: 768–86.

Kapsis, I. (2010). 'The Courts of the European Union', in M. Cini and N. Pérez-Solórzano Borragán (eds), *European Union Politics* (3rd edn). Oxford: Oxford University Press, 176–88.

Kassim, H. (1994). 'Policy Networks, Networks, and European Union Policy Making: A Sceptical View'. *West European Politics*, 17: 15–27.

Kassim, H. (2008). '"Mission Impossible", But Mission Accomplished: The Kinnock Reforms and the European Commission'. *Journal of European Public Policy*, 15: 648–68.

Kassim, H. (2017). 'What's New? A First Appraisal of the Juncker Commission'. *European Political Science*, 16: 14–33.

Kassim, H. and Laffan, B. (2019). 'The Juncker Presidency: The "Political Commission" in Practice'. *Journal of Common Market Studies*, 57: 49–61.

Kassim H. and Le Galès P. (eds) (2010). 'Governing the European Union: Policy Instruments in a Multi-Level Polity'. *West European Politics*, special issue, 33(1): 1–170.

Kassim, H. Peterson, J., Bauer, M. W., Connolly, S. Dehousse, R., Hooghe, L., and Thompson, R. (2013). *The European Commission of the Twenty-First Century*. Oxford: Oxford University Press.

Kassim, H., Connolly, S., Dehousse, R., Rozenberg O., and Bendjaballah, S. (2017). 'Managing the House: The Presidency, Agenda Control and Policy Activism in the European Commission'. *Journal of European Public Policy,* 24: 653–74.

Katzenstein, P. (1996). *The Culture of National Security*. New York: Columbia University Press.

Kelemen, R.D. (2012). 'The Political Foundations of Judicial Independence in the European Union'. *Journal of European Public Policy*, 19(1): 43–58.

Kelemen, R. D. (2019). 'Federalism', in A. Wiener, T. Börzel, and T. Risse (eds), *European Integration Theory* (3rd edn). Oxford: Oxford University Press: 27–42.

Kelemen, R. D. and Schmidt, S. K. (2012). 'Introduction—the European Court of Justice and Legal Integration: Perpetual Momentum?' *Journal of European Public Policy*, 19(1): 1–7.

Keohane, R. (1984). *After Hegemony: Co-operation and Discord in the World Political Economy*. Princeton, NJ: Princeton University Press.

Keohane, R. (1989). 'Neoliberal Institutionalism: A Perspective on World Politics', in R. Keohane (ed.), *International Institutions and State Power*. Boulder, CO, San Francisco, CA, and Oxford: Westview Press, 1–20.

Keohane, R. and Nye, J. S., Jr (1977). *Power and Interdependence: World Politics in Transition*. Boston, MA: Little, Brown.

Khorana, S. and García, M. (2018). *Handbook on the EU and International Trade*. Cheltenham: Edward Elgar.

Kietz, D. and Parkes, R. (2008). 'Justiz- und Innenpolitik nach dem Lissabonner Vertrag', Diskussionspapier, Stiftung Wissenschaft und Politik, 13 May.

Kietz, D. and von Ondarza, N. (2010). 'Willkommen in der Lissabonner Wirklichkeit'. *SWP-Aktuell*, 29 March. Berlin: Stiftung Wissenschaft und Politik.

Knill, C. (2001). *The Europeanization of National Administrations: Patterns of Institutional Change and Persistence*. Cambridge: Cambridge University Press.

Knill, C., Steinebach, Y., and Fernández i Marín, X. (2018). 'Hypocrisy as a Crisis Response? Assessing Changes in Talk, Decisions, and Actions of the European Commission in EU Environmental Policy'. *Public Administration*, 1–15. https://doi.org/10.1111/padm.12542.

Kohler-Koch, B. (1996). 'Catching Up with Change: The Transformation of Governance in the European Union'. *Journal of European Public Policy*, 3: 359–80.

Kohler-Koch, B. and Eising, R. (eds) (1999). *The Transformation of European Governance*. London: Routledge.

Kohler-Koch, B. and Rittberger, B. (2006). 'The "Governance Turn" in EU Studies'. *Journal of Common Market Studies: Annual Review*, 44: 27–49.

Kratochvíl, P. and Sychra, Z. (2019). 'The End of Democracy in the EU? The Eurozone Crisis and the EU's Democratic Deficit'. *Journal of European Integration*, 41: 169–85.

Kreppel, A. (2000). 'Rules, Ideology, and Coalition Formation in the European Parliament: Past, Present, and Future'. *European Union Politics*, 1: 340–62.

Kröger, S. and Friedrich, D. (eds) (2012). *The Challenge of Democratic Representation in the European Union*. Basingstoke: Palgrave Macmillan.

Kronsell, A. (2005). 'Gender, Power and European Integration Theory'. *Journal of European Public Policy*, 12: 1022–40.

531

Krotz, U. (2009). 'Momentum and Impediments: Why Europe Won't Emerge as a Full Political Actor on the World Stage Soon'. *Journal of Common Market Studies*, 47: 555–78.

Kuper, R. (1998). *The Politics of the European Court of Justice*. London: Kogan Page.

Ladrech, R. (1994). 'Europeanization of Domestic Politics and Institutions: The Case of France'. *Journal of Common Market Studies*, 32: 69–88.

Laffan, B. (1997*a*). *The Finances of the European Union*. Basingstoke and London: Macmillan.

Laffan, B. (1997*b*). 'From Policy Entrepreneur to Policy Manager: The Challenge Facing the European Commission'. *Journal of European Public Policy*, 4: 422–38.

Laffan, B. (2014). 'In the Shadow of Austerity: Ireland's Seventh Presidency of the European Union'. *Journal of Common Market Studies*, 52 (Annual Review): 90–8.

Laffan, B. (2019). 'How the EU27 Came to Be'. *Journal of Common Market Studies*, 57 (Annual Review): 13–27.

Laqueur, W. (1972). *Europe since Hitler*. Harmondsworth: Penguin.

Lavenex, S. (2010). 'Justice and Home Affairs: Communitarization with Hesitation', in H. Wallace, M. Pollack, and A. Young (eds), *Policy-Making in the European Union* (6th edn; 7th edn 2015). Oxford: Oxford University Press, 458–77.

Le Galès, P. (2011). 'Policy Instruments and Governance', in M. Bevir (ed.), *The Sage Handbook of Governance*. London: Sage Publications, 142–59.

Lehman, W. (2009). 'The European Parliament', in D. Coen, and J. Richardson, J. (eds), *Lobbying the European Union, Institutions Actors and Issues*. Oxford: Oxford University Press, 39–69.

Lelieveldt, H. and Princen, S. (2011). *The Politics of the European Union* (2nd edn, 2015). Cambridge: Cambridge University Press.

Lenschow, A. (2007). 'Environmental Policy in the European Union: Bridging Policy, Politics, and Polity Dimensions', in K. E. Jørgensen, M. Pollack, and B. Rosamond (eds), *The SAGE Handbook of European Union Politics*. London: SAGE Publications, 413–31.

Leruth, B., Startin, N., and Usherwood, S. (2017). 'Defining Euroscepticism: From a Broad Concept to a Field of Study', in B. Leruth, N. Startin, and S. Usherwood (eds), *The Routledge Handbook of Euroscepticism*. London: Routledge, 3–10.

Leuffen, D., Rittberger, B., and Schimmelfennig, F. (2013). *Differentiated Integration: Explaining Variation in the European Union*. Basingstoke: Palgrave Macmillan.

Lewis, J. (1998). 'Is the "Hard Bargaining" Image of the Council Misleading? The Committee of Permanent Representatives and the Local Elections Directive'. *Journal of Common Market Studies*, 36: 479–504.

Lewis, J. (2000). 'The Methods of Community in EU Decision Making and Administrative Rivalry in the Council's Infrastructure'. *Journal of European Public Policy*, 7: 261–89.

Lewis, J. (2003*a*). 'Informal Integration and the Supranational Construction of the Council'. *Journal of European Public Policy*, 10: 996–1019.

Lewis, J. (2003*b*). 'The Council of the European Union', in M. Cini (ed.), *European Union Politics*. Oxford: Oxford University Press, 148–65.

Lewis, J. (2017). 'The Council of Ministers of the European Union'. *Oxford Research Encyclopaedia of Politics*. DOI:10.1093/acrefore/9780190228637.013.253.

Lindberg, B., Rasmussen, A., and Warntjen, A. (2008). 'Party Politics as Usual? The Role of Political Parties in EU Legislative Decision Making'. *Journal of European Public Policy*, 15: 1107–26.

Lindberg, L. (1963). *The Political Dynamics of European Economic Integration*. Stanford, MD: Stanford University Press; London: Oxford University Press.

Lindberg, L. (1966). 'Integration as a Source of Stress on the European Community System'. *International Organization*, 20: 233–65.

Lindberg, L. and Scheingold, S. (1970). *Europe's Would-Be Polity*. Englewood Cliffs, NJ: Prentice-Hall.

Locher, B. and Prügl, E. (2009). 'Gender and European Integration', in A. Wiener and T. Diez (eds), *European Integration Theory* (2nd edn). Oxford: Oxford University Press, 181–97.

Lodge, J. (ed.) (2005). *The 2004 Elections to the European Parliament*. Basingstoke: Palgrave Macmillan.

Loedel, P. H. (1998). 'Enhancing Europe's International Monetary Power: The Drive Toward a Single Currency', in P.-H. Laurent and M. Marseceau (eds), *The State of the European Union: Vol. 4, Deepening and Widening*. Boulder, CO and London: Lynne Rienner, 243–61.

Lord C. (2001). 'Democracy and Democratization in the European Union', in S. Bromley (ed.), *Governing the European Union*. London: SAGE Publications, 165–90.

Lord, C. (2002). 'Comparing Jacques Delors and Jacques Santer as Presidents of the European Commission. Skill in Supranational Context'. *Politics and Policy*, 30: 324–47.

Lowe, P., Buller, H., and Ward, N. (2002). 'Setting the Next Agenda? British and French Approaches to the Second Pillar of the Common Agricultural Policy'. *Journal of Rural Studies*, 18: 1–17.

Ludlow, P. (Peter) (1991). 'The European Commission', in R. Keohane and S. Hoffmann (eds), *The New European Community: Decision Making and Institutional Change*. Boulder, CO; San Francisco, CA; and Oxford: Westview Press, 85–132.

Ludlow, P. (Piers) (1997). *Dealing with Britain: The Six and the First UK Application to the EEC*. Cambridge: Cambridge University Press.

Lynggaard, K. (2007). 'The Institutional Construction of a Policy Field: A Discursive Institutional Perspective on Change within the Common Agricultural Policy'. *Journal of European Public Policy*, 14: 293–312.

McAllister, R. (2010). *European Union: An Historical and Political Survey* (2nd edn). London: Routledge.

McCormick, J. (2001). *Environmental Policy in the European Union*. Basingstoke: Palgrave Macmillan.

McGowan, L. and Cini, M. (1999). 'Discretion and Politicization in EU Competition Policy: The Case of Merger Control'. *Governance*, 12: 175–200.

McGowan, L. and Wilks, S. (1995). 'The First Supranational Policy in the European Union: Competition Policy'. *European Journal of Political Research*, 28: 141–69.

McKay, D. (2001). *Designing Europe: Comparative Lessons from the Federal Experience*. Oxford: Oxford University Press.

McQueen, M. (1998). 'Lomé Versus Free Trade Agreements: The Dilemma Facing the ACP Countries'. *World Economy*, 21: 421–43.

Machin, A. (2019). 'Changing the Story? The Discourse of Ecological Modernisation in the European Union'. *Environmental Politics*, 28: 208–27.

Magen, A. (2016). 'Cracks in the Foundations: Understanding the Great Rule of Law Debate in the EU'. *Journal of Common Market Studies*, 54: 1050–61.

Mair, P. (2007). 'Political Parties and Party Systems', in P. Graziano and M. Vink (eds), *Europeanization: New Research Agendas*. Basingstoke: Palgrave Macmillan, 154–66.

Mair, P. (2013). *Ruling the Void: The Hollowing of Western Democracy*. London: Verso.

Majone, G. (1991). 'Cross-National Sources of Regulatory Policymaking in Europe and the United States'. *Journal of Public Policy*, 11: 79–106.

Majone, G. (1996). *Regulating Europe*. London: Routledge.

Majone, G. (2001). 'Two Logics of Delegation: Agency and Fiduciary Relations in EU Governance'. *European Union Politics*, 2: 103–22.

Majone, G. (2002). 'The European Commission: The Limits of Centralization and the Perils of Parliamentarization'. *Governance*, 15: 375–92.

Mamadouh, V. and Raunio, T. (2003). 'The Committee System: Powers, Appointments, and Report Allocation'. *Journal of Common Market Studies*, 41: 333–51.

Mancini, G. F. (1991). 'The Making of a Constitution for Europe', in R. Keohane and S. Hoffmann (eds), *The New European Community: Decision Making and Institutional Change*. Boulder, CO; San Francisco, CO; and Oxford: Westview Press, 177–94.

Manners, I. (2002). 'Normative Power Europe: A Contradiction in Terms?'. *Journal of Common Market Studies*, 40: 235–58.

Manners, I. (2007). 'Another Europe is Possible', in K. E. Jørgensen, M. Pollack, and B. Rosamond (eds), *Handbook of European Union Politics*. London: SAGE Publications, 77–95.

Manners, I. (2008). 'The Normative Ethics of the European Union'. *International Affairs*, 84: 45–60.

March, J. G. and Olsen, J. (1984). 'The New Institutionalism: Organizational Factors in Political Life'. *American Political Science Review*, 78: 734–49.

March, J. G. and Olsen, J. (1989). *Rediscovering Institutions: The Organizational Basis of Politics*. New York and London: Free Press.

March, J. G. and Olsen, J. (1996). 'Institutional Perspectives on Political Institutions'. *Governance*, 9: 247–64.

Marks, G. (1993). 'Structural Policy and Multilevel Governance in the EC', in A. Cafruny and G. Rosenthal (eds), *The State of the European Community, Vol. 2: The Maastricht Debates and Beyond*. Boulder, CO: Lynne Rienner; Harlow: Longman, 391–410.

Marks, G., Hooghe, L., and Blank, K. (1996). 'European Integration from the 1980s: State-Centric v Multi-Level Governance'. *Journal of Common Market Studies*, 34: 341–78.

Marsh, D. W. (2009). *The Euro: The Politics of the New Global Currency*. New Haven, CT and London: Yale University Press.

Marsh, D. W. (2013). *Europe's Deadlock: How the Euro Crisis Could be Solved—and Why It Won't Happen*. New Haven, CT and London: Yale University Press.

Matlary, J. H. (1993). 'Towards Understanding Integration: An Analysis of the Role of the State in EC Energy Policy'. Oslo: University of Oslo, Ph.D. thesis.

533

Matlary, J. H. (1997). *Energy Policy in the European Union*. Basingstoke and London: Macmillan.

Matthews, A. (2013). 'The Ciolos CAP Reform', 17 December 2013. http://capreform.eu/the-ciolos-cap-reform/.

Matthews, A. (2018). 'The Greening Architecture in the New CAP', 20 June 2018. http://capreform.eu/the-greening-architecture-in-the-new-cap/.

Matthijs, M. and Blyth, M. (eds) (2015). *The Future of the Euro*. New York: Oxford University Press.

Matthijs, M. and McNamara, K. (2016). 'The Euro Crisis' Theory Effect: Northern Saints, Southern Sinners, and the Demise of the Eurobond'. *Journal of European Integration*, 37: 229–45.

Mayne, R. (1991). 'Gray Eminence', in D. Brinkley and C. Hackett (eds), *Jean Monnet: The Path to European Unity*. Basingstoke and London: Macmillan, 114–28.

Mazey, S. (1992). 'Conception and Evolution of the High Authority's Administrative Services (1952–1956): From Supranational Principles to Multinational Practices', in E. V. Heyen (ed.), *Yearbook of European Administrative History 4: Early European Community Administration*. Baden-Baden: Nomos, 31–47.

Mazey, S. (2012). 'Policy Entrepreneurship, Group Mobilization, and the Creation of a New Policy Domain: Women's Rights and the European Union', in J. Richardson, J. (ed), *Constructing a Policy-Making State? Policy Dynamics in the EU*. Oxford: Oxford University Press, 125–43.

Mazey, S. and Richardson, J. (2015). 'Shooting Where the Ducks Are: EU Lobbying and Institutionalized Promiscuity', in J. Richardson and S. Mazey (eds), *European Union. Power and Policy-Making* (4th edn). Abingdon: Routledge, 419–43.

Menon, A. and Schain, M. (eds) (2006). *Federalism in Europe and the United States*. Oxford: Oxford University Press.

Merlingen, M. (2007). 'Everything is Dangerous: A Critique of "Normative Power Europe"'. *Security Dialogue*, 38: 435–53.

Metcalfe, L. (1992). 'Can the Commission Manage Europe?'. *Australian Journal of Public Administration*, 51: 117–30.

Metcalfe, L. (2000). 'Reforming the Commission: Will Organizational Efficiency Produce Effective Governance?' *Journal of Common Market Studies*, 38: 817–41.

Meunier, S. (2007a). 'Managing Globalization? The EU in International Trade Negotiations'. *Journal of Common Market Studies*, 45: 905–26.

Meunier, S. (2007b). *Trading Voices: The European Union in International Commercial Negotiations*. Princeton, NJ: Princeton University Press.

Middlemass, K. (1995). *Orchestrating Europe: The Informal Politics of European Union, 1973–1995*. London: Fontana.

Milward, A. S. (1984). *The Reconstruction of Western Europe, 1945–51*. London: Routledge.

Milward, A. S. (1992). *The European Rescue of the Nation State*. London: Routledge.

Milward, A. S. and Deighton, A. (eds) (1999). *Widening, Deepening, and Acceleration: The European Economic Community 1957–1963*. Baden-Baden: Nomos.

Mitrany, D. (1943 [1966]). *A Working Peace System*. London: Royal Institute of International Affairs.

Mitrany, D. (1966). 'The Prospect of Integration: Federal or Functional'. *Journal of Common Market Studies*, 4: 119–49.

Mol, A., Spaargaren, G., and Sonnenfeld, D. (2014). 'Ecological Modernisation Theory: Taking Stock, Moving Forward', in S. Lockie, D. Sonnenfeld, and D. Fisher (eds), *Routledge International Handbook of Social and Environmental Change*. Abingdon: Routledge, 15–30.

Monar, J. (2001). 'The Dynamics of Justice and Home Affairs: Laboratories, Driving Factors, and Costs'. *Journal of Common Market Studies*, 39: 747–64.

Monnet, J. (1962). 'A Ferment of Change'. *Journal of Common Market Studies*, 1: 203–11.

Monti, M. (2010). 'A New Strategy for the Single Market: At the Service of Europe's Economy and Society', Report to the President of the European Commission.

Moravcsik, A. (1991a). 'Negotiating the Single European Act'. *International Organization*, 45: 19–56.

Moravcsik, A. (1991b). 'Negotiating the Single European Act', in R. O. Keohane and S. Hoffman (eds), *The New European Community: Decision Making and Institutional Change*. Boulder, CO and Oxford: Westview Press, 41–84.

Moravcsik, A. (1993). 'Preferences and Power in the European Community: A Liberal Intergovernmentalist Approach'. *Journal of Common Market Studies*, 31: 473–524.

Moravcsik, A. (1998). *The Choice for Europe: Social Purpose and State Power from Messina to Maastricht*. Ithaca, NY: Cornell University Press; London: UCL Press.

Moravcsik, A. (2002). 'In Defence of the "Democratic Deficit": Reassessing Legitimacy in the European Union'. *Journal of Common Market Studies*, 40: 603–24.

Moravcsik, A. (2018). 'Preferences, Power and Institutions in Twenty-First-Century Europe'. *Journal of Common Market Studies*. 56: 1648–74.

Moravcsik, A. and Nicolaïdis, K. (1999). 'Explaining the Treaty of Amsterdam: Interests, Influences, Institutions'. *Journal of Common Market Studies*, 37: 59–85.

Moravcsik, A. and Schimmelfennig, F. (2009). 'Liberal Intergovernmentalism', in A. Wiener and T. Diez (eds), *European Integration Theory* (2nd edn). Oxford: Oxford University Press, 67–87.

Moravcsik, A. and Schimmelfennig, F. (2019). 'Liberal Intergovernmentalism', in A. Wiener, T. Börzel, and T. Risse (eds), *European Integration Theory* (3rd edn). Oxford: Oxford University Press: 64–84.

Morgan, S. (2019). 'EU Leaders Claim Victory on 2050 Climate Goal, Despite Polish Snub'. *EurActiv*, 16 December 2019. https://www.euractiv.com/section/climate-environment/news/poland-snubs-climate-neutrality-deal-but-eu-leaders-claim-victory/.

Moser, P. (1996). 'The European Parliament as a Conditional Agenda Setter: What Are the Conditions? A Critique of Tsebelis (1994)'. *American Political Science Review*, 90: 834–8.

Moser, P. (1997). 'A Theory of the Conditional Influence of the European Parliament in the Cooperation Procedure'. *Public Choice*, 91: 333–50.

Mudde, C. and Kaltwasser, C. R. (2017). *Populism; A Very Short Introduction*. Oxford: Oxford University Press.

Müftüler-Bac, M. and McLaren, L. M. (2003). 'Enlargement Preferences and Policy-Making in the European Union: Impacts on Turkey'. *Journal of European Integration*, 25: 17–30.

Mügge, D. (2010). *Widen the Market, Narrow the Competition: Banker Interests and the Making of a European Capital Market*. Colchester: ECPR Press.

Murray-Evans, P. (2018). *Power in North–South Trade Negotiations: Making the European Union's Economic Partnership Agreements*. London: Routledge RIPE Series in Global Political Economy.

National Farmers' Union (NFU) (1996). *Briefing: 1996 US Farm Bill*. London: National Farmers' Union.

Naurin, D. (2015). 'Generosity in Inter-Governmental Relations: The Impact of State Power, Pooling and Socialisation in the Council of the European Union'. *European Journal of Political Research*, 54: 726–44.

Naurin, D. (2018). 'Liberal Intergovernmentalism in the Councils: A Baseline Theory?' *Journal of Common Market Studies*, 56: 1526–43.

Nicolaïdis, K. and Howse, R. (eds) (2001). *The Federal Vision: Legitimacy and Levels of Governance in the United States and the European Union*. Oxford: Oxford University Press.

Nielsen, N. (2019). 'Lobby Register Transparency Talks Collapse'. *EUObserver*, 5 April 2019. https://euobserver.com/institutional/144599.

Niemann, A. (2006). *Explaining Decisions in the European Union*. Cambridge: Cambridge University Press.

Niemann, A. and Schmitter, P. (2009). 'Neofunctionalism', in A. Wiener and T. Diez (eds), *European Integration Theory* (2nd edn). Oxford: Oxford University Press, 45–66.

Niemann, A. and Ioannou, D. (2015). 'EU Economic Integration in Times of Crisis: A Case of Neofunctionalism?' *Journal of European Public Policy*, 22: 196–218.

Niemann, A. and Speyer, J. (2018). 'A Neofunctionalist Perspective on the 'European Refugee Crisis': The Case of the European Border and Coast Guard'. *Journal of Common Market Studies*, 56: 23–43.

Niemann, A., Lefkofridi, Z., and Schmitter, P. (2019). 'Neofunctionalism', in A. Wiener, T. Börzel, and T. Risse (eds), *European Integration Theory* (3rd edn). Oxford: Oxford University Press: 43–63.

Norman, P. (2003). *The Accidental Constitution: The Making of Europe's Constitutional Treaty*. Brussels: EuroComment.

Nousios, P. (2012). 'The Contested Reconstruction of the Belle Époque? Europe 2020, Transnational Capitalism and the Political Economy of Global Restructuring', in P. Nousios, H. Overbeek, and A. Tsolakis (eds), *Globalisation and European Integration: Critical Approaches to Regional Order and International Relations*. Abingdon and New York: Routledge, 243–68.

Novak, S. (2013). 'The Silence of Ministers: Consensus and Blame Avoidance in the Council of the European Union'. *Journal of Common Market Studies*, 51: 1091–107.

Nugent, N. and Rhinard, M. (2015). *The European Commission*. Basingstoke: Palgrave Macmillan.

Nugent, N. and Rhinard, M. (2019). 'The 'Political' Roles of the European Commission'. *Journal of European Integration*, DOI: 10.1080/07036337.2019.1572135

O'Brennan, J. (2006). *The Eastern Enlargement of the European Union*. Abingdon: Routledge.

O'Brennan, J. (2008). *The European Union and the Western Balkans: Stability and Europeanization through Enlargement*. Abingdon: Routledge.

O'Brennan, J. (2013). 'Will Europe End in Croatia?', *Project Syndicate*, 30 June 2013. http://project-syndicate.org/commentary/the-consequences-of-the-eu-s-enlargement-fatigue-by-john-o-brennan.

O'Brennan, J. (2018). 'EU Enlargement to the Western Balkans: Towards 2025 and Beyond',

The Institute of International & European Affairs, 17 May. https://www.iiea.com/publication/iiea-publication-eu-enlargement-to-the-western-balkans-towards-2025-beyond.

Olsen, J. (2002). 'The Many Faces of Europeanization'. *Journal of Common Market Studies,* 40: 921–52.

Olsen, J. (2003). 'Europeanization', in M. Cini (ed.), *European Union Politics.* Oxford: Oxford University Press, 333–48.

O'Neill, O. (2000). *Britain's Entry into the European Community: Report by Sir Con O'Neill on the Negotiations of 1970–1972.* London: Frank Cass.

Orbie, J. and De Ville, F. (2014). 'The European Commission's Neoliberal Trade Discourse since the Crisis: Legitimizing Continuity through Subtle Discursive Change'. *British Journal of Politics and International Relations,* 16: 149–67.

Papadimitriou, D. and Phinnemore, D. (2004). 'Europeanization, Conditionality and Domestic Change: The Twinning Exercise and Administrative Reform in Romania'. *Journal of Common Market Studies,* 42: 619–39.

Parker, C., Karlsson, C., Hjerpe, M., and Linnér, B.-O. (2012). 'Fragmented Climate Change Leadership: Making Sense of the Ambiguous Outcome of COP-15'. *Environmental Politics,* 21: 268–86.

Parker, C. Karlsson, C., and Hjerpe, M. (2017). 'Assessing the European Union's Global Climate Change Leadership: From Copenhagen to the Paris Agreement'. *Journal of European Integration,* 39: 239–52.

Parker, O. (2008). 'Challenging New Constitutionalism in the EU: French Resistance, Social Europe, and Soft Governance'. *New Political Economy,* 13: 397–417.

Parker, O. (2009*a*). 'Why EU, Which EU? Habermas and the Ethics of Postnational Politics in Europe'. *Constellations: An International Journal of Critical and Democratic Theory,* 16: 392–409.

Parker, O. (2009*b*). '"Cosmopolitan Europe" and the EU–Turkey Question: The Politics of a "Common Destiny"'. *Journal of European Public Policy,* 16: 1085–101.

Parker, O. (2012*a*). 'Towards an Ambiguous "Cosmopolitics": Citizens and Entrepreneurs in the European Project'. *International Theory,* 4: 198–232.

Parker, O. (2012*b*). 'Roma and the Politics of EU Citizenship in France: Everyday Security and Resistance'. *Journal of Common Market Studies,* 50: 475–91.

Parker, O. (2013). *Cosmopolitan Government in Europe: Citizens and Entrepreneurs in Postnational Politics.* Abingdon and New York: Routledge.

Parker, O. (2016). 'Teaching (Dissident) Theory in Crisis European Union'. *Journal of Common Market,* 54: 37–52.

Parker, O. (2017). 'Commercializing Citizenship in Crisis EU: The Case of Immigrant Investor Programmes'. *Journal of Common Market Studies,* 55: 332–48.

Parker, O. (2018). 'A Genealogy of EU Discourses and Practices of Deliberative Governance: Beyond States and Markets?'. *Public Administration,* online first. https://doi.org/10.1111/padm.12558.

Parker, O. and Rosamond, B. (2013). '"Normative Power Europe" Meets Economic Liberalism: Complicating Cosmopolitanism Inside/Outside the EU'. *Cooperation and Conflict,* 48: 229–46.

Parker, O. and Tsarouhas, D. (eds) (2018). *Crisis in the Eurozone Periphery: The Political Economies of Greece, Spain, Ireland and Portugal.* London: Palgrave Macmillan.

Patomaki, H. (2013). *The Great Eurozone Disaster: From Crisis to Global New Deal.* London: Zed Books.

Pe'er, G., Dicks, L., Visconti., P., et al. (2014). 'EU Agricultural Reform Fails on Biodiversity'. *Science,* 344(6188): 1090–2.

Pelkmans, J. (1994). 'The Significance of EC-1992', in P.-H. Laurent (ed.), *The European Community: To Maastricht and Beyond.* Special Edition of *The Annals of the American Academy of Political and Social Science,* January: 94–111.

Pelkmans, J. and Winters, L. A. (1988). *Europe's Domestic Market.* London: Routledge.

Peters, B. G. (1997). 'The Commission and Implementation in the European Union: Is There an Implementation Deficit and Why?', in N. Nugent (ed.), *At the Heart of the Union: Studies of the European Commission.* Basingstoke and London: Macmillan, 187–202.

Peters, B. G. and Pierre, J. (2004). 'Multi-Level Governance and Democracy: A Faustian Bargain?', in I. Bache and M. Flinders (eds), *Multi-Level Governance.* Oxford: Oxford University Press, 75–89.

Peterson, J. (1991). 'Technology Policy in Europe: Explaining the Framework Programme in Theory and Practice'. *Journal of Common Market Studies,* 31: 473–524.

Peterson, J. (1992). 'The European Technology Community: Policy Networks in a Supranational Setting', in D. Marsh and R. A. W. Rhodes (eds), *Policy Networks in British Government.* Oxford: Oxford University Press, 226–48.

Peterson, J. (1995*a*). 'Decision Making in the European Union: Towards a Framework for Analysis'. *Journal of European Public Policy,* 2: 69–93.

Peterson, J. (1995*b*). 'Policy Networks and European Union Policy Making: A Reply to Kassim'. *West European Politics*, 18: 389–407.

Peterson, J. (2004). 'Policy Networks', in A. Wiener and T. Diez (eds), *European Integration Theory*. Oxford: Oxford University Press: 117–36.

Peterson, J. (2009). 'Policy Networks', in A. Wiener and T. Diez (eds), *European Integration Theory* (2nd edn). Oxford: Oxford University Press, 105–24.

Peterson, J. (2017). 'Juncker's Political European Commission and an EU in Crisis'. *Journal of Common Market Studies*, 55: 349–67.

Peterson, J. and Bomberg, E. (1993). 'Decision Making in the European Union: A Policy Networks Approach', paper prepared for presentation to the annual conference of the UK Political Studies Association, Leicester, 20–22 April.

Peterson, J. and Bomberg, E. (1999). *Decision Making in the European Union*. Basingstoke: Palgrave Macmillan.

Peterson, J. and Bomberg, E (2003). 'Making Sense of EU Decision Making', in B. Nelsen and A. Stubb (eds), *The European Union: Readings on the Theory and Practice of European Integration* (3rd edn). Basingstoke: Palgrave Macmillan.

Philippart, E. and Edwards, G. (1999). 'The Provisions on Closer Co-operation in the Treaty of Amsterdam'. *Journal of Common Market Studies*, 37: 109–20.

Phinnemore, D. (2010). 'The European Union: Establishment and Development', in M. Cini and N. Pérez-Solórzano Borragán (eds), *European Union Politics* (3rd edn). Oxford: Oxford University Press, 32–47.

Piattoni, S. (ed.) (2015). *The European Union: Democratic Principles and Institutional Architecture in Times of Crisis*. Oxford: Oxford University Press.

Pierre, J. (ed.) (2000). *Debating Governance: Authority, Steering, and Democracy*. Oxford: Oxford University Press.

Pierson, P. (1996). 'The Path to European Integration: A Historical Institutionalist Analysis'. *Comparative Political Studies*, 29: 123–63.

Pierson, P. (1998). 'The Path to European Integration: A Historical Institutionalist Analysis', in W. Sandholtz and A. Stone Sweet (eds), *European Integration and Supranational Governance*. Oxford: Oxford University Press, 27–58.

Piris, J.-C. (2010). *The Lisbon Treaty: A Legal and Political Analysis*. Cambridge: Cambridge University Press.

Poletti, A. and De Bièvre, D. (2014). 'The Political Science of European Trade Policy: A Literature Review with a Research Outlook'. *Comparative European Politics*, 12: 101–19.

Pollack, M. (1997). 'The Commission as an Agent', in N. Nugent (ed.), *At the Heart of the Union: Studies of the European Commission*. Basingstoke and London: Macmillan, 109–28.

Pollack, M. (2003). *The Engines of European Integration: Delegation, Agency and Agenda Setting in the EU*. Oxford: Oxford University Press.

Pollack, M. (2004). 'The New Institutionalisms and European Integration', in A. Wiener and T. Diez (eds), *European Integration Theory*. Oxford: Oxford University Press, 137–56.

Pollack, M. (2019). 'Rational Choice and Historical Institutionalism', in A. Wiener, T. Börzel, and T. Risse (eds), *European Integration Theory* (3rd edn). Oxford: Oxford University Press, 2019, 108–27.

Pollex, J. and Lenschow, A. (2020). 'Many Faces of Dismantling: Hiding Policy Change in Non-Legislative Acts in EU Environmental Policy'. *Journal of European Public Policy*, 27: 20–40.

Porter, B. (1987). *Britain, Europe and the World, 1850–1986: Delusions of Grandeur*. London: Allen & Unwin.

Preston, C. (1995). 'Obstacles to EU Enlargement: The Classical Community Method and the Prospects for a Wider Europe'. *Journal of Common Market Studies*, 33: 451–63.

Preston, C. (1997). *Enlargement and European Integration in the European Union*. London: Routledge.

Prügl, E. (2007). 'Gender and European Union Politics', in K. E. Jørgensen, M. Pollack, and B. Rosamond (eds), *Handbook of European Union Politics*. London: SAGE Publications, 433–48.

Puchala, D. (1975). 'Domestic Politics and Regional Harmonization in the European Communities'. *World Politics*, XXVII: 496–520.

Puetter, U. (2012). 'Europe's Deliberative Intergovernmentalism: The Role of the Council and European Council in EU Economic Governance'. *Journal of European Public Policy*, 19: 161–78.

Puetter, U. (2014). *The European Council and the Council. New Intergovernmentalism and Institutional Change*. Oxford: Oxford University Press.

Putnam, R. (1988). 'Diplomacy and Domestic Politics: The Logic of Two Level Games'. *International Organization*, 42: 427–60.

Radaelli, C. (2003). 'The Europeanization of Public Policy', in K. Featherstone and C. Radaelli (eds), *The Politics of Europeanization*. Oxford: Oxford University Press, 27–56.

537

Radaelli, C. (2004). 'Europeanisation: Solution or Problem?', paper presented to the ESRC/UACES Conference on the *Europeanization of British Politics*, Sheffield Town Hall, 16 July.

Radaelli, C. (2006). 'Europeanization: Solution or Problem?', in M. Cini and A. Bourne (eds), *Palgrave Advances in European Studies*. Basingstoke: Palgrave Macmillan, 56–76.

Radaelli, C. (2008). 'Europeanization, Policy Learning, and New Modes of Governance'. *Journal of Comparative European Policy Analysis*, 10: 239–54.

Radaelli, C. (2020). 'The Europeanization of Member State Policy', in S. Bulmer and C. Lequesne (eds), *The Member States of the European Union* (3rd edn). Oxford: Oxford University Press, 377–98.

Rankin, J. (2019). 'MEPs Reject Two EU Commissioner Candidates'. *The Guardian*, 26 September 2019. https://www.theguardian.com/world/2019/sep/26/meps-reject-two-eu-commissioner-candidates.

Rasmussen, H. (1986). *On Law and Policy in the European Court of Justice: A Comparative Study in Judicial Politics*. Dordrecht: Martinus Nijhoff.

Rasmussen, M. K. (2015). 'The Battle for Influence: The Politics of Business Lobbying in the European Parliament'. *Journal of Common Market Studies*, 53: 365–82.

Rattinger, H. (1994). 'Public Attitudes towards European Integration in Germany and Maastricht: Inventory and Typology'. *Journal of Common Market Studies*, 32: 525–40.

Recchi, E., Favell, A., Apaydin, F., Barbulescu, R., et al. (2019). *Everyday Europe: Social Transnationalism in an Unsettled Continent*. Bristol: Policy Press.

Remling, E. (2018). 'Depoliticizing Adaptation: A Critical Analysis of EU Climate Adaptation Policy'. *Environmental Politics*, 27: 477–97.

Rhodes, R. A. W. (1981). *Control and Power in Central-Local Relations*. Aldershot: Gower.

Rhodes, R. A. W. (1986). *The National World of Local Government*. London: Allen and Unwin.

Rhodes, R. A. W. (1988). *Beyond Westminster and Whitehall: The Sub-Central Governments of Britain*. London: Unwin Hyman.

Rhodes, R. A. W., Bache, I., and George, S. (1996). 'Policy Networks and Policy-Making in the European Union: A Critical Appraisal', in L. Hooghe (ed.), *Cohesion Policy and European Integration*. Oxford: Oxford University Press, 367–87.

Richardson, J. (1996). 'Actor-Based Models of National and EU Policy Making', in H. Kassim and A. Menon (eds), *The European Union and National Industrial Policy*. London and New York: Routledge, 26–51.

Ringe, N. (2010). *Who Decides and How? Preferences, Uncertainty and Policy Choice in the European Parliament*. Oxford: Oxford University Press.

Ripoll Servent, A. (2013). 'Holding the European Parliament Responsible: Policy Shift in the Data Retention Directive from Consultation to Codecision'. *Journal of European Public Policy*, 20: 972–87.

Ripoll Servent, A. (2018). *The European Parliament*. London: Palgrave.

Ripoll Servent, A. and Roederer Rynning, C. (2018). 'The European Parliament: A Normal Parliament in a Polity of a Different Kind'. *Oxford Research Encyclopaedias, Politics*. New York: Oxford University Press, DOI: 10.1093/acrefore/9780190228637.013.152.

Risse, T. (2003). 'The Euro between National and European Identity'. *Journal of European Public Policy*, 10: 487–505.

Risse, T. (2004). 'Social Constructivism and European Integration', in A. Wiener and T. Diez (eds), *European Integration Theory*. Oxford: Oxford University Press, 159–76.

Risse, T. (2009). 'Social Constructivism and European Integration', in A. Wiener and T. Diez (eds), *European Integration Theory* (2nd edn). Oxford: Oxford University Press, 144–60.

Risse, T. (2019). 'Social Constructivism and European Integration', in A. Wiener, T. Börzel, and T. Risse (eds), *European Integration Theory* (3rd edn). Oxford: Oxford University Press, 128–47.

Risse, T. and Wiener, A. (1999). '"Something Rotten" and the Social Construction of Social Constructivism: A Comment on Comments'. *Journal of European Public Policy*, 6: 775–82.

Risse, T., Cowles, M. G., and Caporaso, J. (2001). 'Europeanization and Domestic Change: Introduction', in M. G. Cowles, J. Caporaso, and T. Risse (eds), *Transforming Europe: Europeanization and Domestic Change*. Ithaca, NY, and London: Cornell University Press, 1–20.

Rittberger, B. (2003). 'The Creation and Empowerment of the European Parliament'. *Journal of Common Market Studies*, 41: 203–25.

Rittberger, B. (2005). *Building Europe's Parliament: Democratic Representation beyond the Nation State*. Oxford: Oxford University Press.

Roederer-Rynning, C. (2019). 'The Common Agricultural Policy: A Case of Embedded Liberalism'. *Oxford Research Encyclopaedia Politics*. DOI: 10.1093/acrefore/9780190228637.013.1032.

Roederer-Rynning, C. and Schimmelfennig, F. (2012). 'Bringing Codecision to Agriculture: A Hard Case of Parliamentarization'. *Journal of European Public Policy*, 19: 951–68.

Rosamond, B. (2000). *Theories of European Integration*. Basingstoke: Macmillan.

Rosamond, B. (2002). 'Imagining the European Economy: "Competitiveness" and the Social Construction of "Europe" as an Economic Space'. *New Political Economy*, 7: 157–77.

Rosamond, B. (2003). 'New Theories of European Integration', in M. Cini (ed.), *European Union Politics*. Oxford: Oxford University Press, 109–27.

Rosamond, B. (2007). 'European Integration and the Social Science of EU Studies: The Disciplinary Politics of a Sub-Field'. *International Affairs*, 83: 231–52.

Rosamond, B. (2013). 'Theorizing the European Union after Integration Theory', in M. Cini and N. Pérez-Solórzano Borragán (eds), *European Union Politics* (3rd edn). Oxford: Oxford University Press, 85–102.

Ross, G. (1995). *Jacques Delors and European Integration*. Cambridge: Polity Press.

Roth, S. (2008). *Gender Politics in the Expanding European Union: Mobilization, Inclusion, Exclusion*. New York and Oxford: Berghahn Books.

Ryner, M. (2012). 'Financial Crisis, Orthodoxy, and Heterodoxy in the Production of Knowledge about the EU'. *Millennium: Journal of International Studies*, 40: 647–73.

Ryner, M. and Cafruny, A. (2017). *The European Union and Global Capitalism: Origins, Development, Crisis*. London: Palgrave Macmillan.

Sabatier, P. (1988). 'An Advocacy Coalition Framework of Policy Change and the Role of Policy-Oriented Learning Therein'. *Policy Sciences*, 21: 129–68.

Sabatier, P. (1998). 'The Advocacy Coalition Framework: Revisions and Relevance for Europe'. *Journal of European Public Policy*, 5: 98–130.

Sabel, C. and Zeitlin, J. (2010). *Experimentalist Governance in the European Union: Towards a New Architecture*. Oxford: Oxford University Press.

Sandholtz, W. (1993). 'Choosing Union: Monetary Politics and Maastricht'. *International Organization*, 47: 1–39.

Sandholtz, W. and Stone Sweet, A. (1998). *European Integration and Supranational Governance*. Oxford: Oxford University Press.

Sandholtz, W. and Zysman, J. (1989). '1992: Recasting the European Bargain'. *World Politics*, 42: 95–128.

Saurugger, S. (2013). *Theoretical Approaches to European Integration*. Basingstoke and New York: Palgrave Macmillan.

Sbragia, A. (2003). 'Key Policies', in E. Bomberg and A. Stubb (eds), *The European Union: How Does it Work?* Oxford: Oxford University Press, 111–35.

Scharpf, F. (1989). 'The Joint-Decision Trap: Lessons from German Federalism and European Integration'. *Public Administration*, 66: 239–78.

Scharpf, F. (1998). *Governing in Europe: Effective and Democratic?* Oxford: Oxford University Press.

Scharpf, F. (1999). 'Review Section Symposium: The Choice for Europe: Social Purpose and State Power from Messina to Maastricht. Selecting Cases and Testing Hypotheses'. *Journal of European Public Policy*, 6: 164–8.

Scharpf, F. (2010). 'The Double Asymmetry of European Integration, or Why the EU Cannot Be a Social Market Economy'. *Socio-Economic Review*, 8: 211–50.

Scheinman, L. (1967). 'Euratom: Nuclear Integration in Europe'. *International Conciliation*, no. 563.

Schimmelfennig, F. (2015). 'Europeanization beyond Europe'. *Living Reviews in European Governance*, Vol. 10(1). http://europeangovernance-livingreviews.org/Articles/lreg-2015–1/.

Schimmelfennig, F. and Sedelmeier, U. (2002). 'Theorizing Enlargement: Research Focus, Hypotheses, and the State of Research'. *Journal of European Public Policy*, 9: 500–28.

Schimmelfennig, F. and Sedelmeier, U. (2004). 'Governance by Conditionality: EU Rule Transfer to the Candidate Countries of Central and Eastern Europe'. *Journal of European Public Policy*, 11: 661–79.

Schimmelfennig, F. and Sedelmeier, U. (eds) (2005). *The Europeanization of Central and Eastern Europe*. Ithaca, NY: Cornell University Press.

Schimmelfennig, F. and Sedelmeier, U. (2006). 'The Study of EU Enlargement: Theoretical Approaches and Empirical Findings', in M. Cini and A. Bourne (eds), *Palgrave Advances in European Union Studies*. Basingstoke: Palgrave Macmillan, 96–116.

Schmidt, V. (2006). *Democracy in Europe*. Oxford: Oxford University Press.

Schmidt, V. (2013). 'Democracy and Legitimacy in the European Union Revisited: Input, Output and "Throughput"'. *Political Studies*, 61: 2–22.

Schmidt, V (2014). 'Speaking to the Markets or to the People? A Discursive Institutionalist Analysis of EU Leaders' Discourse during the Eurozone Crisis'. *British Journal of Politics and International Relations*, 16: 188–209.

Schmidt, V. and Wood, M. (2019). 'Conceptualizing Throughput Legitimacy: Procedural Mechanisms of accountability, Transparency, Inclusiveness and Openness in EU Governance', *Public Administration*, online first. https://doi.org/10.1111/padm.12615.

539

Schmitter, P. (1970). 'A Revised Theory of Regional Integration'. *International Organization*, 24: 836–68.

Schneider, G. and Aspinwall, M. (eds) (2001). *The Rules of Integration: Institutionalist Approaches to the Study of Europe*. Manchester: Manchester University Press.

Schütze, R. (2012). *European Constitutional Law*. Cambridge: Cambridge University Press.

Scipioni, M. (2018). 'Failing Forward in EU Migration Policy? EU Integration after the 2015 Asylum and Migration Crisis'. *Journal of European Public Policy*, 25: 1357–75.

Scully, R. M. (1997*a*). 'The European Parliament and the Co-Decision Procedure: A Reassessment'. *Journal of Legislative Studies*, 3: 58–73.

Scully, R. M. (1997*b*). 'The European Parliament and Co-Decision: A Rejoinder to Tsebelis and Garrett'. *Journal of Legislative Studies*, 3: 93–103.

Sedelmeier, U. and Young, A. (2008). 'Editorial: The EU in 2007: Development without Drama, Progress without Passion'. *Journal of Common Market Studies, Annual Review*, 46: 1–5.

Seibicke, H. (2019). 'Gender Expertise in Public Policymaking: The European Women's Lobby and the EU Maternity Leave Directive', *Social Politics: International Studies in Gender, State & Society*. DOI:10.1093/sp/jxz007.

Shackleton, M. and Raunio, T. (2003). 'Co-Decision since Amsterdam: A Laboratory for Institutional Innovation and Change'. *Journal of European Public Policy*, 10: 171–87.

Sharp, M. (1989). 'The Community and the New Technologies', in J. Lodge (ed.), *The European Community and the Challenge of the Future*. London: Pinter, 223–40.

Sharp, M. and Shearman, C. (1987). *European Technological Collaboration*. London: Royal Institute of International Affairs/Routledge and Kegan Paul.

Shotter, J. (2018). 'Poland's Fight with Brussels Backfires'. *The Financial Times,* 27 November.

Siles-Brügge, G. (2014). *Constructing European Union Trade Policy: A Global Idea of Europe*. Basingstoke: Palgrave Macmillan.

Skeete, J.-P. (2017). 'Examining the Role of Policy Design and Policy Interaction in EU Automotive Emissions Performance Gaps'. *Energy Policy*, 104: 373–81.

Skjærseth, J.B. and Wettestad, J. (2009). 'The Origin, Evolution and Consequences of the EU Emissions Trading System'. *Global Environmental Politics*, 9: 101–22.

Smith, J. (1999). *Europe's Elected Parliament*. Sheffield: Sheffield Academic Press/University Association for Contemporary European Studies.

Smith, K. (2000). 'The End of Civilian Power EU: A Welcome Demise or a Cause for Concern?'. *The International Spectator*, 35: 11–28.

Smith, K. (2013). *European Union Foreign Policy in a Changing World* (2nd edn), Cambridge: Polity Press.

Smith, M. E. (1999). 'Rules, Transgovernmentalism, and the Expansion of European Political Cooperation', in W. Sandholtz and A. Stone Sweet (eds), *European Integration and Supranational Governance*. Oxford: Oxford University Press, 304–33.

Smith, M. E. (2000). 'Conforming to Europe: The Domestic Impact of EU Foreign Policy Co-operation'. *Journal of European Public Policy*, 7: 613–31.

Smith, M. E. (2001). 'Diplomacy by Decree: The Legalization of EU Foreign Policy'. *Journal of Common Market Studies*, 39: 79–104.

Smith, M. E. (2003). 'The Framing of European Foreign and Security Policy: Towards a Post-Modern Policy Framework?' *Journal of European Public Policy*, 10: 556–75.

Smith, M. E. (2004). 'Institutionalization, Policy Adaptation and European Foreign Policy Co-operation'. *European Journal of International Relations*, 10: 95–136.

Smith, M. E. (2017). *Europe's Common Security and Defence Policy: Capacity-Building, Experiential Learning and Institutional Change*. Cambridge: Cambridge University Press.

Smith, M. P. (1998). 'Autonomy by the Rules: The European Commission and the Development of State Aid Policy'. *Journal of Common Market Studies*, 36: 55–78.

Spierenburg, D. and Poidevin, R. (1994). *The History of the High Authority of the European Coal and Steel Community: Supranationality in Action*. London: Weidenfeld.

Statham, P., and Trenz, H.-J. (2013). *The Politicization of Europe: Contesting the Constitution in the Mass Media*. Abingdon: Routledge.

Statham, P., and Trenz, H.-J. (2015). 'Understanding the Mechanisms of EU Politicization: Lessons from the Eurozone Crisis'. *Comparative European Politics*, 13: 287–306.

Steinebach, Y. and Knill, C. (2017). 'Still an Entrepreneur? The Changing Role of the European Commission in EU Environmental Policymaking'. *Journal of European Public Policy* 24: 429–46.

Sternberg, C.S. (2013). *The Struggle for EU Legitimacy: Public Contestation, 1950–2005*. Basingstoke: Palgrave Macmillan.

Stevens, C. (1984). *The EEC and the Third World: A Survey. 4: Renegotiating Lomé*. London: Hodder and Stoughton.

Stone Sweet, A. and Sandholtz, W. (1997). 'European Integration and Supranational Governance'. *Journal of European Public Policy*, 4: 297–317.

Stone Sweet, A., Sandholtz, W., and Fligstein, N. (eds) (2001). *The Institutionalization of Europe*. Oxford: Oxford University Press.

Swinbank, A. and Daugbjerg, C. (2006). 'The 2003 CAP Reform: Accommodating WTO Pressures'. *Comparative European Politics*, 4: 47–64.

Szczerbiak, A. and Taggart, P. (eds) (2008). *Opposing Europe? The Comparative Party Politics of Euroscepticism: 2 Vols*, Oxford: Oxford University Press.

Szczerbiak, A. and Taggart, P. (2017). 'Contemporary Research on Euroscepticism: The State of the Art', in B. Leruth, N. Startin, and S. Usherwood (eds), *The Routledge Handbook of Euroscepticism*, London: Routledge, 11–21.

Taggart, P. (1998). 'A Touchstone of Dissent: Euroscepticism in Contemporary Western European Party Systems'. *European Journal of Political Research*, 33: 363–88.

Taggart, P. and Szczerbiak, A. (2018). 'Putting Brexit into Perspective: The Effect of the Eurozone and Migration Crises and Brexit on Euroscepticism in European States'. *Journal of European Public Policy*, 25: 1194–214.

Tallberg, J. (2003). 'The Agenda-Shaping Powers of the EU Council Presidency'. *Journal of European Public Policy*, 10: 1–19.

Tallberg, J. and Johansson, K. M. (2008). 'Party Politics in the European Council'. *Journal of European Public Policy*, 15: 1222–42.

Tamma, P. (2017). 'Future CAP: Court of Auditors Slams 'Ineffective' Greening Measures'. *EurActiv*, 12 December 2017. https://www.euractiv.com/section/agriculture-food/news/future-cap-court-of-auditors-slams-ineffective-greening-measures/.

Thunberg, G. (2019). Speech, United Nations, 23 September 2019. https://news.un.org/en/story/2019/09/1047052.

Tocci, N. (2017). 'From the European Security Strategy to the EU Global Strategy: Explaining the Journey'. *International Politics,* 54: 487–502.

Töller, A. (2010). 'Measuring and Comparing the Europeanization of National Legislation: A Research Note'. *Journal of Common Market Studies*, 48: 417–44.

Tooze, A. (2018*a*). *Crashed: How a Decade of Financial Crisis Changed the World*. UK: Allen Lane.

Tooze, A. (2018*b*). 'The Bank that Nearly Broke Europe'. *Prospect*, September 2018.

Tranholm-Mikkelsen, J. (1991). 'Neofunctionalism: Obstinate or Obsolete? A Reappraisal in the Light of the New Dynamism of the European Community'. *Millennium: Journal of International Studies*, 20: 1–22.

Tsebelis, G. and Garrett, G. (1996). 'Agenda Setting Power, Power Indices, and Decision Making in the European Union'. *International Review of Law and Economics*, 16: 345–61.

Tsebelis, G. and Garrett, G. (2000). 'Legislative Politics in the European Union'. *European Union Politics*, 1: 9–36.

Tsebelis, G. and Garrett, G. (2001). 'The Institutional Foundations of Intergovernmentalism and Supranationalism in the European Union'. *International Organization*, 55: 357–90.

Tsoukalis, L. (1977). *The Politics and Economics of European Monetary Integration*. London: Allen & Unwin.

Turnbull, P. and Sandholtz, W. (2001). 'Policing and Immigration: The Creation of New Policy Spaces', in A. Stone Sweet, W. Sandholtz, and N. Fligstein (eds), *The Institutionalization of Europe*. Oxford: Oxford University Press, 194–220.

Uçarer, E. (2019). 'The Area of Freedom, Security and Justice', in M. Cini and N. Pérez-Solórzano Borragán (eds), *European Union Politics* (6th edn). Oxford: Oxford University Press, 323–42.

Urwin, D. W. (1985). *Western Europe Since 1945: A Short Political History* (4th edn). London and New York: Longman.

Urwin, D. W. (1994). *The Community of Europe: A History of European Integration since 1945* (2nd edn). New York: Longman.

van Apeldoorn, B. (2002). *Transnational Capitalism and the Struggle over European Integration*. London and New York: Routledge.

van Apeldoorn, B and Horn, L. (2019). 'Critical Political Economy', in A. Wiener, T. Börzel, and T. Risse (eds), *European Integration Theory* (3rd edn), Oxford: Oxford University Press, 195–215.

van Apeldoorn, B., Overbeek, H., and Ryner, M. (2003). 'Theories of European Integration: A Critique', in A. Cafruny, and M. Ryner (eds), *A Ruined Fortress? Neoliberal Hegemony and Transformation in Europe*. Lanham, MD: Rowman and Littlefield, 17–46.

van der Veen, M. (2010). 'Ireland Votes "No", Then "Yes" Once More: The Lisbon Treaty Referenda'. *European Union Studies Association (ELISA) Review*, 23: 1. http://citeseerx.ist.psu.edu/viewdoc/download?doi=10.1.1.206.592&rep=rep1&type=pdf.

van Geffen, R. (2016). 'Impact of Career Paths on MEPs' Activities'. *Journal of Common Market Studies*, 54: 1017–32.

Van Munster, R. (2009). *Securitizing Immigration: The Politics of Risk in the EU*. Basingstoke and New York: Palgrave Macmillan.

Vaughan-Williams, N. (2008). 'Borderwork beyond Inside/Outside? Frontex, the Citizen-Detective, and the War on Terror'. *Space and Polity*, 12: 63–79.

Vaughan-Williams, N. (2015). *Europe's Border Crisis: Biopolitical Security and Beyond*. Oxford: Oxford University Press.

Verdun, A. (1999). 'The Role of the Delors Committee in the Creation of EMU: An Epistemic Community?'. *Journal of Common Market Studies*, 34: 531–48.

Versluis, E., van Keulen, M., and Stephenson, P. (2011). *Analyzing the European Union Policy Process*. Basingstoke: Palgrave Macmillan.

Vink, M. and Graziano, P. (2007). 'Challenges of a New Research Agenda', in P. Graziano and M. Vink (eds), *Europeanization: New Research Agendas*. Basingstoke: Palgrave Macmillan, 3–20.

Vollaard, H. (2014). 'Explaining European Disintegration'. *Journal of Common Market Studies*. 52: 1142–59.

Vollaard, H. (2018). *European Disintegration. A Search for Explanations*. Basingstoke: Palgrave Macmillan.

VoteWatch Europe (2013). '20 Years of Co-Decision: A More (Party) Political Parliament, a Less Consensual Council', Special Report. Brussels: VoteWatch Europe, December. http://votewatch.eu/blog/wp-content/uploads/2013/12/votewatch-europe-special-policy-brief-20-years-of-co-decision_final.pdf.

VoteWatch (2019). 'How the Old "Pro-Anti" EU Framing becomes Obsolete after EU Elections', 22 May 2019. https://www.votewatch.eu/blog/how-the-old-pro-anti-eu-framing-becomes-obsolete-after-eu-elections/.

Waever, O. (1996). 'European Security Identities'. *Journal of Common Market Studies*, 34: 103–32.

Wallace, H. (1986). 'The British Presidency of the European Community's Council of Ministers'. *International Affairs*, 62: 583–99.

Wallace, H. (1999). 'Piecing the Integration Jigsaw Together'. *Journal of European Public Policy*, 6: 155–79.

Wallace, W. and Allen, D. (1977). 'Political Co-operation: Procedure as Substitute for Policy', in H. Wallace, W. Wallace, and C. Webb (eds), *Policy-Making in the European Communities*. London: John Wiley and Sons, 227–48.

Wallace, H., Pollack, M., Roederer-Rynning, C., and Young, A. (2015). *Policy-Making in the European Union* (8th edn, 2020). Oxford: Oxford University Press.

Walters, W. and Haahr, J. (2005). *Governing Europe: Discourse, Governmentality, and European Integration*. Abingdon and New York: Routledge.

Waterfield, B. (2011). 'European Parliament Member Resigns over 'Cash for Laws' scandal'. *The Telegraph*. 20 March 2011. https://www.telegraph.co.uk/news/worldnews/europe/eu/8393797/European-Parliament-member-resigns-over-cash-for-laws-scandal.html.

Weale, A. (1999a). *Democracy*. London: Macmillan.

Weale, A. (1999b). 'European Environmental Policy by Stealth: The Dysfunctionality of Functionalism?' *Environment and Planning C: Government and Policy*, 17: 37–51.

Weale, A., Pridham, G., Cini, M., Konstadakopulos, D., Porter, M., and Flynn, B. (eds) (2000). *Environmental Governance in Europe: An Ever Closer Ecological Union?* Oxford: Oxford University Press.

Weatherill, S. (2016). *Cases and Materials on EU Law*. Oxford: Oxford University Press.

Webber, D. (2014). 'How Likely is It that the European Union will Disintegrate? A Critical Analysis of Competing Theoretical Perspectives'. *European Journal of International Relations*, 20: 341–65.

Webber, D. (2016). 'Declining Power Europe: The Evolution of the European Union's World Power in the Early Twentieth Century'. *European Review of International Studies,* 1: 31–52.

Webber, D. (2019a). *European Disintegration? The Politics of Crisis in the European Union*. Basingstoke: Palgrave Macmillan.

Webber, D. (2019b). 'Trends in European Political (Dis)integration. An Analysis of Postfunctionalist and other Explanations'. *Journal of European Public Policy*. 26: 1134–52.

Weiler, J. (1999). *The Constitution of Europe: 'Do the New Clothes have an Emperor' and other Essays on European Integration*. Cambridge: Cambridge University Press.

Wessels, W. (2015). *The European Council*. Basingstoke: Palgrave Macmillan.

Wettestad, J., and Jevnaker, T. (2016). *Rescuing EU Emissions Trading: The Climate Policy Flagship*. Basingstoke: Palgrave Macmillan.

Wettestad, J. and Jevnaker, T. (2019). 'Smokescreen Politics? Ratcheting Up EU Emissions Trading in 2017'. *Review of Policy Research*, 36: 635–59.

Whitaker, R. (2011). *The European Parliament's Committees: National Party Influence and Legislative Empowerment*. London: Routledge.

Whitaker, R. (2019). 'A Case of "You Can Always Get What You Want"? Committee Assignments in the European Parliament'. *Parliamentary Affairs*, 72: 162–81.

Whitman, R. (2002). 'The Fall, and Rise of Civilian Power Europe?'. Australian National University, *National Europe Centre*, Paper No. 16.

Whitman, R. (2016). 'The UK and EU Foreign Security and Defence Policy after Brexit: Integrated, Associated or Detached?' *National Institute Economic Review,* 238: 43–50.

Whitman, R. and Manners, I. (2016). 'Another Theory is Possible: Dissident Voices in Theorising Europe'. *Journal of Common Market Studies*, 54: 3–18.

Wiener, A., Börzel T., and Risse, T. (eds) (2019). *European Integration Theory* (3rd edn). Oxford: Oxford University Press.

Wilks, S. (2015). 'Competition Policy: Defending the Economic Constitution', in H. Wallace, M. Pollack, and A. Young (eds), *Policy-Making in the European Union* (7th edn). Oxford: Oxford University Press, 141–65.

Wille, A. (2013). *The Normalization of the European Commission*. Oxford: Oxford University Press.

Wilson, J. (2012). 'ECB "Ready to Do Whatever it Takes"', *Financial Times*, 26 July.

Wincott, D. (1995). 'Institutional Interaction and European Integration: Towards an Everyday Critique of Liberal Intergovernmentalism'. *Journal of Common Market Studies*, 33: 597–609.

Woll, C. (2006). 'Lobbying in the European Union: From *sui generis* to a Comparative Perspective'. *Journal of European Public Policy*, 13: 456–69.

Woll, C. and Jacquot, S. (2010). 'Using Europe: Strategic Action in Multi-Level Politics'. *Comparative European Politics*, 8: 110–26.

Wurzel, R.W., Connelly, J., and Liefferink, D. (eds) (2017). *The European Union in International Climate Change Politics. Still Taking a Lead?* London: Routledge

Wurzel, R.W., Liefferink, D., and Di Lullo, M. (2019). 'The European Council, the Council and the Member States: Changing Environmental Leadership Dynamics in the European Union'. *Environmental Politics*, 28: 248–70.

Yordanova, N. (2013). *Organising the European Parliament: The Role of Committees and their Legislative Influence*. London: ECPR Press.

Young, A. R. (2000). 'The Adaptation of European Foreign Economic Policy'. *Journal of Common Market Studies*, 38: 93–116.

Young, A. R. (2007). 'Trade Politics Ain't What It Used to Be'. *Journal of Common Market Studies*, 45: 789–811.

Young, A. R. (2017). *TTIP and the New Politics of Trade*. Newcastle: Agenda.

Young, H. (1998). *This Blessed Plot: Britain and Europe from Churchill to Blair*. London: Macmillan.

Young, J. W. (1993). *Britain and European Unity, 1945–1992. Basingstoke:* Macmillan.

Youngs, R. (2004). 'Normative Dynamics and Strategic Interests in the EU's External Identity'. *Journal of Common Market Studies*, 42: 415–35.

Zeitlin, J. (ed.) (2015). *Extending Experimentalist Governance?* Oxford: Oxford University Press.

Zito, A. (1999). 'Task Expansion: A Theoretical Overview'. *Environment and Planning C: Government and Policy*, 17: 19–35.

Zito, A., Burns, C. and Lenschow. A. (2019). 'Is the Trajectory of European Union Environmental Policy Less Certain?' *Environmental Politics*. 28: 187–207.

Zito, A., Burns, C. and Lenschow. A. (2019). 'The Future of European Union Environmental Politics and Policy'. *Environmental Politics*. 29 (special issue).

Glossary

acquis communautaire Often abbreviated simply to *acquis*, a French phrase for which it is difficult to find a precise English translation. A French–English dictionary would define *acquis* as something like 'acquired knowledge' or 'accumulated experience', but the connotation in this phrase is much more like 'heritage'. The *acquis* is the body of laws, policies, and practices that have accumulated over the lifetime of the European Communities, and now the European Union. Any new member state joining the EU has to accept the *acquis* as part of its terms of entry. The adjective '*communautaire*', when applied to the *acquis* or to other nouns, means more than just 'of the (European) community'. It has connotations of something that is in sympathy with the co-operative spirit that informed the original European Community (EC). The term '*communitaire*', which can be found all too frequently in texts on the European Union, is simply an incorrect piece of 'Franglais'.

Benelux An acronym made up of the first parts of the names of the member states: *Be*lgium; the *Ne*therlands; and *Lux*embourg. The governments of these three states adopted a **customs union** while in exile in London in 1944, and extended this to an **economic union** on 1 January 1948.

black box of the state The realist tradition in international relations assumed that relations between states could be understood without analysing the internal politics of the states. It was assumed that each state had a clear and abiding national interest, derived largely from its geographical position in the world and from strategic considerations such as the need to prevent neighbouring states from being able to dominate the region, and the need to defend any colonies and overseas territories that the state might possess. This national interest was assumed to be stronger than any differences between political parties within the country, so that changes of government would produce little lasting change in foreign policy. Therefore, the state could be treated as though it were a 'black box' into which the analyst need not peer.

Bretton Woods In 1944, a major economic conference was held at Bretton Woods in New Hampshire, USA. Agreement was reached on the basis of a post-war international economic and monetary system. The key principles were free trade and monetary stability. Monetary stability was to be achieved by tying the value of national currencies to the US dollar, which in turn was tied to the value of gold at the rate of US\$ 35 per ounce. The **International Monetary Fund (IMF)** was set up to assist in the establishment of the system, and to provide short-term and medium-term loans to states experiencing temporary problems with their balance of payments. The system lasted until 1971, when it collapsed because the United States was forced to devalue the dollar against gold. It was temporarily replaced by the **Smithsonian agreements**.

common market A **customs union**, but with the addition of free movement of factors of production, including capital and labour.

corporatism/corporatist From the Latin verb *corporare*, meaning 'to form into a body'. The process of forming individuals into collective bodies produces corporations, which are artificial persons created by individuals, who authorize the corporation to act on their behalf. Between the wars in Europe, the idea of the 'corporate state' emerged in which representation of the people would not be by geographical constituencies, but through vocational corporations of the employers and employees in each trade and industry. It was seen as an alternative 'third way' between capitalism and communism.

In practice, corporatism came to be most closely associated with the Fascist regime in Italy after 1928, and was widely imitated by other authoritarian regimes. This association discredited the term in the eyes of the Anglo-Saxon states, but the idea still held some resonance in Roman Catholic social thought, hence its revival, without the formal title of corporatism, in the post-war constitutions of some western European states.

customs union   A **free trade area** that has a uniform set of rules on trade with the outside world.

differentiated integration   This is a situation where not all member states participate in the full range of EU policies. Differentiated integration arises in a variety of circumstances. For example, a member state may negotiate a policy opt-out, as occurred with both monetary integration and the Schengen passport-free zone. It may also arise where a member state is deemed not ready to become a full member of an EU arrangement, as also applies to the eurozone and the Schengen zone due to lack of readiness. The situation may also arise where a piece of legislation is adopted according to enhanced co-operation (see Insight 12.2). In general terms, the EU seeks to permit all states to join all policies or legislation at a later stage such that differentiated integration is not exclusionary. Sometimes other terms are used, such as variable-geometry integration or multi-speed integration, but they are different variants of differentiated integration.

dirigiste/dirigisme   A French term that translates literally into English as 'directionism'. It is an economic doctrine that gives a central role to the state in the direction of economic development under capitalism. Typically, the state draws up a national economic plan that acts as a framework within which both state-sector and private-sector enterprises can co-ordinate their decisions on investments. The term 'indicative planning' is often used in English to suggest the same system.

economic union   A **common market** with unified economic and monetary policies.

epistemology   The theory of knowledge; about how knowledge is acquired and validated.

European Investment Bank (EIB)   An EU agency that is charged to provide capital at affordable rates to support projects that contribute to the integration, balanced development, and economic and social cohesion of the member states. It does this by raising funds itself on the capital markets, and then loaning the funds at favourable rates of interest to support projects that further these objectives. It also implements the financial components of agreements under the European development aid policies.

Eurosceptic(ism)   Indicates either qualified or unqualified opposition to the process of European integration (see also Insight 3.2).

free trade area   Member states remove all tariff and quota barriers to trade between themselves, but retain independent trade policies with the outside world.

General Agreement on Tariffs and Trade (GATT)   Negotiated in 1947 and started operation on 1 January 1948. It consisted of a standing conference for the negotiation of tariff cuts, and an agreement that all such cuts would be multilateral, not bilateral. This was embodied in the principle of 'most favoured nation treatment' for all signatories of the agreement: any trade concession extended by one member to another had to be extended to all other members. The GATT held eight rounds of multilateral trade negotiations, culminating in the Uruguay Round, which opened in Punte del Este, Uruguay, in 1986 and was not completed until 1994. It was this round that focused attention on the trade-distorting effects of the EU's Common Agricultural Policy. One of the agreements in the Uruguay Round was the creation of a new World Trade Organization (WTO), which began operation on 1 January 1995. Its functions are: to administer WTO trade agreements; to act as a forum for trade negotiations; to handle trade disputes; to monitor national trade policies; to provide technical assistance and training for developing countries; and to co-operate with other international organizations (*source*: **http://wto.org/**).

Geneva Convention   The term used for a set of Treaties and protocols that set the standards in international law for humanitarian rights

545

during periods of war. There are, in fact, four conventions. They provide, amongst other things, a set of humanitarian standards for dealing with wounded fighters, prisoners of war, civilians, and medical or religious personnel.

International Monetary Fund (IMF)   Set up in 1944: to promote international monetary co-operation; to facilitate the expansion and balanced growth of international trade; to promote stability in exchange rates; to assist in the establishment of a multilateral system of payments in respect of trade between member states; to contribute to the elimination of foreign exchange restrictions; and to provide short-term and medium-term loans to states experiencing temporary balance of payments difficulties. The IMF took on a role in the eurozone rescues in the 2010s (*source*: **http://imf.org/external/about.htm**).

investment capital   Refers to assets that are invested in a country in the form of factories, businesses, etc.

neo-corporatism/neo-corporatist   In the 1970s, academics coined the term 'neo-corporatism' to describe a relationship between the state and organized economic interests that was less formal than **corporatism**, but nevertheless institutionalized patterns of consultation on policy between governments, business, and trade unions in several leading western European states.

ontology   Refers to the nature of being; an underlying understanding of the world.

OPEC   See **Organization of the Petroleum Exporting Countries**.

ordinary legislative procedure (OLP)   A term introduced by the Lisbon Treaty to cover those instances in which the Council of Ministers may decide on legislation by **QMV**, while holding co-decision powers with the European Parliament. The terminology is designed to present this pattern as the default arrangement in EU decision making, while all other arrangements (unanimous voting in the Council and consent or consultation procedures in the European Parliament) are termed 'special legislative procedures'.

ordo-liberalism   Sometimes termed 'German neo-liberalism', referring to a strand in liberal thinking associated with the so-called 'Freiburg school' founded in 1930s Germany. Thinkers associated with this tradition are said to have had an important impact on post-war German politics and also the design and course of aspects of European integration. Ordo-liberals believe in the free market, but emphasize the role of the state or non-politicized public institutional actors (such as the EU) in ensuring that the market works properly. They have, in particular, championed a role for independent public actors in ensuring fair competition and a 'sound' monetary policy based on low inflation (see eg Chapter 20, 'Explaining and Critiquing EMU').

Organization of the Petroleum Exporting Countries (OPEC)   Created at a conference of petroleum-exporting states in Baghdad in 1960. The founder members were Iran, Iraq, Kuwait, Saudi Arabia, and Venezuela. They were later joined by eight other members: Qatar (1961); Indonesia (1962); Libya (1962); the United Arab Emirates (1967); Algeria (1969); Nigeria (1971); Ecuador (1973–92); and Gabon (1975–94). OPEC's objective is to co-ordinate and unify petroleum policies among member countries, in order to secure: fair and stable prices for petroleum producers; an efficient, economic, and regular supply of petroleum to consuming nations; and a fair return on capital to those investing in the industry (*source*: **http://opec.org/**).

***passerelle* clause**   A clause which permits a procedural reform to take place within the EU without the need for a full Treaty reform process. Typically, such a clause would allow the European Council to agree (unanimously) that a particular area of policy making can move from unanimity to **QMV** in the Council of Ministers. First provided for in the Amsterdam Treaty, the number of provisions was extended in the Lisbon Treaty, as well as the requirement for approval by national parliaments added. The first practical use of a *passerelle* provision came in 2004 when, following a five-year transition period after the implementation of the Amsterdam Treaty, the European Council unanimously agreed to move to introduce QMV rules in asylum and immigration policy.

permissive consensus The situation where public levels of support for, or toleration of, European integration gave quite a lot of independence to political elites to adopt European solutions to policy problems. The permissive consensus declined in most member states from the 1990s, as the Maastricht Treaty impacted on core state responsibilities.

pluralism/pluralist In a pluralist system, interest groups lobby the formal institutions to try to get their preferred legislative options. It is a competitive system of seeking influence, but although early pluralist theories suggested that there was a level playing field of competition, it is now generally accepted that some groups have greater resources than others, and so benefit more from this form of interest representation.

policy entrepreneur(ship) A policy actor who seeks to exploit favourable political conditions in order to promote a particular initiative or policy.

politicization The situation whereby the EU or a member state's European policy has become more salient to domestic politics, more contested, and with a wider array of political actors involved. It is a characteristic of the more contested nature of the politics of the EU from the 2010s and contrasts with the earlier **permissive consensus**.

principal–agent theory A branch of rational choice theory that investigates the relationship between institutions that delegate tasks and authority (the principals) and the institutions to which they delegate (the agents). The main concern of principal–agent theory is to investigate the degree to which agents can 'cut slack' so as to achieve a degree of freedom from their principals, freedom that they can use to follow their own agendas rather than the agendas of the principals. Principal–agent theory has been widely used in the investigation of the degree of freedom available to federal agencies in the United States, and in discussion of the relationship of the European Commission to the governments of the member states.

public procurement Purchases of goods and services by governments or other public agencies for use in the public sector, covering everything from paper clips to major projects of civil engineering such as the construction of highways.

qualified majority voting (QMV) A system of voting practised in the Council of Ministers. Until 2014, each member state was given a weighting, which broadly reflected its population size. For a decision to be approved, it was necessary to reach the specific thresholds set down in the Treaties. The rules have been revised over time as a result of institutional reforms and to reflect successive increases in the number of member states. For details of the rules see Chapter 12. QMV is distinct from unanimous voting. Under the latter, all member states must agree before a decision can be taken. Under QMV, by contrast, it is possible for one or a small number of states to be overruled in the Council.

roll-call voting This is the term given to the formal record of voting in the European Parliament or other assemblies. It is often used by researchers to investigate patterns of behaviour on the part of individual elected politicians and the coherence of the party or party grouping to which they belong.

Smithsonian agreements In 1971, the **Bretton Woods** system of international payments, which had been set up at the end of the war, collapsed. It was replaced by a new set of agreements that were signed at the Smithsonian Institute in Washington, DC, in December 1971. Under these arrangements, the US dollar was substantially devalued against all other currencies, and the major central banks of all other states agreed to try to hold the value of their currencies in a range of fluctuation of 2.25 per cent either side of the US dollar, a maximum range of fluctuation of 4.5 per cent. This attempt to restore fixed exchange rates collapsed in March 1973 in the face of extreme speculative pressure, and the world then entered the era of floating exchange rates that we have today.

stagflation Economists used to believe that there was a trade-off between economic growth and inflation. Policies could either promote economic growth, at the price of higher inflation, or they could focus on restraining inflation at the cost of lower rates of economic growth. Governments made policy choices based on this assumption: some aimed for lower growth in return for low inflation; others preferred high rates of inflation in order to promote high rates of growth. However, following the oil crisis in 1973, the trade-off no longer seemed to work. States began to experience the worst of both worlds: stagnation with inflation, or 'stagflation' as it became known.

structure and agency debate A debate in the social sciences about whether or to what extent social structures—such as prevailing ideologies or institutional norms and rules—have primacy over social agency—the ability of individuals or actors to make choices autonomously. Social constructivists and some other critical perspectives (see Chapter 4) would claim that structures and agents are co-constitutive. In other words, structures will place limits on agents, but agents will also sometimes be able to alter particular structures. The position that one takes on this debate relates to the position taken on **ontology** (see also Chapter 4, 'Critical of What?').

subsidiarity Subsidiarity is an ambiguous concept and is taken to mean different things by different political actors. For example, it was interpreted by the British government to mean that action should not be taken at the EU level unless it could be shown that the objectives of the action could be better achieved at that level than at the national level. The German government interprets it more generally to mean that decisions should be taken at the lowest level of government at which they can be made effective. This implies a commitment to internal devolution of power within states.

supranational institution/organization 'Supranational' literally means 'above the national'. A supranational institution or a supranational organization is one that has power or influence going beyond that permitted to it by national governments. An international institution or organization, in contrast, is one that results from the co-operation of national governments, and has no power beyond that permitted to it by those governments.

transgovernmental and transnational networks Links across national boundaries between interest groups and individuals outside of government (transnational) or between departments of national government and individuals working for governments (transgovernmental), which are not monitored or controlled by national foreign offices or other core departments of the executive.

Union method This term relates to mainstream EU business where the Commission typically has the power of initiative, the Council of Ministers and the European Parliament decide on the legislation, and the Court of Justice holds authority as final arbiter on any disputes arising from the Treaties or EU legislation. Prior to implementation of the Lisbon Treaty, the equivalent term used in the academic literature was the Community method, which applied to the practices in the then EC 'pillar' of the EU's former three-pillar architecture (see Chapter 12, 'Treaties'). The Union method does not apply to foreign and security policy, which is treated on a more intergovernmental basis, and has no role for EU law and the Court of Justice, while the Commission and European Parliament have significantly reduced importance.

World Bank (International Bank for Reconstruction and Development or IBRD) Founded in 1944 to give loans to developing states to aid their economic recovery and combat poverty (*source*: http://worldbank.org/).

Abbreviations and Acronyms

ACER	Agency for the Co-operation of Energy Regulators
ACP	African, Caribbean, and Pacific
AFSJ	area of freedom, security, and justice
Agfish	Agriculture and Fisheries Council
AGRI	Agriculture and Rural Development
AKP	Justice and Development Party (Turkey)
ALTER-EU	Alliance for Lobbying Transparency and Ethics Regulation
APEC	Asia–Pacific Economic Co-operation
ASEAN	Association of Southeast Asian Nations
BDB	*Bundesverband Deutscher Banken*
BDI	*Bundesverband der Deutschen Industrie*
Benelux	Belgium, the Netherlands, and Luxembourg
BEREC	Body of European Regulators for Electronic Communications
BSE	bovine spongiform encephalopathy
CAP	Common Agricultural Policy
CdP	*Commissariat du Plan* (French Economic Planning Commission)
CdT	Translation Centre for the Bodies of the European Union
CDU	Christian Democratic Union (Germany)
Cedefop	European Centre for the Development of Vocational Training
CEE	central and eastern Europe
CEEC	Committee for European Economic Co-operation
CEECs	central and eastern European countries
CEN	European Committee for Standardization
CENELEC	European Committee for Standardization of Electrical Products
CEPOL	EU Agency for Law Enforcement Training
CEPS	Centre for European Policy Studies
CET	common external tariff
CETA	Comprehensive Economic and Trade Agreement
CF	Cohesion Fund

CFSP	Common Foreign and Security Policy
CGT	*Confédération Générale du Travail*
CJD	Creutzfeldt-Jakob disease
CJEU	Court of Justice of the European Union
CLIMA	Climate Action
COGECA	General Confederation of Agricultural Co-operatives
COMAGRI	Committee on Agriculture and Rural Development
CONNECT	Communications Networks, Content, and Technology
COP	Conference of the Parties
COPA	Committee of Professional Agricultural Organizations of the European Community
COPS	*Comité Politique et de Sécurité* (see also *PSC*)
CoR	Committee of the Regions and Local Authorities
COREPER	Committee of Permanent Representatives
COREU	*Correspondance Européenne* (Telex link)
CPE	critical political economy
CPVO	Community Plant Variety Office
CSCE	Conference on Security and Co-operation in Europe
CSDP	Common Security and Defence Policy
CSU	Christian Social Union (Germany)
DEVCO	International Co-operation and Development
DG	Directorate General
DIHT	*Deutscher Industrie- und Handelskammertag*
EAFRD	European Agricultural Fund for Rural Development
EASA	European Aviation Safety Agency
EASO	European Asylum Support Office
EAW	European arrest warrant
EBA	European Banking Authority
EBU	European Banking Union
EC	European Community
ECA	European Court of Auditors
ECB	European Central Bank
ECDC	European Centre for Disease Prevention and Control
ECHA	European Chemicals Agency
ECHR	European Convention on Human Rights
ECJ	European Court of Justice
ECOFIN	Economic and Financial Affairs Council
ECSC	European Coal and Steel Community
ECtHR	European Court of Human Rights

ecu	European currency unit
EDA	European Defence Agency
EDC	European Defence Community
EdF	*Electricité de France*
EDF	European Development Fund
EEA	(1) European Economic Area; (2) European Environment Agency
EEAS	European External Action Service
EEC	European Economic Community
EES	European Economic Space
EESC	European Economic and Social Committee
EFC	Economic and Finance Committee
EFCA	European Fisheries Control Agency
EFSA	European Food Safety Authority
EFSF	European Financial Stability Facility
EFSM	European Financial Stabilization Mechanism
EFTA	European Free Trade Association
EIB	European Investment Bank
EIGE	European Institute for Gender Equality
EIOPA	European Insurance and Occupational Pensions Authority
EMCDDA	European Monitoring Centre for Drugs and Drug Addiction
EMCF	European Monetary Co-operation Fund
EMEA	European Medicines Agency
EMF	European Monetary Fund
EMFF	European Maritime and Fisheries Fund
EMS	European Monetary System
EMSA	European Maritime Safety Agency
EMU	economic and monetary union
ENGO	environmental non-governmental organizations
ENISA	European Network and Information Security Agency
ENP	European Neighbourhood Policy
ENPI	European Neighbourhood and Partnership Instrument
EP	European Parliament
EPA	(1) European Parliamentary Assembly; (2) Economic Partnership Agreement
EPC	(1) European Political Community (until 1952); (2) European political co-operation
EPP	European People's Party
EPP–ED	European People's Party and European Democrats
EPSC	European Political Strategy Centre

EPSO	European Personnel Selection Office
ERA	European Railway Agency
ERDF	European Regional Development Fund
ERI	extraterritorial income
ERM	exchange rate mechanism
ERP	European Recovery Programme ('Marshall Plan')
ERT	European Round Table of Industrialists
ERTA	European Road Transport Agreement
ESA	Euratom Supply Agency
ESCB	European System of Central Banks
ESDP	European Security and Defence Policy
ESF	European Social Fund
ESIF	European Structural and Investment Funds
ESM	European Stability Mechanism
ESMA	European Securities and Markets Authority
ESPRIT	European Strategic Programme for Research and Development in Information Technology
ESS	European Security Strategy
ETF	European Training Foundation
ETS	Emissions Trading Scheme
ETUC	European Trade Union Confederation
EU	European Union
EUF	European Union of Federalists
EUGS	EU Global Strategy
eu–LISA	European Agency for the Operational Management of Large-Scale IT Systems in the Area of Freedom, Security, and Justice
EU–OSHA	European Agency for Safety and Health at Work
Euratom	European Atomic Energy Community
EURODAC	EU-wide electronic system for the identification of asylum-seekers
Eurofound	European Foundation for the Improvement of Living and Working Conditions
Eurojust	EU's Judicial Co-operation Unit
Europol	European Police Office
FDP	Free Democrat Party (Germany)
FISMA	Financial Stability, Financial Service, and Capital Markets Union
FRA	European Union Agency for Fundamental Rights
Frontex	European Border and Coast Guard Agency
FSC	Foreign Sales Corporation
FTA	free trade agreement

FYROM	former Yugoslav Republic of Macedonia (now known as North Macedonia)
GAC	General Affairs Council
GAERC	General Affairs and External Relations Council
GATT	General Agreement on Tariffs and Trade
GDP	gross domestic product
GFC	global financial crisis
GHG	greenhouse gas
GM(O)	genetically modified (organism)
GNP	gross national product
GSA	European Global Navigation satellite System Supervisory Authority
GSP	Generalised System of Preferences
HRUFASP	High Representative of the Union for Foreign Affairs and Security Policy
IAR	International Authority for the Ruhr
IAS	Internal Audit Service
IBRD	International Bank for Reconstruction and Development
ICSID	International Centre for Settlement of Investment Disputes
ICTY	International Criminal Tribunal for the Former Yugoslavia
IGC	intergovernmental conference
IIA	inter-institutional agreement
IMF	International Monetary Fund
INTUG	Information Technology User Group
IR	international relations
ISIS	Islamic State
ISS	Institute for Security Studies
ITO	International Trade Organization
JHA	Justice and Home Affairs
JRC	Joint Research Centre
LCD	lowest common denominator
LDC	less developed country
LI	liberal intergovernmentalism
LTRO	Long-Term Refinancing Operations
M5S	Movimento 5 Stelle (Five Star Movement, Italy)
MEP	member of the European Parliament
MFF	multi-annual financial framework
MFN	most favoured nation
MLG	multi-level governance
MoU	Memorandum of Understanding
MP	member of Parliament (Britain)

553

MRP	*Mouvement Républicain Populaire (France)*
NAPs	(1) National Action Plans (for employment) (2) National Allocation Plans (for carbon emissions)
NATO	North Atlantic Treaty Organization
NCEP	National Climate and Energy Plan
NEAR	European Neighbourhood Policy and Enlargement Negotiations
NFU	National Farmers' Union (Britain)
NGOs	non-governmental organizations
NI	new institutionalism
NRPs	National Reform Programmes
NTB	non-tariff barrier
OECD	Organization for Economic Co-operation and Development
OEEC	Organization for European Economic Co-operation
OHIM	Office for Harmonization in the Internal Market
OJ	Official Journal
OLAF	European Anti-Fraud Office
OLP	ordinary legislative procedure
OMC	open method(s) of co-ordination
OMT	outright monetary transaction
ONP	open network provision
OPEC	Organization of Petroleum Exporting Countries
OSCE	Organization for Security and Co-operation in Europe
PEPP	Pandemic Emergency Purchase Programme
PESCO	permanent structured co-operation
PiS	*Prawo i Sprawiedliwość* (Law and Justice Party, Poland)
PJCCM	police and judicial co-operation in criminal matters
PRT	pathogen reduction treatment
PSA	Political Studies Association
PSC	Political and Security Committee (see also COPS)
PTTs	post, telegraph, and telephone companies
QMV	qualified majority voting
REACH	Registration, Evaluation, Authorisation and Restriction of Chemicals
REPA	Regional Economic Partnership Agreement
SAP	stabilization and association process
SCA	Special Committee on Agriculture
SEA	Single European Act
SEM	single European market
SGP	Stability and Growth Pact

SHAPE	Supreme Headquarters Allied Powers Europe
SIS	Schengen Information System
SME	small and medium-sized enterprises
SOE	second-order election
SPD	*Sozialdemokratische Partei Deutschlands* (Social Democratic Party, Germany)
TEC	Treaty Establishing the European Community
TEN	trans-European network
TEU	Treaty on European Union
TFEU	Treaty on the Functioning of the European Union
TiSA	Trade in Services Agreement
TSCG	Treaty on Stability Coordination and Governance
TTIP	Transatlantic Trade and Investment Partnership
UACES	University Association of Contemporary European Studies
UK	United Kingdom
UKIP	UK Independence Party
UN	United Nations
UNICE	Union of Industrial and Employers' Confederations of Europe
US(A)	United States (of America)
USSR	Union of Soviet Socialist Republics
VAT	value added tax
WEU	Western European Union
WTO	World Trade Organization

Chronology

1940s

1945

February Yalta Summit between the United States, the Soviet Union, and Britain; agreed 'spheres of interest' in post-war Europe

May Surrender of Germany ends the war in Europe

September Surrender of Japan; end of the Second World War

1946

September Civil war breaks out in Greece

September Winston Churchill's speech in Zurich in which he calls for a 'United States of Europe'

December European Union of Federalists (EUF) formed

1947

February British government tells US administration that it cannot continue aid to Greece and Turkey

March Truman Doctrine announced in US Congress

March Treaty of Dunkirk signed by Britain and France

April Soviet walkout of Four-Power Council of Foreign Ministers

June Marshall Plan announced

July Committee for European Economic Co-operation (CEEC) set up

1948

January Benelux states commence economic union

March Treaty of Brussels signed by Britain, France, and Benelux states

April Organization for European Economic Co-operation (OEEC) replaces CEEC

May European Congress in The Hague

1949

April Federal Republic of Germany established

April North Atlantic Treaty signed in Washington, DC, setting up the North Atlantic Treaty Organization (NATO)

April International Authority for the Ruhr (IAR) established

May Council of Europe formed

1950s

1950

May Schuman Plan for coal and steel announced (Schuman Declaration)

June Korean War begins

October Pleven Plan for a European Defence Community (EDC) launched

November Council of Europe adopts European Convention on Human Rights

1951

April Treaty of Paris signed, establishing the European Coal and Steel Community (ECSC)

1952

May European Defence Community (EDC) Treaty signed in Paris

July ECSC begins operation

1953

March Draft Treaty for a European Political Community (EPC) adopted

September European Convention on Human Rights comes into force

1954

August EDC Treaty rejected by French National Assembly (collapse of EPC)

October Treaty creating Western European Union (WEU) signed

November Monnet announces that he will not stand for a second term as President of the High Authority of the ECSC

1955

April Spaak memorandum to ECSC states proposing an extension of sectoral integration

April Beyen memorandum on behalf of the Benelux states proposing a general common market

June Messina Conference agrees to set up Spaak Committee to consider future of integration

October Monnet sets up Action Committee for the United States of Europe

1956

March Spaak Report published

May Governments agree Spaak Report

June Start of 'Messina negotiations' based on the Spaak Report

October USSR invades Hungary to put down anti-communist uprising

October Suez crisis: Israel, Britain, and France attack Egypt and occupy Port Said, but forced to withdraw their troops in the face of opposition from the United States

1957

March Completion of 'Messina negotiations'

April Treaties of Rome establishing the European Economic Community (EEC) and European Atomic Energy Community (Euratom) signed

1958

January EEC and Euratom begin operations: Walter Hallstein becomes the first President of the EEC Commission, Louis Armand the first President of the Euratom Commission

July CAP system of common prices agreed at Stresa Conference

1959

January Customs duties within the EEC cut by 10 per cent

1960s

1960

May Acceleration agreement on the common market and Common Agricultural Policy between six EC states

December Organization for Economic Co-operation and Development (OECD) supersedes OEEC

1961

February Paris Summit agrees to set up committee under Christian Fouchet to review co-operation

March Fouchet negotiations begin

July Association Agreement signed with Greece

August Britain, Denmark, and Ireland apply for membership of the EC

December Commission convenes first conference on European regional policy

1962

April Norway applies to join the EEC

July Common Agricultural Policy (CAP) system of common prices agreed at Stresa Conference

December Nassau agreement between Macmillan and Kennedy

1963

January De Gaulle announces his veto of British membership

July First Yaoundé Convention comes into effect

September Association Agreement signed with Turkey

1965

April Merger Treaty signed, agreeing to merge the institutions of the European Coal and Steel Community (ECSC), EEC, and Euratom

July Start of French boycott of the Council of Ministers

1966

January Luxembourg compromise

1967

May Britain, Denmark, and Ireland make a second application for membership of the EC

July Norway makes a second application for membership of the EC

July Sweden applies for EC membership

July Merger Treaty takes effect: Jean Rey is first Commission President for all three communities (ECSC, EEC, Euratom)

December France blocks agreement on opening negotiations with the applicant states

1968

July Customs union completed and common external tariff established

December Commission produces 'Mansholt Plan' for restructuring EC agriculture

1969

December Hague Summit: the 'relaunching of Europe'

1970s

1970

June Membership negotiations begin with Britain, Ireland, Denmark, and Norway

July Franco Malfatti becomes President of the European Commission

October Davignon Report on European political co-operation

1971

January Second Yaoundé Convention signed

February Werner Report on economic and monetary union

March Start of first attempt to move to monetary union with the joint floating of European currencies

March Farmers demonstrate in Brussels against Mansholt Plan. Council of Agricultural Ministers agrees a modified version of the Plan

August Ending of the convertibility of the US dollar into gold marks the collapse of the Bretton Woods international monetary system, closely followed by the collapse of the first experiment with European monetary union

December Smithsonian agreements on international monetary regime to replace Bretton Woods

1972

January Completion of membership negotiations with Britain, Ireland, Denmark, and Norway; Accession Treaties signed

March Sicco Mansholt becomes President of the European Commission

March Start of the 'snake in the tunnel' system of EC monetary co-ordination

March European Parliament (EP) accepts Commission proposals for creation of EC regional policy

May Irish referendum in favour of EC membership

June British pound withdrawn from the 'snake in the tunnel'

September Norwegian referendum rejecting EC membership

October Danish referendum in favour of EC membership

October Paris Summit accepts the case for EC regional policy and requests the Commission to prepare a report on the issue

1973

January François-Xavier Ortoli becomes Commission President

January First enlargement of EC from six to nine member states

February Italy forced to leave the 'snake'

May 'Thomson Report' on regional problems presented to the Council of Ministers

December Organization of Petroleum Exporting Countries (OPEC) oil crisis

1974

January France forced to leave the 'snake'

July Turkish invasion of Cyprus

December Paris Summit: agrees to direct elections to the EP, creation of the European Council, and the creation of the European Regional Development Fund (ERDF)

1975

January ERDF comes into operation

February First Lomé Convention comes into effect

March First European Council meeting in Dublin

June British referendum agrees continued membership of EC

June Greek application for membership of EC

July France rejoins the 'snake'

August Signing of the 'Final Act' at the Conference on Security and Co-operation in Europe (CSCE) in Helsinki

1976

January Commission Opinion on Greek application: not very favourable

April France leaves the 'snake' for the second time

July Opening of Greek accession negotiations

1977

January Roy Jenkins becomes President of the European Commission

March Portuguese application for membership of the EC

July Spanish application for membership of the EC

October Jenkins lecture at the European University Institute, Florence: calls for a new attempt at monetary union

1978

July Bremen European Council agrees to pursue proposal from Schmidt and Giscard for a 'zone of monetary stability in Europe'

October Opening of accession negotiations with Portugal

December Bremen European Council agrees to create the European Monetary System (EMS)

1979

February Opening of accession negotiations with Spain

March EMS begins

May Greek Accession Treaty signed

June First direct elections to the EP

November Dublin European Council: Prime Minister Thatcher demands a British budgetary rebate

December USSR invades Afghanistan

1980s

1980

March Second Lomé Convention comes into effect

June Venice Declaration of the EC member states on the situation in the Middle East

December Second stage of the EMS scheme postponed indefinitely

1981

January Gaston Thorn becomes President of the European Commission

January Greece becomes a member of the EC

October London Report on European Political Co-operation (EPC) published

November Genscher–Colombo Plan calls for a new European Charter to replace the Treaties and form a constitution for the European Communities

1982

June EMS currencies realigned; French socialist government agrees to reform its domestic economic policies and to retreat from its attempts to reflate the economy

1983

January Stuttgart European Council signs Solemn Declaration on European Union

March Further realignment of EMS currencies

1984

February EP approves draft Treaty on European Union (TEU)

March System of quotas for dairy products agreed as part of reform of CAP

June Fontainebleau European Council: British budgetary dispute settled; Dooge Committee on institutional reform set up

June Elections to EP

December Third Lomé Convention signed

1985

January Jacques Delors becomes President of the European Commission

February Brussels European Council: mandates Commission to produce a plan for the single European market

June Cockfield White Paper on the freeing of the internal market

June Portuguese and Spanish Accession Treaties signed

June Milan European Council: 1992 Programme agreed

December Single European Act agreed in principle by heads of government at Luxembourg European Council

1986

January Portugal and Spain join the EC

February Single European Act signed by foreign ministers in Luxembourg (nine states) and, subsequently, The Hague (the remaining three states)

1987

April Turkey applies for EC membership

July Single European Act comes into effect

1988

February Brussels European Council: agrees to a doubling of the structural funds; legal limit placed on increases in spending on agricultural support

June Hanover European Council: sets up the Delors Committee on monetary union

July Jacques Delors makes a speech to the EP in which he predicts that, in ten years' time, 80 per cent of economic legislation will be directed from Brussels; infuriates British Prime Minister Thatcher

September Margaret Thatcher's Bruges speech

1989

January Reformed structural funds, with new policy principles agreed during 1988, come into operation

January Start of revived 'social dialogue' between representatives of employers and trade unions

June Delors Report on monetary union; accepted by heads of government at Madrid European Council

June Elections to EP

July German monetary union

July Austria applies for EC membership

September Start of collapse of communism in eastern Europe

October Delors lectures to the College of Europe in Bruges

December Fourth Lomé Convention signed

December Strasbourg European Council sets up an intergovernmental conference (IGC) to consider institutional changes necessary for completing monetary union

1990s

1990

July Stage 1 of economic and monetary union (EMU) begins

July Cyprus applies for EC membership

July Malta applies for EC membership

August Iraq invades Kuwait

October Reunification of Germany; five new Länder become part of the EC

1991

January Start of IGC on political union

June Start of conflict between federal Yugoslav army and Slovenian separatist forces

July Sweden applies for EC membership

July Agriculture Commissioner MacSharry introduces his proposals for reform of the CAP

November EC imposes sanctions on Yugoslavia

December Maastricht European Council: agrees principles of TEU, and to set up a cohesion fund to assist Greece, Spain, Ireland, and Portugal

1992

January Badinter Commission gives support for recognition of Macedonia and qualified support for Croatian independence

February Maastricht Treaty on European Union signed

March Finland applies for EC membership

May Switzerland applies for EC membership

May MacSharry proposals for reform of CAP agreed by agriculture ministers

June Danish referendum rejects TEU

June WEU Petersberg Declaration commits member states to allocate armed forces to peace keeping and humanitarian tasks in Europe

September French referendum accepts TEU

September British forced to withdraw from exchange rate mechanism of EMS

November Norway applies for EC membership

November Blair House agreement between the EU and the United States on trade in agricultural goods: paves the way for the completion of the Uruguay Round of General Agreement on Tariffs and Trade (GATT) negotiations

December Swiss referendum rejects membership of the European Economic Area (EEA): Swiss government withdraws application for membership of EC

December Edinburgh European Council agrees opt-out for Denmark from single currency

1993

May Second Danish referendum accepts TEU

August The 'narrow bands' of the exchange rate mechanism (ERM) have to be widened to 15 per cent to allow it to survive

November TEU comes into effect

December EU monitors observe Russian elections

1994

January Stage 2 of EMU begins

January Start of European Economic Area (EEA)

January Reforms of structural funds agreed during 1993 come into effect

February Greek government refuses the former Yugoslav Republic of Macedonia access to the port of Salonika

April Hungary applies for EU membership

April Poland applies for EU membership

June Austrian referendum in favour of EU membership

June Corfu European Council agrees to extend internal market to energy and telecommunications

June Elections to EP

October Finnish referendum in favour of EU membership

November Swedish referendum in favour of EU membership

November Norwegian referendum rejects EU membership

1995

January Austria, Finland, and Sweden become members of the EU

January Jacques Santer becomes President of the European Commission

January World Trade Organization (WTO) begins to operate

January CSCE becomes the Organization for Security and Co-operation in Europe (OSCE)

March 'Stability Pact' signed by fifty-two states from western and eastern Europe in an attempt to stabilize the political and security situation in eastern Europe

June Romania applies for EU membership

June Slovak Republic applies for EU membership

October Latvia applies for EU membership

November Estonia applies for EU membership

November Barcelona Conference launches the process that leads to the 'Euro-Med' agreements between the EU and North African and other states bordering the Mediterranean

November Agriculture Commissioner Franz Fischler introduces his proposals for further reform of the CAP; they are subsequently incorporated into *Agenda 2000*

December Lithuania applies for EU membership

December Bulgaria applies for EU membership

December 'New Transatlantic Agenda' agreed between the EU and the United States

December Madrid European Council decides on 'euro' as the name for the single currency

1996

January Czech Republic applies for EU membership

June Slovenia applies for EU membership

March Intergovernmental conference to review TEU officially opens in Turin

September Commission requests that member states extend its mandate in international trade negotiations to cover trade in services; request is refused

December Dublin European Council agrees a 'stability pact' to support monetary union

1997

June Amsterdam European Council: agreement on terms of Treaty of Amsterdam, including to supplement the stability pact with a growth and employment pact; all EU member states commit to the 'Petersberg tasks' as agreed by WEU members in June 1992

July Publication of Commission's Agenda 2000 on eastern enlargement and the reform of the CAP and structural funds

October Treaty of Amsterdam signed

November Special 'jobs summit' held in Luxembourg to work out the principles of the 'co-ordinated strategy for employment' agreed at Amsterdam in June; effectively the 'Luxembourg process' is the first example of the 'open method of co-ordination' (OMC)

1998

March Opening of accession negotiations with Cyprus, Czech Republic, Estonia, Hungary, Poland, and Slovenia

May Special European Council meeting in Brussels to launch the single currency; Wim Duisenberg chosen to be first President of the European Central Bank

December At the end of a bilateral summit at St Malo in France, French President Chirac and British Prime Minister Blair announce their support for the development of a European Security and Defence Policy (ESDP)

1999

January The euro comes into operation, although national notes and coins remain in circulation until 2002

February Negotiations over Agenda 2000 proposals for agriculture begin

March Resignation of the Santer Commission

March Berlin European Council agrees on a financial perspective for 2000–06, reform of CAP and structural funds, and to nominate Romano Prodi as the next President of the Commission

May Treaty of Amsterdam enters into force

May Prodi becomes President of the Commission

June Elections to European Parliament

December Helsinki European Council agrees to open accession negotiations with Bulgaria, Latvia, Lithuania, Malta, Romania, and Slovakia, and also recognizes Turkey as an applicant country; adopts the 'headline goal' of creating a European Rapid Reaction Force by the end of 2003

2000s

2000

March Institutions of ESDP begin provisional operation

March Special European Council held in Lisbon agrees to a new EU strategy on employment, economic reform, and social cohesion, and makes a commitment to turn the EU into 'the most competitive knowledge-based economy in the world' by 2010

June Signing of Cotonou Agreement as successor to Lomé

June Greece gains approval to join single currency

September Danish people vote to reject adoption of the euro

December Nice European Council agrees the Treaty of Nice and formally proclaims the Charter of Fundamental Rights of the European Union

2001

January Greece joins single currency

June Irish people vote to reject the Treaty of Nice

September Terrorist attacks in New York and Washington, DC

September European Council votes to support the United States and to develop EU response following 11 September terrorist attacks

December Laeken European Council adopts the Declaration on the Future of the European Union, preparing the ground for a European Constitution

2002

January Citizens start using euro notes and coins in the twelve participating member states

February Convention on the Future of Europe begins its deliberations in Brussels, chaired by former French President Giscard d'Estaing

December US President Bush identifies an 'axis of evil' that includes Iraq

2003

February Treaty of Nice enters into force

March A coalition of states led by the United States and Britain invades Iraq; France and Germany condemn the invasion

March An EU force replaces the NATO stabilization force in the former Yugoslav Republic of Macedonia

April European Parliament assents to the accession of ten new member states

June Agreement in Council of Ministers on final decoupling of agricultural payments from production

June Giscard d'Estaing presents draft EU Constitution to the European Council

September Swedish people vote to reject adoption of the euro

October Rome IGC convenes to consider draft EU Constitution

November Jean-Claude Trichet replaces Wim Duisenberg as President of the European Central Bank (ECB)

November Eurozone heads of government decide not to impose sanctions on France and Germany for breaching the rules of the stability pact

December Proposals of the Constitutional Convention presented to the European Council

2004

February Commission outlines its proposals for the operation of the structural funds in the period 2007–13

March Terrorist bombings in Madrid

April Adoption of an Internal Market Strategy to improve transposition of EU agreements into national law

May Ten new member states join the EU

June Elections to EP, marked by a record low turnout

June European Council nominates Portuguese Prime Minister José Manuel Durao Barroso as the next President of the Commission

October Treaty establishing a Constitution for Europe signed by the heads of state and government and the EU foreign ministers

November Barroso Commission eventually approved by EP, following resignation of controversial nominee Rocco Buttiglione

November Kok Report on the 'Lisbon Agenda' presented to the Commission

December Heads of government agree to open accession negotiations with Turkey

2005

February Spanish people vote to approve the Constitutional Treaty

April Bulgaria and Romania sign Accession Treaties

May French people vote to reject the Constitutional Treaty

June Dutch people vote to reject the Constitutional Treaty

July Luxembourg people vote to accept the Constitutional Treaty

October EU opens accession negotiations with Croatia and Turkey

December The former Yugoslav Republic of Macedonia given official candidate status

2006

June European Council asks the incoming German presidency for proposals on how to end the constitutional impasse

July European Council agrees to Slovenia joining the eurozone as from 1 January 2007

December Finnish Parliament ratifies the Constitutional Treaty

December Services Directive is adopted by the EP and the Council

2007

January Bulgaria and Romania join the EU

January Slovenia adopts the euro

July Beginning of IGC convened to finalize a 'reform treaty'

October EU summit in Lisbon agrees text on the 'reform treaty'

December 'Lisbon Treaty' formally signed by EU leaders in the Portuguese capital

December Schengen area is extended to include the Czech Republic, Estonia, Hungary, Latvia, Lithuania, Malta, Poland, Slovakia, and Slovenia

2008

January Cyprus and Malta adopt the euro

June Irish people vote to reject the Lisbon Treaty

June European Council urges other member states to continue with the ratification process for the Lisbon Treaty

August Military conflict breaks out between Georgia and Russia

September EU summit condemns Russia's 'disproportionate reaction' in Georgia

December EU announces the creation of an 'eastern partnership' with six former Soviet states (Armenia, Azerbaijan, Belarus, Georgia, Moldova, and Ukraine)

December European Council gives Ireland reassurances over areas of concern in the Lisbon Treaty and the Irish government agrees to hold a new referendum by the end of 2009

December EU leaders agree to cut greenhouse gas emissions by 20 per cent by 2020

December Montenegro applies for EU membership

2009

January Slovakia adopts the euro

April Albania applies for EU membership

June EP elections held

July Iceland applies for EU membership

September Heads of government appoint Herman Van Rompuy as first President of the European Council and nominate Baroness Catherine Ashton for the post of High Representative of the Union for Foreign Affairs and Security Policy

September EP votes in favour of a second five-year term for Commission President Barroso

October Irish people vote to accept the Lisbon Treaty in a second referendum

October New socialist government in Greece reveals fiscal position worse than thought

December Lisbon Treaty comes into effect

December Serbia applies for EU membership

2010s

2010

February New Commission takes office headed by President Barroso

April Eurozone members agree a financial assistance package for Greece

May EU and IMF agree financial package for Greece

June Formal adoption of Europe 2020 strategy

June Iceland given official candidate status

November Financial assistance package for Ireland agreed

December Montenegro given official candidate status

2011

October Second assistance package for Greece

November Mario Draghi replaces Trichet as ECB President

December European Council agrees a new set of fiscal rules, but Britain refuses to sign up

2012

March The Treaty on Stability Coordination and Governance (TSCG, or Fiscal Compact) is signed by all the EU member states except Britain and the Czech Republic.

March Serbia given candidate status

June Spain requests assistance to recapitalize its banking sector

June Cyprus requests financial assistance

June Accession negotiations start with Montenegro

October EU awarded Nobel Peace Prize

2013

January British Prime Minister David Cameron pledges a referendum on membership of EU

March Financial assistance package given to Cyprus

April Catherine Ashton brokers deal over Kosovo

May Agreement reached on reform of Common Fisheries Policy, covering 2014–20

June Agreement reached between European Commission, EP, and Council of Ministers on reform of the CAP covering 2014–20

July Croatia joins EU

November EU budget for 2014 and the multiannual financial framework for 2014–20 agreed

November Seventh European environmental action programme adopted, covering 2014–20

2014

January Accession negotiations begin with Serbia

February The EU condemns Russia's annexation of Crimea, a part of Ukraine

May Elections to European Parliament

June Albania given candidate status

July The European Parliament elects Jean-Claude Juncker as Commission President, using the 'spitzenkandidaten' process for the first time

2015

July Third assistance package is agreed for Greece

November Terrorist attack in Paris leads to tightened security in Schengen zone

December One million asylum seekers arrive over the course of the year, leading to 'refugee crisis'

2016

March Turkey–EU agreement reached on reducing irregular migration

June UK people vote to leave the EU in referendum

2017

January Italian conservative Antonio Tajani becomes President of the EP following Martin Schulz's resignation

March Sixtieth anniversary of Treaty of Rome and adoption of 'Rome Declaration'

March UK's EU withdrawal process (under Article 50) begins

September Comprehensive Economic and Trade Agreement (CETA) with Canada enters into force

December Permanent Structured Cooperation (PESCO) framework for defence cooperation agreed

December Commission launches measures over Polish rule of law reforms

2018

February Draft Withdrawal Agreement between EU and UK published

July EU fines Google for unfair market practices

August Greece exits third bailout package

2019

February EU–Japan free trade agreement enters into force

March EU agrees to extend UK withdrawal date beyond 29 March

May Elections to EP

June Court of Justice of the European Union (CJEU) ruling against Poland on rule of law

July Ursula von der Leyen elected (by European Parliament) as first female President of European Commission and David Sassoli elected President of EP

November Christine Lagarde replaces Draghi as President of the ECB

December Boris Johnson's Conservatives win UK general election on 'Get Brexit done' platform

2020

January The UK leaves the European Community on 31 January

 Take your learning and understanding further by downloading an interactive timeline from the online resources www.oup.com/uk/bache5e.

General Index

coins, Euro 162, 385, 387, 396, 565, 566
Cold War 89, 90, 93, 96, 97, 100, 101, 104, 108, 116, 120, 150, 154, 160, 164, 335, 343, 434, 435, 451, 459, 490, 504, 508, 509
co-legislation 213, 236, 259, 274, 280, 285, 294, 295, 326
Cold War 89–90, 93–7, 100–1, 104, 108, 116, 120, 150, 154, 160, 164, 335, 343, 434–5, 451, 459, 481, 490, 504, 508–9
collective-action problem 416
College of Commissioners 39, 165, 173, 239, 244, 255, 285–6, 296, 349, 427
collegiality principle 242, 244, 265, 268, 272, 275
colonialism 118, 335, 457–8
colonies 118, 456–8, 463, 465, 474, 544
Comitology case 246, 302–4
command and control structure 30, 35, 108, 309, 480, 490
Commissariat du Plan (CdP) 97, 98, 118, 549
Commission see European Commission
Commission Directorates-General (DGs) 239, 242, 244, 273, 322, 422, 424, 427, 432, 446
Commission on Human Rights (CHR) 93
Commission v. Greece case (2000) 308
Commissioner for External Relations 482–3
Commissioners-Designate hearings 285–6
Committee on Agriculture and Rural Development (COMAGRI) 302, 406, 550
Committee of Permanent Representatives (COREPER) 39, 211, 257–9, 268–71, 274, 276, 327, 345, 550
Committee of Professional Agricultural Organizations (COPA) 321, 550
Committee of the Regions and Local Authorities (CoR) 209, 211, 215, 216, 221, 222, 236, 301, 550
Common Agricultural Policy (CAP) 15, 27, 28, 125, 127, 130, 131, 135, 141, 144, 158, 159, 164, 165, 199, 226, 283, 284, 296, 308, 320, 325, 334, 340, 353, 399–413, 419, 420, 522, 527, 528, 534, 541, 549, 558, 561, 563–5, 568

common commercial policy (CCP) 230, 271, 338, 457, 460–4, 469–70, 473, 476
common external tariff (CET) 125, 127, 549
Common Fisheries Policy (CFP) 158, 167, 230, 306, 338, 568
Common Foreign and Security Policy (CFSP) 31, 155, 157, 168–70, 175, 176, 182, 190, 194, 198, 206, 208–10, 212, 225, 227–31, 233–6, 238, 252, 253, 260, 266–9, 281, 295, 300, 337, 339–42, 346, 347, 358, 468, 476, 477, 479–83, 486–94, 498, 504, 508, 527, 550
Common Security and Defence Policy (CSDP) 168, 175, 176, 182, 190, 194, 198, 337, 341, 342, 347, 468, 477, 479–84, 486, 487, 489–94, 498, 508, 550
Commonwealth of Nations 91, 503
communism 8, 89, 91, 93–5, 101, 104, 108, 130, 134, 140, 150, 154–5, 161, 163, 169, 176, 321, 403, 434, 459, 474, 479, 495, 498, 501, 505–6, 509, 513, 544, 562
communitarization 168, 436, 451, 453, 532
Community gross domestic product (GDP) 186, 352, 353, 381, 383, 386, 389, 458, 506, 553
Community Plant Variety Office (CPVO) 252, 550
Comoros 466
compensation 306, 307, 403, 529
competencies catalogue 229–31, 236, 267, 339, 436
competition 30, 31, 49, 53, 60, 72, 74, 102, 103, 113, 116, 122, 132, 143, 145, 225, 226, 230, 238–40, 247, 248, 251, 292, 299, 307, 338–40, 344, 346, 348–50, 353–5, 358, 359, 361, 362, 366, 367, 374, 399, 400, 425–7, 458, 518, 529, 533, 535, 543, 546 see also dumping
competitiveness 35, 70, 174, 225, 248, 264, 266, 267, 321, 340, 343, 349–54, 356, 357, 365, 372, 392, 409, 472, 504, 539
Competitiveness Council 266–7
complaints 364, 422, 464
Comprehensive Economic and Trade Agreement (CETA) 472, 549, 569
concentration principle 102–3

Conciliation Committees 210, 218–21, 223, 249, 293–4
Confederation Générale du Travail (CGT) 367, 550
Conference of Presidents 279, 296
Conference on Security and Co-operation in Europe (CSCE) 134, 164, 478, 479, 493, 550, 560, 564
confidentiality 325, 477
conglomerates 103, 188
consent procedure 220, 224, 234, 241–2, 282
conservation 230, 231, 338
Conservative Party (UK) 91, 101, 131, 141, 194–5, 290–1, 569
Constitution for Europe 177, 184, 566
Constitutional Treaty 56, 172, 176, 178–81, 183–5, 206, 282, 369, 566–7
constitutionalism 394, 527, 536
constitutionalization 74, 311, 313
'constructive abstention' 168, 228
constructivism 3, 4, 13, 28, 51, 53, 66–73, 75, 79, 81, 83–5, 268, 270–1, 275, 295, 375, 473, 487, 488, 493, 502, 508, 514, 520, 528, 538, 548
consultancy firms 320, 368
consultation procedure 220, 222, 224, 281, 293, 296, 304, 546
Consultative Assembly of the Council of Europe 108, 126
Consultative Committee of the European Coal and Steel Community 209
contamination 303, 304
contracts 143, 350, 362, 364, 365
convergence criteria 70, 161–2, 381–4
co-operation procedure 220, 282, 285, 293, 304
Cook Islands 466
COPA (Committee of Professional Agricultural Organizations 321, 550
Copenhagen Conference of the Parties' (COP) meeting 424, 429, 550
Copenhagen criteria (1993) 179, 263, 415, 424, 459, 498, 501, 508, 510, 536
copyright 324, 370, 521
CoR (Committee of the Regions and Local Authorities) 209, 211, 215, 216, 221, 222, 236, 301, 550
Corbyn, J. 74

579

O

Author Index